Georgetown
District of Columbia

Marriage and Death Notices

1801-1838

Wesley E. Pippenger

WILLOW BEND BOOKS
2008

WILLOW BEND BOOKS
AN IMPRINT OF HERITAGE BOOKS, INC.

Books, CDs, and more—Worldwide

For our listing of thousands of titles see our website
at
www.HeritageBooks.com

Published 2008 by
HERITAGE BOOKS, INC.
Publishing Division
100 Railroad Ave. #104
Westminster, Maryland 21157

Copyright © 2004 Wesley E. Pippenger

All rights reserved. No part of this book may be reproduced or transmitted in any form or by any means, electronic or mechanical, including photocopying, recording or by any information storage and retrieval system without written permission from the author, except for the inclusion of brief quotations in a review.

International Standard Book Numbers
Paperbound: 978-1-58549-945-8
Clothbound: 978-0-7884-7243-5

Georgetown, D.C.
MARRIAGE AND DEATH NOTICES
1801 to 1838

Georgetown, D.C., Marriage and Death Notices, 1801-1838

INTRODUCTION

Marriage and death notices in newspapers provide genealogical information that is oftentimes not found elsewhere. They range from those containing limited or routine data to the bizarre.

These notices, taken from different newspapers, are generally presented verbatim as found in the newspaper. However, these transcripts have been shortened for instances where the notice contains lengthy editorial comments or scripture. Newspapers presented here are on microfilm which is available from the Library of Congress, Washington, D.C. Citations to the source newspaper include paper code, date of issue, and page, e.g. "WF, 2 JAN 1801, p. 2."

The following newspapers have been used:

CG *Columbian Gazette*, July 2, 1829 through March 30, 1833, succeeds the *Georgetown Columbian, District Advertiser, and Commercial Gazette*. Library of Congress reading room film #3048, order #NP4175. Printed and published by Benjamin Homans, on Tuesday, Thursday and Saturday. Located opposite the Mayor's office and Semmes' Tavern, and on High Street near Bridge Street (1833).

CDA *[Georgetown] Columbian, and District Advertiser*, January 2 through December 25, 1827. Library of Congress film #NP4136. The *Columbian & District Advertiser* continues *The Columbian*, which was established November 16, 1826. The *Columbian & District Advertiser* became the *Georgetown Columbian, and District Advertiser* on either March 2 or 6, 1827. Published semi-weekly (Tuesday and Friday), by Samuel S. Rind, on Jefferson Street, three doors below David English's Hardware Store in Georgetown, D.C.

DFR *The Daily Federal Republican*, January 3, 1814 to December 31, 1814. Library of Congress film #NP2182. Published in Washington Street, near the Union Tavern.

IA *[Georgetown] Independent American*, published 1809-1811. Library of Congress film #NP2013, reading room film #2891. Initially published Tuesdays, Thursdays and Saturdays by Edgar Patterson. For the period July to December 1810 publication changed to Wednesdays and Saturdays.

M *The Metropolitan*. Library of Congress film #NP4203, for January 2, 1821 through December 11, 1826. Title established January 26, 1820, and absorbed the National Messenger on May 22, 1821. Published tri-weekly (Tuesday, Thursday and Saturday) through March 11, 1823; semi-weekly (Tuesday and Friday) through January 11, 1826 with a few exceptions. With the issue of May 20, 1823 shows "Printed and Published on Tuesdays and Fridays, on Jefferson-street, Georgetown, D.C., three doors below David English's Hardware Store, by Samuel [Seabrook] Rind." Due to a labor problem, the issue of February 27, 1825, was printed as two broadside pages. Published by William Alexander Rind, Jr. Beginning January 21,

Georgetown, D.C., Marriage and Death Notices, 1801-1838

1826, published weekly (Saturday).

MS   *The Messenger (and Town and City Commercial Gazette).* Library of Congress film #NP4191. Published April 17, 1816 to October 24, 1817. Published by James C. Dunn & Co. Title established April 17, 1816. Frequency varies from semi-weekly (Wednesday and Saturday), and tri-weekly (Tuesday, Thursday and Saturday). Continued as the *National Messenger,* October 27, 1817, with new numbering.

NM   *The National Messenger.* Library of Congress film #NP4586. Copies from January 1 through May 21, 1821. Title established October 27, 1817 as *The Messenger.* Published tri-weekly (Monday, Wednesday and Friday). Absorbed by *The Metropolitan,* May 22, 1821. Published by James C. Dunn.

PA   *The Potomac Advisor and Metropolitan Intelligencer* (Georgetown), July 13-December 31, 1837, and January 1-February 12, 1838. Title established July 19, 1837. When Thomas Turner bought the establishment of *The Metropolitan,* he used this new title but continued the volume numbering of that publication. Printed each Monday, Wednesday and Friday. Price six dollars per annum, payable quarterly. In the issue of Monday, February 5, 1838, we find "This Office for Sale!" Thomas Turner seeks to sell the newspaper. The paper's operation soon closed.

T   *The United States Telegraph* (Washington), published by Duff Green (1832) and by John S. Meehan (1826).

WF   *Washington Federalist* (Georgetown), January 2, 1801 through December 31, 1809. Title established September 25, 1800. Frequency of publication varies. Publication is daily from January 2 through February 24, 1801 (during session of Congress); publication is tri-weekly February 26 through December 4, 1801. Publication is again daily from December 7, 1801 to May 5, 1802 (during session of Congress). Publication is then tri-weekly for the period May 7, 1802 through July 11, 1804, and semi-weekly from July 16, 1804. Initially printed by William Alexander Rind, for himself and John Stewart.

1802, MAR 22	Mr. Prentiss having sold his concern in this paper, it will be continued under the firm of William A. Rind & Co.
1802, DEC 29	The office of the *Washington Federalist* removed to the Brick House, in Washington Street, lately occupied by Mr. Bushby, a few doors south of the Union Tavern, Georgetown.
1803, MAY 30	The partnership of William A. Rind & Co. is this day dissolved by mutual consent. All persons indebted to the firm of Rind & Prentiss, or William A. Rind & Co., are requested to make immediate payment to William A. Rind, who will continue to conduct the paper as usual.
1804, SEP 8	Charles Prentiss, formerly one of the proprietors of this paper, has engaged to commence, this week, the rendering to us of editorial assistance.
1804, DEC	The paper was reduced to two pages in length for a short term,

Georgetown, D.C., Marriage and Death Notices, 1801-1838

1808, AUG 11	appearing twice weekly on Wed. and Sat. It was sometimes being printed on Tuesday; switching which day of the week it was printed occasionally afterward. "This is the last number of the *Washington Federalist* that will appear in my name, or in which I shall be interested. I have sold the Establishment to Mr. Jonathan S. Findlay, for some time past connected with the editorial department, who will continue the publication ... While too many of my nominal patrons have chilled by ardour by the coldness of neglect, and embarrassed my exertions by their want of punctuality; others have stretched out towards me the hand of liberal beneficence—supported me beneath the pressure of adversity, and helped to dissipate the gloom which sometimes thickened round me ... W.A. Rind."
1808, AUG 13	The paper was printed and published three times a week by Jonathan S. Findlay. "Price five dollars per annum payable in advance," is noted on issue #1080.

Wesley E. Pippenger
Arlington, Virginia
Fall 2003

Georgetown, D.C., **Marriage and Death Notices, 1801-1838**

STREET NAMES CHANGED

Modern readers are easily confused with Georgetown street locations given in early newspapers. The streets were renamed in October 1880,[1] as they were renamed to be in line those already within the City of Washington.

Street hitherto called--	
North street, as	Twenty-sixth street
Monroe street, as	Twenty-seventh street
Mill street, as	Twenty-seventh street
Rock street, as	Rock street
Montgomery street, as	Twenty-eighth street
Greene street, as	Twenty-ninth street
Washington street, as	Thirtieth street
Jefferson street, as	Jefferson street
Congress street, as	Thirty-first street
Valley street, as	Valley street
High street, as	Thirty-second street
Potomac street, as	Potomac street
Market street, as	Thirty-third street
Frederick street, as	Thirty-fourth street
Fayette street, as	Thirty-fifth street
Lingan street, as	Thirty-sixth street
Warren street, as	Thirty-seventh street
Water street, as	Water street
South street, as	South street
Grace street, as	Grace street
Needwood street, as	L street
Aqueduct street, as	Pennsylvania avenue
Bridge street, as	M street
Olive street, as	Olive street
Prospect street, as	Prospect street
Gay street, as	N street
First street, as	N street
Dunbarton street, as	Dunbarton street
Beall street, as	O street
Second street, as	O street
West street, as	P street
Third street, as	P street
Stoddard street, as	Q street
Fourth street, as	Q street
Fifth street, as	R street

---

[1] Report of the Commissioners of the District of Columbia, Annual Report, Fiscal Year 1881, p 19, October 4, 1880, "Ordered, . . That hereafter the streets of that part of the District of Columbia known as Georgetown will be known on the official records of the District of Columbia by the following names, to wit "

Georgetown, D.C., **Marriage and Death Notices, 1801-1838**

Sixth street, as	S street
Seventh street, as	T street
Eighth street, as	U street
Road street, as	U street

The official numbers of the houses on the streets above mentioned will be as follows, to wit: Houses on the north and east sides of streets will bear odd numbers; houses on the south and west sides of streets will bear even numbers. Each number will be considered equivalent to a front of *twenty* feet. Of houses fronting on streets running north and south, the houses on the northern corners will be numbered as follows, to wit:

At corner of Water street	1000 and 1001
L street	1100 and 1101
M street	1200 and 1201
N street	1300 and 1301
O street	1400 and 1401
P street	1500 and 1501
Q street	1600 and 1601
R street	1700 and 1701
S street	1800 and 1801
T street	1900 and 1901
U street	2000 and 2001

From these corner houses the numbers will proceed in regular order by addition of two for each front of *twenty* feet on each side of the street until the next street of those just mentioned is arrived at.

Of houses fronting on streets running east and west, the houses on the western corners will be numbered as follows, to wit:

At corner of Twenty-sixth street	2600 and 2601
Twenty-seventy street	2700 and 2701
Twenty-eighth street	2800 and 2801
Twenty-ninth street	2900 and 2901
Thirtieth street	3000 and 3001
Thirty-first street	3100 and 3101
Thirty-second street	3200 and 3201
Thirty-third street	3300 and 3301
Thirty-fourth street	3400 and 3401
Thirty-fifth street	3500 and 3501
Thirty-sixth street	3600 and 3601
Thirty-seventh street	3700 and 3701

From these corner houses the numbers will proceed in regular order by addition of two for each front of *twenty* feet on each side of the street until the next street of those just mentioned is arrived at.

The surveyor of the District of Columbia is hereby directed to make a survey of that part of the District of Columbia above referred to, and to fix the number of each house in accordance with the requirements of this order. While the survey is in progress he will notify the inhabitants of each house of its official number, and will furnish to each house a painted sign of inexpensive pattern bearing the numbers. Upon completing the survey he will make two identical plats of the same, showing the names of the streets and the location and number of each house; one of these plats will be furnished to the Commissioners of the District of Columbia, and the other will be kept in the records of the surveyor's office, together with a copy of this order.

The expenses of the survey and of purchasing the painted signs will be paid from the appropriation for general contingent expenses of the District of Columbia.

Georgetown, D.C., **Marriage and Death Notices, 1801-1838**

EARLY MINISTERS (1801-1838)

Numerous ministers are found mentioned in the newspaper marriage notices. Researchers may find more about a marriage if the minister can be tied to an area church that has records surviving from the period. Some early 19th century ministers can be linked with a religion or an area church, as below:

Addison, Walter Dulany .... St. John's Episcopal (Georgetown)
Allen, Ethan .... Christ Episcopal (Washington)
Amiss, John L. .... Dumbarton Methodist (Georgetown)
Andrews, Wells .... First Presbyterian (Alexandria, D.C.)
Baker, Daniel .... Second Presbyterian (Washington)
Balch, Stephen Bloomer ...... Bridge Street Presbyterian (Georgetown)
Balch, Thomas Bloomer ...... Presbyterian
Baxter, Roger .... St. Mary's Catholic (Alexandria, D.C.)
Bear, John .... Foundry Methodist (Washington)
Breckenridge, John .... Presbyterian (Bladensburg, Md.)
Brooke, John Thompson ...... Christ Episcopal (Georgetown)
Brown, Obadiah Bruen .... First Baptist (Washington)
Bunn, Seely .... 4th Street Methodist (Washington)
Burch, Thomas .... Foundry Methodist (Georgetown, Washington)
Campbell, John N. .... Presbyterian (Georgetown)
Chalmers, John .... Trinity M.E. Circuit (Fairfax Co., Va.)
Childs, John .... Methodist Episcopal (Montgomery Co., Md.)
Cone, Spencer Houghton ..... Baptist (Alexandria, D.C.)
Cornelius, Samuel .... Baptist (Alexandria, D.C.)
Dade, Townsend .... Episcopal (Alexa., D.C.; Montgomery Co., Md.)
Danforth, Joshua N. .... 4th Presbyterian (Washington)
Davis, John .... Dumbarton, Foundry (Georgetown; Washington)
Davis, Samuel H. .... Foundry Methodist (Washington)
Deagle, Matthew .... St. Peter's Catholic (Washington)
Douglass, Sutherland .... St. John's Episcopal (Georgetown)
Dubuisson, Stephen L. .... Trinity Catholic (Georgetown)
Emory, John .... Foundry Methodist (Washington)
Evans, French S. .... Foundry Methodist (Washington)
Fairclough, Joseph William .... St. Mary's Catholic (Alexandria, D.C.)
Fechtig, Lewis R. .... Methodist Episcopal
Fenwick, Benedict J. .... Trinity Catholic (Georgetown)
Fenwick, Enoch .... St. Mary's Catholic (Alexandria, D.C.)
Foxall, Henry .... Methodist (Georgetown)
Furlong, Henry .... Dumbarton Methodist (Georgetown)
Gantt, Edward .... Episcopal (Georgetown, Washington Parish)
Gibson, William Lewis .... St. Paul's Episcopal (Alexandria, D.C.)
Grassi, John A. .... Trinity Catholic (Georgetown)
Grey, H.H. .... Christ Episcopal (Georgetown)
Guest, Job .... Methodist (Georgetown; Alexandria, D.C.)

Georgetown, D.C., Marriage and Death Notices, 1801-1838

Hamilton, William . . . . Dumbarton, Foundry (Georgetown; Washington)
Hanson, James M. . . . . Dumbarton Methodist (Georgetown)
Harrison, Elias . . . . First Presbyterian (Alexandria, D.C.)
Hawley, William H. . . . . St. John's Episcopal (Washington)
Hemphill, Andrew . . . . 4th Street Methodist (Washington)
Hildt, George . . . . 4th Street Methodist, Foundry (Washington)
Hoff, John F. . . . . Christ Episcopal (Georgetown)
Jackson, William M. . . . . St. Paul's Episcopal (Alexandria, D.C.)
James, John Waller . . . . St. John's Episcopal (Georgetown)
Jones, Joseph H. . . . . First Baptist (Washington)
Laurie, James . . . . Presbyterian (Washington)
Lucas, James . . . . St. Peter's Catholic (Washington)
Keith, Reuel . . . . Episcopal (Georgetown; Alexandria, D.C.)
McCann, James . . . . Dumbarton Methodist (Georgetown)
McCormick, Alexander . . . . Christ Episcopal (Washington)
McElroy, John . . . . Holy Trinity Catholic (Georgetown)
McIlvaine, Charles P. . . . . Christ Episcopal (Georgetown)
McVean, James . . . . Presbyterian (Georgetown)
Matthews, William . . . . St. Patrick's Catholic (Washington)
Mines, John . . . . Presbyterian (Cabin John & Bethesda, Md.)
Moore, Jeremiah . . . . Second Baptist (Washington)
Muir, James . . . . First Presbyterian (Alexandria, D.C.)
Neale, Francis Ignatius . . . . Holy Trinity Catholic (Georgetown)
Norris, Oliver . . . . Christ Episcopal (Alexandria, D.C.)
Pitts, John . . . . Trinity Methodist Episcopal (Alexandria, D.C.)
Post, Reuben . . . . First Presbyterian (Washington)
Rice, Luther . . . . First Baptist (Washington)
Roberts, Robert R. . . . . Dumbarton Methodist (Georgetown)
Robbins, Isaac . . . . Trinity Methodist Episcopal (Alexandria, D.C.)
Roszel, Stephen George . . . . . . Methodist Episcopal (Georgetown; Baltimore, Md.)
Ryland, William . . . . 4th Street Methodist (Georgetown; Washington)
Sargent, Thomas F. . . . . Dumbarton Methodist (Georgetown)
Sayrs, John Johnson . . . . St. John's Episcopal (Georgetown)
Shinn, Asa . . . . Dumbarton, Foundry (Georgetown; Washington)
Slaughter, Philip . . . . Christ Episcopal (Georgetown)
Slicer, Henry . . . . Dumbarton Methodist (Georgetown)
Smith, David (C) . . . . African near St. Peter's (Washington)
Snethen, Nicholas . . . . Dumbarton Methodist (Georgetown)
Tippett, Charles B. . . . . Dumbarton Methodist (Georgetown)
Tyng, Stephen Higginson . . . . . . St. John's Episcopal (Georgetown)
Vinton, Robert S. . . . . Dumbarton Methodist (Georgetown)
Watters, William . . . . Methodist Episcopal (Georgetown)
Waugh, Beverley . . . . Dumbarton Methodist (Georgetown)
Wells, Joshua . . . . 4th Street Methodist (Washington)
Wilmer, William Holland . . . . St. Paul's Episcopal (Alexandria, D.C.)
Wilson, Norval . . . . 4th Street Methodist (Georgetown, Washington)
Young, Benjamin A. . . . . Catholic (P.G. Co., Md.; Georgetown)

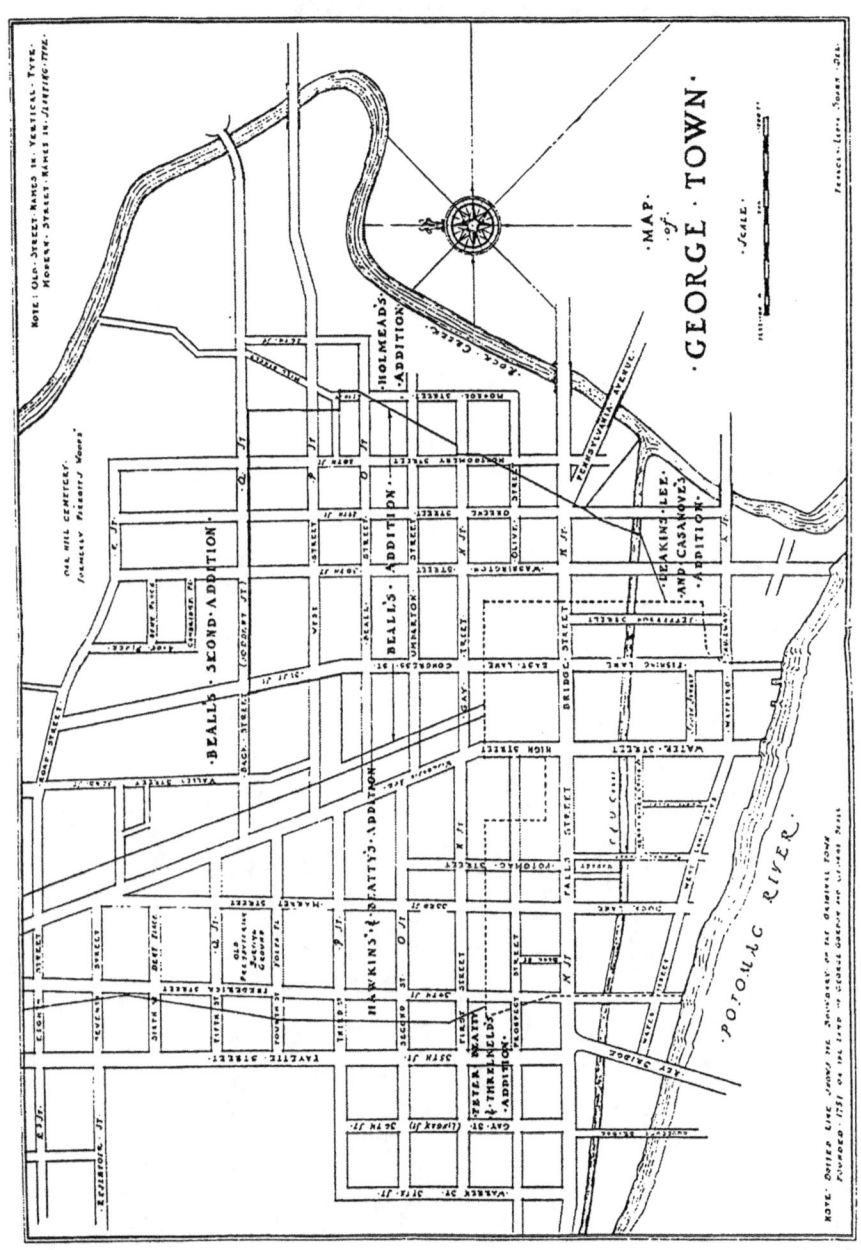

Georgetown, D.C., **Marriage and Death Notices, 1801-1838**

MARRIAGE AND DEATH NOTICES

WASHINGTON FEDERALIST
January 2, 1801, to December 31, 1809

DIED, on board the frigate *United States*, on the 31st Dec. [i.e. 31 DEC 1800], Lieut. WILLIAM M'CLEARY, of the Marine Corps. [WF, Sat., 28 FEB 1801, p. 2]

Married, Sunday Evening [i.e. 15 MAR 1801], by the Rev. Mr. M'Cormack, Maj. DAVID HOPKINS, Marshal of Md., to Miss ISABELLA FORD, a young Lady lately from Jamaica. [WF, Tues., 17 MAR 1801, p. 2]

DIED—at Edinburgh, (Scotland) the Reverend HUGH BLAIR, D.D., Professor of Rhetoric and Belles Letters in the University of Edinburgh. [WF, Tues., 17 MAR 1801, p. 2]

MARRIED—Last Thursday evening [i.e. 7 MAY 1801] by the Right Reverend Bishop Carroll, ROBERT GOODLOE HARPER, Esq., to Miss CARROLL, daughter of Charles Carroll, Esq., of *Carrollton*. [WF, Thurs., 14 MAY 1801, p. 2]

DIED, at Savannah, on the 9th ult. [i.e. 9 APR 1801], after a short illness, CHARLES FRANCIS COUGNACQ, a most celebrated French physician. [WF, Sat., 16 MAY 1801, p. 2]

DIED, on the 18 ult. [i.e. 18 APR 1801], on Patterson's creek, Hampshire Co., Va., MATTHIAS A. HERNSMON, a native of Germany, aged, by the most accurate accounts 125 years.—He lived upon low diet, and drank but little ardent spirits, had three wives in Germany, and one in this country. [WF, Thurs., 21 MAY 1801, p. 2]

DIED.—On the 11th of May [i.e. 11 MAY 1801], at Bermuda, whither she had retired for the restoration of her health, Mrs. BINGHAM, consort of the Hon. William Bingham, of Philadelphia. [WF, Mon. 1 JUN 1801, p. 2]

DIED. — At Salem, (Mass.) [no date], GEORGE BRAXTON, Esq., of Va., aged 38. [WF, Mon. 1 JUN 1801, p. 2]

DIED.—At Lancaster on Thursday last [i.e. 11 JUN 1801], FREDERICK AUGUSTUS MUGHLENBURG, Receiver General of the Land-Office. [WF, Mon. 15 JUN 1801, p. 2]

DIED.—At Lancaster [no date], JOHN WILKES KITTERA, late a member of the House of Representatives of the United States. [WF, Mon. 15 JUN 1801, p. 2]

Died, on Tuesday, the 8th inst. [i.e. 8 SEP 1801], universally lamented by those who knew her, in the 59th year of her age, Mrs. ANN BAYLEY, consort of Col. Thomas Bayl[e]y, of Accomac[k] Co., Va. [WF, Fri. 25 SEP 1801, p. 2]

Georgetown, D.C., **Marriage and Death Notices, 1801-1838**

MARRIED—On Thursday last [i.e. 8 OCT 1801], by the Rev. Mr. Reed, Mr. BRICE SELBY, to Miss KITTY MARKER—both of Williamsburgh, Montgomery Co. [WF, Mon. 12 OCT 1801, p. 2]

DIED, at Washington City, on the 19th inst. [i.e. 19 OCT 1801], Mrs. ESTHER FROST, wife of Amariah Frost, Esq. Her remains were interred in the Presbyterian Churchyard in Georgetown. [WF, Mon. 26 OCT 1801, p. 2]

MARRIED, on Friday the 30th of October [i.e. 30 OCT 1801], by the Rev. Mr. Clarkson, Mr. STEPHEN PLEASONTON, late of the State of Delaware, to Miss MOLLY HOPKINS, daughter of John Hopkins, Esq., of Lancaster Co., Pa. [WF, Fri. 13 NOV 1801, p. 2]

MARRIED, last evening [i.e. 26 NOV 1801], by the Rev. Stephen B. Balch, Mr. EDGAR PATTERSON, Merchant, to the amiable Miss MARGARET SUTER, both of this place. [WF, Fri. 27 NOV 1801, p. 2]

MARRIED, on Thursday evening last [i.e. 10 DEC 1801], at *Rock Hill*, by the Rev. Mr. Gantt, Lieut. ROBERT RANKIN, Adjt. of the Marine Corps, to Miss ELIZABETH SCOTT, daughter of the late Gustavus Scott, Esq. [WF, Sat., 12 DEC 1801, p. 2]

DIED—Yesterday morning [i.e. 18 DEC 1801], about two o'clock at the Seven Buildings, Miss JANE GARDNER, a young lady whose suavity of disposition and amiable manners endeared her to all her connections and acquaintances. [WF, Sat., 19 DEC 1801, p. 2]

MARRIED—last evening [i.e. 21 JAN 1802], at *Bush Hill*, Va. by the Rev. Mr. Davis, JOHN C. SCOTT, Esq., of George-Town, to Miss ANN LOVE, *Sallisbury*, Va. [WF, Fri. 22 JAN 1802, p. 2]

DIED on the night of the 10th inst. [i.e. 10 FEB 1802], in Geo. Town, Mrs. REBECCA STODDERT, the wife of Maj. Benjamin Stoddert, late secretary of the Navy of the United States of America. Her remains moved from her late dwelling on Saturday, 11 o'clock, A.M. to Addison's Chapel, in Prince George's Co., attended by an unusual number of carriages and horsemen: in the grave yard there they were decently and solemnly deposited ... [WF, Tues., 16 FEB 1802, p. 2]

Departed this life, last Tuesday morning [i.e. 23 FEB 1802], at nine o'clock, after three weeks illness, Mrs. HELEN RENNER, wife of Mr. Daniel Renner of this town, in the 21st year of her age, she was the daughter of Mr. Daniel Fowler of Annapolis; dutiful as a daughter, loving as a wife, and affectionate as a Sister, were striking traits to her character. Her remains, attended by a disconsolate husband, and a numerous train of relations & friends, were interred in the Presbyterian burying ground on the 24th inst. She met the approach of the King of terrors, in a manner, worthy of imitation. Feb. 26. [WF, Sat., 27 FEB 1802, p. 2]

DIED.—On Tuesday last [i.e. 2 MAR 1802], Mrs. JONES, wife of Mr. Edward Jones, principal clerk in the Treasury department.—She was an affectionate mother, and has left a young family to deplore her loss. [WF, Fri. 5 MAR 1802, p. 2]

Georgetown, D.C., **Marriage and Death Notices, 1801-1838**

DIED.—On Wednesday [i.e. 3 MAR 1802], Mr. EDWARD BLACKBURN, printer, a young man of amiable disposition and engaging manners; in the 21st year of his age. [WF, Fri. 5 MAR 1802, p. 2]

Married on Thursday last [i.e. 4 MAR 1802], Mr. SAMUEL TREAT, late of Boston, to Miss LETTICE M. NAYLOR of this district. [WF, Tues., 9 MAR 1802, p. 2]

Married, on Sunday evening [i.e. 7 MAR 1802], Mr. JOHN CHRISTIAN BAUM, to the amiable Miss CATHARINE COKENDEFFER, both of George-Town. [WF, Wed. 10 MAR 1802, p. 2]

In our paper of Friday last, we mentioned the death of Mrs. Jones, wife of Mr. Edward Jones, of the Treasury Department. It is with pain that we now announce the death of their eldest daughter, Miss MARIA JONES, a young Lady of an affectionate heart ... She closed her eyes, in the sleep of death on the morning of the 10th inst. [i.e. 10 MAR 1802], and was yesterday interred in the Presbyterian burying ground in George-town, attended by a bereaved and disconsolate father, and many respectable friends and acquaintances, whose countenances, and tears, evinced the sorrow of their hearts ... [WF, Fri. 12 MAR 1802, p. 2]

DIED.— at N.Y., on Saturday Morning last [i.e. 6 MAR 1802], after a severe illness of several weeks, Mr. JOHN WARD FENNO, formerly proprietor and editor of this Gazette. *Bronson's Gazette.* [WF, Fri. 12 MAR 1802, p. 2]

Died, on Thursday the 11th inst. [i.e. 11 MAR 1802], the Hon. NARSWORTHY HUNTER, Esq., delegate to Congress from the Mississippi Territory. He was interred in the Presbyterian burying ground in George-Town, with every mark of respect due to his public character.—The Vice President and members of the Senate, the Speaker, and members of the House of Representatives, with many respectable citizens formed the procession which followed him to the silent tomb. [WF, Wed. 17 MAR 1802, p. 3]

Married at Newport, (R.I.) [no date], Mr. ISRAEL LORING, of Washington, Merchant, to Mrs. FRANCES DEAN. [WF, Fri. 19 MAR 1802, p. 2]

Died suddenly on Monday evening last [i.e. 22 MAR 1802], NOTLEY YOUNG, Esq., one of the oldest inhabitants of the City of Washington. His loss will be sincerely lamented not only by his family, but by all who had the pleasure of his acquaintance. In the death of Mr. Young, the city has lost one of its most active and useful friends. He was yesterday interred in the Catholic burying ground, attended by a large concourse of the most respectable inhabitants of the City and George-Town. [WF, Thurs., 25 MAR 1802, p. 2] ☞ The Funeral Service for the late NOTLEY YOUNG, Esq., will be performed and a sermon preached at the Catholic Church in George-Town, on Wednesday the 7th inst., to commence at Ten o'Clock in the forenoon. [WF, Tues., 6 APR 1802, p. 2]

Died yesterday morning [i.e. 25 MAR 1802], Mr. JAMES ORME, age 75. [WF, Fri. 26 MAR 1802, p. 2]

Georgetown, D.C., Marriage and Death Notices, 1801-1838

Died, lately [no date] at Trenton, N.J., RICHARD HOWEL, Esq., late Governor of that State ... a native of Delaware ... [WF, Fri. 14 MAY 1802, p. 3]

MARRIED—On Sunday the 9th inst. [i.e. 9 MAY 1802], at the City of Washington, Mr. JOHN P. VAN NESS, Esq., Member in Congress, from the state of New-York, to Miss MARCIA [BURNES], of that city—The gentleman estimable for private worth and political integrity—the lady celebrated for the splendor of her fortune, but much more enviable and respected for the purity of her mind, and the unaffected sweetness of her temper and manners. *Aurora*. [WF, Wed. 26 MAY 1802, p. 2]

Winchester, June 23. MARRIED—Capt. JOHN HEISKELL, of this town, (late of the U. States army) to the amiable Miss ANN SOWERS, daughter of Mr. Jacob Sowers, of *Buckmarsh*, Frederick Co. [WF, Fri. 2 JUL 1802, p. 2]

DIED on Wednesday last, the 7th inst. [i.e. 7 JUL 1802], Mrs. LETITIA JACK, wife of Mr. John Jack of the City of Washington, in the 26th year of her age, universally lamented. In her were blended those christian and domestic virtues which rendered her a blessing to her family—a tedious and painful illness had reconciled her to the inevitable blow.—She has left three children to mourn with their disconsolate father the loss they have sustained. [WF, Wed. 14 JUL 1802, p. 2]

DIED—On Saturday the 7th inst. [i.e. 7 AUG 1802], at *Mount Eagle*, near Alexandria, the Right Honorable and Rev. BRIAN LORD FAIRFAX, aged nearly seventy-six years. [WF, Fri. 13 AUG 1802, p. 3]

DIED at *Windsor*, in Lancaster Co., Pa., Mrs. DYER, on the 10th inst. [i.e. 10 SEP 1802], wife of William Dyer, carpenter, of the city of Washington. [WF, Wed. 22 SEP 1802, p. 3]

DIED, In George Town, on Monday night the 18th inst. [i.e. 18 OCT 1802], Mrs. ELIZABETH BRODHAG, consort of Mr. Charles Brodhag, aged 34 years. She has left three disconsolate Children to mourn her untimely end ... [WF, Fri. 22 OCT 1802, p. 3]

DIED— On the 1st inst. [i.e. 1 OCT 1802], at Charleston, S.C., Mr. FRANCIS KEARNES, formerly a resident of George Town. [WF, Fri. 22 OCT 1802, p. 3]

DIED]—On Tuesday the 26th ult. [i.e. 26 OCT 1802], at Westmoreland court-house, JOHN JAMES MAUND, Esq., of *Nomony-Hall*. When in the act of pleading a cause, in which he appeared much interested, he dropped in a kind of apoplexy and expired in a few hours ... [WF, Fri. 19 NOV 1802, p. 3]

Married, on Thursday last [i.e. 9 DEC 1802], W.O. SPRIGG, Esq., of George Town, to the amiable Miss ELIZA GANTT, daughter of Levi Gantt, Esq., of Prince George's Co. [WF, Wed. 15 DEC 1802, p. 3]

On Thursday last [i.e. 30 DEC 1802], was married by the Rev. Mr. Balch, Mr. JOSEPH E. ROWLES, of Geo. Town, to the amiable and accomplished Mrs. HANNAH E. FITZHUGH, of Loudoun Co., Va. [WF, Mon. 3 JAN 1803, p. 3]

Georgetown, D.C., **Marriage and Death Notices, 1801-1838**

Departed this life, on Friday morning the 21st of January [i.e. 21 JAN 1803], in the 57th year of his age, HARDAGE LANE, Esq., of Montgomery Co., Md. He was a kind neighbor, a friend to the poor, and a good citizen—he has left a large family to mourn his death and their loss. [WF, Wed. 2 FEB 1803, p. 3]

DIED on the 6th inst. [i.e. 6 FEB 1803], Mrs. MARY BURROWS, wife of Col. W.W. Burrows, aged 37 years and 6 months. [WF, Mon. 7 FEB 1803, p. 3]

MARRIED, on Tuesday the 8th inst. [i.e. 8 FEB 1803], by the Rev. M.L. Weems, Dr. JOSIAS H. M'PHERSON, of Montgomery Co., to the amiable Miss ELIZABETH B. HANSON, daughter of Maj. Samuel Hanson, of Charles Co. [WF, Wed. 16 FEB 1803, p. 3]

MARRIED—last Tuesday the 22d inst. [i.e. 22 MAR 1803], by the Rev. M. Scott, THOMAS BROOKE, Esq., of Prince George's Co., to the amiable and truly accomplished Miss ELIZABETH BOWIE, daughter of Walter Bowie, Esq., of said county. [WF, Wed. 30 MAR 1803, p. 3]

MARRIED, at N.Y., April 20th [i.e. 20 APR 1803], by the Right Revd. Bishop Provost, Mr. JOHN CALDWELL, of that city, merchant, to Miss HIGINBOTHAM, of Md. [WF, Mon. 25 APR 1803, p. 3]

Richmond, April 20, 1803. Mr. WYNDHAM GRYMES, whom we mentioned in our last Gazette, being wounded in a duel with Mr. Terrel, died on Friday [i.e. 22 APR 1803] about two in the afternoon ... [WF, Wed. 27 APR 1803, p. 3]

DIED, at Detroit, on the 11th inst. [i.e. 11 APR 1803], JOHN F. HAMTRAMCK, Esq., Colonel of the 1st Regiment, in the Army of the United States. He was a native of Canada, joined the American Army in 1775, and continued in that service nearly 27 years—as a Disciplinarian he was exemplary—as a Gentleman and an Officer highly respectable.—Having merited the approbation of General Washington, he received from him the most honorable testimonials. *Pittsburg Gazette*. [WF, Mon. 9 MAY 1803, p. 3]

MARRIED—At Princeton, (N.J.) [no date], JOHN M. PINTARD, Esq., late Consul of the United States at Madeira, to Miss ELIZA SMITH, daughter of the Revd. Dr. Smith, President of the College of New-Jersey. [WF, Mon. 16 MAY 1803, p. 3]

Married on Saturday Evening [i.e. 14 MAY 1803], by the Rev. Mr. Wiley, Mr. EDWARD JONES, to the amiable Miss LOUISA MAWS. [WF, Wed. 18 MAY 1803, p. 3]

Departed this life, the 11th inst. [i.e. 11 MAY 1803], in the 40th year of his age, at his seat in St. Mary's Co., HENRY TUBMAN, Esq. ... [WF, Wed. 18 MA 1803, p. 3]

Died at Philadelphia, on the 9th of May [i.e. 9 MAY 1803], at half past 11 o'clock in the evening, Gen. STEPHENS THOMPSON MASON, one of the Senators from the state of Virginia in the Congress of the United States. His funeral took place on Tuesday evening, on which occasion the offices of the federal and state governments, and of the militia of the state of Pa., and the militia legion under arms were invited to attend. *Phil. pap.* [WF, Wed. 18 MAY 1803, p. 3]

Died in the city of Washington on Sunday the 8th inst. [i.e. 8 MAY 1803], Mrs. DIANE MARIA RAY, wife of James Ray, Esq., and daughter of the late Col. Straham of the British Army ... [WF, Wed. 18 MAY 1803, p. 3]

MARRIED, last evening [i.e. 31 MAY 1803], Lieut. JAMES THOMPSON, Paymaster of the Marine Corps, to Miss BURROWS, daughter of Col. Burrows, Commandant of the Marines, all of Washington. [WF, Wed. 1 JUN 1803, p. 3]

DIED on the 6th ult. [i.e. 6 MAY 1803], at his seat, (*Belville*) near Nashville, in the state of Tennessee, Capt. EDWARD BUTLER, of the 2d regiment of Infantry in the army of the U. States ... In 1791 he joined the army under the command of Gen. St. Clair, with the rank of Captain .... [H]is older brother, Maj. Thomas Butler, (now the oldest Colonel in the army of the U. States) was dangerously wounded, and left on the field of battle .... [WF, Fri. 3 JUN 1803, p. 3]

DIED at Barbadoes [no date], THOMAS DICK, Esq., of Bladensburg, Md., in the 28th year of his age. Nearly two years he had been laboring under a consumption; for the relief of which he was seeking the benign influence of a warmer climate. He has left a widow and an infant son to lament the irreparable loss of an affectionate husband and father ... [WF, Wed. 8 JUN 1803, p. 3]

MARRIED, at Philadelphia on Tuesday, the 31st May [i.e. 31 MAY 1803], by the Rev. Dr. Wharton, Mr. WILLIAM WEEMS, of Calvert Co., Md., to Miss MARY KINSEY, of Burlington, N.J., daughter of the late Chief Justice Kinsey. [WF, Fri. 17 JUN 1803, p. 2]

MARRIED, last evening [i.e. 16 JUN 1803], by the Rev. Dr. Gantt, Capt. SIBALD, of Ga., to Miss COX, of Georgetown. [WF, Fri. 17 JUN 1803, p. 3]

DIED, at New-Haven [no date], SAMUEL BISHOP, Esq., Collector of the District of New-Haven, aged 80. At the same place, Mr. JOHN BISHOP, aged [35]. [WF, Wed. 17 AUG 1803, p. 3]

☞ On sabbath evening, the 14th inst. [i.e. 14 AUG 1803], were married by the Rev. Jeremiah Moore, the Rev. WILLIAM CLINGAN, a Baptist Minister of Taneytown, Md., to the respectable widow SARAH DARBY; at her residence near Seneca, in Montgomery Co. [WF, Mon. 22 AUG 1803, p. 3]

DIED, in the City of Washington on the 9th inst. [i.e. 9 AUG 1803], Mrs. LYDIA STORY, late of Charleston near Boston, Consort of William Story, formerly of Boston, Mass. ... [WF, Wed. 24 AUG 1803, p. 3]

DIED, at George-Town, on Saturday evening the 3d inst. [i.e. 3 SEP 1803], Mrs. ELIZABETH EVANS, Consort of Evan Evans, who was remarkable during her life time for her philanthropy—a professor of the Christian religion ... And on the morning [i.e. 4 SEP

Georgetown, D.C., **Marriage and Death Notices, 1801-1838**

1803] following her only son, Mr. JAMES HARRISON, aged 23 years, expired after a short but very severe illness. He has left an affectionate wife two little boys and many other relations to weep for his untimely fate. Mr. Harrison had served in a military capacity in the army of his Country for a short period. He died a commissioned officer of the Washington City Light Infantry Company ... And on the morning of the 5th he was interred, at Rock creek church burying ground, with military honors, by the light Infantry Company and the Regimental Staff officers ... [WF, Wed. 7 SEP 1803, p. 3]

Married last Evening [i.e. 29 SEP 1803], by the Rev. Mr. Balch, Mr. THOMAS PRYSE, of Georgetown, to Miss ELIZABETH JONES, of Washington. [WF, Fri. 30 SEP 1803, p. 3]

DIED—at Philadelphia, on the 13th inst. [i.e. 13 SEP 1803], Com. BARRY ... He was one of that little band of naval heroes, who first hoisted the flag of the American Navy, in the year 1775, & to his valor our country owed much of the honor she acquired on the seas during the revolutionary war ... *Phil. pap.* [WF, Fri. 30 SEP 1803, p. 3]

Married on Monday Evening, 3d inst. [i.e. 3 OCT 1803], by the Rev. Dr. Gantt, Mr. JOHN HAMAN, to Mrs. MARY ANN MITCHELL, both of this place. [WF, Wed. 5 OCT 1803, p. 3]

MARRIED, on Tuesday last [i.e. 23 OCT 1803], by the Revd. Mr. Davis, JEREMIAH WILLIAMS, Esq., of Georgetown, to Miss STEWART, the amiable daughter of Hugh Stewart, Esq., of Fairfax Co., Va. [WF, Mon. 31 OCT 1803, p. 2]

Richmond, October 29, 1803. DEATH! On Wednesday last [i.e. 26 OCT 1803], departed this life, in the 83d year of his age, EDMUND PENDLETON, Esq., the venerable President of the Court of Appeals of this state ... *Virg. Gaz.* [WF, Mon. 7 NOV 1803, p. 3]

MARRIED—On Tuesday the 22d inst. [i.e. 22 NOV 1803], by the Rev. Mr. Rahauser at Hagers Town, Mr. DANIEL BUSSARD, Merchant of Georgetown, to the amiable Miss CATHARINE KNO[W]LE, of Washington Co., Md. [WF, Wed. 30 NOV 1803, p. 3]

MARRIED. On Thursday 29th Dec. [i.e. 29 DEC 1803], by the Rev. Bishop White, THOMAS MANNERS, Esq., Captain in his Brittanic Majesty's 49th regiment of foot, to Miss MARY RUSH, daughter of Dr. Rush, of this city. *Phil. True Amer.* [WF, Wed. 4 JAN 1804, p. 3]

MARRIED. On Thursday the 1st December [i.e. 1 DEC 1803], at Savannah, in Georgia, JOHN MACPHERSON BERRIEN, Esq., Attorney at Law, to Miss ELIZA ANCIAUX, the only daughter of Nicholas Anciaux, Esq. [WF, Wed. 4 JAN 1804, p. 3]

MARRIED, last evening [i.e. 31 JAN 1804], by the Rev. Mr. Balch, ELIAS B. CALDWELL, Esq., Attorney at Law, and Clerk of the Supreme Court of the United States, of Georgetown, to Miss BOYD, only daughter of the late Archibald Boyd, Esq., dec., of Washington. [WF, Wed. 1 FEB 1804, p. 3]

MARRIED, on Thursday the 9th inst. [i.e. 9 FEB 1804], by the Right Rev. Bishop Claggett, RICHARD WELLS BRASHEARS, Esq., of Upper Marlboro, to the amiable Miss BERRY,

Georgetown, D.C., **Marriage and Death Notices, 1801-1838**

only daughter of Zachariah Berry, Esq., of Prince-George's Co. [WF, Fri. 17 FEB 1804, p. 3]

MARRIED, at Mecklenburg Court-House, Va., on the 22d inst. [i.e. 22 MAR 1804], FREDERICK HAMME, Esq., of that place, to the amiable Mrs. BUTLER, of N.C. [WF, Fri. 30 MAR 1804, p. 3]

Married, in England [no date], Mr. MASON, to a Miss CARPENTER, "A good partnership for undertaking to build a *family house*." [WF, Fri. 6 APR 1804, p. 3]

Longevity.—Died, on Tuesday, the 3d of April [i.e. 3 APR 1804], at the Alms-house of Philadelphia, DOROTHY DUSAN, aged 105 years: She had suffered her toe nails to grow until some of them had nearly encompassed her foot. [WF, Fri. 6 APR 1804, p. 3]

MARRIED on Thursday evening last [i.e. 19 APR 1804], by the Rev. Mr. Fenwick, Mr. JOSEPH THAW, to Miss ELEANOR SCOTT, both of this place. [WF, Mon. 23 APR 1804, p. 3]

MARRIED.—on Saturday evening last [i.e. 21 APR 1804], by the Rev. Mr. Gant, Mr. ELIE PETER PLEURY, to Miss ELIZABETH SANFORD, both of this place. [WF, Wed. 25 APR 1804, p. 3]

MARRIED.—About the middle of January last [i.e. ? JAN 1804], ROBERT SEMPLE, Esq., late an officer in the army of the United States to the amiable Miss ELIZA TURNBULL, of the Bayou of West Florida. [WF, Wed. 25 APR 1804, p. 3]

DIED.—On Sunday last [i.e. 29 APR 1804], Col. RICHARD BARNES, of St. Mary's Co., Md. In the death of this respectable citizen his friends have sustained a mournful, and his country, an irreparable loss. His will declares all his negroes, amounting to between three and four hundred, free three years after his death, provided they behave themselves well. [WF, Fri. 4 MAY 1804, p. 3]

MARRIED.—On Sunday last [i.e. 29 APR 1804], by the Rev. Mr. Balch, Mr. DANIEL RAPPINE, Bookseller, to Miss CHARLOTTE OSBORNE, both of this City. [WF, Fri. 4 MAY 1804, p. 3]

DIED.—At the City of Washington on the 7th ult. [i.e. 7 APR 1804], Mrs. ELIZA BETTERTON, wife of Mr. Benjamin Betterton, late of Philadelphia ... [WF, Fri. 11 MAY 1804, p. 3]

MARRIED last evening [i.e. 15 MAY 1804], by the Rev. Mr. Neal, Mr. T. DIXON, to Miss C. KALDENBACK, both of this town. [WF, Wed. 16 MAY 1804, p. 3]

Norfolk, May 15. Died on the 10th inst. [i.e. 10 MAY 1804], at the house of Mr. John Nivison, in this borough, in the 35th year of his age, JOHN STRATTON, Esq., of the county of Northampton, & late a Representative to Congress for the district of Accomack. [WF, Wed. 23 MAY 1804, p. 3]

Georgetown, D.C., **Marriage and Death Notices, 1801-1838**

MARRIED.—last evening [i.e. 29 MAY 1804], by the Rev. S.B. Balch, Mr. JACOB MO[U]NTZ, Merchant of George-Town, to the amiable Miss PARMELIA BELT, daughter of Mr. Benjamin Belt, District of Columbia. [WF, Wed. 30 MAY 1804, p. 3]

DIED.—On Saturday evening the 2d of June [i.e. 2 JUN 1804], Mr. JOHN MARCH, Stationer and Bookseller, and for several years a respectable inhabitant of this place. [WF, Mon. 4 JUN 1804, p. 3]

DIED, on the 28th ult. [i.e. 28 MAY 1804], Mr. JOHN BURCHAN of Washington city, leaving a sorrowful aged mother and other relatives to mourn their loss. His remains were attended the next day by numerous friends and neighbors to the Presbyterian new burying ground in Georgetown, where he was interred ... [WF, Fri. 15 JUN 1804, p. 3]

DEATH. Departed this life on the 25th ult. [i.e. 25 MAY 1804], at his residence in Charles Co., Capt. WILLIAM GODFREY ADAMS ... [WF, Fri. 22 JUN 1804, p. 3]

MARRIED.—Yesterday evening [i.e. 1 JUN 1804], by the Rev. Mr. Bunn, Mr. JOHN WIRT, to Miss SALLY RENSHAW, all of George-Town. [WF, Mon. 2 JUL 1804, p. 3]

Died, at Geneva, on the 9th April [i.e. 9 APR 1804], after a short illness, Mons. NECKER, formerly French minister of Finance. [WF, Mon. 9 JUL 1804, p. 3]

Married at Alexandria [i.e. 7 JUL 1804], on Saturday evening last by the Rev. Thomas Davis, GEORGE WASHINGTON PARKE CUSTIS, Esq., to Miss MOLLY FITZHUGH, daughter of Wm. Fitzhugh, Esq., of that place. [WF, Wed. 11 JUL 1804, p. 3]

MARRIED on Tuesday evening the 9th inst. [i.e. 9? JUL 1804], by the Rev. Mr. M'Cormick, Mr. SAMUEL POLK, of Somerset Co., Md., to Miss IRVING GILLIS, of Washington City. [WF, Mon. 16 JUL 1804, p. 3]

Philadelphia, July 12 ... The greatest man in America has this morning [i.e. 12 JUL 1804] fallen in a duel! Gen. [Alexander] HAMILTON ... Early this morning he, and Col. Burr, settled an affair of honour at Hoboken. Hamilton fell the first shot ... [also see July 20, 1804, Fri., pp. 2-3, in his 48th year, and has left Mr. Hamilton with eight children, four boys and four girls; will reproduced in issue of July 23, 1804, Mon., p. 2] [WF, Mon. 16 JUL 1804, p. 3]

DIED—at the City of Washington on Tuesday the 24th inst. [i.e. 24 JUL 1804], CHARLES deKRAFFT, Surveyor and Draftsman of the Treasury Department. [WF, Sat., 27 JUL 1804, p. 3]

On Friday the 20th inst. [i.e. 20 JUL 1804], departed this life, Mr. JUDSON COOLIDGE BURGESS, of Prince George's Co., in the 22d year of his age. [WF, Wed. 1 AUG 1804, p. 3]

DIED—on Tuesday last [i.e. 31 JUL 1804], in the 38th year of her age, Mrs. MARY TUNNICLIFF, wife of Mr. William Tunnicliff, on Capitol Hill. [WF, Sat., 4 AUG 1804, p. 3]

Georgetown, D.C., **Marriage and Death Notices, 1801-1838**

Departed this transitory life, on Wednesday last [i.e. 1 AUG 1804], after a lingering illness, MARIA SHARP, a teacher in the Young Ladies Academy: in her death, female youth have to bewail the loss of an able, attentive, and tender teacher; the community at large, that of a very useful member—she was recommendable for her unfeigned piety, suavity of manners, and integrity of conduct. [WF, Wed. 8 AUG 1804, p. 3]

DIED—on Wednesday last, the 8th inst. [i.e. 8 AUG 1804], Mr. JESSE DEWEES, merchant of this place. [WF, Sat., 11 AUG 1804, p. 3]

Yesterday afternoon [i.e. 22 AUG 1804], the Printing Office of Mr. Way, in the City, was struck by lightning, and a very promising youth, JOHN M'DONALD, an apprentice, killed ... [WF, Thurs., 23 AUG 1804, p. 2]

DIED—on Thursday last [i.e. 30 AUG 1804], at George-Town, Mrs. MARY LAIRD, wife of Mr. John Laird, Merchant. [WF, Sat., 1 SEP 1804, p. 3]

DIED—on the morning of Tuesday last [i.e. 28 AUG 1804], after a short but severe illness, Mr. FRANCIS M'CLURE, printer, in Washington. On Wednesday morning he was interred in the public burying ground east of the Capitol. Having been a member of one of the Masonic Lodges and also of the Light Infantry Company, a procession was formed for the purpose of accompanying the Corpse to the place of interment, of which the following is the order ... reading the burying ground 'till near two. Having arrived there the body was deposited in the grave, and the burial service was read in an impressive manner by the Rev. Mr. M'Cormick ... [WF, Sat., 1 SEP 1804, p. 3]

Departed this life on the 26th of August [i.e. 26 AUG 1804], after a short illness, Miss ELIZABETH DONCASTLE, who resided in this town for upwards of twenty years; esteemed by all that knew her for her sincerity, piety and manly sense ... [WF, Wed. 12 SEP 1804, p. 3]

Died lately [no date], in George Town, Col. CHARLES BEATTY. [WF, Wed. 26 SEP 1804, p. 3]

Departed this life on the 20th inst. [i.e. 20 SEP 1804], JAMES PAXTON, late of Trenton, N.J., aged 55 years. [WF, Wed. 26 SEP 1804, p. 3]

The loss the public has sustained by the death of Dr. GUSTAVUS RICHARD BROWN of Port-Tobacco, is irreparable to the present generation ... [WF, Sat., 13 OCT 1804, p. 3]

Doctor ALEXANDER MITCHELL, to whose memory these few lines are dedicated by the hand of friendship, was a native of Scotland. He removed early to this country, where he finished his medical education. He died at Bladensburg on the 28th day of September last [i.e. 28 SEP 1804], in the 36 year of his age ... Dr. Mitchell, tho' for several weeks laboring under a severe ague and fever, could not be prevailed on to relax from his professional avocations, which were uncommonly great ... He was called for to a poor man on a rainy night, when a high fever was just yielding to a profuse perspiration. In this dangerous

Georgetown, D.C., **Marriage and Death Notices, 1801-1838**

situation he braved the inclemency of the weather, to visit his patient, and never recovered from the shock ... [WF, Sat., 13 OCT 1804, p. 3]

MARRIED on Tuesday Evening last [i.e. 8 JAN 1805], by the Right Rev. Bishop Neale, Capt. IGNATIUS MANNING, of St. Mary's Co., Md., to Miss MARY SEWALL, the 2d daughter of Capt. C. Sewall of Alexandria Co., Columbia. [WF, Sat., 12 JAN 1805, p. 2]

MARRIED—on the 7th inst. [i.e. 7 APR 1805], by the Rev. Mr. Sayers, Mr. CHARLES COOLIDGE, of Boston, to Miss HETTY TEMPLEMAN, of Georgetown. [WF, Wed. 10 APR 1805, p. 2]

DIED, in George-Town, on Monday last [i.e. 3 JUN 1805], after a short but painful illness, Miss ANNE HEUGHES. A firm and vigorous faith in her Redeemer deprived Death of his Sting, and the Grave of its horrors ... Her Funeral Discourse will be delivered in the Episcopal Church by the Rev'd. Mr. Sayrs next Sunday at half past 10 A.M. [WF, Wed. 5 JUN 1805, p. 2]

Married, on Monday evening last [i.e. 18 NOV 1805], by the Revd. Mr. Balch, Mr. PETER MEEM, age 69, to Mrs. M'FEE, age 54, both of George-Town. [WF, Thurs., 21 NOV 1805, p. 2]

DIED, at his house at Windsor, (Conn.) on the 26th Nov. [i.e. 26 NOV 1807], at 12 o'clock, OLIVER ELLSWORTH, aged 62 years ... [WF, Wed. 23 DEC 1807, p. 2]

MARRIED on Wednesday evening the 20th inst. [i.e. 20 JUL 1808], by the Rev. Mr. Lawrie, Mr. JEHIEL CROSSFIELD, printer, to Miss MARGARET ELEANOR TOWNSEND TRIPLETT, both of the City of Washington. [WF, Sat., 22 JUL 1808, p. 2]

MARRIED—on Tuesday Evening the 26th inst. [i.e. 26 JUL 1808], by the Rev. Mr. Sargent, Mr. JOSEPH THAW, to the amiable Miss ELIZA WOODSIDE, daughter of Mr. John Woodside, clerk in the Treasury Department. [WF, Sat., 30 JUL 1808, p. 3]

OBITUARY. Rarely doth the record of death receive upon its dark list, a kindred spirit to the beloved and amiable consort of Richard Harrison, Esq., auditor of the Treasury of the United States. The melancholy duty to enrol on its gloomy page the name of Mrs. ANN HARRISON, the victim of a long and most severe illness .... [WF, Wed. 3 AUG 1808, p. 2]

In consequence of the death of one of the Publisher's [William A. Rind] Children, the appearance of the paper has been delayed till this Evening. [WF, Wed. 3 AUG 1808, p. 2]

DIED yesterday morning [i.e. 24 AUG 1808], Mrs. NANCY LOVE, wife of Mr. Charles Love, of this town. She was blest with an amiable sweetness of temper. Her heart was genuous and liberal. She possessed the tender sensibilities of human nature, and an indulgent husband found in her an endearing and affectionate wife. [WF, Thurs., 25 AUG 1808, p. 2]

Was married on Tuesday Evening last [i.e. 6 SEP 1808], in this Town, by the Rev. Thomas Sargent, JOHN B. PATTON, Esq., to the amiable Miss REBECCA BUTCHER, daughter

Georgetown, D.C., Marriage and Death Notices, 1801-1838

of Mr. Jonathan Butcher—all of Alexandria. [Note: Corrected in issue September 10, 1808, p. 2, to the daughter of Mr. Job Butcher, of Philadelphia] [WF, Thurs., 8 SEP 1808, p. 2]

MARRIED, on Wednesday the 28th ult. [i.e. 28 SEP 1808], at the Friend's Meeting House in Washington, Mr. ARNOLD BOONE, of Montgomery Co., to Miss BETSEY SHOEMAKER, of the District of Columbia ... [WF, Sat., 1 OCT 1808, p. 3]

MARRIED, on Sunday evening last [i.e. 16 OCT 1808], by the Rev. Mr. Sargeant, Mr. NINIAN BEALL, of Washington City, to Miss RACHEL GROVES, of Georgetown. [WF, Tues., 18 OCT 1808, p. 3]

MARRIED, on Tuesday evening [i.e. 15 NOV 1808], by the Reverend Mr. M'Cormick, NICHOLAS ROOSEVELT, Esq. of the City of N.Y., to Miss LATROBE, daughter of B.H. Latrobe, Esq., Surveyor of the Public Buildings of the United States. [WF, Thurs., 17 NOV 1808, p. 3]

DIED—on Saturday morning the 19th inst. [i.e. 19 NOV 1808], Mrs. SIMMONS, wife of William Simmons, Accountant of the War Department. [WF, Tues., 22 NOV 1808, p. 3]

DIED last Friday morning [i.e. 25 NOV 1808], at his seat near Green Castle, in Franklin Co., Maj. Gen. ROBERT JOHNSTON, aged fifty eight years ... [WF, Sat., 3 DEC 1808, p. 3]

DIED, on the 15th October [i.e. 15 OCT 1808], at Westham, Middlesex (Eng.), Dr. JAMES ANDERSON, well known for his numerous workings on Agriculture, Political Economy, &c. [WF, Thurs., 29 DEC 1808, p. 3]

MARRIED, at Annapolis, on Tuesday the 27th ult. [i.e. 27 DEC 1808], by the Rev. Mr. Judd, Mr. ROBERT GETTY, merchant of this town, to Miss MARGARET WILMOT, of the former place. [WF, Thurs., 5 JAN 1809, p. 3]

MARRIED, on Thursday last [i.e. 29 DEC 1808], by the Rev. Mr. M'Cormick, Mr. GEORGE BALTZER, of this town, to Miss SUSANNA WEBB, eldest daughter of Thomas Webb, Esq., of *Lowe's Rest*, Montgomery Co., Md. [WF, Thurs., 5 JAN 1809, p. 3]

MARRIED on Tuesday evening, the 17th inst. [i.e. 17 JAN 1809], by the Rev. Mr. John Fenwick, Mr. JAMES MURRAY, to the amiable and accomplished Miss SARAH GREEN, both of Charles Co. [WF, Thurs., 19 JAN 1809, p. 3]

Departed this life on Monday morning, the 9th inst. [i.e. 9 JAN 1809], in this place, Capt. THOMAS CHILTON, of Loudoun Co., Va. ... [WF, Thurs., 19 JAN 1809, p. 3]

DIED, on the 15th inst. [i.e. 15 JAN 1809], at his seat in Bladensburg, BENJAMIN LOWNDES, Esq., aged 59 ... [WF, Thurs., 19 JAN 1809, p. 3]

Among those whom death has taken out of this transitory life, the name of Mr. JOHN HENDERSON, who expired on the 15th inst. [i.e. 15 JAN 1809], in the 40th year of his age,

Georgetown, D.C., **Marriage and Death Notices, 1801-1838**

is added to the list. Mr. Henderson was, in the strictest sense of the word, an honest man ... [WF, Thurs., 19 JAN 1809, p. 3]

Departed this life on the night of the 17th inst. [i.e. 17 JAN 1809], at his residence in Port Tobacco, Charles Co., Dr. JOHN DYSON, who was on that day forty one years of age.—In him shone forth with uncommon lustre all the social affections of husband, father, brother and friend for in his death, his disconsolate widow and infant children have lost a kind tender husband, and affectionate father ... [WF, Sat., 28 JAN 1809, p. 3]

MARRIED, on Monday evening last [i.e. 6 FEB 1809], by the Rev. Mr. Balch, Mr. WILLIAM FLEMING REED to Miss CHARLOTTE AUGUSTA MATILDA STENGER. [WF, Thurs., 9 FEB 1809, p. 2]

MARRIED—on Thursday evening last [i.e. 16 FEB 1809], by the Rev. Mr. Mathews, Mr. THOMAS JOHNSON, to Miss TERESA DIXON. [WF, Sat., 18 FEB 1809, p. 3]

Georgetown, D.C., **Marriage and Death Notices, 1801-1838**

GEORGETOWN INDEPENDENT AMERICAN
July 29, 1809 to January 5, 1811

MARRIED, on Thursday evening, the 27th inst. [i.e. 27 JUL 1809], by the Rev. Mr. Balch, Mr. STEPHEN RIGDEN, to Miss ELIZABETH GLOYD, both of this place. [IA, Sat., 29 JUL 1809, p. 3]

Departed this life, on Saturday the 6th inst. [i.e. 6 AUG 1809], after a severe and painful indisposition, which she bore with Christian fortitude, Mrs. SARAH M'MAHON, the amiable and much beloved consort of Mr. William M'Mahon, of Cumberland, Md. [IA, Sat., 25 AUG 1809, p. 3]

DIED, on Saturday the 16th inst. [i.e. 16 SEP 1809], Mrs. SARAH SMITH, the amiable consort of Maj. Walter Smith, of this town, and daughter of Mr. and Mrs. Hoffman, of the city of Baltimore, in the 26th year of her age. Her funeral procession, exceeded by no former example in this town, for number or respectability, moved from her late dwelling about 4 o'clock, P.M., on the 17th, to the Episcopal church, where after the appropriate introductory services, a discourse suited to the solemn occasion was delivered by the Rev. Mr. Addison, grounded on these impressive words, "Nevertheless not my will, but thine be done." Her remains were after the service, removed to the Presbyterian burying ground, where they were laid to rest ... [IA, Tues., 19 SEP 1809, p. 3]

MARRIED, on Thursday evening, the 21st ult. [i.e. 21 SEP 1809], by the Rev. Mr. Streight, of Winchester, Capt. FIELDER LUCKETT, of Alexandria, to the truly amiable Miss ELIZABETH WILLIS, youngest daughter of Mr. Rich. Willis, of Jefferson Co., Va. [IA, Tues., 3 OCT 1809, p. 3]

MARRIED, at Baltimore, by the Rt. Rev. Bishop Carroll, WM. LEE, Esq., of this Town, to Miss MARY L. HOLLIDAY, of that city. [IA, Thurs., 12 OCT 1809, p. 3]

Married, in this town, on Tuesday evening last [i.e. 10 OCT 1809], by the Rev. Mr. Wiley, JOHN R. WILSON, Esq., of New York, to Miss HARRIOT BALCH, of this place. [IA, Thurs., 12 OCT 1809, p. 3]

DIED, on the 9th ult. [i.e. 9 SEP 1809], after a short illness, Mrs. BARCLAY, wife of the Rev. Francis Barclay, Rector of William & Mary Parish, St. Mary's County. [IA, Thurs., 12 OCT 1809, p. 3]

DIED.—On board the ship Powhatan, on the passage from London, Mrs. CHARLOTTE S. GAMBLE, wife of John Gamble, Esq., of Richmond. [IA, Sat., 4 NOV 1809, p. 2]

MARRIED, by the Rev. Walter D. Addison, on Thursday evening last [i.e. 3 NOV 1809], at the seat of Robert Beverly, Esq., Mr. THOMAS ROBERTSON, merchant, to Miss JANE BRADSHAW BEVERLY, both of this place. [IA, Tues., 7 NOV 1809, p. 3]

Georgetown, D.C., **Marriage and Death Notices, 1801-1838**

DIED, yesterday morning [i.e. 10 NOV 1809], about 5 o'clock, after a long and painful illness, which he bore with great fortitude, ROBERT PETER, Jun., of this town. His friends and acquaintances are requested to attend his funeral this evening at 3 o'clock. His funeral sermon will be delivered tomorrow, in the Presbyterian Church, at 11 o'clock, forenoon. [IA, Sat., 11 NOV 1809, p. 3]

Died, at Augusta, on the 23d ult. [i.e. 23 OCT 1809], Mr. DAVID BULL, of Hartford in Connecticut, but who has for a few years past, been a respectable merchant of that place.—This worthy young man had been on a summer's tour to the northward, and on his return he stopped a few days in Charleston, S.C., which place he left on Monday the 16th and the next day was attacked with a slight fever—he continued his journey, however, and arrived at that place on Friday greatly indisposed, medical aid was immediately called in, but the disease had then become too obstinate to yield to the skill of the physician, and on Monday, he closed his connexion with temporal things ... [IA, Tues., 14 NOV 1809, p. 2]

Died, in Pennsylvania Hospital, on the 9th inst. [i.e. 9 NOV 1809], ELEANOR CRAVAN; she was admitted about thirty-two years since a *destitute stranger*, very much deranged in her mind ... [IA, Tues., 14 NOV 1809, p. 2]

DIED, on the 16th of October [i.e. 16 OCT 1809], at his seat in Cornwallis's Neck, Charles Co., Maryland, after a long and acute illness, CHARLES PYE, Esq., in the 40th year of his age, leaving a widow and five children. [IA, Tues., 14 NOV 1809, p. 3]

DIED, at Georgetown, on the 13th inst. [i.e. 13 NOV 1809], at an advanced age, HENRY DARNALL, Esq., an ancient and respectable resident of Frederick Co., Maryland. In the death of this worthy gentleman the poor have to lament the loss of their best friend and patron.—His hand was ever open to relieve the distressed and indigent. His truly edifying and christian conduct uniformly exhibited through life is universally known and admired by the respectable and extensive circle of his acquaintance. He bore his short and painful illness with a christian fortitude ... [IA, Thurs., 16 NOV 1809, p. 3]

MARRIED.—On Thursday evening last [i.e. 16 NOV 1809], by the Rev. Mr. Balch, Mr. JOHN TURNER, to Miss ELIZABETH KURTZ, of this town. [IA, Sat., 18 NOV 1809, p. 3]

MARRIED, on Sunday evening last [i.e. 19 NOV 1809], by the Rev. Mr. Boswell, Mr. SIMEON MATLOCK, to Miss SARAH Y. DOVE, both of Washington. [IA, Tues., 21 NOV 1809, p. 3]

DIED, in the city of Washington on the 29th Nov. 1809, CALEB SWAN, Esq., late Paymaster General of the United States army—was a Revolutionary officer and from his known integrity and merit was appointed by General Washington in the year 1793 to that confidential office. [IA, Sat., 2 DEC 1809, p. 3]

MARRIED.—On Tuesday evening last [i.e. 5 DEC 1809], by the Rev. Mr. Addison, Capt. GEORGE PETER, of Georgetown, to Miss ANN PLATER, Daughter of Thomas Plater, Esq., of *Greenwood*, District [of] Columbia. [IA, Sat., 9 DEC 1809, p. 3]

Georgetown, D.C., **Marriage and Death Notices, 1801-1838**

DIED, at Georgetown, on the 6th inst. [i.e. 6 DEC 1809], in the 29th year of her age, Mrs. SUSANNA CARBERRY, widow of the late John B. Carberry. She was an endearing and most beloved friend—and throughout a long and fatiguing illness, her pious resignation gave a rare and exemplary proof of the efficiency of virtue ... [IA, Sat., 9 DEC 1809, p. 3]

Departed this life on Sunday night last [i.e. 17 DEC 1809], after a short illness, in the thirty-third year of her age, Mrs. CATHERINE MOUNTZ, consort of Mr. John Mountz, Jun., of this Town. [IA, Tues., 19 DEC 1809, p. 3]

MARRIED, on Tuesday evening the 19th inst. [i.e. 18 DEC 1809], by the Rev. Mr. Addison, Mr. JOHN R. RITTENHOUSE, to Miss HARRIOTT BEVERLEY, sister of Robert Beverley, Esq., of this place. [IA, Thurs., 28 DEC 1809, p. 3]

MARRIED, on Sunday evening last [i.e. 14 JAN 1810], by the Rev. Mr. Foxall, Mr. JOHN FRANK, Printer, of Washington City, to Miss MARY TUTTLE, of this town. [IA, Tues., 16 JAN 1810, p. 3]

MARRIED, On Tuesday the 23d inst. [i.e. 23 JAN 1810], by the Rev. Mr. Balch, Mr. BAPTISE MAUPIN to Miss CATHARINE FLISSET, both of Washington. [IA, Thurs., 25 JAN 1810, p. 3]

MARRIED, on Tuesday the 30th ult. [i.e. 30 JAN 1810], by the Rev. Mr. Balch, Mr. PHILIP BUSSARD, to Miss MARGARET HAZEL, all of this town. [IA, Thurs., 1 FEB 1810, p. 3]

DIED, on Tuesday evening last [i.e. 8 FEB 1810], after a lingering illness which he bore with resignation, Mr. ANDREW HOOVER, a respectable citizen of this town. He has left a wife and several small children to deplore his loss. [IA, Thurs., 15 FEB 1810, p. 3]

Departed this life at Chillicothe, on the 20th ult. [i.e. 20 JAN 1810], of a dropsical complaint, in the 27th year of his age, Dr. RICHARD BROWN, son of the late William Brown of Alexandria ... [IA, Thurs., 15 FEB 1810, p. 3]

MARRIED, on Thursday evening last [i.e. 15 FEB 1810], by the Rev. Mr. Balch, Mr. JEREMIAH DUFIEF, to Mrs. MARY WELLS, both of this town. [IA, Sat., 17 FEB 1810, p. 3]

MARRIED, on Sunday evening last [i.e. 25 FEB 1809], by the Rev. Mr. Addison, Mr. WILLIAM GRAYSON, of this place, to Miss MARY THRELKELD, daughter of John Threlkeld, Esq., of *Burleath*, District of Columbia. [IA, Sat., 3 MAR 1809, p. 3, and Tues., 6 MAR 1810, p. 3]

DEATHS. In the City of Washington, on the 17th inst. [i.e. 17 MAR 1810], in the 55th year of her age, Mrs. ELLENOR SPEAKE, formerly of Charles [County]. [IA, Thurs., 22 MAR 1810, p. 3]

Georgetown, D.C., **Marriage and Death Notices, 1801-1838**

DIED, on Thursday last [i.e. 29 MAR 1810], in this place, in the 19th year of her age, Miss JANE PETER. To her friends and relations her loss is great; to herself the change immortal gain ... [IA, Sat., 31 MAR 1810, p. 3]

DIED, in Georgetown, last evening [i.e. 18 MAY 1810], Mr. ROBERT SUTER, aged 31, lat of the city of Baltimore. His funeral will take place at 5 o'clock, P.M., tomorrow, from the house of Mr. Alexander Suter, in Bridge street, which his friends and acquaintances are requested to attend without further notice. [IA, Sat., 19 MAY 1810, p. 3]

DIED, at Higham (Mass.), Major General BENJAMIN LINCOLN. How great and how good this compatriot of Washington was, the present generation know; the historian has recorded; and posterity will delight to remember. [IA, Sat., 19 MAY 1810, p. 3]

MARRIED.—On Thursday evening last [i.e. 17 MAY 1810], by the Rev. Mr. Addison, Mr. THOMAS B. DASHIEL, to the amiable Miss KEZIAH A. COUZINS, both of W. city. [IA, Tues., 22 MAY 1810, p. 3]

MARRIED.—On Tuesday evening the 22d inst. [i.e. 22 MAY 1810], by the Rev. Mr. Addison, Mr. JEREMIAH W. BRONAUGH, to Miss ELIZABETH H. MITCHELL, daughter of the late Capt. John Mitchell, all of this place. [IA, Thurs., 31 MAY 1810, p. 3]

MARRIED.—On Tuesday evening last [i.e. 29 MAY 1810], by the Rev. Mr. Balch, Mr. PETER RETTER to Mrs. TERESA LYON, all of this place. [IA, Thurs., 31 MAY 1810, p. 3]

MARRIED.—On Tuesday evening last [i.e. 29 MAY 1810], by the Rev. Mr. Addison, Doct. GEORGE CLARK, to Miss MARIA BEVERLEY, daughter of Robert Beverley, Esq. [IA, Sat., 2 JUN 1810, p. 3]

MARRIED.—On Thursday evening the 31st ult. [i.e. 31 MAY 1810], by the Reverend Francis Neale, Mr. JOHN SHERLOCK, to Miss SARAH ANN POOLE, all of this place. [IA, Tues., 5 JUN 1810, p. 3]

Died, in Philadelphia, on the 13th inst. [i.e. 13 JUN 1810], Maj. DENNIS HART, formerly an officer in the British army. [IA, Sat., 16 JUN 1810, p. 3]

Married, on Tuesday evening the 12th inst. [i.e. 12 JUN 1810], by the Rev. S.B. Balch, Mr. WILLIAM PEERCE, to Miss HARRIET T. GAITHER, eldest daughter of Mrs. Mary Gaither, all of this place. [IA, Sat., 23 JUN 1810, p. 3]

MARRIED, on Sunday last [i.e. 24 JUN 1810], by the Rev. Stephen Bloomer Balch, Mr. REUBEN WHIPS, to Miss NANCY LAYLAND, both of this place. [IA, Tues., 26 JUN 1810, p. 3]

MARRIED.—On Monday evening the 16th inst. [i.e. 16 JUL 1810], by the Rev. Mr. Fenwick, THOMAS C. BOARMAN, to Miss MARY LOUISA BOARMAN, all of this place. [IA, Wed. 25 JUL 1810, p. 3]

Georgetown, D.C., **Marriage and Death Notices, 1801-1838**

MARRIED.—By the Rev. Walter D. Addison, on Sunday evening last [i.e. 22 JUL 1810], Mr. PETER LEXIS, to the amiable Miss ANN HILLSANDERS, both of this place. [IA, Sat., 28 JUL 1810, p. 3]

DIED, yesterday [i.e. 31 JUL 1810], about 3 o'clock P.M., SAMUEL DAVIDSON, Esq., aged 63 years, and many years a respectable inhabitant of this town. His friends are invited to attend the funeral this evening at five o'clock, from his late residence at the Union Tavern. August 1, 1810. [IA, Wed. 1 AUG 1810, p. 3]

DIED. In Washington city, yesterday morning [i.e. 4 SEP 1810], Col. JOHN WHITING, of the fifth regiment of the United States' infantry, aged about 54. He has left behind him a numerous family of children to lament his loss—a loss which nothing on this side of heaven can compensate. Honest, frank and manly, he was esteemed and beloved by all who knew him. With the ardent feelings of a revolutionary soldier he blended that genuine philanthropy which endears its possessor to all mankind. *National Intelligencer.* [IA, Wed. 5 SEP 1810, p. 3]

Married, on Sunday last [i.e. 16 SEP 1810], by the Rev. Mr. Hoskins, Mr. TOBIAS MATTHEWS of the city of Washington, to the amiable & accomplished Miss SARAH ANN BOOSE, of Prince George's Co., Md. [IA, Wed. 19 SEP 1810, p. 3]

Died, in New York, on Wednesday afternoon last [i.e. 19 SEP 1810], in the 38th year of his age, Mr. JAMES CHEETHAM, editor of the *American Citizen.* [IA, Wed. 26 SEP 1810, p. 3]

Died, at Scituate, (Mass.) on the 13th inst. [i.e. 13 SEP 1810], Hon. WM. CUSHING, aged 77, one of the associate Justices of the U.S. Court. [IA, Wed. 26 SEP 1810, p. 3]

DIED, on Tuesday last [i.e. 2 OCT 1810], at Georgetown, Col., WILLIAM AUGUSTINE WASHINGTON, in the 53d year of his age. The character of this gentleman is righteously portrayed in the short but descriptive expression of "the most amiable man." [IA, Sat., 6 OCT 1810, p. 3]

DIED. On Sunday last [i.e. 4 NOV 1810, suddenly, in Hampton, Com. SAMUEL BARRON, of the United States Navy, and late commander of a squadron in the Mediterranean. Com. Barron, was one of those Americans, who French violence and injustice, induced to quit the peaceable and lucrative merchant service, to meet the enemy of his country in arms, at that honorable epoch of American history, the year 1798. He was first appointed commander of the Augusta brig, a vessel equipped by the citizens of Norfolk, and in compliment to whom, their favorite barron was appointed to command ... was appointed to command in the Mediterranean against the bay of Tripoli ... Within a few months past, he was appointed to the superintendence of the naval arsenal at Gosport, an employment which he accepted, and would discharge with advantage to the service, and with credit to himself ... [IA, Wed. 7 NOV 1810, p. 3]

Georgetown, D.C., **Marriage and Death Notices, 1801-1838**

DIED, on the 13th inst. [i.e. 13 NOV 1810], Mrs. DELAPLANE, consort of Mr. Joseph Delaplane, of this town, leaving an affectionate husband and two children to lament their irreparable loss. [IA, Wed. 14 NOV 1810, p. 3]

Schooner *Hamilton*, [Capt.] Boyd, on her passage to Barbadoes from this place, was run down on the night of the 16th ult. [i.e. 16 OCT 1810], by a British man of war, and so materially injured, that from 130 to 150 barrels of flour were thrown overboard.
—On the 22d of the same month [i.e. 22 OCT 1810], within two day's sail of Turk's Island, Mr. GEORGE MOUNTZ (merchant of this place, and supercargo of the above vessel), was unfortunately washed overboard, and drowned. The loss of this amiable young man, is an event deeply to be regretted by every friend of genuine merit. He was an ornament to society, and bid fair to be an honor to his country. [IA, Wed. 23 NOV 1810, p. 3]

MARRIED.—On Thursday evening [i.e. 6 DEC 1810], Mr. DAVID SOMERVILLE, to Miss JANE UNDERWOOD, both of Washington. [IA, Tues., 11 DEC 1810, p. 3]

MARRIED, in Baltimore, on Friday evening last [i.e. 7 DEC 1810], Mr. RICHARD HOBURG, to Miss ELIZABETH RICE, of Georgetown, [Columbia]. [IA, Tues., 11 DEC 1810, p. 3]

DIED, at Leesburg, (Va.) on Saturday morning last [i.e. 8 DEC 1810], Mr. EDWARD CARTER STANARD, Editor and proprietor of the *Spirit of '76*. He has left a widow and two children to bemoan his loss. [IA, Thurs., 13 DEC 1810, p. 3]

Departed this life on the 17th inst. (Dec.) [i.e. 17 DEC 1810], in the 44th year of her age, Mrs. SARAH RUSSEL CONTEE, wife of the Rev. Dr. Benjamin Contee. This lady gave in the dawn of youth a presage of that sweetness, goodness and excellence, which increasing years happily improved and matured. She was exemplary and estimable in every walk in which she was engaged through life—lovely and beloved. Her death is deeply felt and sincerely lamented. [IA, Thurs., 27 DEC 1810, p. 3]

Departed this life in the month of November last, of a pulmonary complaint, in the Island of Barbados, Mr. WILLIAM S. BELT, Jr., of this town. He bore a lingering and cruel disease, with the mild and calm resignation of a christian ... [IA, Sat., 29 DEC 1810, p. 3]

MARRIED, on Thursday, 20th ult. [i.e. 20 DEC 1810], Mr. JAMES CASSIN, Merchant, to Miss T. DEAKINS, daughter of Leonard Deakins, Esq., all of this place. [IA, Sat., 5 JAN 1811, p. 3]

MARRIED, Tuesday the 1st January [i.e. 1 JAN 1811], Mr. SAMUEL FITZHUGH, Merchant of this place, to Miss ELEANOR CHISHOLM, of Washington City. [IA, Sat., 5 JAN 1811, p. 3]

Georgetown, D.C., **Marriage and Death Notices, 1801-1838**

THE DAILY FEDERAL REPUBLICAN
January 3, 1814, to March 31, 1816

Married in Baltimore, on Tuesday evening last [i.e. 4 JAN 1814], by the Most Reverend Archbishop Carroll, ROBERT Y. BRENT, Esq., of the City of Washington, to Miss ELIZA L. CARRERE, daughter of John Carrere, Esq., of that city. [DFR:7 JAN 1814, p. 3]

Died, on Sunday morning the 9th inst. [i.e. 9 JAN 1814], in the 54th year of her age, Mrs. MARY MITCHELL, consort of the late Capt. John Mitchell. [DFR:17 JAN 1814, p. 3]

Married on the 18th inst. [i.e. 18 JAN 1814], at French Town, by the Rev. Mr. Farrell, PHILIP HARDING, Esq., cashier of the Elkton Bank of Maryland, to the amiable and accomplished Miss AMELIA GILES, daughter of the late Thomas Giles, both of Elkton. [DFR:25 JAN 1814, p. 3]

Married, near Middleburg, Va., on the 5th inst. [i.e. 5 JAN 1814], by the Rev. Wm. Williamson, LLOYD NOLAND, Esq., to Miss ANN W. POWELL, daughter of Burr Powell, all of Loudoun Co. [DFR:29 JAN 1814, p. 3]

Married on the 3d inst. [i.e. 3 FEB 1814], by the Rev. Mr. Gibson, the Rev. WALTER D. ADDISON, to Mrs. REBECCA MACKALL, daughter of William Bayly, Esq., of Prince George's Co. [DFR:7 FEB 1814, p. 3]

Departed this life on Tuesday the 8th inst. [i.e. 8 FEB 1814], after a lingering illness, Mrs. ANN PETER, the wife of Capt. George Peter, in the 23d year of her age. In the death of this excellent lady, her relatives, her friends, and society, have sustained an irreparable & painful loss ... [DFR:10 FEB 1814, p. 3]

Obituary. Died lately at Lexington, (Kentucky) Miss CAROLINE LAURENS SMITH, youngest daughter of the Rev. Dr. Samuel S. Smith, formerly president of Princeton College ... [DFR:17 FEB 1814, p. 3]

Married, at Rockville, Montgomery Co., on the 15th inst. [i.e. 15 FEB 1814], by the Rev. Mr. Read, JOHN STRODE, Esq., of Martinsburgh, Va., to Miss ELIZA MARTIN, daughter of Honore Martin, Esq., of the former place. [DFR:18 FEB 1814, p. 3]

Married on Tuesday evening the 15th inst. [i.e. 15 FEB 1814], by the Rev. Mr. Wilmer, Mr. HENRY O. MIDDLETON, of this town, to Miss ANN H. TOLSON, daughter of Francis Tolson, Esq., of Prince George's Co., Md. [DFR:22 FEB 1814, p. 3]

Married on Saturday last [i.e. 26 FEB 1814], by the Rev. Mr. Brown, Col. LAVAL, of the first light dragoons, to Miss SOPHIE VILLARD, daughter of A.J. Villard, of Washington City. [DFR:4 MAR 1814, p. 3]

Georgetown, D.C., **Marriage and Death Notices, 1801-1838**

Died, on the 23d of February [i.e. 23 FEB 1814], at *Sully*, in Fairfax Co., Va., the seat of Francis L. Lee, Esq., Mrs. JANE BEVERLY, consort of Carter Beverly, Esq. The most amiable, and truly interesting lady, was cut off at only a few days notice. She met her end with pious resignation, and has gone to the awful audit, with those rare excellencies that prepared for alike for the prosperity and adversity that marked her course in this life. She has left a numerous young progeny to the kindness of the world, with the inviting recommendation of her many virtues. [DFR:5 MAR 1814, p. 3]

Died, in the city of Philadelphia, on the 2d inst. [i.e. 2 MAR 1814], the Rev. GEORGE RICHARDS. [DFR:8 MAR 1814, p. 3]

Died, on Wednesday evening the 23d ult. [i.e. 23 FEB 1814] at the advanced age of 90 years, Dr. UPTON SCOTT, a native of Ireland, but for more than 60 years a most distinguished inhabitant of this city. Society seldom mourns the loss of a more excellent and valuable member, than the venerable man whose decease we now record. Through the course of a life, protracted far beyond the ordinary span of human existence, his career has been one unbroken tenor of virtue, dignity, and usefulness. Pure in his principles, discerning in his judgment, unshaken in his attachments, he has been the hereditary counselor and friend of many generations, and has enjoyed the successive confidence and affection of grandsire, son and father, who have been successively enlightened by his wisdom, and ennobled by his friendship. [DFR:8 MAR 1814, p. 3]

Departed this life, on Wednesday, the 2d inst. [i.e. 2 MAR 1814], in the 13th year of his age, JOHN HENRY CHAPMAN, eldest son of Maj. Henry H. Chapman, of Charles Co. ... [DFR:17 MAR 1814, p. 3]

Obituary. Died, 4 o'clock on the 21st inst. [i.e. 21 MAR 1814], at the residence of her eldest son, Gen. Walter Smith, Mrs. ESTHER SMITH, relict of Dr. Walter Smith, aged 70 years. Mrs. Smith was among the oldest and most respectable inhabitants of this town ... Those of her children whose contiguity of residence gave them the opportunity to witness the removal of a mother "loved so long," and who had, by their fond and affectionate attentions, woven themselves intimately with every fibre of her heart, received from her dying lips the most dignified of all legacies ... [DFR:24 MAR 1814, p. 3]

Died on Monday night last [i.e. 28 MAR 1814], at *Green Hill*, the seat of Thomas Plater, Esq., Master GEORGE PETER, eldest son of Capt. George Peter, in the fourth year of his age ... [DFR:1 APR 1814, p. 3]

Married, on Tuesday the 12th inst. [i.e. 12 APR 1814], by the Rev. Mr. Matthews, Mr. CHRISTOPHER ANDREWS, of Washington city, to Miss HENRIETTA MARIA WEBB, daughter of Mr. Thos. Webb, of Montgomery Co. [DFR:15 APR 1814, p. 3

The following obituary notice of the Hon. SAMUEL ALLYNE OTIS, late Secretary of the Senate of the United States, is copied from the *Boston Paladium*. This much lamented fellow-citizen was son of the late Hon. James Otis, of Barnstable, whose life was devoted to the service of his country, and brother of the celebrated scholar, statesman and patriot of the same name, who led the way to the American revolution. Imbued with a strong

Georgetown, D.C., Marriage and Death Notices, 1801-1838

attachment to the principles of his father, and eldest brother, and liberally educated under their influence, Mr. Otis was himself an early and decided friend to the liberties of his country. In 1776, he was chosen a Representative for Boston, and afterwards to the Convention which framed the Constitution of Mass. ... [DFR:7 MAY 1814, p. 3]

Died on Monday last [i.e. 2 MAY 1814] at Philadelphia, after a short illness, the Hon. NICHOLAS GILMAN, senator of the United States from New-Hampshire. [DFR:9 MAY 1814, p. 3]

Married on Thursday evening, 5th inst. [i.e. 5 MAY 1814], by the Rev. Francis Moore, Mr. JOSEPH DELAPLANE to Miss JULIANA HINKLE, daughter of Mr. Samuel Hinkle, of Jefferson Co., Va. [DFR:17 MAY 1814, p. 3]

Died in Boston on the 11th inst. [i.e. 11 MAY 1814], the Hon. ROBERT TREAT PAINE, Æt. eighty-four years. He was late one of the judges of the Supreme Court—had filled many other important offices—was one of the earliest advocates of our Revolution, and before his disease was one of the very few distinguished surviving statesmen who signed the declaration of Independence. He remained faithful to the end. [DFR:24 MAY 1814, p. 3]

Married, on the 19th inst. [i.e. 19 MAY 1814], by the Rev. Mr. Balch, Mr. WM. THOMSON, to the amiable Miss ELIZABETH BALTZER, both of this town. [DFR:25 MAY 1814, p. e]

Married. In Newport, on the 17th inst. [i.e. 17 MAY 1814], by the Rev. Mr. Towle, Capt. ROBERT D. WAINWRIGHT, of the U.S. Marines, to Miss JUARIA M. AUCHMUTY, eldest daughter of the late Robert N. Auchmuty, Esq., of Newport. [DFR:30 MAY 1814, p. 3]

Married. At Mount Hope, (Bristol) on Monday evening the 16th inst. [i.e. 16 MAY 1814], by the Rev. Mr. White, Lieut. RAYMOND H.J. PERRY, of the U.S. Navy, to Miss MARY ANN D'WOLFE, daughter of James D'Wolfe, Esq., of Bristol. [DFR:30 MAY 1814, p. 3]

Married on Sunday evening, 5th inst. [i.e. 5 JUN 1814], by the Rev. Mr. Balch, Mr. DANIEL KURTZ, to Miss MARY LYON, both of this town. [DFR:7 JUN 1814, p. 3]

Died, at Wiscasset, in Maine, on Wednesday, 8th inst. [i.e. 8 JUN 1814], suddenly, after having been the day previous in the exercise of his official duties on the bench of the supreme Judicial court, the Hon. SAMUEL SEWALL, Chief Justice of Mass. ... He was, in the year 1800, appointed a Judge of the Supreme Judicial Court in which station he remained until, on the lamented death of the late Chief Justice Parsons, he was promoted to the highest judicial office in the Commonwealth ... [DFR:18 JUN 1814, p. 3]

Died, at Sandwich, on Friday last [i.e. 17 JUN 1814], Mr. JOSEPH GREENLIEF, bookseller, of this place [Boston]. He, with several other gentlemen, was amusing himself by shooting at a mark, and when in the act of stooping with a pistol in his hand, it accidentally went off and lodged the contents in his head. [DFR:21 JUN 1814, p. 3]

Death. Seldom have we to perform a task so painful, as the one in recording the death of

Georgetown, D.C., **Marriage and Death Notices, 1801-1838**

Mr. JOHN DICKSON, the Editor of the *Petersburg Intelligencer*. In announcing the departure of this truly valuable member of society, we acknowledge our inability to portray his deserving character—but feel a conviction that some zealous and more adequate pen, will hereafter reward the merits of our deceased fellow citizen. *Petersburg Republican*. [DFR:23 JUL 1814, p. 3]

Married at *Rosedale*, on Thursday the 21st inst. [i.e. 21 JUL 1814], by the Rev. Dr. Addison, JOHN GREEN, Esquire, of Md., to Miss ANN FORREST, second daughter of the late Gen. Uriah Forrest. [DFR:28 JUL 1814, p. 3]

Canandaigua [N.Y.], July 19. Death of Gen. Swift.—We have received the orders of Maj. Gen. Brown and Brig. Gen. P.B. Porter, dated Queenston Heights, July 12, announcing, that on Tuesday evening July 12 [i.e. 12 JUL 1814], Brig. Gen. JOHN SWIFT, of Palmyra, in this Co., was killed, in a most perfidious manner, by one of the enemy ... The General's body was taken to the American side of the Niagara, and on Wednesday last, at 6 o'clock, interred with the honors due to his rank ... [DFR:29 JUL 1814, p. 3]

Departed this life on Sunday the 31st July [i.e. 31 JUL 1814] at *Rich Hill*, his farm in Charles Co., Md., Mr. JOHN CHANDLER COX, aged about 28 years. In the death of Mr. Cox, his relatives have lost a tender and affectionate brother, and long will his friends and neighbors remember and lament his early end. [DFR:9 AUG 1814, p. 3]

Obituary. Departed this life, after a short but most severe illness of three days, on the 3d day of August, 1814, Mrs. ELIZABETH RINGGOLD, consort of Mr. Richard Ringgold of Chester Town, Kent Co., Md. ... [DFR:11 AUG 1814, p. 3]

Married on Thursday evening last [i.e. 11 AUG 1814], by the Rev. Mr. Neal, Mr. WILLIAM P. NOWLAND, to Miss MARY NORRIS, both of this town. [DFR:13 AUG 1814, p. 3]

Died on the 25th July [i.e. 25 JUL 1814], in Sassafras Neck, Cecil Co., Md., aged 27 years, Dr. DAVID DAVIS, son of the late Naylor Davis, of Prince George's Co. [DFR:13 AUG 1814, p. 3]

Obituary. Died on the evening of the 23d ult. [i.e. 23 AUG 1814] at his residence, *Kingston Hall*, Maj. HENRY JAMES CARROLL, of Somerset Co., Md., in the 47th year of his age ... [DFR:6 SEP 1814, p. 3]

Obituary. Died, on the 3d inst. [i.e. 3 SEP 1814], deeply lamented, Mrs. MARY B. TYLER, aged 28—consort of George Tyler, Esqr., of Prince George's Co. In the death of this amiable woman, society is deprived of a bright example of the domestic virtues—her numerous friends of one, who was endeared to them by many acts of unaffected kindness and zealous friendship, and three lovely children mourn the loss of a mother's watchful tenderness, in marking the progress of infant reason and forming their minds to piety and virtue. [DFR:23 SEP 1814, p. 3]

Obituary. Died, on the 14th day of August [i.e. 14 AUG 1814], in Charles Co., (Md.) Mrs. MARY LOUISA BOARMAN, consort of Mr. T.C. Boarman, and daughter of Mrs. Sarah T.

Georgetown, D.C., **Marriage and Death Notices, 1801-1838**

Boarman, of Charles Co., aged 22 years—In stating her death, it is but justice to add, that her loss is a subject of lamention to more than her relations; besides depriving her family of an innocent and virtuous member ... Mrs. Mary L. Boarman, left to lament her loss, a loving consort and an innocent child of only 4 years old. [DFR:1 OCT 1814, p. 3]

Departed this life on the 27th of October [i.e. 27 OCT 1814], in the 37th year of her age, after severe and protracted suffering, Mrs. REBECCA B. MAGRUDER, wife of Alexander C. Magruder, Esq. ... But for the four little cherubs she bequeathed to his care and affection ... [DFR:2 NOV 1814, p. 3]

Died, yesterday morning [i.e. 14 NOV 1814], of a pulmonary disorder, Mr. ROBERT LAMB, formerly of the house of *Maynard & Lamb*, Boston. ☞ The friends and acquaintance of the deceased, are respectfully requested to attend his funeral, this evening at 4 o'clock, from Mrs. Coolidge's, Bridge-street. [DFR:15 NOV 1814, p. 3]

Married, on the 10th inst. [i.e. 10 NOV 1814], by the Rev. Mr. Slemmers, Mr. WILLIAM DONE, son of Col. John Done, to Miss CHARLOTTE HAYNIE, all of Somerset Co., Md. [DFR:22 NOV 1814, p. 3]

Yesterday [i.e. 23 NOV 1814], a little after 1 o'clock, a message was received by the House of Representatives from the Senate, announcing the death of the Vice President of the United States [ELBRIDGE GERRY]. After the usual proceedings in such cases, the house adjourned. Mr. Gerry had left his lodgings earlier than common, after breakfast, to pay some visits, before taking his seat in the Senate. He was taken unwell at the last house he stopped at, and got into the back to return to his lodgings. When the driver stopped, though the distance was short, his Excellency groaned and expired before he was got into the house. Such are the circumstances of this melancholy event as related to us. [DFR:24 NOV 1814, p. 2]

Married on Thursday evening last [i.e. 24 NOV 1814], by the Rev. Mr. Balch, Mr. RICHARD WELLS, to Miss ELIZABETH BAILEY, all of this place. [DFC:28 NOV 1814, p. 3]

Married last evening [i.e. 29 DEC 1814], by the Rev. Mr. Brown, Mr. JAMES PENNINGTON, of Georgetown, to Miss ANNE MINCHER, of Washington City. [DFR:30 DEC 1814, Friday, p. 3]

Departed this life on Wednesday the 14th inst. [i.e. 14 DEC 1814], at his seat at *Mount Welby*, Prince George's Co., Md., sincerely and deservedly lamented by his family and friends, SAMUEL DeBUTTS, aged sixty-three years, a native of Sligo, in the Kingdom of Ireland, and many years a respectable citizen of these states. [DFR:5 JAN 1815, Thursday, p. 3]

Died, at Bladensburg, on Wednesday morning [i.e. 4 JAN 1815], in her 53d year, after a short illness, Mrs. DOROTHA LOWNDES, relict of Benjamin Lowndes, deceased. She was a lady of exemplary virtue and unsullied parity, whose departed excellence will be forever remembered and long lamented by a family of affectionate children. [DFR:6 JAN 1815, Friday, p. 3]

Georgetown, D.C., Marriage and Death Notices, 1801-1838

The frequency of deaths which have lately taken place at Alexandria, Bladensburg, and the neighborhood, by the progress of a malignant complaint resembling the Spotted Fever, has been such as to excite no little alarm. Not a day elapses that we do not hear of the death of some valuable member of society, under its fatal influence. [DFR:6 JAN 1815, Friday, p. 3]

Married, on Tuesday evening last [i.e. 31 JAN 1815], by the Rev. Mr. Balch, Mr. JOHN GULICK, of Princeton, N.J., to Miss MARGARET Y. WILEY, daughter of the late Rev. David Wiley, of this place. [DFR:2 FEB 1815, Thursday, p. 3]

MARRIED, on Tuesday evening last [i.e. 21 FEB 1815], by the Rev. Mr. Greentree, Mr. WM. DEMENT, Jr., of Charles Co., Md., to Miss JULIA E. KENNEDY, of this place. [DFR:23 FEB 1815, Thursday, p. 3]

Departed this life on the 22d inst. [i.e. 22 FEB 1815], at his residence in Washington City, SAMUEL HANSON BAKER, in the 43d year of his age ... [DFR:25 FEB 1815, Saturday, p. 3]

Died, in N.Y., on the 23d ult. [i.e. 23 FEB 1815], ROBERT FULTON, Esq., proprietor of the Steam-Boats. [DFR:1 MAR 1815, Wednesday, p. 3]

Departed this life on Monday morning, the 20th ult. [i.e. 20 FEB 1815], in his 56th year, Maj. THOMAS BEATTY, of this town.—A revolutionary officer, he distinguished himself during the perilous conflict for independence. He ha left an "extended circle of sympathy" to lament the death of the affectionate husband and father, the sincere friend and patriot. [DFR:2 MAR 1815, Thursday, p. 3]

DIED, on the 11th inst. [i.e. 11 MAR 1815], after a short illness, Mr. RICHARD WEEMS, of Prince George's Co., Md., aged 19 years. [DFR:16 MAR 1815, Thursday, p. 3]

From the *Fredericktown Herald*. Departed this life, at *Honey-wood*, in Berkeley Co., Va., on Sunday the 5th inst. [i.e. 5 MAR 1815], Mrs. JANE COLSTON, wife of Edward Colston, Esq., and daughter of the late Charles Marshall, Esq., of Fauquier Court-house ... [DFR:20 MAR 1815, Monday, p. 3]

MARRIED, on Thursday last [i.e. 16 MAR 1815], at the seat of Chas. W. Hanson, Esq., by the Right Rev. Bishop Kemp, the Hon. THOS. P. GROSVENOR, to Miss MARY J. HANSON. [DFR:22 MAR 1815, Wednesday, p. 3]

DIED, on Friday the 24th [i.e. 24 MAR 1815], after a severe illness of ten days, which she bore with truly Christian fortitude, Miss REBECCA P. TAYLOE, second daughter of Col. John Tayloe, of *Mount Airy*, Va. In the death of this young lady, who had scarcely reached her seventeenth year, an extensive circle of relatives and friends are involved in deep affliction ... [DFR:31 MAR 1815, Friday, p. 3]

DIED, at Alexandria, Pa., on the 12th inst. [i.e. 12 MAR 1815], the Rev. DAVID BARD, member of Congress from Pa. The deceased was on his return from Washington—was in apparent good health on Tuesday evening preceding his dissolution, but he was not permitted to reach his own residence before he was summoned to another world. He breathed his last at the house of Dr. Buchanan, his son-in-law, at 11 o'clock, A.M. [DFR:31 MAR 1815, Friday, p. 3]

Died, on the 17th Sept. [i.e. 17 SEP 1814], the Bey of Tunis—It was the last day of Ramadan (the Mahometan Lent) and this prince had fasted during 24 years ... [DFR:1 APR 1815, Saturday, p. 3]

Departed this life, after a short illness, Mrs. SARAH MACKEY, relict of Alexander Mackey. Her friends and acquaintance are particularly invited to the funeral this afternoon at four o'clock. [DFR:5 APR 1815, Wednesday, p. 3]

Married, at Alexandria, on the 4th of April [i.e. 4 APR 1815], by Dr. Muir, the Rev. JAMES LAURIE, of the city of Washington, to Mrs. ELIZABETH B. HALL, of the former place. [DFR:7 APR 1815, Friday, p. 3]

MARRIED, at Alexandria, on Sunday evening last [i.e. 2 APR 1815], by the Rev. Mr. Robbins, Mr. RICHARD THOMPSON, of this place, to Miss LYDIA HORNER, of the former place. [DFR:8 APR 1815, Saturday, p. 3]

Communicated. DIED, on Wednesday, the 5th inst. [i.e. 5 APR 1815] after a severe illness of 9 days, which she bore with christian fortitude, Mrs. MARY KING, consort of Mr. Joseph King, of this place.—She has left an affectionate husband, infant son, aged mother, and an extensive circle of relations and friends to lament her loss. She resigned her soul to her God, and met death with perfect resignation. [DFR:12 APR 1815, Wednesday, p. 3]

MARRIED, on Thursday evening last [i.e. 13 APR 1815], by the Rev. James Higgins, Capt. THOMAS GIST, to Miss HARRIET DORSEY, both of Frederick Co. [DFR:15 APR 1815, Saturday, p. 3]

MARRIED, on Thursday evening last [i.e. 20 APR 1815], in Montgomery Co., Md., by the Rev. Mr. Dashiells, Mr. ALEXANDER SUTER, of Washington City (D.C.), to Miss SUSANNAH READ, daughter of the Rev. Thomas Read, of the former place. [DFR:25 APR 1815, Tuesday, p. 3]

Communicated. DIED, at the Wood-Yard, in Prince George's Co., Md., on Sunday last [i.e. 30 APR 1815], Mrs. HANNAH WEST, in the 82d year of her age. Her funeral was attended on Tuesday by a large collection of her friends and neighbors, who thus testified a respect most justly due to her memory, and a sermon delivered by the Right Rev. Bishop Claggett. Her death was remarkably sudden. She was well and cheerful at breakfast, and expired about mid-day without any apparent pain or uneasiness. She had passed a long and eventful life, engaged in an extended sphere of duty, and had lived to weep over the cold remains of many of her dearest relatives, surviving most of her children and several grand children ... [DFR:2 MAY 1815, Tuesday, p. 3]

DIED, on the 21st ult. [i.e. 21 APR 1815], after a long & painful illness, FRANCIS

Georgetown, D.C., **Marriage and Death Notices, 1801-1838**

LOWNDES, Esq., an highly respectable citizen of this town, in the 65th year of his age. [DFR:6 MAY 1815, Saturday, p. 3]

DIED, at Fredericktown, Md., on Tuesday last [i.e. 2 MAY 1815], JOHN HANSON THOMAS, Esq., of that place. [DFR:6 MAY 1815, Saturday, p. 3]

We feel our full share in common with all our fellow citizens, in that deep concern which every man possessing the heart of an American, or the slightest pretensions to taste must feel for the death of Dr. DAVID RAMSAY, of Charleston, S.C. ... cut off by a violent death, in the 67th year of his age ... a native of New Jersey ... [DFR:19 MAY 1815, Friday, p. 3]

DIED, at his seat in Piscataway Forest, Prince George's Co., on the 20th April [i.e. 20 APR 1815], in the 32d year of his age, Dr. CHARLES EVERSFIELD, of an attack of the prevailing epidemic, in which he suffered for five days most excessive pain with the utmost fortitude and resignation ... [DFR:20 MAY 1815, Saturday, p. 3]

Died, at Winchester, (N.Y.) on Sunday last [i.e. 14 MAY? 1815], VALENTINE MORRIS. Com. Morris was appointed under the Adams' administration to the command of the squadron for the Mediterranean, and he was one of the first victims to the malignant spirit of Thomas Jefferson ... *Poulson's Philadelphia American*. [DFR:23 MAY 1815, Tuesday, p. 3]

MARRIED, last evening [i.e. 26 MAY 1815], by the Rev. Mr. Addison, Mr. DAWSON P. BURGESS, to Mrs. HENRIETTA CRAIG, the former of Culpeper Co., Va., the latter of this place. [DFR:27 MAY 1815, Saturday, p. 3]

DIED.—On Saturday, the 27th ult. [i.e. 27 MAY 1815], at Halifax Court-house, MATHEW CLAY, member of Congress from Campbell District. [DFR:10 JUN 1815, Saturday, p. 3]

DIED, on the 7th inst. [i.e. 7 JUN 1815], Gen. ROGER NELSON, of Hagerstown, after a long illness and incredible suffering, borne with unexampled fortitude. [DFR:15 JUN 1815, Thursday, p. 3]

MARRIED, on Thursday evening last [i.e. 15 SUN 1815], by the Rev. Mr. Wilmer, Mr. WM. W. CLAGETT, of this place, to Miss ANN PAGE, daughter of Charles Page, Esq., of Alexandria. [DFR:20 JUN 1815, Tuesday, p. 3]

Obituary. DIED, in Somers Town, (Eng.) [no date], Mr. JAMES PELLER MALCOLM, F.S.A., author of "Londinium Redivivum; or an Ancient History and Modern Description of London" ... at the advanced age of 72 ... [DFR:7 JUL 1815, Friday, p. 3]

DIED, on Saturday evening, July 8th [i.e. 8 JUL 1815], after a long illness, Mrs. ISABELLA HOLTZMAN, wife of William Holtzman, aged 24 years and 3 months. [DFR:11 JUL 1815, Tuesday, p. 3]

Married, on Tuesday last [i.e. 11 JUL 1815], Mr. JAS. ENTWISLE, to Mrs. M.A. MASON, both of the Theatre. [DFR:13 JUL 1815, Thursday, p. 3]

Georgetown, D.C., **Marriage and Death Notices, 1801-1838**

DIED, in Washington City, on Saturday the 22d inst. [i.e. 22 JUL 1815], THOMAS BAKER, formerly merchant of this place, after a lingering illness of nearly six months. [DFR:26 JUL 1815, Wednesday, p. 3]

Melancholy Accident.—On Saturday afternoon the 15th inst. [i.e. 15 JUL 1815], the house of Mr. THOMAS KELLY, on *Carroll's Manor*, in Baltimore Co., was struck with lightning, and Mr. Kelly himself, who was in the house, was immediately deprived of life, while the rest of the family, although at a small distance from him, were uninjured. Mr. Kelly has left a wife and 12 children, to deplore their loss. *Federal Gazette*. [DFR:29 JUL 1815, Saturday, p. 2]

DIED.—Sunday evening the 6th inst. [i.e. 6 AUG 1815], after a lingering and painful illness, JOHN SMITH, Esq., Post Captain in the United States Navy. [DFR:11 AUG 1815, Friday, p. 3]

Died, at Philadelphia, on the 8th inst. [i.e. 8 AUG 1815], after an illness of 10 days, Col. RALPH ISAACS, in the 48th year of his age. [DFR:16 AUG 1815, Wednesday, p. 3]

MARRIED, On Tuesday the 22d inst. [i.e. 22 AUG 1815], by the Rev. Mr. Norris, Mr. ISAAC K. HANSON, of Washington City, to the amiable Miss MARIA H. JONES, of Georgetown. [DFR:28 AUG 1815, Monday, p. 3]

DROWNED, on Sunday morning last [i.e. 10 SEP 1815], while in the act of stepping from the Potomac Bridge on board the Steam-Boat, Mr. JOHN HINES, Printer, of Winchester, Va. [DFR:30 AUG 1815, Wednesday, p. 3; DFR:12 SEP 1815, Tuesday, p. 3]

(Communicated.) DIED, on Sunday evening last [i.e. 3 SEP 1815], in the 28th year of her age, Mrs. SARAH D. SEMMES, consort of Mr. Joseph Semmes, of Georgetown. She was afflicted with a long lingering sickness, which she bore with great christian fortitude and submission—Her loss is severely felt by her surviving affectionate husband and friends. [DFR:6 SEP 1815, Wednesday, p. 3]

MARRIED, In Hagerstown, Md., on the 5th inst. [i.e. 5 SEP 1815], Mr. THOMAS MUSTIN, of the War Department, to Miss SOPHIA WESTERN HELM, daughter of the late Thomas Helm, Esq., of Hagerstown. [DFR:12 SEP 1815, Tuesday, p. 3]

Died, suddenly, yesterday morning [i.e. 13 SEP 1815], in the 73d year of his age, the Right Reverend SAMUEL PROVOOST, D.D., Bishop of the Protestant Episcopal Church in the state of New York ... *New York paper*. [DFR:14 SEP 1815, Thursday, p. 3]

MARRIED, On Thursday evening last [i.e. 14 SEP 1815], at Greenleaf's Point, by the Rev. O.B. Brown, Mr. R.H.L. VILLARD, to Miss M.A. MULHOLLEN, both of this place. [DFR:20 SEP 1815, Wednesday, p. 3]

MARRIED, On Tuesday last [i.e. 3 OCT 1815], at the seat of Mr. Joshua Dyall, by the Rev. Mr. Redman, Mr. HENRY BELL, of Prince George's Co., to Miss MARGARET LANHAM, of Montgomery Co., Md. [DFR:7 OCT 1815, Saturday, p. 3]

Georgetown, D.C., **Marriage and Death Notices, 1801-1838**

MARRIED, On Tuesday, the 3d inst. [i.e. 3 OCT 1815], by the Rev. Mr. Jackson, MORDECAI CLINTON JONES, to Miss ELIZABETH ARMSTRONG, third daughter of Maj. John Armstrong, all of St. Mary's Co., Md. [DFR:17 OCT 1815, Tuesday, p. 3]

(Communicated.) DIED, at Georgetown, on Tuesday last [i.e. 10 OCT 1815], Miss LETITIA BROOKE, in the 32d year of her age ... [DFR:17 OCT 1815, Tuesday, p. 3]

From the *Wilmington Gazette*, Oct. 12. COMMUNICATION ... WM. S. HASELL, Esq., the Editor of this *Gazette* is no more! He expired on Friday last [i.e. 6 OCT 1815], after a severe and excruciating sickness of six days ... He leaves a disconsolate wife ... [DFR:25 OCT 1815, Wednesday, p. 3]

DIED.—At Colrain, Mass., on the 3d inst. [i.e. 3 OCT 1815], Mr. THOMAS BELL, son of Mr. Walter and Mrs. Sally Bell, in the 28th year of his age ... Mr. Bell had been for some time in Mr. Thompson's Tavern without taking any active part in the exercises ... [DFR:26 OCT 1815, Thursday, p. 3]

OBITUARY. Departed this life in the city of Washington on Monday night last [i.e. 30 OCT 1815], WALTER HELLEN, Esq., aged 49 years—many years a resident and a very respectable citizen of the District of Columbia. After a tedious illness, through all the vicissitudes of which, his mind was strengthened and supported by a truly christian fortitude, and a firm reliance on a saving redeemer. He has left a widow, four children, and society to mourn his loss. [DFR:2 NOV 1815, Thursday, p. 3]

Philadelphia, Nov. 6. DIED, on Wednesday the first inst. [i.e. 1 NOV 1815], in the 65th year of his age, EDWARD TILGHMAN, Esq., of this city, Counselor at Law ... Mr. Tilghman descended from an old and respectable family in the state of Maryland ... [DFR:10 NOV 1815, Friday, p. 3]

DIED.—At Fire Place, L.I., Mr. ALEXANDER FISHER, a native of Richmond, Va., and Student of Yale College. He perished with cold, wet and fatigue, on board the sloop *Richmond Packet*, Capt. Egbert, from Richmond for New-York, which struck on the bar near Smith's Inlet on Saturday [i.e. 4 NOV 1815] ... [DFR:11 NOV 1815, Saturday, p. 3]

DIED, On the 30th ult. [i.e. 30 OCT 1815], DAVID SLATER, Esq., of Prince George's Co., Md., in the 49th year of his age. he deceased was an amiable and useful member of society, and in the less expanded circles of private and domestic life, honest, sincere, tender & benevolent. [DFR:15 NOV 1815, Wednesday, p. 3]

Married, on Tuesday evening, the 14th inst. [i.e. 14 NOV 1815], at *Locust Grove*, Prince William Co., Va., by the Rev. Mr. Mathews, Mr. GEORGE SWEENY, of the City of Washington, to Miss MARY S.C. HOOE, daughter of the late Bernard Hooe, Sen., Esq., of the former place. [DFR:17 NOV 1815, Friday, p. 3]

Died, yesterday morning [i.e. 28 NOV 1815], in Washington City, after a lingering illness, Mr. JOSEPH MAGUIRE. Previous to being attacked by this illness, he had been employed, at different times, in important situations the duties of which several capacities

Georgetown, D.C., **Marriage and Death Notices, 1801-1838**

he discharged with expedition and accuracy. He has left, besides a tender mother, a numerous circle of relatives and friends to lament his loss. [DFR:29 NOV 1815, Wednesday, p. 3]

Baltimore, Dec. 4. DIED, yesterday [i.e. 4 DEC 1815] about six o'clock in the morning, the Most Reverend Doctor JOHN CARROLL, Arch-Bishop of Baltimore, in the 80th year of his age ... [DFR:5 DEC 1815, Tuesday, p. 3]

MARRIED, on Sunday evening last [i.e. 3 DEC 1815], by the Rev. Mr. McCormick, Mr. EDWARD SIMMONS LEWIS, to Miss SUSAN JEAN WASHINGTON, daughter of Lund Washington, Esq., all of Washington City. [DFR:6 DEC 1815, Wednesday, p. 3]

MARRIED, on Sunday evening last [i.e. 3 DEC 1815], by the Rev. Mr. Addison, Mr. LEWIS JOHNSON, to Mrs. ANN REINAGLE, daughter of Mr. P.L. Duport, all of this town. [DFR:6 DEC 1815, Wednesday, p. 3]

DIED, on Monday evening last [i.e. 4 DEC 1815], at the seat of her brother, Alexander C. Hanson, Esq., MARY JANE GROSVENOR, wife of Thomas P. Grosvenor, Esq., aged twenty-five years. The disease which terminated her life at this early age, was that destroying angel of our country-women, a consumption. On the 13th of July last, she ruptured a blood vessel in her lungs, which was followed by nearly five months of decline ... [DFR:8 DEC 1815, Friday, p. 3]

DIED, on Tuesday morning last [i.e. 19 DEC 1815], in the forty-ninth year of his age, Dr. BENJAMIN SMITH BARTON, Professor of the Theory and Practice of Medicine, and of Natural History and Botany, in the University of Pennsylvania. *Philadelphia Paper.* [DFR:25 DEC 1815, Monday, p. 3]

Departed this life on the 12th inst. [i.e. 12 DEC 1815], at his seat in St. Mary's Co., Md., Col. HENRY NEALE, (one of the few remaining veterans of '76) in the 64th year of his age, after a short but severe illness, thro' which was exemplified, that patient fortitude and christian resignation, the strong characteristics of his protracted and well spent life; leaving an affectionate wife and children, with a numerous and most respectable acquaintance to lament the awful separation. [DFR:27 DEC 1815, Wednesday, p. 3]

DEATH. Departed this life, last evening [i.e. 29 DEC 1815], after a lingering illness, Mr. JOHN MORRISON, Printer. His friends and acquaintances are requested to attend his funeral from Farmer's Tavern, on High Street, tomorrow at 3 o'clock. [DFR:30 DEC 1815, Saturday, p. 3]

DIED.—In England, T. EVANS, Esq., and W. MIDDLEMORE, Esq., bankers, at Nottingham, and partners through life in different extensive concerns—the former, while engaged at a game of chess with one of his daughters, and the latter, who was previously indisposed, never spoke after he received the account of his partner's death. [DFR:5 JAN 1816, Friday, p. 3]

DIED.—On Monday 1st of January 1816, after a severe illness of three weeks, Miss JANE

Georgetown, D.C., **Marriage and Death Notices, 1801-1838**

EASTON, in the eighteenth year of her age ... [DFR:8 JAN 1816, Monday, p. 3]

MARRIED.—In Dumfries, by the Rev. Mr. Lemmon, on the evening of the 31st December [i.e. 31 DEC 1815], INMAN HORNER, Esq., to Miss MARY HENDERSON, youngest daughter of Alexander Henderson, Esq., deceased. [DFR:10 JAN 1816, Wednesday, p. 3]

MARRIED, on the 24th December, 1815, by the Rev. Mr. Brown, Mr. ALEXANDER GRAHAM, of Philadelphia, to Miss SARAH CLEMENTSON, of Georgetown, D.C. [DFR:10 JAN 1816, Wednesday, p. 3]

Communicated. DIED, in this town, Mr. C. FOX, on Thursday last [i.e. 4 JAN 1816], and early next day his brother, Mr. B. FOX. Both were afflicted with a lingering sickness, which they bore with exemplary fortitude ... Their two coffins were deposited side by side in the same grave, next to those of two amiable sisters the daughters of Mr. B. FOX. The sorrow of the two widows and their helpless children might be imagined but cannot be described. [DFR:10 JAN 1816, Wednesday, p. 3]

DIED.—In Boston, Mass. [no date], after a short illness, the Rev. JOHN LATHROP, D.D., aged 76 years.—The Venerable pastor of the second church in this town ... [DFR:11 JAN 1816, Thursday, p. 3]

Communicated. DIED.—At *Worton*, Kent Co., on the 21st of Dec. [i.e. 21 DEC 1816], after a severe & painful illness, Col. JOHN BORDLEY, son of the late John Beale Bordley, Esq., of Philadelphia. Col. Bordley was an ardent lover of his country, and a zealous defender of her liberties; he was a kind husband, a tender affectionate father, an indulgent master and above all, he lived and died a pious christian ... [DFR:12 JAN 1816, Friday, p. 3]

MARRIED.—On the 11th inst. [i.e. 11 JAN 1816], by the Rev. Mr. Redmond, D.P. NOLAND, Esq., of Loudoun Co., Va., to Miss CAROLINE F. HARDING, daughter of Edward Harding, Esq., of Montgomery Co., Md. [DFR:13 JAN 1816, Saturday, p. 3]

MARRIED.—On last evening [i.e. 18 JAN 1816], by the Rev. Dr. Muir of Alexandria, Mr. JAMES C. WILSON, merchant of Baltimore, to Miss ANNA E.B. BALCH, daughter of the Rev. S.B. Balch of this place. [DFR:19 JAN 1816, Friday, p. 3]

MARRIED.—On Thursday the 18th inst. [i.e. 18 JAN 1816], by the Rev. Mr. Day, Mr. JOSEPH JACKSON, merchant of this town, to Miss RACHAEL PLUMMER, daughter of Yate Plummer, of Frederick Co. [DFR:24 JAN 1816, Wednesday, p. 3]

DIED, suddenly, in the borough of Lancaster [Pa.], on Monday night last [i.e. 15 JAN 1816], in the 76th year of his age, ANDREW GRAFF, Esq., a very worthy and respectable character. He was born in Lancaster and served for many years as an Associate Judge of the county. *Lancaster, Pa., Jan. 17.* [DFR:24 JAN 1816, Wednesday, p. 3]

OBITUARY. On the 18th inst. [i.e. 18 JAN 1816], departed this life, at his father's seat, in Bedford, Va., Maj. JOHN REID, of the United States army, the well known aid of Gen. Jackson, in his transactions against the Creeks and the British. The evening preceding that on which he died, he was in the finest health and spirits. About midnight he complained of chilliness; medical assistance was called in before breakfast, and additional aid was sent for during the day, but all to no purpose, the disease very hour visibly increased; in the evening the warn bath was about to be applied, but suspended on account of his exhausted condition, he was turned over on his side for temporary relief, and appeared to sink into a gentle sleep; but he awoke no more; the ethereal spirit had forsaken its mansion, and the hero who had, for his country's sake, fearlessly braved the cannon and the sabre on the 8th January, 1815, fell victim to a fever of 21 hours continuance, on the 18th January, 1816. Would that he could have lived at least long enough to complete the history which he had announced to the world, and in the composition of which he was busily engaged. His loss is the more to be deplored by his family, as it is the second it has experienced this year: for th day after the major arrived from Washington, whither he had accompanied his beloved General, he saw his sister Maria, a blooming young girl of eighteen, expire. Imagine, then, reader, if though canst, the poignant anguish his aged father, his disconsolate mother, his bereaved consort, and his other relations, must feel at his death! Social and agreeable in private life, gallant in the field, in integrity he had but few equals and no superior. [DFR:3 FEB 1816, Saturday, p. 3]

Communicated. Departed this life on the 13th ult. [i.e. 13 JAN 1816], at his residence in Fauquier Co., Va., Major SAMUEL ASHBY, in the forty-third year of his age ... [DFR:9 FEB 1816, Friday, p. 3]

MARRIED, on the 8th inst. [i.e. 8 FEB 1816], by the Rev. Mr. Francis Neale, Mr. HENRY HOWARD, to Mrs. MARGARET BRINKMAN, both of this place. [DFR:10 FEB 1816, Saturday, p. 3]

MARRIED, on Thursday evening last [i.e. 8 FEB 1816], by the Rev. Mr. Roszel, Mr. WILLIAM WEIGHTMAN, of Alexandria, to Miss ELIZABETH SHERLEY, of this place. [DFR:10 FEB 1816, Saturday, p. 3]

OBITUARY. DIED.—On Thursday, the 8th inst. [i.e. 8 FEB 1816], at about 4 o'clock, in the morning, in the 35th year of her age, at her father's residence in this town, after a sharp conflict of about thirty hours, Mrs. MARY GEORGE, consort of Rev. Enoch George, an Elder in the Methodist Church ... as a mother, her little children will weep at the recollection of her guardian care, her fond solicitude, and maternal love. [DFR:10 FEB 1816, Saturday, p. 3]

Communicated. DIED, on the 10th inst. [i.e. 10 FEB 1816], at 7 o'clock in the morning, in the 57th year of her age, Mrs. MARGARET FOXALL, consort of the Rev. Henry Foxall, of this place ... For twenty years, and upwards, death was engaged in undermining the life of our departed friend ... [DFR:14 FEB 1816, Wednesday, p. 3]

MARRIED, on the 15th inst. [i.e. 15 FEB 1816], by the Rev. Mr. M'Cormick, Mr. JAMES TOWNLEY, to Miss SARAH KNOWLES, daughter of Mr. Henry Knowles, of Georgetown. [DFR:19 FEB 1816, Monday, p. 3]

Georgetown, D.C., **Marriage and Death Notices, 1801-1838**

DIED.—On Sunday the 10th inst. [i.e. 10 FEB 1816], at Richmond, after a short illness, and in the humble but firm hope of a blessed immortality, through the merits of her redeemer, Mrs. JUDITH RANDOLPH, third daughter of the late Thomas Mann Randolph, Esq., of *Tuckahoe*, and relict of the late Richard Randolph, Esq., of *Bizarre*, in the county of Cumberland ... [DFR:14 MAR 1816, Thursday, p. 3]

DIED, yesterday the 15th inst. [i.e. 15 MAR 1816], at his seat in this place, THOMAS TURNER, Esq., late Accountant of the Navy Department—His friends and acquaintances are invited to attend his funeral at 4 o'clock this afternoon. [DFR:16 MAR 1816, Saturday, p. 3]

DIED, in London, on the 29th of December last [i.e. 29 DEC 1815], PHINEAS BOND, Esq., for many years Consul General of His Britannic Majesty, for the Middle and Southern States of America. Mr. Bond was a native of Philadelphia ... [DFR:19 MAR 1816, Tuesday, p. 3]

DIED, last Thursday night [i.e. 21 MAR 1816], about 12 o'clock, in the 41st year of her age, Mrs. MARY FELL STUART, consort of the honorable Philip Stuart, a representative of Congress from the state of Maryland ... She has left a disconsolate husband & eight children ... [DFR:25 MAR 1816, Monday, p. 3]

MARRIED.—On the 20th November [i.e. 20 NOV 1815], Mr. GEORGE WEST, of Giles, (Va.) aged 106 years, to Mrs. MARY GARDNER, of Monroe, aged 80 ... [DFR:26 MAR 1816, Tuesday, p. 3]

Georgetown, D.C., **Marriage and Death Notices, 1801-1838**

THE MESSENGER (AND TOWN AND CITY COMMERCIAL GAZETTE)
April 17, 1816, to October 24, 1817

DIED, on Monday night last [i.e. 15 APR 1816], after a lingering illness, GERARDUS WILEY, (aged 19 years,) second son of the late David Wiley, Esq., of this town ... [MS:17 APR 1816, Wednesday, p. 3]

On Sunday, the 31st of March, 1816, departed this life, near Fredericksburg, Va., in the 72d year of his age, the venerable FRANCIS ASBURY, bishop of the Methodist episcopal church. Of him it may be said, 'a great man has fallen in Israel,' having labored in his Lord's Vineyard, more than fifty years ... [MS:17 APR 1816, Wednesday, p. 3]

DIED, in Georgetown, D.C., on Sunday morning, the 21st inst. [i.e. 21 APR 1866], Mr. ALEXANDER MACKEY, aged about 75. He was formerly of the city of Philadelphia, but has for the last fifteen years been an inhabitant of Georgetown. [MS:27 APR 1816, Saturday, p. 3]

DIED, in Georgetown, D.C. on Tuesday the 23d inst. [i.e. 23 APR 1816], Miss ANNE TAYLOR GREEN GUSTINE, (aged 17 years) youngest daughter of Dr. Gustine. Her complaint was of a pulmonary kind. She was confined several months; during which time she displayed an exemplary fortitude and christian like resignation ... [MS:27 APR 1816, Saturday, p. 3]

CAPT. JAMES LAWRENCE. A monument is now erecting in Trinity Church, to the memory of the much lamented Lawrence. It represents a broken column of white marble of the Doric order, the cap of which is broken off and rests on the base. On the plinth in front is the following inscription: "In Memory of / Captain JAMES LAWRENCE, / of the United States Navy, who fell / on the first day of June, 1813, in the 32d year / of his age, / In the action between the frigates *Chesapeake* / and *Shannon* ..." *N.Y. Gazette*. [MS:8 MAY 1816, Wednesday, p. 3]

DEPARTED this life, yesterday morning, the 10th inst. [i.e. 10 MAY 1816], Mrs. ISABELLA KING, in the 75th year of her age. Her friends and acquaintance are requested to attend her funeral this afternoon, at 5 o'clock, at the dwelling of her son, William King, jun., in Jefferson-street. [MS:11 MAY 1816, Saturday, p. 3]

Died, at Athens, in New-York, on his way home from this city, with his family, the hon. SAMUEL DEXTER, of Mass. His illness was very short. A great and good man has departed from amongst us; he is lost to his county; but his noble example will never be forgotten. His name will live in history; his death will be lamented, and his memory honoured by every patriot in the land. *National Intelligencer*. [MS:11 MAY 1816, Saturday, p. 3]

MARRIED, on Tuesday evening [i.e. 21 MAY 1816], by the Rev. Mr. Addison, WM. BEVERLEY RANDOLPH, Esq., of Va., to Miss SARAH LINGAN, eldest daughter of the

Georgetown, D.C., **Marriage and Death Notices, 1801-1838**

late Gen. Lingan, of Md. [MS:25 MAY 1816, Saturday, p. 3]

DIED, At his residence, in Schoharie Co., Capt. THOMAS MACHIN, member of the order of Cincinnati, aged 72 years. He was a British officer at the battle of Minden, and an American during the whole revolutionary war. The chain across the Hudson, at West Point, was constructed under his direction, and he had the honor of being wounded in the defense of Bunker-Hill, and severely in the defense of Fort-Montgomery. In the camp and in retirement, his qualifications were holden in very high consideration. [MS:1 JUN 1816, Saturday, p. 3]

CENOTAPH. Erected at Wiscasset to the memory of the late Justice SAMUEL SEWALL (in Latin) ... [MS:1 JUN 1816, Saturday, p. 4]

Richmond yesterday [i.e. 4 JUN 1816] lost one of her best and most beloved citizens, in the person of WILLIAM MARSHALL, Esq., the commonwealth's attorney for this city, the clerk of the federal court for this district, and one of the ablest practitioners at the bar of Virginia. He died of a lingering indisposition. He was a man of that sterling worth, that the whole world saw and felt it ... *Richmond Compiler* [MS:5 JUN 1816, Wednesday, p. 3]

MARRIED, in this place, on Thursday evening, the 6th inst. [i.e. 6 JUN 1816], by the Rev. Mr. Balch, Mr. GARRETT HEYER, of N.Y., to Miss HARRIET SIFFERT, of Baltimore. [MS:8 JUN 1816, Saturday, p. 3]

MARRIED, on Sunday evening last [i.e. 2 JUN 1816], by the Rev. Mr. Balch, Mr. THOMAS ORME, to Miss SARAH KURTZ, both of this town. [MS:8 JUN 1816, Saturday, p. 3]

MARRIED, on Sunday evening last [i.e. 2 JUN 1816], at Broad Creek, Md., by the Rev. Mr. Young, Mr. JOHN WEIGHTMAN, merchant, of Washington, to Miss SIDNEY LYLES, daughter of the late Col. Lyles. [MS:8 JUN 1816, Saturday, p. 3]

MARRIED, on Tuesday evening the 28th ult. [i.e. 28 MAY 1816] by the Rev. Mr. Ryland, Mr. CRAVEN P. BEEDING, merchant of Georgetown, to Miss ROSETTA L. LACKLAND, daughter of the late James Lackland, Esq., of Montgomery Co., Md. [MS:8 JUN 1816, Saturday, p. 3]

MARRIED, on Thursday evening last [i.e. 20 JUN 1816], by the Rev. Mr. Balch, JOHN WILEY, Esq., Recorder of this City, to Miss SALLY CLAGETT, of this place. And, Mr. JOHN HOLTZMAN to Miss NEWTON, both of this place. [MS:22 JUN 1816, Saturday, p. 3]

MARRIED, on the 2d inst. [i.e. 2 JUL 1816], by the Rev. Mr. M'Cormick, Mr. CHRISTOPHER BYRNE, Printer, to Miss MARIA FARRELL, all of Wash'n. [MS:10 JUL 1816, Wednesday, p. 3]

DIED, at Beaufort, in S.C., on the 30th ult. [i.e. 30 JUN 1816], the Hon. PAUL HAMILTON, late Secretary of the Navy of the United States. Let us respect the memory of this truly honourable and estimable man. He has departed from a world for which his openhanded benevolence and warm hearted disposition almost unfitted him. *National Intelligencer.* [MS:13 JUL 1816, Saturday, p. 3]

DIED, at Maj. Wm. Gholson's in Brunswick Co., Va., on Thursday last [i.e. 11 JUL 1816], of a lingering disease, Hon. THOMAS GHOLSON, a Representative in Congress from the state of Virginia; as upright a politician, and as righteous a man, perhaps, as ever has filled a place in this sublunary scene. [MS:17 JUL 1816, Wednesday, p. 3]

MARRIED, in Baltimore, on the 13th inst. [i.e. 13 JUL 1816], by the Rev. Mr. Neal, Mr.REZIN ORME, of this town, to Miss MARGARET THOMAS, of the former place. [MS:20 JUL 1816, Saturday, p. 3]

DIED, on Sunday last [i.e. 18 AUG 1816], in Washington, after a long and painful illness, Maj. G. ANDREWS. The warm benevolence of his heart, and his merits as a citizen endeared him to all who knew him. [MS:21 AUG 1816, Wednesday, p. 3]

MARRIED, on Tuesday evening last [i.e. 27 AUG 1816], by the Rev. Mr. Grassi, the Hon. WM. GASTON, of N.C., to Miss ELIZA WORTHINGTON, of this town. [MS:4 SEP 1816, Wednesday, p. 3]

MARRIED, by Rev. Mr. Addison [no date], Mr. RICHARD H. FITZHUGH, to Miss MARY ANN MARBURY, both of this town. [MS:4 SEP 1816, Wednesday, p. 3]

MARRIED.—On Wednesday evening last [i.e. 11 SEP 1816], by the Rev. Mr. Grassi, Mr. JOSEPH SEMMES, to Mrs. BEATTY (widow of the late Maj. Beatty) all of this town. [MS:14 SEP 1816, Saturday, p. 3]

MARRIED, on Thursday evening [i.e. 12 SEP 1816], by the Rev. Mr. Greentree, Mr. SAMUEL TUCKER, to Miss MELINDA HOSKINS, all of this place. [MS:14 SEP 1816, Saturday, p. 3]

MARRIED, last evening [i.e. 27 SEP 1816], by the Rev. Mr. Balch, Mr. ULYSSES WARD, of this place, to Miss SUSANA VULINDA BEALL, of Prince George's Co., Md. [MS:28 SEP 1816, Saturday, p. 3]

MARRIED.—On Tuesday evening last [i.e. 8 OCT 1816], by the Rev. Mr. Balch, Dr. JOHN OTT, to Miss ANN CRUIKSHANK, both of this place. [MS:12 OCT 1816, Saturday, p. 3]

MARRIED, in Baltimore, on Tuesday evening last [i.e. 8 OCT 1816], by the Rev. Mr. Hempill, Mr. THOMAS WOODWARD, of this town, to Miss OCTAVIA ROZZELL, of the former place. [MS:12 OCT 1816, Saturday, p. 3]

MARRIED.—On Thursday, the 10th inst. [i.e. 10 OCT 1816], at Leesburg, Va., Mr. G. RICHARDS, of this town, to Mrs. ANN B. SAUNDERS, of the former place. [MS:23 OCT 1816, Wednesday, p. 3]

MARRIED, in Washington City [c.15 OCT 1816], by the Rev. Mr. M'Cormick, Mr. THOS.

Georgetown, D.C., **Marriage and Death Notices, 1801-1838**

R. WALTER, to Miss MARY WINTERS, all of that place. [MS:23 OCT 1816, Wednesday, p. 3]

DIED, on Wednesday, the 16th inst. [i.e. 16 OCT 1816], in the 25th year of his age, Mr. JOSEPH HARRIS, of the Baltimore and Philadelphia Theatres. He submitted to the distresses of a long and painful illness ... His disease originated from the exertion of that pure patriotism, which led so many of the youth of Baltimore to its protection, in the hour of danger—having served as a volunteer in the glorious defence of Fort M'Henry. His remains were interred yesterday morning, attended by the Rev. Bishop Kemp, who performed the service, and a numerous assemblyage of his former associates and friends, who evinced, by the poignancy of their feelings, how sensibly they felt his loss. [MS:23 OCT 1816, Wednesday, p. 3]

DIED, in England [no date], JOHN HAZERENTINE, whitesmith, aged 56 ... [MS:23 OCT 1816, Wednesday, p. 3]

DIED, in Hannan's Town, on Tuesday night [i.e. 27 AUG 1816], at a very advanced age, JOHN REEDER, a well known black man, as having been many years captain of the Charles Town Maroons. He is the person who in the year 1781, after a most severe personal conflict, killed the robber *Three-Fingered Jack,* who was supposed by the negroes to be possessed of supernatural powers, and seemed invulnerable from all attacks. In consequence of this service Reeder received an annual stipend from the government of this island. He did not know his exact age, but said only a few days ago that he was a stout boy at the first peace with the Maroons in the year 1730. *Kingston, Jam. paper, 3d ult.* [MS:23 OCT 1816, Wednesday, p. 3]

DIED, on Friday afternoon [i.e. 25 OCT 1816], in the 74th year of his age, Mr. DAVID POE, a native of Ireland, and for the last forty years, a resident of Baltimore. Mr. Poe was an early and decided friend of American liberty, and was actively engaged in promoting that cause during the revolutionary war. He died as he lived, a zealous republican regretted by an extensive circle of relatives and friends. [MS:26 OCT 1816, Saturday, p. 3]

DIED, at New-York, on Wednesday afternoon last [i.e. 23 OCT 1816], JOHN T. BAINBRIDGE, Esq., Clerk of the Marine Court, and brother to Com. Bainbridge. [MS:26 OCT 1816, Saturday, p. 3]

DIED, on Wednesday last [i.e. 6 NOV 1816], after a long and distressing illness, MORDECAI M. MORGAN, of this town. [MS:9 NOV 1816, Saturday, p. 3]

DIED, lately [no date] at Port-au-Prince, St. Domingo, of a bilious fever, Mr. JAMES ORR, aged 34, a native of the county of Wexford, Ireland, and recently of this city ... Mr. Orr had been a Lieutenant in the British army, and distinguished himself in all the memorable battles fought under Lord Wellington in Spain; from whence, with the hostile band under General Ross, he was transported to our shores, there to spread devastation and conflagrate our infant metropolis ... he abandoned his companions in arms at Bladensburg, and repaired to Baltimore ... *Baltimore American* [MS:9 NOV 1816, Saturday, p. 3]

Georgetown, D.C., **Marriage and Death Notices, 1801-1838**

MARRIED.—On Tuesday evening November 5th [i.e. 5 NOV 1816], at the seat of Benjamin Berry, Esq., in P. George's Co., by the Rev. Mr. Burch, Mr. T.B. DASHIEL, of Washington, to Miss MARY B. BEALL, of the former place. [MS:13 NOV 1816, Wednesday, p. 3]

MARRIED, on Monday evening last [i.e. 18 NOV 1816], by the Rev. Mr. Addison, JOHN NELSON, Esq., of Frederick-town, to Miss FRANCES HARRIETT BURROWS, of Washington. [MS:23 NOV 1816, Saturday, p. 3]

MARRIED, at Baltimore, on Tuesday evening the 12th inst. [i.e. 12 NOV 1816], by the Rev. Mr. Glendy, BARNABY BARNES, Esq., of Philadelphia, to Miss CHRISTIANA PECHIN, eldest daughter of Maj. William Pechin, of Baltimore. [MS:23 NOV 1816, Saturday, p. 3]

MARRIED, in Amelia Co., Va., on Wednesday the 6th inst. [i.e. 6 NOV 1816], by the Rev. Mr. Logan, Dr. JAMES H. CONWAY, to Miss AUGUSTA GILES, eldest daughter of William B. Giles, Esq. [MS:23 NOV 1816, Saturday, p. 3]

DIED.—At six o'clock last evening [i.e. 26 NOV 1816], in the 45th year of his age, after a long and painful illness, Mr. WILLIAM CRAWFORD, the proprietor of the Union Tavern, of this town. In the death of this valuable and enterprising citizen, society is deprived of a useful member; the town has lost an active and zealous friend; and his afflicted wife and children are bereaved of a most affectionate and tender husband and parent. His remains will be deposited in the Church burying ground, on Thursday the 28th inst., at 2 o'clock in the afternoon, on which occasion his friends and acquaintances are respectfully invited to attend. [MS:27 NOV 1816, Wednesday, p. 3]

DIED.—On Sunday last [i.e. 24 NOV 1816], Mr. JOHN CRUIKSHANK, after a short illness. The amiable disposition and correct deportment of this young gentleman endeared him to all who knew him. [MS:27 NOV 1816, Wednesday, p. 3]

DIED, in Norfolk [no date], Mrs. RACHEL GLENN, wife of Mr. Thomas Glenn of that borough, few ladies, says the *Norfolk Beacon*, have ever quit this life with higher claims to the affectionate remembrance of her friends. In the same place, Mrs. LOUISA COLVERT, wife of Mr. Colvert, of the firm of *Colvert & Cobb*, aged nineteen, and eldest daughter of Mr. Glenn—thus has this gentleman been deprived of an affectionate wife and daughter in the course of a few days. [MS:27 NOV 1816, Wednesday, p. 3]

MARRIED.—On Tuesday evening, the 26th inst. [i.e. 26 NOV 1816], by the Rev. Francis Neal, Mr. GEORGE KING, (son of Mr. Charles King) to Miss SUSANNA MARIA FORD, all of this town. [MS:30 NOV 1816, Saturday, p. 3]

DIED.—On Wednesday morning last [i.e. 4 DEC 1816], in the 23d year of his age, Mr. ANDREW M'KELDEN, Book-keeper of the Bank of Columbia.—He has left a wife, infant son, and numerous train of relatives, to lament his early death. On Thursday all that was mortal of him, was carried to its last above, the grave ... [MS:7 DEC 1816, Saturday, p. 3]

MARRIED.—On Tuesday last [i.e. 3 DEC 1816], by the Rev. Wm. Waters, Mr. DAVID

Georgetown, D.C., **Marriage and Death Notices, 1801-1838**

ENGLISH, Jun., merchant of this town, to Miss MARY SLADE, of Alexandria. [MS:10 DEC 1816, Tuesday, p. 3]

DIED.—In Washington, on Sunday last [i.e. 8 DEC 1816], JOHN CAMPBELL, Esq., formerly of St. Louis, in the Missouri territory. To an amiable disposition, Mr. Campbell united a pleasing suavity of manner, which rendered him a most agreeable companion to his friends. To his children he was indeed a father in every sense of the word. Mr. C. had resided but a few years in Washington, and from the active interest he took in its welfare, added much to its appearance, by having constructed several elegant and useful buildings. [MS:10 DEC 1816, Tuesday, p. 3]

DIED, on Friday last [i.e. 6 DEC 1816], in Charles Co., Mr. T.F. RATCLIFFE, aged 18 years, son of Mr. Joseph Ratcliffe, of this town. [MS:10 DEC 1816, Tuesday, p. 3]

DIED, in Boxborough, by the accidental discharge of a fowling piece, Mr. — HOPGOOD, merchant. A person came into the store of the deceased to fix the flint in his gun, and while engaged in hammering it, it went off. The ball entered the back part of Mr. H's head, and came out of his forehead. [MS:10 DEC 1816, Tuesday, p. 3]

DIED, Mr. HUGGINS, hair dresser, well known by the title of *Emperor*, put a period to his existence by cutting his throat. This shocking act was perpetrated in Albany, where Mr. H. had gone on a visit to his friends. [MS:10 DEC 1816, Tuesday, p. 3]

DIED, suddenly, on Wednesday morning [i.e. 11 DEC 1816], at 3 o'clock, Mr. CHARLES FLORIS, in the 60th year of his age. Mr. Floris was a venerable old foreigner, who was much respected for his amiable qualities, and died universally lamented. His friends and acquaintances are invited to attend his funeral this evening, at 3 o'clock. [MS:12 DEC 1816, Thursday, p. 3]

DIED, on Friday last [i.e. 6 DEC 1816], on his passage from Havana, in the 17th year of his age, Mr. JESSE LEAKIN, a youth of great promise, and universally respected by all who knew him. [MS:12 DEC 1816, Thursday, p. 3]

DIED, at New Orleans, on the 5th of Nov. last [i.e. 5 NOV 1816], after a short illness of four weeks, Maj. DANIEL CARMICK, of the U.S. marine corps. *Baltimore American*. [MS:12 DEC 1816, Thursday, p. 3]

DIED, in Murfreesboro', N.C., on the 23d ult. [i.e. 23 NOV 1816], after a few days illness, Master ALEXANDER FERGUSON, late a resident of Boston, aged 15. [MS:12 DEC 1816, Thursday, p. 3]

Washington, (Penn.), Dec. 19. DIED.—Yesterday evening [i.e. 18 DEC 1816], of a fracture in the scull bone, NATHANIEL WOODS, of Buffalo township—Nathaniel and his wife, on Sunday the 1st inst., fell in with a stranger, at Mr. Caldwell's tavern on the Wheeling road, about one mile from his residence. The stranger, Nathaniel and his wife, left the tavern together, about 7 or 8 o'clock in the evening, with the intention of coming by way of Woods' house to Washington, where Nathaniel worked. On the road, the stranger put his great

Georgetown, D.C., **Marriage and Death Notices, 1801-1838**

coat round Mrs. Woods, the night being cold. Nathaniel took umbrage at this rudeness, and gave the coat two or three rents—about which they quarreled at Woods' door, where the stranger gave Nathaniel a violent blow on the head, about three inches above the left eye, with a stone and then made his escape. Wood continued going about until Saturday last, refusing the necessary surgical aid, when he lost his reason. His scull was trespanned on Saturday evening, and a number of fractured pieces extracted, which had perforated the membranes of the brain. But a mortification had taken place. [MS:28 DEC 1816, Saturday, p. 2]

MARRIED.—On the 25th inst. [i.e. 25 DEC 1816], by the Rev. Mr. Ryland, Mr. HENRY GAITHER, to Miss ARIE ANN HEUGHES, both of Georgetown. [MS:31 DEC 1816, Tuesday, p. 3]

MARRIED, on Tuesday evening [i.e. 7 JAN 1817], by the Rev. Mr. Balch, Mr. WM. I. BRONAUGH, Jr., of Loudoun Co., Va., to Miss MARY C. MITCHELL, of this place. [MS:9 JAN 1817, Thursday, p. 3]

Obituary. Departed this life on the 6th inst. [i.e. 6 JAN 1817], at her seat in the District of Columbia, Mrs. SUSANNA P. ROBERTS, in the 36th year of her age. She has left a mourning affectionate husband, and disconsolate children! The character of this lady would have been read, even by the passing stranger, in the sobs and grief of her afflicted family, relatives and neighbours. An impressive funeral sermon was delivered by the Rev. Mr. Balch. [MS:11 JAN 1817, Saturday, p. 3]

DIED.—In Canandaigua, N.Y. [no date], Mr. JOHN STOUT; his death was occasioned by burns received at the recent loss of his house by fire. [MS:16 JAN 1817, Thursday, p. 3]

DIED, in Albany [no date], Mrs. CATHALINA, wife of Mr. John H. Wendell. [MS:16 JAN 1817, Thursday, p. 3]

It is with no ordinary feelings, that we announce to our readers the departure from the world of ALEXANDER JAMES DALLAS, the Secretary of the Treasury, who died at two o'clock on Thursday morning last [i.e. 16 JAN 1817], of a sudden attack of a disease to which he was subject ... *National Intelligencer.* [MS:21 JAN 1817, Tuesday, p. 3]

DIED, at Fort Warren, yesterday morning [i.e. 22 JAN 1817], of a pluretick fever, Capt. ARMSTRONG IRVINE, of the United States Regiment of Light Artillery, son of the late Brigadier General Irvine, of Pa. [MS:23 JAN 1817, Thursday, p. 3]

MARRIED.—On Thursday evening last [i.e. 23 JAN 1817] , by the Rev. Mr. M'Cormick, Mr. JOHN RENNER, to Miss ELIZA AUSTIN, all of this place. [MS:25 JAN 1817, Saturday, p. 3]

DIED.—In this town, last week, in the 17th year of her age, Miss MARY WILEY. Miss W. had for a long time been confined by a pulmonary complaint, during all her tedious illness, a murmur never escaped her, she looked as serene and placid in death, as if she had been asleep ... [MS:28 JAN 1817, Tuesday, p. 3]

Georgetown, D.C., **Marriage and Death Notices, 1801-1838**

MARRIED.—On Tuesday evening last [i.e. 28 JAN 1817], by the Rev. Mr. Balch, SAMUEL J. POTTS, to Miss MARY ANN ROSS, all of this place. On the same evening, Dr. M'SHEERRY, of Virginia, to Miss ANN KING, of this town. [MS:30 JAN 1817, Thursday, p. 3]

OBITUARY. Departed this life on Tuesday evening [i.e. 28 JAN 1817], suddenly, Mr. SINGLETON OWENS. [MS:30 JAN 1817, Thursday, p. 3]

DIED, yesterday morning [i.e. 29 JAN 1817], at 3 o'clock, Dr. GUSTINE, the younger. [MS:30 JAN 1817, Thursday, p. 3]

MARRIED.—On Tuesday last [i.e. 4 FEB 1817], by the Rev. Stephen B. Balch, Mr. CHARLES CRUIKSHANK, to Miss MARTHA BROWN. [MS:7 FEB 1817, Friday, p. 3]

MARRIED, in Baltimore, on the 2d inst. [i.e. 2 FEB 1817], by the Rev. Mr. Hagerty, Mr. JAMES COCHRAN, Printer, to Miss ELIZA C. CEBRULAR, all of that place. [MS:14 FEB 1817, Friday, p. 3]

MARRIED, in S.C., on the 1st inst. [i.e. 1 FEB 1817], Mr. STEPHEN LYON, to Miss REBECCA LAMB. [MS:14 FEB 1817, Friday, p. 3]

MARRIED, in New York [no date], by the Rev. Mr. Clarke, Col. CHARLES K. GARDNER, Adjt. Gen. of the Northern Division of the U. States Army, to Miss ANN ELIZA M'LEAN, daughter of John M'Lean, Esq., Q.M. General of the State of New York. [MS:14 FEB 1817, Friday, p. 3]

OBITUARY. In New York [no date], Mrs. COX, wife of Mr. William Cox, of Middleton, Orange Co. Mrs. Cox had just been giving some nourishment to a sick husband, and had sat down by the fire, apparently as well as usual. She told her daughter she felt very strange, and did not know but she was dying. Her daughter assisted her to bed—she still complained of feeling very strange, and of being excessively cold all over. Her daughter went to the bed and took hold of her hands, but her breath was departing, and she immediately breathed her last. [MS:14 FEB 1817, Friday, p. 3]

DIED, in Wilmington, (Vt.) [no date], Mr. GEORGE REYNOLDS, of this town, found frozen to death within 30 rods of the house to which he was going, his horse standing by the body, with the bridle round the neck of Mr. Reynolds. [MS:14 FEB 1817, Friday, p. 3]

MARRIED, on Thursday evening last [i.e. 13 FEB 1817], by the Rev. Mr. Neale, Mr. LIONEL JAMES LARKIN, to Miss MARY A. NEWTON, all of this place. [MS:17 FEB 1817, Monday, p. 3]

MARRIED, on Saturday evening last [i.e. 15 FEB 1817], by the Rev. Mr. Balch, Mr. JACOB CLARKSON, to Miss ELIZA ANN COLLEY, both of Newburyport, Mass. [MS:19 FEB 1817, Wednesday, p. 3]

DIED, in Baltimore, on Saturday evening last [i.e. 15 FEB 1817], after a short illness,

Georgetown, D.C., **Marriage and Death Notices, 1801-1838**

Mr. JAMES LINVILL, aged 25 years. [MS:21 FEB 1817, Friday, p. 3]

DIED.—In London [no date], Col. JOHN HAMILTON, formerly his Britannic Majesty's Consul for Virginia and North Carolina. [MS:12 MAR 1817, Wednesday, p. 3]

DIED, at Baltimore [no date], after a short illness, the Honorable JOSEPH HOPPER NICHOLSON, aged 47 years, Chief Judge of the 6th Judicial District, and judge of the Court of Appeals in Md. [MS:12 MAR 1817, Wednesday, p. 3]

MARRIED.—On Thursday evening last [i.e. 20 MAR 1817], by the Rev. Mr. Greentree, Mr. BENJAMIN BOSWELL, to Miss WINDFORD FIELDING, all of this town. [MS:26 MAR 1817, Wednesday, p. 3]

DIED.—On Wednesday evening last [i.e. 16 APR 1817], Mrs. ALICE RIGGS, wife of Mr. Elisha Riggs, Merchant of this place. [MS:18 APR 1817, Friday, p. 3]

MARRIED.—On Thursday evening [i.e. 17 APR 1817], at Rockville, by the Rev. Mr. Searle, JOHN LACEY, of Georgetown, to Miss EMILY M. LODGE, of the former place. [MS:23 APR 1817, Wednesday, p. 3]

MARRIED.—On Tuesday evening last [i.e. 22 APR 1817], by the Rev. Mr. M'Cormick, Mr. JAMES S. BRIDGES, of Georgetown, to Miss MARY M'KIM, of Washington City. [MS:25 APR 1817, Friday, p. 3]

MARRIED.—On Thursday evening last [i.e. 24 APR 1817], by the Rev. S.B. Balch, Mr. WILLIAM KNOWLES, to Miss JEANNET BARREN, both of this place. [MS:30 APR 1817, Wednesday, p. 3]

DIED.—At *Belmont* [no date], the seat of Alexander Contee Hanson, THOMAS P. GROSVENOR, Esq., member of Congress. Mr. G. was a statesman of no ordinary talents' a tear is due to his memory; although our opposite in politics, he was held in the highest estimation by us. The *Federal Republican* of the 26th inst., contains a beautiful eulogy upon the death of this truly amiable gentleman. It speaks of him as he really was. [MS:30 APR 1817, Wednesday, p. 3]

DIED, in the District of Maine [no date], after a short illness of four days, Maj. Gen. CYRUS KING, formerly a member of the House of Representatives—aged 44 years. [MS:5 MAY 1817, Monday, p. 3]

MARRIED.—On Thursday evening last [i.e. 8 MAY 1817], by the Rev. Mr. Ryland, Mr. WILLIAM COOK, of this place, to Miss MARY BEALL. [MS:12 MAY 1817, Monday, p. 3]

DIED.—In Baltimore, on Friday last [i.e. 9 MAY 1817], after a lingering illness, Miss ANN SMITH, daughter of Gen. J. Smith of that city.—She was a young lady of uncommon attainment, and had scarcely reached her 18th year, when she was snatched from this world of sorrow. [MS:12 MAY 1817, Monday, p. 3]

Georgetown, D.C., **Marriage and Death Notices, 1801-1838**

DIED.—In Richmond [c.7 MAY 1817], Col. DAVID LAMBERT, in the 67th year of his age. [MS:14 MAY 1817, Wednesday, p. 3]

DIED, in Norfolk [no date], Maj. PETER NESTELL, an old revolutionary officer. [MS:14 MAY 1817, Wednesday, p. 3]

DIED.—Yesterday [i.e. 20 MAY 1817], JAMES BLOOMER BALCH, youngest son of Samuel Turner, Esq., of this place. [MS:21 MAY 1817, Wednesday, p. 3]

MARRIED.—On Tuesday evening last [i.e. 20 MAY 1817], at *Analostan*, the seat of Gen. John Mason, by the Rev. Mr. Hawley, C.C. JAMISON, Esq., of Baltimore, to Miss ANN E.M.JOHNSON. [MS:23 MAY 1817, Friday, p. 3]

MARRIED.—On Thursday morning last [i.e. 22 MAY 1817], by the Rev. Mr. Grassi, Mr. BERNARD SPALDING, to Miss ANN FORD, all of this place. [MS:26 MAY 1817, Monday, p. 3]

DIED.—On the morning of the 15th inst. [i.e. 14 MAY 1817], at his residence in Baltimore, ELI SIMKINS ... The luxury of doing good was his reward: he sought no other ... *National Intelligencer*. [MS:28 MAY 1817, Wednesday, p. 3]

MARRIED.—Last Saturday evening [i.e. 24 MAY 1817], by the Rev. Mr. Burch, Mr. FREDERICK HEVNER, to Miss MARY COOKESEY, both of this place. [MS:30 MAY 1817, Friday, p. 3]

MARRIED.—On Tuesday evening last [i.e. 3 JUN 1817], by the Rev. Mr. Balch, Mr. GEORGE W. DASHIELL, to Miss DEBORAH BEALL, all of Washington. [MS:6 JUN 1817, Friday, p. 3]

DIED.—At Philadelphia, 1st inst. [i.e. 1 JUN 1817], Dr. THOMAS H. CUSHING, one of the Assistant Surgeons of the U.S. ship *Franklin*—a gentleman much esteemed in his professional and private character. He was interred on Monday afternoon, with military honors. [MS:9 JUN 1817, Monday, p. 3]

MARRIED, last evening [i.e. 10 JUN 1817], by the Rev. Mr. Ryland, Mr. HENRY B. BLAGROVE, to Miss GRACY N. RATCLIFFE, all of this place. [MS:11 JUN 1817, Wednesday, p. 3]

MARRIED.—In Ontario Co., on the 16th ult. [i.e. 16 MAY 1817], Mr. EZEKIEL FOLSOM, aged thirteen years, to Miss LUCY FITCH, aged sixteen years, daughter of the Rev. Ebenezer Fitch, D.D., late President of Williams College. [MS:18 JUN 1817, Wednesday, p. 3]

DIED, on Wednesday morning, the 18th inst. [i.e. 18 JUN 1817], between the hours of one and two, in the 71st year of his age, the Most Rev. LEONARD NEALE, Archbishop of

Georgetown, D.C., **Marriage and Death Notices, 1801-1838**

Baltimore, and successor, in the Archiepiscopal See to the late Most Rev. Dr. John Carroll, after a short and painful illness of only 36 hours. [MS:20 JUN 1817, Friday, p. 3]

MARRIED.—On Tuesday evening last [i.e. 17 JUN 1817], in Alexandria, by the Rev. Wm. H. Wilmer, Mr. FIELDER R. DORSETT, of this town, to Miss ANN M'REA, of the former place. [MS:23 JUN 1817, Monday, p. 2]

MARRIED.—On the evening of the 25th inst. [i.e. 25 JUN 1817], by the Rev. Mr. Ryland, Mr. WM. SIMMONS, to Mrs. ELIZABETH SHAW, both of Washington. [MS:30 JUN 1817, Monday, p. 3]

MARRIED, last Wednesday [i.e. 30 JUL 1817], in Washington City, by the Rev. Mr. Matthews, Mr. SAMUEL BARKLEY, of Alexandria, to Miss TERESIA C. JEMESON, of Charles Co., Md. [MS:1 AUG 1817, Friday, p. 3]

Died on the 2d of July [i.e. 2 JUL 1817], at Cape Henry (Hayti) the *Prince of Hayti*, in the 40th year of his age. [MS:4 AUG 1817, Monday, p. 3]

Died, on the 9th of June [i.e. 9 JUN 1817], at Cape Henry (Hayti) Capt. JOHN TAYLER, of Salisbury, late master of the brig *Phebe*, of Newburyport. [MS:4 AUG 1817, Monday, p. 3]

Died, on the 20th inst. [i.e. 20 JUL 1817], at Poughkeepsie, in the state of New-York, JAMES HAMILTON, Esq., of the Woodlands, near this city.—This gentleman, with a princely fortune, appeared in society without ostentation or parade. In his intercourse with the world he was modest, liberal, and unassuming; and a most affectionate relative and friend. [MS:4 AUG 1817, Monday, p. 3]

MARRIED.—On Tuesday evening, the 5th inst. [i.e. 5 AUG 1817], by the Rev. Mr. Fenwick, Mr. BLUNTT CLEMENTS, to Miss ELIZA HYDE, both of this town. [MS:8 AUG 1817, Friday, p. 3]

DIED, at Natchez, (M.T.) on the 23d of July last [i.e. 23 JUL 1817], after an illness of three weeks, Mr. ANDREW HASLET, formerly of Baltimore. [MS:20 AUG 1817, Wednesday, p. 3]

DIED.—At Richmond, Va., on Sunday last [i.e. 17 AUG 1817] in the 19th year of her age, Mrs. MARIA D. TRUEHEART, wife of Mr. Daniel Trueheart, Esq., one of the editors of the *Compiler*. Mrs. Trueheart was a lady of uncommon excellence—beloved by her relations, valued and esteemed by her friends, she died universally lamented. [MS:22 AUG 1817, Friday, p. 3]

DIED.—At Rockaway, (N.Y.) on Saturday last [i.e. 23 AUG 1817], Mr. HOLLMAN, late manager of the Theatre Charleston, S.C. [MS:29 AUG 1817, Friday, p. 3]

MARRIED, on Tuesday evening, 16th inst. [i.e. 16 SEP 1817], by the Rev. Dr. Hunter, Mr. WM. Y. WETZEL, to Miss MARY HOLTZMAN, both of Georgetown. [MS:19 SEP 1817, Friday, p. 3]

Georgetown, D.C., **Marriage and Death Notices, 1801-1838**

MARRIED, on Tuesday, the 2d inst. [i.e. 2 SEP 1817], by the Rev. Mr. Reed, Mr. HORATIO WILLCOXEN, to Miss ANN R. GAITHER, all of Montgomery Co., Md. [MS:19 SEP 1817, Friday, p. 3]

MARRIED.—At Rockville, Montgomery Co. [no date], BRIG SELBY, Esq., to Miss CAROLINE SAUNDERS. [MS:29 SEP 1817, Monday, p. 3]

MARRIED, in Nantucket [no date], Mr. JOHN KNOWLES, to Miss SUSAN HALL. [MS:29 SEP 1817, Monday, p. 3]

MARRIED, in Boston [no date], Mr. V. FRENCH, (merchant,) to Miss CAROLINE FRENCH. [MS:29 SEP 1817, Monday, p. 3]

DIED.—In Norfolk, (Va.) [no date], Mr. JOHN DAUL, also, Mr. ELISHA HOWARD. [MS:29 SEP 1817, Monday, p. 3]

DIED, in Hampton, (Va.) [no date], WILLIAM W. WAYMOUTH, packet master between Norfolk and New-York. [MS:29 SEP 1817, Monday, p. 3]

MARRIED, on the 23d inst. [i.e. 23 SEP 1817], at the seat of Thomas T. Somervell, Esq., Prince George's, Md., by the Rev. Mr. Williston, the Rev. THOMAS HORRELL, of Berkeley, Va., to Miss ANN SOMERVELL. [MS:1 OCT 1817, Wednesday, p. 3]

MARRIED.—At Alexandria [c.23 SEP 1817], by the Rev. Mr. Griffith, Mr. GEORGE JACOBS, to Miss SARAH A. CHILDS, all of that place. [MS:3 OCT 1817, Friday, p. 2]

MARRIED, yesterday evening [i.e. 7 OCT 1817], by the Rev. Mr. Ryland, Mr. STEPHEN LANCASTER, to Miss SARAH BECK, both of Washington. [MS:8 OCT 1817, Wednesday, p. 2]

MARRIED.—On Tuesday evening last [i.e. 21 OCT 1817], at Union Mills, Montgomery Co., Md., by his father, (the Rev. Thomas Read,) Mr. ROBERT READ, of this district, to Miss JANE LYNN LACKLAND, daughter of the late James Lackland, Esq., of the former place. [MS:24 OCT 1817, Friday, p. 3]

Georgetown, D.C., **Marriage and Death Notices, 1801-1838**

NATIONAL MESSENGER
January 1, 1821, through May 21, 1821

MARRIED.—On Tuesday evening last [i.e. 6 JAN 1821], by the Rev. Mr. McCormick, Mr. GEORGE A. BARNES, to Miss SUSAN C. PHILLIPS, all of Prince George's Co., Md. [NM:12 JAN 1821, Friday, p. 3]

MARRIED, on Tuesday the 9th inst. [i.e. 9 JAN 1821], by the Rev. Thomas B. Balch, D.D., Mr. STERLING GRESHAM, of the General Land Office, to Miss MARY ELIZA WINGARD, daughter of the late Abraham Wingard, of this place. [NM:19 JAN 1821, Friday, p. 3]

MARRIED, on Thursday the 18th inst. [i.e. 18 JAN 1821], by the Rev. Mr. Addison, JOSEPH PEARSON, Esq., to Miss CATHERINE WORTHINGTON, daughter of Dr. Charles Worthington of this place. [NM:22 JAN 1821, Monday, p. 3]

MARRIED, at Philadelphia, on Tuesday evening, the 16th inst. [i.e. 16 JAN 1821], by the Right Rev. Bishop Conwell, Mr. ATHANASIUS FORD, of the City of Washington, to Miss MARY ANN, daughter of Gen. William Duncan, of the former place. [NM:24 JAN 1821, Wednesday, p. 3]

MARRIED, on Tuesday the 23d inst. [i.e. 23 JAN 1821], by the Rev. S.B. Balch, LEWIS G. DAVIDSON, Esq., to Miss ELIZA CRAWFORD, daughter of the late Mr. William Crawford, all of this place. [NM:29 JAN 1821, Monday, p. 3]

MARRIED, at Baltimore, on Tuesday evening last [i.e. 6 FEB 1821], by the Rev. Dr. Roberts, Mr. WILLIAM QUYNN, of this place, to Miss MARGARET BRANSON, of the former place. [NM:9 FEB 1821, Friday, p. 3]

MARRIED, in Wilmington, Del., on the 1st inst. [i.e. 1 FEB 1821], by the Rev. Dr. Read, Mr. JOSEPH CHEESELY, to Miss ANN PHILIPS, alias Springer, BOTH BLIND! [NM:14 FEB 1821, Wednesday, p. 3]

DIED, on Friday evening last [i.e. 9 FEB 1821], in her sixteenth year, Miss SABRE JET BAKER, eldest daughter of Mr. Zachariah Baker of this place. The deceased possessed a singular excellence of character: her disposition was mild and amiable; her piety ardent and exemplary; her death has deprived society of one of its brightest female ornaments; her acquaintances of a sincere and affectionate friend—and her afflicted parent of one in whom he had placed his greatest hope of earthly happiness. [NM:14 FEB 1821, Wednesday, p. 3]

DIED.—Near Charlotte Hall, Md., at the residence of Mrs. Mary Sothoron, on the 16th of January [i.e. 16 JAN 1821], NELL COURCEY, a negro woman, aged 130. She had been deaf and totally blind for the last 16 years of her life, but enjoyed uninterrupted health till a very few days previous to her dissolution. Also, at the residence of the late John Chapelier, SARAH, a negro woman aged 105. Both these old women were born in Saint

Georgetown, D.C., **Marriage and Death Notices, 1801-1838**

Mary's Co., where their births are on record, and where they were generally known. [NM:16 FEB 1821, Friday, p. 3; M:17 FEB 1821, Saturday, p. 3]

Died, in this town on Monday evening last [i.e. 19 FEB 1821], Mr. CHARLES REDHEIFFER, of Philadelphia. [NM:21 FEB 1821, Wednesday, p. 3]

DIED.—At his late residence, near New-Market, in Frederick Co., Md., on the evening of the 7th inst. [i.e. 7 FEB 1821], the reverend JOHN PITTS, long an itinerant minister in the Methodist Episcopal Church, leaving a widow and six children to bemoan their irreparable bereavement. [NM:23 FEB 1821, Friday, p. 3; M:22 FEB 1821, Thursday, p. 3]

MARRIED, on Tuesday evening last [i.e. 27 FEB 1821], by the Rev. Mr. Decheaux, Mr. JAMES H. NEWTON, to Miss ANN E., daughter of Mr. Richard Smith, Merchant of this town. [NM:5 MAR 1821, Monday, p. 3]

DIED, in Charles Co., Md., on the 18th inst. [i.e. 18 FEB 1821], after a short and painful illness, Mrs. E.A. BRAWNER, wife of Mr. Robert Brawner, leaving to her bereaved friends the great consolation of her having parted from them with christian resignation to her Maker's will. [NM:5 MAR 1821, Monday, p. 3]

DIED.—On Monday morning last [i.e. 2 APR 1821], Mr. JOHN WINTER, printer, in the 62d year of his age, a native of Philadelphia, but for a long time a resident of Alexandria. [NM:6 APR 1821, Friday, p. 2]

MARRIED.—On Thursday evening last [i.e. 5 APR 1821], by the Rev. Mr. Ware, Mr. TILLEY, to Miss MARY McLEOD, all of this place. [NM:9 APR 1821, Monday, p. 3]

MARRIED.—On Tuesday the 13th ult. [i.e. 13 MAR 1821], by the Rev. Mr. McElroy, Mr. BERNARD BRIEN, of Washington, to Mrs. ELIZA O'BRIEN, of Georgetown. [NM:13 APR 1821, Friday, p. 3]

MARRIED.—At Alexandria, on Sunday last [i.e. 8 APR 1821], Mr. ISAAC COOPER, Grocer (aged 86), to Miss NANCY (aged 19) his housekeeper—both of that place. [NM:13 APR 1821, Friday, p. 3]

DIED.—On Saturday last [i.e. 14 APR 1821], in the 47th year of her age, Mrs. MARY BRUFF, relict of the late Dr. Bruff. She had long suffered with a pulmonary affection—and breathed her last in prayer and praise. [NM:18 APR 1821, Wednesday, p. 3]

DIED, on Friday last [i.e. 13 APR 1821], Mrs. PARSONS, the affectionate consort of Mr. William Parsons, of this place. [NM:18 APR 1821, Wednesday, p. 3]

DIED.—At Hartford, Conn., on the 7th of April [i.e. 7 APR 1821], ELISHA BABCOCK, Esq., 37 years proprietor and publisher of *The American Mercury*. [NM:18 APR 1821, Wednesday, p. 3]

Georgetown, D.C., **Marriage and Death Notices, 1801-1838**

DIED, at Alexandria, on the 10th inst. [i.e. 10 APR 1821], of a pulmonary complaint, which had gradually undermined her constitution, Miss ANN ELLEN CRANCH, aged 21 years, eldest daughter of the Hon. William Cranch, Chief Judge of this District. [NM:18 APR 1821, Wednesday, p. 3]

DIED, in New York, on Thursday evening [i.e. 12 APR 1821], MARIA LOUISA, daughter of the late Philip Jacobs, Esq., aged 2 years and 2 months. [By this death, the Orphan Asylum will receive the handsome sum of about $50,000, agreeable to the will of the late Mr. Jacobs.] [NM:18 APR 1821, Wednesday, p. 3]

DIED, in Middleborough [no date], the venerable JOHN ALDEN, in his 103d year. His great grandfather, whose name he bore, as did also his grandfather and father, was one of the first settlers of New England, being one of the number who accompanied the Rev. Mr. Robinson from Europe to America, in 1620, and is said to have been the man who first stepped upon the Plymouth Rock. His grandmother was the daughter of Mr. Peregrine White, who was the first English male born in New-England. Mr. Alden was married young, and his first wife, by whom he had 5 children, died at the age of 27. By his second and last wife he had fourteen children. His descendants are 19 children, 62 grand-children, 134 great-grand children, and several of the 5th generation; 47 of this number, we believe, have deceased, and 172 are now living. [NM:18 APR 1821, Wednesday, p. 3]

DIED, at Aberdeen, in Scotland, on the 18th of September last [i.e. 18 SEP 1820], in the 45th year of his age, Mr. JAMES OGILVIE, the Orator; whither he went to take the title and possession of the estate of Lord Finlater, to which he had recently become the lawful heir. He had distinguished himself in that as well as in this country by the powers of his eloquence, and in some of the European journals his public performances are mentioned with great commendation. [NM:18 APR 1821, Wednesday, p. 3]

DIED, at Norfolk [no date], the Rev. SAMUEL LOW, late Rector of Christ Church in that Borough. [NM:18 APR 1821, Wednesday, p. 3]

DIED, on the 10th inst. [i.e. 10 APR 1821], at his seat, in Stafford Co., Va., deeply regretted by his bereaved family, neighbors, and friends, JOHN T. BROOKS, Esq., President of the Farmers' Bank in Fredericksburg. [NM:18 APR 1821, Wednesday, p. 3]

DIED.—Yesterday morning [i.e. 1 MAY 1821], about 10 o'clock, after a short illness, WILLIAM S. RADCLIFFE, Esq., son of Jacob Radcliffe, Esq., formerly mayor of the city of New York. He was an officer in the army during the late war and for some time past resided in the city of Washington. [NM:2 MAY 1821, Wednesday, p. 3]

MARRIED.—in Georgetown, on Sunday evening, the 6th inst. [i.e. 6 MAY 1821], by the Rev. Mr. McElroy, Mr. JOHN B. HASKINS, of St. Mary's Co., to Miss MARY, daughter of Mr. Joseph Crown, of the former place. [NM:9 MAY 1821, Wednesday, p. 3]

Georgetown, D.C., **Marriage and Death Notices, 1801-1838**

THE METROPOLITAN
January 2, 1821, through December 11, 1826

MARRIED, on Monday evening last [i.e. 25 DEC 1820], by the Rev. S.B. Balch, Judge TOMPKINS, of the House of Representatives, to Miss ELIZABETH H. DAVIS, of this town. [M:2 JAN 1821, Tuesday, p. 3]

DIED, on Monday the first day of January [i.e. 1 JAN 1821], after a long and tedious illness, which she bore with christian fortitude and pious resignation, Miss BARBARA BOHRER [sic Borher], daughter of Mrs. Mary M. Bohrer, of this Town. [M:2 JAN 1821, Tuesday, p. 3]

MARRIED, in Harford Co., on the 26th ult. [i.e. 26 DEC 1820], by the Rev. Mr. Stevenson, Mr. JOHN MOLTON, to Miss MARY NEVIL. [M:9 JAN 1821, Tuesday, p. 3]

DIED, in Harford Co., on the 29th ult. [i.e. 29 DEC 1820], Mr. JOHN MOLTON. About 10 o'clock on the evening on which he was married, (the 26th) he was suddenly taken ill, and remained entirely void of speech for two days, when he expired—and thus exchanged the nuptial bed, for the darksome and the dreary tomb. [M:9 JAN 1821, Tuesday, p. 3]

DIED.—In Tredyffrin township, on Saturday, the 23d ult. [i.e. 23 DEC 1820], Mr. EDWARD WOODMAN, aged about 70 years of age. The deceased was found on the barn floor, too badly hurt to speak. It appeared that he had been pitching down wheat from the mow, that a rail broke on which he stood, and that he fell a considerable distance and bruised himself so that he died. He survived but a few minutes after being found. Mr. Woodman was a soldier of the Revolution, and bore the character of an upright man. [M:9 JAN 1821, Tuesday, p. 3]

DIED, in Eastbradford [no date], Mrs. ENTRIKEN, at a very considerable age. She was found in the morning dead in her bed, her arms folded on her breast, seeming to have departed without a pang or the least struggle. [M:9 JAN 1821, Tuesday, p. 3]

DIED, in Trenton, on Friday evening last [i.e. 5 JAN 1821], JAMES LINN, Esq., late Secretary of State of the state of New-Jersey, and formerly a Representative in Congress. [M:11 JAN 1821, Thursday, p. 3]

DIED, in Cambridge, Mass., on Monday evening, the 1st [i.e. 1 JAN 1821], WILLIAM GAMAGE, M.D., in the 76th year of his age ... [M:11 JAN 1821, Thursday, p. 3]

DIED.—At Natchitoches, on the 9th ult. [i.e. 9 DEC 1820], Captain JOHN FOWLER, late U.S. Factor at Sulphur fork of Red River, and for many years a citizen of this town—after an illness of five months. [M:16 JAN 1821, Tuesday, p. 3]

MARRIED.—on Thursday evening [i.e. 18 JAN 1821], by the Right Rev. Bishop Conwell, ATHANASIUS FORD, Esq., of the city of Washington, to Miss MARY ANN, eldest daughter of Gen. William Duncan, of this city. *Philadelphia Paper.* [M:23 JAN 1821, Tuesday, p. 3]

Georgetown, D.C., **Marriage and Death Notices, 1801-1838**

MARRIED, on Thursday the 18th inst. [i.e. 18 JAN 1821], by the Rev. Mr. Addison, JOSEPH PEARSON, Esq., to Miss CATHERINE WORTHINGTON, daughter of Dr. Charles Worthington of this place. [M:23 JAN 1821, Tuesday, p. 3]

MARRIED.—On Tuesday evening last [i.e. 23 JAN 1821], by the Rev. S.B. Balch, LEWIS GRANT DAVIDSON, Esq., to Miss ELIZA, daughter of the late William Crawford, Esq., all of this place. [M:27 JAN 1821, Saturday, p. 3]

DIED.—On Sunday morning last [i.e. 4 FEB 1821], in the 12th year of her age, MARTHA, daughter of Mr. William Calder, Merchant, of this place. She was a lovely and most interesting child, and was just blooming into beauty, when the fell destroyer nipt the bud. During a severe illness, she bore up with a meekness and sweetness of disposition, aided by religion, which must have afforded great consolation to her distressed parents in so trying an hour. [M:6 FEB 1821, Tuesday, p. 3]

MARRIED, at Baltimore on Tuesday evening last [i.e. 6 FEB 1821], by the Rev. Dr. Roberts, Mr. WILLIAM QUYNN of this town, to Miss MARGARET BRANSON, of the former place. [M:10 FEB 1821, Saturday, p. 3]

Departed this life yesterday evening [i.e. 19 FEB 1821], Mr. CHARLES REDHEIFFER, of Philadelphia. His funeral will take place at 4 o'clock this evening, from the house of Mr. Heabner, on Bridge-street. [M:20 FEB 1821, Tuesday, p. 3]

Died, at Boston, on the 10th inst. [i.e. 10 FEB 1821], JAMES PRINCE, Esq., marshal of the district; a faithful public officer, and a valuable citizen. [M:20 FEB 1821, Tuesday, p. 3]

Died, at Chelmsford, England [no date], Mrs. MARY NAFTEL, of the Society of Friends, who had traveled much in America to promulgate the gospel. [M:20 FEB 1821, Tuesday, p. 3]

DIED.—In Paris [no date], M. TALIEN, aged 54, one of the most noted characters of the French Revolution ... he was an actor of some eminence at Bordeaux, and married one of the most elegant and accomplished women in France. [M:20 FEB 1821, Tuesday, p. 3]

DIED, in England [no date], WILLIAM HAYLEY, Esq., the venerable poet, aged 75. He was the author of the "Lives of Milton," Cowper and Romney, the "Triumphs of Temper," several odes and some dramatic works. [M:20 FEB 1821, Tuesday, p. 3]

MARRIED.—By the Rev. Mr. Rowan, in Alexandria, on Tuesday evening last [i.e. 20 FEB 1821], GIDEON DAVIS, Esq., of this town, to Miss MARIA W., daughter of Wm. Rhodes, Esq., of the former place. [M:24 FEB 1821, Saturday, p. 3]

MARRIED, on Tuesday evening last [i.e. 27 FEB 1821], by the Rev. Mr. Dethroux, Mr. JAMES H. NEWTON, to Miss E., daughter of Mr. Richard Smith, merchant of this place. [M:3 MAR 1821, Saturday, p. 3]

Georgetown, D.C., **Marriage and Death Notices, 1801-1838**

Communicated.—DIED in this town [no date], Mrs. EUNICE RUTHERFORD, wife of Capt. Alexander Rutherford, aged 40 years. By the death of Mrs. R. her relatives and acquaintance have lost a kind and affectionate friend, and they may weep for her loss, but thanks be to God, she was prepared by grace for death, and has gone to that place where the weary are at rest forever. [M:12 APR 1821, Thursday, p. 3]

DIED, at Norfolk, on the Evening of April 5th [i.e. 5 APR 1821], the Rev. SAMUEL LOW, late rector of Christ Church, in that Borough. [M:12 APR 1821, Thursday, p. 3]

DIED.—In Italy [no date], LOUIS CAUIRE, a Frenchman. He dressed himself in the Oriental costume, and presented himself at the hermitage of St. Savour, near Mount Vesuvius, announcing to the hermit his wish to pass a few days under his hospitable room. On the next day, he requested the hermit to accompany him to the crater of the volcano, and as soon as they reached it, plunged into its insatiable abyss, leaving the hermit in a state of horror and surprise more easily to be conceived than expressed. [M:12 APR 1821, Thursday, p. 3]

DIED, on Saturday last [i.e. 14 APR 1821], in the 47th year of her age, Mrs. MARY BRUFF, relict of the late Dr. Bruff. This lady had long suffered with that most distressing and tedious of all diseases, a pulmonary affection—yet she bore up under her afflictions with a patience which the religion of our blessed redeemer alone enables us to exercise. She exhorted all around her to meet her in heaven, and exclaimed the moments she had to live were tedious—she breathed her last in prayer and praise. [M:17 APR 1821, Tuesday, p. 3]

DIED.—In Greenland, on Wednesday morning [i.e. 18 APR? 1821], JOHN WEEKS, Esq., a highly valued and respectable citizen, aged 64 years.—The circumstances attending the death of Mr. Weeks we understand are as follows. He had been laboring on his farm the day previous, with Daniel Hodgkin, a man about 50, who had lived in his family thirteen years.—On going home at sunset Mr. Weeks directed Hodgkin to fodder the cattle, and he obeyed without hesitation. On returning to the house, he stepped up stairs, and brought down a musket which he had previously loaded, and entered the sitting room of Mr. Weeks, saying "Now, Deacon, I am going to kill you." —Mr. Weeks retreated to another apartment, shut the door and held it by the latch. Hodgkin then discharged the musket through the door, and the ball entering his left side passed through the abdomen and lodged in his right side; and he fell, mortally wounded ... Weeks had been for many years a Deacon of the Congregational church in Greenland; and lately accepted the appointment of a Trustee of Hampton Academy ... The verdict of a jury was "wilful murder" by Hodgkin, who was committed to prison in this town, to await his trial at the next term of the Superior Court to be holden in Exeter in September. [M:24 APR 1821, Tuesday, p. 3]

Communicated ... Mrs. NANCY R. TEBBS, consort of Foushee Tebbs, Esq., of Dumfries, Va., and daughter of the late Gurdin Chapin, Esq., of this town, had scarce completed her 17th year, when on the 21st inst. [i.e. 21 APR 1821], the mandate of the Almighty was issued calling her to himself ... *Alexandria Paper*. [M:28 APR 1821, Saturday, p. 3]

MARRIED, in Baltimore [no date], by the Rev. G.S. Roszel, Dr. SAMUEL X. JENNINGS, Jr., to Miss ELIZABETH H. OWINGS. [M:5 MAY 1821, Saturday, p. 3]

Georgetown, D.C., **Marriage and Death Notices, 1801-1838**

DIED.—In the City of London [no date], the Rev. JOSEPH BENSON, aged 73, formerly of St. Edmund Hall, Oxford, and for upwards of 50 years a distinguished minister among the Wesleyan Methodists. For many years, Mr. Benson has been the Editor of the Methodist Magazine, a work of very great repute. [M:5 MAY 1821, Saturday, p. 3]

MARRIED.—In this town on Sunday evening the 6th inst. [i.e. 6 MAY 1821], by the Rev. Mr. M'Elroy, Mr. JOHN B. HASKINS, of St. Mary's Co., to Miss MARY, daughter of Joseph Crown, of the former place. [M:12 MAY 1821, Saturday, p. 3]

MARRIED, last evening [i.e. 11 MAY 1821], at Washington, by Rev. —, Mr. C.P. SENGSTACK, to Miss CATHERINE HALLER, both of this place. [M:12 MAY 1821, Saturday, p. 3]

MARRIED.—On Friday evening last [i.e. 18 MAY 1821], by the Rev. S.B. Balch, Mr. HENRY OULD, to Miss ELIZABETH C. PEIRCE, both of this place. [M:22 MAY 1821, Tuesday, p. 3]

DIED.—On Wednesday the 23d inst. [i.e. 23 MAY 1821], in Montgomery Co., (Md.) Miss CAROLINE THOMAS, daughter of Mr. John Thomas, 3d. She had been afflicted with a pulmonary consumption upwards of two years. It may truly be said that she died a sincere believer in Jesus Christ—at her latest breath she proclaimed to all around her, that she felt the witness within her that she accepted of her divine Master, and should shortly be in glory with him. [M:2 JUN 1821, Saturday, p. 3]

MARRIED.—On Sunday evening, May 27 [i.e. 27 MAY 1821], by the Rev. Mr. M'Cormick, Mr. JAMES WILSON, printer, to Miss MARIA SOPHIA MARKS, all of Washington city. [M:5 JUN 1821, Tuesday, p. 3]

DIED.—On Tuesday, the 5th inst. [i.e. 5 JUN 1821], at the residence of his son, Mr. ROBERT ROSS, a native of Ireland, in the 89th year of his age. [M:7 JUN 1821, Thursday, p. 2]

MARRIED.—At Belfast, Me. [no date], Mr. ALEXANDER CLARK, aged 75, to Miss ANNA CAIN, age 25. [M:16 JUN 1821, Saturday, p. 3]

DIED.—On the 16th inst. [i.e. 16 JUN 1821], at the residence of his father, in Prince George's Co., Md., Mr. SAMUEL T. GODMAN, in the 23d year of his age.—He possessed a kindness of disposition, that rendered him companionable to all ... [M:19 JUN 1821, Tuesday, p. 3]

DIED, suddenly, on Wednesday morning last [i.e. 13 JUN 1821], at New York, Mrs. ALSOP, late of the London Theatres. Mrs. A. was the daughter of the late celebrated English actress, Mrs. Jordon. [M:19 JUN 1821, Tuesday, p. 3]

DIED, in England, on the 25th of April last [i.e. 25 APR 1821], the Earl of Carhampton, in the 78th year of his age. He was distinguished in early life as the opponent of Mr. Wilkes' and known in the letters of Junius and in the recorded scenes of that day by the name of

Georgetown, D.C., **Marriage and Death Notices, 1801-1838**

Colonel Luttrell. He left no issue and is succeeded by his brother. [M:19 JUN 1821, Tuesday, p. 3]

MARRIED.—On Tuesday evening last [i.e. 19 JUN 1821], by the Rev. Beverley Waugh, Mr. SMITH TWYFORD, to Miss CATHERINE MURPHY, both of Georgetown. [M:26 JUN 1821, Tuesday, p. 3]

MARRIED.—On Thursday evening last [i.e. 5 JUN 1821], by the Rev. Mr. Balch, Mr. WILLIAM H. BOSWELL, Printer, to Miss ELIZABETH H. FLETCHER, all of this place. [M:7 JUL 1821, Saturday, p. 3]

MARRIED.—At Florence, Italy [no date], Ferdinand 3d, Grand Duke of Tuscan, brother of the Emperor of Austria, to the Princess Maria Ferdinanda Amelia Xaifre, of Saxony. The Bridegroom is in his 52d, and the bride in her 25th year. [M:7 JUL 1821, Saturday, p. 3]

DIED, at Brainerd, in the Cherokee nation, on the 7th inst. [i.e. 7 JUN 1821], the Rev. SAMUEL WORCESTER, D.D., of Salem, aged 50. Having been advised by Physicians to take a voyage and journey for the benefit of his health, he left Boston for New-Orleans at the commencement of the present year. He suffered much from a boisterous passage ... [M:7 JUL 1821, Saturday, p. 3]

MARRIED, on Sunday evening last [i.e. 15 JUL 1821], by the Rev. Mr. Tyng, Mr. PETER SYMINGTON, to Miss KATHARINE BRUNER, all of this place. [M:17 JUL 1821, Tuesday, p. 3]

DIED.—On the 18th inst. [i.e. 18 JUL 1821], in Georgetown, at the Ladies Academy, of which she was a member, Miss SUSAN WIGHTT, aged 20 years. Her expectation of death during two months of a hopeless disease, did not alter for a moment, her ordinary gaiety, sweetness, and peace of mind, fruits of a life conformable, in every point, to the perfection of the faith which had made her devote herself to God, and to the education of the female youth, in that respectable institution. [M:21 JUL 1821, Saturday, p. 3]

MARRIED.—In the village of Homer, Cortland Co., on the evening of the 14th inst. [i.e. 14 JUL 1821], by the Rev. Alfred Bennett, after a short but pleasant courtship of one evening, Mr. THOMAS STONE, aged 45, to Miss DESIRE WING, aged 20 years. [M:7 AUG 1821, Tuesday, p. 3]

DIED.—In Cahaba, Alabama, a few days since [no date], Col. JOHN TAYLOR, Receiver of Public Monies, and formerly Member of Congress from the state of South-Carolina. [M:9 AUG 1821, Thursday, p. 3]

DIED.—At *Cedar Point*, Charles Co., on the 4th inst. [i.e. 4 AUG 1821], Mr. ABNER RITCHIE, formerly of this town, aged 27 years. [M:21 AUG 1821, Tuesday, p. 3]

DIED.—On the 17th inst. [i.e. 17 AUG 1821], at the Cotton Manufactory between this place and Alexandria, Mr. STEPHEN S. HOVEY, cabinet-maker, formerly of near Salem, Mass., and for two years past a resident of this place. [M:25 AUG 1821, Saturday, p. 3]

Georgetown, D.C., **Marriage and Death Notices, 1801-1838**

DIED.—At the Little Falls, D.C., on the 2d inst. [i.e. 2 AUG 1821], JOHN HOWE, formerly of or near Boston, (Mass.) and a soldier in the late war. [M:30 AUG 1821, Thursday, p. 3]

DIED, in this town, on the 24th inst. [i.e. 24 AUG 1821], JAMES NELSON, a native of Ireland. [M:30 AUG 1821, Thursday, p. 3]

DIED.—At Germantown, on Saturday night last [i.e. 25 AUG 1821], GEORGE ALLEN, Esq.—This gentleman had lately arrived in this city, on a visit to his daughters, at a respectable boarding school. His death was very sudden ... His remains were deposited in the Episcopal burying ground, attended by a large and highly respectable assemblage of the inhabitants of Germantown ... He has left a wife and a large family of children. — *Philadelphia National Gazette.* [M:1 SEP 1821, Saturday, p. 3]

DIED, at New-Orleans, in the 24th year of his age [no date], LEWIS COZENS, Esq., son of Doctor Cozens of this city.—Mr. Cozens had chosen for this profession the law, and was a young gentleman of no ordinary mind and capacity—he was just in a way to realize for himself both fortune and fame, when death put a period to his career ... The news of his death has been peculiarly agonizing to his family—his parents, wife, brothers and sisters, and an interesting little daughter, were anxiously expecting his arrival, when the blighting intelligence reached their ears. [M:8 SEP 1821, Saturday, p. 3]

MARRIED.—On Thursday evening 6th inst. [i.e. 6 SEP 1821], by the Rev. Mr. M'Elvaine, W.J. DAVIDSON, merchant, to Miss MARY ANN, daughter of Henry Upperman, Esq., all of this place. [M:13 SEP 1821, Thursday, p. 3]

DIED.—At North Kingstown, on the 21st ult. [i.e. 21 AUG 1821], Miss LUCY GARDNER, daughter of Mr. James Gardner, in the 20th year of her age.—She was taken suddenly with a violent bleeding at her mouth, nose and ears, and expired in about three minutes after the commencement of the bleeding. [M:13 SEP 1821, Thursday, p. 3]

MARRIED.—At Willingford, Conn. [no date], Mr. JOSEPH DOOLITTLE, to Miss MARY BRONSON. Mr. SAMUEL MOSS to Miss BETSY DOOLITTLE. Mr. ROSWELL DOOLITTLE, to Miss POLLY MOSS; Mr. LEMUEL DOOLITTLE, to Miss DUODEMA MATTOOM. [These Doolittles have done a good deal.] *Hartford Paper.* [M:20 SEP 1821, Thursday, p. 3]

DIED.—In Portland [no date], Miss CAROLINE J. KENDALL, aged 17 years. She was recovering from a fit of sickness, of which she had been ill some time. Finding her strength had increased, she visited the circus on Wednesday evening. Not long after she had got seated, she became faint, and before she could be removed from the circus expired. [M:27 SEP 1821, Thursday, p. 3]

DIED.—In Prince George's Co., Md., on the 24th inst. [i.e. 24 SEP 1821], at half past 6 o'clock, P.M., in the 58th year of his age, JAMES BECK, Sr., of a pulmonary complaint, which he bore with christian patience and fortitude for nearly seven years. The Methodist Episcopal Church has lost one who belonged to her society thirty years. He was an

Georgetown, D.C., **Marriage and Death Notices, 1801-1838**

affectionate husband, an indulgent parent, a kind neighbor, and a good master. [M:29 SEP 1821, Saturday, p. 3]

DIED.—On Thursday evening last [i.e. 27 SEP 1821], at York-Haven, after an illness of about one week, Dr. CHRISTOPHER STODDART, formerly of this place. [M:2 OCT 1821, Tuesday, p. 3]

MARRIED.—On Thursday evening last [i.e. 4 OCT 1821], by the Rev. Dr. Balch, Mr. WILLIAM WATKINS, to Miss MARY TILLEY, all of this place. [M:6 OCT 1821, Saturday, p. 3]

MARRIED.—At Preston, England [no date], Mr. JOHN PENNY, to Miss ISABELLA PENNY. [M:9 OCT 1821, Tuesday, p. 3]

DIED.—In Alexandria [no date], of a Malignant Fever, contracted in that town, JAMES H. DULANEY, Esq., a young gentleman much and deservedly esteemed.—Mr. D. was delicate and refined in his sentiments, lofty, generous, and noble in his disposition ... We since understand the authorities are fencing off the infected district. [M:11 OCT 1821, Thursday, p. 3]

Another Revolutionary Hero Gone! DIED.—On Saturday morning [i.e. 6 OCT 1821] at his residence near Germantown, the venerable Commodore MURRAY, the senior officer of the Navy of the United States. [M:11 OCT 1821, Thursday, p. 3]

DIED.—On Thursday night [i.e. 11 OCT 1821], after a very short illness, of malignant fever, Mr. WILLS HOLT, Printer, of this Borough, but more recently a Grocer ... *American Beacon (Norfolk).* [M:13 OCT 1821, Saturday, p. 3]

Communicated.—Died very suddenly in this town, on Tuesday evening the 9th inst. [i.e. 9 OCT 1821], Mr. GEORGE KING, Senr., in the 63d year of his age ... [M:16 OCT 1821, Tuesday, p. 3]

Died, on Sunday night last [i.e. 14 OCT 1821], after a short illness, Mr. THOMAS C. HODGES, a highly respected merchant of this town. [M:16 OCT 1821, Tuesday, p. 3]

DIED.—On Sunday morning [i.e. 14 OCT 1821], after a short illness, ISAAC BURNESTON, in the fifty-third year of his age. Few men were better known or more deservedly esteemed in Baltimore than Mr. Burneston ... [M:18 OCT 1821, Thursday, p. 3]

MARRIED.—On Thursday evening the 18th inst. [i.e. 18 OCT 1821], by the Rev. Mr. Tyng, THOMAS COOK, Esq., of Washington City, to Mrs. CATHARINE WILSON, of Philadelphia. [M:20 OCT 1821, Saturday, p. 3]

DIED.—On Wednesday morning last [i.e. 17 OCT 1821], after a short illness, in the 18th year of his age, JOSEPH DOYNE, relative and adopted son of Mr. Joseph Semmes of this place ... [M:20 OCT 1821, Saturday, p. 3]

Georgetown, D.C., **Marriage and Death Notices, 1801-1838**

DIED.—On Monday evening last [i.e. 22 OCT 1821], Mrs. CAROLINE, wife of Mr. Horatio Scott, merchant of our town. This lady was at that time of life when society became interested in her—she was a mother and a wife, and amiable and interesting in both. She went to Alexandria to minister to her mother, and to pay to her the last sad rites of humanity; and while in these praiseworthy offices she took the malignant fever which occasioned her death. [M:25 OCT 1821, Thursday, p. 3]

DIED,—On Sunday last [i.e. 21 OCT 1821], Mr. S. COLLINGWOOD, merchant in Water-street. Mr. C. has resided long among us, and always sustained a most irreproachable character. [M:25 OCT 1821, Thursday, p. 3]

DIED.—In Philadelphia [no date], Mrs. SUSAN BLAIR, only daughter of Mr. William Shippen and relict of the Rev. Samuel Blair, who left our transitory world, October 11th, 1821 ... [M:25 OCT 1821, Thursday, p. 3]

DIED, yesterday morning [i.e. 19 OCT? 1821], at 4 o'clock, Mr. E. SALOMON, Cashier of the U.S. Branch Bank, in this city. *N.O. Gazette*. [M:27OCT 1821, Saturday, p. 3]

DIED, at Newport [no date], MEREAH BRENTON, a woman of colour, better known by the name of Aunt Merea Coggeshell. When the twenty eight pirates were hung, in the year 1723, on Gravelly point, in Newport, she was of sufficient age to be carried to see that awful spectacle, and recollected seeing them in the carts. [M:3 NOV 1821, Saturday, p. 2]

DIED.—In this town, on Sunday the 4th inst. [i.e. 4 NOV 1821], Mr. JOHN TRAVERS, aged 72 years, an old and respectable inhabitant of this place. [M:6 NOV 1821, Tuesday, p. 3]

DIED.—In Baltimore, on Sunday evening last [i.e. 4 NOV 1821], in the 45th year of his age, WILLIAM BRUFF, Esqr., a gentleman of talents and integrity. [M:10 NOV 1821, Saturday, p. 3]

DIED.—At his residence six miles south of Nashville [no date], JESSE MAXWELL; for many years a citizen of that county. He was a soldier in the revolution, a sterling patriot, a good citizen, and discharged with much credit all the relations of life. [M:10 NOV 1821, Saturday, p. 3]

DIED.—In Wilmington, (Del.) on the 2d inst. [i.e. 2 NOV 1821], HENRY W. PHYSIC ... [M:15 NOV 1821, Thursday, p. 3]

MARRIED.—Last week [no date], by the Rev. Dr. Balch, Mr. JOSEPH HOWARD, of Virginia, to Miss SARAH ROBERTSON, of this place. [M:20 NOV 1821, Tuesday, p. 3]

Communicated. DIED.—In this town, on Saturday morning last [i.e. 17 NOV 1821], in the 31st year of her age, after a very short, but distressing illness, Mrs. ELIZABETH ARNY, wife of Joseph Arny, Confectioner, and eldest daughter of Mr. William Hide, residing near Bromsgrove, Worcestershire (England) ... [M:20 NOV 1821, Tuesday, p. 3]

Georgetown, D.C., **Marriage and Death Notices, 1801-1838**

MARRIED.—On Tuesday evening last [i.e. 20 NOV 1821], by the Rev. Mr. McElroy, Mr. PETER BRADY, to Miss ANN RAINSFORD, all of this place. [M:24 NOV 1821, Saturday, p. 3]

MARRIED.—On Thursday evening, 22d inst. [i.e. 22 NOV 1821], by the Rev. Mr. Addison, Lieut. J. SMITH, U.S. Army, to Miss MARY REBECCA, youngest daughter of General M. Bayly, of this district. [M:27 NOV 1821, Tuesday, p. 3]

DIED.—At Lancaster, Pa., on the 20th inst. [i.e. 20 NOV 1821], after an illness of eight days, Mr. HENRY G. GRAEFF, in the 20th year of his age. His friends in this city condole sincerely with his parents and relatives in this severe and unexpected affliction. [M:27 NOV 1821, Tuesday, p. 3]

Communicated. DIED.—On the 25th inst. [i.e. 25 NOV 1821], at her father's house in Georgetown, Miss SALLY FORD, aged about 20 ... She was Nun of the order of Emmitsburg, & trained in her assimilated virtues under the auspices of the accomplished, fatherly and tender superior of the order, Mr. DuBois ... [M:29 NOV 1821, Thursday, p. 3]

DIED.—In this town [no date], Major H.H. CHAPMAN, a soldier of the Revolution, and very highly esteemed and respected in private life. He had filled various public offices in the State of Md., whence he removed about two years ago. A wife and nine children mourn the loss of their natural protector and guardian. [M:8 DEC 1821, Saturday, p. 3]

DIED, on the 8th ult. [i.e. 8 NOV 1821], in Alabama, Major THOMAS FREEMAN, of Washington, Mississippi, for many years Surveyor General of Public Lands south of Tennessee river. [M:8 DEC 1821, Saturday, p. 3]

Died, on the 29th ult. [i.e. 29 NOV 1821], Mr. CONSTANTINE PETIT DeCLAVILLE, aged 72 years and 20 days, a native of Chartres in France, he was a French officer during seven years in the East Indies, emigrated to this country at the time of the French revolution, and was for several years a teacher of the French language at the College of Athens, Georgia ... *Georgia Chronicle.* [M:20 DEC 1821, Thursday, p. 3]

MARRIED.—On Thursday evening last [i.e. 20 DEC 1821], by the Rev. Mr. McIlvaine, Dr. WILLIAM JONES, of Washington, to Miss SARAH, daughter of Thos. Corcoran, Esq., of this place. [M:22 DEC 1821, Saturday, p. 3]

DIED.—At *Weston,* the residence of Thomas L. M'Kenny, Esq., at 5 o'clock in the afternoon of the 25th inst. [i.e. 25 DEC 1821], Mrs. HANNAH BURNESTON, of Chester Town, Eastern Shore of Md., in the 68th year of her age ... [M:29 DEC 1821, Saturday, p. 3]

Died, in Washington City [no date], Mrs. MARGARETTA KING, relict of the late Nicholas King, Esq. [M:29 DEC 1821, Saturday, p. 3]

Departed this transitory life, we hope for a blessed immortality, on Saturday the 8th inst. [i.e. 8 DEC 1821], after a few days of severe sickness and suffering, Mr. GEORGE S. BAKER,

Georgetown, D.C., **Marriage and Death Notices, 1801-1838**

aged 34 years, leaving a wife and six children, a mother, brothers and sisters, and numerous friends ... *Baltimore paper.* M:3 JAN 1822, Thursday, p. 3]

DIED.—At N. Haven, on the 19th inst. [i.e. 19 DEC 1821], where she had been several weeks, under the surgical aid of Dr. Smith, Mrs. MIMA BURR, aged 60, wife of Mr. Samuel Burr, of Bridgeport, Conn. ... [M:5 JAN 1822, Saturday, p. 3]

DIED, in Portland [Me.] on Saturday last [i.e. 5 JAN 1822], Mr. JOHN DAVIS, 2d mate of the brig *Mentor*, a native of Sweden, aged about 40. Whilst in the act of taking off the main-topmast cross-tree, it being defective, gave way, and precipitated him about 50 feet upon the deck, which killed him instantly. [M:10 JAN 1822, Thursday, p. 3]

DIED.—Yesterday morning [i.e. 11 JAN 1822], at nine o'clock, ANDREW ROSS, Esq., Chief Clerk in the Office of the 5th Auditor of the Treasury Department. His friends and acquaintances are invited to attend his funeral from his late dwelling on Bridge street, this afternoon, at half past 3 o'clock. [M:12 JAN 1822, Saturday, p. 3]

DIED.—At Upper Marlborough, Prince George's Co., on the night of the 12th inst. [i.e. 12 JAN 1822], after an illness of five days, Mr. RICHARD K. SCOTT, a respectable merchant of that place, leaving a family and many friends to lament his loss. [M:15 JAN 1822, Tuesday, p. 3]

DIED.—On the 8th of January [i.e. 8 JAN 1822], after a long and lingering illness, Mr. JOSEPH HUSLER, aged 41 years.—He has left a wife and 6 children to lament the loss of a fond parent and an affectionate husband. [M:19 JAN 1822, Saturday, p. 3]

DIED.—At Hagerstown, Jan. 12th, 1822, PETER BAZLIN, a man of colour, formerly the servant of Col. John Rea, of Savanna, aged upwards of one hundred and ten years. He perfectly recollected the war in which the colonies were engaged with the Yamasees, Cherokees, Creeks, and other Indian nations, which ended in 1720. And was employed in assisting to erect forts on the river Savanna before the arrival from England of General Oglethorpe, who built the city of Savanna, on the site of Yomacraw, an Indian village. [M:19 JAN 1822, Saturday, p. 3]

MARRIED.—On Tuesday evening, January 1st [i.e. 1 JAN 1822], by E. Hall, Esq., Mr. THOMAS BODELY, to Miss ALMIRA FORCE, both of Woodstock, Mass. [M:22 JAN 1822, Tuesday, p. 3]

MARRIED.—In Hancock, Vermont [no date], Mr. IRA COOPER, to Miss BETSEY GOODENOUGH ... [M:22 JAN 1822, Tuesday, p. 3]

MARRIED.—On Thursday evening the 17th inst. [i.e. 17 JAN 1822], by the Rev. Mr. Breckenridge, Mr. PAOLI BROWN, of Baltimore, to Miss REBECCA D., daughter of Edward Magruder, Esq., of Prince George's Co., Md. [M:26 JAN 1822, Saturday, p. 3]

Georgetown, D.C., **Marriage and Death Notices, 1801-1838**

MARRIED.—On Tuesday 21st of Jan. [i.e. 21 JAN 1822], in *Mount Terling*, Crawford Co., Indiana, by the Rev. Mr. Webster, Mr. NATHANIEL McRIM, to Miss MARY A. ASHWORTH, all formerly of the City of Washington. [M:31 JAN 1822, Thursday, p. 3]

MARRIED.—On Tuesday evening last [i.e. 29 JAN 1822], by the Rev. Mr. Detau, Mr. JAMES DREWRY, of Washington City, to Miss LOUISA COLLINS, of this place. [M:31 JAN 1822, Thursday, p. 3]

MARRIED.—On the 8th of Jan. [i.e. 8 JAN 1822], by the Rev. Mr. Reed, AQUILLA S. STINCHCOMB, Esq., of Georgetown, D.C., to the amiable Miss ANN CREIGHTON, of Dorchester Co., E.S. of Md. [M:31 JAN 1822, Thursday, p. 3]

DIED.—In the City of Washington, on Monday morning the 21st ult. [i.e. 21 JAN 1822], after a lingering and protracted illness, aged about 53 years, Mrs. ELIZABETH BEALL, consort of Mr. Robert B. Beall, and daughter of Benjamin S. Berry, Senr., Esq., of Prince George's Co., Md. [M:2 FEB 1822, Saturday, p. 3]

DIED.—At his residence on the 1st inst. [i.e. 1 FEB 1822], Mr. ELISHA LANHAM, of a painful and lingering disease; long a respectable inhabitant of this place. [M:5 FEB 1822, Tuesday, p. 3]

DIED, in Haverhill [no date], Mr. JOHN WHITING, aged 94.—He was born in Chester, N.H., Feb. 22nd, 1728, and is said to have been the first white male child in that settlement. At the age of twelve, he removed to Haverhill. In 1743, he was engaged as an artisan in the expedition to Cape Breton, when the important fortress of Louisburg yielded to the undisciplined valor of the New-England militia ... At eighty-two he had a new set of teeth ... his mother died at the advanced age of 99 ... [M:21 FEB 1822, Thursday, p. 2]

OBITUARY.—Col. JOHN IRWIN, of Brush-Hill, breathed his last on the 15th ult. [i.e. 15 FEB 1822], having attained the 83rd year of his age. His death was occasioned by repeated attacks of apoplexy. [M:2 MAR 1822, Saturday, p. 3]

MARRIED.—At Springfield near Snow-Hill, Md., on the 20th ult. [i.e. 20 FEB 1822], by the Rev. T.B. Balch, Esq., IRVING SPENCE, Esq., to Miss MARGARET ROBBINS, daughter of the Hon. Judge Robbins, all of that place. [M:9 MAR 1822, Saturday, p. 3]

MARRIED.—On Tuesday evening last [i.e. 12 MAR 1822], by the Rev. Dr. Laurie, GEORGE R. GAITHER, Esq., merchant of Georgetown, to Miss HANNAH, second daughter of Abraham Bradley, Jr., Esq., of Washington City. [M:14 MAR 1822, Thursday, p. 3]

MARRIED.—On Tuesday evening last [i.e. 12 MAR 1822], by the Rev. Mr. Kurtz, Mr. THOMAS S. LAMDEN, to Miss ANN JONES—all of this city [Baltimore]. [M:19 MAR 1822, Tuesday, p. 3]

Georgetown, D.C., **Marriage and Death Notices, 1801-1838**

MARRIED.—On Tuesday evening last [i.e. 12 MAR 1822], by the Rev. Mr. Kurtz, Mr. LOUIS CHASTEAU, to Miss MARY M'CONNELL—also of this city [Baltimore]. [M:19 MAR 1822, Tuesday, p. 3]

DIED.—On the 12th inst. [i.e. 12 MAR 1822], in this town, Mrs. LYDIA ANN TYLER, daughter of the late Mr. John Bridges, in the 34th year of her age. She was a dutiful and affectionate daughter.—She suffered much from severe afflictions, which she bore with great resignation and fortitude and died in a firm belief of a happy immortality. [M:21 MAR 1822, Thursday, p. 3]

DIED.—At New York [no date], a few days ago, ABRAHAM I. DURYEE, M.D., grandson of John Barnes, Esq., Collector of the port of Georgetown, in the 28th year of his age ... [M:23 MAR 1822, Saturday, p. 3]

DIED.—On Saturday night [i.e. 23 MAR 1822], after a long illness, Col. SAMUEL LANE, a worthy officer of the army during the late war, and, for several years past, Commissioner of the Public Buildings at the seat of government. Col. Lane bore his protracted illness with great firmness, and met death with a degree of fortitude which a few display at that trying hour. A numerous connexion and large circle of friends lament his loss. [M:26 MAR 1822, Tuesday, p. 3]

DIED.—On Wednesday last [i.e. 20 MAR 1822], Miss ANN HYATT, daughter of Mr. Seth Hyatt, Sen., of Prince George's Co., Md. ... [M:26 MAR 1822, Tuesday, p. 3]

MARRIED.—On Thursday, the 21st inst. [i.e. 21 MAR 1822], by the Rev. Mr. Henshaw, Mr. JOSEPH B. TENNISON, to Miss CATHARINE GOLDSMITH, all of this city. *Baltimore Patriot.* [M:28 MAR 1822, Thursday, p. 3]

DIED.—In Buckingham, Pa., on the 13th inst. [i.e. 13 MAR 1822], ABIGAIL, daughter of Jacob Harman, aged 14 years ... She was subject to fits, and about sunrise on the morning of her death, Mr. Harman her only surviving parent, and his housekeeper were engaged at the barn, and the young lady was left in bed and no other person in the house ... [M:30 MAR 1822, Saturday, p. 3]

DIED.—In Washington, on Wednesday last [i.e. 10 APR 1822], Mrs. MARY DASHIEL, wife of Thomas B. Dashiel, Esq., of the Treasury Department. Mrs. D. Was a lady of highly interesting manners, and in her domestic circle her virtues were most conspicuous ... [M:13 APR 1822, Saturday, p. 3]

DIED.—On Saturday the 20th inst. [i.e. 20 APR 1822], in the 52d year of her age, Mrs. SUSAN MONROE WASHINGTON, wife of Mr. Lund Washington, of this city, after a painful and lingering illness of seven months ... *National Intelligencer.* [M:30 APR 1822, Tuesday, p. 3]

MARRIED.—On the 16th ult. [i.e. 16 APR 1822], at the farm of Solomon Davis, Esq., in Montgomery Co., Md., Dr. SAMUEL TURNER, formerly of this place, and now resident of

Georgetown, D.C., **Marriage and Death Notices, 1801-1838**

Loudoun Co., Va., to Miss AMANDA M.F. WILLIAMS, of the latter place. [M:14 MAY 1822, Tuesday, p. 3]

MARRIED, at Lexington, Ky., on the 22d ult. [i.e. 22 APR 1822], by the Rev. G.T. Chapman, MARTIN DURALD, Esq., of New Orleans, to Miss SUSAN H. CLAY, eldest daughter of Henry Clay, Esq. [M:14 MAY 1822, Tuesday, p. 3]

Died, at Summerset county [Somerset Co., Md.?] [no date], Mrs. WINDER, relict of the late General Levin Winder. [M:16 MAY 1822, Thursday, p. 3]

MARRIED, on Thursday evening last [i.e. 16 MAY 1822], by the Rev. Mr. B. Waugh, Mr. GEORGE THOMPSON, to Miss SARAH ANN HAYWOOD, all of this place. [M:18 MAY 1822, Saturday, p. 3]

DIED.—On the 10th inst. [i.e. 10 MAY 1822], in this town, Mrs. MARY HEDGES, wife of Nicholas Hedges. Mrs. H. had long labored under a pulmonary affection, which she bore up against the most pious resignation. [M:21 MAY 1822, Tuesday, p. 2]

DIED, at Richmond yesterday morning [i.e. 20 MAY 1822], JOHN WOOD, Esq., a native of Scotland, but more than twenty years a resident of the United States.—He is most celebrated as a profound Mathematician, but he is also known for his travels in Switzerland, and certain political tracts which he has written in America ... [M:21 MAY 1822, Tuesday, p. 2]

DIED.—On the 26th inst. [i.e. 26 MAY 1822], at his seat near this place, in the 66th year of his age, General HENRY CARBERY, a distinguished officer of the Revolution. In that struggle for the emancipation of his country, he received a wound in the side from a musket ball, which could not be extracted without endangering his life, and it was no doubt the cause of his death, after remaining in him forty odd years ... [M:30 MAY 1822, Thursday, p. 3]

MARRIED, in North Carolina [no date], the Rev. EDWARD BIRD, aged 83, and weighing 100 lbs., to Miss ELIZA CHERRY, aged 75, and weighing 200 lbs. [M:4 JUN 1822, Tuesday, p. 3]

OBITUARY.—Died, at Oxford, N.Y., on the 16th inst. [i.e. 16 MAY 1822], of a short illness, Col. BENJAMIN THROOP, Æ 80. The deceased was one of the few remaining patriots, who gave liberty and independence to his country. In 1777, he led a hundred warriors of the Moegan tribe to Canada ... [M:4 JUN 1822, Tuesday, p. 3]

Married, on Thursday evening last [i.e. 6 JUN 1822], by the Rev. Mr. McIlvain, Mr. WM. HAYMAN, Jr., of this town, to Miss JOHANNA, daughter of Samuel Lane, Esq., of Frederick county (Md.) [M:8 JUN 1822, Saturday, p. 3]

Married, on Tuesday evening last [i.e. 4 JUN 1822], by the Rev. Mr. Waugh, Mr. JOHN WILSON, Jr., to Miss CHARLOTTE MOYERS, all of this place. [M:8 JUN 1822, Saturday, p. 3]

Died, in Baltimore [no date], sailing Master GEORGE ULRICK, of the United States Navy. The deceased commanded one of the five gunboats which made a gallant defense, a few days previous to the siege of New Orleans, and was one of the last to surrender to the overwhelming force opposed to them. Mr. Ulrick maintained in life the character of a brave and intelligent officer. [M:11 JUN 1822, Tuesday, p. 3]

MARRIED.—In Albany [no date], the Rev. CHARLES S. STEWART, of the Theological Seminary at Princeton, to Miss HARRIET B. TIFFANY. The new married couple are attached to the mission family about to depart for the Sandwich Islands. After the solemnization of their union, a collection was taken up, amounting to nearly $120, to aid in the outfit of this family. [M:13 JUN 1822, Thursday, p. 3]

DIED, on Wednesday evening the 5th inst. [i.e. 5 JUN 1822], in Prince William Co., Va., of a lingering consumption, Mrs. GRACY ANN BLAGROVE, wife of Henry B. Blagrove, Printer, in the 25th year of her age. She has left a husband and two infants to mourn their irreparable loss. [M:13 JUN 1822, Thursday, p. 3]

DIED.—Suddenly yesterday morning [i.e. 17 JUN 1822], Mrs. REBECCA SHOEMAKER. The friends of the deceased are requested to attend her funeral from the [residence] of Mr. Trueman Beck, in Jefferson street this morning at 10 o'clock. [M:18 JUN 1822, Tuesday, p. 3]

MARRIED.—In New York, on Friday morning last [i.e. 14 JUN 1822], Maj. GEORGE McGLASSIN, of Philadelphia, to Miss ABBY P. JONES, daughter of Samuel Jones, Esq., of Lebanon Springs, Columbia Co., N.Y. [M:20 JUN 1822, Thursday, p. 3]

MARRIED.—At Baltimore on Tuesday evening last, the 18th inst. [i.e. 18 JUN 1822], by the Rev. Mr. Kurtz, Mr. JOSEPH ARNY, of this town, to Miss CAROLINE HENRIETTA VON WEISENSKE, niece to Charles G. Boehm, of that city. [M:22 JUN 1822, Saturday, p. 3]

DIED.—In the town of Livingston, on Sunday morning last [i.e. 23 JUN 1822], Col. JOHN McKINSTY, aged 77 ... [M:25 JUN 1822, Tuesday, p. 3]

DIED.—On Monday the 15th inst. [i.e. 15 JUL 1822], at Upper Marlborough, Mrs. SARAH BEANES, consort of Dr. William Beanes, of that place, in the 72d year of her age ... [M:23 JUL 1822, Tuesday, p. 3]

DIED, in this City [no date], of the brain fever, ROBERT H. SHANKLIN, from some of the northern States; he appeared to be about 24 years of age. [M:23 JUL 1822, Tuesday, p. 3]

Capt. JAMES POE, died at his residence, near Chambersburgh, Franklin county (Pa.) [no date], in about the 70th year of his age ... [M:27 JUL 1822, Saturday, p. 3]

MARRIED.—Near *Vansville*, Prince George's Co., Md., on Thursday evening last [i.e. 25 JUL 1822], by the Rev. Mr. Adylott, Mr. THOMAS MITCHELL, to Miss MATILDA JONES, both of that county. [M:30 JUL 1822, Tuesday, p. 3]

Georgetown, D.C., **Marriage and Death Notices, 1801-1838**

MARRIED.—On Thursday evening last [i.e. 15 AUG 1822], by the Rev. B. Waugh, Mr. JAMES C. DUNN, printer of the *Congressional Examiner*, to Miss ELIZA RATCLIFF, all of this place. [M:17 AUG 1822, Saturday, p. 3]

DIED.—At his seat near Montgomery Court House, Md., on Saturday, Aug. 10th [i.e. 10 AUG 1822], in the 54th year of his age, ROBERT B. MAGRUDER, Esq.—His bereaved widow and a large circle of relatives and friends will long lament the loss of an uncommonly excellent husband and friend ... [M:20 AUG 1822, Tuesday, p. 3]

DIED, on Tuesday last [i.e. 20 AUG 1822], Mrs. LOUISA MASON, daughter of Richard Harrison, Esq., 1st Auditor of the Treasury, and consort of George Mason, Esq. Mrs. Mason was one of those delicate and lovely flowers which bloom but for a little while and then depart ... [M:22 AUG 1822, Thursday, p. 3]

MARRIED.—In Johnstown, N.Y., on the 1st of January last [i.e. 1 JAN 1822], Mr. JOHN JOHNS, son of Mr. John Johnson Johns, joiner, to Miss JANE JOHNSON, daughter of Judge Jonathan Johnson, all of Johnston.—Ceremony performed by the Rev. Mr. James J. Jackson, Rector of St. John's Church. [M:5 SEP 1822, Thursday, p. 3]

DIED.—In Norfolk on Thursday last [i.e. 3 SEP 1822], Mrs. CANTELO, a lady whose charitable disposition and amiable manners were proverbial—The poor have lost one of their best friends, and her dependents the kindest mistress. Mrs. C. was peculiarly distinguished for the virtues which adorn her sex, and we trust she has gone to that mansion where her virtues will meet their reward. [M:5 SEP 1822, Thursday, p. 3]

Married, at Philadelphia, on Sunday evening [i.e. 1 SEP 1822], by the Rev. Dr. Abercrombie, PETER GRAYSON WASHINGTON, Esq., of Washington City, to Miss MARGARET, daughter of the late Gen. Wm. McPherson, of Philadelphia. [M:7 SEP 1822, Saturday, p. 3]

DIED, in the City of Washington, on Wednesday evening last [i.e. 4 SEP 1822], JOSIAH MEIGS, Esq., Commissioner of the General Land Office. [M:7 SEP 1822, Saturday, p. 3]

DIED.—At Harper's Ferry, a few days ago [no date], after a short illness, Col. JACINT LAVAL, aged about 60 years. Col. Laval came to this country during our Revolutionary war, as a cornet of dragoons in the French army under Gen. Rochambeau. He served to the end of the war with that gallantry which is the characteristic of his name, and carried to his grave honorable scars of the wounds he received in battle. [M:12 SEP 1822, Thursday, p. 3]

DIED.—In Washington on Sunday morning [i.e. 15 SEP 1822], in the 28th year of his age, the Rev. SAMUEL H. DAVIS, of the Methodist Episcopal Church.—Mr. Davis was a clear, succinct and forcible expounder of the tenets of his office master, as well as a pious and zealous Christian, he was universally loved and esteemed by his congregation ... [M:17 SEP 1822, Tuesday, p. 3]

Georgetown, D.C., **Marriage and Death Notices, 1801-1838**

DIED.—On Monday the 16th inst. [i.e. 16 SEP 1822], WILLIAM GRAYSON, a promising child of Lund Washington, Jr., aged nine months. [M:19 SEP 1822, Thursday, p. 2]

DIED, on Thursday afternoon [i.e. 19 SEP 1822], in Georgetown, after an illness of ten or fifteen days, Mrs. MACOMB, the excellent and much respected wife of General Alexander Macomb. In her death society has lost one of its brightest ornaments, and her bereaved husband and family, the spring of all their happiness. [M:21 SEP 1822, Saturday, p. 3]

DIED, at Raleigh in N.C. [no date], Miss ANN ELIZA GALES, sister of Joseph Gales, Esqr., of this District. She was a young lady of fascinating manners, and of the most kindly and sweet disposition—Actively alive to all those feelings which render the worth of the sex so proverbial ... [M:28 SEP 1822, Saturday, p. 3]

MARRIED.—On the 26th inst. [i.e. 26 SEP 1822], by the Rev. Mr. Addison, Dr. HORACE WELLFORD, of Richmond Co., Va., to REBECCA, the second daughter of Thomas Plater, Esq., of Georgetown, D.C. [M:1 OCT 1822, Monday, p. 3]

DIED.—On Tuesday evening [i.e. 1 OCT 1822], in the 19th year of her age, Mrs. ELIZA CHANDLER, of Annapolis. In the same fortnight the husband and the wife have descended to the tomb! Beauty, intelligence, and amiability, combined to render the character of this excellent woman interesting to all who knew her, and to make her loss irreparable to her friends.—*Intelligencer*. [M:5 OCT 1822, Saturday, p. 2]

DIED, in this city, on Friday night last [i.e. 4 OCT 1822], of a severe but short illness, JOHN LAW, Esq., aged about 30 years, Attorney at Law. In him our city has sustained the loss of one of its earliest, most respectable and most useful citizens. *Intelligencer*. [M:8 OCT 1822, Tuesday, p. 3]

DIED, on the 3d inst. [i.e. 3 OCT 1822], at his residence near Brookville, Montgomery Co., Md., THOMAS MOORE, a most respectable member of the Society of Friends, and Principal Engineer to the Board of Public Works of Virginia. [M:8 OCT 1822, Tuesday, p. 3]

MARRIED.—On Tuesday evening last [i.e. 8 OCT 1822], by the Rev. Mr. Waugh, BROOK WILLIAMS, Esq., to Miss REBECCA BECK, all of this place. [M:10 OCT 1822, Thursday, p. 3]

MARRIED.—On Thursday last [i.e. 10 OCT 1822], by the Rev. Dr. Balch, WILLIAM LAIRD, son of John Laird, Esq., to Miss HELLEN DUNLOP, daughter of James Dunlop, Esq., all of this place. [M:12 OCT 1822, Saturday, p. 3]

Communicated. To a large circle of friends and acquaintances, the painful intelligence of the death of Doctor GEORGE CLARKE, was made known on Thursday morning. This excellent, amiable, pious man, expired on Saturday last [i.e. 5 OCT 1822], in Essex Co., Va., whither he had gone to render professional services to a family of afflicted relatives ... [M:12 OCT 1822, Saturday, p. 3]

Georgetown, D.C., **Marriage and Death Notices, 1801-1838**

MARRIED, at Burlington, N.J., on the 8th inst. [i.e. 8 OCT 1822], by the Rev. Dr. Wharton, the Rev. CHARLES P. M'ILVAINE, of Georgetown, D.C., to EMILY, daughter of William Doxe, Esq., of the former place. *National Intelligencer.* [MP15 OCT 1822, Tuesday, p. 3]

DIED, on Thursday, 10th [i.e. 10 OCT 1822], WILLIAM LEVELY, Watch Maker, after a most severe illness of six months, which he bore with the most perfect resignation to the will of his Maker. During all his suffering he never was heard to complain: he has left a wife and an aged mother, brother, and sisters to deplore his loss. [M:15 OCT 1822, Tuesday, p. 3]

DIED, Yesterday morning [i.e. 16 OCT 1822], after a short illness, Mr. FREDERICK CANA, grocer, a native of Germany. The deceased was a very industrious and useful citizen, and much respected for his correct deportment. [M:17 OCT 1822, Thursday, p. 3]

DIED, in this city, on the evening of the 12th inst. [i.e. 12 OCT 1822], after a severe illness, which he sustained with fortitude and resignation, Mr. JAMES WATSON, in the 94th year of his age, leaving an afflicted widow, and a numerous and distressed family, to lament his loss, by which they are bereaved of an affectionate parent and an earthly protector ... [M:17 OCT 1822, Thursday, p. 3]

MARRIED.—On Thursday last [i.e. 17 OCT 1822], by the Rev. Mr. Lethaux, Mr. BALAAM BERCH, to Miss ELIZABETH NOWLAN, all of this place. [M:19 OCT 1822, Saturday, p. 3]

MARRIED.—On the 15th inst. [i.e. 15 OCT 1822], by the Rev. Mr. McCormick, Mr. JOHN C. ROBINSON, to Miss ELIZA CHARLES, both of this city. *National Intelligencer.* [M:19 OCT 1822, Saturday, p. 3]

DIED.—At the farm of John Speed, Esq., near Louisville, (Ky.) on the 3d inst. [i.e. 3 OCT 1822], H.C. LEWIS, late a resident of Philadelphia. He was professional a Printer, and a man of education ... [M:19 OCT 1822, Saturday, p. 3]

DIED, on Thursday last [i.e. 17 OCT 1822], at Pinebush, in the town of Montgomery, (N.Y.,) Capt. ARCHIBALD HUNTER, aged about twenty-eight. The Circumstances of Captain Hunter's death are somewhat remarkable. As he was opening a cow, supposed to have been poisoned in some way or other, he received a slight wound on the hand which became immediately impregnated with the poison, and in less than an hour it was diffused over the whole system, in consequence of which he died in about ten days time. Some hogs, which eat of the flesh of the cow, also died. [M:22 OCT 1822, Tuesday, p. 3]

Departed this life on Friday [i.e. 18 OCT 1822], at Mr. Shekell's Tavern, Georgetown: Mr. THOMAS FRAZER, son of Mr. Frazer of Alexandria Co., (D.C.). In the character of this truly amiable young man, was concentrated—all we admire and love,—he was meek natures child, a constant votary of innocence ... [M:24 OCT 1822, Thursday, p. 3]

Communicated. DIED, on Sunday last [i.e. 27 OCT 1822], after a short illness, Mr. WILLIAM MORGAN, Jr., aged 19 years ... [M:29 OCT 1822, Tuesday, p. 3]

DIED, in Gloucester Township, New Jersey, on the evening of the 20th inst. [i.e. 20 OCT 1822], Mr. SAMUEL EVANS, a respectable young man, after a very short illness. What renders this dispensation peculiarly trying is, that he was engaged to be married to a worthy young woman in the neighborhood and had passed Friends' meeting only the Second day previous to his decease. [M:29 OCT 1822, Tuesday, p. 3]

DIED, on Woodbury, on the 20th inst. [i.e. 20 OCT 1822], WILLIAM SAILER, Esq., Post Master at that village. [M:29 OCT 1822, Tuesday, p. 3]

MARRIED, on Thursday 24th inst. [i.e. 24 OCT 1822], by the Rev. Mr. Balch, ALEXANDER RAY, Esq., to Miss HANNAETT, daughter of the late Andrew Ross, all of this place. [M:31 OCT 1822, Thursday, p. 3]

MARRIED, at Pittsburg, Pa., October 8th [i.e. 8 OCT 1822], at the United States arsenal, by the Rev. Joseph M'Elroy, Lieut. JAMES HEPBURN, of the U.S. Army, to Miss ANN E., eldest daughter of Dr. Hanson Catlett. [M:31 OCT 1822, Thursday, p. 3]

DIED, at Naples [no date], where he was for the benefit of his health, on the 25th of August last, WILLIAM THURSTON, Esq., of Boston, Counselor at Law. Few persons in proportion to their means of doing good had taken a more active part in works of public and private charity than this useful citizen. [M:31 OCT 1822, Thursday, p. 3]

DIED.—At Lebanon, Conn. [no date], Miss HEPZIBAH STRONG, age 67. When a blooming girl of 19, and on the eve of being married, she received a fall and injured the spiral marrow, and for the space of 48 years, never walked, or was able to raise her head from the pillow—most of the time also unable to bear the least noise or light. [M:31 OCT 1822, Thursday, p. 3]

DIED.—On Thursday night last [i.e. 31 OCT 1822], CHARLES W. DAWSON, Esq.—A gentleman whose social qualities and amiable disposition endeared to him a very large circle of friends.—Mr. D. was on the eve of marriage with a lovely and interesting young lady, when the fell destroyer laid him low. [M:2 NOV 1822, Saturday, p. 3]

DIED, at Bladensburg, on Monday evening, 28th inst. [i.e. 28 OCT 1822], after a short illness, Mr. HENRY T. TILLEY, aged about 28 years. In the death of this young man his family and all who knew his worth, have sustained an irreparable loss. [M:2 NOV 1822, Saturday, p. 3]

DIED.—On the 5th inst. [i.e. 5 NOV 1822], at the residence of Mr. Wm. Clarke, in this place, of the dysentery, Mr. EDWARD S. LIVINGSTON, in the 22d year of his age, a native of Gloucester Co., Va. [M:7 NOV 1822, Thursday, p. 3]

MARRIED.—On Tuesday evening last [i.e. 12 NOV 1822], by the Rev. Mr. Balch, Mr. HENRY UPPERMAN, Sen.., aged 80 years, to Miss MARGARET GIBBS, aged 65 years, all of this place ... [M:14 NOV 1822, Thursday, p. 3]

Georgetown, D.C., **Marriage and Death Notices, 1801-1838**

MARRIED.—At *Rose Hill*, (near Rockville, Md.) on Tuesday evening last [i.e. 12 NOV 1822], by the Rev. Thos. Read, ROBERT READ, Esq., of this town, to Miss FRANCES REBECCA, daughter of Ignatius Davis, Esq., of Frederick Co., Md. [M:16 NOV 1822, Saturday, p. 3]

MARRIED.—On Thursday the 7th inst. [i.e. 7 NOV 1822], by the Rev. Mr. Hoskinson, Mr. REZIN BECK, formerly of this town, to Miss ELIZABETH ANN, daughter of Mr. Nathan Walker, of Prince George's Co., Md. [M:16 NOV 1822, Saturday, p. 3]

DIED.—On Thursday evening last [i.e. 21 NOV 1822], after a protracted and painful illness, Mr. THOMAS KNOWLES, of this Town, in the 33d year of his age. In the several relations of husband, father, son, and brother, he was affectionate and kind; and as a member of society, without reproach ... His friends and acquaintance, and those of the family, are invited to attend his funeral, from his late residence on Bridge-street, this evening, at 3 o'clock. [M:23 NOV 1822, Saturday, p. 3]

DIED.—On Monday 4th Nov. [i.e. 4 NOV 1822], at Craney Island, Dr. SAMUEL R. TREVETT, Junr., of Boston, Surgeon in the U.S. Navy, aged 38. He was attached to the Sloop of War *Peacock*, Capt. Cassin, just arrived from a cruise in the West Indies ... [M:23 NOV 1822, Saturday, p. 3]

DIED.—On Sunday evening last [i.e. 24 NOV 1822], Mr. SAMUEL HARRIS, Printer, of Washington City, in the 22nd year of his age; respected while living, and regretted when dead, by all who were acquainted with him. [M:26 NOV 1822, Tuesday, p. 3]

Beginning with the issue of 7 DEC 1822, published for P. Brunet, three doors below the Farmers' and Mechanics Bank, with much improved format and type style.

MARRIED.—On Thursday the 28th inst. [i.e. 28 NOV 1822], at *Shirley*, the seat of Hill Carter, Esqr., by the Rev. Bishop Moore, Mr. EDMOND F. WICKHAM, to Miss LUCY CARTER. [M:7 DEC 1822, Saturday, p. 3]

MARRIED.—In Georgetown, on 30th Dec. [i.e. 30 DEC 1822], by the Rev. Mr. M'Ilvaine, Mr. JACOB FADELY, Jr., to Miss CHARITY ANN GOSSUM, both of Loudoun Co., Va. [M:2 JAN 1823, Thursday, p. 3]

DIED.—In this town, on Sunday morning last [i.e. 29 DEC 1822], Col. ELIE WILLIAMS, in the 73 year of his age. The venerable subject of this obituary notice has left to all who knew him a long life full of those virtues which adorn character and benefit society, to command their respectful remembrance ... He fell a victim to his zeal for the accomplishment of a great national work, in the forwarding of which he was engaged during the last summer. A few days before his death, he signed, with his colleagues, the report of the Commissioners for the survey of the Potomac river, in reference to the contemplated canal; and it may be esteemed a great public loss that he was not spared to urge, with his experience and judgment, that important object before the Md. Legislature, of which he was a member at the time of his death ... [M:2 JAN 1823, Thursday, p. 3]

Georgetown, D.C., **Marriage and Death Notices, 1801-1838**

Killed, in an engagement with the pirates, on the 9th of November last [i.e. 9 NOV 1822], JAMES DENNY, quarter-gunner of the United States' schooner *Alligator*, aged 30years, son of Capt. John Denny, (an officer of the revolution,) deceased, late of Albany. His capacity as gunner, rendered it unnecessary for him to engage with the pirates in an open boat; but he readily volunteered his services, and perished in the same boat with Lieut. Allen. [M:2 JAN 1823, Thursday, p. 3]

MARRIED, at Canterbury, (England) [no date], Mr. JAMES PORTER, Sen'r. to Mrs. CATHARINE BARGE, being his sixth wife! [M:7 JAN 1823, Tuesday, p. 3]

Married, at St. Mary's Church, Lancaster, (England) [no date], Mr. WILLIAM ARNOLD, a blithesome swain of 73, to Mrs. S. THORNTON, a brisk widow of 68; the lovely bride was conducted to the altar by her son, a sprightly youth of 43. [M:7 JAN 1823, Tuesday, p. 3]

Married, in Charleston, (N.N.) [no date], Mr. JOHN P. BARBER, to Miss ELLEN BELLOWS. [M:7 JAN 1823, Tuesday, p. 3]

Married, in Washington, (Vt.) [no date], Hon. DANIEL PEASLEE, aged 49, to Miss LUCY PEPER, aged 17. [M:7 JAN 1823, Tuesday, p. 3]

The melancholy intelligence of the death of WILLIAM LOWNDES, comes upon us with a painful and sudden shock. We had been prepared to hear of this suffering for, months for years; and Hope had pointed to some distant period for the return of death. But Lowndes is dead! ... Mr. Lowndes died on the 27th of October last [i.e. 27 OCT 1822] on board the ship *Moss*, on his passage from Philadelphia to London, in the forty-third year of his age. His family were around him ... *Charleston City Gazette*. [M:21 JAN 1823, Tuesday, p. 2]

Communicated.—Died on Sunday morning, 19th inst. [i.e. 19 JAN 1823], negro YARROW, aged (according to his account) 136 years! He was interred in the corner of his garden, the spot where he usually resorted to pray.—Yarrow resided in this town upwards of 60 years—it is known to all who knew him, that he was always industrious, honest and moral—the early part of his life he met with several losses by loaning money, which he never got, but he persevered in industry and economy, and accumulated some Bank stock and a house and lot, on which he lived comfortable in his old age.—Yarrow was never known to eat of swine, nor drink ardent spirits. [M:23 JAN 1823, Thursday, p. 3]

DIED.—In this city on Wednesday, the 15th inst. [i.e. 15 JAN 1823], of pulmonary consumption, Capt. JAMES H. BALLARD, of the U.S. 4th Regt. of Artillery. Capt. Ballard was a native of Mass. During the late war with Great Britain, he served with distinguished reputation in the rifle corps on the northern frontier, and was subsequently an Aid-de-Camp to General Miller. His remains were interred with military and masonic honors, on the Gracis of Fort St. Mark.—*East Florida Herald*. [M:6 FEB 1823, Thursday, p. 2]

MARRIED.—On Sunday evening last [i.e. 9 FEB 1823], by the Rev. Mr. Deteaux, Mr. JAMES M'CLEISH, of Alexandria, to Miss ELIZABETH RIGDEN, of this place. [M:11 FEB 1823, Tuesday, p. 3]

Georgetown, D.C., **Marriage and Death Notices, 1801-1838**

Departed this life on Sunday morning last [i.e. 23 FEB 1822], Mrs. ELIZABETH PINKNEY, consort of Jonathan Pinkney, Esq., Cashier of the Farmers' Bank of Md., in the fifty-fifth year of her age. [M:1 MAR 1823, Saturday, p. 3]

MARRIED.—On Sunday, 2d inst. [i.e. 2 MAR 1822], by the Rev. Mr. Balch, Mr. BENJAMIN MAYFELD, to Miss SUSANNA WRIGHT, eldest daughter of Mr. John Wright, Unitarian Minister, all of Georgetown. [M:4 MAR 1823, Tuesday, p. 3]

MARRIED.—On Tuesday evening last [i.e. 4 MAR 1822], by the Rev. Mr. Balch, Mr. JOHN P. WETHEREL, of Georgetown, to Miss SARAH ELLEN THOMSON, of Waterford, Va. [M:6 MAR 1823, Thursday, p. 3]

DIED.—On Monday evening last [i.e. 3 MAR 1823], at 11 o'clock, Dr. NINIAN MAGRUDER; long a high-respected citizen of this town. [M:6 MAR 1823, Thursday, p. 3]

DIED.—At *Hayes*, near this place on Monday the 3d inst. [i.e. 3 MAR 1823], JAMES DUNLOP, Esq., in the 68th year of his age. The deceased has resided, for almost 40 years in Georgetown, and its vicinity, and was deservedly regarded as one of its most honored and worthy citizens ... [M:14 MAR 1823, Friday, p. 3]

DIED.—In East Haddam, Conn. [no date], Mr. THOMAS BURNS, aged 49. He was one of the unfortunate sufferers with Capt. Riley, on the great desert of Sahara. [M:14 MAR 1823, Friday, p. 3]

MARRIED.—Last evening [i.e. 3 APR 1823], by the Rev. C.P. McIlvaine, Mr. WM. SHAW, to Miss CATHARINE GRANT, both of this place. [M:4 APR 1823, Friday, p. 3]

MARRIED, at Alexandria on Sunday evening last [i.e. 20 APR 1823], by the Rev. Isaac Robbins, Mr. WILLIAM QUINN of Georgetown, to Mrs. LOUISA R. WHITTINGTON, of Alexandria. [M:25 APR 1823, Friday, p. 3]

MARRIED, in Washington, on the 11th inst. [i.e. 11 APR 1823], by the Rev. Mr. Chalmers, Mr. LUND WASHINGTON, Sen'r., to Miss SALLY, daughter of the late Mr. John Johnson, of Worcester Co., Md., near Snow Hill. [M:25 APR 1823, Friday, p. 3]

MARRIED, on Tuesday evening last [i.e. 22 APR 1823], by the Rev. Mr. Matthews, MICHEL ESPERANCE HERSANT, Esq., Eleve Vice Consul to France, to Miss MARY CECILIA THOMPSON, only daughter of Col. James Thompson, of this city. [M:25 APR 1823, Friday, p. 3]

MARRIED, on Tuesday evening [i.e. 22 APR 1823], by the Rev. Mr. Baker, Mr. JOEL SIMPSON, of Montgomery Co., to Miss ANGELICA LENOX, of this place. [M:25 APR 1823, Friday, p. 3]

DIED, at his lodgings in this city, yesterday [i.e. 24 APR 1823], Col. JAMES MORRISON, of Kentucky, a gentleman of high character for his probity and patriotism. [M:25 APR 1823, Friday, p. 3]

MARRIED, on the 4th inst. [i.e. 4 MAY 1823], by the Rev. Thomas G. Allen, Mr. WILLIAM HOLT, of this place, to Miss MARY D. LITTON, of Montgomery County. [M:6 MAY 1823, Tuesday, p. 3]

MARRIED.—On Monday evening last [i.e. 5 MAY 1823], by the Rev. Mr. M'Elroy, MADISON NELSON, Esq., to Miss JOSEPHINE MARCILLY, all of this city. [M:9 MAY 1823, Friday, p. 3]

DIED.—On Saturday morning last [i.e. 3 MAY 1823], Mr. JOHN WILLIAM MILLER, in the 84th year of his age, an upright and respectable citizen of this city.—*Fredericktown Herald*. [M:9 MAY 1823, Friday, p. 3]

MARRIED, in this place on Thursday evening, 12th inst. [i.e. 12 MAY 1823], by the Rev. Mr. M'Ivaine, Dr. JOHN M. THOMAS, of Frederick Co., (Md.) to Miss CATHARINE C. TURNER, daughter of the late Thomas Turner, Esq. [M:16 MAY 1823, Friday, p. 3]

MARRIED, in Washington on the 13th inst. [i.e. 13 MAY 1823], by the Rev. Mr. Lucas, Mr. JOHN A. DONOHOO, to Miss HARRIET MINCHIN, both of that place. [M:16 MAY 1823, Friday, p. 3]

DIED, on the 6th inst. [i.e. 6 MAY 1823], at the house of St. George Tucker, Esq. in Williamsburg, Va., where she was on a visit, Mrs. REBECCA CARY, relict of the late Wilson Miles Cary, in about the 66th year of her age. [M:16 MAY 1823, Friday, p. 3]

DIED, yesterday morning [i.e. 15 MAY 1823], at the Navy Yard, in this City, JOHN V. THOMAS, formerly printer and bookseller of Alexandria, and for more than a quarter of a century, a citizen of this District. [M:16 MAY 1823, Friday, p. 3]

DIED, in this city, on the evening of the 11th inst. [i.e. 11 MAY 1823], Mr. JOHN GREEN, formerly Manager of the Richmond and Southern Theatres. It was his unhappy destiny to be the voluntary agent of his own destruction. This fatal act was executed under circumstances of composure and deliberation too painful for description ... *Richmond paper*. [M:16 MAY 1823, Friday, p. 3]

Obituary.—Departed this life, on the 11th April last [i.e. 11 APR 1823], at the Island of St. Thomas, whither he had gone for the benefit of his health, HENRY LAMSON, of this city, in the 37th year of his age. Mr. L. was a native of Haverhill, Mass., but for the last 12 years a native of Baltimore. About two years since he was attacked by pulmonary affection; on the appearance of which, yielding to medical advice, he abandoned all thoughts of business, and gave himself up wholly to the recovery of his heath ... [M:20 MAY 1823, Tuesday, p. 3]

DIED.—Yesterday morning [i.e. 2 JUN 1823], Mrs. HANNAH CORCORAN, consort of Thomas Corcoran, Esq. The friends of the family are invited (without further notice) to attend her funeral at 5 o'clock this afternoon. [M:3 JUN 1823, Tuesday, p. 3]

Georgetown, D.C., **Marriage and Death Notices, 1801-1838**

MARRIED.—On Thursday evening last [i.e. 5 JUN 1823], in Petersburg, by the Rev. John N. Campbell, of Washington City, Mr. NATHANIEL SNELSON, to the interesting Miss LUCY ANN, daughter of Robert Bolling, Esq., of this town. [M:7 JUN 1823, Saturday, p. 3]

DIED.—In Nantucket [no date], FREDERICK ALLEN, aged 13, son of David Allen, Esq. His death was occasioned by having accidently swallowed, some months since, a half dollar. [M:7 JUN 1823, Saturday, p. 3]

Died, in Middlesex, Vt., May 12 [i.e. 12 MAY 1823], drowned in the North Branch, a stranger by the name of HENRY CROSBY, a native of Charlestown, N.H. ... [M:7 JUN 1823, Saturday, p. 3]

MARRIED.—By the Rev. Dr. Glendy, on the evening of Monday last [i.e. 2 JUN? 1823], Mr. HENRY HAZEL, merchant of Georgetown, to Miss JANE RAYMOND, of Baltimore. [M:10 JUN 1823, Tuesday, p. 3]

Married, at Annapolis [no date], HENRY M. STEELE, Esq., of Dorchester Co., to Miss MARIA LLOYD, second daughter of Francis S. Key, Esq., of this Town. [M:10 JUN 1823, Tuesday, p. 3]

Married, on the 5th inst. [i.e. 5 JUN 1822], by the Rev. Mr. McCormick, Mr. PETER GRIFFIN, to Miss CAROLINE BRISCOE, both of Washington city. [M:10 JUN 1823, Tuesday, p. 3]

DIED.—At Baltimore on the 4th inst. [i.e. 4 JUN 1823], Mr. JOHN OLIVER—a gentleman who is spoken of in the Baltimore papers in the highest terms of eulogy, as a man distinguished for the excellence of his morals and the purity of his virtue. [M:10 JUN 1823, Tuesday, p. 3]

Obituary.—General HENRY LIVINGSTON, was born January 19, 1752, and died, at his residence, in the Manor of Livingston, (New York) Monday, May 26, 1823. On the Wednesday following, his remains were deposited in the family vault, in the village churchyard, attended by a numerous concourse of mourning relatives and friends. *Northern Whig.* [M:10 JUN 1823, Tuesday, p. 3]

MARRIED, on the 5th inst. [i.e. 5 JUN 1823], by the Rev. Mr. Campbell, Doctor ELIJAH R. CRAVEN, of this city, to Miss SARAH E. LANDRETH, daughter of John Landreth, Esq., of Somerset Co., Md. [M:13 JUN 1823, Friday, p. 3]

MARRIED, on Tuesday evening the 10th inst. [i.e. 10 JUN 1823], by the Rev. Mr. Hawley, Mr. JAMES MONTGOMERY, of the Treasury Department, to Miss ELIZA VIRGINIA SMOOT, daughter of the late Alexander Smoot, Esq., all of this place. [M:13 JUN 1823, Friday, p. 3]

Married.—In Hampton, on Thursday evening last [i.e. 3 JUN 1823], by the Rev. Mr. Gilliam, Mr. JOSEPH A. REPITON, of Williamsburg, to Miss ELIZA BROUGH, daughter of William Brough, Esq., of the former place. [M:8 JUL 1823, Tuesday, p. 2]

*Georgetown, D.C., * **Marriage and Death Notices, 1801-1838**

DIED, on Sunday last [i.e. 3 AUG 1823], of a short but very severe illness, Mr. JOHN KNOWLES, son of Mr. Henry Knowles of this town.—Mr. Knowles was a worthy and industrious citizen, a most affectionate husband, and kind father, and in all the relative duties of life his conduct was proverbial.—It affords the greatest consolation to his numerous relatives and friends, to know that he departed this life in the full assurance of a blessed immortality to come. [M:5 AUG 1823, Tuesday, p. 3]

DIED, on Sunday last [i.e. 3 AUG 1823], ELOISA, daughter of Mr. Lawrence Greatrake, a peculiarly beautiful and interesting child. [M:5 AUG 1823, Tuesday, p. 3]

Married.—At Capt. Blasdell's, opposite Alexandria, yesterday [i.e. 7 AUG 1823], by the Rev. I. Robbins, Mr. JAMES KIDWELL, to Mrs. ELIZABETH WHEELER, both of Fairfax county. [M:8 AUG 1823, Friday, p. 3]

Married.—On Tuesday last [i.e. 5 AUG 1823], by the Rev. Mr. Fairclough, Mr. LEWIS C. LABILLE, to Miss MARY O'NEAL, both of this place. [M:8 AUG 1823, Friday, p. 3]

DIED, on Sunday the 27th ult. [i.e. 27 JUL 1823], at the house of Mr. William I. Bronaugh, Loudoun Co., Va., Miss REBECCA A. TOWNSEND, of this town, after a protracted illness which she bore with great patience—her death is sincerely lamented by her relatives and acquaintances. [M:8 AUG 1823, Friday, p. 3]

Died.—At Philadelphia, on the 6th of August [i.e. 6 AUG 1823], in the 45th year of his age, Mr. PETER C. KONKLE, Printer, of the firm of *Sisk & Konkle*. [M:12 AUG 1823, Tuesday, p. 3]

Died [no date], universally lamented at his residence in Montgomery (County), Col. GEORGE MAGRUDER, in the 57th year of his age. Col. Magruder was ill only 24 hours, he was formerly of our town, and much esteemed for his many virtues. [M:15 AUG 1823, Friday, p. 3]

DIED, at the house of his father, in Washington, on the 24th of July [i.e. 24 JUL 1823], Mr. BASIL W. BEALL, of the Treasury Department, in the 27th year of his age. His complaint was a pulmonary affection, which had formerly threatened him, but for time past had left room for better hopes ... [M:15 AUG 1823, Friday, p. 3]

DIED, in Washington, on the 6th inst. [i.e. 6 AUG 1823], aged 24 years, Mrs. ELIZA W. HUTTON, wife of Mr. James Hutton, of the Navy Commissioner's Office, and daughter of James Leander Cathcart, Esq. She has left an infant son, whose loss though great, he cannot feel .... [M:15 AUG 1823, Friday, p. 3]

DIED, at Thompson's Island, on the 28th of July last [i.e. 28 JUL 1823], after a short illness, JOSHUA TOWNLEY, Esq., of Elizabeth Town (N.J.) [M:15 AUG 1823, Friday, p. 3]

DIED.—In this city, on Saturday [i.e. 16 AUG 1823], WALKER TENNISON, aged 13 years, son of Mr. Joshua Tennison. [M:22 AUG 1823, Friday, p. 3]

Georgetown, D.C., **Marriage and Death Notices, 1801-1838**

Died.—At Leesburg [no date], STEPHEN C. ROSZELL, Esq., aged 48, after an illness of seven days. Mr. Roszell was a man of decided firmness, strict integrity, kind and charitable.—He was a member of the Legislature of Virginia for several sessions, and a magistrate for the county of Loudoun for a number of years. [M:2 SEP 1823, Tuesday, p. 3]

DIED, in Murfreesborough, North Carolina, on Thursday the 21st inst. [i.e. 21 AUG 1823], the Rev'd. SAMUEL WELLS, aged 58 years, leaving a disconsolate widow, and a large circle of friends, to deplore their loss. Mr. Wells has been for many years a pious and much esteemed Minister of the Gospel, in the Methodist Episcopal Church, and will be remembered with veneration by the citizens of Murfreesborough and its vicinity. [M:2 SEP 1823, Tuesday, p. 3]

DIED.—On Saturday last [i.e. 30 AUG 1823], Mr. HENRY STEWART, a young gentleman of the most amiable disposition and obliging manners. [M:2 SEP 1823, Tuesday, p. 3]

MARRIED, on Tuesday evening last [i.e. 22 SEP 1823], by the Rev. Mr. Addison, Dr. OTHO M. LINTHICUM, to Miss ANN E. MAGRUDER, second daughter of George B. Magruder, Esq., all of this place. [M:9 SEP 1823, Tuesday, p. 3]

MARRIED, on Tuesday evening last [i.e. 2 SEP 1823], by the Rev. Mr. Little, Mr. JOHN WHITE, to Miss SARAH C. HENSON, all of this place. [M:9 SEP 1823, Tuesday, p. 3]

DIED [no date], at the residence of her father, Joseph Forrest, Esq., Mrs. SOPHIA DeBUTTS, a lady universally loved and esteemed. [M:9 SEP 1823, Tuesday, p. 3]

MARRIED.—On Tuesday evening last [i.e. 23 SEP 1823], by the Rev. Mr. Post, Mr. WILLIAM WILLIAMSON, of Washington, to Miss JANE WHANN, youngest daughter of the Rev. Dr. Stephen B. Balch, of this town. [M:26 SEP 1823, Friday, p. 3]

DIED.—In Washington, yesterday evening [i.e. 25 SEP 1823], after a short illness, the Rev. LEWIS R. FECHTIG, of the Methodist Episcopal Church, and presiding elder of the Baltimore District.—Mr. F. was a pious and eloquent divine, and calculated to do great good in the service of his divine master. [M:26 SEP 1823, Friday, p. 3]

DIED [no date], at the residence of his father in Loudoun Co., Va., Mr. ALEXANDER GRAYSON, in the 24th year of his age. In the vigor of health and in the morning of life, inexorable death has born to the grave the subject of this obituary, and left his numerous friends and relatives to bewail with unavailing sorrow the loss of that promise, which his intelligence, integrity and uncommon manliness had given. [M:26 SEP 1823, Friday, p. 3]

DIED.—In this town at the house of his brother-in-law, Eban Stout, Esq., on the 30th Sept. [i.e. 30 SEP 1823], FRANCIS HOPKINSON, Esq. (youngest son of the late Hon. Francis Hopkinson, one of the signers of the declaration of Independence) in the 44th year of his age. His benevolent feelings and genuine warmth of heart endeared him to a large circle of friends and acquaintances in this town, who sincerely sympathize with his afflicted relatives, in the loss they have sustained. It may be consolatory to his friends at a distance

Georgetown, D.C., **Marriage and Death Notices, 1801-1838**

to know that the most tender and unremitted attention was shown him throughout his illness, by an affectionate sister, a skillful physician, and many warmly attached friends. [M:3 OCT 1823, Friday, p. 3]

Norfolk, Oct. 6.—We announce with regret, the death of one of our oldest, most respectable and most useful citizens, ROBERT BROUGH, Esq'r., for many years an active member and President of the Common Council of this Borough, and at the time of his death senior Magistrate of Norfolk County ... He was a useful member of the Methodist Church. He died on Friday night last [i.e. 3 OCT 1823], after an illness of about two weeks. [M:10 OCT 1823, Friday, p. 3]

MARRIED, on Wednesday evening [i.e. 15 OCT 1823], by the Rev. Mr. McIlvaine, Mr. JOHN HARRY, of Hagerstown, Md., to Miss HARRIET ELIZA WILLIAMS, of this town. [M:17 OCT 1823, Friday, p. 3]

On Saturday last [i.e. 18 OCT 1823] the body of a man named MICHAEL McCLOSKEY was found near the mud machine at the wharf supposed to have fallen in accidentally in the night preceding. [M:21 OCT 1823, Tuesday, p. 3]

DIED, on Saturday morning last [i.e. 18 OCT 1823], Mrs. ELIZABETH E. ELLIOT, aged 28 years, wife of Mr. William Elliot, of Washington City, and eldest daughter of the Rev. Robert Little ... [M:21 OCT 1823, Tuesday, p. 3]

MARRIED.—On Thursday evening, the 16th inst. [i.e. 16 OCT 1823], by the Rev. Mr. Harrison, Col. ARCHIBALD HENDERSON, commandant of the U.S. marine corps, to ANNA MARIA, second daughter of Anthony Charles Cazenove, Esq., of this place. *Alexandria Herald*. [M:24 OCT 1823, Friday, p. 3]

Died.—On Friday evening last [i.e. 17 OCT 1823], after a severe illness, in the 53d year of her age, Mrs. ROSANNA RHODES, wife of William Rhodes, Esq., of this place.—*Alexandria Herald*. [M:24 OCT 1823, Friday, p. 3]

Married.—In Montgomery Co., on the 23rd inst. [i.e. 23 OCT 1823], Mr. ANTHONY FRAZER, of Alexandria Co., D.C., to Miss PRESHA LEE, daughter of Mr. Daniel Lee, of the former place. [M:28 OCT 1823, Tuesday, p. 3]

MARRIED.—On Tuesday evening last [i.e. 28 OCT 1823], by the Rev. S.B. Balch, Mr. RICHARD R. SHECKELL, to Miss HARRIET BOHRER, daughter of Abraham Bohrer, Esq., of this town. [M:31 OCT 1823, Friday, p. 3]

Dr. W.R. COZENS, an eminent physician and intelligent gentleman, was killed on Wednesday evening last [i.e. 29 OCT 1823], by a fall, while returning home. The night was unusually dark, and it is thought he missed his way. [M:31 OCT 1823, Friday, p. 3]

On Tuesday evening [i.e. 28 OCT 1823], Mr. BENTZ, a sail-maker, fell from the Sail Loft of Mr. Clementson, into the street, and was instantly killed. [M:31 OCT 1823, Friday, p. 3]

Georgetown, D.C., **Marriage and Death Notices, 1801-1838**

HENRY T. BEATTY, Esq., and Midshipman WEEMS, of this town, have both fallen victims to the yellow fever. The one died in the service of his country, of a disease contracted in a foreign clime; the other at New Orleans. Both gentlemen were much esteemed for their rare virtues, and social and endearing qualities ... *Iris* [M:31 OCT 1823, Friday, p. 3]

MARRIED.—On Wednesday, 31st ult. [i.e. 31 OCT 1823], by the Rev. Dr. Balch, Mr. J.L. SMITH, of Newburyport, to Miss SOPHIA PEABODY, daughter of Gen. John Peabody of this place. [M:7 NOV 1823, Friday, p. 3; lic. on the 29th]

MARRIED.—Last evening [i.e. 20 NOV 1823], by the Rev. Mr. McKann, Mr. NOAH B. KEELER, of Vermont, to Mrs. RACHEL REEDER, of this place. [M:21 NOV 1823, Thursday, p. 3]

DIED.—On Wednesday the 19th inst. [i.e. 19 NOV 1823], after a painful illness of three weeks, Master CHARLES E. LANHAM, a youth of much promise, and son of the late Elisha Lanham. [M:21 NOV 1823, Thursday, p. 3]

DIED.—On Saturday last [i.e. 22 NOV 1823], Mr. WM. THOMPSON, Sen'r., one among our oldest and most respectable inhabitants. He was a kind husband and affectionate parent, with a heart always open to relieve the necessities of his fellow-beings ... [M:25 NOV 1823, Tuesday, p. 3]

DIED.—On Saturday last [i.e. 22 NOV 1823], Mr. JAMES REDMAN, an old and respectable inhabitant.—Mr. R. had been employed for some years as Collector of the County Taxes, and was remarkable for punctuality and a faithful discharge of all his duties. [M:25 NOV 1823, Tuesday, p. 3]

DIED, at Philadelphia, on Monday, the 17th inst. [i.e. 17 NOV 1823], in the 78th year of his age, JOHN MARK, Esq., of that city ... [M:25 NOV 1823, Tuesday, p. 3]

MARRIED.—On the 27th inst. [i.e. 27 NOV 1823], by the Rev. Mr. Allen, Mr. SAMUEL R. GAITHER, to Miss MARIA, eldest daughter of Frederic R. Gaither, Esq., all of Montgomery Co., Md. [M:2 DEC 1823, Tuesday, p. 3]

DIED.—On Tuesday evening last [i.e. 25 NOV 1823], at *Grassland*, near Georgetown, D.C., DAVID LUFBOROUGH, Esq., in the 85th year of his age. The deceased preserved, to the last, a sound and vigorous intellect, which the physical infirmities, attending extreme old age had not impaired. His great pleasure was in books tough attentive to those friends who called upon him, and readily and freely engaging in conversation. The characteristics of the mind and conduct of the deceased were great independence, integrity, and sacred regard for the truth. [M:2 DEC 1823, Tuesday, p. 3]

Mr. DeGREUHM, Minister Resident of his Majesty the King of Prussia to the United States, Knight of the Order of the Red Eagle, departed this life on Monday morning the 1st inst. [i.e. 1 DEC 1823], at about five o'clock, at his late residence in this town. [M:5 DEC 1823, Friday, p. 3]

Georgetown, D.C., **Marriage and Death Notices, 1801-1838**

Communicated. DIED.—On Sunday evening last [i.e. 7 DEC 1823], at the residence of her mother on Bridge-street, Miss ELEANOR CAMPBELL STEWART, aged 22—a native of Scotland, but for several years a resident of Georgetown; her mind was richly stored with every grace that could embellish her sex ... [M:9 DEC 1823, Tuesday, p. 3]

DIED, in Washington, on the 5th inst. [i.e. 5 DEC 1823], of a pulmonary disorder, Dr. ELISHA CRAVEN, a gentleman universally esteemed. Dr. C. combined in himself, the gentleman, scholar, and scientific physician, and had he not fallen a victim to the disease which is making such rapid inroad upon the American community, he wold have attained that eminence, to which his rare talents entitled him. [M:9 DEC 1823, Tuesday, p. 3]

DIED, on Saturday last [i.e. 6 DEC 1823], CATHARINE, daughter of Major Stull, a beautiful and interesting child, aged two years. [M:9 DEC 1823, Tuesday, p. 3]

DIED.— In this town [no date], BENJ. F. HOMANS, Esq., 1st chief clerk of the Navy Dept.—Mr. Homans had a heart made up of sincerity and benevolence, serving his fellow man to the uttermost. [M:12 DEC 1823, Friday, p. 3]

DIED, on Tuesday last [i.e. 9 DEC 1823], LUKE MARBURY, a free colored man, aged about 60. Luke was much esteemed for his good qualities, being an example to his colored brethren of honesty, sobriety, and correct dealing. [M:12 DEC 1823, Friday, p. 3]

MARRIED.—On the 21st inst. [i.e. 21 DEC 1823], by the Rev. Dr. Balch, Mr. BENJAMIN CLARKE, to Mrs. E. HARRIS. [M:30 DEC 1823, Tuesday, p. 3]

DIED.—On the 26th ult. [i.e. 26 NOV 1823], at the residence of her son, Gustavus Thompson, in Queen Anne's Co., Mrs. NANCY THOMPSON, after a short but most distressing illness. She was in her 57th year, and from her youth was a member of, and strictly devoted to, the Presbyterian system of religion ... [M:30 DEC 1823, Tuesday, p. 3]

MARRIED.—Last evening [i.e. 15 JAN 1824], by the Rev. Mr. McIlvaine, Mr. BENJAMIN HOMANS, of the Navy Department, to Miss EMILY WRIGHT, eldest daughter of Mr. T.C. Wright, all of this town. [M:16 JAN 1824, Friday, p. 3]

MARRIED.—On Tuesday evening last [i.e. 20 JAN 1824], by the Rev. Mr. Hawley, Mr. JOHN PASKIN, to Miss DOROTHY DeGILSIE, all of Washington City. [M:23 JAN 1824, Friday, p. 3]

MARRIED.—On Tuesday last [i.e. 27 JAN 1824], by the Rev. Doctor Balch, Capt. JAMES MITCHELL, of Alexandria, to Miss MARGARET THOMPSON, of this place. [M:30 JAN 1824, Friday, p. 3]

MARRIED.—On Tuesday, 27th inst. [i.e. 27 JAN 1824], by the Rev. Mr. Johnson, TOWNSHEND McVAUGH, Esq., of Loudoun, to Miss KAREN H. THRIFT, of Fairfax Co., (Va.) [M:30 JAN 1824, Friday, p. 3]

Georgetown, D.C., **Marriage and Death Notices, 1801-1838**

DIED.—On the 11th of December last [i.e. 11 DEC 1823], near Birmingham in England, in the sixty-fourth year of his age, the Rev. HENRY FOXALL, of Georgetown, District of Columbia. Mr. Foxall had gone on a visit to England, the land of his birth, and expected to have returned to America, his adopted country, this spring. His health was very good up to the attack, which was of the bilious type, that terminated his existence. His illness was short, not were his sufferings considered acute ... Death was to him but the portal of life, and he entered it as he had often encouraged others, during the course of a long and sincerely faithful ministry in the Methodist Church, to enter it. Mr. Foxall was blest with both the means and disposition to be useful, and he was never found wanting in whatever was required of him as a neighbor, citizen, or friend ... His purse, in various ways was their auxiliary support. In this city is to be found a monument of his bounty.—The Foundry Chapel, so called, was built by him, and presented to the society ... *Washington Republican*. [M:13 FEB 1824, Friday, p. 3]

DIED.—On Saturday night, the 14th inst. [i.e. 14 FEB 1824], in the 73d year of his age, RICHARD O'BRIEN, Esq., late Consul General of the United States to the Barbary Powers ... He was, in succession, an active and experienced seaman, a successful adventurer in the privateering exploits of the Revolution, a brave commander in the regular naval service, a captive slave in Algiers, Consul General to Barbary, member of the Pa. Legislature, a worthy farmer, and lastly, an ardent party politician ... [M:20 FEB 1824, Friday, p. 3]

Married, at Cornwall, on the 27th ult. [i.e. 27 JAN 1824], by the Rev. Mr. Smith, JOHN R. RIDGE, an Indian of the Cherokee tribe, and late member of the Foreign Mission School, to Miss SALLY B. NORTHROP, aged 19, daughter of Mr. John P. Northrop, late Steward of the F.M. School. [M:24 FEB 1824, Tuesday, p. 3]

MARRIED.—On Thursday evening last [i.e. 19 FEB 1824], by the Rev. Mr. Baker, Mr. JOHN ADAMS, to Miss MATILDA MITCHEL. [M:24 FEB 1824, Tuesday, p. 3]

DIED.—After a protracted illness, at his lodgings in this City, yesterday [i.e. 1 MAR 1824], the Hon. WILLIAM LEE BALL, aged about 45, for several years past, and at the time of his death, a Representative on Congress, from the State of Virginia. Mr. B. united to the social and amiable qualities which made him the delight of his friends, powers of intellect, which, though seldom called forth, were effective whenever exerted in his public station. *National Intelligencer*. [M:2 MAR 1824, Tuesday, p. 2]

MARRIED.—On Tuesday evening the 23d inst. [i.e. 23 MAR 18240, by the Rev. Mr. M'Cann, Mr. THOMAS PAINE, of Fairfax Co., Va., to Miss ELLEN GRIFFIN, of this place. [M:26 MAR 1824, Friday, p. 3]

DIED.—On Friday evening last [i.e. 19 MAR 1824], after a short illness, HENRY FLEETE, a colored man, in the 63d year of his age.—Henry was beloved by all who knew him, for honesty and correct dealing. He died in the triumph of faith ... [M:26 MAR 1824, Friday, p. 3]

Georgetown, D.C., **Marriage and Death Notices, 1801-1838**

MARRIED.—On Thursday evening the 25th inst. [i.e. 25 MAR 1824], by the Rev. Mr. Adams, Mr. JAMES PAYNE, to Miss HANNAH HUGHES, all of Fairfax Co., Va. [M:30 MAR 1824, Tuesday, p. 3]

DIED, on the 30th ult. [i.e. 30 MAR 1824], WILLIAM WILSON, the venerable President of the Bank of Baltimore ... *American Farmer*. [M:6 APR 1824, Tuesday, p. 3]

MARRIED, on the 11th inst. [i.e. 11 APR 1824], at *Perrywood*, Prince George's Co., Md., by the Rev. Mr. Tyng, ROBERT ELLIS, Esq., of the Treasury Department, to Miss MARY M., daughter of Clement Brooke, Esq. [M:16 APR 1824, Friday, p. 3]

MARRIED, on Tuesday evening last [i.e. 13 APR 1824], by the Rev. Dr. Balch, Mr. GEORGE PIERCE, to Mrs. HARRIET HYER, all of this place. [M:16 APR 1824, Friday, p. 3]

MARRIED, on Monday evening last [i.e. 12 APR 1824], by the Rev. Mr. M'Ilvaine, Mr. PHILIP COKELY, of Fredericksburg (Va.) to Miss FRANCES, youngest daughter of Mrs. Ann Freeman of Washington City. [M:16 APR 1824, Friday, p. 3]

DIED, at Frederick-town, Md., on Monday evening last [i.e. 12 APR 1824], Mr. WM. RITCHIE, of Wm., aged about forty-four years. [M:16 APR 1824, Friday, p. 3]

DIED, suddenly in Philadelphia [no date], Miss MATILDA, eldest daughter of Mr. Hathwell, of the Theatre. [M:20 APR 1824, Tuesday, p. 3]

MARRIED, in Philadelphia, on Tuesday the 20th inst. [i.e. 20 APR 1824], by the Rev. Philip F. Mayer, Mr. WILLIAM MECHLIN, of Washington, (D.C.) to Miss SOPHIA, daughter of the late George Wagner, of this city. [M:23 APR 1824, Friday, p. 3]

DIED.—On Wednesday last [i.e. 21 APR 1824], in the 5th year of her age, MARY ANN, daughter of Jonathan Elliott, Esq., Editor of the *Washington Gazette*. [M:23 APR 1824, Friday, p. 3]

MARRIED, on Thursday last [i.e. 22 APR 1824], by the Rev. Mr. Addison, CHARLES HAY, Esq., Chief Clerk in the Navy Department, to LUCY, eldest daughter of Walter S. Chandler, Esq., of this town. [M:27 APR 1824, Tuesday, p. 3]

MARRIED, on Thursday, 22d inst. [i.e. 22 APR 1824], by the Rev. Mr. Bench, Mr. JAMES SINCLAIR, to the amiable and accomplished Miss EMILY SAUNDERS, both of Loudoun Co., Va. [M:4 MAY 1824, Tuesday, p. 3]

MARRIED.—On the 4th May [i.e. 4 MAY 1824], by the Rev. Mr. Gilles, Mr. SAMUEL CHILDS, merchant, Benedict, Charles Co., to Miss ELIZABETH LAMAR, of Prince George's County. [M:11 MAY 1824, Tuesday, p. 3]

Georgetown, D.C., **Marriage and Death Notices, 1801-1838**

MARRIED.—On Thursday the 20th inst. [i.e. 20 MAY 1824], by the Rev. Mr. Hawley, JAMES BAKER, Esq., Acting Consul General of his Britannic Majesty, to CATHARINE, daughter of John Tayloe, Esq. [M:25 MAY 1824, Tuesday, p. 3]

MARRIED.—On Tuesday evening last [i.e. 18 MAY 1824], by the Rev. O.B. Brown, Mr. GREENBURY GAITHER, to Miss MARGARET BRULEY, all of Washington city. [M:25 MAY 1824, Tuesday, p. 3]

MARRIED, at Alexandria, on Tuesday evening, the 18th inst. [i.e. 18 MAY 1824], by the Rev. Mr. Norris, Lieut. DAVID VAN NESS, of the U.S. Army, to JULIA ANN ELIZA, youngest daughter of Wm. Yeaton, Esq., of that place. [M:25 MAY 1824, Tuesday, p. 3]

On Monday, the 24th of May, 1824, General WILLIAM H. WINDER, departed this life, in the 49th year of his age ... [M:28 MAY 1824, Friday, p. 3]

MARRIED.—On Thursday evening, 27th inst. [i.e. 27 MAY 1824], by the Rev. Dr. Laurie, Mr. FRANCIS SEAWELL, to Miss MARY MACKEY, daughter of William Mackey, Esq., of this town. [M:1 JUN 1824, Tuesday, p. 3]

MARRIED.—On Thursday evening last [i.e. 27 MAY 1824], by the Rev. Mr. Hamilton, Rev. CHARLES A. DAVIS, to Miss CHARLOTTE WILLIAMS, both of Washington City. [M:1 JUN 1824, Tuesday, p. 3]

MARRIED, yesterday morning [i.e. 31 MAY 1824], at half past 6 o'clock, by the Rev. Wm. Hamilton, Mr. JAMES A. KENNEDY, to Miss SUSAN COBB, all of Washington City. [M:1 JUN 1824, Tuesday, p. 3]

MARRIED, in Dayton, Ohio [no date], Mr. CONRAD REED, to Miss CATHARINE WEAVER. [M:1 JUN 1824, Tuesday, p. 3]

DIED, yesterday morning [i.e. 3 JUN 1824], in the 44th year of her age, Mrs. CHARLOTTE MYERS, consort of Mr. John Myers.—It may be said of the deceased that she lived the christian life and died in full assurance of further happiness—she has left a number of relations and friends to lament her loss. [M:4 JUN 1824, Friday, p. 3]

DIED.—On Saturday last [i.e. 29 MAY 1824], in Alexandria, GEORGE F. THORNTON, Esq., of King George Co., Va., in the 31st year of his age. Mr. Thornton had been afflicted three or four years by a disease which terminated very suddenly. [M:4 JUN 1824, Friday, p. 3]

DIED, at Philadelphia, on Friday, 20th May last [i.e. 21? MAY 1824], after a protracted illness, which he bore with christian fortitude, Mr. LEONARD ECKLIN, aged 92 years.—Mr. E. was a truly pious man and has left a numerous offspring to lament their irreparable loss. [M:4 JUN 1824, Friday, p. 3]

DIED.—Yesterday morning [i.e. 7 JUN 1824], at his residence near Queen's Chapel, RICHARD JAMISON, formerly collector of this District, at the advanced age of ninety three, his funeral will take place this morning at 10 o'clock at the Catholic Burying Ground in this town. [M:8 JUN 1824, Tuesday, p. 4]

MARRIED.—On Thursday evening [i.e. 10 JUN 1824], by the Rev. James McCann, Mr. NATHANIEL MARDEN, to Miss MARY ANN, eldest daughter of John Lutz, Esq., all of this place. [M:15 JUN 1824, Tuesday, p. 3]

MARRIED.—On Friday evening the 18th inst. [i.e. 18 JUN 1824], by the Rev. Dr. S. Balch, Mr. JAMES WILLIAMS, to Miss SUSAN ARNOLD, all of this place. [M:22 JUN 1824, Tuesday, p. 3]

DIED.—On Friday evening last [i.e. 25 JUN 1824], after a short illness, FLORIDE, only daughter of Samuel J. Potts, Esq., of this town, aged 16 months. [M:29 JUN 1824, Tuesday, p. 3]

DIED, of an apoplectic stroke, at his residence in this town, on the 27th June, inst. [i.e. 27 JUN 1824], THOMAS WILSON, Esq., of Dullatur, Scotland, in his 66th year. He was a man of the most unbounded philanthropy, liberal principles, and strict moral rectitude ... His numerous friends in Scotland belonged chiefly to that literary and scientific circle which has illustrated the city of Edinburgh. They valued his attainments, and still more the qualities of his heart. But, of all those who knew him and loved him, there is none who owes as deep a debt of reverence and gratitude to his memory as the author of this article. On the death of his [the author's] father, Theobald Wolfe Tone, Mr. Wilson, who had been his friend, adopted his children, and brought them up with the kindness and generosity of a second parent. In the course of time, the only survivor amongst them became doubly his by his marriage with their mother. [M:2 JUL 1824, Friday, p. 3]

DIED, on the 28th inst. [i.e. 28 JUN 1824], aged 50 years, JOSEPH SCATTERGOOD, of the Northern Liberties, a Member of the Religious Society of Friends ... *Philadelphia paper*. [M:2 JUL 1824, Friday, p. 3]

DIED.—On Friday 2d inst. [i.e. 2 JUL 1824], at the residence of her sister in Anne Arundel Co., (Md.) in the 23d year of her age, Mrs. ANN DEVINY, consort of Mr. Charles Deviny, of Washington city ... [M:9 JUL 1824, Friday, p. 3]

MARRIED.—On Sunday the 11th inst. [i.e. 11 JUL 1824], by the Rev. Mr. Hawley, Mr. ANDREW M. LAUB, to Miss ELIZA UPPERMAN, both of this place. [M:13 JUL 1824, Tuesday, p. 3]

MARRIED.—In Woodstock, Va. [no date], by the Rev. J. Mayer, Mr. DANIEL GETZ, aged sixty-five, to Miss ANN FRYMAN, aged fifteen. The son of the groom had previously married a sister of the bride. [M:13 JUL 1824, Tuesday, p. 3]

DIED.—On the 3d of July [i.e. 3 JUL 1824], at her residence near the Cool Springs, St. Mary's Co., Md., after a short illness, Mrs. ELIZABETH DIXON, in the 80th year of her age. [M:20 JUL 1824, Tuesday, p. 3]

Georgetown, D.C., **Marriage and Death Notices, 1801-1838**

DIED.—At New-Mills (N.J.) [no date], in the 38th year of his age, CHARLES LACEY, Esq., a Lieutenant in the navy of the United States, formerly a resident of our town ... [M:23 JUL 1824, Friday, p. 3]

DIED, on board the U.S. ship *Hornet*, lying off Old Point Comfort [no date], THOMAS N. MANN, Esq., Diplomatic Agent from this government of Guatemala. His complaint was of a pulmonary character, which as is usual in that disease, flattered him to the last moment with a promise of returning health. His remains were landed at Old Point yesterday afternoon, at 4 o'clock; minute guns being fired from the ship from the ship from the time the corpse left her side until it reached the shore. [M:23 JUL 1824, Friday, p. 3]

It is with deep concern that we announce the death of Captain HENRY KEELE, of the sloop *Sally*, of this port, who was lost overboard on his homeward passage from the Island of St. Thomas on the 22d inst. [i.e. 22 JUL 1824], in lat. 32, long. 74, faring heavy gale from the N.E.... Capt. Keele was a native of this town ... He has left a wife and numerous offspring to whom his death is a truly calamitous dispensation. *Norfolk Herald.* [M:3 AUG 1824, Tuesday, p. 3]

DIED.—On his passage from Marseilles to this country [no date], JAMES CRAWFORD, Esq., a young gentleman, who, had he been spared to mature years, would doubtless have become an honor to the country and an ornament to the town which gave him birth. Mr. C. had qualified himself for the practice of law ... [M:13 AUG 1824, Friday, p. 3]

DIED.—Suddenly, at Fredericktown, Md., on his way home from Bath, by the eruption of a blood vessel, on Saturday evening last [i.e. 7 AUG 1824], L.H. JOHNS, Esq., in the 46th year of his age, long a respectable and enterprising citizen of Georgetown. He has left a wife and a large family, with a numerous train of relations and warm friends, to lament his loss. [M:13 AUG 1824, Friday, p. 3]

It has become our duty to announce the death of CÆSAR A. RODNEY, Minister of the United States to Buenos Ayres. He died suddenly, on the 10th of June [i.e. 10 JUN 1824], at six in the morning, and was buried with appropriate marks of respect on the following day. His family were to take passage for Philadelphia, on board of a vessel which was to sail a few days thereafter. *National Intelligencer.* [M:13 AUG 1824, Friday, p. 3]

DIED.—In London [no date], Miss CRACHAMI, the celebrated Sicilian dwarf, aged 10 years. She weighed only five pounds—her exact height was 19½ inches, and her limbs in proportion. [M:17 AUG 1824, Tuesday, p. 3]

DIED, in Paris [no date], Gen. MURRAY, aged 85 years, 60 of which he had been in the British service in different parts of the world. He was twelve years a prisoner in France during Napoleon's reign. [M:17 AUG 1824, Tuesday, p. 3]

DIED, in Dublin [no date], Mr. SHEEKLETON, demonstrator of anatomy to the royal College of surgeons ... [M:17 AUG 1824, Tuesday, p. 3]

Georgetown, D.C., **Marriage and Death Notices, 1801-1838**

Departed this life, yesterday afternoon, (13th August [1824]), CHARLES GOLDSBOROUGH, Jr., Esq., of Talbot Co., near Easton, Md., in the 46th year of his age. [M:20 APR 1824, Friday, p. 2]

DIED.—In Howard Co., [Mo.] on the 6th July [i.e. 6 JUL 1824], JOSEPH JONES MONROE, Esq., (brother to the President of the United States) ... *Missouri Intelligencer.* M:27 AUG 1824, Friday, p. 3

DIED, Yesterday morning [i.e. 9 SEP 1824], Mr. WILLIAM CALDER, a native and resident of this town, in the 37th year of his age. During his illness, which was short, but severe, he continually manifested a strong hope in Jesus, on whom he rested as his Saviour, and an entire resignation to the sovereign will of Him who is Lord of all. On his bereaved wife and children the dispensation falls heavy; they knew his worth, and will feel his loss. ☞ The friends and acquaintances of Mr. William Calder, and of the family, are requested to attend his funeral this afternoon at 4 o'clock. [M:10 SEP 1824, Friday, p. 3]

MARRIED.—On Tuesday the 10th inst. [i.e. 10 AUG? 1824], by the Rev. Mr. McCann, Mr. TARLTON T. HENDERSON, of Fairfax Co., to Miss JANE S. JACKSON, of Middleburg, Loudoun Co., Va. [M:14 SEP 1824, Tuesday, p. 3]

DIED.—Yesterday morning [i.e. 13 SEP 1824], in the 58th year of his age, SAMUEL HUTCHINSON, a native of Ireland, for many years a resident of Washington City; in his death an amiable family, the society of which he was a member, and the community at large, have suffered a loss not to be repaired ... [M:14 SEP 1824, Tuesday, p. 3]

MARRIED.—On Wednesday evening, Sept. 15th [i.e. 15 SEP 1824], by the Rev. Mr. McCann, Mr. THOMAS HOLTZMAN, to Miss CHRISTIANA GOSZLER, second daughter of George A. Goszler, Esq., all of this place. [M:17 SEP 1824, Friday, p. 3]

DIED.—On the 13th inst. [i.e. 13 SEP 1824], in the twenty-third year of her age, Miss MARTHA PLATER, daughter of Thomas Plater, Esq., of this Town, highly esteemed by all who knew her ... [M:17 SEP 1824, Friday, p. 3]

DIED.—On Sunday last [i.e. 12 SEP 1824], at his late residence in Anne Arundel Co., in the 84th year of his age, Major WILLIAM BROGDEN, a truly venerable and respectable member of the community. Mr. B. served in the cause of his country during the revolutionary war, and subsequently as a member of the Legislature of Md. [M:17 SEP 1824, Friday, p. 3]

DIED.—In this town on Thursday the 16th inst. [i.e. 16 SEP 1824], Mr. ISAAC OWENS, Jr., merchant, a young gentleman very much esteemed for the excellence of his disposition, and benevolence of his heart. As a husband he was most kind and attentive, and as a son, an affectionate and dutiful one—and the loss which his relatives have sustained by his death, will not easily be replaced. [M:21 SEP 1824, Tuesday, p. 3]

Georgetown, D.C., **Marriage and Death Notices, 1801-1838**

DIED, in Philadelphia, on the 17th inst. [i.e. 17 SEP 1824], Mr. THOMAS JEFFERSON, of the Theatre, a young gentleman of excellent acquirements and most accomplished manners ... [M:21 SEP 1824, Tuesday, p. 3]

DIED, on Wednesday 22d ult. [i.e. 22 SEP? 1824], JAMES CRAWFORD BURGESS, aged 12 months, youngest child of Richard Burgess, Esq., of this place ... [M:24 SEP 1824, Friday, p. 3]

DIED.—In this town on Saturday last [i.e. 25 SEP 1824], after a short but severe illness, Mrs. DAWES, wife of Mr. Benjamin Dawes, a lady much esteemed for her excellent qualities and amiable disposition. [M:28 SEP 1824, Tuesday, p. 3]

Died, in Duplin country, N.C. [sic], on the 1st ult. [i.e. 1 AUG? 1824], Mr. JACOB MATTHEWS, aged 108 years. Until a few months before his death he retained almost the vigor of youth, his sight was perfect, and he could talk ten or fifteen miles a day. Seven years ago, his wife died, aged 100 years; they had been married about 80 years. [M:28 SEP 1824, Tuesday, p. 3]

DIED.—Yesterday morning [i.e. 7 OCT 1824], at *Oakland*, THOMAS A. BROOKE, Esq., a gentleman loved, esteemed and admired for those virtues which adorn the human character ... [M:8 OCT 1824, Friday, p. 3]

DIED.—On Friday the 1st inst. [i.e. 1 OCT 1824], at 2 o'clock, at *Clover Hill*, his residence, within a few miles of the Metropolis of St. Mary's Co., Mr. EDWARD MILLARD, in the 30th year of his age ... [M:8 OCT 1824, Friday, p. 3]

MARRIED.—On Sunday evening last [i.e. 31 OCT 1824], by the Rev. Mr. Detheu, Mr. JOHN BURROWS, to Miss ELIZABETH BATEMAN, both of this place. [M:2 NOV 1824, Tuesday, p. 3]

DIED.—On Wednesday evening last [i.e. 27 OCT 1824], CATHERINE, wife of Mr. Richard Smith, and daughter of Mr. Enoch Spaulding, in the 27th year of her age. [M:2 NOV 1824, Tuesday, p. 3]

MARRIED.—On Tuesday evening last [i.e. 23 NOV 1824], by the Rev. M'Ivaine, Mr. SAMUEL FEARSON, merchant, to Miss ELIZABETH THECKER, all of this place. [M:26 NOV 1824, Friday, p. 3]

DIED, in this town last week [no date], Mrs. HARRIET, wife of Mr. John Holtzman, Collector. She was a lady much esteemed for her worth and excellence. [M:21 DEC 1824, Tuesday, p. 3]

DIED.—On Sunday last [i.e. 19 DEC 1824], Mrs. ELIZABETH WATERS. Mrs. Waters had attained a good age, and spent her life in works of piety and usefulness. [M:21 DEC 1824, Tuesday, p. 3]

Georgetown, D.C., Marriage and Death Notices, 1801-1838

MARRIED.—At Milford, Montgomery Co., Md., on Thursday evening, 23d inst. [i.e. 23 DEC 1824], by the Rev. Mr. Dunn, Captain GEORGE MASON CHICHESTER, of Loudoun Co., Va., to Miss MARY, eldest daughter of Washington Bowie, Esq. [M:31 DEC 1824, Friday, p. 3]

MARRIED.—On Tuesday evening last [i.e. 28 DEC 1824], by the Rev. Mr. McCann, Mr. JOHN DIXON, to Miss ANN LIPSCOMB, all of this place. [M:31 DEC 1824, Friday, p. 3]

DIED.—In New Brunswick, (N.J.) [no date], in the 79th year of his age, the Rev. Dr. JOHN H. LIVINGSTON, Professor of Theology in the Theological Seminary, of the Reformed Protestant Dutch Church. The death of this venerable servant of God, was a serene and happy as his life had been calm and dignified ... [M:11 FEB 1825, Friday, p. 3]

DIED.—Yesterday morning [i.e. 14 FEB 1825], at the house of Mr. Barnes where she had resided for near 30 years, Mrs. RATCLIFFE, a lady much esteemed for her benevolence and social virtue. She was in perfect health only a few minutes before her death. [M:15 FEB 1825, Tuesday, p. 3]

MARRIED.—On the 14th inst. [i.e. 14 FEB 1825], by the Rev. Mr. Hawley, EDMOND KIRBY, Esq., of the United States Army, to Miss ELIZA A. BROWN, daughter of Major General Jacob Brown. [M:18 FEB 1825, Friday, p. 3]

MARRIED.—On Thursday the 24th Feb. [i.e. 24 FEB 1825], by the Rev. Mr. Allen, Mr. SAMUEL T. NICHOLS, to Miss SARAH, daughter of Mr. Wm. O'Neale, Esq., of Montgomery Co., Md. [M:1 MAR 1825, Tuesday, p. 3]

MARRIED.—On Wednesday last [i.e. 23 FEB 1825], by the Rev. Mr. McCann, HENRY BARRON, Esq., of Prince William (Va.) to Miss REBECCA LATIMER, of this place. [M:1 MAR 1825, Tuesday, p. 3]

DIED.—In this town on Tuesday [i.e. 22 FEB 1825], last of a lingering disease, WILLIAM CLAGGET, Esq., a clerk in the War Department. Mr. C. bore his illness with all becoming fortitude and resignation, and yielded his life to him who gave it without a murmur. [M:1 MAR 1825, Tuesday, p. 3]

DIED.—In Washington, on Saturday last [i.e. 26 FEB 1825], Mrs. SARAH WILSON, in the 70th year of her age. Mrs. Wilson had long kept one of the first boarding houses in the Metropolis, and was proverbial for her courteous behavior, bland and affable manners—as a mother she was affectionate and attentive, and as a friend, warm hearted and sincere. She was ever the benefactoress of the poor ministering to their necessities and wants to the utmost of her ability. [M:1 MAR 1825, Tuesday, p. 3]

MARRIED, on Wednesday evening last [i.e. 2 MAR 1825], by the Rev. Mr. Addison, Mr. ARCHIBALD CUNNIGIN to Mrs. JANE WILSON, all of this place. [M:4 MAR 1825, Friday, p. 3]

Georgetown, D.C., **Marriage and Death Notices, 1801-1838**

DIED.—At Alexandria, on the evening of the 25th [i.e. 25 FEB 1825], after a protracted illness, RICHARD H. LITLE, Druggist of that place, in the death of this worthy man the Town, the society of which he was a member and his family have suffered a loss not easily to be repaired. [M:4 MAR 1825, Friday, p. 3]

DIED.—On Tuesday evening last [i.e. 1 MAR 1825], at the residence of Benne S. Pigman, Esq., of this city, Mrs. ELIZABETH JORDAN SHANKS, formerly of St. Mary's Co., Md., in the 53d year of her age. [M:4 MAR 1825, Friday, p. 3]

DIED, on Friday last [i.e. 25 FEB 1825], in this city, Mrs. SUSAN DOLL, widow of Mr. John Doll, deceased. [M:4 MAR 1825, Friday, p. 3]

DIED, on Monday last [i.e. 28 FEB 1825], at the residence of Mr. David Boyd, Mr. MICHAEL MYERS, an old citizen of this city. [M:4 MAR 1825, Friday, p. 3]

Departed this life on the 5th of February [i.e. 5 FEB 1825], after an illness of ten days, in the 78th year of his age, the Rev. J.C.H. HELMUTH, D.D., senior of the Evan. Luth. Synod of Pa. The deceased was a native of Germany, and was educated at Halle ... Before the corpse was removed from Zion's church, the Rev. Mr. Demure, one of the pastors of the church, delivered a pathetic address ... The corpse was then deposited in a vault in front of the altar, in St. Michael's Church ... [M:4 MAR 1825, Friday, p. 3]

DIED.—On Wednesday afternoon [i.e. 6 APR 1825], in Frederick, Md., after an illness of a few days, MATTHIAS BARTGIS, Esq., aged 74 years. Mr. Bartgis was the original proprietor of the printing establishment of the *Republican Gazette*. [M:12 APR 1825, Tuesday, p. 3]

DIED.—In this Town, on the 28th inst. [i.e. 28 APR 1825], JOHN ERMANTINGER, aged 38 years, formerly of Switzerland but for several years past a resident of New York. [M:3 MAY 1825, Tuesday, p. 3]

MARRIED.—On Tuesday evening 3d inst. [i.e. 3 MAY 1825], by the Rev. Mr. Guest, Mr. WM. D. BARROTT, to Miss ANN E. MEIM. [M:6 MAY 1825, Friday, p. 3]

MARRIED.—On Thursday evening, 12th inst. [i.e. 12 MAY 1825], by the Rev. Mr. Hawley, JEREMIAH ATWATER TOWNSEND, Esq., merchant of New York, to Miss MARIA CLARISSA, eldest daughter of Elijah Mix, Esq., of this place. [M:13 MAY 1825, Friday, p. 3]

MARRIED.—On Tuesday evening last [i.e. 10 MAY 1825], by the Rev. Wm. Ryland, Mr. GIDEON BEALL, of the Treasury Department, to Miss ANN F. WESTON, daughter of the late Capt. Weston, of Alexandria, D.C. [M:13 MAY 1825, Friday, p. 3]

MARRIED.—In Baltimore, on Tuesday evening, the 10th inst. [i.e. 10 MAY 1825], by the Rev. Mr. Henshaw, Mr. EDWARD INGLE, merchant of Washington, to Miss JULIA PECHIN, daughter of Col. Wm. Pechin, of the former place. [M:13 MAY 1825, Friday, p. 3]

Georgetown, D.C., **Marriage and Death Notices, 1801-1838**

DIED.—Lately in New York [no date], Mr. WALTER HUGHS, of the Theatre, formerly known in this and other towns of Virginia, as a performer of respectable talents. Mr. H. was a native of England, and originally educated for, and had practiced at, the bar in that country ... *Norfolk Herald.* [M:13 MAY 1825, Friday, p. 3]

MARRIED.—Yesterday evening [i.e. 19 MAY 1825], by the Rev. Mr. Addison, Mr. GEORGE A. ADAMS, to Miss DEBORAH WATERS, all of this place. [M:20 MAY 1825, Friday, p. 3]

MARRIED.—On Tuesday evening last [i.e. 17 MAY 1825], by the Rev. Mr. Cloreviere, LUKE EDWARD LAWLESS, Esq., of St. Louis, Miss. [sic], to the Baroness GREUHM. [M:20 MAY 1825, Friday, p. 3]

DIED.—In this town on Wednesday last [i.e. 18 MAY 1825], WALTER S. CHANDLER, Esq., one among our oldest and most respectable inhabitants. Mr. C. was proverbial for every virtue which adorns the human character,—his remains were attached to the grave yesterday by an immense concourse of citizens, all of whom manifested the deepest sorrow at the loss of so much genuine worth. [M:20 MAY 1825, Friday, p. 3]

DIED.—On the 19th inst. [i.e. 19 MAY 1825], at noon of an affection of the lungs, Mrs. ELIZA ROBERTSON, consort of the late Samuel Robertson, Esq., of the U.S. Navy, leaving an interesting family of five children who, about four years since had to mourn the death of a peculiarly indulgent and loving father ... Her sickness was severe; she died calmly. [M:24 MAY 1825, Tuesday, p. 3]

DIED.—At Barboursville, in the State of Virginia, on the 16th inst. [i.e. 16 MAY 1825], Col. THOMAS BARBOUR, (Father to the present Secretary of War) in the 90th year of his age. He was an ardent Whig of the Revolution, and, except his venerable contemporary Mr. Jefferson, was the last survivor of the Members of the House of Burgesses of Virginia; which, in 1769, made the first protest against the stamp act in which the Revolution began. Col. B. has been, during his whole life, possessed of the unbounded confidence of his fellow citizens, having repeatedly represented them in the Legislative Body. For the last sixty years he has discharged, with great assiduity and integrity, the duties of civil magistrate. The length of his service, in that capacity, may be illustrated by the fact that four times he had become in successive cycles, entitled (as senior magistrate) to the Sheriffalty of the Co., and at his death had just completed the fifth revolution or succession, and was again in nomination for the office. Useful, active and faithful as a public man, his private life was no less exemplary. [M:24 MAY 1825, Tuesday, p. 3]

MARRIED.—On Tuesday evening last [i.e. 24 MAY 1825], by the Rev. Mr. Guest, Mr. CHARLES BRADLEY, of New Haven, Conn., to Miss MARIA BEALL, of this place. [M:27 MAY 1825, Friday, p. 3]

DIED.—In Washington City, on Tuesday night last [i.e. 31 MAY 1825], after an illness of long duration, ELIAS B. CALDWELL, Esq., Attorney at Law, and Clerk of the Supreme Court of the United States, which office he had filled for a number of years. Mr. C. Was one of the oldest and most respected of the residents of this city, and has left, besides his

Georgetown, D.C., Marriage and Death Notices, 1801-1838

disconsolate family, a large circle of friends, who will seriously deplore his loss. *National Intelligencer.* [M:3 JUN 1825, Friday, p. 3]

MARRIED.—On Thursday evening last [i.e. 2 JUN 1825], by the Rev. Dr. Staughton, JOHN BOOSE, Esq., to Miss SARAH OSBORN, all of the District of Columbia. [M:7 JUN 1825, Tuesday, p. 3]

MARRIED.—On Thursday evening last [i.e. 30 JUN? 1825], at Norfolk, by the Rev. Mr. Smith, Lieut. HENRY D. SCOTT, of the U.S. Navy, to Miss CLARISSA, daughter of George Wilson, Esq., of Norfolk. [M:8 JUL 1825, Friday, p. 3]

MARRIED.—On Thursday, the 7th inst. [i.e. 7 JUL 1825], in this City, GEORGE GRAHAM, Esq., Commissioner of the General Land Office, to Miss JANE LOVE WATSON, eldest daughter of the late James Watson, Esq., of Washington. [M:12 JUL 1825, Tuesday, p. 2]

MARRIED,—In Montgomery Co., Md. [no date], Col. GEORGE PETER, Representative in Congress, to Miss SARAH FREELAND. [M:12 JUL 1825, Tuesday, p. 2]

DIED.—In Washington on Wednesday evening last [i.e. 13 JUL 1825], ELIZA HANCOCK, infant daughter of General Jessup, a beautiful and interesting child. [M:15 JUL 1825, Friday, p. 3]

MARRIED.—On Tuesday evening last [i.e. 26 JUL 1825], by the Rev. Mr. Mathews, Mr. THOMAS CROWLEY, to Miss JULIET GOODWIN, all of Washington. [M:29 JUL 1825, Friday, p. 3]

MARRIED.—On Wednesday the 20th inst. [i.e. 20 JUL 1825], by the Rev. Mr. Barnes, Mr. SAMUEL LATIMER, of Charles Co., Md., to Miss CHARLOTTE A. BARRON, of Prince William, Va. [M:2 AUG 1825, Tuesday, p. 3]

DIED.—In Washington City, on Wednesday morning last [i.e. 3 AUG 1825], after an illness of five months, Mr. JOHN POOR, in the 65th year of his age. [M:5 AUG 1825, Friday, p. 3]

DIED.—In the Mediterranean after a short illness [no date], Lieut. H.S. GARDINER, of the U.S. Marine Corps ... [M:9 AUG 1825, Tuesday, p. 3]

DIED, in Chestertown, Md., on Monday 1st inst. [i.e. 1 AUG 1825], Mrs. REBECCA TILDEN, widow of the late John Tilden, Esq.—mourned by a large circle of relatives and friends, and lamented by all who had the pleasure of her acquaintance. [M:12 AUG 1825, Friday, p. 2]

DIED.—At Mogadore, 30th June [i.e. 30 JUN 1825], Rais Bel Cassine, so well known by the character drawn of him in Capt. Riley's narrative ... [M:30 AUG 1825, Tuesday, p. 3]

DIED.—On Friday morning the 9th inst. [i.e. 9 SEP 1825], WILLIAM MACKEY, Jr., Merchant of this place, of a lingering illness which he sustained with Christian firmness and resignation, in the 23d Year of his age. [M:13 SEP 1825, Tuesday, p. 3]

Georgetown, D.C., **Marriage and Death Notices, 1801-1838**

DIED.—Yesterday [i.e. 12 SEP 1825], at his Father's house, on Bridge-street, SAMUEL RAWLINGS, aged 26 years. The friends and acquaintances of the family are invited to attend his funeral, this day, at 4 o'clock. [M:13 SEP 1825, Tuesday, p. 3]

DIED.—in Georgetown on the 5th inst. [i.e. 5 SEP 1825], REZIN PAUL SHIPLEY, an old and respectable resident of this place, aged 56 years, 5 months; a citizen of unblemished character and sterling integrity. He has left a disconsolate and affectionate widow and 5 children to mourn their irreparable loss ... Peace be to his manes ... [M:16 SEP 1825, Friday, p. 3]

DIED.—At *Bloomingdale* [no date], Mr. WILLIAM SUMMERFIELD, father of the late Rev. J. Summerfield. [M:23 SEP 1825, Friday, p. 2]

MARRIED.—On Thursday the 22d inst. [i.e. 22 SEP 1825], by the Rev. Mr. Dubuison, Mr. JAMES COLBORN, to Miss SUSAN NEWTON, all of this place. [M:27 SEP 1825, Tuesday, p. 3]

MARRIED.—On Thursday evening 22d inst. [i.e. 22 SEP 1825], at the residence of E. Mix, Esq., Georgetown, by the Rev. Mr. Campbell, JOHN HOLMES OFFLEY, Esq., of Smerna, to Miss CATHARINE VANRENCELEAR HEATON, of Mount Pleasant, New York. [M:30 SEP 1825, Friday, p. 3]

DIED, on Friday morning last [i.e. 23 SEP 1825], on board the United States frigate *Constellation*, in this harbor, Midshipman CHARLES F. SHOEMAKER. Mr. S. came to his death in consequence of a wound from a pistol bullet, received in a duel with a brother officer, of the same ship (whose name we purposely omit) on Thursday evening, at Fort Nelson, being the nearest landing place from the frigate.—He fell at the first fire, having received his adversary's ball in the right side, a little above the hip bone, and survived only a few hours. *Norfolk Herald*. [M:30 SEP 1825, Friday, p. 3]

DIED, at Nottoway C.H., in this state, on the 31st ult. [i.e. 31 AUG 1825], Lieut. ALBERT G. WALL, of the U.S. Navy. *Norfolk Herald*. [M:30 SEP 1825, Friday, p. 3]

DIED.—Yesterday morning [i.e. 6 OCT 1825], after an illness of two days, THOS. HYDE, son of Mr. John Wells, Jr., of the Treasury Department, aged nine years and nine months. The friends of the family are invited to attend the funeral this morning 7th inst., at 10 o'clock precisely. [M:7 OCT 1825, Friday, p. 3]

DIED.—At *Stepney*, in the county of Prince William, Va., on Monday, the 26th September [i.e. 26 SEP 1825], in the 54th year of her age, Mrs. HARRIET BROOKE, wife of Edmund Brooke, Esq., of Georgetown, D.C. And on the following Wednesday, 28th, at the same place, in her 22nd year, Miss T.E. BROOKE, daughter of the former—both having left home a few days previously (in perfect health) on a visit to their friends in Virginia ... [M:7 OCT 1825, Friday, p. 3]

Georgetown, D.C., **Marriage and Death Notices, 1801-1838**

MARRIED.—In this Town, last Evening [i.e. 10 OCT 1825], by the Rev. C.R. Brown, Mr. THOMAS G. PRETTYMAN, to Miss MARY PELTON, both of Alexandria. [M:11 OCT 1825, Tuesday, p. 3]

DIED.—On Saturday night last [i.e. 8 OCT 1825], MARY GERALDINE, youngest daughter of Mr. John Wells, Jr., of the Treasury Department, aged eighteen months. [M:11 OCT 1825, Tuesday, p. 3]

MARRIED.—On Thursday evening last [i.e. 13 OCT 1825], by the Rev. Mr. Guest, Dr. JAMES S. GUNNELL, of Washington, to Miss HELLEN M., daughter of Capt. Leonard Mackall of this town. [M:18 OCT 1825, Tuesday, p. 3]

MARRIED.—On Tuesday the 18th inst. [i.e. 18 OCT 1825], by the Rev. Mr. Kurtz, Dr. MEREDITH HELM, of this town, to Miss ELIZABETH ORNDORFF, of Washington Co., Md. [M:25 OCT 1825, Tuesday, p. 3]

MARRIED.—On Thursday the 20th inst. [i.e. 20 OCT 1825], by the Rev. Mr. Smith, Mr. JACOB STAHL, of Hanover, to Miss MARY ANN ELLEN RISWICK, of this town. [M:28 OCT 1825, Friday, p. 3]

MARRIED.—On Tuesday evening the 25th inst. [i.e. 25 OCT 1825], by the Rev. Mr. Kielly of Washington City, Mr. T. O'DONOGHUE, Merchant, to Miss SARAH HUTCHINSON, both of this town. [M:28 OCT 1825, Friday, p. 3, marriage date changed to Wednesday the 26th in issue of 1 NOV 1825]

MARRIED.—On Tuesday evening last [i.e. 25 OCT 1825], by the Rev. Mr. Guest, Mr. JAMES WILLIAMS, of Alexandria, to Miss MATILDA, eldest daughter of Mr. Robert Simmonds of this place. [M:28 OCT 1825, Friday, p. 3]

MARRIED.—On Sunday evening last [i.e. 30 OCT 1825], by the Rev. Mr. Guest, Mr. JOSEPH STEINGASSER, of this place, to Mrs. CAROLINE BURTON, formerly of Baltimore. [M:1 NOV 1825, Tuesday, p. 2]

DIED.—In Baltimore, on Friday last [i.e. 28 OCT 1825], JAMES MOSHER, Jr., Esq., of this town.—He was an inestimable and enterprising citizen and much beloved by his fellow townsmen. He fell a victim in the prime of life and usefulness to that lingering disease, consumption. Mr. Mosher acted for some time as Secretary to President Monroe and enjoyed his full confidence. [M:1 NOV 1825, Tuesday, p. 2]

MARRIED, on Tuesday evening last [i.e. 1 NOV 1825], by the Rev. Mr. Addison, GEORGE G. BREWER, Esq., of the City of Annapolis, to Miss SUSAN ANN HARWOOD, of Georgetown, D.C. [M:4 NOV 1825, Friday, p. 3]

MARRIED.—On Thursday the 3rd inst. [i.e. 3 NOV 1825], by the Rev. Mr. Guest, Mr. JOHN H. KING, Merchant of this place, and Miss ELLEN, daughter of the late Elias Harrott, deceased, of Carlisle, Pa. [M:11 NOV 1825, Friday, p. 3]

Georgetown, D.C., **Marriage and Death Notices, 1801-1838**

MARRIED, in Washington, on Tuesday the 8th inst. [i.e. 8 NOV 1825], by the Rev. Reily, Mr. SERAPHIM MASI, to Miss CATHARINE A. BRADFORD, daughter of Capt. C. Bradford, all of that place. [M:11 NOV 1825, Friday, p. 3]

MARRIED, in Rockville, Md., on Tuesday evening the 1st inst. [i.e. 1 NOV 1825], by the Rev. Thomas G. Allen, Mr. THOMAS GRIFFITH, to Miss ELIZABETH GRIFFITH, daughter of Col. Lyde Griffith. [M:11 NOV 1825, Friday, p. 3]

MARRIED, on Tuesday evening the 1st inst. [i.e. 1 NOV 1825], in Brookville, by the Rev. Thomas G. Allen, Mr. WM. I. DORSEY, to Miss SUSAN R. ROBERTSON. [M:11 NOV 1825, Friday, p. 3]

DIED.—In this town on Tuesday last [i.e. 8 NOV 1825], Mr. FRANCIS I. FENWICK, after a short but severe illness. Mr. F. was the surveyor of the town and Co., and was much esteemed for his estimable qualities. [M:11 NOV 1825, Friday, p. 3]

Hon. WILLIAM GRAY, died in Boston on Friday morning last [i.e. 4 NOV 1825], aged 75. He was a wealthy and highly respectable merchant, of unostentatious, affable and plain manners, and one of the parents of the India trade ... He has left a family of which any father would be proud. [M:11 NOV 1825, Friday, p. 3]

DIED.—On Tuesday last [i.e. 15 NOV 1825], JOHN, infant son of Wm. Laird, Esq., of this town. [M:22 NOV 1825, Tuesday, p. 3]

MARRIED.—In this town, on the 15th inst. [i.e. 15 NOV 1825], by the Rev. Mr. Dougherty, Mr. JOSEPH W. GREENWELL, to Miss LYDIA ANN, daughter of Henry Coalter, Esq., of Annapolis. [M:25 NOV 1825, Friday, p. 3]

MARRIED.—On Tuesday last [i.e. 29 NOV 1825], by the Rev. Dr. Balch, Mr. LOUIS S. TSCHIFFELEY, of the Treasury Department, to Miss ELIZA MILLER, youngest daughter of the late Peter Miller, Esq., deceased. [M:2 DEC 1825, Friday, p. 3]

DIED.—In Georgetown, D.C., on the 30th ult. [i.e. 30 NOV 1825], in the 26th year of his age, JOHN B. BROOKS, eldest son of Mr. Joseph Brooks. For several years, a student of Georgetown College, he was eminently distinguished for the constant regularity of his department. After completing his classical studies, he was admitted a candidate for the Religious Society, whose members conduct that literary institution ... [M:2 DEC 1825, Friday, p. 3]

DIED, on Monday last [i.e. 28 NOV 1825], Mrs. ELIZABETH McCUTCHEON, an old and respectable inhabitant of this town. [M:2 DEC 1825, Friday, p. 3]

DIED, in Washington [no date], after a short illness, ELIZABETH ANN MARIA, only daughter of B.O. Tyler, Esq., of Washington, aged about 7 years. [M:2 DEC 1825, Friday, p. 3]

Georgetown, D.C., **Marriage and Death Notices, 1801-1838**

MARRIED.—In Norfolk, Va. [no date], by the Rev. Mr. Seixas, Mr. PHILIP I. COHEN, of the house of J.I. Cohen & Brothers, to Miss AUGUSTA, daughter of Moses Myers, Esq. [M:4 JAN 1826, Wednesday, p. 3]

MARRIED.—On Thursday last [i.e. 5 JAN 1826], at Elkridge Landing, by the Rev. Mr. Shane, Mr. JOHN DENTY, of that place, to Miss MARIA BARBOUR, of this district. [M:11 JAN 1826, Wednesday, p. 3]

DIED.—In this town, on Saturday last [i.e. 11 FEB 1826], in the ninety-sixth year of his age, JOHN BARNES, Collector of this port. Throughout his long and well spent life, he managed to conciliate the esteem and kind feelings of every acquaintance. In the disposition of his property, he made such bequests as will forever endear his name to the poor. After freeing and providing legacies for the maintenance of his slaves, the remainder of his estate was left to build a Poor's House, and make provision for the annual support of the same. Mr. Barnes was a native of the city of Norwich, in England, but came to New York some years prior to the revolution. When New York was taken by the British, he removed up the North River; he returned to the city after the restoration of peace. When Congress removed to Philadelphia, Mr. Barnes settled in that city, and in 1800 removed to this town. [M:18 FEB 1826, Saturday, p. 3]

DIED.—On the 6th inst. [i.e. 6 FEB 1826], in the 18th year of his age, Mr. DAVID L. CHAPMAN, son of the late Henry H. Chapman, Esq. In the death of this youth, an affectionate family have been sorely afflicted ... [M:18 FEB 1826, Saturday, p. 3]

DIED.—Last evening [i.e. 17 FEB 1826], of the prevailing cold, Mr. GEORGE CLEMENTSON, Book keeper of the Bank of Columbia, an old and much esteemed resident. [M:18 FEB 1826, Saturday, p. 3]

DIED.—On Tuesday last [i.e. 14 FEB 1826], Mr. THOS. DIXON, in the 56th year of his age, hackney coach driver, an honest and respectable citizen. [M:18 FEB 1826, Saturday, p. 3]

DIED.—On Monday [i.e. 13 FEB 1826], Mr. NALLY, in the 93d year of his age. [M:18 FEB 1826, Saturday, p. 3]

DIED.—On Friday s'night [i.e. 17 FEB 1826], Mrs. CARMICHAEL, in the 89th year of her age, long a worthy and respectable member of the Presbyterian Church. [M:18 FEB 1826, Saturday, p. 3]

DIED.—On Tuesday [i.e. 14 FEB 1826], WALTER NEWTON, in the 39th year of his age, who had long acted as a magistrate in the county. [M:18 FEB 1826, Saturday, p. 3]

DIED.—Yesterday morning [i.e. 17 FEB 1826], after a severe illness of only five days, Mr. RICHARD ROSS, formerly of St. Mary's Co., Md., aged about 28. [M:18 FEB 1826, Saturday, p. 3]

Georgetown, D.C., **Marriage and Death Notices, 1801-1838**

DIED.—In Washington, on Monday last [i.e. 13 FEB 1826], Mrs. MARY MOULDER, wife of John N. Moulder, Esq., of the Treasury Department, a lady much esteemed for her benevolence and private worth. [M:18 FEB 1826, Saturday, p. 3]

MARRIED.—At *Cedar Hill*, Prince George's Co., on Tuesday, 21st inst. [i.e. 21 FEB 1826], by the Rev. Mr. Tyng, ROBERT BOWIE, Esq., to Miss MARGARET H.W. FRENCH, daughter of George French, Esq., of Washington Co., Md. [M:4 MAR 1826, Saturday, p. 3]

MARRIED.—On Thursday last [i.e. 16 MAR 1826], by the Rev. Mr. Guest, Mr. JEREMIAH ORME, merchant, to Miss ELLINOR, daughter of Thomas Hyde, Esq., all of this place. [M:18 MAR 1826, Saturday, p. 2]

MARRIED.—On Thursday evening 16th inst. [i.e. 16 MAR 1826], by the Rev. Mr. Guest, Mr. THOMAS CICLE, of Georgetown, to Miss ELIZA, eldest daughter of the late Morris Lambert, of Washington City, D.C. [M:25 MAR 1826, Saturday, p. 2]

MARRIED.—On Tuesday evening last [i.e. 21 MAR 1826], by the Rev. Mr. Hawley, Mr. WILLIAM HURDLE, to Miss ELIZABETH ADAMS (both of this town). [M:25 MAR 1826, Saturday, p. 2]

DIED.—Departed this life on the 13th [i.e. 13 MAR 1826], at *Wilua*, Cecil Co., Md., after a long illness which she bore with fortitude 'trusting in Him who giveth and taketh away,' Mrs. ANNA MARIA MACKALL, consort of Benjamin Mackall, formerly of this place. [M:25 MAR 1826, Saturday, p. 2]

DIED. *Here sheer hulk, likes poor Tom Bowline.* On Friday 24th ult. [i.e. 24 MAR 1826], in the Asylum for the poor of this town, DANIEL B. TWINE, formerly a respectable ship master out of the port of Baltimore. The hand of misfortune had fallen heavily on old Twine, as he was familiarly termed; nevertheless he was a noble, generous, and gallant son of Neptune ... The old fellow had many of the attributes of his brother [ship] *Tom Bowline* ... [M:1 APR 1826, Saturday, p. 3]

At the house of Mr. Joseph Yager, Miss CATHARINE MILLER, of Woodstock, Va., in the 23d year of her age. The cause of this lady's death is truly heart rending; about two months ago she left Woodstock, Va., the place of her nativity, and came to Baltimore, accompanied by her father, to learn the business of a Milliner. On Thursday, the 16th inst., she felt unwell, and went upstairs to get her bonnet, and as she related before her death, seeing a bottle on the mantle-piece, and thinking that it was Lavender Compound, (that being in the house,) she took one swallow, and then getting another quantity in her mouth, (she suspecting something wrong,) spit it out, when to her astonishment, it proved to be Corrosive Sublimate; she immediately complained of feeling great pain, a glass of water was handed her, she drank it; she then went to Mr. John West's, Marsh market space, where medical aid was immediately called in, but all to no effect; she suffered excruciating pain, until the eighth day after this circumstance [i.e. 24 MAR 1826], when her spirit left the tenement of clay for a better world ... [M:1 APR 1826, Saturday, p. 3]

Georgetown, D.C., **Marriage and Death Notices, 1801-1838**

DIED. Departed this life early on Wednesday morning the 19th inst. [i.e. 19 APR 1826], after a long and protracted illness which she bore with christian fortitude and resignation, Mrs. JANE CLARK, in the 38th year of her age, consort of the Rev. Samuel Clark, and daughter of Ruben and Ruth Mitchel, of Dorchester Co., eastern shore of Md.; and for the last 23 years of her life a regular member of the Methodist Episcopal Church. [M:22 APR 1826, Saturday, p. 3]

OBITUARY. Died.—In this town, on Tuesday morning the 2d inst. [i.e. 2 MAY 1826], Mrs. MARY O. ENGLISH, the wife of Mr. David English, Jun., aged 27 years. The amiable and excellent lady, presented in herself a most striking combination of those various virtues, which adorn and beautify the human character ... Mrs. English was for the last ten years of her life an exemplary member of the Methodist Church ...She has left a disconsolate husband and four children, with large circle of affectionate relatives to mourn in irreparable loss. [M:6 MAY 1826, Saturday, p. 3]

DIED.—In this town on Sunday evening last [i.e. 30 APR 1826], after seven days illness, of a severe attack of the bilious pleurisy, THOMAS KURTZ, aged 43 years and 4 mo., long a citizen of this town, and for the last nine years a resident of Indiana. [M:6 MAY 1826, Saturday, p. 3]

MARRIED.—On Thursday the 4th inst. [i.e. 4 MAY 1826], by the Rev. Dr. Balch, ALEXANDER CARMICHAEL, a gay young Adonis of 85, to Mrs. SUSANNA PIERCE, a blooming Hebe of 69, all of this town ... [M:13 MAY 1826, Saturday, p. 3]

MARRIED.—In Kent Co., Eastern Shore of Md., on Tuesday evening last [i.e. 9 MAY 1826], by the Rev. Thomas Smith, ANTHONY BANNING, Esq., of this Co., to Mrs. MARIA RINGGOLD, of the former county. [M:13 MAY 1826, Saturday, p. 3]

MARRIED.—On Thursday evening last [i.e. 11 MAY 1826], at W. House, by the Rev. Mr. Hotchkiss, Lieut. CHARLES LOWNDES, of the U.S. Navy, to Miss SARAH S., daughter of the Hon. Edward Lloyd. [M:13 MAY 1826, Saturday, p. 3]

OBITUARY. Died, in Washington on Wednesday evening last [i.e. 10 MAY 1826], ALEXANDER C. MITCHELL, Esq., son of J. Mitchell, Esq., formerly agent for American prisoners at Halifax (N.S.) ... During the war and some time prior, Mr. M. was very advantageously known as a political writer on the side of the Republican party. He has left an amiable wife, to bemoan her loss, and numerous sincere friends who mingle their regrets with hers. [M:13 MAY 1826, Saturday, p. 3]

OBITUARY. Died.—at New-Harmony, on the 4th inst. [i.e. 4 JUN 1826], in the 54th year of his age, of acute inflamation of the liver, GEORGE SCOTT, late of Georgetown, D.C., formerly of Davenport, G.B. [M:10 JUN 1826, Saturday, p. 3]

MARRIED.—In Rehoboth [no date], by Allen Hunt, Esq., Mr. ABEL CARPENTER, to Miss ABBEY W. BLISS. [M:1 JUL 1826, Saturday, p. 2]

Georgetown, D.C., **Marriage and Death Notices, 1801-1838**

MARRIED.—At *Tudor Place*, on Tuesday 2[7th June, by] the Rev. Mr. Addison, Lieut. W.G. WILLIAMS [of the U.S. Ar]my, to Miss AMERICA PINKNEY PETER, dau. [of Thomas] Peter, Esq., of this town. [M:13 JUL 1826, Saturday, p. 3]

Obituary. A correspondent at West Point, informs us of the decease of PIERRE TRINQUE, sword master, United States Military Academy, West Point, aged 42 years, who died on the 27th inst. [i.e. 27 JUN 1826]. This gentleman commenced his career in the French Army, at nine years of age; was in most of the campaigns during the French war, and particularly distinguished himself at the battle of A[?]col; served as aid-de-camp to General Lavalette at St. Domingo ... [M:13 JUL 1826, Saturday, p. 3]

Departed this life on the 29th June 1826, in St. Joseph's Church, Philadelphia, while attending divine service, Mrs. SUSANNAH MALBRO, aged 64 years, wife of John Malbro of Georgetown, D.C., who was, while living, a pious and upright wife, friend and neighbour, and an affectionate mother—she died the death of the righteous, whose last end is peace. [M:15 JUL 1826, Saturday, p. 3]

MARRIED.—At Philadelphia [no date], Mr. JOSEPH JEFFERSON, to Mrs. CORNELIA FRANCES BURK. If this interesting young lady discourses as harmoniously in Matrimony, as she warbles sweetly in the Theatre, Mr. J. will have a delightful time. [M:5 AUG 1826, Saturday, p. 3]

DIED.—On Tuesday last [i.e. 8 AUG 1826], THOMAS COOK, Esq., an old and respectable inhabitants of this District.—Mr. Cook professed Deism, was an exemplary, moral and upright citizen, and yielded himself up calmly and collectedly, adhering to his faith to the last. [M:12 AUG 1826, Saturday, p. 3]

DIED.—In this place on Saturday last, the 5th inst. [i.e. 5 AUG 1826], Mr. HENRY KING, aged about 70 years. [M:12 AUG 1826, Saturday, p. 3]

DIED.—At the residence of her son-in-law, J.S. Findley, near Lexington, Lafayette Co., Missouri, on Wednesday, the 21st of June [i.e. 21 JUN 1826], Mrs. MARGARET DARGEN, a native of Md., and for many years, a resident in the District of Columbia, aged about 66 years. She had been for nearly 40 years a professing member of the Methodist Episcopal Church ... [M:12 AUG 1826, Saturday, p. 3]

MARRIED.—On Thursday evening last [i.e. 7 SEP 1826], by the Rev. Doctor Balch, Mr. THOMAS DAWSON, to Miss MARY HALES, all of this place. [M:9 SEP 1826, Saturday, p. 3]

MARRIED.—On Tuesday the 19th inst. [i.e. 19 SEP 1826], at the house of Judge Dade, in Dumfries, Va., by the Rev. Mr. Dougherty, Mr. ROBERT A. SLYE, of the Navy Commissioner's Office, to Miss ROBERTA, second daughter of the late Gwynn Baylor, Esqr., of the former place. [M:23 SEP 1826, Saturday, p. 3]

Georgetown, D.C., Marriage and Death Notices, 1801-1838

MARRIED.—In Windsor, Vermont [no date], Mr. BARON SLOW, Editor of the *Columbian Star*, published in Washington, to Miss ELIZABETH L. SKINNER, of Windsor, Vt. [M:23 SEP 1826, Saturday, p. 3]

MARRIED.—At Boston [no date], HENRY J. FINN, Esq., Manager of the Boston Theatre, to Miss ELIZABETH POWELL, second daughter of the late Snelling Powell, Esq., a former Manager. [M:23 SEP 1826, Saturday, p. 3]

DIED.—On Tuesday last [i.e. 19 SEP 1826], Master WILLIAM SEATON, youngest son of W.W. Seaton, Esq., one of the Editors of the *National Intelligencer*. The unhappy cause of his death was owing to a fall form his horse. He was an unusually intelligent and interesting child for his years, and bid fair to have been a comfort to his parents and an honor to his country. [M:23 SEP 1826, Saturday, p. 3]

DIED.—At Pittsburgh, on the 13th inst. [i.e. 13 SEP 1826], Mr. JOHN MARSHALL, Founder, aged 77 years. He was a native of Renfrewshire, Scotland, and emigrated to America in 1768. He cast the first cannon made in the United States, during the Revolutionary war, at Capt. Charles Ridgely's works, Md. He also gave the first draft of a boring mill for boring cannon. [M:23 SEP 1826, Saturday, p. 3]

DIED.—At Philadelphia, on Saturday morning [i.e. 16 SEP 1826], in the 56th year of his age, of a lingering illness, Mr. GEORGE GILLINGHAM, Professor of Music. [M:23 SEP 1826, Saturday, p. 3]

TRIBUTE OF FRIENDSHIP, JOSEPH PETER PICOT DeCLORIVIERE, deceased on the 29th of September [i.e. 29 SEP 1826], at the monastery of the Visitation in Georgetown, was descended of a noble family in the province of Brittany in France. Since the year 1344, his ancestors are mentioned with distinction, in the history of this province in the religious civil and military careers. Joseph Peter Picot, the subject of the present notice, was born near Brons on the 4th of November 1768. At the epoch of the revolution which brought Lewis XVI to the scaffold, he took a decided part in defense of the rights of his country and of humanity, and so many were his feats of valor, and so undaunted his courage, that he deserved to receive in the year 1800, from the hands of Charles the present King of France, in the name of his brother Lewis XVIII, the decorations of the order of St. Lewis. Like many of his fellow officers, when the army of Lavendee was disbanded, he went to England, and afterwards came to this Co., which in those days of confusion and anarchy, so frequently proved the asylum of the brave and of the virtuous. After having spent several years in different avocations, honorably supporting a life, which would have been lulled in affluence in his native country, determined in 1808 to enter the Seminary in Baltimore, and having performed the usual course of prepatory studies, was admitted in 1812 to the holy order of Priesthood. The most venerable Dr. Carroll, who then occupied the archepiscopal see of Baltimore, with his usual prudence and sagacity discerned his merit, and immediately commissioned him to share the labors of the extensive congregation of Charleston, in South Carolina ... In 1819, when Charleston became an Episcopal See, Mr. de Cloriviere returned to the Diocese of Baltimore ... [and appointed] to the important charge of Director of the monastery of the visitation in Georgetown ... [M:14 OCT 1826, Saturday, p. 3]

MARRIED.—On Thursday evening last [i.e. 2 NOV 1826], by the Rev. Mr. Addison, Mr. EDWARD B. GANTT, to Miss [Jane] CHANDLER, daughter of the late Walter Chandler, Esq., of this town. [M:4 NOV 1826, Saturday, p. 3]

MARRIED, in Washington [no date], by the Rev. Mr. Matthews, Captain T. CARBERRY, of Washington, to Miss MARY H. MANNING, of Loudoun Co., Va. [M:4 NOV 1826, Saturday, p. 3]

DIED.—In Washington City, on the 25th Oct. [i.e. 25 OCT 1826], after a short illness, Mrs. MARY LAMBERT, aged 46 yrs., consort of the late Morris Lambert, deceased. [M:4 NOV 1826, Saturday, p. 3]

DIED.—In Washington City, on Thursday last [i.e. 2 NOV 1826], after an illness of eight days, Mr. CHARLES BUDDY, aged about 32 years, formerly of Germantown, near Philadelphia, Pa. [M:4 NOV 1826, Saturday, p. 3]

DIED.—In Washington, on Sunday, the 29th October [i.e. 29 OCT 1826], in the 12th year of his age, RICHARD, the third son of the Hon. Richard Rush, Secretary of the Treasury. [M:4 NOV 1826, Saturday, p. 3]

DIED, suddenly on Friday last [i.e. 8 DEC 1826], in the 29th year of his age, Mr. GEORGE CLEMENTSON, book binder. Mr. C. was a young man of fine feelings and integrity of principle. [M:11 DEC 1826, Monday, p. 3]

Georgetown, D.C., **Marriage and Death Notices, 1801-1838**

THE UNITED STATES TELEGRAPH (Washington)
Various Dates

DIED, On Saturday evening last [i.e. 4 FEB 1826], after three days illness of the prevailing cold, JOHN BARNES, Esq., aged ninety four years, Collector of the port of Georgetown, in this District ... [T:10 FEB 1826, p. 2]

MARRIED, in Georgetown, D.C., on Tuesday evening last [i.e. 7 MAR 1826], by the Rev. Mr. Balch, Doctor R.H. BEATTY, of Hancock, Md., to Miss MARY C. OTT, daughter of the late Doctor John Ott, of the former place. [T:10 MAR 1826, p. 3]

DIED, on Monday, the 13th inst. [i.e. 13 MAR 1826], at the residence of Mr. James Kincaid, Georgetown, D.C., Mrs. MARY ANN S. PATTON, relict of the late James Patton, Esq., of *Clifton Lodge*, Fairfax Co., Va., in the 52d year of her age, after a protracted and painfully distressing illness ... [T:14 MAR 1826, p. 3]

MARRIED, last evening [i.e. 11 APR 1826], by the Rev. Mr. Smith, Mr. ZACHARIAH M. OFFUT, to Miss ELIZA ANN REMINGTON, daughter of Mr. Wm. Remington, all of Georgetown. [T:12 APR 1826, p. 3]

MARRIED, on Thursday last [i.e. 20 APR 1826], by the Rev. Mr. Chalmers, Mr. ANDREW E. THOMPSON, of Georgetown, to Miss ELIZABETH SIMPSON, of Montgomery Co., Md. [T:24 APR 1826, p. 3]

DIED, on the 7th inst. [i.e. 7 MAY 1826], in Georgetown, after an illness of [illegible] which she bore with Christian fortitude, Miss MARY KIRK, eldest daughter of the late M.T. Kirk. [T:15 MAY 1826, p. 3]

DIED, on Saturday, the 12th inst. [i.e. 13? MAY 1826], JAMES WALKER, youngest son of Mr. David Walker, of Georgetown, District of Columbia. [T:22 MAY 1826, p. 3]

MARRIED, on Saturday morning last [i.e. 27 MAY 1826], at Georgetown, in the District of Columbia, by the Rev. Septimus Tuston, Major-General ALEXANDER MACOMB, of the United States' Army, to Mrs. HARRIET B. WILSON, daughter of the Rev. Dr. Walsh, Pastor of the Presbyterian Church in that place. [T:29 MAY 1826, p. 3]

DIED, at New Harmony, Indiana, on the 4th ult. [i.e. 4 MAY 1826], in the 54th year of his age, of acute inflammation of the liver, GEORGE SCOTT, late of Georgetown, D.C., but formerly at Davenport, England. He was a member of the neighboring community of Feiba Peveli. [T:8 JUN 1826, p. 3]

MARRIED, in St. Mary's Co., Md., on the 7th inst. [i.e. 7 JUN 1826], by the Rev. James Neale, Mr. MATTHEW M'LEOD, to ELIZABETH H. MANNING, both of Georgetown. [T:19 JUN 1826, p. 3]

MARRIED, in Georgetown, by the Rev. Mr. Keith, on Thursday evening the 22d inst. [i.e. 22 JUN 1826], the Rev. WILLIAM LOUIS MARSHALL, of Fauquier Co., Va., to Miss ANN KINLOCH LEE, daughter of the late Gen. Henry Lee. [T:30 JUN 1826, p. 3]

MARRIED, at *Tudor Place*, on Tuesday 27th June [i.e. 27 JUN 1826], by the Rev. Mr. Addison, Lieut. W.G. WILLIAMS, of the United States Army, to Miss AMERICA PINKNEY PETER, daughter of Thomas Peter, Esq., of Georgetown, D.C. [T:6 JUL 1826, p. 3]

DIED, in Georgetown, D.C., on Saturday, the 19th inst. [i.e. 19 AUG 1826], Mrs. ELIZABETH THRELKELD, consort of John Threlkeld, Esq., aged 55 years and 7 months. [T:23 AUG 1826, p. 3]

Georgetown, D.C., **Marriage and Death Notices, 1801-1838**

COLUMBIAN & DISTRICT ADVERTISER
January 2 to February 27, 1827

DIED. In this town, on Saturday last [i.e. 6 JAN 1827], Mr. JOHN S. HUTCHINSON, from one of the Southern States. Having lately taken up his residence with us, he fell victim to an intermittent fever, which terminated his existence in a few weeks. [CDA, Tues., 9 JAN 1827, p. 3]

Col. UPTON BEALL died in the 57th year of his age, on the 25th of last month [i.e. 25 JAN 1827] at Rockville, Md. He had been Clerk of Montgomery County Court upwards of 30 years, and has left a wife and three children. [CDA, Fri. 2 FEB 1827, p. 2]

DIED, at Upper Sandusky, on Tuesday, the 2d of January [i.e. 2 JAN 1827], the celebrated chief of the Wyandot nation, *Between-the-Logs*. He was eminent for his eloquence and the conspicuous relation he held to the Nation as their chief speaker.—He lived and died a friend to the American government. He was the first that embraced religion among his brethren and the nation; from his firm piety, he was appointed a leader and afterwards an Exhorter in the Methodist E. Church, in each of these, as in every other station, he filled with dignity and faithfulness. He died in the full triumph of the Christian faith, and with his last breath declared the goodness of God. [CDA, Fri. 2 FEB 1827, p. 3]

DIED.—In Georgetown, in the 58th year of her age, Miss MARY BROOK, after a short illness which she bore with christian fortitude. [CDA, Tues., 13 FEB 1827, p. 3]

DIED.—On Saturday night last [i.e. 10 FEB 1827], after a painful and distressing illness of six weeks, which he bore with great patience and fortitude, Mr. SAMUEL McINTIRE, of Washington, in the 64th year of his age. [CDA, Tues., 13 FEB 1827, p. 3]

Georgetown, D.C., **Marriage and Death Notices, 1801-1838**

GEORGETOWN COLUMBIAN, AND DISTRICT ADVERTISER
March 6 to December 25, 1827

DIED.—In this town, on Saturday evening the 3d inst. [i.e. 3 MAR 1827], HENRY GOSZLER, of Anthony, dec'd., in the 46th year of his age. [CDA, Tues., 13 MAR 1827, p. 2]

MARRIED.—On Thursday last [i.e. 15 MAR 1827], by the Rev. Mr. Green, Mr. GRAFTON POWEL, of Poolsville, (Md.) to Miss MARGARET ANN SCRIVNER, of Georgetown, D.C. [CDA, Fri. 23 MAR 1827, p. 3]

MARRIED.—In the City of Washington, on Tuesday evening, the 17th inst. [i.e. 17 MAR 1827], by the Rev. Mr. Ryland, E.J. WEED, Esq., Quarter Master of the Marine Corps, to Miss ARABELLA E. M'LEAN, eldest daughter of the Hon. John M'Clean [sic], Postmaster General of the United States. [CDA, Fri. 30 MAR 1827, p. 3]

Communicated. OBITUARY. DIED.—On the 29th inst. [i.e. 29 MAR 1827], Mrs. SARAH WATROUS, at the very advanced age of 94 years.—She retained her intellectual powers unimpaired until a few hours of her death—as she lived, so she died, an unshaken believer in the religion of Jesus Christ, in the full prospect of a happy immortality. [CDA, Fri. 30 MAR 1827, p. 3]

MARRIED.—At Analostan Island, on Wednesday evening the 4th inst. [i.e. 4 APR 1827], by the Rev. Mr. Addison, Lieut. SAMUEL COOPER, of the U.S. Army, to Miss SARAH MARIA, daughter of Gen. John Mason. [CDA, Tues., 10 APR 1827, p. 3]

MARRIED.—On Thursday evening last [i.e. 5 APR 1827], by the Rev. Mr. Addison, JOHN MASON, Jr., Esq., Secretary of the Legation of the U.S. at Mexico, to CATHERINE, eldest daughter of Maj. Gen. Macomb. [CDA, Tues., 10 APR 1827, p. 3]

DIED.—At his residence in N.Y., on Sunday the 29th [i.e. 29 APR 1827], the Hon. RUFUS KING, in the 73 year of his age. [CDA, Fri. 4 MAY 1827, p. 2]

DIED.—On Sunday the 29th [i.e. 29 APR 1827], at Philadelphia, the Hon. Judge TILGHMAN, in the 71st year of his age. [CDA, Fri. 4 MAY 1827, p. 2]

MARRIED.—At Baltimore, on Thursday evening last [i.e. 3 MAY 1827], by the Rev. Mr. Pise, Mr. RICHARD WRIGHT, of Washington, to Miss MARY JOSEPHINE, daughter of Mr. William V. Jinkins, of the former place. [CDA, Tues., 8 MAY 1827, p. 3]

MARRIED.—On Thursday evening last [i.e. 10 MAY 1827], by the Rev. Mr. Davis, Mr. THOMAS CONNOR, to Miss JEMIMA B. WELLS, late of Prince George's Co., Md. [CDA, Tues., 15 MAY 1827, p. 2]

Georgetown, D.C., **Marriage and Death Notices, 1801-1838**

MARRIED.—On Sunday evening last [i.e. 13 MAY 1827], by the Rev. Mr. Baker, Mr. JOHN DEWDNEY, late of England, to Miss HANNAH CAMMACK, of Washington. [CDA, Tues., 15 MAY 1827, p. 2]

Communicated. DIED, on board the brig *Olympia,* of this port, on the 21st of April last [1827], Capt. JOHN SOUTHER, aged 30 years.—For many years a respectable ship master from this port ... [CDA, Tues., 15 MAY 1827, p. 3]

MARRIED, in Liverpool, Capt. DUFFEY, of the brig *Laura,* to Miss HAMILTON, the celebrated Sailoress of that vessel. She has resumed female attire, but threatens if affairs are not well conducted on board, she will turn Jack Tar again, and take command. [CDA, Fri. 18 MAY 1827, p. 2]

DIED.—At the residence of the Right Rev. Dr. Conwell, Catholic Bishop of Philadelphia, the Rev. R. BAXTER, in the 36th year of his age. As a classical scholar, as an orator, and as a divine, he had but few equals, and hardly any superiors; but the qualities of his heart were superior to his other endowments ... [CDA, Fri. 1 JUN 1827, p. 3]

SUICIDE.—A well-dressed, good looking young man, was found dead on Tuesday last [i.e. 29 MAY 1827], suspended by a silk handkerchief, near Mount Vernon Tavern, on the Lancaster and Philadelphia turnpike. From papers found in his possession, it is thought his surname was DOLL. [CDA, Fri. 1 JUN 1827, p. 4]

MARRIED.—On the 31st ult. [i.e. 31 MAY 1827], by the Rev. Norwell Wilson, Mr. HORATIO N. STEELE, of Alexandria, to Miss MARY RAY, of Georgetown. [CDA, Tues., 5 JUN 1827, p. 3]

MARRIED.—On Tuesday evening the 12th inst. [i.e. 12 JUN 1827], by the Rev. Dr. Balch, Mr. ANDREW LOCKE, to Miss SARAH HUNTER, both of this place. [CDA, Fri. 15 JUN 1827, p. 2]

DIED.—On the 2d of April [i.e. 2 APR 1827], at New Orleans, in the 21st year of his age, Lieut. SAMUEL H. RIDGELY, eldest son of Col. Charles S. Ridgely, of Anne Arundel Co. The death of this young man has penetrated the hearts of his family with a shaft of the most bitter affliction, and has cast a gloom over all who had the pleasure of his acquaintance. He had but just entered upon the busy scene of life, (having the past year graduated at West Point) when he was attacked by a pulmonary disease, which baffled the skill of eminent practitioners, and a voyage to a milder climate was recommended as a last resort; but this too has failed, and grave has closed over one who promised fair to be an ornament and bright example to any society ... [CDA, Fri. 15 JUN 1827, p. 2]

MARRIED.—In Washington on Sunday last [i.e. 18 JUN 1827], by the Rev. Mr. M'Cormick, Mr. JOHN GODFREY HAMMER, late of Germany, to Miss ELIZABETH GIBBON, of the former place. [CDA, Tues., 26 JUN 1827, p. 3]

Georgetown, D.C., **Marriage and Death Notices, 1801-1838**

MARRIED.—On Wednesday the 3d of August [i.e. 3? AUG 1827], by the Rev. Mr. Johnson, Mr. GEORGE BEARD, to Miss MARY, eldest daughter of the late Capt. R. Dye, both of Fairfax Co., Va. [CDA, Fri. 10 AUG 1827, p. 3]

Communicated. OBITUARY. Died.—2d inst. [i.e. 2 AUG 1827], at Mr. Gooding's on the Capitol Hill, Mr. JOHN KING, he was a native of Virginia but has lived in Georgetown and Washington for the last 23 years, and has been employed by the Brick Layers of those cities, who testify to his honest and industrious course throughout. A large and respectable assemblage of mechanics accompanied his remains to the Catholic burial ground near Georgetown where his funeral obsequies were performed by the Rev. Mr. Smith. [CDA, Fri. 14 AUG 1827, p. 3]

DIED.—In this town on Monday night [i.e. 1 OCT 1827], after a short illness, Mr. JOHN WILSON, Sen., an old and respectable citizen of this place. [CDA, Tues., 2 OCT 1827, p. 3]

DIED.—On the 22d ult. [i.e. 22 SEP 1827], at *Friend's-Loss*, Montgomery Co., Mr. WILLIAM RATRIE; aged 76 years, a native of Scotland, but for upwards of 30 years a respectable inhabitant of this town. [CDA, Tues., 2 OCT 1827, p. 3]

MARRIED. On the 25th ult. [i.e. 25 SEP 1827], at Western River, Culpeper Co., Va., by the Rev. Mr. Jones, Mr. WILLIAM BUSSARD, of Georgetown, D.C., to Miss MARY ANN, eldest daughter of John C. Scott, Esq. [CDA, Fri. 12 OCT 1827, p. 3]

DIED.—On the 13th inst. [i.e. 13 OCT 1827], in the 25th year of her age, Mrs. SARAH S., wife of Mr. I.S. NICHOLLS, of this place ... [CDA, Tues., 16 OCT 1827, p. 3]

From the *Baltimore American*, October 13. ... the death [no date] of Col. JOHN EAGER HOWARD, the distinguished Patriot and Soldier of the Revolution. He departed this life at half past eight o'clock last night. [CDA, Tues., 16 OCT 1827, p. 3]

Death of Mr. Emmet.—It is with feelings of the deepest regret that we record the death of THOMAS ADDIS EMMIT, Esq., who has stood in the front rank of eminent American Jurists, and whose gigantic legal attainments and powerful eloquence have thrown such lustre over the bar of New York ... He was sitting in Court yesterday, in the forenoon, in apparent health, and was conversing only a few moments before the event. He was observed to lean forward with his head resting on his hand, or on his table, and when spoken to, was found to be entirely insensible ... A litter was prepared for his removal on which he was carried to his house in Hudson Square .... We are told that Wednesday was the anniversary of Mr. Emet's [sic] arrival in this country, 20 years ago; a singular coincidence. [CDA, 20 NOV 1827, p. 3]

MARRIED.—On Thursday evening [i.e. 20 DEC 1827], by the Rev. Mr. Wilson, Mr. CHARLES BOSTON, of Baltimore, to Miss MARTHA ANN DAVIS, of this place. [CDA, 25 DEC 1827, p. 3]

Georgetown, D.C., **Marriage and Death Notices, 1801-1838**

COLUMBIAN GAZETTE
July 2, 1829 to March 30, 1833

MARRIAGE. In Charleston, S.C. [no date], Lieut. E.C. RUTLEDGE, of the U.S. Navy, to REBECCA, daughter of the late Hon. William Lowndes. [CG, Thurs., 2 JUL 1829, p. 3]

DEATHS. In Baltimore, on Friday, the 19th inst. [i.e. 19 JUN 1829], aged forty years, Mrs. SARAH PRESBURY, wife of Mr. Geo. G. Presbury, of Baltimore, and daughter of the late Thomas Gassaway Howard. [CG, Thurs., 2 JUL 1829, p. 3]

DEATHS. In Kittery, Me., on Friday, the 19th inst. [i.e. 19 JUN 1829], Lieut. AUGUSTUS CUTTS, of the U.S. Navy, aged thirty-six years. In the death of Lieut. Cutts, the service has lost an excellent officer. [CG, Thurs., 2 JUL 1829, p. 3]

MARRIED. In Washington, on Tuesday, 7th inst. [i.e. 7 JUL 1829], by the Rev. Mr. Post, Mr. JOHN ANDERSON, Printer, to Miss ANN THOMPSON, all of that City. [CG, Thurs., 9 JUL 1829, p. 3]

MARRIED. On Thursday evening, the 2d inst. [i.e. 2 JUL 1829], by the Rev. Dr. Lawrie, Mr. CHARLES COLTMAN, to Miss MARY ANN DRUMMOND, all of that city. [CG, Thurs., 9 JUL 1829, p. 3]

MARRIED, at Baltimore, on Thursday, the 2d inst. [i.e. 2 JUL 1829], by the Right Rev. Archbishop Whitfield, J.M. MONTOYA, Esq., Charges des Affaires from the United States of Mexico to Miss EMILY E. WHELAN, of Baltimore. [CG, Thurs., 9 JUL 1829, p. 3]

DIED. In Washington City, on Wednesday evening last, Mrs. ELIZA GRAY, wife of Stephen W. Gray, Esq., of the General Post Office Department, in the 47th year of her age. [CG, Thurs., 9 JUL 1829, p. 3]

DIED. In Washington City [no date], Mr. JOHN SKIPPON, a worthy and industrious man.
    On the 20th ult. [i.e. 20 JUN 1829], at Charlestown, Cecil Co., Md., Dr. FRANCIS LeBARON, Apothecary General of the U.S. Army during the late war.
    On Tuesday night last [i.e. 7 JUL 1829], Mr. RUSSEL HILL, Merchant of Petersburg, Va., a man universally beloved and esteemed.
    At Arkansas on Sunday morning, 24th May [i.e. 24 MAY 1829], Maj. WILLIAM McLELLAN, Superintendent of Indian Affairs for the Choctaw Indians West of the Mississippi.
    In the City of New York on Tuesday evening [i.e. 7 JUL 1829], Mr. JOHN COTTON, aged twenty-nine years, the unfortunate man who lost his arms in the American brig *Patriot*, in an engagement off the Island of Cuba, with a piratical schooner, in September 1822.
    In Petersburg, on Wednesday last, 24th inst. [i.e. 24 JUN 1829], Mr. THOMAS F. DRUMMOND, merchant of that place.

Georgetown, D.C., **Marriage and Death Notices, 1801-1838**

On the 24th ult. [i.e. 24 JUN 1829], at Lebanon, Ohio, of a typhus fever, CHARLES R. SHERMAN, Esq., one of the Judges of the Supreme Court of that State.

In Norfolk [no date], Capt. JAMES MACKENZIE, commander of the Revenue Cutter *Wasp*. [CG, Thurs., 9 JUL 1829, p. 3]

MARRIED. On the 5th inst. [i.e. 5 JUL 1829], by the Rev. Mr. Jackson, of Leesburg, at *Oak Hill*, the residence of James Monroe, late President of the United States, in Loudoun Co., Va., LLOYD N. ROGERS, Esquire, of Md., to HORTENSIA MONROE, daughter of George Hay, Judge of the U.S. for the Eastern District of Virginia. [CG, Sat., 11 JUL 1829, p. 3]

MARRIED. In Baltimore [no date], Mr. WILLIAM KEPLINGER, to Miss MARY ANN, second daughter of Peter Cline, Esquire. [CG, Sat., 11 JUL 1829, p. 3]

MARRIED [no date]. GARDINER G. HOWLAND, Esquire, Merchant, of N.Y., to Miss LOUISA, daughter of J. Meredith, Esquire, of Baltimore. [CG, Sat., 11 JUL 1829, p. 3]

DIED. In Alexandria [no date], after a lingering illness, Mr. ALEXANDER M. JOHNSON, aged 21 years—youngest son of the late Capt. Dennis Johnson. [CG, Sat., 11 JUL 1829, p. 3]

DIED. At Baltimore, on the 4th inst. [i.e. 4 JUL 1829], Miss ELIZABETH ALCOCK, aged 69 years, a native of England, but for the last 59 years a resident of that City. [CG, Sat., 11 JUL 1829, p. 3]

MARRIED. On Wednesday last, the 1st inst. [i.e. 1 JUL 1829], at *Liberty Hall*, King William Co., Va., Capt. BEVERLY KENNON, of the U.S. Navy, to Miss BETSEY CLAIBORNE, daughter of the late Dandridge Claiborne, Esq., of that county. [CG, Tues., 14 JUL 1829, p. 3]

MARRIED. At *Berkley*, in Charles City Co., on the 8th inst. [i.e. 8 JUL 1829], Col. ANDREW PICKENS, of Ala., to Miss MARY NELSON. [CG, Tues., 14 JUL 1829, p. 3]

MARRIED. In Alexandria, on Thursday last [i.e. 9 JUL 1829], by the Rev. Jacob Larkin, Mr. LEMUEL N. MURRAY, to Miss MARY CARROL. [CG, Tues., 14 JUL 1829, p. 3]

MARRIED. On Thursday evening last [i.e. 9 JUL 1829], by the Rev. Jacob Larkin, Mr. BENJAMIN CAWOOD, to Miss MARY ANN McGEE, all of that place [Alexandria]. [CG, Tues., 14 JUL 1829, p. 3]

DIED. At Limington, Me. [no date], MARY HOWE, aged 103 years and 4 months. She has left a husband a few weeks younger than herself, with whom she lived in the marriage state about 84 years. [CG, Tues., 14 JUL 1829, p. 3]

DIED. At the Naval Hospital, near Pensacola, on the 10th June [i.e. 10 JUN 1829], Midshipman N.G.C. SLAUGHTER, of the U.S. Navy, a citizen of the District of Columbia. [CG, Tues., 14 JUL 1829, p. 3]

Georgetown, D.C., **Marriage and Death Notices, 1801-1838**

DIED. At Wheeling, Va., on the 5th inst. [i.e. 5 JUL 1829], GEORGE PANNELL, aged about fifty-six years, long a respectable resident of Baltimore. He was reared and educated in Baltimore. [CG, Tues., 14 JUL 1829, p. 3]

DIED. Departed this life, in this town, on the 6th inst. [i.e. 6 JUL 1829], Mrs. JANE LOWNDES, consort of the late Francis Lowndes, Sr., aged 74; after an indisposition of several years, which she bore with christian fortitude—much lamented by her family, and by all who had the pleasure of her acquaintance. [CG, Thurs., 16 JUL 1829, p. 3]

DIED. In Northampton Co., Va., on the 3d inst. [i.e. 3 JUL 1829], Dr. GEORGE P. JACOB, in the 24th year of his age. [CG, Thurs., 16 JUL 1829, p. 3]

DIED. At Fredericksburg, on the 12th inst. [i.e. 12 JUL 1829], after a lingering illness, aged 62, Mr. BENJAMIN PARKE, master Commissioner of the Chancery Court. [CG, Thurs., 16 JUL 1829, p. 3]

DIED. At Battletown, Frederick Co., Va., on the 7th inst. [i.e. 7 JUL 1829], Mrs. MARIA C. BYRD, wife of Mr. Thomas Taylor Byrd, Merchant, of that place, and elder daughter of Judge M'Mechen, of Baltimore. [CG, Thurs., 16 JUL 1829, p. 3]

DIED. In Baltimore, on the 9th inst. [i.e. 9 JUL 1829], ALEXANDER, third son of Jonathan Mauro, in the 30th year of his age. [CG, Thurs., 16 JUL 1829, p. 3]

MARRIED. In Alexandria, on Sunday evening last [i.e. 12 JUL 1829], Mr. JOHN F. COHAGEN, of Fairfax Co., Va., to Miss SARAH E., daughter of Robert Guest, Esq., of Charles Co., Md. [CG, Sat., 18 JUL 1829, p. 3]

MARRIED. In Baltimore, on the 30th ult. [i.e. 30 JUN 1829], Dr. AUGUSTUS J. SCHWARTZE, Jr., to Miss ELIZABETH A.K. WATTS, both of that City. [CG, Sat., 18 JUL 1829, p. 3]

MARRIED. In Baltimore, on the 14th inst. [i.e. 14 JUL 1829], Mr. SAMUEL JONES, Jr., to Miss ANN E. FORMAN. [CG, Sat., 18 JUL 1829, p. 3]

DIED. On the 13th inst. [i.e. 13 JUL 1829], at his house [on] Hudson street, N.Y., WILLIAM COLEMAN, Esq., late senior Editor of the *New York Evening Post*, in the 64th year of his age. [CG, Sat., 18 JUL 1829, p. 3]

MARRIED. In New York, on the 12th inst. [i.e. 12 JUL 1829], Mr. CHRISTOPHER HALL, of Norfolk, to Mrs. SARAH JONES. [CG, Tues., 21 JUL 1829, p. 3]

MARRIED. In Norfolk [no date], Mr. W. WOODWARD, to Miss S.A.W. OWENS, also Mr. THOMAS CLARKE, Merchant, of York Co., to Miss ROBINSONOVA, eldest daughter of Robert C. Jennings. [CG, Tues., 21 JUL 1829, p. 3]

MARRIED. In Baltimore [no date], Mr. J.R. BOARDLY, to Miss FRANCES P., daughter of the late Samuel Hanson Baker, of Washington City. [CG, Tues., 21 JUL 1829, p. 3]

Georgetown, D.C., **Marriage and Death Notices, 1801-1838**

MARRIED. On the 29th of Decr. 1828, by J.W. Brodie, Esq., H. LEVELY, of Baltimore, to HARRIET F.B. DeLaROCHE, of the Island of Jamaica.—*Philadelphia Aurora*. [CG, Tues., 21 JUL 1829, p. 3]

DIED. On Sunday the 12th inst. [i.e. 12 JUL 1829], Mrs. MARTHA HATTON, consort of Mr. John Hatton, of Isle of Wight Co. [CG, Tues., 21 JUL 1829, p. 3]

DIED. At 3 o'clock, on Friday afternoon, 17th inst. [i.e. 17 JUL 1829], CHARLES RIDGELY, of Hampton, late Governor of Md., in the 70th year of his age. [CG, Tues., 21 JUL 1829, p. 3]

DIED. In Philadelphia [no date], MARGARET OVERN, in the 81st year of her age. [CG, Sat., 25 JUL 1829, p. 3]

DIED [no date]. BARCLAY WARTERMAN, in the 22d year of his age. [CG, Sat., 25 JUL 1829, p. 3]

DIED [no date]. Mrs. PRUDENCE WILLIAMS, consort of William J. Williams. [CG, Sat., 25 JUL 1829, p. 3]

DIED [no date]. In the 63d year of her age, Mrs. ANNA M'PHAIL, widow of John M'Phail, late merchant of that city [Philadelphia]. [CG, Sat., 25 JUL 1829, p. 3]

MARRIED. In Philadelphia, on the 22d inst. [i.e. 22 JUL 1829], Capt. GEORGE C. READ, of the U.S. Navy, to ELIZABETH, daughter of the late Com. Richard Dale. [CG, Tues., 28 JUL 1829, p. 3]

DIED. In Washington, yesterday [i.e. 27 JUL 1829], WILLIAM HENRY, son of Mr. Thomas Fillebrown, Jr., age 7 months. Funeral this morning at 9 o'clock, which the friends of the family are respectfully invited to attend. [CG, Tues., 28 JUL 1829, p. 3]

DIED. On Thursday afternoon, the 23d inst. [i.e. 23 JUL 1829], Mrs. GRACE HURST, age 36 years, consort of Mr. John Hurst, of the War Department [CG, Tues., 28 JUL 1829, p. 3]

MARRIAGE. In Baltimore, on the 28th inst. [i.e. 28 JUL 1829], Mr. NATHAN SHEPPARD, to HONORIA, daughter of the late William Howell, Esq. [CG, Thurs., 30 JUL 1829, p. 3]

MARRIAGE. At Brownville, N.Y., on the 14th inst. [i.e. 14 JUL 1829], Lieut. D.H. VINTON, of the Army, to Miss PAMELA, daughter of the late Maj. Gen. Jacob Brown. [CG, Thurs., 30 JUL 1829, p. 3]

DIED. In Washington, on Sunday morning last [i.e. 26 JUL 1829], Mr. ALONZO BROOKE, age 23 years. [CG, Thurs., 30 JUL 1829, p. 3]

DIED. At New Haven, Conn., on the 20th inst. [i.e. 20 JUL 1829], Mr. JAMES M. WILLEY, son of the Hon. Calvin Willey, of Tolland. [CG, Thurs., 30 JUL 1829, p. 3]

Georgetown, D.C., **Marriage and Death Notices, 1801-1838**

DIED. Mrs. ANN H. LEE, of Georgetown, the widow of Gen. Henry Lee, of the Revolution, died on the morning of the 26th [i.e. 26 JUL 1829], at *Ravensworth*, the residence of W.H. Fitzhugh, surrounded by her family and friends. Her death is such as might have been expected from her life—exhibiting the resignation and composure of a practical Christian ... *Alex. Gazette*. [CG, Thurs., 30 JUL 1829, p. 3]

MARRIED. At Baltimore, on the 26th ult. [i.e. 26 JUL 1829], JAMES E. KILBOURN, of N.Y., to Miss ELIZABETH TENNISON, of Baltimore. [CG, Sat., 1 AUG 1829, p. 2]

MARRIED. In Philadelphia, on the 27th ult. [i.e. 27 JUL 1829], SAMUEL MERRICK, to Miss MARY HAMILTON, daughter of the late Jas. Gamble, Esq., all of that place. [CG, Sat., 1 AUG 1829, p. 2]

DIED. In Prince George's Co., Md., on the 23d ult. [i.e. 23 JUL 1829], Mr. JOHN A. EDELEN, aged 26. [CG, Sat., 1 AUG 1829, p. 2]

DIED. In Philadelphia, on the 25th ult. [i.e. 25 JUL 1829], JOHN R. BAKER, Esq., merchant, of that city, aged 67. [CG, Sat., 1 AUG 1829, p. 2]

DIED. At the Navy Yard, Brooklyn, (N.Y.) [no date], Mrs. ANNA CHAUNCEY, mother of Com. Chauncey, aged 88. [CG, Sat., 1 AUG 1829, p. 2]

DIED. At Marseilles, on the 29th May [i.e. 29 MAY 1829], the Rev. MICHAEL DuBOURG EGAN, nephew of the first Catholic Bishop of Philadelphia, and late President of Mount St. Mary's Seminary at Emmitsburg, Md., aged 29. [CG, Sat., 1 AUG 1829, p. 2]

MARRIED. In Washington, on the 26th ult. [i.e. 26 JUL 1829], Mr. ELI E. WILLIAMS, to Mrs. SARAH COOK, both of that place. [CG, Tues, 4 AUG 1829, p. 2]

MARRIED. In Washington, on the 23d ult. [i.e. 23 JUL 1829], by the Rev. William Ryland, the Rev. FRENCH S. EVANS, to Miss GEORGIANA CLINTON, third daughter of Mr. Wm. O'Neale, of that city. [CG, Tues, 4 AUG 1829, p. 2]

DIED. At his residence in Montgomery Co., near Rockville, Md., on the night of the 28th ult. [i.e. 28 JUL 1829], greatly respected by all who knew him, Mr. BENNETT CLEMENTS, aged 72 years. [CG, Tues, 4 AUG 1829, p. 2]

DIED. After an illness of about ten days [no date], Mrs. MARY DICKEY, aged 53. [CG, Tues, 4 AUG 1829, p. 2]

DIED. Near Carrol, in Greenfield township, on the 22d inst. [i.e. 22 JUL 1829], at 6 o'clock, A.M., Mr. THOMAS HENEY, late Postmaster at West Union, Ohio Co., Va., in the 42d year of his age. [CG, Tues, 4 AUG 1829, p. 2]

DIED. On the 25th ult. [i.e. 25 JUL 1829], after a short but severe illness, Maj. WILLIAM TRIMBLE, of Pleasant Township, Ohio, aged about 59 years. Maj. Trimble was one of the first settlers of this county, and his usefulness was not excelled by any, having at an early

Georgetown, D.C., Marriage and Death Notices, 1801-1838

period been chosen by the people, to represent them in the state Legislature. [CG, Tues, 4 AUG 1829, p. 2]

DIED. In Bristol, R.I., on the 16th inst. [i.e. 16 JUL 1829], Mr. NICHOLAS CAMPBELL, in the 97th year of his age. Mr. Campbell was born in the Island of Malta, but has been a citizen of this town for the last 54 years. He came to this country previous to the American Revolution, and was one of the memorable Boston Tea Party, who committed one of the first acts of resistance to British oppression by the destruction of a cargo of Tea in Boston Harbor, and commenced that glorious struggle which terminated in our National Independence. [CG, Tues, 4 AUG 1829, p. 2]

MARRIED. In Washington, on Monday evening last [i.e. 3 AUG 1829], by the Rev. Mr. Danforth, Mr. CHARLES F. WOOD, to Miss ARIANE ELLIS. [CG, Thurs., 6 AUG 1829, p. 2]

MARRIED. At Avignon, (Md.) on the 4th inst. [i.e. 4 AUG 1829], Mr. F. HARRISON, U.S. Assistant Civil Engineer, to Miss LYDIA REBECCA, daughter of Peter Levering, Esq., of Baltimore. [CG, Thurs., 6 AUG 1829, p. 2]

DIED. Near Cincinnati, (Ohio,) on the 23d ult. [i.e. 23 JUL 1829], in the 87th year of his age, PETER KEMPER. He was an officer in the Revolutionary War, and at the siege of York, where the contest was decided, and where he received a British grapeshot, the mark of which he carried to his grave. [CG, Thurs., 6 AUG 1829, p. 2]

DIED. At his residence in Edenton, (N.C.) on Tuesday, the 28th ult. [i.e. 28 JUL 1829], after a few days illness, the Rev. HENRY HOLMES, of the Methodist Episcopal Church. [CG, Thurs., 6 AUG 1829, p. 2]

MARRIED. In N.Y. [no date], Mr. JOHN B. PENDLETON, of Boston, to Miss ELIZA M. BLYDENBURG, daughter of Mr. Samuel Blydenburg, of N.Y. [CG, Sat., 8 AUG 1829, p. 3]

MARRIED. At Philadelphia [no date], by the Rev. Mr. Abercrombie, Mr. S.H. CHAPMAN, to Miss ELIZABETH, daughter of Mr. Joseph Jefferson, Comedian. [CG, Sat., 8 AUG 1829, p. 3]

DIED. In Washington, on Sunday last [i.e. 2 AUG 1829], at the residence of Capt. Barry, near the Navy Yard, after a painful and protracted illness of several months, Mr. PIERCE NAGLE, a native of Cork in Ireland, and recently of Prince George's Co., Md. [CG, Sat., 8 AUG 1829, p. 3]

DIED. At Havana, on the 2d June last [i.e. 2 JUN 1829], Mr. CHARLES T. MONAHAN, a native of Hagerstown, Md., in the 23d year of his age. [CG, Sat., 8 AUG 1829, p. 3]

DIED. In Philadelphia, on the 3 inst. [i.e. 3 AUG 1829], after a long protracted illness, WILLIAM GORDON, Esq., aged 32, late U.S. Consular Commercial Agent, at Aux Cayes, Hayti. [CG, Sat., 8 AUG 1829, p. 3]

Georgetown, D.C., **Marriage and Death Notices, 1801-1838**

DIED. On the 5th [i.e. 5 AUG 1829], MARY CATHARINE CLAVIER, aged 73 years. [CG, Sat., 8 AUG 1829, p. 3]

DIED [no date]. HENRY CHILD, in the 77th year of his age. [CG, Sat., 8 AUG 1829, p. 3]

DIED [no date]. MARY ANN, daughter of Joseph Lewis, aged 18 months. [CG, Sat., 8 AUG 1829, p. 3]

MARRIED. At Newcastle, Del., on Thursday evening last [i.e. 6 AUG 1829], by the Rev. Mr. Bell, the Rev. JOSHUA N. DANFORTH, Pastor of the Fourth Presbyterian Church in Washington, to Mrs. JANE J. WHILDEN, daughter of Thomas Janvier, Esq., of the former place. [CG, Tues., 11 AUG 1829, p. 3]

MARRIED. In Ogden, N.Y. [no date], the Rev. NATHANIEL W. FISHER, to Miss MARTHA MARIA, daughter of Rufus Graves, Esq., of Amherst, Mass. [CG, Tues., 11 AUG 1829, p. 3]

DIED. At Plaistow, N.H., on the 9th ult. [i.e. 9 JUL 1829], Col. JOSEPH WELCH, an officer and soldier of the Revolution, in the 87th year of his age. [CG, Tues., 11 AUG 1829, p. 3]

DIED. In Newburyport, Mass., on the 1st inst. [i.e. 1 AUG 1829], the Hon. DUDLEY A. TYNG, in the 69th year of his age, father of the Rev. Stephen H. Tyng, Rector of St. Paul's Church, in Philadelphia. [CG, Tues., 11 AUG 1829, p. 3]

DIED. In New York, on the 20th ult. [i.e. 20 JUL 1829], Mr. GEORGE RELPP, merchant, of the firm of *Relp, M'Intire and Co.*, of Charleston. [CG, Tues., 11 AUG 1829, p. 3]

DIED. At Camden, S.C., on the 20th ult. [i.e. 20 JUL 1829], Capt. GEORGE COOPER, in the 70th year of his age—a soldier and patriot of the Revolution. [CG, Tues., 11 AUG 1829, p. 3]

DIED. In London, on the 15th of June [i.e. 15 JUN 1829], Mr. THOMAS WILSON, an eminent merchant and banker, of the house of *Thomas Wilson & Son*. [CG, Tues., 11 AUG 1829, p. 3]

MARRIED. In N.Y., 6th inst. [i.e. 6 AUG 1829], WILLIAM LAMB, Esq., attorney at law, to Miss MARGARET K., younger daughter of William Wilson, Esq., of the former place. [CG, Thurs., 13 AUG 1829, p. 2]

MARRIED. On the 19th ult. [i.e. 19 JUL 1829], JOHN BREDIN, Esq., Editor of the *Butler Repository*, to Miss NANCY McCLELAND, daughter of George McCleland, of Franklin, Venango county [N.Y.]. [CG, Thurs., 13 AUG 1829, p. 2]

MARRIED. At Charleston, S.C., on the 23d ult. [i.e. 23 JUL 1829], JOHN KITCHELL, Esq., of Philadelphia, to Miss MARGARET SWEENY, of Charleston. [CG, Thurs., 13 AUG 1829, p. 2]

DIED. In this town, on Monday evening last [i.e. 10 AUG 1829], after a protracted illness, which she bore with exemplary fortitude, Mrs. REBECCA HYDE, consort of Mr. Thomas Hyde, in the 59th year of her age. [CG, Thurs., 13 AUG 1829, p. 2]

DIED. At Geneva, in Switzerland, on the 29th of May [i.e. 29 MAY 1829], the great and celebrated Philosopher, Sir HUMPHREY DAVY, in the 51st year of his age. [CG, Thurs., 13 AUG 1829, p. 2]

DIED. At Vera Cruz, on the 19th of June [i.e. 19 JUN 1829], Mrs. SARAH WILSON SOULNIER, Spouse of Mr. John Soulnier, merchant in that city, formerly of Philadelphia. [CG, Thurs., 13 AUG 1829, p. 2]

DIED. At his residence in Loudoun Co., Va., a few days since [no date], TOMMY TOMSON, a black man, aged 130 years. He was born and lived in Virginia, and retained his mental and physical faculties, to a few days previous to his decease. [CG, Thurs., 13 AUG 1829, p. 2]

DIED. In Washington City, on Monday last [i.e. 10 AUG 1829], after a few yours illness, JAMES JOSEPH, son of Mr. James Wilson, Printer, aged 6 years and 3 months ... [CG, Thurs., 13 AUG 1829, p. 2]

MARRIED. At Rossburg, Md., on Tuesday evening last [i.e. 11 AUG 1829], by the Rev. Reuben Post, Mr. JOSEPH STETTINIUS, of Washington, to Miss HELEN DAVIS, of the former place. [CG, Sat., 15 AUG 1829, p. 3]

DIED. At Tenly Town, Montgomery Co., Md., on the 9th inst. [i.e. 9 AUG 1829], DANIEL VANDERHOOF, of Oneida Co., N.Y., aged 28 years. [CG, Sat., 15 AUG 1829, p. 3]

DIED. At Port Tobacco, Charles Co., Md., on the 5th inst. [i.e. 5 AUG 1829], Mrs. ANN MASON, in the 78th year of her age. [CG, Sat., 15 AUG 1829, p. 3]

DIED. At Montpelier, France, on the 22d of May [i.e. 22 MAY 1829], where he had gone for the benefit of his health, JOHN BOULIN, in the 23d year of his age, late of the firm of *Boulin & Ferratun* of N.Y. [CG, Sat., 15 AUG 1829, p. 3]

DIED. In Fredericksburg, Va., on the 10th inst. [i.e. 10 AUG 1829], after a short illness, Mr. BENJAMIN B. WHITTEMORE, junior partner in the *House of Whittemore & Co.*, in the 24th year of his age. [CG, Sat., 15 AUG 1829, p. 3]

MARRIED. On Sunday evening, the 16th inst. [i.e. 16 AUG 1829], by the Rev. Dr. Balch, CHARLES E. MIX, Esq., of New Haven, Conn., to Miss CATHARINE S., third daughter of Henry Upperman, Esq., of this place. [CG, Tues., 18 AUG 1829, p. 3]

MARRIED. In London, on the 13th of June [i.e. 13 JUN 1829], A.G. RALSTON, Esq., of Philadelphia, to ELIZA, eldest daughter of Timothy Wiggin, Esq., of Harley street. [CG, Tues., 18 AUG 1829, p. 3]

Georgetown, D.C., **Marriage and Death Notices, 1801-1838**

MARRIED. In N.Y., on the 12th inst. [i.e. 12 AUG 1829], by the Rev. Dr. Broadhead, Mr. OLIVER HULL, to Miss REBECCA ANN, daughter of Orlando Harriman, merchant, all of that city. [CG, Tues., 18 AUG 1829, p. 3]

DIED. In the City of Washington, on Tuesday last [i.e. 11 AUG 1829], at half past 12 o'clock, Mrs. SARAH ROWEN LYNDALL. Mrs. L. was born in the City of Philadelphia, September 8, 1759, where she resided until a few years past, when she came to Washington to live with her son. [CG, Tues., 18 AUG 1829, p. 3]

DIED. On the 11th inst. [i.e. 11 AUG 1829], near the town of Harrisburg, Pa., JACOB BOMBERGER, at the advanced age of 85, and on the succeeding day his remains were decently interred in Sharer's burial ground. The deceased was known as "old Bomberger," and we believe made more noise in the world preaching, singing and sounding his trumpet for the last 40 years, than any individual now living. He was constantly engaged in traveling through the country, sounding his trumpet exhorting and denouncing. His zeal carried him among the North Western Indians, where he was kindly treated and whence he returned not long since, with his rugged frame fairly worn out and exhausted. The deceased was a native of Lancaster Co. [CG, Tues., 18 AUG 1829, p. 3]

DIED. At Portobello, Scotland, on the 11th June [i.e. 11 JUN 1829], Mrs. MARY MORRISON, sister of the late Archibald Gracie, of N.Y., aged 73 years. [CG, Tues., 18 AUG 1829, p. 3]

DIED. In Hagerstown, on the 9th inst. [i.e. 9 AUG 1829], Mrs. MARY INGLIS, late of Baltimore, in the 85th year of her age. [CG, Tues., 18 AUG 1829, p. 3]

DIED. At Catawissa, Columbia Co., N.Y., on the 6th inst. [i.e. 6 AUG 1829], Mr. PHILIP RUPERT, in the 92d year of his age.—The subject of this notice was the father of Leonard Rupert, Esq., one of the associate Judges of that county; and has left a numerous progeny, having had thirteen sons and daughters, eleven of whom have survived him. [CG, Tues., 18 AUG 1829, p. 3]

DIED. In Annapolis, Md. [no date], after a short but severe illness, Mrs. MATILDA CHASE, widow of the late Thomas Chase, leaving three children. [CG, Tues., 18 AUG 1829, p. 3]

DIED. At his residence in Chillicothe, Ohio, on the tenth inst. [i.e. 10 AUG 1829], Dr. EDWARD TIFFIN, in the 64th year of his age. The deceased was a native of England, and settled in Berkeley Co., in the state of Virginia, as a practicing physician. Shortly after this state (then a part of the N.W. territory, so called) was opened for settlement, he removed to this town, then in its infancy, and erected the first house that was covered with a shingle roof! In 1799, he was elected a member of the territorial legislature, in which capacity he continued to serve until he was chosen a member of the convention that formed the Constitution of Ohio—of which body he was President. When in 1803, the constitution of the state went into operation, he was called to the first executive office under it, by a very flattering vote of the people ... He has left to deplore his loss, a widow, and five children, a number of near relatives, and an extensive circle of public and private acquaintances. On the succeeding afternoon his mortal remains were committed to the

Georgetown, D.C., **Marriage and Death Notices, 1801-1838**

tomb, attended by a large concourse of the citizens of the town and of the adjoining neighborhood. [CG, Thurs., 20 AUG 1829, p. 2]

DIED. At Pasto, Colombia, (in South America) [no date], Col. JOHN FERRIAR, commander of the Battalion of Carabobia, and son of the late Dr. Ferriar, of Manchester, Eng. [CG, Thurs., 20 AUG 1829, p. 2]

DIED. On the 7th inst. [i.e. 7 AUG 1829], in the vicinity of Leesburg, Va., MALCOLM DOWNS, in the 19th year of his age, and on the same day, HAMILTON M., brother of Malcolm, in his 18th year, both of bilious fever. [CG, Thurs., 20 AUG 1829, p. 2]

DIED. In Wilmington, (N.C.) on the 5th inst. [i.e. 5 AUG 1829], Mrs. MARY CAMPBELL, aged forty-three years, relict of Mr. Fenneth [sic] Campbell. [CG, Sat., 22 AUG 1829, p. 2]

DIED. On the 6th inst. [i.e. 6 AUG 1829], Mr. JOHN B. HARRIS, aged 28. [CG, Sat., 22 AUG 1829, p. 2]

DIED. In Bladen Co., N.C. [no date], Mr. ISAAC SESSUMS, aged upwards of 80 years. On the day before his death, he walked sixteen miles, and on the following morning he rose and was proceeding to his daily labour, when after walking about 100 yards, he sunk down and died without a groan. [CG, Sat., 22 AUG 1829, p. 2]

DIED. In Bladen Co., N.C., on the 3d inst. [i.e. 3 AUG 1829], Mr. EDWARD REVES, aged 103 years. He was one of three living within seven miles of each other, whose aggregate ages amounted to 305 years. The others are still living. [CG, Sat., 22 AUG 1829, p. 2]

DIED. In Washington, on the 21st inst. [i.e. 21 AUG 1829], Mrs. ELIZA WOODSIDE, the wife of John Woodside, of the Treasury Department, Comptroller's Office. [CG, Tues., 25 AUG 1829, p. 2]

DIED. At his residence in Williamson Co., near Harpeth, Tenn., on the 10th of May 1829, in the 74th year of his age, Mr. MINOS CANNON, Sr. He was a native of Md., where he engaged, when a youth, in the Revolutionary war; shared the dangers of the Battle of Brandywine, and several others. Nor did he lay aside his arms until he witnessed the surrender of the British army at Yorktown. [CG, Tues., 25 AUG 1829, p. 2]

DIED. On the 19th inst. [i.e. 19 AUG 1829], at *Morven*, his residence, near Leesburg, Va., in the 29th year of his age, JOHN SWANN. [CG, Tues., 25 AUG 1829, p. 2]

DIED. In the city of New York, on the 16th inst. [i.e. 16 AUG 1829], of apoplexy, MANUEL TEIXEIRA D'AGRELLA, Esq., aged 57 years, late of the Island of Madeira. [CG, Tues., 25 AUG 1829, p. 2]

DIED. At Pensacola, on the 21st July [i.e. 21 JUL 1829], CORA FLORIDA RIDGELY, infant daughter of Com. Charles G. Ridgely, aged about nine months. [CG, Tues., 25 AUG 1829, p. 2]

Georgetown, D.C., **Marriage and Death Notices, 1801-1838**

DIED. In Baltimore, on the 15th inst. [i.e. 15 AUG 1829], after a lingering illness, MARY, second daughter of the Rev. Dr. Wyatt, aged 7 year and 9 months. [CG, Tues., 25 AUG 1829, p. 2]

MARRIED. At New Berlin, Chenango Co., N.Y., on the 9th inst. [i.e. 9 AUG 1829], Col. CHARLES W. SIMONS, of the State of Ohio, to Miss ELIZA C. DEWEY, of the former place, and lately from Brunswick, Me. [CG, Thurs., 27 AUG 1829, p. 3]

MARRIED. At Gosport, on the 16th inst. [i.e. 16 AUG 1829], Lieut. GEORGE S. BLAKE, of the Navy, (of Mass.) to Miss MARY A.A. BARRON, youngest daughter of Com. James Barron, of the Navy. [CG, Thurs., 27 AUG 1829, p. 3]

DIED. In Washington, on the 24th inst. [i.e. 24 AUG 1829], after a severe and protracted illness, MARY, consort of Lemuel Townsend, aged 59 years. [CG, Thurs., 27 AUG 1829, p. 3]

DIED. In Baltimore, on Saturday evening last [i.e. 22 AUG 1829], after a long and severe illness, Mr. RICHARD JONES, of Prince George's Co., Md., beloved and esteemed by all who had the pleasure of his acquaintance. [CG, Thurs., 27 AUG 1829, p. 3]

DIED. On the 23d inst. [i.e. 23 AUG 1829], in the 61st year of his age, after a lingering and most painful illness, which he bore with the greatest fortitude, JOHN BEALE DAVIDGE, A.M.M.D., Professor of Anatomy in the University of Maryland. [CG, Thurs., 27 AUG 1829, p. 3]

DIED. In Wells, Ver. [no date], Capt. ICHABOD MITCHEL, aged 84, a soldier of the revolution. [CG, Thurs., 27 AUG 1829, p. 3]

DIED. In Iredell Co., N.C. [no date], Mr. WILLIAM MURDOCK, aged 90. He had been married 60 and has lived on the plantation where he died 65 years. He served in the revolutionary war. [CG, Thurs., 27 AUG 1829, p. 3]

DIED. At New Orleans, on the 1st inst. [i.e. 1 AUG 1829], Mr. LEONARD BOSWELL, late of Methuen, Mass. [CG, Thurs., 27 AUG 1829, p. 3]

DIED. On the 3d inst. [i.e. 3 AUG 1829], Mr. HUGH M'CLASKEY, a native of Lancaster Co., Pa. [CG, Thurs., 27 AUG 1829, p. 3]

DIED. On the 3d inst. [i.e. 3 AUG 1829], WILLIAM M. SAUL, Esq., late Cashier of the Bank of Orleans. [CG, Thurs., 27 AUG 1829, p. 3]

DIED. In Cincinnati, Ohio, on the 18th inst. [i.e. 18 AUG 1829], Mr. JOHN DAVIES, aged 85. Mr. Davies was a native of England, and had only recently returned from a visit to two daughters, who have long resided in Washington, and who must have been gratified to behold their aged parent once more on this side of the grave. [CG, Sat., 29 AUG 1829, p. 2]

Georgetown, D.C., **Marriage and Death Notices, 1801-1838**

MARRIAGE. At Philadelphia, on Thursday evening, the 27th inst. [i.e. 27 AUG 1829], WILLIAM STAUGHTON, D.D., to ANN C., daughter of Mr. James Peale, all of that city. [CG, Tues., 1 SEP 1829, p. 3]

DIED. In Washington, on Saturday [i.e. 29 AUG 1829], ARMISTEAD MASON, and on Sunday morning, ANN THORNTON MASON, two fine promising children, aged about 10 and 11 years, of Richard B. Mason, Esq., of that city. [CG, Tues., 1 SEP 1829, p. 3]

DIED. On the evening of the 26th ult. [i.e. 26 AUG 1829], after a severe illness of 17 days, Mrs. ANN THOMAS, wife of George Thomas, Esq., Teller of the Bank of the Metropolis, in the 20th year of her age. [CG, Tues., 1 SEP 1829, p. 3]

DIED. At his residence in Montgomery Co., Md., on the 27th ult. [i.e. 27 AUG 1829], at 10 o'clock in the morning, AQUILLA LANHAM, Esq., in the 46th year of his age; at 5 o'clock in the afternoon of the same day, his sister Miss ELIZA LANHAM, aged 50. [CG, Tues., 1 SEP 1829, p. 3]

DIED. On the morning of the 28th [i.e. 28 AUG 1829], at the residence of Charles A. Burnett, in Georgetown, where she had been but a few days, on a visit, Miss MARCIA M. LANHAM, in the 38th year of her age. Thus have fallen by the stroke of death, in the short space of 24 hours, an affectionate brother and two sisters, whose loss will be long lamented by their relatives and a numerous acquaintance. [CG, Tues., 1 SEP 1829, p. 3]

MARRIED. In Washington [no date], Mr. RICHARD REYNOLDS, of N.Y., to Miss EMELINE M. CHESTER. [CG, Thurs., 3 SEP 1829, p. 2]

MARRIED. At Providence, R.I. [no date], Lt. EDWARD J. JOHNSON, of the U.S. Navy, to Miss EMILY DODGE. [CG, Thurs., 3 SEP 1829, p. 2]

DIED. At Alexandria, D.C., on Friday evening the 28th ult. [i.e. 28 AUG 1829], Mrs. MARY CRUSE, eldest daughter of the late Peter Hoffman, of Baltimore. [CG, Thurs., 3 SEP 1829, p. 2]

DIED. At Mobile, on the 7th ult. [i.e. 7 AUG 1829], the Rev. WM. H. JUDD, of the Protestant Episcopal Church, a native of New London, Conn. [CG, Thurs., 3 SEP 1829, p. 2]

DIED. In Bedford, Pa., on the 25th ult. [i.e. 25 AUG 1829], Mr. JOSEPH PATTERSON, of Baltimore, generally known as "Patterson the Gambler." His disease was violent and his dissolution rapid ... [CG, Thurs., 3 SEP 1829, p. 2]

DIED. In Philadelphia, on the 30th ult. [i.e. 30 AUG 1829], JONATHAN FOWLE, Esq. [CG, Thurs., 3 SEP 1829, p. 2]

DIED. On the 25th ult. [i.e. 25 AUG 1829], at Williamsport, Pa., ESPY VAN HORNE, late of the U.S. House of Representatives. [CG, Thurs., 3 SEP 1829, p. 2]

Georgetown, D.C., **Marriage and Death Notices, 1801-1838**

MARRIED. In East Randolph, (Vt.) [no date], MOSES PARSONS, aged 85, to MARTHA WENTWORTH, aged 70; two Revolutionary characters. [CG, Sat., 5 SEP 1829, p. 2]

DIED. In Washington City, on the 31st ult. [i.e. 31 AUG 1829], Mrs. MASON, wife of Richard B. Mason, Esq., and on the 2d inst., VIRGINIA, daughter of Mr. M., aged six years. [CG, Sat., 5 SEP 1829, p. 2]

DIED. On Friday last [i.e. 28? AUG 1829], at his late residence in Calvert Co., DANIEL KENT, lately a member of the Senate of Maryland, in the 47th year of his age, in the vigor of life, and in the midst of his usefulness. [CG, Sat., 5 SEP 1829, p. 2]

DIED. In Baltimore, on the 25th August last [i.e. 25 AUG 1829], in the 75th year of his age, Col. RICHARD WATERS, a soldier of the Revolution. He entered the army at the commencement of the war, and continued faithfully to discharge his duty until its close. [CG, Sat., 5 SEP 1829, p. 2]

MARRIED. On Thursday evening, the 3d inst. [i.e. 3 SEP 1829], by the Rev. Mr. Campbell, Mr. JOSEPH S. WILSON, to Miss ELIZABETH U. MOULDER, daughter of J.N. Moulder, Esq., both of Washington City. [CG, Tues., 8 SEP 1829, p. 3]

MARRIED. In Albany, N.Y., on the 1st inst. [i.e. 1 SEP 1829], Lieut. JAMES T. HOMANS, of the U.S. Navy, to Miss ELIZABETH KAY, daughter of James Kay, Esq., of that city. [CG, Tues., 8 SEP 1829, p. 3]

DIED. At Bedford, Pa., on the 30th ult. [i.e. 30 AUG 1829], Mrs. SARAH M. KING, consort of Mr. George King, of Charles, of Washington City. [CG, Tues., 8 SEP 1829, p. 3]

DIED. At his residence in Radnor township, Chester Co., Pa., on the 2d inst. [i.e. 2 SEP 1829], very suddenly, Gen. WILLIAM BROOKE, an officer of the Revolution. [CG, Tues., 8 SEP 1829, p. 3]

DIED. In Holme's Hole (Me.) [no date], THEODORE PARSONS, Esq., aged 73 years, a soldier of the Revolution. [CG, Tues., 8 SEP 1829, p. 3]

DIED. At the residence of her sister, in Harford Co., on Monday last [i.e. 31 AUG? 1829], Mrs. MARGARET BARNEY, consort of John H. Barney, Esq., of Baltimore. [CG, Tues., 8 SEP 1829, p. 3]

DIED. In N.Y., on the 30th ult. [i.e. 30 AUG 1829], JAMES HERON, Esq., of the firm *J. & J.E. Heron*, of Richmond, a gentleman of great worth and high respectability. [CG, Tues., 8 SEP 1829, p. 3]

MARRIAGE. On the 2d inst. [i.e. 2 SEP 1829], at *Poplar Plain*, Caroline Co., Va., WILLIAM WERTENBAKER, Esq., of the University of Virginia, to Miss LOUISA TIMBERLAKE, daughter of Mr. Lewis Timberlake. [CG, Thurs., 10 SEP 1829, p. 3]

Georgetown, D.C., **Marriage and Death Notices, 1801-1838**

MARRIAGE. In Alexandria, on Tuesday [i.e. 8 SEP 1829], SAMUEL J. DUNCAN, of Lincoln Co., Me., to Miss ANN JANE COATS, of Alexandria. [CG, Thurs., 10 SEP 1829, p. 3]

MARRIED. At Medford, near Boston, on the 3d inst. [i.e. 3 SEP 1829], CHARLES FRANCIS ADAMS, Esq., son of Ex-President Adams, to ABBY, daughter of the Hon. Peter C. Brooks. [CG, Thurs., 10 SEP 1829, p. 3]

DIED. On Thursday, the 3d inst. [i.e. 3 SEP 1829], in the 63d year of his age, Mr. JOHN DOBBYN, a native of Ireland, but for many years a resident of this District. [CG, Thurs., 10 SEP 1829, p. 3]

DIED. At the residence of his father, in Geneva, N.Y. [no date], DELANO SWIFT, son of Gen. J.G. Swift, aged 17 years. [CG, Thurs., 10 SEP 1829, p. 3]

DIED. In King & Queen Co., Va., on the 2nd of this month [i.e. 2 SEP 1829], JOHN BOULWARE, aged twenty-three, a tutor in the Columbian College. [CG, Thurs., 10 SEP 1829, p. 3]

DIED. At the residence of Mr. Josiah Biscoe, St. Mary's Co., Md. [no date], the Rev. HENRY N. HOTCHKISS, rector of William and Mary Parish, in the 29th year of his age. [CG, Thurs., 10 SEP 1829, p. 3]

DIED. At N.Y., on Sunday morning last [i.e. 6 SEP 1829], the Rev. MATTHIAS BRUEN, Pastor of the Bleecker Street Presbyterian Church, after one week's illness. [CG, Thurs., 10 SEP 1829, p. 3]

DIED. At Chapofa, near Tallahassee, Fla., on the 5th August [i.e. 5 AUG 1829], the Rev. HORATIO NELSON GRAY, formerly Rector of Christ Church, Georgetown, D.C. ... His delicate frame being found unequal to the duties of the ministry in this climate he was induced, by the advice of his physicians, to accept a mission to the milder of Florida under the region direction of the Dom. and For. Mis. Society of the Prot. Ep. Church in the U. States ... [CG, Thurs., 10 SEP 1829, p. 3]

DIED. In Philadelphia, on Tuesday the 1st of September [i.e. 1 SEP 1829], FELICIA LIBERIA HEMANS, first and only child of Rev. R.R. Gurley, Secretary of the American Colonization Society, aged ten months. [CG, Thurs., 10 SEP 1829, p. 3]

DIED, while on a visit with her parents to *Bloomsbury*, the seat of Judge Plater, in St. Mary's Co., Md., on the 2d inst. [i.e. 2 SEP 1829], SOPHIA P., daughter of Wm. G. and Sophia Ridgely, of this Town, in the 10th year of her age ... [CG, Sat., 12 SEP 1829, p. 3]

DIED. *Another Soldier of the Revolution gone!*—Died at his residence in the County of Buckingham, on Monday the 31st of August [i.e. 31 AUG 1829], after a lingering and painful disease of some months, Mr. ARTHUR MOSELEY, in the 69th year of his age. Mr. Moseley was in several battles during the Revolution, throughout the whole of which he was distinguished for his zealous and patriotic devotion, to those great principles of Liberty,

Georgetown, D.C., **Marriage and Death Notices, 1801-1838**

which constitute the broad and solid basis of our government. [CG, Tues., 15 SEP 1829, p. 3]

DIED. In this town on Thursday Morning [i.e. 17 SEP 1829], EDWARD JONES, Esq., late Chief Clerk in the Treasury Department, aged 74 years and 9 months. [CG, Sat., 19 SEP 1829, p. 2]

DIED. In Philadelphia, on the 15th inst. [i.e. 15 SEP 1829], Mr. ABRAHAM SMALL, in the 65th year of his age, for many years an eminent Bookseller in that place. [CG, Sat., 19 SEP 1829, p. 2]

DIED. In Baltimore on the 14th inst. [i.e. 14 SEP 1829], Mrs. JANE BIRKHEAD, wife of Dr. Solomon Birkhead, in the 72d year of her age. [CG, Sat., 19 SEP 1829, p. 2]

DIED. In Louisville, Ky. [no date], Dr. JOSEPH BUCHANAN, in the 44th year of his age, after an illness of 11 days, of a bilious remittent fever. Dr. B. was editor of the *Louisville Focus*. [CG, Sat., 19 SEP 1829, p. 2]

DIED. On Tuesday the 8th inst. [i.e. 8 SEP 1829], at St. Clairsville, Ohio, Mr. DAVID IRWIN, and a young man, his apprentice, named ELIJAH JOHNSON. The young man had gone into a well, which had been shut up some time. When about half way down he fell to the bottom, and remained silent. Mr. Irwin, not knowing the cause of his fall, went in after him and also fell. It was thus that the presence of noxious gas in the well was ascertained ... Mr. Irwin, was formerly resident in Wheeling, and was universally respected as a most worthy citizen ... [CG, Tues., 22 SEP 1829, p. 2]

DIED. At Montgomery, Ala., on the 30th ult. [i.e. 30 AUG 1829], Mr. OTHO BELT, in the 40th year of his age, a native of Washington City. [CG, Tues., 22 SEP 1829, p. 2]

MARRIED. In Washington, on the 14th inst. [i.e. 14 SEP 1829], Mr. S.J. TODD, to LEAH ANN, daughter of Thomas H. Gillis, Esq. [CG, Thurs., 24 SEP 1829, p. 3]

MARRIED [no date]. Dr. GEO. B. McKNIGHT, of the U.S. Navy, to Miss MARTHA H. PROUT. [CG, Thurs., 24 SEP 1829, p. 3]

DIED. At Marlborough, P.G. Co., Md., on the 18th inst. [i.e. 18 SEP 1829], JULIUS FORREST, Esq., Attorney at Law, in the 31st year of his age, son of the late Richard Forrest, Esq. [CG, Thurs., 24 SEP 1829, p. 3]

DIED. In Baltimore, on the 22d inst. [i.e. 22 SEP 1829], Mr. THOMAS POWERS, formerly of Washington City, in the 23d year of his age. [CG, Thurs., 24 SEP 1829, p. 3]

DIED. In Washington, on the 21st inst. [i.e. 21 SEP 1829], Mr. EDWARD S. LEWIS, in the 35th year of his age, a member of the Board of Aldermen and many years a clerk in the third Auditor's Office. [CG, Thurs., 24 SEP 1829, p. 3]

Georgetown, D.C., **Marriage and Death Notices, 1801-1838**

MARRIED. In Alexandria, on the 22d inst. [i.e. 22 SEP 1829], Mr. JAMES M'KENZIE, to Miss SARAH EVELETH, second daughter of Thomas Sanford, Esq., of that place. [CG, Sat., 26 SEP 1829, p. 3]

MARRIED. On the 22d inst. [i.e. 22 SEP 1829], Mr. WILLIAM HUBBLE, to Miss ANN R., eldest daughter of Spencer Jackson, Esq., of Fairfax Co., Va. [CG, Sat., 26 SEP 1829, p. 3]

MARRIED. In Baltimore [no date], the Rev. JOHN HOFFMAN, of Taneytown, to Miss ANN MARGARET, daughter of John Reese, Esq. [CG, Sat., 26 SEP 1829, p. 3]

DIED. In Washington, on the 22d inst. [i.e. 22 SEP 1829], Mr. JOHN L. BELL, a native of Sacket's Harbor, N.Y., aged 23 years 6 months. [CG, Sat., 26 SEP 1829, p. 3]

DIED [no date]. Miss MARY B. STELLE, in the 26th year of her age. [CG, Sat., 26 SEP 1829, p. 3]

DIED. At Bellefontaine, Mo., on the 2d inst. [i.e. 2 SEP 1829], Maj. JOHN WHISTLER, of the U.S. Army, aged 71. [CG, Sat., 26 SEP 1829, p. 3]

DIED. In Baltimore, on the 23d inst. [i.e. 23 SEP 1829], WILLIAM JESSOP, Sen., Esq., in the 75th year of his age. [CG, Sat., 26 SEP 1829, p. 3]

DIED. On the 16th inst. [i.e. 16 SEP 1829], Mrs. REBECCA GRIFFITH, wife of Capt. David Griffith, and eldest daughter of Daniel James, in the 24th year of her age. [CG, Sat., 26 SEP 1829, p. 3]

DIED. At Elk Ridge, on the 24th inst. [i.e. 24 SEP 1829], THOMAS NORRIS, of Thomas. [CG, Sat., 26 SEP 1829, p. 3]

MARRIED. In Littleton, Mass. [no date], JOHN S.C. KNOWLTON, Esq., Editor of the *Lowell Journal*, to Miss ANNA W. HARTWELL. [CG, Tues., 29 SEP 1829, p. 2]

MARRIED. In Newburyport, Mass. [no date], Lieut. GEORGE F. PEARSON, of the U.S. Navy, to Miss ELLEN JACKSON. [CG, Tues., 29 SEP 1829, p. 2]

DIED. In Fredericksburg, Va., on the 24th inst. [i.e. 24 SEP 1829], Mr. JOHN PITTMAN, formerly of Alexandria. [CG, Tues., 29 SEP 1829, p. 2]

DIED. In New Orleans, on the 3d inst. [i.e. 3 SEP 1829], of the prevailing fever, Mrs. LIONEL AUGUSTA HAYES, late of Philadelphia. [CG, Tues., 29 SEP 1829, p. 2]

DIED. In Fredericktown, Md., on the 23d inst. [i.e. 23 SEP 1829], the Rev. JONATHAN HELFENSTEIN, in the 46th year of his age, for man years Pastor of the German Reformed Church of that place. [CG, Tues., 29 SEP 1829, p. 2]

Georgetown, D.C., **Marriage and Death Notices, 1801-1838**

DIED. On Wednesday, the 2d of September [i.e. 2 SEP 1829] at his residence, *Park House,* near Albion, Ill., RICHARD FLOWER, Esq., aged 68 years. He was a distinguished emigrant from England. [CG, Tues., 29 SEP 1829, p. 2]

DIED. In Philadelphia, on the 25th inst. [i.e. 25 SEP 1829], SAMUEL WETHERILL, Esq., in the 66th year of his age. [CG, Tues., 29 SEP 1829, p. 2]

DIED. In New York, on the 19th [i.e. 19 SEP 1829], very suddenly, Dr. JOHN DENNY, assistant Surgeon U.S. Navy, aged 26. [CG, Tues., 29 SEP 1829, p. 2]

DIED. In Farmington, Conn., on the 21st inst. [i.e. 21 SEP 1829], Mrs. MARY H. NORTON, aged 27, wife of John T. Norton, Esq., of Albany, and daughter of Hon. Timothy Pitkin. [CG, Tues., 29 SEP 1829, p. 2]

DIED. In Lymington, (Md.) LAZARUS ROWE, aged 104. His wife, who died last spring, was born the same year with her husband, (1725). They were married at the age of eighteen, and consequently lived together eighty six years. They reared a numerous family, and saw their descendants of the fifth generation. Their youngest son is now a pensioner of the revolutionary army. In early life the old man was a soldier in the French and Indian wars: he was at the taking of Louisburg in 1745. Afterwards he belonged to Captain Rogers' company of Rangers in New Hampshire, and was often in Indian battles; was taken captive; and was once on the point of being burned to death by the savages, when he escaped by an almost super-human effort. He was in the bloody engagement near Lake George, September 6th, 1755, when the French commander, Baron Dieskau, was killed. He was also under Col. Munroe, at the capitulation of Fort William Henry, in 1757. He retained, to his last days, a vivid recollection of the terrific scenes of that siege and capitulation, and of the massacre that followed. [CG, Tues., 29 SEP 1829, p. 2]

DIED. In Alexandria, on the 29th inst. [i.e. 29 SEP 1829], Mrs. MARY RICKETTS, widow of the late John Thomas Ricketts, in the 66th year of her age. [CG, Thurs., 1 OCT 1829, p. 2]

DIED. On Saturday last [i.e. 26 SEP 1829], in the 65th year of his age, Mr. JOHN CRANSTON, a native of Rhode Island, but for the last forty years a respectable inhabitant of Alexandria. He has left a wife and eight children to mourn his loss. [CG, Thurs., 1 OCT 1829, p. 2]

DIED. In Bushwick, Long Island, on the 25th ult. [i.e. 25 SEP 1829], GARDNER THOMAS, Esq., Purser U.S. Navy, in the 52d year of his age. Few men have passed through life more esteemed, or left a memory behind more highly cherished, than Mr. Thomas. [CG, Thurs., 1 OCT 1829, p. 2]

DIED. At his residence, near Lebanon, Ohio, on the 3d ult. [i.e. 3 SEP 1829], MATHIAS CORWIN, Esq., formerly Speaker of the House of Representatives of the State of Ohio, and more recently one of the Associate Judges for the county of Warren. [CG, Thurs., 1 OCT 1829, p. 2]

Georgetown, D.C., **Marriage and Death Notices, 1801-1838**

DIED. In Philadelphia, on the 28th ult. [i.e. 28 SEP 1829], Mr. FRANCIS WRIGLEY, Printer, in the 86th year of his age. Mr. Wrigley was one of the oldest printers in the United States, and printed for the Old Congress while sitting in Philadelphia, and accompanied them from that city to Baltimore, where he printed the "Old Continental Money," which was at that time in circulation.—He was a man celebrated for his kindness and generosity, particularly towards those of his profession—was the first to visit the sick and dying, and endeavoring to administer comfort and relief to the helpless widow. [CG, Sat., 3 OCT 1829, p. 3]

MARRIED. In this town, on Thursday evening, 1st inst. [i.e. 1 OCT 1829], the Hon. HENRY JOHNSON, late Governor of Louisiana, to ELIZABETH, daughter of the late Philip Barton Key, Esq. [CG, Tues., 6 OCT 1829, p. 2]

MARRIED. In Randolph, Ver., on the 22d ult. [i.e. 22 SEP 1829], Mr. GEORGE P. WILLIAMS, Tutor in Kenyon College, to Miss ELIZABETH EDSON. [CG, Tues., 6 OCT 1829, p. 2]

DIED. At the residence of his father, Bristol, R.I., on the 27th ult. [i.e. 27 SEP 1829], the Rev. GEORGE GRISWOLD, eldest surviving son of the Right Rev. A.V. Griswold, and late Rector of Christ Church, Alexandria, D.C. [CG, Tues., 6 OCT 1829, p. 2]

DIED. In Edenton, N.C., on the 29th ult. [i.e. 29 SEP 1829], Mr. JOHN P. NORFLEET, in the 31st year of his age. [CG, Tues., 6 OCT 1829, p. 2]

MARRIED. In Alexandria, on Sunday evening the 4th inst. [i.e. 4 OCT 1829], Mr. SAMUEL J. STAPLES, of Norfolk, Va., to Mrs. MARY BIRD, of the former place. [CG, Thurs., 8 OCT 1829, p. 2]

DIED. In Alexandria, on the 5th inst. [i.e. 5 OCT 1829], Mrs. CATHARINE GRAY, in the 86th year of her age. [CG, Thurs., 8 OCT 1829, p. 2]

DIED. In Fredericksburg, Va. [no date], Mr. PETER HORD, long a respectable merchant of that place. [CG, Thurs., 8 OCT 1829, p. 2]

DIED. In Philadelphia, on the 4th inst. [i.e. 4 OCT 1829], Mr. GEORGE HOBSON, Merchant, in the 65th year of his age. [CG, Thurs., 8 OCT 1829, p. 2]

DIED. On the 5th inst. [i.e. 5 OCT 1829], Mrs. M.B. CAREY, in the 61st year of her age, wife of Mathew Carey, Esq. [CG, Thurs., 8 OCT 1829, p. 2]

MARRIED. In Washington, on Wednesday evening last [i.e. 7 OCT 1829], by the Rev. Mr. Brown, Capt. BENJAMIN F. SPENCER, to Miss PRUDENCE, eldest daughter of Mr. Samuel Hills, of Baltimore. [CG, Sat., 10 OCT 1829, p. 3]

MARRIED. In Baltimore, on the 6th inst. [i.e. 6 OCT 1829], JAMES BEATTY, Jr., to ELIZABETH, daughter of Philip Laurenson. [CG, Sat., 10 OCT 1829, p. 3]

Georgetown, D.C., **Marriage and Death Notices, 1801-1838**

DIED. At Brooklyn, N.Y., on Monday evening [i.e. 5 OCT 1829], of a disease of the heart, Capt. HENRY W. KENNEDY, in the 33d year of his age, a native of Bucks Co., Pa. Captain K. resigned his commission in the U.S. Marine Corps, in November 1816, after which he entered the Buenos Ayrean service, and then that of the Chilian, in which he lost his eye-sight by a wound received in an engagement between the Chilians and Peruvians. He returned to the United States in 1820. In 1821, Captain K. was appointed Sutler of the Marines under the command of Col. Gamble, at the Navy Yard at Brooklyn. [CG, Sat., 10 OCT 1829, p. 3]

DIED. In Baltimore, on the 6th inst. [i.e. 6 OCT 1829], Mrs. RUHAMAH PINDALL, relict of the late Hon. James Pindall, of Virginia. [CG, Sat., 10 OCT 1829, p. 3]

MARRIED. On Tuesday, the 6th inst. [i.e. 6 OCT 1829], on South River, Mr. LEWIS I. BROOKS, of this town, to Miss MARGARET, daughter of Mr. James Davidson, of Anne Arundel County. [CG, Tues., 13 OCT 1829, p. 3]

MARRIED. In Washington, on Sunday, 11th inst. [i.e. 11 OCT 1829], by the Rev. S. Cornelius, Mr. HENRY TARLTON, to Miss SUSANNA B. SMITH, all of Alexandria, D.C. [CG, Thurs., 15 OCT 1829, p. 3]

DIED. At his residence in Sampson Co., (N.C.) on Tuesday, the 26th ult. [i.e. 26 SEP 1829], Gen. GABRIEL HOLMES, formerly Governor of North Carolina, and latterly one of her Representatives in the Congress of the United States, in the sixty-first year of his age. [CG, Thurs., 15 OCT 1829, p. 3]

DIED. At Valparaiso, in May last [i.e. MAY 1829], on board the U.S. Ship *Vincennes*, Mid. JOSHUA W. LARKIN, aged 20, son of Samuel Larkin, Esq., of Portsmouth, N.H. [CG, Thurs., 15 OCT 1829, p. 3]

DIED. At Callao, in June last [i.e. JUN 1829], on board the U.S. Frigate *Brandywine*, Mid. JAMES MARCUS PREVOST, in the 26th year of his age, acting sailing master of the B. and son of the late John B. Prevost, Esq. [CG, Thurs., 15 OCT 1829, p. 3]

MARRIED. In Philadelphia, on Tuesday, 13th inst. [i.e. 13 OCT 1829], Mr. GEORGE H. SMOOT, of Alexandria, to Mrs. CATHARINE COOK, of the former place. [CG, Sat., 17 OCT 1829, p. 3]

DIED. In Cocke Co., (Tenn.) Col. THOMAS GRAY, aged 84, counselor at law. He commenced his professional career in the year 1761, and made his last speech in the Circuit Court of Cocke County at July term, 1826, before the Hon. Edward Scott, then presiding, in which he addressed the jury in an animated and forcible argument of more than half an hour in length.—He held, under the English government, the office of council for the crown in the province of Virginia, as early as 1765.—He was several years a distinguished member of the legislature of North Carolina, and held, under a commission from Gen. Washington, the office of Attorney for the United States, for the Tennessee district, in the year 1797. [CG, Sat., 17 OCT 1829, p. 3]

Georgetown, D.C., **Marriage and Death Notices, 1801-1838**

MARRIED. At Fortress Monroe, on the 7th inst. [i.e. 7 OCT 1829], Lieut. WILLIAM MAYNADIER, of the United States' Army, to Mrs. SARAH EVELETH. [CG, Tues., 20 OCT 1829, p. 3]

DIED. At his residence in Prince George's Co., Md. [no date], Col. WILLIAM DENT BEALL, in the 75th year of his age. He was a worthy and distinguished Officer of the Revolutionary Army, and had served his country faithfully in various capacities, his last public service being in the Legislature of the State. He was as firm in the Council as brave in the field. [CG, Tues., 20 OCT 1829, p. 3]

DIED. At his residence in Prince William Co., Va., on Thursday evening, 15th inst. [i.e. 15 OCT 1829], the Hon. WILLIAM A.G. DADE, Judge of the Northern Neck District, a gentleman possessing great dignity, exceeding quickness of apprehension, patient to the uttermost, bland, passionless, cautious and inflexible in the performance of his professional duties. Judge Dade had been elected a member of the Virginia Convention, but resigned the situation on account of his health. [CG, Thurs., 22 OCT 1829, p. 3]

DIED. In Washington, on Tuesday, the 20th inst. [i.e. 20 OCT 1829], Mrs. PHEBE HORNER, late of Alexandria, D.C., in the 65th year of her age. [CG, Thurs., 22 OCT 1829, p. 3]

DIED. In Philadelphia, on the 17th inst. [i.e. 17 OCT 1829], Mrs. CAROLINE R.H. CORBIN, in the 29th year of her age, wife of Robert Corbin, of Virginia, and daughter of Joseph Sims, of Washington. [CG, Thurs., 22 OCT 1829, p. 3]

DIED. On the 16th inst. [i.e. 16 OCT 1829], at the residence of Mr. Robert E. Steed, in Norfolk, Miss JULIANA W. LEONARD, of Alexandria, and niece of Mrs. Steed. She was sick about fifteen days, and had just entered her fifteenth year. [CG, Thurs., 22 OCT 1829, p. 3]

MARRIED. On Thursday evening last [i.e. 22 OCT 1829], by the Rev. Mr. Vinton, Mr. WILLIAM H. EDES, late of Baltimore, to Miss MARTHA, daughter of Mr. Joseph Ratcliff, of Washington. [CG, Sat., 24 OCT 1829, p. 3]

DEATH. On Sunday, Oct. 18 [i.e. 18 OCT 1829], Gen. SAMUEL RINGGOLD, of Washington Co., in the 60th year of his age. His remains were interred at Fountain Rock, attended by mourning relatives and sincere friends, and a respectable assemblage of his fellow citizens. [CG, Sat., 24 OCT 1829, p. 3]

MARRIED. In this Town, on the 21st inst. [i.e. 21 OCT 1829], by the Rev. Mr. Brooke, JAMES S. MORSELL, Esq., Judge of the Circuit Court of the District of Columbia, to Mrs. MARY ANN FITZHUGH, daughter of William Marbury, Esq., of this Town. [CG, Tues., 27 OCT 1829, p. 3]

MARRIED. In Washington, on Thursday evening last [i.e. 22 OCT 1829], GIBSON F. HILL, Esq., of Eatonton, Ga., to MARY ANN, eldest daughter of Ezekiel Macdaniel, Esq. [CG, Tues., 27 OCT 1829, p. 3]

Georgetown, D.C., **Marriage and Death Notices, 1801-1838**

MARRIED. On Thursday, the 15th inst. [i.e. 15 OCT 1829], Mr. EDWARD SULLIVAN, of this Town, to Miss ANN LYNCH, of Washington. [CG, Tues., 27 OCT 1829, p. 3]

MARRIED. On the 22d inst. [i.e. 22 OCT 1829], in Fairfax Co., Va., by the Rev. Wm. O. Lumsdon, of Alexandria, Mr. JAMES TUCKER, to Miss ANN PAYNE, both of the District. [CG, Tues., 27 OCT 1829, p. 3]

DIED. In Washington, on the 22d inst. [i.e. 22 OCT 1829], Mr. JACOB LEONARD, Silversmith. [CG, Tues., 27 OCT 1829, p. 3]

DIED. In Charleston, S.C., on the 13th of this month [i.e. 13 OCT 1829], EVAN D. JONES, eldest son of the late Edward Jones, Esq., of this Town. [CG, Tues., 27 OCT 1829, p. 3]

MARRIED. In this Town, on Tuesday evening [i.e. 27 OCT 1829], by the Rev. Mr. Brooke, Mr. BASIL H. WARING, eldest son of Mr. Basil Waring of Washington City, to Miss SARAH, only daughter of Mr. John Bennett, deceased. [CG, Sat., 31 OCT 1829, p. 2]

MARRIED. In Washington City, on Thursday evening [i.e. 29 OCT 1829], by the Rev. Wm. W. Wallace, Mr. RICHARD W. CLAXTON, Printer, of this town, to Miss CATHARINE ANN, only daughter of Capt. Ignatius Luckett, of Md., deceased. [CG, Sat., 31 OCT 1829, p. 2]

DIED. In this town on Tuesday morning last [i.e. 27 OCT 1829], Mr. BASIL RAGAN, in the 66th year of his age, an old resident of the town and a respectable member of the Methodist Episcopal Church. A funeral discourse will be delivered on the occasion of his death tomorrow morning in the Methodist Episcopal Church, by the Rev. R.S. Vinton. [CG, Sat., 31 OCT 1829, p. 2]

DIED. At the residence of Judge Martin, on Coosawatchie, on the 24th Sept. [i.e. 24 SEP 1829], GEORGE W. McGEHEE, Professor of Mathematics in the University of Georgia, in the 28th year of his age. [CG, Sat., 31 OCT 1829, p. 2]

MARRIED. In Washington, on Thursday morning last [i.e. 29 OCT 1829], at the residence of W.H. Jenifer, THOMAS GRIFFITH, Indian Agent at Natchitoches, to Miss CATHARINE, daughter of the late James Patton, Esq., British Vice Consul of Alexandria, D.C. [CG, Tues., 3 NOV 1829, p. 2]

DIED. In Washington, on Thursday morning [i.e. 29 OCT 1829], Mr. JOHN BELL, aged 52 years, a native of Northamptonshire, England. [CG, Tues., 3 NOV 1829, p. 2]

DIED. In Washington, on Friday evening last [i.e. 30 OCT 1829], after a short illness, in the 31st year of his age, Mr. WILLIAM L. KENNEDY, Merchant of that city and lately of Alexandria, D.C. [CG, Tues., 3 NOV 1829, p. 2]

DIED. In Baltimore, on the 30th ult. [i.e. 30 OCT 1829], in the 48th year of his age, RICHARD H. DOUGLASS, a highly respectable merchant of that place. [CG, Tues., 3 NOV 1829, p. 2]

Georgetown, D.C., **Marriage and Death Notices, 1801-1838**

DIED. At Boston, on Tuesday 27th ult. [i.e. 27 OCT 1829], JOHN COFFIN JONES, aged 82, for many years an eminent merchant of that city. [CG, Tues., 3 NOV 1829, p. 2]

DIED. In London [no date], Mr. J. REEVES, King's Printer; he has left above £200,00 to different connexions. He had no child of his own. [CG, Tues., 3 NOV 1829, p. 2]

MARRIED. In Washington, on Thursday, the 29th ult. [i.e. 29 OCT 1829], Dr. HENRY HAW, of this Town, to Miss ELIZA BROWN, youngest daughter of Jesse Brown, Esq., of Washington. [CG, Thurs., 5 NOV 1829, p. 2]

MARRIED. On Thursday evening last [i.e. 5 NOV 1829], by the Rev. Walter D. Addison, THOMAS FRANCIS PURCELL, Esq., of Virginia, to Miss MATHILDA COX, daughter of Col. John Cox, of this Town. [CG, Sat., 7 NOV 1829, p. 2]

MARRIED. In Baltimore, on Tuesday, the 3d inst. [i.e. 3 NOV 1829], by the Rev. James Whitfield, Archbishop of Baltimore, JEROME NAPOLEON BONAPARTE, son of Jerome Bonaparte, and grandson of William Patterson, Esq., of Baltimore, to SUSAN MAY, only daughter of the late Benjamin Williams, of that City. [CG, Sat., 7 NOV 1829, p. 2]

MARRIED. On Tuesday, the 3d inst. [i.e. 3 NOV 1829], Dr. HENRY W. BAXLEY, to Miss ANNABELLA, only daughter of Col. Peter Little, of Baltimore County. [CG, Sat., 7 NOV 1829, p. 2]

MARRIED [no date]. JOHN R. YATES, to RACHEL, eldest daughter of Samuel Harden, all of Baltimore. [CG, Sat., 7 NOV 1829, p. 2]

DIED. On the 30th of September [i.e. 30 SEP 1829], on board the Sloop *Splendid*, lying off Caesar's Creek, (Florida,) GREGORY WEEMS, M.D., formerly of this Town. The remains of the deceased were carried to Indian Key, and there interred. [CG, Sat., 7 NOV 1829, p. 2]

DIED. In Washington, on the 7th inst. [i.e. 7 NOV 1829], Mrs. MARGARET MOORE, consort of Mr. James Moore, of the Treasury Department, aged 51 years. [CG, Tues., 10 NOV 1829, p. 2]

DIED. At Huntingfield, in Kent Co., Md., on the 2d inst. [i.e. 2 NOV 1829], Gen. PHILIP REED, a patriot of the Revolution. [CG, Tues., 10 NOV 1829, p. 2]

MARRIED. In Washington, on the 3d inst. [i.e. 3 NOV 1829], by the Rev. Mr. Deagle, Mr. DAVIS F. MORICE, to Miss MARY ANN M'CANN, both of that city. [CG, Thurs., 12 NOV 1829, p. 2]

MARRIED. In Washington, on Monday last [i.e. 9 NOV 1829], by the Rev. Wm. A. Smallwood, Dr. WILLIAM L. WHARTON, of the U.S. Army, to Miss ELEANOR JONES, second daughter of Col. David Brearley, of that city. [CG, Thurs., 12 NOV 1829, p. 2]

Georgetown, D.C., **Marriage and Death Notices, 1801-1838**

DIED. In Washington City, on the 8th inst. [i.e. 8 NOV 1829], Mr. JOHN S. MacCUBBIN, in the 36th year of his age. [CG, Thurs., 12 NOV 1829, p. 2]

DIED. In Charles Co., Md., on the 3d inst. [i.e. 3 NOV 1829], Mr. ROBERT CRAIN, in the 68th year of his age. For thirty years he was a Justice of the Peace for that Co., and for many years a Judge of the Levy Court in the same county. [CG, Thurs., 12 NOV 1829, p. 2]

MARRIED. In this town, on Thursday evening last [i.e. 12 NOV 1829], by the Rev. W.D. Addison, Mr. JOHN DAVIS, merchant, to Miss MARY E. DAVIS, all of Georgetown. [CG, Sat., 14 NOV 1829, p. 2]

MARRIED. In Baltimore, on the 12th inst. [i.e. 12 NOV 1829], JAMES J. CORNER, to ELIZABETH ANN WIGHT, both of that city. [CG, Sat., 14 NOV 1829, p. 2]

MARRIED. In Boston, on the 12th inst. [i.e. 12 NOV 1829], Mr. ELIJAH WILLIAMS, Jr., merchant, formerly of Baltimore, to Miss MARY, daughter of Benjamin Bangs, Esq. [CG, Sat., 14 NOV 1829, p. 2]

DIED. At Port Mahon, on the 24th Sept. [i.e. 24 SEP 1829], Lt. WILLIAM H. HOMER, of the U.S. ship *Delaware*, a native of Boston. [CG, Sat., 14 NOV 1829, p. 2]

MARRIED. In Norfolk, on Thursday the 12th inst. [i.e. 12 NOV 1829], Com. JAMES BARRON, Commandant of the Navy Yard at Gosport, to Miss MARY ANN, eldest daughter of Mr. John Wilson, of Portsmouth, Va. [CG, Thurs., 19 NOV 1829, p. 3]

MARRIED. On the 22d of July last [i.e. 22 JUL 1829], at the Island of Timos, in the Archipelago, the Rev. JONAS KING, one of the American agents in Greece, to Miss ANN ASPASIA MENGUS, (A Greek lady) of Smyrna. [CG, Thurs., 19 NOV 1829, p. 3]

MARRIED. In Washington, on Tuesday evening last [i.e. 17 NOV 1829], Dr. HENRY HUNTT, to Miss ANN MARIA RINGGOLD, daughter of Tench Ringgold, Esq., Marshal of the District. [CG, Sat., 21 NOV 1829, p. 3]

MARRIED [no date]. Mr. RANDOLPH B. REEVES, of Alexandria, to Miss ELLEN ELLIOT, of Washington. [CG, Sat., 21 NOV 1829, p. 3]

MARRIED. In Washington, on Tuesday evening last [i.e. 17 NOV 1829], Mr. JOHN A. REMINGTON, of this Town, to Miss MARY ELIZABETH PARSONS, of Brunswick, N.J. [CG, Sat., 21 NOV 1829, p. 3]

MARRIED. In Washington, on the evening of the 19th inst. [i.e. 19 NOV 1829], by the Rev. Mr. Campbell, Capt. THOMAS F. HUNT, of the U.S. Army, to Mrs. DORCAS L. LOVELL, daughter of the late Ezekial King, Esq., of that city. [CG, Tues., 24 NOV 1829, p. 3]

MARRIED. At Timsbury, Ire., J. DUDDEN, Esq., of Temple Cloud, to Mrs. EDGELL, mother of Dr. Edgell, of Chew. There were present at the wedding two fathers, one

Georgetown, D.C., **Marriage and Death Notices, 1801-1838**

mother, one mother-in-law, one father-in-law, one son, one daughter, one daughter-in-law, one son-in-law, one grandfather, one grand-daughter, two nieces, two nephews, two uncles, three first cousins, and one second cousin—yet there were only six persons present, and the bride and bridegroom no kin before marriage! [Will some of our readers favor us with an explanation of this riddle, for it puzzles our ingenuity.] [CG, Tues., 24 NOV 1829, p. 3]

MARRIED. In Fredericksburg, Va., on Thursday evening the 19th inst. [i.e. 19 NOV 1829], by the Rev. Edward C. McGuire, Mr. THOMAS W. GRAY, of Culpeper, to Miss SARAH W., daughter of Mr. Fielding Lucas, of F. [CG, Tues., 24 NOV 1829, p. 3]

DIED. [Communicated.] Departed this life, on the 25th of September last [i.e. 25 SEP 1829], at his mother's residence, in Charles Co., Md., Mr. WALTER DYSON, in the 17th year of his age ... Mr. Dyson, at the time of his decease was a member of the Academy at Charlotte Hall, as also of the Washington Society, which is attached thereto ... [CG, Tues., 24 NOV 1829, p. 3]

DIED. At Dublin, on the 16th of September [i.e. 16 SEP 1829], after a few days of severe illness, JAMES HAMILTON, Esq., author of the Hamiltonian system of teaching languages, in the 60th year of his age. [CG, Tues., 24 NOV 1829, p. 3]

DIED. At Paris, on the 7th of October [i.e. 7 OCT 1829], Mr. SELIGMAN MICHAL, Grand Rabbi of the Israelite persuasion at the age of 95 years. All the Israelite population of the capital followed his funeral to the cemetery of Pere LaChaise. M. Deutz, the grand Rabbi of the Central Consistory, pronounced his funeral oration on the tomb in praise of the eminent qualities of the deceased. [CG, Tues., 24 NOV 1829, p. 3]

DIED. In Boston, on Saturday morning 14th inst. [i.e. 14 NOV 1829], Col. GERRY FAIRBANKS, aged 50. By the death of Col. F., society is deprived of an active and useful member, the circle of private friendship has lost a respectable and faithful companion, and a family is bereaved of an affectionate husband, father and brother. [CG, Tues., 24 NOV 1829, p. 3]

MARRIED. In Baltimore, on the 22d inst. [i.e. 22 NOV 1829], Mr. THOMAS IRONS, to Mrs. ANN JOYCE. [CG, Thurs., 26 NOV 1829, p. 3]

MARRIED. On the 24th [i.e. 24 NOV 1829], REZIN HAMMOND SNOWDEN, Esq., of Anne Arundel Co., Md., to MARGARET, eldest daughter of John M'Fadon, Esq. [CG, Thurs., 26 NOV 1829, p. 3]

MARRIED. On the 25th [i.e. 25 NOV 1829], Mr. CHARLES TAYLOR, to Miss NANCY KEERL. [CG, Thurs., 26 NOV 1829, p. 3]

MARRIED. In Washington, on the 21st inst. [i.e. 21 NOV 1829], Mr. WASHINGTON BACON, to Miss PRUDENCE D. LOCKE, both of that City. [CG, Sat., 28 NOV 1829, p. 2]

Georgetown, D.C., **Marriage and Death Notices, 1801-1838**

MARRIED. In Baltimore, on the 25th inst. [i.e. 25 NOV 1829], Mr. ISAAC CLARKE, of Washington City, to Miss MARY AUGUSTA, daughter of the late Thomas Everitt, Esq., of Baltimore. [CG, Sat., 28 NOV 1829, p. 2]

MARRIED. In Boston [no date], Hon. BENJAMIN GORHAM, Member of Congress, to Mrs. MARGARET C. COLES, daughter of the late Hon. John Coffin Jones. [CG, Sat., 28 NOV 1829, p. 2]

MARRIED. In Washington, on the 26th ult. [i.e. 26 NOV 1829], Dr. BAILY WASHINGTON, Surgeon U.S. Navy, to Miss ANN MATILDA LEE, daughter of the late Richard Bland Lee, Esq. [CG, Tues., 1 DEC 1829, p. 2]

MARRIED. On the 22d ult. [i.e. 22 NOV 1829], Mr. WILLIAM BIRD, of Alexandria, to Miss MARGARET VIRGINIA SULLIVAN, of Washington. [CG, Tues., 1 DEC 1829, p. 2]

MARRIED. On the 23d ult. [i.e. 23 NOV 1829], Mr. JOHN W. SMITH, to Miss REBECCA W. CAMPBELL, eldest daughter of Mr. William Campbell, of Alexandria. [CG, Tues., 1 DEC 1829, p. 2]

MARRIED. In Alexandria, on the 24th ult. [i.e. 24 NOV 1829], Mr. WILLIAM ATWELL, to Mrs. SUSAN ROTCH, of that town. [CG, Tues., 1 DEC 1829, p. 2]

MARRIED. On the 26th ult. [i.e. 26 NOV 1829], Capt. WM. Y. STEWART, of Prince George's Co., Md., to Miss ANN M. HODGKIN, of Alexandria. [CG, Tues., 1 DEC 1829, p. 2]

MARRIED. In Charleston, (S.C.) on the 19th ult. [i.e. 19 NOV 1829], Lieut. THOMAS PETIGRU, of the U.S.N., to Miss MARY ANN LaBRUCE. [CG, Tues., 1 DEC 1829, p. 2]

DIED. At Smithville, (N.C.), 10th ult. [i.e. 10 NOV 1829], Dr. GEORGE C. CLITHERALL, of the U.S.A., aged 49 years. [CG, Tues., 1 DEC 1829, p. 2]

DIED. In Alexandria, on the 1st inst. [i.e. 1 DEC 1829], Mr. JOHN GRUBER. [CG, Thurs., 3 DEC 1829, p. 2]

MARRIED. In Washington, on the 1st inst. [i.e. 1 DEC 1829], Mr. WILLIAM GARDNER, to Mrs. MATILDA AUSTIN, both of that City. [CG, Sat., 5 DEC 1829, p. 3]

MARRIED. In Baltimore, on the 1st inst. [i.e. 1 DEC 1829], CALEB B. LITTIG, to JANE R., youngest daughter of Jonathan Harrison, Esq. [CG, Sat., 5 DEC 1829, p. 3]

MARRIED [no date]. Mr. JOHN B. CANNON, to MATILDA JANE, only daughter of John Mitchell, Esq. [CG, Sat., 5 DEC 1829, p. 3]

MARRIED. In Anne Arundel Co., Md. [no date], JOHN S. TYSON, Counselor at Law, to RACHAEL, youngest daughter of the late John Snowden, Esq. [CG, Sat., 5 DEC 1829, p. 3]

Georgetown, D.C., **Marriage and Death Notices, 1801-1838**

DIED. In Washington City, on the 1st inst. [i.e. 1 DEC 1829], Mr. JOHN B. BRUNET, aged 37 years. Mr. B. was a native of France, but for the last ten years had resided in the District of Columbia. [CG, Sat., 5 DEC 1829, p. 3]

DIED. In Washington, on the 3d inst. [i.e. 3 DEC 1829], of a pulmonary affection, Mrs. MARY NAIRN, widow of the late James Nairn. [CG, Sat., 5 DEC 1829, p. 3]

DIED. In Philadelphia, on the 2d inst. [i.e. 2 DEC 1829], the Rev. WILLIAM ASHMEAD, Pastor of the Second Presbyterian Church in Charleston, S.C. [CG, Sat., 5 DEC 1829, p. 3]

DIED. Suddenly, on the 28th ult. [i.e. 28 NOV 1829], in the 60th year of her age, Mrs. ANN WASHINGTON, the consort of the late Hon. Bushrod Washington, one of the Judges of the Supreme Court of the United States. The bereavement which this lady experienced on the 26th ult. [i.e. 26 NOV 1829, Dr. Baily Washington] only two days before, on the death of a husband to whom she was entirely devoted, and whose existence the event has proved was identified with her own, left her without a desire to live, and she fell a martyr to intensity of attachment which she had manifested with an undeviating constancy and enthusiasm during the forty years of their union ... The gaieties and festivities of life were, however, cut short in 1815 by the death of her beloved mother ... Two days after his death she started from the city with a nephew and niece, Mr. and Mrs. John Washington, on her sorrowful return home, determined, however, as she said, to follow exactly the advice of her dear husband; they had proceeded only four or five miles on the Darby Road, when she complained of feeling indisposed, and before the carriage which conveyed her, could be driven to a farm house, on the road side, the vital spark was totally extinguished. Her remains have followed those of her husband to be deposited in the family vault at *Mount Vernon. National Gazette.* [CG, Sat., 5 DEC 1829, p. 3]

DIED. At City Point, Va., suddenly, on the 1st inst. [i.e. 1 DEC 1829], on board the Ship *Anacreon*, Capt. WILSON BOUSH, of the Revenue Service, and many years previous a skillful and intelligent ship master of Norfolk. [CG, Tues., 8 DEC 1829, p. 3]

DIED. At Baton Rouge, La., Oct. 25th [i.e. 25 OCT 1829], ISAAC HUGHES TYLER, Esq., of Louisville. He went to the former place to unite himself to the daughter of the Hon. H.H. Gurley. On his arrival he was seized with the yellow fever, which terminated his existence in three days. [CG, Tues., 8 DEC 1829, p. 3]

DIED. The Hon. THOMAS B. REED, Senator in Congress from the State of Mississippi, died at Lexington, Ky., on the 26th ult. [i.e. 26 NOV 1829], of a pulmonary disease. Mr. R. was on his way to Washington to take his seat in the Senate, when he was arrested by the illness that terminated his career. Mr. R. was in the meridian of life, was a gentleman of fine talents, and greatly esteemed by his friends. [CG, Thurs., 10 DEC 1829, p. 3]

DIED. The venerable RICHARD HARRISON, one of the oldest and most respectable members of the Bar in this City, died yesterday [i.e. 6 DEC 1829]. He has descended to the grave, full of years and honors, and the purity of his whole life has adorned the practice, and reflected light upon a profession to which his best faculties have ever been

Georgetown, D.C., **Marriage and Death Notices, 1801-1838**

assiduously devoted. The Superior Court and the Court of Sessions adjourned as soon as the event was announced, to testify their high sense of his exalted worth. *Jour. Com.,* Dec. 7. [CG, Thurs., 10 DEC 1829, p. 3]

MARRIED. In Washington City, on the 8th inst. [i.e. 8 DEC 1829], Mr. WILLIAM FORD, to Miss ELIZABETH DOUGLASS, both of that City. [CG, Sat., 12 DEC 1829, p. 3]

DIED. At Philadelphia [no date], at the house of Andrew Spence, St. Andrew's Square, (near *Bush Hill*,) PETER WHITESIDE, aged 76 years, formerly Merchant in Philadelphia, and the confidential Secretary and partner of Robert Morris during the trying and eventful period of the Revolution. [CG, Sat., 12 DEC 1829, p. 3]

MARRIED. In Newport, (R.I.) [no date], the Hon. DUTEE J. PEARCE, Representative in Congress from that State, to Miss HARRIET, daughter of the late John L. Ross, Esq., of Newport. [CG, Tues., 15 DEC 1829, p. 3]

DIED. In Washington City, on the 12th inst. [i.e. 12 DEC 1829], the Rev. WILLIAM STAUGHTON, D.D., President of the Georgetown College, in Kentucky, and formerly President of the Columbian College in this District. [CG, Tues., 15 DEC 1829, p. 3]

DIED. In Scituate, (Mass.) on the 6th inst. [i.e. 6 DEC 1829], Mr. JOHN ELLIOTT, aged 100 years, a soldier of the Revolutionary War, in which he served seven years. [CG, Tues., 15 DEC 1829, p. 3]

DIED. In Portsmouth, (N.H.) [no date], the Hon. JAMES SHEAFE, formerly a Senator in Congress, aged 74. [CG, Tues., 15 DEC 1829, p. 3]

DIED. In Cincinnati, (Ohio,) on the 3d inst. [i.e. 3 DEC 1829], of inflammation of the brain, after an illness of ten days, WM. MONROE M'LEAN, aged eight years and nine months, youngest son of Judge John M'Lean, of that City. [CG, Tues., 15 DEC 1829, p. 3]

MARRIED. In this town, on Tuesday evening last [i.e. 15 DEC 1829], by the Rev. Mr. Vinton, Mr. SAMUEL ROSE, to Miss CAROLINE CRAIG, both of this town. [CG, Sat., 19 DEC 1829, p. 3]

MARRIED. In Va., on Tuesday evening last [i.e. 15 DEC 1829], by the Rev. Wm. O. [Lumsdon], Mr. WILLIAM NELSON, of Va., to Miss ANN, daughter of Jacob Payne, Esq., of this district. [CG, Sat., 19 DEC 1829, p. 3]

MARRIED. In Washington, on the 15th inst. [i.e. 15 DEC 1829], Mr. JOSEPH H. DAWES, to Miss MARGARET MOORE. [CG, Sat., 19 DEC 1829, p. 3]

MARRIED. In Portsmouth, Va., on the 10th inst. [i.e. 10 DEC 1829], GABRIEL GALT, Naval Store Keeper at the U.S. Navy Yard Gosport, to Miss ELIZABETH B. BROWNE, daughter of the late James Browne, Esq., of Norfolk Co. [CG, Sat., 19 DEC 1829, p. 3]

Georgetown, D.C., **Marriage and Death Notices, 1801-1838**

MARRIED. In N.Y., on the 12th inst. [i.e. 12 DEC 1829], the Hon. DANIEL WEBSTER, of Boston, Senator in Congress from Mass., to Miss CAROLINE, youngest daughter of the late Herman LeRoy, Esq., of New York. [CG, Sat., 19 DEC 1829, p. 3]

MARRIED. At Pensacola, on the 25th ult. [i.e. 25 NOV 1829], Mr. THOMAS COOPER, of Va., to Miss HARRIET JOSEPHINE PARSONS, of Washington City. [CG, Sat., 19 DEC 1829, p. 3]

DIED. At Key West, Fla., on the 11ult. [i.e. 11 NOV 1829], Col. EDGAR MACON, Counselor and Attorney at Law. Col. M. was a native of Va. and a near relative of the Venerable ex-President Madison. [CG, Sat., 19 DEC 1829, p. 3]

DIED. In Philadelphia, on the 18th inst. [i.e. 18 DEC 1829], WILLIAM SEAL, M.D., Assistant Surgeon of the U.S. Navy, in the 24th year of his age, of consumption ... [CG, Tues., 22 DEC 1829, p. 3]

DIED. At Chester, Delaware Co., (Penn.) on the 15th inst. [i.e. 15 DEC 1829], WILLIAM ANDERSON, Esq., in the 67th year of his age. Mr. Anderson acted a conspicuous and highly honorable part in our Revolutionary struggle—he was at the siege of Yorktown and surrender of Cornwallis. He served throughout the campaign with honor to himself and advantage to his country. He was a citizen of Delaware county for many years, has represented the county in the Congress of the U. States several times, held the appointment of Judge of the Courts of Delaware Co., and at the time of his decease was attached to the Custom House department. [CG, Tues., 22 DEC 1829, p. 3]

MARRIED. In Baltimore, on Tuesday evening last [i.e. 22 DEC 1829], Mr. WILLIAM DEAN, merchant, of this Town, to Miss MARGARET, youngest daughter of Thomas Norris, of Thomas. [CG, Thurs., 24 DEC 1829, p. 2]

DIED. In this Town, on Monday last [i.e. 21 DEC 1829], at Mr. J. Hammett's Tavern, on High Street, BENJAMIN L. KNOX, Stone Cutter, about 25 or 30 years of age. He was a native of Maine, and was in the employ of the Chesapeake and Ohio Canal Company. The writer of this witnessed his exit from time to eternity; and it may alleviate the grief of his relatives and friends, to learn that, tho' far distant from his native home, he received from the hands of strangers every kindness and attention, during a lingering indisposition of seven weeks. [CG, Thurs., 24 DEC 1829, p. 2]

DIED. In N.Y., on the 17th inst. [i.e. 17 DEC 1829], after an illness of several weeks, Midshipman HELMUTH J. GAEDIKE, of the U.S. Navy, aged 23 years and 4 months. [CG, Thurs., 24 DEC 1829, p. 2]

MARRIED. On the 15th inst. [i.e. 15 DEC 1829], at Falling Spring, Alleghany Co., Va., JOHN H. PLEASANTS, Esq., Senior Editor of the *Richmond Whig*, to Miss MARY L., daughter of Henry Massie, Esq., of the former place. [CG, Tues., 29 DEC 1829, p. 3]

Georgetown, D.C., **Marriage and Death Notices, 1801-1838**

MARRIED. At St. Louis, on the 2d inst. [i.e. 2 DEC 1829], Capt. JOHN B. CLARK, of the 3d Regiment U.S. Infantry, to Miss HENRIETTA C., daughter of Mr. Alexander Sanford, of Baltimore, Md. [CG, Tues., 29 DEC 1829, p. 3]

DIED. In Baltimore, on the 27th inst. [i.e. 27 DEC 1829], in the 50th year of his age, NICHOLAS G. RIDGELY, Esq., for many years a high respectable merchant, of the late firm of *Macdonald and Ridgely*, of that City. [CG, Tues., 29 DEC 1829, p. 3]

DIED. At Bristol, Pa., on the 18th inst. [i.e. 18 DEC 1829], after a short indisposition, of a bilious fever, JACOB GILLINGHAM, in the seventeenth year of his age, and at Rocklesstown, N.J., of the same disease, on the morning of the 19th inst., MATTHIAS GILLINGHAM, in the twenty-ninth year of his age.—It is but about five weeks since, we had to record the decease of Moses Gillingham, the father of these young men ... residing at different places ... carried together at the same funeral, and laid by each other's side in the same grave. [CG, Tues., 29 DEC 1829, p. 3]

DIED. In Baltimore, on the 29th inst. [i.e. 29 DEC 1829], Mr. WM. MUNDAY, in the 78th year of his age. He entered the Revolutionary army as a private soldier, in the New York line, and rose, by regular gradations to the rank of Lieutenant. [CG, Thurs., 31 DEC 1829, p. 2]

DIED. On the 19th inst. [i.e. 19 DEC 1829], at Mr. Newell's Hotel, Mount Vernon, Ohio, Mr. ROBERT GRAY, aged about 20 years. This young man was a student at Kenyon College, and a native of Fredericksburg, Va., where his relatives reside. [CG, Thurs., 31 DEC 1829, p. 2]

MARRIED, in Alexandria, on the 25th ult. [i.e. 25 DEC 1829], the Rev. THOMAS J. DORSEY, of the Baltimore Conference, to Miss JANE PRINCE, eldest daughter of the Rev. I. Robbins, of Alexandria. [CG, Sat., 2 JAN 1830, p. 3]

MARRIED, in this Town, on the 29th ult. [i.e. 29 DEC 1829], by the Rev. Mr. Armstrong, Dr. RUFUS H. SPEAKE, of Washington, to Miss ELIZA W., daughter of the late John Vinson, Esq., of Montgomery Co., Md. [CG, Sat., 2 JAN 1830, p. 3]

DIED, in Washington, on the 30th ult. [i.e. 30 DEC 1829], Mr. JOHN LEITCH. [CG, Sat., 2 JAN 1830, p. 3]

DIED, in N.Y., on the 27th ult. [i.e. 27 DEC 1829], the Rev. JOHN M. MASON, D.D., aged 69 years, one of the most celebrated divines of the age ... [CG, Sat., 2 JAN 1830, p. 3]

DIED, in Bedford Co., Va., on the 19th ult. [i.e. 19 DEC 1829], of a pulmonary consumption, CALOHILL MENNIS, aged 33 years, late a member of the Virginia Convention. [CG, Sat., 2 JAN 1830, p. 3]

DIED, in Norfolk, Va., on the 27th ult. [i.e. 27 DEC 1829], Capt. ROGER QUARLES, for many years a highly respectable and intelligent ship master, and during the War commander of the Privateer *Roger*. [CG, Sat., 2 JAN 1830, p. 3]

Georgetown, D.C., **Marriage and Death Notices, 1801-1838**

DIED, on the 25th ult. [i.e. 25 DEC 1829], at Fort Norfolk, Mr. WILLIAM SEYMOUR, in the 49th year of his age, U.S. Military Store Keeper. [CG, Sat., 2 JAN 1830, p. 3]

MARRIED, on the 24th December last [i.e. 24 DEC 1829], Dr. SEPTIMUS J. COOK, of Bladensburg, to Miss ANN REBECCA, daughter of Mr. George Beall, all of Prince George's Co., Md. [CG, Thurs., 7 JAN 1830, p. 2]

MARRIED, in Baltimore, on the 28th Dec. [i.e. 28 DEC 1829], AUGUSTUS J. PLEASANTON, of the U.S. Army, to Miss CAROLINE DUGAN, of Philadelphia. [CG, Thurs., 7 JAN 1830, p. 2]

MARRIED, at Milford, on Tuesday evening last [i.e. 5 JAN 1830], Capt. JAMES EDELIN, of the Marines, to MARGARET, daughter of the late Francis Toulson, Esq. [CG, Thurs., 7 JAN 1830, p. 2]

DIED, in Washington on the 2d inst. [i.e. 2 JAN 1830], of a pulmonary disease, which he bore with great fortitude and christian resignation, Mr. THOMAS MITCHELL, late of this Town, who, when living, had only to be known to be esteemed ... [CG, Thurs., 7 JAN 1830, p. 2]

DIED, at *Mount Air*, near Piscataway, (Md.) on the 30th ult. [i.e. 30 DEC 1829], CAROLINE, daughter of Dr. Benedict I. Semmes, in the 3d year of her age. [CG, Thurs., 7 JAN 1830, p. 2]

DIED, in Philadelphia, on the 30th ult. [i.e. 30 DEC 1829], after a long and painful illness, ISAAC JONES, Esq., in the 78th year of his age. He was an active soldier of '76, under our illustrious Washington, who, for his devoted patriotism, bestowed upon him a commission, which duty he discharged with devoted zeal. [CG, Thurs., 7 JAN 1830, p. 2]

DIED, in Boston, on the 29th ult. [i.e. 29 DEC 1829], Hon. EDWARD H. ROBBINS, Judge of Probate for Norfolk Co., and formerly Lieutenant Governor of Mass. [CG, Thurs., 7 JAN 1830, p. 2]

DIED, in Woodford Co., Ky., on the 4th ult. [i.e. 4 DEC 1829], Mrs. ELIZABETH WATKINS, widow of Henry Watkins, her second husband, in the 80th year of her age. She was the mother of Henry Clay. [CG, Thurs., 7 JAN 1830, p. 2]

MARRIED. *June and January.* In Pittsylvania Co., Va., on the 17th Dec. [i.e. 17 DEC 1829], Mr. MOORE LUMPKINS, aged 80, to Miss CATHERINE RICHARDSON, in the 18th year of her age. In Johnson Co., N.D., on the 20th Dec. [i.e. 20 DEC 1829], Mr. WILLIAM FORT, aged 66, to Mrs. ELIZABETH WHITFELD, aged 38. [CG, Sat., 9 JAN 1830, p. 3]

(From the *Alexandria Gazette*). Wholesale Work.—On the 17th ult. [i.e. 17 DEC 1829], Mr. GEORGE BEARD to Miss JANE DISNEY; on the 29th ult. [i.e. 29 DEC 1829], Mr. QUINTON BARKER to Miss LUCRETIA KEENE; on the 31st ult. [i.e. 31 DEC 1829], Mr. LEVI BURNE to Miss JANE CATHERINE COFFER.—[no date], Mr. JOHN H. KIDWELL to Miss PRICILLA ROBEY.—[no date], Mr. JAMES BAGGETT, of Loudoun Co.,

Georgetown, D.C., **Marriage and Death Notices, 1801-1838**

to Miss MARY KIDWELL.—[no date], Mr. REUBEN ROUZIE to Mrs. ELEANOR POWELL; on the 5th inst. [i.e. 5 JAN 1830], Mr. JOHN W. DAVIS to Miss NANCY LYNN of Prince William Co. All the rest of Fairfax, and all of them married by the Rev. James Reid. [CG, Sat., 9 JAN 1830, p. 3]

MARRIED, in Boston [no date], M. de WALESKI, formerly Colonel in the Imperial Army of France, to Mrs. ANN F. HUMPHREYS, of Boston. [CG, Sat., 9 JAN 1830, p. 3]

MARRIED, on the 5th inst. [i.e. 5 JAN 1830], by the Rev. Mr. Gibbon, ENOCH W. SMALLWOOD, of Port Tobacco, Md., to Miss JANETT B., second daughter of George Phillips, of Washington City. [CG, Sat., 9 JAN 1830, p. 3]

MARRIED, on Saturday morning [i.e. 2 JAN 1830], at N.Y., by the Rev. George Upfold, JAMES F. SWIFT, United States' Civil Engineer, to MARIA FARQUHAR, daughter of Mr. Jephson. [CG, Sat., 9 JAN 1830, p. 3]

DIED, on the second inst. [i.e. 2 JAN 1830], in the 60th year of his age, JACOB SPERRY, Esq., one of the Aldermen of the city of Philadelphia. [CG, Sat., 9 JAN 1830, p. 3]

DIED, at Delphia, county of Delaware, N.Y., on the 28th ult. [i.e. 28 DEC 1829], the Hon. EBENEZAR FOOTE, in the 75th year of his age. Descended from a respectable family in Connecticut, he in early life entered the army and fought under General Washington for the Independence of his country. After having much to his credit discharged the duties of a member of the Legislature, both in the Senate and Assembly of New York, he has been for many years first Judge of the county of Delaware. [CG, Sat., 9 JAN 1830, p. 3]

DIED, in Washington, on Saturday evening last [i.e. 9 JAN 1830], after a long and most afflicting illness, Mr. JOHN CONNELL, for many years a Messenger in the Treasury Department, in the 40th year of his age. [CG, Tues., 12 JAN 1830, p. 3]

MARRIED, in this town, on Monday evening, 11th inst. [i.e. 11 JAN 1830], by the Rev. S.B. Balch, Mr. EDWARD CLEMENTSON, to Mrs. CHRISTINE CLARK, both of this place. [CG, Thurs., 14 JAN 1830, p. 3]

MARRIED, in Washington, on Monday the 11th inst. [i.e. 11 JAN 1830], by the Rev. W. Matthews, Mr. DAVID MOOR to Miss ELIZABETH BROOKS. [CG, Thurs., 14 JAN 1830, p. 3]

MARRIED, on Tuesday evening, the 12th inst. [i.e. 12 JAN 1830], by the Rev. Mr. Campbell, Mr. JOHN THOMAS CLEMENTS, to Mrs. ELIZA LARNER, both of Washington. [CG, Thurs., 14 JAN 1830, p. 3]

MARRIED, on the 5th inst. [i.e. 5 JAN 1830], by the Rev. Mr. Jones, at *Summerseat*, the residence of Hon. Clement Dorsey, in Md., the Hon. WILLIAM D. MARTIN, a Representative in Congress from S.C., to Miss SALLY MARIA DORSEY, daughter of the Hon. Clement Dorsey, Representative in Congress from Md. [CG, Thurs., 14 JAN 1830, p. 3]

Georgetown, D.C., **Marriage and Death Notices, 1801-1838**

MARRIED, at Princeton, N.J., on the 22d ult. [i.e. 22 DEC 1829], Mr. ALFRED WHARTON CLIFTON, son of the late Col. Franklin Wharton, of Washington City, to Miss ADELAIDE PASSAGE, daughter of John Passage, Esq., of the former place. [CG, Thurs., 14 JAN 1830, p. 3]

MARRIED, in Alexandria, on Sunday evening last [i.e. 10 JAN 1830], by the Rev. I. Robbins, Mr. JOHN WATSON, of Baltimore, to Mrs. CAROLINE E. KEFFER, of Alexandria. [CG, Thurs., 14 JAN 1830, p. 3]

MARRIED, on the 29th ult. [i.e. 29 DEC 1829], by the Rev. Wm. Jackson, Mr. LINDSAY, of Old Point Comfort, to Miss MARY CATON, of Alexandria. [CG, Thurs., 14 JAN 1830, p. 3]

MARRIED, on the 31st ult. [i.e. 31 DEC 1829], by the Rev. J.W. Fairclough, Mr. WM. POMERY, to Miss JANE, eldest daughter of the late Alexander Bagget, of Alexandria. [CG, Thurs., 14 JAN 1830, p. 3]

MARRIED, on the 7th inst. [i.e. 7 JAN 1830], by Rev. J.W. Fairclough, Mr. MAURICE HURLIHY, to Miss ANN O'NEAL, both of Alexandria. [CG, Thurs., 14 JAN 1830, p. 3]

MARRIED, on Thursday, 3d December [i.e. 3 DEC 1829], by the Rev. S. Cornelius, Mr. WM. D. SELECMAN, to Miss MARGARET, daughter of Thomas Selecman, all of Fairfax Co., Va. [CG, Thurs., 14 JAN 1830, p. 3]

DIED, on Tuesday morning [i.e. 12 JAN 1830], at half past 3 o'clock, after a lingering and distressing illness, which she bore with the fortitude which a Christian's hope can alone inspire, Mrs. JULIET A.C. MacGILL, in the 26th year of her age, consort of Mr. Thomas MacGill. [CG, Thurs., 14 JAN 1830, p. 3]

DIED, on the 29th November 1829, SOPHIA COVINGTON, aged about 16 months, youngest daughter of Jno. A. Smith, Esq., of Washington City. [CG, Thurs., 14 JAN 1830, p. 3]

DIED, in the state of Illinois [no date], at her father's house, Mrs. JULIA COOK, relict of the late Daniel P. Cook. [CG, Thurs., 14 JAN 1830, p. 3]

MARRIED, in Washington, on Tuesday evening last [i.e. 12 JAN 1830], Mr. THOMAS SCOTT, of Fauquier Co., Va., to Miss ADELINE SELVY, of Washington. [CG, Sat., 16 JAN 1830, p. 3]

MARRIED, in Baltimore, on Wednesday morning [i.e. 13 JAN 1830], Mr. A.C. GIBBS, of Washington, to Miss ELIZA L., daughter of Dr. H.H. Hayden, of the former place. [CG, Sat., 16 JAN 1830, p. 3]

DIED, in Washington, on Tuesday night [i.e. 12 JAN 1830], Miss ELIZABETH TABBS, after a protracted illness of nearly twelve months. [CG, Sat., 16 JAN 1830, p. 3]

Georgetown, D.C., **Marriage and Death Notices, 1801-1838**

DIED, on Thursday [i.e. 14 JAN 1830], Maj. JOHN DAVIDSON, in the 60th year of his age. Also, MARGARET VANHORN GIBSON, in the 17th year of her age, daughter of Mr. Joseph Gibson, of Washington. [CG, Sat., 16 JAN 1830, p. 3]

MARRIED, at *Stonington*, Montgomery Co., Md., on the 16th inst. [i.e. 16 JAN 1830], Mr. FRANCIS G. BLACKFORD, of Washington City, to Miss ANNA MARIA STONE, of the former place. [CG, Tues., 19 JAN 1830, p. 3]

DIED, in Washington, on the 14th inst. [i.e. 14 JAN 1830], at his residence near the Navy Yard, Mr. LAWSON PEARSON, long a resident of that city, aged 59 years. [CG, Tues., 19 JAN 1830, p. 3]

DIED, in Baltimore, on Thursday, the 14th inst. [i.e. 14 JAN 1830], MARY, consort of Wm. Lorman, in the 59th year of her age. [CG, Tues., 19 JAN 1830, p. 3]

DIED, in Washington, on the 14th inst. [i.e. 14 JAN 1830], of a pulmonary disease, Mr. ARCHIBALD DOBBIN, in the 67th year of his age, a native of Ireland, and for many years a respectable citizen of Baltimore. [CG, Thurs., 21 JAN 1830, p. 3]

DIED, at *Green Hill*, Prince George's Co., Md., on the 17th inst. [i.e. 17 JAN 1830], WILLIAM DUDLEY DIGGES, Esq., in the 39th year of his age. [CG, Thurs., 21 JAN 1830, p. 3]

OBITUARY. Died at Gambier, Ohio, on Friday night the 8th inst. [i.e. 8 JAN 1830], of mortification, produced by premature confinement, Mrs. MARY W. FITCH, aged 22, second daughter of Thomas C. Wright, of this Town, and wife of the Rev. C.W. Fitch, one of the Professors of Kenyon College ... Mrs. F. was pious from principle, was several years a member of the Episcopal Church, and beloved wherever she was known. [CG, Thurs., 21 JAN 1830, p. 3]

DIED, in Washington, on Wednesday night last [i.e. 20 JAN 1830], after a long and painful illness, which he bore with patience and christian resignation, Capt. WILLIAM B. DYER, in the 59th year of his age. [CG, Sat., 23 JAN 1830, p. 3]

DIED, in Alexandria, on Thursday, the 21st inst. [i.e. 21 JAN 1830], JOHN MARSHALL CLAGETT, second son of Horatio Clagett, Esq., in the twenty-third year of his age. [CG, Sat., 23 JAN 1830, p. 3]

DIED, in Richmond, Va., on the 16th inst. [i.e. 16 JAN 1830], after a painful and protracted illness, in the 38th year of his age, JOHN MACRAE, Esq., of Fauquier Co.—a distinguished Officer during the last War, a lawyer of brilliant promise, and a member of the late State Convention. [CG, Sat., 23 JAN 1830, p. 3]

MARRIED, in Martinsburg, Va., on Tuesday evening 19th inst. [i.e. 19 JAN 1830], JOHN T. EVANS, Esq., of Ky., to Miss SUSAN, daughter of Capt. James Maxwell, of the former place. [CG, Tues., 26 JAN 1830, p. 3]

Georgetown, D.C., **Marriage and Death Notices, 1801-1838**

MARRIED, in Fredericksburg, Va., on the 19th inst. [i.e. 19 JAN 1830], Mr. JAMES P. CORBIN, of *Farley Vale,* to Miss JANE C. WELLFORD; also on the same evening, Dr. GEO. F. CARMICHAEL to Miss MARY C. WELLFORD, daughters of John S. Wellford, of Fredericksburg. [CG, Tues., 26 JAN 1830, p. 3]

DIED, in Washington, on Sunday morning last [i.e. 23 JAN 1830], at the residence of his son-in-law, Mr. Charles G. Wilcox, after an illness of ten days, in the full possession of all his faculties, JOHN MITCHELL, Esq., in the 79th year of his age, formerly an eminent merchant of Philadelphia, a patriotic Whig of the Revolution of sterling integrity and unbounded benevolence. [CG, Tues., 26 JAN 1830, p. 3]

DIED, at his residence in Alexandria, on the 14th inst. [i.e. 14 JAN 1830], in the 42d year of his age, NATHANIEL S. WISE, Esq., for many years a Lawyer and Magistrate of that city. [CG, Tues., 26 JAN 1830, p. 3]

DIED, on the 22d inst. [i.e. 22 JAN 1830], at *Barnaby Manor,* his residence, Prince George's Co., Mr. ANTHONY ADDISON, formerly of this Town, aged 76 years. [CG, Thurs., 28 JAN 1830, p. 3]

DIED, in Philadelphia, on Monday, 25th inst. [i.e. 25 JAN 1830], SUSANNAH POULSON, wife of Zachariah Poulson, Editor of the *American Daily Advertiser.* [CG, Thurs., 28 JAN 1830, p. 3]

DIED, yesterday [i.e. 27 JAN 1830], at 4 o'clock, after a short illness, in the 76th year of his age, THOMAS CORCORAN, Esq. Though not a native of Georgetown, Mr. Corcoran was amongst the oldest and most respected of its inhabitants; being ever esteemed as an honorable, useful and enterprising citizen, having filled the various offices of Magistrate, Mayor and Postmaster, with great credit to himself, and to the entire satisfaction of the public. He leaves behind him many relatives and descendants to mourn over his departure, and many friends, who will long cherish the recollection of his worth as an excellent citizen, a warm friend, and a zealous advocate of the cause of his Redeemer. The poor too, whom he never forgot, in the best days of his prosperity, will long have cause to mourn the loss of a generous and sincere friend. His friends and acquaintances are invited to attend his funeral, on Friday evening next, at ½ past 3 o'clock, from his late residence on Bridge Street. [CG, Thurs., 28 JAN 1830, p. 3]

DIED, on Thursday afternoon [i.e. 28 JAN 1830], of a bilious pleurisy, DANIEL RENNER, Esq., for many years a respectable citizen of this town. The funeral will take place this afternoon, at 3 o'clock, which the friends and acquaintances of the deceased are respectfully invited to attend without further notice. [CG, Sat., 30 JAN 1830, p. 3]

MARRIED, in this Town, on Thursday evening last [i.e. 28 JAN 1830], by the Rev. Mr. Brooke, Mr. DANIEL KENT, of Calvert Co., Md., to Miss CHARITY MARGARETTA, second daughter of Horatio Jones, Esq. [CG, Tues., 2 FEB 1830, p. 3]'

MARRIED, in Frederick, Md. [no date], Mr. DAVID GILBERT, to Miss MARGARET KOONTZ; also Mr. CHARLES W. TODD, to Miss MARCELLEA BONHAM; also, Mr. HUGH

Georgetown, D.C., **Marriage and Death Notices, 1801-1838**

CUNNINGHAM to Miss REBECCA GETTINGER; and Mr. HENRY YOKEY to Miss MARY JACOBS. [CG, Tues., 2 FEB 1830, p. 3]

MARRIED, in Martinsburg, Va. [no date], Mr. THORNTON C. DUNHAM, to Miss LOUISA WORLEY. [CG, Tues., 2 FEB 1830, p. 3]

MARRIED, in Chatham, Va., on the 20th ult. [i.e. 20 JAN 1830], Mid. JOHN RANDOLPH BRYAN, of the U.S. Navy, to Miss ELIZABETH COALTER, daughter of the Hon. Judge Coalter. [CG, Tues., 2 FEB 1830, p. 3]

MARRIED, in Spotsylvania, Va., on the 21st ult. [i.e. 21 JAN 1830], ALEXANDER G. JENKINS, to Miss ALICE E. COURTER. [CG, Tues., 2 FEB 1830, p. 3]

DIED, in this Town, last Thursday morning (28th ult.) [i.e. 28 JAN 1830], MATTHEW GREENTREE, aged about 73 years. [CG, Tues., 2 FEB 1830, p. 3; see lengthy obituary in issue of Sat., 6 FEB 1830, p. 3]

DIED, in Washington, on Saturday evening last [i.e. 30 JAN 1830], of a pulmonary complaint, ELEANOR BARRY, second daughter of Capt. Edward Barry, of that city. [CG, Tues., 2 FEB 1830, p. 3]

DIED, at Baton Rouge, La., on the 8th ult. [i.e. 8 JAN 1830], Mrs. LUCY GURLEY, the amiable, affectionate and devoted wife of the Hon. H.H. Gurley, member of Congress from that state. [CG, Tues., 2 FEB 1830, p. 3]

DIED, in Alexandria, on Sunday morning last [i.e. 31 JAN 1830], in the 43d year of her age, Mrs. JANE DIXON, long a resident of that city. [CG, Thurs., 4 FEB 1830, p. 3]

DIED, at *Bush Hill*, near Alexandria, on the 26th ult. [i.e. 26 JAN 1830], Mrs. ELEANOR DOUGLASS SCOTT, wife of Richard M. Scott, in the 23d year of her age. [CG, Thurs., 4 FEB 1830, p. 3]

Another of the old Revolutionary Patriots gone!—At Schohariekill, N.Y., on Monday, the 28th ult. [i.e. 28 DEC 1829?], Capt. HENRY BECKER, in the 84th year of his age. [CG, Thurs., 4 FEB 1830, p. 3]

DIED, in Amherst, Erie Co., N.Y. [no date], Maj. FREDERICK MILLER, aged upwards of 70 years. Major Miller was a soldier of the revolution, and an officer in the late war. He was one of the first settlers of that county, and very generally respected. [CG, Thurs., 4 FEB 1830, p. 3]

DIED, in Baltimore, on Sunday evening last [i.e. 31 JAN 1830], ISAAC GARRETSON, Esq., Senior Purser in the United States Navy, aged 63 years. [CG, Thurs., 4 FEB 1830, p. 3]

DIED, in Fredericktown, Md., on the 20th ult. [i.e. 20 JAN 1830], Dr. WILLIAM ADAMS, age unknown, but from circumstances, supposed to be upwards of 100 years. He was a native

Georgetown, D.C., **Marriage and Death Notices, 1801-1838**

of Ireland, where he resided till qualified for the practice of Medicine. At the age of twenty he removed to America (during the French war of 1744-63,) and was for some time surgeon in the service of Sir Wm. Johnston, the British Colonial Agent for Indian Affairs, in the (now) State of New York. For more than seventy years he was a practicing physician, and, for a greater part of that time, a resident in the city of Schenectady ... [CG, Thurs., 4 FEB 1830, p. 3]

DIED, at his residence near Woodville, in Culpeper Co., Va., on the 16th ult. [i.e. 16 JAN 1830], Col. JOHN SLAUGHTER, in the 71st year of his age; leaving a widow, twelve grown children, and a number of grand-children, to lament his death. Col. S. entered the army at the age of 16, was in the actions of Trenton and Princeton; and in 1777 volunteered in the late Major Long's Company to join the chosen Regiment of Riflemen, which Morgan was directed to raise. He was present at Still Water, and witnessed the surrender of Burgoyne. He was for 45 years an active magistrate, and at the time of his death High Sheriff of the County for the second time. [CG, Thurs., 4 FEB 1830, p. 3]

DIED, at Camden, S.C., on the 21st ult. [i.e. 21 JAN 1830], full of years and of honors, Capt. BENJAMIN CARTER, in the 75th year of his age, the last of the old soldiers of Camden. He was truly a patriot, and soldier of the Revolutionary War. He fought in the battles of Brandywine and Germantown, where he was wounded; he wintered with the American army at Valley Forge; was at Gates' defeat near Camden; and was among the patriots that harassed Lord Cornwallis, and compelled him, after many skirmishes, to retreat through North Carolina. He fought at the battles of Hobkirk-hill and the Eutaw Springs; was at the taking of Fort Mott; and joined the knot of officers who united under an oak tree near M'Cord's Ferry, and swore that they would be revenged on the British for hanging Col. Hayne.—He was brave and active throughout the whole of the Revolution; for he served occasionally under Gen. Sumter and Gen. Marion, and wound up his useful life by many benevolent acts. [CG, Thurs., 4 FEB 1830, p. 3]

MARRIED, in Fredericksburg, Va., on Thursday, the 28th ult. [i.e. 28 JAN 1830], Mr. WILLIAM N. WELLFORD, of that town, to Mrs. REBECCA P.F. FAUNTLEROY, of *Laneville*, King and Queen; also, in the same place on the 4th inst., Mr. THOMAS FENNALL, of that place, to Miss ANN FRANCES BULLARD, of King George Co. [CG, Tues., 9 FEB 1830, p. 3]

MARRIED, at *Montauverd*, the residence of Maj. George Peter, Montgomery Co., Md., on the 2d inst. [i.e. 2 FEB 1830], JOHN P.C. PETER, Esq., to ELIZABETH JANE, only daughter of the late James Henderson, Esq., of Williamsburg, Va. [CG, Tues., 9 FEB 1830, p. 3]

MARRIED, in Alexandria, D.C., on Thursday evening last [i.e. 4 FEB 1830], Mr. GEORGE F. HUGLE, to Miss SARAH H. CARLIN, both of that town. [CG, Tues., 9 FEB 1830, p. 3]

MARRIED, in Martinsburg, Va., on Thursday, the 28th ult. [i.e. 28 JAN 1830], Mr. WILLIAM S. MORRISON, to Miss VIRGINIA H. BAKER; at the same place, and on the same day, Mr. JAMES FISHER, to Miss CATHARINE RAMSBURGH. [CG, Tues., 9 FEB 1830, p. 3]

Georgetown, D.C., **Marriage and Death Notices, 1801-1838**

MARRIED, in Fredericktown, Md., on Monday, the 1st inst. [i.e. 1 FEB 1830], the Rev. FRANCIS A. McNEILL, to Miss MARY CRONISE. [CG, Tues., 9 FEB 1830, p. 3]

MARRIED, in Hagerstown, Md., on Sunday evening, 31st ult. [i.e. 31 JAN 1830], Mr. JOHN WEIS, to Miss ADELINE G. LANCASTER. [CG, Tues., 9 FEB 1830, p. 3]

MARRIED, in Baltimore, on Tuesday evening, 26th ult. [i.e. 26 JAN 1830], Mr. HENRY DUNDORE, to Miss ELIZA WEST. [CG, Tues., 9 FEB 1830, p. 3]

DIED, in Washington, on Saturday morning last [i.e. 6 FEB 1830], after a long and painful illness, which he bore with manly philosophy, MICHAEL O'CONNER, aged about thirty-five. The deceased was a native of Ireland, and of the City of Dublin, in which he was bred to the Law. He was a gentleman of fine talents and warm feelings ... [CG, Tues., 9 FEB 1830, p. 3]

DIED, in Alexandria, D.C., on the 4th inst. [i.e. 4 FEB 1830], Mr. THEODORE GIBBS, in the 39th year of his age, long an honest and respectable citizen of that place. [CG, Tues., 9 FEB 1830, p. 3]

DIED, in Fredericktown, Md., on the 1st inst. [i.e. 1 FEB 1830], in the 54th year of his age, Mr. HENRY SINN, of that town. [CG, Tues., 9 FEB 1830, p. 3]

DIED, on Saturday, 30th ult. [i.e. 30 JAN 1830], at *Long Meadows,* four miles from Hagerstown, Md., Mr. RICHARD WISE; on the same day, Mrs. RIDENOUR, consort of Mr. Jacob Ridenour, of Harrystown, Md., and, on Sunday morning, 31st ult., Mrs. COLIFLOWER, consort of George Coliflower, merchant, in Hagerstown, Md. [CG, Tues., 9 FEB 1830, p. 3]

MARRIED, by the Rev. Mr. Grundick of the Catholic Church, at the residence of Benjamin M. Piatt, Esq., Logan Co., Ohio, on the 14th inst. [i.e. 14 JAN 1830], his eldest daughter, Miss H.J. PIATT, to Mr. RALPH RUNKLE, merchant, late of N.J. *Cincinnati Gazette, Jan. 26.* [CG, Thurs., 11 FEB 1830, p. 3]

MARRIED, in Washington, on the 7th inst. [i.e. 7 FEB 1830], by the Rev. Mr. McCormick, Mr. OVERTON PRATHER, of Prince George's Co., to Miss ANN ELIZABETH CARRICO, of that place. [CG, Thurs., 11 FEB 1830, p. 3]

DIED, in Washington on the 4th inst. [i.e. 4 FEB 1830], in the 24th year of her age, Mrs MARY MILLER, of pulmonary consumption, with which she had suffered for four months. [CG, Thurs., 11 FEB 1830, p. 3]

DIED, on Monday [i.e. 8 FEB 1830], TOBIAS SIMPSON, (a colored man) for many years past the faithful, vigilant, and respected servant of the Senate of the United Sates. His age is supposed to have been about 50 years. [CG, Thurs., 11 FEB 1830, p. 3]

Georgetown, D.C., **Marriage and Death Notices, 1801-1838**

DIED, in Alexandria, on the 12th of January last [i.e. 12 JAN 1830], Mr. ALLEN KELLOG, aged 25—a native of Litchfield, Conn.; highly respected by all who knew him. [CG, Thurs., 11 FEB 1830, p. 3]

DIED, at his residence in Baltimore Co., Md., on Friday last [i.e. 5 FEB 1830], Col. PETER LITTLE, for many years past (until this session) a Representative in Congress of the United States, and a most faithful and useful one. [CG, Thurs., 11 FEB 1830, p. 3]

DIED. [Mr.] WILLIS, the famous bugle man and leader of the West Point band, died at that post on Monday [i.e. 8 FEB 1830], and was buried with the honors of war. [CG, Thurs., 11 FEB 1830, p. 3]

DIED, in New Haven, Conn., on the 3d inst. [i.e. 3 FEB 1830], Col. JARED MANSFELD, LL.D., aged 71, for several years Surveyor General of the United States, and Professor of Natural Philosophy in the military Academy at West Point. [CG, Thurs., 11 FEB 1830, p. 3]

MARRIED, in Richmond, Va., on the 4th inst. [i.e. 4 FEB 1830], Mr. WM. B. DABNEY, to Miss CECILIA B. WHITING, all of that city. [CG, Sat., 13 FEB 1830, p. 3]

MARRIED, at Rio de Janeiro, W.H.C'C. WRIGHT, consul U.S.A., to ELIZA L., daughter of the late John Warner, consul of the United States at Havana. [CG, Sat., 13 FEB 1830, p. 3]

DIED, at Parsonsfield, Me., Mrs. NANCY McINTIRE, aged 33, wife of the Hon. Rufus McIntire, Member of Congress from the State of Maine. [CG, Sat., 13 FEB 1830, p. 3]

DIED, at Brownville, N.Y., on Tuesday, February 2d [i.e. 2 FEB 1830], at the residence of her son, Mayor Samuel Brown, Mrs. ABBE BROWN, the mother of the late Gen. Jacob Brown, aged 78 years, after a protracted illness of many years. [CG, Sat., 13 FEB 1830, p. 3]

MARRIED, in Winchester, Va., on the 4th inst. [i.e. 4 FEB 1830], OBED WAITE, Esq., Mayor of that place, to Miss SARAH STUART, daughter of the late Dr. Daniel Stuart, of *Ossian Hall*, Fairfax Co. On the same day, the Rev. LEWIS EICHELBERGER, Pastor of the Lutheran Congregation, Winchester, to Miss MARY ANN MILLER, daughter of John Miller, Esq., of the same place. [CG, Tues., 16 FEB 1830, p. 2]

DIED, in Winchester, on Thursday last [i.e. 11 FEB 1830], Mr. WILLIAM R. SHINDLER, a native of Shepherdstown, and formerly of Martinsburg, Va. [CG, Tues., 16 FEB 1830, p. 2]

DIED, on the 1st inst. [i.e. 1 FEB 1830], at his residence in Greensboro', Georgia, Hon. THOMAS W. COBB, one of the Judges of the Superior Courts of Georgia, and late a member of the United States Senate. [CG, Thurs., 18 FEB 1830, p. 2]

Georgetown, D.C., **Marriage and Death Notices, 1801-1838**

MARRIED, in Baltimore, on Tuesday evening last [i.e. 16 FEB 1830], SAMUEL CARUSI, of Washington, D.C., to ADELINE S., second daughter of John McLean, Esq., of Baltimore. Also, on the same evening, Dr. SOLOMON BIRCKHEAD, to Mrs. OGDEN, both of Baltimore. [CG, Sat., 20 FEB 1830, p. 2]

DIED, in Baltimore, on Thursday morning last [i.e. 18 FEB 1830], in the 89th year of his age, Col. JAMES HINDMAN. [CG, Sat., 20 FEB 1830, p. 2]

MARRIED, in Baltimore, on Thursday, the 13th inst. [i.e. 13 FEB 1830], at Friend's Meeting House, Dr. THOMAS WORTHINGTON, of Harford Co., to ELIZABETH GILLINGHAM, of that city. [CG, Tues., 23 FEB 1830, p. 2]

MARRIED, on Thursday evening [i.e. 18 FEB 1830], Mr. GEORGE A. DAVIS, to Miss ELIZABETH MOORE. [CG, Tues., 23 FEB 1830, p. 2]

MARRIED, on the 18th inst. [i.e. 18 FEB 1830], in Harford Co., Md., DANIEL RAYMOND, Esq., of Baltimore, to SARAH, daughter of the late Mr. Isaac R. Amos. [CG, Tues., 23 FEB 1830, p. 2]

DIED, in this town, on the 18th inst. [i.e. 18 FEB 1830], JOHN HENRY WIRT, only child of H.W. Tilley, aged ten months and four days. [CG, Tues., 23 FEB 1830, p. 2]

DIED, on Tuesday last, at the residence of his mother, in Baltimore, HENRY D. SCOTT, late Lieut. in the U.S. Navy, in the 37th year of his age. He left a widow and a large circle of relations and friends to mourn his loss. [CG, Tues., 23 FEB 1830, p. 2]

MARRIED, in Alexandria, on the 23d inst. [i.e. 23 FEB 1830], Capt. SAMUEL HILTON, of Washington, to Miss CATHERINE STEEL, of Alexandria. [CG, Thurs., 25 FEB 1830, p. 3]

MARRIED, on the 18th inst. [i.e. 18 FEB 1830], R.S. BURKE, of Fairfax Co., Va., to Miss MARY ANN McDENICK, of Alexandria. [CG, Thurs., 25 FEB 1830, p. 3]

DIED, at Alexandria, on the 21st inst. [i.e. 21 FEB 1830], SAMUEL HAWKINS, an attorney at law, in the 26th year of his age. [CG, Thurs., 25 FEB 1830, p. 3]

DIED, at N.Y., on Wednesday last [i.e. 17 FEB 1830], Col. HENRY RUTGERS, in the 35th year of his age ... the body was conveyed from his residence in Jefferson street to the Dutch Church in Nassau street ... [CG, Thurs., 25 FEB 1830, p. 3]

DIED ... the intelligence of the death of NATHANIEL H. CARTER, Esq., of this city, who expired at Marseilles on the 2d January [i.e. 2 JAN 1830]. Mr. Carter was well known in the city of N.Y., where he commenced his career ... [text continues] [CG, Thurs., 25 FEB 1830, p. 3]

MARRIED, in Washington City, on Tuesday evening last [i.e. 23 FEB 1830], by the Rev. Mr. Matthews, Mr. WILLIAM PETERS, to Miss MARY ANN REX, all of that city. [CG, Sat., 27 FEB 1830, p. 3]

Georgetown, D.C., **Marriage and Death Notices, 1801-1838**

MARRIED, in Alexandria, on Thursday evening, 18th inst. [i.e. 18 FEB 1830], Mr. JOHN POSTON, of Loudoun Co., Va., to Miss ANN JANE, daughter of Mr. John Major of Alexandria. [CG, Sat., 27 FEB 1830, p. 3]

MARRIED, in Washington, on the 25th ult. [i.e. 25 FEB 1830], Hon. AUGUSTINE H. SHEPPERD, a Representative in Congress from N.C., to Miss MARTHA TURNER, youngest daughter of the late Samuel Turner, formerly of this town. [CG, Thurs., 4 MAR 1830, p. 3]

DIED, in Alexandria, D.C., on Monday evening, the 1st inst. [i.e. 1 MAR 1830], in the 65th year of her age, Mrs. ELIZABETH MUIR, relict of the late Dr. James Muir, former pastor of the 1st Presbyterian church in that town. [CG, Thurs., 4 MAR 1830, p. 3]

DIED, at his residence in Jericho, L.I., on the evening of the 27th ult. [i.e. 27 FEB 1830], in the 82d year of his age, ELIAS HICKS, a member of the Society of Friends, an eminent Minister of the Gospel, in which he labored about 60 years. His disorder was paralytic, of about two weeks continuance. [CG, Thurs., 4 MAR 1830, p. 3]

MARRIED, on Thursday evening, 4th inst. [i.e. 4 MAR 1830], by the Rev. Dr. Balch, Dr. HEZEKIAH MAGRUDER, to Miss HARRIET L., second daughter of Joel Cruttenden, Esq., all of this town. [CG, Sat., 6 MAR 1830, p. 3]

DIED, in N.Y., on Tuesday morning [i.e. 2 MAR 1830], Capt. HENRY CAHOONE, Commander of the Revenue Cutter *Alert*, aged 55 years. [CG, Sat., 6 MAR 1830, p. 3]

MARRIED, in Alexandria, D.C., on Thursday night last [i.e. 4 MAR 1830], Mr. MARTIN L. TILSON, of Plymouth, Mass., to Miss FRANCIS B., daughter of John G. Gray, Esq., of Alexandria. [CG, Tues., 9 MAR 1830, p. 3]

MARRIED, on the 4th of January [i.e. 4 JAN 1830], at the house of Isaac Cox Barnet, Esq., Consul of the United States at Paris, by the Right Rev. President Marron, one of the Pastors of the Protestant Reformed Church, GEORGE WASHINGTON GREENE, Esq., of R.I., (Grandson of the late distinguished American General of that name,) to Miss CARLOTTA, daughter of Louis Slorzosi, Esq., of Rome. [CG, Tues., 9 MAR 1830, p. 3]

DIED, on Thursday morning last [i.e. 4 MAR 1830], FRANCIS K. ADDISON, son of the Rev. Walter D. Addison, of Georgetown, in the 14th year of his age, after a short but severe illness. [CG, Tues., 9 MAR 1830, p. 3]

DIED, in London [no date], Lady LEE O'MEARA, the wife of Barry O'Meara. This lady's first husband was Capt. Donnellan, who was executed for poisoning Sir Theodosius Boughton, by the juice of laurel leaves. With the exception of an annuity of one thousand pounds to her husband, secured by marriage settlement, Lady Lee has left the whole of her fortune to her daughter by her former husband. She was affectionately attached to Mr. O'Meara, and during her illness, refused all medicine unless given to her by him. [CG, Tues., 9 MAR 1830, p. 3]

Georgetown, D.C., **Marriage and Death Notices, 1801-1838**

DIED, in Raleigh, N.C., on the 5th inst. [i.e. 5 MAR 1830], the Right Rev. JOHN STARK RAVENSCROFT, D.D., Bishop of the Protestant Episcopal Church in N.C., in the 58th year of his age. [CG, Sat., 13 MAR 1830, p. 3]

DIED, in Alexandria, on the 11th inst. [i.e. 11 MAR 1830], Mrs. LOUISA E. VIOLETT, consort of Mr. Robert G. Violett, and only daughter of Mr. James English, aged 27 years. [CG, Sat., 13 MAR 1830, p. 3]

DIED, in Baltimore, on the 7th inst. [i.e. 7 MAR 1830], Mrs. JANE YOUNG, in the 67th year of her age, formerly of Philadelphia. [CG, Sat., 13 MAR 1830, p. 3]

DIED, on the 9th inst. [i.e. 9 MAR 1830], Mrs. CATHERINE PALMER, wife of Edward Palmer, in the 40th year of her age. [CG, Sat., 13 MAR 1830, p. 3]

MARRIED, at Washington, on the 4th inst. [i.e. 4 MAR 1830], by the Rev. Ethan Allen, WILLIAM M. MANADIER, Esq., to Miss CATHERINE S. BROWN, both of Alexandria. [CG, Thurs., 18 MAR 1830, p. 3]

DIED, in N.Y., on Sunday last [i.e. 14 MAR 1830], after an illness of only three or four days, the Rev. JOSEPH S. CHRISTMAS, Pastor of the Bowery Presbyterian Church in that City ... [CG, Thurs., 18 MAR 1830, p. 3]

MARRIED, at Schenectady, N.Y., on Friday evening, 12th inst. [i.e. 12 MAR 1830], Mr. SAMUEL JONES, 2d, to Mrs. ECHIE McINTOSH, pursuant to the 9th, 10th and 11th sec. of art. 1, title 1, chap. VIII, part 2, book 2, p. 138, 139, 140 and 141, 1st edition, printed by P. & V.B. copy right secured by A.C. Flagg, Esq., Secretary of State. *Schenectady Cabinet.* [CG, Sat., 20 MAR 1830, p. 3]

DIED, in Washington, on Thursday Morning, 18th inst. [i.e. 18 MAR 1830], JAMES FOSTER SWIFT, U.S. Civil Engineer, and son of Gen. J.G. Swift, aged 24 years. [CG, Sat., 20 MAR 1830, p. 3]

DIED, on Wednesday, 17th inst. [i.e. 17 MAR 1830], Mr. JOSIAS TAYLOR, one of the oldest inhabitants of Washington, aged 43 years. [CG, Sat., 20 MAR 1830, p. 3]

DIED, on Wednesday, 17th inst. [i.e. 17 MAR 1830], Mr. LAWRENCE MURPHY, a native of Ireland, aged about 40 years. [CG, Sat., 20 MAR 1830, p. 3]

DIED, at the Mansion Hotel in Washington, on the 21st inst. [i.e. 21 MAR 1830], in the 28th year of her age, Mrs. CORNELIA L. RIDGELY, consort of Com. Charles G. Ridgely, of the Navy, and grand-daughter of the late Chancellor Livingston of N.Y. [CG, Thurs., 25 MAR 1830, p. 3]

DIED, in Washington, on the 19th inst. [i.e. 19 MAR 1830], Mr. ABRAHAM CHANEY, in the 23d year of his age. His death was sudden—excessive pain from an ear-ache induced him to take frequent and rather large doses of laudanum, which had been standing for a long time, and had thereby acquired much additional activity. Ignorance of this fact proved fatal to him, and should be remembered as a caution to all who use or employ useful but potent medicine. [CG, Thurs., 25 MAR 1830, p. 3]

MARRIED, in this Town, on Thursday evening last [i.e. 25 MAR 1830], by the Rev. Mr. Vanlommell, Mr. BENNET H. SEWALL, to Miss MARY T. MANNING, both of this place. [CG, Sat., 27 MAR 1830, p. 2]

OBITUARY. Died on the morning of the 7th inst. [i.e. 7 MAR 1830], at La Fourche, La., the residence of the Hon. Henry Johnson, late Governor of Louisiana, LOUISA, a twin daughter of the late Philip B. Key, of this District, in the 18th year of her age. The disease which in five days cut down, in the midst of its bloom and beauty, this lovely flower, was inflammatory fever ... [CG, Sat., 27 MAR 1830, p. 2, and Sat., 12 JUN 1830, p. 3]

DIED, in Boston [no date], of consumption, GARAFILIA MOHALBY, aged 12, an orphan from Greece, who was receiving education and support in a benevolent family in that city. [CG, Tues., 30 MAR 1830, p. 2]

DIED, at his residence in Hanover Co., Va. [no date], after an illness of a few days, in the 68th year of his age, Dr. JAMES LYONS, formerly an eminent physician of Richmond. [CG, Tues., 30 MAR 1830, p. 2]

DIED, in Liverpool, Eng., on the 27th January [i.e. 27 JAN 1830], Mrs. MAURY, consort of James Maury, Esq., late Consul of the United States for that port. [CG, Tues., 30 MAR 1830, p. 2]

DIED, in Springfield, Mass. [no date], EDWARD PYNCHON, Esq., aged 56. Upon the death of his father, in 1802, he succeeded him in the offices of Town Clerk and Treasurer, Parish Clerk and Treasurer, County Treasurer, and County Register of Deeds, to which offices he has been regularly re-elected. From the year 1608 the offices of County Treasurer and County Register, have been filled by some one of the family.—*[This may be called rotation in office.]*. [CG, Thurs., 1 APR 1830, p. 2]

DIED, in Washington, on the 31st ult. [i.e. 31 MAR 1830], Mr. JOHN RUSTICK, aged 28 years. [CG, Sat., 3 APR 1830, p. 2]

DIED, in Alexandria, on the 31st ult. [i.e. 31 MAR 1830], in the 76th year of his age, JOHN LONGDEN, one of the oldest and most esteemed citizens of that place, and a soldier of the Revolutionary War. [CG, Sat., 3 APR 1830, p. 2]

DIED, on the 30th ult. [i.e. 30 MAR 1830], Mrs. MARY ANN HEINEMAN, in the 85th year of her age. [CG, Sat., 3 APR 1830, p. 2]

DIED, at his residence in Bedford, Pa., on the 27th ult. [i.e. 27 MAR 1830], of an affection of the stomach, the Hon. JOHN TOD, one of the associate Judges of the Supreme Court of Pa. [CG, Sat., 3 APR 1830, p. 2]

Georgetown, D.C., **Marriage and Death Notices, 1801-1838**

DIED, in Charleston, S.C., on the 28th ult. [i.e. 28 MAR 1830], of gout in the stomach, STEPHEN ELLIOTT, Esq., aged fifty-eight.—The Charleston papers speak in the highest terms of praise of the character, talents, and attainments of Mr. Elliott. He was a member of many learned Societies,—the principal conductor and one of the largest contributors to the *Southern Review*,—and connected with almost every public scheme having for its ends general improvement and intellectual cultivation. The death of such a man is a public calamity, in whatever section he may reside. [CG, Tues., 6 APR 1830, p. 2]

DIED, in Iredell Co., N.C., on the 17th ult. [i.e. 17 MAR 1830], Maj. MUSSENDINE MATTHEWS, in the 77th year of his age, an officer, and an ardent supporter of his country rights, during the Revolutionary War. [CG, Tues., 6 APR 1830, p. 2]

DIED, in Washington City, on the 2d inst. [i.e. 2 APR 1830], H. THOMPSON RANKIN, in the 24th year of his age, formerly of Alexandria. [CG, Tues., 6 APR 1830, p. 2]

MARRIED, in this Town, on Tuesday evening last [i.e. 6 APR 1830], by the Rev. Dr. Balch, Capt. RICHARD CRUIKSHANK, to Miss ANN JANE, second daughter of Wm. Mackey, Esq., all of this place. [CG, Thurs., 8 APR 1830, p. 3]

MARRIED, in Baltimore, on the 5th inst. [i.e. 5 APR 1830], Col. ISAAC A. COLES, of Albemarle, Va., to Mrs. JULIA ANN RANKIN, daughter of the late Gen. Stricker. [CG, Thurs., 8 APR 1830, p. 3]

MARRIED, in Fredericksburg, on the 5th inst. [i.e. 5 APR 1830], H. SKIPWITH, Esq., of Mecklenburg Co., Va., to Mrs. LELIA ROBERTSON, of La. [CG, Thurs., 8 APR 1830, p. 3]

MARRIED, in Richmond, on the 1st inst. [i.e. 1 APR 1830], Mr. JOHN G. HULL, of Fredericksburg, to Miss HARRIET W., daughter of Mr. Harvey Shore, of the former place. [CG, Thurs., 8 APR 1830, p. 3]

DIED, in Baltimore, on the 3d inst. [i.e. 3 APR 1830], Mrs. MARY JANE CARR, wife of Lt. John S. Nicholas, of the U.S. Navy, and daughter of the late John Hollins, Esq. [CG, Thurs., 8 APR 1830, p. 3]

DIED, near Prince Fredericktown, Calvert Co., Md., on the 20th of March [i.e. 20 MAR 1830], a colored man named BASIL, aged 114 years. (Certified on the best authority.) [CG, Thurs., 8 APR 1830, p. 3]

DIED, in Richmond, on the 4th inst. [i.e. 4 APR 1830], Mrs. MILLY STONE, in the 63d year of her age, widow of the late Wm. S. Stone, of Fredericksburg. [CG, Thurs., 8 APR 1830, p. 3]

DIED, in Georgetown, Del., on the 1st inst., [i.e. 1 APR 1830] the Hon. NICHOLAS RIDGELY, Chancellor of the State of Delaware, in the 72d year of his age. In the morning he was actively engaged in the discharge of his official functions in the Court of Chancery; in the afternoon of the same day was taken suddenly ill, and almost immediately expired. [CG, Sat., 10 APR 1830, p. 3]

Georgetown, D.C., **Marriage and Death Notices, 1801-1838**

DIED, in Washington, on the 7th inst. [i.e. 7 APR 1830], Mrs. CLARISSA HOOVER, consort of Mr. Michael Hoover, in the 29th year of her age. [CG, Sat., 10 APR 1830, p. 3]

MARRIED, in Alexandria, on the 6th inst. [i.e. 6 APR 1830], Mr. BENJAMIN P. SMITH, of Washington, to Miss MATILDA R. PRICE, of Alexandria. [CG, Tues., 13 APR 1830, p. 3]

MARRIED, in Fredericksburg, on the 8th inst. [i.e. 8 APR 1830], Mr. ALEXANDER A. MUSE, to Miss CATHARINE MAYER; Mr. JOHN L. KNIGHT, to Miss ELLEN MATHESON, all of Fredericksburg. [CG, Tues., 13 APR 1830, p. 3]

MARRIED, in Hagerstown [no date], Mr. JOHN SUTER to Mrs. CATHARINE MARTIN; Mr. DAVID SWOPE, to Miss MARIA RENNER. [CG, Tues., 13 APR 1830, p. 3]

MARRIED, in N.Y., on the 6th inst. [i.e. 6 APR 1830], BYAM KERBY STEVENS, Esq., to FRANCES, only daughter of the Hon. Albert Gallatin. [CG, Tues., 13 APR 1830, p. 3]

MARRIED, at Poughkeepsie, N.Y., on the 6th inst. [i.e. 6 APR 1830], Dr. BENJAMIN R. TINSLAR, of the U.S. Navy, to JANE CATALINA, daughter of John Van Benthuysen, Esq. [CG, Tues., 13 APR 1830, p. 3]

MARRIED, at Augusta, Ga. [no date], DAVID E. TWIGGS, of the U.S. Army, to Miss ELIZABETH WAKE, daughter of Col. John W. Hunter. [CG, Tues., 13 APR 1830, p. 3]

DIED, in Baltimore, on the 9th inst. [i.e. 9 APR 1830], THOMAS ROSS, aged 50, long known as an active and efficient Police Officer. [CG, Tues., 13 APR 1830, p. 3]

DIED, in Orwigsburg, Pa., on the 6th inst. [i.e. 6 APR 1830], in the 46th year of his age, the Hon. SAMUEL D. FRANKS, late President Judge of the 12th Judicial District. [CG, Tues., 13 APR 1830, p. 3]

DIED, on board the U.S. ship *Guerriere*, at Valparaiso, on the 3d of January last [i.e. 3 JAN 1830], Midshipman LUCIUS MILLER, youngest son of Maj. Thomas R. Miller, of Washington City. On the following day, his remains, attended by the officers of the *Guerriere*, and a large concourse of American and English residents at Valparaiso, were interred, with military honors, in the Catholic cemetery of that City ... [CG, Thurs., 15 APR 1830, p. 3]

MARRIED, in Alexandria, on the 14th inst. [i.e. 14 APR 1830], by the Rev. S. Cornelius, Mr. JOHN T. RIORDAN, to Miss ELIZABETH P. JACKSON, all of that place. [CG, Sat., 17 APR 1830, p. 3]

DIED, in Washington City, on Thursday last [i.e. 22 APR 1830], ELIZA HACKETT, aged 32 years. [CG, Sat., 17 APR 1830, p. 3]

Georgetown, D.C., **Marriage and Death Notices, 1801-1838**

DIED, in Baltimore, on Thursday last [i.e. 15 APR 1830], Mrs. SIDNEY JANE VAN WYCK, aged 25 years, wife of John C. Van Wyck, and second daughter of the Hon. Judge M'Mechen. [CG, Sat., 17 APR 1830, p. 3]

DIED, at Bath, (England) [no date], Mrs. FORTUNE GIFFORD, wife of Mr. Gifford, of Great Pulteney Square, daughter of the late Wm. Randolph, Esq., of Bristol, and cousin to the Hon. John Randolph, and to the Hon. Thomas Jefferson, late President of the United States.—*Belfast Chronicle, March 20.* [CG, Sat., 17 APR 1830, p. 3]

MARRIED, in Norfolk, Va., on the 15th inst. [i.e. 15 APR 1830], Lieut. ROBERT B. CUNNINGHAM, of the U.S. Navy, to Miss ANN H., eldest daughter of Dr. Robert B. Stark, of that Borough. [CG, Tues., 20 APR 1830, p. 3]

DIED, in Washington, on Saturday last [i.e. 17 APR 1830], the Hon. ALEXANDER SMITH, Representative in Congress from the State of Virginia, aged about 65 years. [CG, Tues., 20 APR 1830, p. 3]

MARRIED, at *Neabsco*, Prince William Co., Va., on the 15th inst. [i.e. 15 APR 1830], Mr. SAMUEL S. RIND, of this town, to Miss REBECCA MONTGOMERY, daughter of the late Rev. Zebulon Kankey. [CG, Thurs., 22 APR 1830, p. 3]

MARRIED, in Washington, on the 15th inst. [i.e. 15 APR 1830], Mr. CHARLES OWENS, of Calvert Co., Md., to Miss WINIFRED SPAULDING, of Washington. [CG, Thurs., 22 APR 1830, p. 3]

MARRIED, in Washington, on the 20th inst. [i.e. 20 APR 1830], Col. JOHN H. HUNTER, of Murfreesborough, N.C., to Miss MARY E. BROWN, daughter of the Rev. O.B. Brown, of Washington. [CG, Thurs., 22 APR 1830, p. 3]

DIED, in this town, at five o'clock, A.M., yesterday [i.e. 21 APR 1830], Mrs. BRIDGET FAHEY, in the 55th year of her age, nearly 30 years of which she has been a respectable resident of this town. ☞ The friends of the deceased, and those of her son-in-law, Mr. Connelly, are requested to attend her funeral at 4 o'clock, P.M., this day, from the residence of her son-in-law, S. Rainey, High street, opposite Mr. M'Candless' tavern. [CG, Thurs., 22 APR 1830, p. 3]

DIED, in Philadelphia, on the 17th inst. [i.e. 17 APR 1830], JOHN D. GODMAN, M.D., Professor of Anatomy, Natural History, &c., aged 32 years. Few men of his years had attained so high and enviable a reputation as Dr. Godman; he has left behind him works that will establish his fame as a scholar and a physician. [CG, Thurs., 22 APR 1830, p. 3]

MARRIED, in Philadelphia, on the 15th inst. [i.e. 15 APR 1830], Dr. EDWARD DICKINSON, of Hadley, (Mass.) to Miss CATHARINE JONES, daughter of the late Edward Jones, Esq., of this town. [CG, Sat., 24 APR 1830, p. 3]

DIED, in Baltimore, on the 21st inst. [i.e. 21 APR 1830], Maj. REUBEN ROSS, in the 49th year of his age, a useful and enterprising citizen. [CG, Sat., 24 APR 1830, p. 3]

Georgetown, D.C., **Marriage and Death Notices, 1801-1838**

MARRIED, in Alexandria, on the 20th inst. [i.e. 20 APR 1830], Capt. CHARLES DEARBORN, to Miss ELIZABETH MARKLEY, daughter of the late Capt. Markley, all of that place. [CG, Tues., 27 APR 1830, p. 3]

DIED, in Charleston, (S. Carolina), on the 16th inst. [i.e. 16 APR 1830], Mrs. MARIETTA KEITH, wife of the Rev. Reuel Keith, D.D., Professor of the Theological Seminary, near Alexandria, D.C., and formerly of this town. [CG, Tues., 27 APR 1830, p. 3]

DIED, in Washington, on the 25th inst. [i.e. 25 APR 1830], Mrs. SARAH BURKE, relict of the late James Burke, Printer. [CG, Tues., 27 APR 1830, p. 3]

DIED, in N.Y., on the 21st inst. [i.e. 21 APR 1830], Col. THOMAS BARCLAY, late British Consul General to the U.S. in the 77th year of his age. He was respected and esteemed by all who knew him. [CG, Tues., 27 APR 1830, p. 3]

MARRIED, in Washington City, on Tuesday, the 27th inst. [i.e. 27 APR 1830], Mr. WILLIAM JOHNSON, to Miss SIDNEY TWEEDY, both of that City. [CG, Thurs., 29 APR 1830, p. 3]

MARRIED, on the 25th inst. [i.e. 25 APR 1830], Mr. GODFREY L. DeGILSE, to Miss MARY E. HARRISON, both of Washington. [CG, Thurs., 29 APR 1830, p. 3]

MARRIED, in Alexandria, on the 22d inst. [i.e. 22 APR 1830], Mr. JOHN MORGAN, to Miss BARBARA MYERS, both of that place. [CG, Thurs., 29 APR 1830, p. 3]

DIED, in Washington City, on the 25th inst. [i.e. 25 APR 1830], Mr. SAMUEL HARKNESS, in the 68th year of his age, after a lingering illness of several months. Mr. H. was a native of Ireland, emigrated to this country when 18, and for the last 30 years has been an active and useful citizen of Washington. [CG, Thurs., 29 APR 1830, p. 3]

DIED, on the 25th inst. [i.e. 25 APR 1830], Mr. ROBERT BROWN, an old and respectable inhabitant of the Navy Yard Hill. [CG, Thurs., 29 APR 1830, p. 3]

DIED, at *Audley*, her residence, in Frederick Co., Va., on Good Friday, the 9th of April, 1830, in the 65th year of her age, Mrs. BETTY CARTER, relict of the late Mr. Charles Carter, and only daughter of the only sister of the Father of his country, Gen. George Washington. [CG, Thurs., 29 APR 1830, p. 3]

MARRIED, in Alexandria, on the 27th ult. [i.e. 27 APR 1830], Mr. NOBLE JOHNSON, of Charles Co., Md., to Miss MARY ANN, daughter of Mr. William Morgan, of Alexandria. [CG, Sat., 1 MAY 1830, p. 3]

DIED, in Boston [no date], the Hon. DANIEL COBB, aged 81, a soldier of the Revolution, who filled, during his life, many civil offices with honor to himself and usefulness to the State of Mass. He was for several years Speaker of the House of Representatives, President of the Senate, and Member of Congress. In 1809, he was Lieutenant Governor of the State, and was afterwards a member of the Council Board. [CG, Sat., 1 MAY 1830, p. 3]

Georgetown, D.C., **Marriage and Death Notices, 1801-1838**

DIED, on Friday night, the 16th ult. [i.e. 16 APR 1830], at his late residence in Culpeper Co., Va., the Rev. JAMES GARNETT, Sen., in about the 87th year of his age. He was a zealous and faithful preacher of the gospel, in the Baptist church, for upwards of fifty years. [CG, Sat., 1 MAY 1830, p. 3]

MARRIED, in Alexandria, on the 27th ult. [i.e. 27 APR 1830], Mr. JOHN NORRISS, to Miss EMELINE ZIMMERMAN, both of that place. [CG, Tues., 4 MAY 1830, p. 2]

MARRIED, in this town, on Wednesday evening last [i.e. 28 APR 1830], by the Rev. Mr. Vanlommel, JOHN A. KING, Esq., to Mrs. FRANCES BRONAUGH; and at the same time and place, JAMES D. KING, Esq., of the Treasury Department, to Miss MARY ALPHONSA, daughter of Thomas G. Slye, Esq., of Washington. [CG, Tues., 4 MAY 1830, p. 2]

DIED, in Washington, on the 29th ult. [i.e. 29 APR 1830], Mr. WILLIAM TODD, formerly of N.Y., but for nine months past a resident of Washington. [CG, Tues., 4 MAY 1830, p. 2]

DIED, in Alexandria, on the 30th ult. [i.e. 30 APR 1830], Miss REBECCA KING, aged 35 years. [CG, Tues., 4 MAY 1830, p. 2]

DIED, at his residence in Montgomery Co., Md., on the 1st inst. [i.e. 1 MAY 1830], Col. THOMAS PLATER, aged about 58 years; a gentleman of the most estimable character, and for a long time, until within a few years past, a resident of this District. [CG, Tues., 4 MAY 1830, p. 2]

MARRIED, in Washington City, on the 2d inst. [i.e. 2 MAY 1830], Mr. HORACE WEYBORN, to Miss SUSAN DARLEY, both of Alexandria. [CG, Thurs., 6 MAY 1830, p. 3]

MARRIED, in Lycoming Co., Pa., on Thursday, the 8th ult. [i.e. 8 APR 1830], at 3 o'clock, A.M., by Samuel Morris, Esq., Mr. JOHN RYNEARSON, to Miss CATHARINE COLNER, of Muncy Township, Lycoming. (At 12 o'clock at night the bridegroom came, he knocked, the door opened, and his betrothed saddled her horse and rode eight miles through a wilderness country, in the dead hour of the night, &c.) [CG, Thurs., 6 MAY 1830, p. 3]

DIED, in this town, on Tuesday afternoon last [i.e. 4 MAY 1830], Miss ELIZABETH YOUNG, second daughter of Mr. Edgar Patterson, aged 16 years. [CG, Thurs., 6 MAY 1830, p. 3]

DIED, at his residence in the Navy Yard, Washington City, on the 2d inst. [i.e. 2 MAY 1830], in the 60th year of his age, Capt. EDWARD BARRY, one of the oldest Sailing Masters in the service, and a correct, vigilant, and faithful officer. [CG, Thurs., 6 MAY 1830, p. 3]

DIED, in Lyndeborough, N.H., on the 15th ult. [i.e. 15 APR 1830], NATHAN GREEN, aged about 75 ... He is supposed to have possessed an estate to the amount of from 20 to $30,000, and yet he probably never ate what by others would have been deemed a comfortable meal of victuals, or wore a decent garment in his life! He had no family; but

Georgetown, D.C., Marriage and Death Notices, 1801-1838

lived a recluse, and died without any to lament his departure. He had many poor relations, to whom he left only very trifling legacies, but divided the bulk of his property between two nephews less needy ... [CG, Thurs., 6 MAY 1830, p. 3]

DIED, in Washington City, on the 1st inst. [i.e. 1 MAY 1830], Mr. SIMON CANTWELL, a native of the county of Limerick, Ire., aged 68 years. [CG, Sat., 8 MAY 1830, p. 3]

DIED, in Bladensburg, on the 29th ult. [i.e. 29 APR 1830], Dr. REZIN B. VAN HORN, in the 31st year of his age. [CG, Sat., 8 MAY 1830, p. 3]

DIED, in Baltimore, on the 5th inst. [i.e. 5 MAY 1830], after a long and severe illness, which he bore with Christian fortitude and resignation, Col. JERU BOULDIN, of that City, in the 70th year of his age. The venerable citizen has thus closed a long and useful life, distinguished by a meritorious performance of all the duties of a man and a citizen. For 20 years he held the office of City Surveyor, and for the last two, the appointment of County Surveyor was added, and the duties of both were always promptly and faithfully performed. Though legally exempt from military service, he bore arms in defense of his country during the war, and commanded a troop of cavalry at North Point. His numerous acquaintances remember him with sorrow, as a true patriot and a most excellent man. [CG, Sat., 8 MAY 1830, p. 3]

MARRIED, in Baltimore, on the 6th inst. [i.e. 6 MAY 1830], Mr. P.M. HOLBROOK, Merchant, of Washington City, to Miss CHRISTINA, daughter of Mr. Frederick Crey, of Baltimore. [CG, Tues., 11 MAY 1830, p. 3]

DIED, in Alexandria, on the 30th ult. [i.e. 30 APR 1830], Mr. JOHN D. BROWN, in the 48th year of his age; of the late firm of *Thomas Janney & Co.*, of that place. [CG, Tues., 11 MAY 1830, p. 3]

DIED, on the 15th ult. [i.e. 15 APR 1830], at *Cedar Hill*, Prince William Co., Va., Mr. WILLIAM L. SCOTT, in the 28th year of his age, formerly a merchant in Alexandria. [CG, Tues., 11 MAY 1830, p. 3]

DIED, in Baltimore, Md., on Sunday last, the 9th inst. [i.e. 9 MAY 1830], SAMUEL HOLLINGSWORTH, Esq., in the 74th year of his age; for many years a highly respectable merchant and worthy citizen. [CG, Thurs., 13 MAY 1830, p. 3]

DIED, at Key West, in April last [i.e. APR 1830], WILLIAM TRUXTUN, Esq., only remaining son of the late Com. Truxton, of the U.S. Navy. [CG, Thurs., 13 MAY 1830, p. 3]

MARRIED, in this Town, on Thursday evening last [i.e. 13 MAY 1830], by the Rev. Mr. Amiss, Mr. JENKIN THOMAS, to Miss ELIZA, eldest daughter of Mr. William Parsons, all of this place. [CG, Sat., 15 MAY 1830, p. 3]

MARRIED, in N.Y., on the 5th inst. [i.e. 5 MAY 1830], the Rev. MATTHEW M. FULLERTON, of Hagerstown, Md., to Miss ANN DURYEE, daughter of the late Isaac Heyer, of N. York. [CG, Sat., 15 MAY 1830, p. 3]

Georgetown, D.C., **Marriage and Death Notices, 1801-1838**

DIED, in this Town, on Thursday evening last [i.e. 13 MAY 1830], in the 59th year of his age, DANIEL BUSSARD, Esquire, a Member of the Board of Alderman, and one of our oldest and most respected citizens. Mr. Bussard has long been known as an enterprising and industrious merchant, sustaining all the relations in life with credit to himself and utility to his fellow citizens. He bore one of the most excruciating disorders to which the human frame is subject, with uncommon fortitude; and amidst all his sufferings was never known to complain. By his family and relatives, his loss will be poignantly felt—by the public at large, deeply regretted. ☞ The funeral will take place this afternoon, at half past four o'clock, from his late residence on Third street. The friends and acquaintance of the family are respectfully invited to attend without further notice. [CG, Sat., 15 MAY 1830, p. 3]

MARRIED, in this town, on the 11th inst. [i.e. 11 MAY 1830], by the Rev. Mr. Brooke, Dr. BENJAMIN H. STRATTON, of Mount Holly, (N.J.,) to Miss EMELINE N., daughter of Samuel Whitall, Esq. [CG, Tues., 18 MAY 1830, p. 3]

DIED, in Washington City, on the 13th inst. [i.e. 13 MAY 1830], in the 62d year of her age, Mrs. MARGARET CRAIG, wife of John D. Craig, of the Patent Office. [CG, Tues., 18 MAY 1830, p. 3]

DIED, at his residence in Somerset Co., Md., on the 3d inst. [i.e. 3 MAY 1830], in the 68th year of his age, JOHN LANDRETH, Esq., a native of Scotland, but for 40 years a resident of this country. [CG, Tues., 18 MAY 1830, p. 3]

MARRIED, in Cumberland Co., (Pa.) on the 18th inst. [i.e. 18 MAY 1830], Mr. DANIEL WETHERSPOON, of Franklin Co., to Miss MASSA ANN CAROTHERS, of the former place. [CG, Sat., 22 MAY 1830, p. 3]

DIED, in Washington City, on Thursday last [i.e. 20 MAY 1830], Mr. JAMES MILTON, late of Jefferson Co., Va. [CG, Sat., 22 MAY 1830, p. 3]

DIED, in Washington City, on Sunday morning last [i.e. 23 MAY 1830], Miss MARTHA HOBAN, eldest daughter of Capt. James Hoban. [CG, Tues., 25 MAY 1830, p. 3]

DIED, in Cambridge, (Md.) on the 21st inst. [i.e. 21 MAY 1830], of apoplexy, WILLIAM H. FITZHUGH, Esq., of *Ravensworth*, Fairfax Co., Va. [CG, Tues., 25 MAY 1830, p. 3]

MARRIED, at Augusta, (Georgia,) on the 9th inst. [i.e. 9 MAY 1830], Capt. GEORGE W. GARDINER, of the U.S. Artillery, to Miss FANNY P. FOWLER, daughter of Lieut. Fowler. [CG, Thurs., 27 MAY 1830, p. 3]

MARRIED, on the 17th inst. [i.e. 17 MAY 1830], Dr. ELIJAH COONS, of Tuscumbia, (Ala.,) to Miss EFFE M'ARTHUR, daughter of Gen. Duncan M'Arthur, of Ohio. [CG, Thurs., 27 MAY 1830, p. 3]

DIED, on the 20th inst. [i.e. 20 MAY 1830], at the residence of her father, in Charles Co., (Md.) Miss FRANCES WATHEN, in the 40th year of her age. [CG, Thurs., 27 MAY 1830, p. 3]

Georgetown, D.C., **Marriage and Death Notices, 1801-1838**

DIED, on the 24th ult. [i.e. 24 MAY 1830], near Bainbridge, (Ohio,) Mr. WILLIAM TAYLOE, in the 86th year of his age; leaving 14 children, 124 grandchildren, and 75 great grand children.—He was a native of Monmouth Co., N. Jersey.—*Scioto Gazette.* [CG, Thurs., 27 MAY 1830, p. 3]

MARRIED, in Washington City, on the 25th inst. [i.e. 25 MAY 1830], Mr. ELEXIUS SIMMS, to Miss EURYDICE FRANZONI, both of that City. [CG, Sat., 29 MAY 1830, p. 3]

MARRIED, on Thursday last [i.e. 27 MAY 1830], THOMAS M. NEWELL, Esq., of the U.S. Navy, to Miss HETTY R. ADAMS, both of Ga. [CG, Sat., 29 MAY 1830, p. 3]

MARRIED, in N.Y., on the 6th inst. [i.e. 6 MAY 1830], STEWART BROWN, Jr., Merchant of that City, to Miss MARY ANN ABBOTT, eldest daughter of Henry R. Abbott, late of England. [CG, Sat., 29 MAY 1830, p. 3]

DIED, in Washington, on Sunday last [i.e. 30 MAY 1830], of pulmonary complaint, with which she had been afflicted about twelve months, Mrs. MATILDA ADAMS, in the 34th year of her age, consort of Mr. John Adams, Jr. [CG, Tues., 1 JUN 1830, p. 2]

MARRIED, in Albany, (N.Y.) [no date], GOUVERNEUR MORRIS WILKINS, Esq., to Miss CATHARINE VAN RENSSELAER, daughter of the Hon. Stephen Van Rensselaer. [CG, Tues., 8 JUN 1830, p. 3]

DIED, at his residence in Anne Arundel Co., (Md.) on the 26th ult. [i.e. 26 MAY 1830], REZIN ESTEP, Esq., in the 67th year of his age. [CG, Tues., 8 JUN 1830, p. 3]

MARRIED, at *Bush Hill*, (the seat of R.M. Scott, Esq.) near Alexandria, on the 3d inst. [i.e. 3 JUN 1830], WILLIAM H. FOOTE, Esq., of *Hayfield*, to Miss MARY SCOTT, only daughter of the late D.W. Scott, Esq., of Virginia. [CG, Thurs., 10 JUN 1830, p. 3]

MARRIED, in Baltimore, on Tuesday morning, 8th inst. [i.e. 8 JUN 1830], the Rev. SAMUEL G. WINCHESTER, of Philadelphia, to Miss GRACE, youngest daughter of Alexander Mactier, Esq., of Baltimore. [CG, Thurs., 10 JUN 1830, p. 3]

MARRIED, in Alexandria, on the 8th inst. [i.e. 8 JUN 1830], Mr. LEVI HURDLE, to Miss LYDIA R., eldest daughter of Capt. Uriah Jenkins, all of that place. [CG, Sat., 12 JUN 1830, p. 3]

MARRIED, in Baltimore, on Thursday morning, 10th inst. [i.e. 10 JUN 1830], Mr. ISAAC SMITH HOMANS, of Washington, to SARAH, daughter of Col. Thomas Sheppard, of Baltimore. [CG, Sat., 12 JUN 1830, p. 3]

DIED, at *Mount Erin*, near Alexandria, on the 8th inst. [i.e. 8 JUN 1830], JAMES FRANCIS TRACY, a native of Dublin, Ire.; he emigrated to this country in 1822. [CG, Sat., 12 JUN 1830, p. 3]

Georgetown, D.C., **Marriage and Death Notices, 1801-1838**

DIED, on Saturday morning, the 6th of March [i.e. 6 MAR 1830], at the residence of Gov. Johnson, near Thibodeauxville, Miss., LOUISA E. KEY, daughter of the late Philip B. Key, of Georgetown, D.C., after an illness of five days ... [CG, Sat., 12 JUN 1830, p. 3]

Died, in Georgetown, on Tuesday the 1st inst. [i.e. 1 JUN 1830], after a short but painful illness, Mr. JOHN BUCHANAN, in the 32d year of his age. The deceased was a native of Tyron[e] Co., Ire., and a graduate of Trinity College, Dublin; he was possessed of excellent mental endowments ... his mortal remains [were] deposited in the Episcopal burying ground, in the town in which he died ... [CG, Thurs., 17 JUN 1830, p. 3]

DIED, on the 5th inst. [i.e. 5 JUN 1830], at the residence of his son-in-law, Mr. Lewis Collins, in Maysville, Ky., Maj. VALENTINE PEERS, one of the very few surviving officers of the Revolutionary Army, aged 74 years. Maj. Peers emigrated to America from Ireland, his native country, a short time previous to the commencement of the war for Independence on the part of the colonies. Though then a youth, having imbibed those principles of liberty which characterize the intelligent part of his countrymen, he ardently espoused the cause of the oppressed colonists; and throughout the arduous struggle which ensued, he bore an active, distinguished, and useful part. [CG, Thurs., 17 JUN 1830, p. 3]

DIED, at Norfolk, on Saturday [i.e. 12 JUN 1830], after a short but violent attack of inflammatory sore throat, Col. WILLIAM ANDERSON, of the U.S. Marine corps. As an officer, he signalized himself as commander of Marines on board the U.S. frigate *United States*, under Com. Decatur, in the memorable battle which resulted in the capture of H.B.M. frigate *Macedonian* ... Col. Anderson was a native of Pa. [CG, Thurs., 17 JUN 1830, p. 3]

MARRIED, in Baltimore, on Thursday morning [i.e. 17 JUN 1830], THOMAS J. HODSON, of Washington City, to MARGARET, only daughter of the late Willis Vincent, of Dorchester Co., Md. [CG, Sat., 19 JUN 1830, p. 3]

MARRIED, on Thursday evening last [i.e. 17 JUN 1830], by the Rev. Mr. Brooke, Mr. BAZIL BRAWNER, to Mrs. ELEANOR H. SEMMES, all of this town. [CG, Tues., 22 JUN 1830, p. 3]

MARRIED, in Washington, on Sunday morning [i.e. 20 JUN 1830], the Rev. ROBERT ASH, of Charleston, Va., to HENRIETTA MARIA, daughter of the late Thomas G. Addison, Esq., of Md. [CG, Tues., 22 JUN 1830, p. 3]

MARRIED, in Alexandria, on the 17th inst. [i.e. 17 JUN 1830], by the Rev. Mr. Larkin, Mr. CORREL HUMPHREYS, of Canton, Conn., to Miss CATHARINE A. GLASGOW, of Middleburg, Va. [CG, Tues., 22 JUN 1830, p. 3]

MARRIED, at Kingston, N.J., on the 15th inst. [i.e. 15 JUN 1830], Dr. J.S. DUNN, of Princeton, and formerly of Washington, to SUSAN ANN, daughter of Robert Bayles, of Kingston. [CG, Tues., 22 JUN 1830, p. 3]

MARRIED, in Washington, on the 17th inst. [i.e. 17 JUN 1830], Mr. PATRICK F. NASH, of that city, to Miss ELIZABETH BARNES, of Charles Co., Md. [CG, Thurs., 24 JUN 1830, p. 3]

DIED, suddenly, on the morning of the 18th inst. [i.e. 18 JUN 1830], ELIZABETH CROGHAN, youngest daughter of Gen. Jesup, aged sixteen months and one day. [CG, Thurs., 24 JUN 1830, p. 3]

DIED, in Alexandria, on Sunday morning last [i.e. 19 JUN 1830], after a long and painful illness, Mrs. ANN AVERY, in the 54th year of her age. [CG, Thurs., 24 JUN 1830, p. 3]

DIED, in Washington, on Wednesday 23d inst. [i.e. 23 JUN 1830], Mrs. LEAH IRVING, late of Somerset Co., Md., relict of Dr. Levin Irving, in the 73d year of her age. [CG, Sat., 26 JUN 1830, p. 3]

MARRIED, at Terre Haute, (Ind.,) on the 3d inst. [i.e. 3 JUN 1830], Hon. THOMAS HOLDSWORTH BLAKE, a member of the last Congress, to Miss SARAH LINTON. [CG, Tues., 29 JUN 1830, p. 3]

DIED, in this town, on Monday morning, 14th inst. [i.e. 14 JUN 1830], after a few days sickness, Mrs. MARGARET CASSIN, in the 41st year of her age, wife of Com. Stephen Cassin, of the U.S. Navy. [CG, Tues., 29 JUN 1830, p. 3]

DIED, in this town, yesterday morning [i.e. 30 JUN 1830], Miss BRIDGET CONNOLLY, in the 20th year of her age, after a lingering illness of several months ... ☞ The funeral will take place this afternoon, at 5 o'clock, from her late residence at the corner of Frederick and Market streets; her friends and acquaintances are respectfully invited to attend, without further notice. [CG, Thurs., 1 JUL 1830, p. 3]

DIED, in Alexandria, on the 28th ult. [i.e. 28 JUN 1830], Miss LUCINDA HERBERT. [CG, Thurs., 1 JUL 1830, p. 3]

MARRIAGE, in Alexandria, on Thursday evening last [i.e. 1 JUL 1830], JOHN P. DENNY, Esq., of Washington City, to Miss LUCINDA CONSTANTIA, only daughter of Mrs. Jane Crandell, of Alexandria. [CG, Sat., 3 JUL 1830, p. 3]

DIED, in Portsmouth, N.H. [no date], Hon. ELIJAH HALL, aged 67. He was a Lieutenant in the Navy in the Revolutionary war, sailed under Paul Jones in the *Ranger*, and has been, for several years, Naval Officer at Portsmouth. [CG, Sat., 3 JUL 1830, p. 3]

MARRIED, in Washington, on the 1st inst. [i.e. 1 JUL 1830], Dr. SIDNEY W. SMITH, of Alexandria, to Miss RACHEL B., youngest daughter of the late John Hesselius, of Baltimore. [CG, Thurs., 8 JUL 1830, p. 3]

MARRIED, on Saturday evening the 3d inst. [i.e. 3 JUL 1830], Mr. HENRY W. SWEETING, of Baltimore, to Miss ELLEN McCUBBIN, of that City. [CG, Thurs., 8 JUL 1830, p. 3]

Georgetown, D.C., **Marriage and Death Notices, 1801-1838**

MARRIED, near Rockville, Md., on the 29th ult. [i.e. 29 JUN 1830], Mr. GEORGE B. KNOWLES, of this town, to Miss LAURANER, daughter of James B. Higgins. [CG, Thurs., 8 JUL 1830, p. 3]

MARRIED, in N.Y., on the 30th ult. [i.e. 30 JUN 1830], Lieut. THOMAS R. GERRY, of the U.S. Navy, to HANNAH GREENE, daughter of the late Peter P. Gould. [CG, Thurs., 8 JUL 1830, p. 3]

MARRIED, on the 1st inst. [i.e. 1 JUL 1830], JEAN GERMAIN SAMUEL ADAMS DANNENY, Esq., Knight of the Royal Order of the Legion of Honor, Consul of France for the port of Philadelphia, to Miss MARIE ALEXANDRINE, eldest daughter of Mr. Durant St. Andre, Consul General of France for the United States. [CG, Thurs., 8 JUL 1830, p. 3]

MARRIED, on the 30th ult. [i.e. 30 JUN 1830], Lieut. THEODORUS BAILEY, of the U.S. Navy, to Miss SARAH ANN PLATT, of that City. [CG, Thurs., 8 JUL 1830, p. 3]

MARRIED, in Philadelphia, on the 27th ult. [i.e. 27 JUN 1830], Lieut. FREDERICK A. NEVILLE, of the U.S. Navy, to Miss ANN CATHARINE, eldest daughter of Robert Kennedy, Esq., Naval Storekeeper of that City. [CG, Thurs., 8 JUL 1830, p. 3]

DIED, in Albany [no date], in the 34th year of his age, NICHOLAS F. BECK, Esq., Adjutant General of the State of N.Y. [CG, Thurs., 8 JUL 1830, p. 3]

DIED, in Medfield, Mass. [no date], Deacon JONATHAN WIGHT, aged nearly 96. He was one of a family of 14 children, whose ages have averaged more than 83 years. [CG, Thurs., 8 JUL 1830, p. 3]

DIED, on the 9th ult. [i.e. 9 JUN 1830], at Marie, near Quebec, NOUVELLE BEAUCE JACQUES GAGNE, and MAGDALINE MORIN, his wife, both 77 years old. These two persons were born the same day, baptized the same day, made their first communion the same day, died and were buried the same day. [CG, Thurs., 8 JUL 1830, p. 3]

MARRIED, on the 4th inst. [i.e. 4 JUL 1830], in Washington, Mr. ROBERT J. SIMONDS, to Miss CORNELIA ANN GAILLARD, both of Washington City. [CG, Sat., 10 JUL 1830, p. 3]

MARRIED, on the 18th ult. [i.e. 18 JUL 1830], at the residence of Henry Carrington, Esq., of Charlotte, Va., the Rev. JAMES W. ALEXANDER, of Trenton, N.J., to Miss ELIZABETH C. CABELL, daughter of the late Dr. George Cabell, of Richmond. [CG, Sat., 10 JUL 1830, p. 3]

MARRIED, on the 24th ult. [i.e. 24 JUN 1830], at the residence of J.S. Benham, Esq., Ohio, Mr. ISRAEL L. LUDLOW, of Cincinnati, to Miss HELEN ADELA SLACUM, daughter of the late George W. Slacum, of Alexandria. [CG, Sat., 10 JUL 1830, p. 3]

Georgetown, D.C., **Marriage and Death Notices, 1801-1838**

MARRIED, in Fayetteville, N.C., on the 30th ult. [i.e. 30 JUN 1830], JOHN W. SANFORD, Esq., Cashier of the U.S. Branch Bank, to Miss MARGARET HALLIDAY, eldest daughter of the late Robert Halliday, Esq. [CG, Sat., 10 JUL 1830, p. 3]

DIED, in Alexandria, on the 26th ult. [i.e. 26 JUN 1830], after a long and painful illness, in the 56th year of his age, Mr. DANIEL WRIGHT, a useful and respectable citizen of that place. [CG, Sat., 10 JUL 1830, p. 3]

DIED, in Alexandria, on Thursday [i.e. 8 JUL 1830], after a short illness, Mrs. MARY WHITTLE, consort of Thomas Whittle. [CG, Sat., 10 JUL 1830, p. 3]

MARRIED, in Washington, on Thursday [i.e. 8 JUL 1830], by the Rev. Allen, Mr. FREDERICK SPICER, to Miss MARIA BUFORD, all of that City. [CG, Tues., 13 JUL 1830, p. 3]

MARRIED, at Sharpsburg, Md., on the 24th ult. [i.e. 24 JUN 1830], the Rev. JOHN ALEXANDER ADAMS, of the District of Columbia, to Mrs. MARY ANN RITCHIE, of the former place. [CG, Tues., 13 JUL 1830, p. 3]

DIED, on board the U.S. ship *Peacock*, (Capt. E.R. McCall,) at sea, on the 23d of June [i.e. 30 JUN 1830], of yellow fever, contracted at Matanzas, Lieut. WILLIAM T. TEMPLE, of Caroline Co., Va.—He entered the service of his country on the 1st September 1811—and was promoted to the rank of Lieutenant 1st of April, 1818. Mr. T. was a highly meritorious officer, and much esteemed by those associated with him on public duty. [CG, Tues., 13 JUL 1830, p. 3]

DIED, on board the U.S. ship *Peacock*, on the 22d of June [i.e. 22 JUN 1830], at sea, of yellow fever, contracted at Matanzas, Mr. NELSON R. BAKER, Midshipman of the U.S. Navy, a native of Md. He entered the service 1st November, 1828, was much esteemed by his brother officers, and promised to be an acquisition to the Navy. [CG, Tues., 13 JUL 1830, p. 3]

MARRIED, in Alexandria, on the 8th inst. [i.e. 8 JUL 1830], Mr. JAMES FORTUNE, of Baltimore, to Miss MARY SANE, of Alexandria. [CG, Thurs., 15 JUL 1830, p. 3]

MARRIED, at Fredericksburg, Va., on Tuesday morning last [i.e. 13 JUL 1830], Mr. A.D. BECKWITH, Printer, of Washington City, to Miss ADELAIDE CARTER, of the former place. [CG, Thurs., 15 JUL 1830, p. 3]

DIED, at Hillsborough, Loudoun Co., Va., on the 4th inst. [i.e. 4 JUL 1830], SOLOMON PARSONS, in the 53d year of his age, a native of Mass. [CG, Thurs., 15 JUL 1830, p. 3]

DIED, at Annapolis, on Tuesday last [i.e. 13 JUL 1830], in the 28th year of her age, Mrs. EUPHEMIA ANDERSON, daughter of Mr. Joseph Anderson, Sr., of the Philadelphia, Baltimore and Washington Theatres. She has left, besides her aged parents, her brothers and sisters, two young and interesting daughters to lament her death. [CG, Sat., 17 JUL 1830, p. 3]

Georgetown, D.C., **Marriage and Death Notices, 1801-1838**

MARRIED, in Washington, on Tuesday evening, the 13th inst. [i.e. 13 JUL 1830], by the Rev. Mr. Robb, Mr. S.C. ROSZELL, to Miss MARY JANE CHALMERS, daughter of the Rev. John Chalmers, all of that City. [CG, Tues., 20 JUL 1830, p. 3]

MARRIED, in Portsmouth, (N.H.) [no date], Midshipman JOHN JACKSON WHITE, U.S. Navy, of this town, to Miss SARAH H. PEARSE. [CG, Tues., 20 JUL 1830, p. 3]

DIED, in Washington City, on Sunday morning last [i.e. 18 JUL 1830], Mrs. MARY ANN HICKEY, aged 54 years, relict of the late James Hickey, an old and respectable inhabitant of that City. [CG, Tues., 20 JUL 1830, p. 3]

DIED, in Washington, on Monday last [i.e. 19 JUL 1830], Mr. JOHN STREET, aged 42 years; a native of England, but for 10 or 12 years an industrious citizen of Washington, where he has left a widow and three small children. [CG, Thurs., 22 JUL 1830, p. 3]

DIED, in Providence, R.I., on the 12th inst. [i.e. 12 JUL 1830], Mr. GEORGE SCHAFFER, aged 46, Professor of Dancing, and one of the most celebrated wits and wags of the age. [CG, Thurs., 22 JUL 1830, p. 3]

MARRIED, in Washington City, on the 21st inst. [i.e. 21 JUL 1830], by the Rev. Mr. Keppler, Mr. WILLIAM H. PERKINS, to Miss SUSAN DYER, daughter of the late Capt. Wm. Dyer, both of that City. [CG, Sat., 24 JUL 1830, p. 3]

MARRIED, in N.Y., on the 14th inst. [i.e. 14 JUL 1830], by the Rev. A. Verren, DOMINIQUE D'ARBEL, Esq., of France, to Mad'selle ADELAIDE CHARLOTTE WOLDEMARINE HUYGENS, daughter of his Excellency the Chevalier Huygens, Envoy Extraordinary and Minister Plenipotentiary of his Majesty the King of the Netherlands to the United States. [CG, Sat., 24 JUL 1830, p. 3]

MARRIED, at Cincinnati, on the 8th inst. [i.e. 8 JUL 1830], Dr. HAYWARD, of Boston, to Miss SARAH ANN M'LEAN, daughter of the Hon. John M'Lean. [CG, Sat., 24 JUL 1830, p. 3]

MARRIED, at Dayton, Ohio, on the 29th June [i.e. 29 JUN 1830], JOHN G. WORTHINGTON, Esq., of Cincinnati, to Miss ELIZABETH PHILLIPS, daughter of Horatio G. Phillips, Esq. [CG, Sat., 24 JUL 1830, p. 3]

DIED, in Washington City, on the 22d inst. [i.e. 22 JUL 1830], after a short illness, Mrs. SARAH TUEL, aged about 48 years. [CG, Sat., 24 JUL 1830, p. 3]

DIED, in Washington City, on the 20th inst. [i.e. 20 JUL 1830], after a severe and painful illness, MARIA, youngest daughter of Joseph P. M'Corkle, aged 16 months. [CG, Sat., 24 JUL 1830, p. 3]

DIED, in N.Y., on the 19th inst. [i.e. 19 JUL 1830], after a short but severe illness, Lieut. ALEXANDER M. MULL, of the U.S. Navy. [CG, Sat., 24 JUL 1830, p. 3]

Georgetown, D.C., **Marriage and Death Notices, 1801-1838**

DIED, in Lancaster, Pa., on the 8th inst. [i.e. 8 JUL 1830], in the 77th year of his age, Mr. JEREMIAH MOSHER, a General in the militia of that State. He was a native of the town of Roxbury, adjacent to the City of Boston, and was one of the earliest who armed in vindication of the liberties of his country. [CG, Sat., 24 JUL 1830, p. 3]

MARRIED, in Washington, on the 22d inst. [i.e. 22 JUL 1830], Mr. JAMES WALKER, to ANN SOPHIA, eldest daughter of Mr. George Cover, all of that city. [CG, Thurs., 29 JUL 1830, p. 3]

DIED, in Washington, on the 24th inst. [i.e. 24 JUL 1830], Mrs. ANN FENWICK, relict of the late Richard Fenwick, aged about 73 years. [CG, Thurs., 29 JUL 1830, p. 3]

DIED, on the 18th inst. [i.e. 18 JUL 1830], of bilious remittent fever, BENJAMIN Y. WEBB, of Montgomery Co., Md. [CG, Thurs., 29 JUL 1830, p. 3]

DIED, in Alexandria, on the 26th inst. [i.e. 26 JUL 1830], Mr. MAURICE HERBERT, son of the late Thomas Herbert, Esq., aged 34 years. [CG, Thurs., 29 JUL 1830, p. 3]

DIED, on the 27th [i.e. 27 JUL 1830], Mr. NICHOLAS HINGSTON, in the 81st year of his age, a native of Devonshire, Eng., but for the last 40 years a respectable citizen of Alexandria. [CG, Thurs., 29 JUL 1830, p. 3]

MARRIED, in Washington, on the 25th inst. [i.e. 25 JUL 1830], Mr. WILLIAM COX, of Prince George's Co., Md., to Miss B.A. WALCH, of Washington. [CG, Sat., 31 JUL 1830, p. 3]

MARRIED, at Cincinnati, Ohio, on the 20th inst. [i.e. 20 JUL 1830], Mr. JOHN STETTINIUS, of Washington, to Miss MARY LONGWORTH, eldest daughter of Nicholas Longworth, Esq. [CG, Sat., 31 JUL 1830, p. 3]

MARRIED, on Monday, 26th ult. [i.e. 26 JUL 1830], by the Rev. Mr. Van Lomel, Mr. JOHN WHITE, of Emmitsburg, to Miss MARY O'BRIEN, eldest daughter of Mrs. Brien [sic] of this town. [CG, Tues., 3 AUG 1830, p. 2]

MARRIED, on Thursday, 29th ult. [i.e. 29 JUL 1830], by the Rev. Dr. Balch, Mr. CHARLES J. GRAENACHER, to Miss MARGARET McCLELLAND, all of this town. [CG, Tues., 3 AUG 1830, p. 2]

MARRIED, on the 15th ult. [i.e. 15 JUL 1830], Hon. W.T. NUCKOLLS, Member of Congress from South Carolina, to Miss SUSAN DAUKINS, daughter of Gen. E.D. of Union District, S.C. [CG, Tues., 3 AUG 1830, p. 2]

DIED, in Washington, on the 23d ult. [i.e. 23 JUL 1830], Mrs. MARY COOPER, aged 24 years. [CG, Tues., 3 AUG 1830, p. 2]

Georgetown, D.C., Marriage and Death Notices, 1801-1838

DIED, in Boston, on the 25th ult. [i.e. 25 JUL 1830], Dr. JOHN D. WELLS, Professor of Anatomy and Surgery in the University of Maryland, in the 31st year of his age. [CG, Tues., 3 AUG 1830, p. 2]

Departed this life, on Saturday last [i.e. 31 JUL 1830], in the 58th year of her age, Mrs. MARY ANN HAW, consort of John S. Haw, Esq., of Georgetown ... [CG, Thurs., 5 AUG 1830, p. 2]

DIED, in Washington, on the 3d inst. [i.e. 3 AUG 1830], at the residence of her son-in-law, Edward Ingle, Mrs. CATHERINE PECHIN, wife of Col. William Pechin, of Baltimore. [CG, Sat., 7 AUG 1830, p. 3]

DIED, on the 31st ult. [i.e. 31 JUL 1830], Mr. PHILIP MARTIN, in the 47th year of his age. [CG, Sat., 7 AUG 1830, p. 3]

MARRIED, in Washington City, on the 1st inst. [i.e. 1 AUG 1830], Mr. SAMUEL KEEP, of Boston, to Miss JULIA, daughter of Capt. Peter Lenox. [CG, Tues., 10 AUG 1830, p. 3]

DIED, in this Town, on Sunday evening last [i.e. 8 AUG 1830], Mr. WILLIAM THOMPSON. [CG, Tues., 10 AUG 1830, p. 3]

DIED, yesterday [i.e. 9 AUG 1830], Mr. JAMES WHARTON. [CG, Tues., 10 AUG 1830, p. 3]

DIED, on Sunday morning last [i.e. 7 AUG 1830], at the residence of Mr. Robert Y. Brent, near the City of Washington, GEORGE GRAHAM, Esq., Commissioner of the General Land Office. [CG, Tues., 10 AUG 1830, p. 3]

DIED, at Portsmouth, N.H., lately [no date], Hon. J.S. SHERBURNE, Judge of the United States District Court, aged 73. Judge Sherburne was an aid-de-camp to Gen. Whipple, in the Revolutionary war, and lost his left leg by a cannon shot at the battle of Butt's Hill, in Rhode Island, under the immediate command of Maj. Gen. Sullivan. He died in the mansion of his father, in the same chamber in which he was born. [CG, Thurs., 12 AUG 1830, p. 3]

MARRIED, on Wednesday evening, the 11th inst. [i.e. 11 AUG 1830], by the Rev. Dr. Laurie, Mr. EDWARD FARRIGUE, to Miss ELIZA MILLER, of Georgetown, D.C. [CG, Sat., 14 AUG 1830, p. 3]

DIED, on the evening of the 10th inst. [i.e. 10 AUG 1830], at the City Hotel, after an illness of eight days, SAMUEL KEEP, Esq., of Washington, D.C., a native of Boston, and formerly Agent of the United States at Pensacola, in the 26th year of his age. The unfortunate subject of this notice, was married on the 1st inst. [i.e. 1 AUG 1830] to an interesting young lady of Washington, which place he left the next day with his wife and her two sisters, to visit his parents in Boston. Intending to leave Baltimore on the morning of the 3d for Philadelphia, Mr. Keep rose about three o'clock to observe the state of the weather, and to make the necessary arrangements. Between three and four o'clock, before the persons who usually attend the bar were up, he called on the porter for a glass of cider.—By one of those unaccountable oversights, which in the best regulated establishments may sometimes occur, a bottle of *Corrosive Sublimate* had been left in the bar, which the porter by mistake drew for cider. A small portion of it was drunk by Mr. Keep, and produced immediate vomiting. As soon as the poisonous nature of the draught was discovered, two eminent physicians were called in. Their attentions were unremitting during the whole course of his sickness: and the family of Mr. Barnum could not have been more assiduous than they were in every possible effort to avert the fatal result of the accident which they so deeply deplored. The strongest hopes were entertained of the recovery of Mr. Keep until Monday last, when symptoms of mortification appeared, which terminated in his death. This statement has been submitted to the family of the deceased, and meets their approbation.—*Baltimore Chronicle.* [CG, Sat., 14 AUG 1830, p. 3]

DIED, on Saturday evening, the 14th inst. [i.e. 14 AUG 1830], a little before 8 o'clock, at his late residence in this city, Gen. PHILIP STUART, in the 71st year of his age ... *National Intelligencer.* [CG, Tues., 17 AUG 1830, p. 3]

MARRIED, on Wednesday evening last [i.e. 18 AUG 1830], by the Rev. W.W. Wallace, Mr. EDWARD W. COLLINS, to Miss MARTHA B. CLAXTON, all of this town. [CG, Sat., 21 AUG 1830, p. 3]

DIED, in Washington, on the 19th inst. [i.e. 19 AUG 1830], Mr. JOHN B. MARKWARD, in the 29th year of his age. [CG, Sat., 21 AUG 1830, p. 3]

DIED, at Alexandria, D.C., on Saturday the 17th inst. [i.e. 14? AUG 1830], after thirteen days illness, in the fifty-fifth year of his age, Mr. JAMES ENGLISH, for many years a respectable merchant of that place; a man who bore the ills of life without a murmur; the same in prosperity and adversity. He died as he had lived, calmly—resigned to his fate. [CG, Sat., 21 AUG 1830, p. 3]

DIED, on Saturday, the 14th inst. [i.e. 14 AUG 1830], at his late residence in Prince George's Co., Md., THOMAS MAGRUDER, Esq., in the 54th year of his age. [CG, Sat., 21 AUG 1830, p. 3]

MARRIED, in Washington, on Thursday, the 19th inst. [i.e. 19 AUG 1830], by the Rev. Mr. Ryland, Mr. WILLIAM A. REEDER, of Georgetown, to Miss ELIZABETH POWERS, of Washington City. [CG, Tues., 24 AUG 1830, p. 3]

DIED, at N.Y., on Sunday evening [i.e. 22 AUG 1830], in the 90th year of his age, Col. MARINUS WILET, a patriot of the Revolution, and a most upright and estimable citizen. [CG, Thurs., 26 AUG 1830, p. 3]

DIED, on the 8th August [i.e. 8 AUG 1830], near the Sweet Springs, Va., WILLIAM H. PETER, a Midshipman in the Navy of the U.S., in the 24th year of his age. He had been suffering for 12 months under a rapid pulmonary disease, contracted on the Mediterranean station, and had gone to the Virginia Springs with a delusive hope of an amendment of his health. [CG, Thurs., 26 AUG 1830, p. 3]

Georgetown, D.C., **Marriage and Death Notices, 1801-1838**

DIED, at Fort Armstrong, Rock Island, Upper Mississippi, on the 27th July ult. [i.e. 27 JUL 1830], Dr. JOHN GALE, Surgeon U.S. Army, aged 33 years—an officer whose medical skill was surpassed by few of his profession. [CG, Thurs., 26 AUG 1830, p. 3]

DIED, on the 12th inst. [i.e. 12 AUG 1830], at his residence on the Sassafras river, the Rev. SAMUEL SITGREAVES, Rector of St. Steven's Parish, Cecil, and Shrewsbury Parish, Kent, Md. Mr. Sitgreaves was a son of the late Hon. Samuel Sitgreaves, formerly a distinguished member of Congress from Philadelphia. [CG, Thurs., 26 AUG 1830, p. 3]

MARRIED, at Cincinnati, Ohio, on the 17th inst. [i.e. 17 AUG 1830], Mr. GEORGE A. BENDER, of Hagerstown, Md., to Miss JEMIMA HALES, youngest daughter of Col. Charles Hales. [CG, Sat., 28 AUG 1830, p. 3]

MARRIED, at West River, Md., on the 24th inst. [i.e. 24 AUG 1830], WILLIAM STEWART, Esq., of Philadelphia, to KATHARINE, daughter of the late Com. A. Murray. [CG, Tues., 31 AUG 1830, p. 3]

MARRIED, at New Orleans, on the 29th ult. [i.e. 29 JUL 1830], Gen. ELEAZER W. RIPLEY, of East Feliciana, to Mrs. AURELIA DAVIS, of the parish of St. Francisville. [CG, Tues., 31 AUG 1830, p. 3]

MARRIED, on Wednesday, the 7th July [i.e. 7 JUL 1830], at Swansea, Wales, by Dr. Cohen, under the special sanction of the Very Rev. Dr. Solomon Hirschel, DAVID I. COHEN, Esq., of Baltimore, U.S.A., to HARRIET T., daughter of the late Jacob Cohen, Esq. [CG, Thurs., 2 SEP 1830, p. 3]

MARRIED, in Washington, on the 26th ult. [i.e. 26 AUG 1830], Mr. GILBERT D. KEAN, to Mrs. HARRIET R. JONES, all of that City. [CG, Thurs., 2 SEP 1830, p. 3]

MARRIED, in Baltimore, on the 31st ult. [i.e. 31 AUG 1830], Mr. JOHN J. BERRET, to Miss LAURA HOPKINSON, daughter of the late Francis Hopkinson, Esq., all of that city. [CG, Sat., 4 SEP 1830, p. 3]

DIED, at his residence on the heights of Georgetown, on the night of the 30th ult. [i.e. 30 AUG 1830], JOHN THRELKELD, Esq., in the 73d year of his age. Being born and having resided during his life on the spot where he died, and having always indulged in a frank and unreserved intercourse with society, his merits are so generally known and appreciated, that eulogium may be superfluous ... Before the separation of this County from Md., he represented his fellow citizens in the Legislature of that State. Subsequently for many years, and up to the period of his death, he was in the Commission of the Peace and a member of the Levy Court ... It will be recollected, by many, that some years since, while yet in the enjoyment of his patrimonial estates, on the occasion of a severe winter, and much apprehended suffering, on the part of the poor, from the scarcity of fuel, besides his own numerous direct charities to the sufferers, he gave to those benevolent citizens who actively interested themselves on the occasion, the unlimited use of his woods ... A few days before his death he was in active and hale health, and gave a promise of lengthened life: and has since fallen a victim to imprudent exposure, and an insuperable aversion to medical relief ... [CG, Sat., 4 SEP 1830, p. 3]

DIED, on Sunday, July 4th [i.e. 4 JUL 1830], at her house in Upper George Street, Montague Square, London, at the age of 84 years, Mrs. ANNE PENN, relict of the late John Penn, Esq., formerly Governor, and one of the hereditary proprietors of Pa. [CG, Tues., 7 SEP 1830, p. 3]

DIED, at Norfolk, on the 28th ult. [i.e. 28 AUG 1830], Dr. GEORGE BALFOUR, in the 60th year of his age. [CG, Tues., 7 SEP 1830, p. 3]

DIED, in Baltimore, on the 3d inst. [i.e. 3 SEP 1830], in the 56th year of his age, HALL HARRISON, Esq., merchant of the firm of *Harrison & Sterett*. [CG, Tues., 7 SEP 1830, p. 3]

DIED, in Annapolis, on the 31st ult. [i.e. 31 AUG 1830], in the 23d year of her age, Mrs. JANETTA WELLS, consort of George Wells, Jr., Esq. [CG, Tues., 7 SEP 1830, p. 3]

DIED, on the 31st ult. [i.e. 31 AUG 1830], Mrs. LETITIA PHILLIPS, consort of Mr. John Phillips. [CG, Tues., 7 SEP 1830, p. 3]

MARRIED, in Washington, on the 7th inst. [i.e. 7 SEP 1830], Mr. MICHAEL LOMAX, of Fredericksburg, Va., to Miss SOPHRONIA A. SMITH, of Alexandria. [CG, Thurs., 9 SEP 1830, p. 3]

MARRIED, in Washington, the 2d inst. [i.e. 2 SEP 1830], Mr. CHARLES GREEN, of Alexandria, D.C., to Miss ELIZABETH JANE HAISLIP, of Charles Co., Md. [CG, Thurs., 9 SEP 1830, p. 3]

MARRIED, at St. Michael's Church, Liverpool, on the 29th July last [i.e. 29 JUL 1830], HUGH CHARLES SMITH, Esq., of Alexandria, to ISABELLA, third daughter of Archibald Keightly, of that place. [CG, Thurs., 9 SEP 1830, p. 3]

MARRIED, in Claremont, N.H., on the 30th ult. [i.e. 30 AUG 1830], JOSEPH THORNTON ADAMS, Esq., Editor of the *Boston Centinel*, to Miss SUSAN P. JARVIS, daughter of Dr. Leonard Jarvis, of Claremont. [CG, Thurs., 9 SEP 1830, p. 3]

DIED, at Elk Ridge, Md., on the 4th inst. [i.e. 4 SEP 1830], WILLIAM S. MOORE, Esq., formerly a respectable Merchant of Baltimore. [CG, Thurs., 9 SEP 1830, p. 3]

DIED, on the 6th inst. [i.e. 6 SEP 1830], at Cooperstown, N.Y., HARRIET, wife of the Rev. C.S. Stewart, of the U.S. Navy ... The foundation of the disease which has brought her to an early grave, was laid at the Sandwich Islands, when a member, for three years, of the Christian Mission there. [CG, Tues., 14 SEP 1830, p. 3]

Georgetown, D.C., **Marriage and Death Notices, 1801-1838**

DIED, near the Navy Yard, Washington, on the 9th inst. [i.e. 9 SEP 1830], Mrs. CATHARINE CAMALIER, consort of Mr. Vincent Camalier. [CG, Tues., 14 SEP 1830, p. 3]

DIED, at the residence of her father, John Duvall, Esq., near Nottingham, Md., on the 25th July [i.e. 25 JUL 1830], in the 25th year of her age, Mrs. SUSAN B. SANGSTON, wife of Capt. John A. Sangston. [CG, Tues., 14 SEP 1830, p. 3]

DIED, in Washington, on the 7th inst. [i.e. 7 SEP 1830], JOHN H. RUNNELLS, Esq., Surgeon Dentist, aged 35 years, a native of Boston, but for some years a resident of Alexandria. [CG, Tues., 14 SEP 1830, p. 3]

DIED, at Portsmouth, N.H., on the 6th inst. [i.e. 6 SEP 1830], JOSHUA HAVEN, a very respectable Merchant of Philadelphia. [CG, Tues., 14 SEP 1830, p. 3]

DIED, in this town [no date], at the residence of his grand-mother, in the 25th year of his age, WARRINGTON FLEET, a resident of Washington. His complaint was of a pulmonary nature, and had confined him to his bed about three months. He was a colored man, endowed by nature with so many good qualities, that his death is sincerely lamented by others than those of his own caste, who chanced to know him. [CG, Tues., 14 SEP 1830, p. 3]

MARRIED, on the 6th inst. [i.e. 6 SEP 1830], by the Rev. W.W. Wallace, Mr. WILLIAM B. SHEPPARD, to Miss MARY ANNA SOUTHALL, all of Georgetown, D.C. [CG, Thurs., 16 SEP 1830, p. 3]

MARRIED, at *Locust Grove*, Charles Co., Md., on the 9th inst. [i.e. 9 SEP 1830], PETER WOOD CRAIN, Esq., Attorney at Law, to Miss ELIZABETH JENIFER, only daughter of the late Thomas M. Fowler. [CG, Thurs., 16 SEP 1830, p. 3]

DIED, on Tuesday evening last [i.e. 14 SEP 1830], Mrs. JULIAN, wife of Mr. Tobias Nixdorff, in the 36th year of her age. Her friends and acquaintances are respectfully invited to attend her funeral, this evening, at four o'clock, from her late residence on High street. [CG, Thurs., 16 SEP 1830, p. 3]

DIED, in Washington City, on Sunday, September the 12th [i.e. 12 SEP 1830], after a short but severely painful illness, which was borne with the fortitude and resignation of a Christian, Mrs. SARAH A. MINOR, in the 41st year of her age. [CG, Thurs., 16 SEP 1830, p. 3]

Departed this life, in the 36th year of his age, at Fairfax, in Culpeper Co., ROBERT PATTON, Esq., of Fredericksburg: His death was occasioned by hemorrhage from the lungs, commencing on the evening of the 11th, and recurring, at intervals, from that period until he expired, on the morning of the 13th [i.e. 13 SEP 1830]. He left home but a few days since, in his usual health, on a visit to Culpeper; whither he was drawn, by the session of the Superior Court, on professional business. [CG, Thurs., 16 SEP 1830, p. 3]

Georgetown, D.C., **Marriage and Death Notices, 1801-1838**

DIED, at *Milton Hill*, Charles Co., Md., on the 3d inst. [i.e. 3 SEP 1830], Mrs. MARY G. HEARD, consort of Edward I. Heard, Esq., in the 47th year of her age. [CG, Thurs., 16 SEP 1830, p. 3]

DIED, at Wilmington, Del. [no date], SAMUEL S. GRUBB, Esq., in the 28th year of his age. [CG, Thurs., 16 SEP 1830, p. 3]

MARRIED, in Washington, on the 16th inst. [i.e. 16 SEP 1830], Mr. NELSON JARBOE, to Miss CATHRINE, daughter of Mr. John O. Moore, of Pa. [CG, Tues., 21 SEP 1830, p. 3]

DIED, in this Town, early on Saturday morning, the 18th inst. [i.e. 18 SEP 1830], of the Croup, MARGARET ELIZABETH, youngest child of John B. and Rebecca A. Gray, aged 17 months and 8 days. [CG, Tues., 21 SEP 1830, p. 3]

DIED, at his residence on Mill Creek, S.C., on the 4th inst. [i.e. 4 SEP 1830], the Hon. ROBERT STARK, Secretary of State of South Carolina, in the 68th year of his age. [CG, Tues., 21 SEP 1830, p. 3]

DIED, in Fairfax Co., Va., on the 14th inst. [i.e. 14 SEP 1830], THOMAS LINDSAY, Esq., in the 80th year of his age. [CG, Tues., 21 SEP 1830, p. 3]

MARRIED, at Port Mahon, on the 16th July [i.e. 16 JUL 1830], Lieut. E. RIDGEWAY, of the U.S. Navy, to the Senorita MARIA RUSI, eldest daughter of George T. Ladico, Esq., U.S. Consul at that place. Mr. HORATIO N. ROBINSON, of N.J., to Miss CATALINA BUSQUET, youngest daughter of Gen. Busquet, of the Spanish Army. [CG, Sat., 25 SEP 1830, p. 2]

MARRIED, in Alexandria, on the 21st inst. [i.e. 21 SEP 1830], THOMAS ROGERS, Esq., to Miss E.S. CHAMBLIN, daughter of Charles Chamblin, Esq., both of Loudoun Co., Va. [CG, Sat., 25 SEP 1830, p. 2]

DIED, at Buffalo, N.Y., on the 8th inst. [i.e. 8 SEP 1830], MYNDERT M. DOX, Esq., late Collector of that port, and a Captain in the U.S. Army, during the late war. [CG, Sat., 25 SEP 1830, p. 2]

DIED, at Wapatomaka, Ohio [no date], Maj. JONATHAN CASS, father of Gov. Cass. [CG, Sat., 25 SEP 1830, p. 2]

MARRIED, in Washington, on the 23d inst. [i.e. 23 SEP 1830], Lieut. GEORGE D. RAMSAY, of the U.S. Army, to Miss FRANCES W. MUNROE, youngest daughter of Thomas Munroe, Esq. [CG, Tues., 28 SEP 1830, p. 2]

MARRIED, in Annapolis, on the 22d inst. [i.e. 22 SEP 1830], ALFRED W. CAVANLY, Esq., of Ill., to Miss SARAH A. WHETCROFT, of the former place. [CG, Tues., 28 SEP 1830, p. 2]

Georgetown, D.C., **Marriage and Death Notices, 1801-1838**

MARRIED, in Alexandria, on the 22d inst. [i.e. 22 SEP 1830], Mr. JOSEPH BOUIS, of Baltimore, to Miss ELIZA HUBHALL, of Alexandria. [CG, Tues., 28 SEP 1830, p. 2]

MARRIED, at the residence of Gen. William Clark, in Mo., on the 5th inst. [i.e. 5 SEP 1830], Maj. STEPHEN N. KEARNEY, of the U.S. Army, to Miss MARY RADFORD. [CG, Tues., 28 SEP 1830, p. 2]

Another Revolutionary Patriot Gone! Departed this life, at his residence in Prince George's Co., Md., on the 16th inst. [i.e. 16 SEP 1830], Col. JOSEPH CROSS, in the 75th year of his age. Of him it may be truly said, as it was of the Chevalier Bayard, that "he was a man without fear and without reproach." [CG, Tues., 28 SEP 1830, p. 2]

DIED, a few days ago, at Mrs. Clarke's, in Albemarle, Hon. GEORGE HAY, U.S. Judge for the Eastern District of Virginia, and son-in-law of James Monroe, late President of the United States. A letter received in Washington, on Sunday, announces the decease, on Thursday last, the 23d inst. [i.e. 23 SEP 1830], at the family residence in Loudoun Co., Va., of Mrs. MONROE, the respected consort of Ex-President Monroe. [CG, Tues., 28 SEP 1830, p. 2]

DIED, at the Navy Yard Hill, Washington, on the 21st inst. [i.e. 21 SEP 1830], Mr. VALENTINE CONNER, aged 39 years. [CG, Tues., 28 SEP 1830, p. 2]

DIED, on the 20th inst. [i.e. 20 SEP 1830], Mrs. ANN CARROLL, relict of the late Nicholas Carroll, Esq., of Annapolis, in the 69th year of her age. [CG, Tues., 28 SEP 1830, p. 2]

DIED, on the 14th inst. [i.e. 14 SEP 1830], in the County of Hanover, Va., at the advanced age of 87 years, Mrs. LUCY NELSON, widow of the distinguished Revolutionary Patriot, Gen. Thomas Nelson, of Virginia. Mrs. N. left, at the time of her death, 119 descendants living. [CG, Tues., 28 SEP 1830, p. 2]

DIED, at the residence of her father, near Manchester, S.C., on the 14th inst. [i.e. 14 SEP 1830], Mrs. MARY REBECCA McDUFFIE, consort of the Hon. George McDuffie, and daughter of Richard Singleton, Esq. [CG, Tues., 28 SEP 1830, p. 2]

MARRIED, on Tuesday evening last, the 28th inst. [i.e. 28 SEP 1830], by the Rev. Mr. Vanlomell, Mr. CHARLES HUTCHINS, to Mrs. CECELIA RAGAN, both of this place. [CG, Thurs., 30 SEP 1830, p. 3]

DIED, at Valparaiso, on the 8th April last [i.e. 8 APR 1830], of a pulmonary complaint, Mr. JOHN HOMANS, second son of the late Benjamin Homans, of the Navy Department, Washington; had he lived two days longer, he would have completed his 27th year ... He embarked in his usual health, in February 1829, on board the U.S. Frigate *Guerriere*, and held until the time of his death, the honorable and responsible station of Secretary to the Commander of the U.S. Naval forces in the Pacific ... His remains repose in the Protestant cemetery. [CG, Thurs., 30 SEP 1830, p. 3]

Georgetown, D.C., **Marriage and Death Notices, 1801-1838**

DIED, in Washington, on the 28th ult. [i.e. 28 SEP 1830], Mrs. MARY ORR, wife of the Rev. Isaac Orr. [CG, Sat., 2 OCT 1830, p. 3]

DIED, in Alexandria, on the 30th ult. [i.e. 30 SEP 1830], Mrs. JACOBINA McCUTCHEN, aged 80 years, a native of Scotland. [CG, Sat., 2 OCT 1830, p. 3]

DIED, at *Stony Point*, the residence of his son, near Yorktown, Va., on the 22d ult. [i.e. 22 SEP 1830], in the 72d year of his age, DAVID MEADE RANDOLPH, Esq., formerly Marshal of Virginia, who in the days of his prosperity was as remarkable for his hospitality as for the manners of an urbane gentleman. He contributed much, both in person and purse, to the promotion of our Revolution. He died suddenly of gout to the stomach. [CG, Sat., 2 OCT 1830, p. 3]

MARRIED, in Washington, on the 26th ult. [i.e. 26 SEP 1830], Mr. JOHN KELLY, to Miss MARIA McPHEARSON. [CG, Tues., 5 OCT 1830, p. 3]

MARRIED, in Washington, on the 12th ult. [i.e. 12 SEP 1830], Mr. PETER HALL, to Miss SUSAN GATES, both of Alexandria. [CG, Tues., 5 OCT 1830, p. 3]

MARRIED, in Alexandria, on Thursday morning last [i.e. 30 SEP 1830], Mr. JOHN F.M. LOWE, of Prince George's Co., Md., to Mrs. SOPHIA E. LEONARD, daughter of the late Abraham Faw, Esq., of Alexandria. [CG, Tues., 5 OCT 1830, p. 3]

MARRIED, on Thursday evening last [i.e. 30 SEP 1830], Mr. FRANCIS RUTHERFORD, to Miss FRANCES TOLER. [CG, Tues., 5 OCT 1830, p. 3]

MARRIED, on Thursday evening last [i.e. 30 SEP 1830], Mr. JOSEPH GRIMES, to Mrs. MARGARET BARNES, all of Alexandria. [CG, Tues., 5 OCT 1830, p. 3]

DIED, in Washington, on the 2d inst. [i.e. 2 OCT 1830], Mrs. MARGARET CAREY, aged 73 years. [CG, Tues., 5 OCT 1830, p. 3]

DIED, at Pensacola, on the 10th ult. [i.e. 10 SEP 1830], after a few days illness, of Yellow Fever, Lieut. CARY H. HANSFORD, U.S. Navy, of Norfolk, in the 24th year of his age. [CG, Tues., 5 OCT 1830, p. 3]

MARRIED, in Washington, on Thursday evening, the 7th inst. [i.e. 7 OCT 1830], by the Rev. F.S. Evans, Mr. LEMUEL WILLIAMS, to Miss LYDIA BATES, all of that city. [CG, Tues., 12 OCT 1830, p. 3]

DIED, at Boston, on Sunday [i.e. 3? OCT 1830], JOHN P. BOYD, Naval Officer, for the port of Boston and Charlestown, and formerly Brigadier General in the army of the U.S. [CG, Tues., 12 OCT 1830, p. 3]

DIED, in Washington, on Sunday morning [i.e. 10 OCT 1830], Mrs. MARY G. BRADLEY, daughter of William J. Hall, of Alexandria, deceased, and relict of Abraham Bradley, Jr. [CG, Tues., 12 OCT 1830, p. 3]

Georgetown, D.C., **Marriage and Death Notices, 1801-1838**

DIED, on Sunday afternoon [i.e. 10 OCT 1830], Capt. PETER MILLS, a native of N.Y., and an Officer of the Revolution, aged 104 years. [CG, Tues., 12 OCT 1830, p. 3]

DIED, on September 19 [i.e. 19 SEP 1830], in Mercer Co., Ky., Col. GABRIEL SLAUGHTER, formerly Lieut. Governor, and for near four years, acting Governor of Kentucky. [CG, Tues., 12 OCT 1830, p. 3]

MARRIED, at *Rock Hill*, on the 12th inst. [i.e. 12 OCT 1830], by the Rev. Mr. Hawley, Mr. JOHN B. HOLMEAD, to Miss JANE J., eldest daughter of Thomas W. Pairo, Esq., all of that District. [CG, Sat., 16 OCT 1830, p. 3]

DIED, in Alexandria, on the 7th inst. [i.e. 7 OCT 1830], in the 28th year of his age, Mr. JAMES MATTHEWS, a native of Scotland, but for several years past a respectable resident of that town. [CG, Sat., 16 OCT 1830, p. 3]

MARRIED, in Washington, on Tuesday the 12th inst. [i.e. 12 OCT 1830], Mr. ROBERT T. RAMSAY, to Mrs. ELIZA MARBURY, both of Alexandria. [CG, Thurs., 21 OCT 1830, p. 3]

DIED, in Washington, on Monday morning [i.e. 18 OCT 1830], after a painful illness of ten days, Mr. WILLIAM BLAIR, a Clerk in the General Post Office, and brother-in-law to Judge McLean. He was amiable, pious, and exemplary in the relations which render man valuable. He left a disconsolate widow and four children. [CG, Thurs., 21 OCT 1830, p. 3]

DIED, at Port Tobacco, Md., on the 15th inst. [i.e. 15 OCT 1830], of bilious fever, after an illness of nine days, Mr. JAMES WILSON, Printer, of Washington City. His loss is much lamented by his numerous relatives. [CG, Thurs., 21 OCT 1830, p. 3]

MARRIED, in Washington, on the 18th inst. [i.e. 18 OCT 1830], Gen. DANIEL S. DONELSON, of Tenn., to Miss MARGARET, daughter of the Hon. John Branch, Secretary of the Navy. [CG, Sat., 23 OCT 1830, p. 3]

MARRIED, in Alexandria, on the 17th [i.e. 17 OCT 1830], Capt. ROBERT BURROWS, of Md., to Miss SOPHIA BROWN, of Alexandria. [CG, Sat., 23 OCT 1830, p. 3]

MARRIED, at Princeton, on the 19th inst. [i.e. 19 OCT 1830], W.K. McDONALD, Esq., of Alexandria, D.C., Attorney at Law, to HANNAH M., youngest daughter of Rev. James Carnahan, D.D., President of the College of New Jersey. [CG, Sat., 23 OCT 1830, p. 3]

DIED, on the 5th inst. [i.e. 5 OCT 1830], after a very severe illness of about two weeks, in the 68th year of his age, Maj. WILLIAM BROADUS, of Harper's Ferry. Major Broadus was a native of Culpeper Co., Va. In 1824, he obtained from President Monroe the appointment of Paymaster at Harper's Ferry, which post he held until his death, with credit to himself, and to the satisfaction of the people generally. [CG, Sat., 23 OCT 1830, p. 3]

DIED, in Fredericksburg, Va., on the 17th inst. [i.e. 17 OCT 1830], Mr. JOHN P. LITTLE, Merchant, aged 45. [CG, Sat., 23 OCT 1830, p. 3]

Georgetown, D.C., **Marriage and Death Notices, 1801-1838**

DIED, in Alexandria, on the 20th inst. [i.e. 20 OCT 1830], Mrs. ALICE L. WATERHOUSE. [CG, Sat., 23 OCT 1830, p. 3]

DIED, at Portsmouth, N.H., on the 28th Sept. [i.e. 28 SEP 1830], Col. JOHN LANGDON STORER. He has been for the last two years attached to the Department of the General Post Office in this city, where he had many friends, by whom his death will be sincerely deplored ... [CG, Sat., 23 OCT 1830, p. 3]

MARRIED, in Washington, on the 21st inst. [i.e. 21 OCT 1830], Mr. WALTER WARDER, to Miss ANN S., daughter of Joseph Gibson. [CG, Tues., 26 OCT 1830, p. 3]

MARRIED [no date]. Mr. ALEXANDER LAMMOND, to Miss MARGARET ANN McINTIRE, both of Alexandria. [CG, Tues., 26 OCT 1830, p. 3]

DIED, in Nanjemoy, Md., on the 16th inst. [i.e. 16 OCT 1830], Mrs. ELIZABETH SHEPHERD, relict of Capt. Thomas Shepherd, formerly of Charles Co., Md. [CG, Tues., 26 OCT 1830, p. 3]

DIED, in Philadelphia, on the 19th inst. [i.e. 19 OCT 1830], Mrs. ANN BROWN, wife of Hon. James Brown, our late Minister to France. [CG, Tues., 26 OCT 1830, p. 3]

MARRIED, in Washington, on the 23d inst. [i.e. 23 OCT 1830], Mr. WILLIAM THORN, to Miss HANNAH KING, both of that city. [CG, Thurs., 28 OCT 1830, p. 3]

DIED, in Alexandria, on the 22d inst. [i.e. 22 OCT 1830], Mr. SAMUEL BROWN, Ship Carpenter, in the 45th year of his age. [CG, Thurs., 28 OCT 1830, p. 3]

MARRIED, in Middleburg, Loudoun Co., Va., on the 21st inst. [i.e. 21 OCT 1830], Lieut. THOMAS S. HAMERSLEY, of the U.S. Navy, to Mrs. EMILY A. NOLAND. [CG, Sat., 30 OCT 1830, p. 3]

DIED, at Shawneetown, Ill., on the 14th inst. [i.e. 14 OCT 1830], after a painful illness of one week, the Hon. JOHN McLEAN, a Senator in Congress from that State. [CG, Sat., 30 OCT 1830, p. 3]

MARRIED, in Alexandria, on the 28th ult. [i.e. 28 OCT 1830], CHARLES L. POWELL, Esq., of Loudoun Co., Va., to Miss SELINA, eldest daughter of John Lloyd, Esq., of Alexandria. [CG, Tues., 2 NOV 1830, p. 3]

MARRIED, in Washington, on the 28th ult. [i.e. 28 OCT 1830], JOHN FAGAN, Esq., of N.Y., to Miss MARY H., daughter of the late George Ironside, Esq., of Washington. [CG, Tues., 2 NOV 1830, p. 3]

MARRIED, in Bladensburg, on the 26th ult. [i.e. 26 OCT 1830], Mr. ZADOK McKNEW, of Washington, to Miss ELIZABETH ANN, daughter of E. Evans, Esq., of the former place. [CG, Tues., 2 NOV 1830, p. 3]

Georgetown, D.C., **Marriage and Death Notices, 1801-1838**

MARRIED, in Washington, on Monday evening last [i.e. 1 NOV 1830], Mr. BEVERLEY C. SANDERS, to Miss CHARLOTTE, daughter of the late Toppan Webster, Esq. [CG, Thurs., 4 NOV 1830, p. 3]

DIED, at his residence in the Territory of Arkansas, on the 16th September [i.e. 16 SEP 1830], EDWARD W. DUVAL, Esq., aged about 40 years, formerly of Washington, and late Indian Agent for the Cherokees. [CG, Thurs., 4 NOV 1830, p. 3]

DIED, at New Orleans, on the 14th ult. [i.e. 14 OCT 1830], after a painful illness of eleven days, Mr. THOMAS LEE, (of the firm of *T. & G.M. Lee*), a native of the city of Baltimore, and for several years a respectable inhabitant of N. Orleans. [CG, Thurs., 4 NOV 1830, p. 3]

DIED, on the 14th ult. [i.e. 14 OCT 1830], after a long and painful disease, Mr. ZENON ROMAN, a brother of the governor elect of this state [Louisiana] ... [CG, Thurs., 4 NOV 1830, p. 3]

DIED, at Cincinnati, Ohio, on the 23d ult. [i.e. 23 OCT 1830], in the 40th year of her age, Mrs. MARGARET BECK, wife of Truman Beck, Hatter. She was a native of Georgetown, D.C. [CG, Sat., 6 NOV 1830, p. 3]

DIED, on Sunday night, the 7th inst. [i.e. 7 NOV 1830], Mrs. REBECCA M.K. RIND, consort of Mr. Samuel S. Rind. The friends and acquaintances of the deceased are respectfully invited to attend the funeral this afternoon, at half past 2 o'clock, from the residence of Mr. Wm. A. Rind, sen., on Cherry Street. [CG, Tues., 9 NOV 1830, p. 3]

MARRIED, in this town, on Thursday last [i.e. 4 NOV 1830], Col. JAMES KEARNEY, U.S. Topographical Engineer, to Miss LOUISA O'REILY, daughter of the late Henry O'Reily, Esq. [CG, Thurs., 11 NOV 1830, p. 3]

MARRIED, in Washington, on Thursday evening [i.e. 4 NOV 1830], Mr. WILLIAM A. GORDON, of the War Department, to Miss GLORVINA BLAKE, daughter of the late Dr. James H. Blake. [CG, Thurs., 11 NOV 1830, p. 3]

MARRIED, on Thursday evening [i.e. 4 NOV 1830], Mr. THOMAS K. GRAY, to Miss ELEANOR NALLY, both of Washington. [CG, Thurs., 11 NOV 1830, p. 3]

MARRIED, in Washington, on Sunday evening [i.e. 7 NOV 1830], Mr. ISRAEL STEWART, to Miss ELIZA WAYSON, both of that place. [CG, Thurs., 11 NOV 1830, p. 3]

MARRIED, in Alexandria, on Thursday evening [i.e. 4 NOV 1830], Mr. FRANCIS BURDETT JONES, of N.Y., to Miss HARRIET WRIGHT, of Alexandria. [CG, Thurs., 11 NOV 1830, p. 3]

MARRIED, on Thursday evening [i.e. 4 NOV 1830], Mr. JOHN W. KING, to Miss ANN CHILDS, both of Alexandria. [CG, Thurs., 11 NOV 1830, p. 3]

MARRIED, on Thursday evening [i.e. 4 NOV 1830], Mr. GEORGE GLASGOW, to Miss HANNAH JACOBS, both of Alexandria. [CG, Thurs., 11 NOV 1830, p. 3]

MARRIED, on Tuesday, 2d inst. [i.e. 2 NOV 1830], THOMAS S. HERBERT, M.D., to Miss CAMILLA A., daughter of the late Denton Hammond, Esq., all of Anne Arundel Co., Md. [CG, Thurs., 11 NOV 1830, p. 3]

MARRIED, on Tuesday, 2d inst. [i.e. 2 NOV 1830], Mr. EDWARD W. OWEN, to Miss ELIZABETH ANN, only daughter of Nathaniel [Clagget], Esq., all of Montgomery Co., Md. [CG, Thurs., 11 NOV 1830, p. 3]

DIED, at North Bend, Ohio, on the 30th ult. [i.e. 30 OCT 1830], JOHN CLEVES SYMMES HARRISON, Esq., aged 32, eldest son of Gen. Wm. H. Harrison. He died at his father's residence, after an illness of a few days, from which no danger was apprehended until a few hours before his death. He was a much esteemed and most excellent citizen, in the prime of youth and manhood. His afflicted widow is the only child of Gen. Z.M. Pike. [CG, Thurs., 11 NOV 1830, p. 3]

MARRIED, in Washington, on Thursday, the 11th inst. [i.e. 11 NOV 1830], by the Rev. Dr. Matthews, Mr. CHARLES STRAHAN, of that city, to Miss SUSAN H. SWEENY, daughter of the late George Sweeny, Esq., of Prince William Co., Va. [CG, Sat., 13 NOV 1830, p. 3]

DIED, at his residence in Montgomery Co., Md., on Thursday morning, Nov. 4, 1830, Mr. PATRICK ORME, aged 61 years 9 months and 27 days. In early life the deceased became a subject of the renovating influence of Divine grace ... [CG, Sat., 13 NOV 1830, p. 3]

DIED, in Fredericksburg, on Monday morning, the 8th inst. [i.e. 8 NOV 1830], in the 35th year of her age, Mrs. SARAH ANN MILLER, consort of Benjamin M. Miller, leaving a husband and two children to mourn their irreparable loss ... [CG, Sat., 13 NOV 1830, p. 3]

MARRIED, at Easton, Talbot Co., Md., on Tuesday, the 9th inst. [i.e. 9 NOV 1830], the Rev. STEPHEN B. BALCH, of this town, to Mrs. JANE PARROTT, of Easton, and formerly of Georgetown. [CG, Thurs., 18 NOV 1830, p. 3]

MARRIED, in Philadelphia, on Thursday evening last [i.e. 11 NOV 1830], by the Right Rev. Bishop White, CHARLES H. CARTER, Esq., of Va., to ROSALIE EUGENIA, daughter of George Calvert, Esq., of Prince George's Co., Md. [CG, Thurs., 18 NOV 1830, p. 3]

MARRIED, in Boston, on the 4th inst. [i.e. 4 NOV 1830], WILLIAM LEE, Esq., late 2nd Auditor of the Treasury Department, Washington, to Mrs. ANN McLEAN, widow of the late John McLean, Esq. [CG, Thurs., 18 NOV 1830, p. 3]

MARRIED, at *Friendship*, near Georgetown, on Thursday evening, the 18th inst. [i.e. 18 NOV 1830], by the Rev. Mr. Brooke, Mr. MAYNADIER MASON, to Miss MARY VIRGINIA FRENCH, daughter of the late Mr. Charles French. [CG, Sat., 20 NOV 1830, p. 3]

Georgetown, D.C., **Marriage and Death Notices, 1801-1838**

MARRIED, in Washington, on the 17th inst. [i.e. 17 NOV 1830], JOHN R. NOURSE, son of Col. Michael Nourse, to Miss LUCRETIA C. SKINNER, youngest daughter of the Rev. I.L. Skinner. [CG, Sat., 20 NOV 1830, p. 3]

MARRIED, in Alexandria, on the 16th inst. [i.e. 16 NOV 1830], Mr. JOHN MUIR, of that place, to Miss LYDIA ROBINSON, of Fauquier Co., Va. [CG, Sat., 20 NOV 1830, p. 3]

MARRIED, in Alexandria [no date], Mr. IGNATIUS CARUSI, to Miss MARY JANE HOLLEYWOOD, both of Alexandria. [CG, Sat., 20 NOV 1830, p. 3]

DIED, at Rockville, Md., on Tuesday evening, 16th inst. [i.e. 16 NOV 1830], Miss CATHERINE CLEMENTS, daughter of the late Bennett Clements, after a protracted illness, which she endured with great resignation. [CG, Sat., 20 NOV 1830, p. 3]

DIED, in Washington, on Thursday, 18th inst. [i.e. 18 NOV 1830], Mr. LOUIS F. SMITH, Jeweller and Silversmith, aged 25 years, formerly of Baltimore. [CG, Sat., 20 NOV 1830, p. 3]

MARRIED, in Washington, on the 18th inst. [i.e. 18 NOV 1830], Mr. CHRISTOPHER LANSDAL, to JULIA ANN WELLS, both of that place. [CG, Tues., 23 NOV 1830, p. 3]

DIED, in Washington, on the 19th inst. [i.e. 19 NOV 1830], JOHN R. SMITH, Esq., of Philadelphia, brother of Samuel H. Smith, Esq., the President of the U.S. Branch Bank. [CG, Tues., 23 NOV 1830, p. 3]

DIED, on the 3d inst. [i.e. 3 NOV 1830], SAMUEL HARRISON, Esq., aged 84 years. [CG, Tues., 23 NOV 1830, p. 3]

DIED, in Va., on the 12th inst. [i.e. 12 NOV 1830], WILLIAM DANDRIDGE, Esq., late Cashier of the Bank of Virginia. [CG, Tues., 23 NOV 1830, p. 3]

MARRIED, at Newburgh, on the 9th inst. [i.e. 9 NOV 1830], Lieut. EDWARD C. ROSS, Assistant Professor of Mathematics, U.S. Military Academy, to ANN DEWITT, youngest daughter of the late Gen. James Clinton. [CG, Thurs., 25 NOV 1830, p. 3]

MARRIED, in Baltimore, on the 20th inst. [i.e. 20 NOV 1830], JOHN H. JANNEY, Esq., of Alexandria, to Miss MARGARET, daughter of the late Jesse Tyson, of Baltimore. [CG, Thurs., 25 NOV 1830, p. 3]

MARRIED, in Prince George's Co., Md., on the 21st inst. [i.e. 21 NOV 1830], Mr. PETER Q. BARTLETT, to Miss LABINA EMERSON, both of Alexandria. [CG, Thurs., 25 NOV 1830, p. 3]

DIED, in Baltimore, suddenly, on Saturday morning last [i.e. 20 NOV 1830], Lieut. JONATHAN W. SHERBURNE, of the U.S. Navy. [CG, Thurs., 25 NOV 1830, p. 3]

Georgetown, D.C., **Marriage and Death Notices, 1801-1838**

DIED, in Washington [no date], Mrs. MARY PETER, wife of Mr. Wm. Peter, in the 56th year of her age. [CG, Thurs., 25 NOV 1830, p. 3]

DIED [no date]. Mr. JOHN CALNAN[2]. [CG, Thurs., 25 NOV 1830, p. 3]

MARRIED, in Washington [no date], by the Rev. Mr. Danforth, Mr. JOHN CLOKEY, to Miss MARCIA STANDAGE. [CG, Sat., 27 NOV 1830, p. 3]

MARRIED, in this town, on Thursday evening, the 18th inst. [i.e. 18 NOV 1830], by the Rev. Mr. Vanlommel, Mr. GEORGE W. VARNELL, of Alexandria, to Miss MARY A.C. GIBSON, of this place. [CG, Sat., 27 NOV 1830, p. 3]

MARRIED, in Prince George's Co., Md., on the 23d inst. [i.e. 23 NOV 1830], Mr. CLEMENT B. HILL, to Mrs. ANN MARIA BERRY, both of that county. [CG, Sat., 27 NOV 1830, p. 3]

DIED, at Vincent's Orphan Asylum, on the 24th inst. [i.e. 24 NOV 1830], Sister MARY JAMES, (Catherine Cecilia Tyler, of Boston,) in the 19th year of her age. [CG, Sat., 27 NOV 1830, p. 3]

MARRIED, on the 25th inst. [i.e. 25 NOV 1830], by the Rev. Mr. Vanlommel, Mr. WILLIAM P. SHAW, merchant, Georgetown, to Miss MARY ELEANOR GANNON, both of the same place. [CG, Tues., 30 NOV 1830, p. 3]

DIED, at Norfolk, Va., on the 25th inst. [i.e. 25 NOV 1830], in the 52d year of his age, Col. ANDREW J. McCONNICO, Postmaster of that place. [CG, Tues., 30 NOV 1830, p. 3]

DIED, at Dayton, Ohio, on the 18th ult. [i.e. 18 NOV 1830], Gen. WILLIAM M. SMITH, Attorney at Law, and Representative elect in the next Legislature. [CG, Thurs., 2 DEC 1830, p. 3]

DIED, in Prince William Co., Va., on the 19th ult. [i.e. 19 NOV 1830], Mrs. CLARINDA SCOTT, in the 56th year of her age, formerly a resident of Alexandria, and widow of Jesse Scott, for many years a merchant in Dumfries. [CG, Thurs., 2 DEC 1830, p. 3]

DIED, at Norfolk, Va., on the 27th ult. [i.e. 27 NOV 1830], Capt. JOHN MYERS, aged 42, eldest son of Moses Myers, Esq., and formerly a merchant in Baltimore. [CG, Thurs., 2 DEC 1830, p. 3]

DIED, at Boston, on Saturday last [i.e. 27 NOV 1830], the Hon. AARON HILL, formerly Postmaster of that city. [CG, Sat., 4 DEC 1830, p. 3]

DIED, at Chicago, Ill. [no date], Dr. ALEXANDER WOLCOTT, U.S. Indian Agent at that place. [CG, Sat., 4 DEC 1830, p. 3]

---

[2] The *National Intelligencer*, of 23 NOV 1830, notes that Mr Calnan died in Washington on Nov 22nd

Georgetown, D.C., **Marriage and Death Notices, 1801-1838**

DIED, in this town, yesterday morning [i.e. 8 DEC 1830], after a long illness, Mr. ANDREW M. KIRK, of the Treasury Department, aged 35 years. His friends and acquaintances are respectfully invited to attend his funeral, without further invitation, from his residence in Cherry Alley, this afternoon, at half past 3 o'clock. [CG, Thurs., 9 DEC 1830, p. 3]

DIED, in Alexandria, on Sunday last [i.e. 5 DEC 1830], Mr. JOHN FRANCIS WISE, in the 26th year of his age. [CG, Thurs., 9 DEC 1830, p. 3]

MARRIED, in Alexandria, on the 7th inst. [i.e. 7 DEC 1830], JOHN H. MARBURY, Esq., of Prince George's Co., Md., to Miss ELIZA C. FENDALL, youngest daughter of Capt. B.T. Fendall, of Alexandria. [CG, Sat., 11 DEC 1830, p. 3]

MARRIED, on the 2d inst. [i.e. 2 DEC 1830], by the Rev. L.I. Gilliss, Mr. JAMES MAGRUDER, Jr., to Miss ELIZABETH A.T. RIGGS, all of Montgomery Co., Md. [CG, Sat., 11 DEC 1830, p. 3]

DIED, in Washington City, yesterday morning [i.e. 10 DEC 1830], Mrs. CAROLINE CATHARINE, wife of Capt. Joseph L. Kuhn, of the U.S. Marine Corps. The friends of Capt. K. are respectfully invited to attend the funeral, which will take place, from his residence, tomorrow, at 1 o'clock, P.M. [CG, Sat., 11 DEC 1830, p. 3]

DIED, at New London, Conn., on the 3d inst. [i.e. 3 DEC 1830], Mrs. SARAH PERRY, widow of the late Christopher R. Perry, and mother of the late Com. O.H. Perry, of the U.S. Navy. [CG, Sat., 11 DEC 1830, p. 3]

DIED, in Nansemond Co., Va., on the 29th ult. [i.e. 29 NOV 1830], Dr. PHILLIP BARRAND, in the 73d year of his age; an eminent physician and highly respected citizen of Norfolk for many years. [CG, Sat., 11 DEC 1830, p. 3]

DIED, at Norfolk, Va., on the 4th inst. [i.e. 4 DEC 1830], COPELAND PARKER, Esq., Surveyor of the Customs for that port. [CG, Sat., 11 DEC 1830, p. 3]

DIED, in Alexandria, on the 8th inst. [i.e. 8 DEC 1830], Mrs. FANNY CHATHAM, in the 40th year of her age, consort of Mr. Henry Chatham. [CG, Sat., 11 DEC 1830, p. 3]

DIED, at his residence in Montgomery Co., Md., on the 2d inst. [i.e. 2 DEC 1830], THOMAS CRAMPHIN, aged 90 years and 10 months. [CG, Sat., 11 DEC 1830, p. 3]

MARRIED, in Washington, on Thursday last [i.e. 9 DEC 1830], Mr. JAMES JOHNSTON, to Miss MARY ANN B., the only daughter of Capt. Blunt, of Alexandria. [CG, Tues., 14 DEC 1830, p. 3]

DIED, at his residence in Amelia Co., on the 4th inst. [i.e. 4 DEC 1830], WILLIAM B. GILES, late Governor of Virginia, aged 69 years. [CG, Tues., 14 DEC 1830, p. 3]

DIED, in Alexandria, on the 3d inst. [i.e. 3 DEC 1830], Mrs. MARY ANN WISE, aged 66 years. [CG, Tues., 14 DEC 1830, p. 3]

Georgetown, D.C., **Marriage and Death Notices, 1801-1838**

DIED, in Albany, on Thursday morning last [i.e. 9 DEC 1830], Gen. MATTHEW TROTTER. Gen. T. was an officer of the Revolution; he was engaged with Gen. Peter Gansevoort and Col. Marinus Willet, at the battle of Fort Stanwix. He was subsequently, we believe, an Aid to Maj. Gen. Lord Stirling. At the close of the War he engaged in the mercantile business in that city, and was for some years Captain of a sloop which sailed between that city and New York. He held several places as one of the Municipal Authorities of that city. When Lafayette arrived in this Country, in 1824, Gen. Trotter was deputed, jointly with Gen. John H. Wendell, on behalf of the Corporation of Albany, to proceed to New York and invite him to the hospitalities of that city ... [CG, Thurs., 16 DEC 1830, p. 3]

DIED, in Annapolis, on Sunday morning last [i.e. 12 DEC 1830], the Rev. GEORGE WELLS, a Minister of the Associated Methodist Church, and long a resident of that city, after a tedious illness, during which he evinced the efficacy of the faith he had professed in softening a dying pillow. A large concourse attended his remains to the grave. [CG, Thurs., 16 DEC 1830, p. 3]

MARRIED, at Rockville, Md., on the 13th inst. [i.e. 13 DEC 1830], Mr. WILLIAM CLINE, to Miss ROSANNA N. WINDSOR, both of Alexandria. [CG, Sat., 18 DEC 1830, p. 3]

DIED, in Washington, on the 16th inst. [i.e. 16 DEC 1830], Col. SAMUEL HANSON, of Samuel, in the 78th year of his age. [CG, Sat., 18 DEC 1830, p. 3]

DIED, in Alexandria, on the 15th inst. [i.e. 15 DEC 1830], Mr. FRANCIS HAGAN, aged 76 years, a native of Fairfax Co., Va. [CG, Sat., 18 DEC 1830, p. 3]

MARRIED, at *Solona,* on Tuesday evening, the 21st inst. [i.e. 21 DEC 1830], by the Rev. J.L. Amiss, Mr. ALFRED G. CARTER, of Ky., to Miss ELIZABETH L. CARTER, daughter of Mrs. Ann B. Maffitt, of Fairfax Co., Va. [CG, Thurs., 23 DEC 1830, p. 3]

MARRIED, at the University of Virginia, on the 15th inst. [i.e. 15 DEC 1830], by the Rev. Mr. Bowman, Dr. GESSNER HARRISON, Professor of Ancient Languages, to Miss ELIZA, daughter of George Tucker, Esq., Professor of Moral Philosophy &c. [CG, Sat., 25 DEC 1830, p. 3]

MARRIED, in this town, on the 26th inst. [i.e. 26 DEC 1830], by the Rev. J.L. Amiss, Mr. JOSEPH DAW, to Miss ELIZABETH TRUEMAN, daughter of the late William Shanks, all of this town. [CG, Thurs., 30 DEC 1830, p. 3]

MARRIED, in Washington, on the 21st inst. [i.e. 21 DEC 1830], Mr. WILLIAM L. BAILEY, to Miss JANE ELIZA MOLDEN, both of Alexandria. [CG, Thurs., 30 DEC 1830, p. 3]

MARRIED, in Alexandria, on the 23d inst. [i.e. 23 DEC 1830], Mr. CHARLES TAYLOR, to Miss ROSETTA TATSAPAUGH, both of that place. [CG, Thurs., 30 DEC 1830, p. 3]

MARRIED [no date]. Mr. JOHN LANPHIER, of Middleburg, Va., to Miss ANN G. MARTIN, of Alexandria. [CG, Thurs., 30 DEC 1830, p. 3]

Georgetown, D.C., **Marriage and Death Notices, 1801-1838**

MARRIED, in Washington, on the 3d inst. [i.e. 3 JAN 1831], Mr. JAMES S. COLLARD, of Fairfax Co., Va., to Miss ELIZA BOSWELL, of the former place. [CG, Sat., 8 JAN 1831, p. 3]

MARRIED, at Norfolk, on Thursday evening, 30th ult. [i.e. 30 DEC 1830], the Hon. TIMOTHY CHILDS, Member of Congress for the State of N.Y., to Mrs. LOUISA S. DICKINSON, of Norfolk, Va. [CG, Sat., 8 JAN 1831, p. 3]

DIED, at Jerusalem, Palestine, on the 3d August last [i.e. 3 AUG 1830], CORNELIUS BRADFORD, Esq., American Consul at Lyons, France, and formerly of N.Y. [CG, Sat., 8 JAN 1831, p. 3]

DIED, at Fort Washington, on the 23d ult. [i.e. 23 DEC 1830], Mr. ANDREW LEWIS, a native of France, in the 79th year of his age. [CG, Sat., 8 JAN 1831, p. 3]

DIED, in Washington, on the 29th ult. [i.e. 29 DEC 1830], Mr. HONORE JULLIEN, aged 70; a native of France, and one of the first settlers in Washington. [CG, Sat., 8 JAN 1831, p. 3]

DIED, on the 30th ult. [i.e. 30 DEC 1830], Mrs. ELIZA B. PROUT, in the 21st year of her age, wife of Mr. Jonathan Prout, and eldest daughter of the late Samuel N. Smallwood, Esq. [CG, Sat., 8 JAN 1831, p. 3]

DIED, in Alexandria, on the 24th ult. [i.e. 24 DEC 1830], Mr. SAMUEL TENNESSON, in the 54th year of his age. [CG, Sat., 8 JAN 1831, p. 3]

DIED, on the 30th ult. [i.e. 30 DEC 1830], Maj. HORACE FIELDS, in the 56th year of his age; long a respectable inhabitant of that town [Alexandria]. [CG, Sat., 8 JAN 1831, p. 3]

DIED, on the 4th inst. [i.e. 4 JAN 1831], Capt. DAVID BLACK, one of the oldest and most respectable inhabitants of Alexandria. [CG, Sat., 8 JAN 1831, p. 3]

DIED, at the residence of her brother, Robert D. Sewall, on the 1st inst. [i.e. 1 JAN 1831], Mrs. MARY BRENT KEY, aged 22 years, wife of Philip B. Key, and daughter of the late Robert Sewall, Esq., of *Poplar Hill*, Prince George's Co., Md. [CG, Sat., 8 JAN 1831, p. 3]

Departed this life, on Thursday, December 30th [i.e. 30 DEC 1830], at half past 3, A.M., in the 16th year of her age, AGNES CABELL WIRT, youngest daughter of William Wirt of Baltimore. [CG, Sat., 8 JAN and Tues., 11 JAN 1831, p. 3]

DIED, at Brooklyn, N.Y., on Friday evening, 31st ult. [i.e. 31 DEC 1830], after a short illness, Master Commandant SAMUEL W. ADAMS, of the U.S. Navy, aged 43. [CG, Sat., 8 JAN 1831, p. 3]

DIED, in Washington, on Thursday evening last [i.e. 6 JAN 1831], after a short illness, in the 60th year of his age, Mr. WILLIAM EMACK, one of the earliest settlers in that city. [CG, Tues., 11 JAN 1831, p. 3]

Georgetown, D.C., **Marriage and Death Notices, 1801-1838**

DIED, in Washington, on the 11th inst. [i.e. 11 JAN 1831], in the 56th year of her age, Mrs. JANE JEFFERSON, consort of Mr. Joseph Jefferson, Sen., of the Theatre. [CG, Tues., 18 JAN 1831, p. 3]

DIED, in Baltimore, on Sunday morning, the 9th inst. [i.e. 9 JAN 1831], in the 81st year of his age, ROBERT WALSH, a native of Ireland, and for the last 60 years a respectable inhabitant of that city. [CG, Tues., 18 JAN 1831, p. 3]

DIED, in Brunswick, Me., on Sunday, the 26th of December 1830, Mr. WILLIAM TRUE HARMON, in the 22d year of his age, formerly a resident of Alexandria. [CG, Tues., 18 JAN 1831, p. 3]

MARRIED, in this town, on Tuesday evening, 18th inst. [i.e. 18 JAN 1831], by the Rev. J.L. Amiss, Mr. WILLIAM GARDINER, to Miss MARY C. DIDENHOVER, all of Georgetown. [CG, Thurs., 20 JAN 1831, p. 3]

MARRIED, on Tuesday evening, the 18th [i.e. 18 JAN 1831], Mr. WILLIAM HARDY, to Mrs. SARAH RAGAN, both of this town. [CG, Thurs., 20 JAN 1831, p. 3]

MARRIED, in Washington, on Tuesday morning, 18th inst. [i.e. 18 JAN 1831], by the Rev. O.B. Brown, Mr. THOS. B. ABBETT, of Philadelphia, to Miss MARY ANN, only daughter of Mr. D. Appler, of Washington. [CG, Thurs., 20 JAN 1831, p. 3]

DIED, at his residence in Georgetown, in the 83d year of his age, at half past one o'clock, A.M., on Wednesday the 19th inst. [i.e. 19 JAN 1831], ALEXANDER MACOMB, Esq., father of Major General Macomb. Few men in their day have been more active, useful, and enterprising. Mr. Macomb was a citizen of New York, and had the honor of representing that City in the Legislature of the State, at the time of the adoption of its Constitution, after the Revolutionary struggle ... During the war with Great Britain, he testified his devotion to the Republic by sending into the field six sons, to assist in asserting those rights, and maintaining those principles, which the statesmen of the Revolution successfully advocated, and the Heroes of that day so nobly fought and bled to establish. He has left a disconsolate widow, a numerous progeny, and many friends to mourn his loss. ☞ His funeral will take place THIS DAY, Thursday the 20th January, at half past three o'clock, from his late residence in First Street, where his friends and acquaintances are respectfully invited to attend. [CG, Thurs., 20 JAN 1831, p. 3]

DIED, in Alexandria, at one o'clock, on Tuesday morning [i.e. 18 JAN 1831], EDWARD STABLER, in the 62d year of his age. No man knew Edward Stabler who did not admire the virtues of his heart, the purity of his life and conduct, and the sterling integrity of his principles ... [CG, Thurs., 20 JAN 1831, p. 3]

DIED, in this town, on Thursday, the 20th inst. [i.e. 20 JAN 1831], Mrs. ELIZABETH FULTON, in the 99th year of her age. ☞ The friends and acquaintances of the deceased are respectfully invited to attend her funeral, on Sunday (tomorrow) at ½ past 3 o'clock, from her late residence at Mrs. Crawford's, on Beall Street. [CG, Sat., 22 JAN and Tues., 25 JAN 1831, p. 3]

Georgetown, D.C., **Marriage and Death Notices, 1801-1838**

DIED, on Friday, the 14th inst. [i.e. 14 JAN 1831], MARY ROBERTSON, in the 89th year of her age. The deceased suffered in body during a protracted illness of several months, but closed her long life in perfect mind and peace. [CG, Sat., 22 JAN 1831, p. 3]

MARRIED, in Alexandria, on the 20th inst. [i.e. 20 JAN 1831], SAMUEL H. JANNEY, to Miss ELIZABETH, daughter of Samuel Mann, all of that place. [CG, Tues., 25 JAN 1831, p. 3]

DIED, in Alexandria, on Saturday last [i.e. 22 JAN 1831], Mrs. ELLEN BURNS, aged 33 years, wife of Mr. Benj. Burns, of Washington City, and daughter of the late Benjamin Thomas. [CG, Thurs., 27 JAN 1831, p. 3]

MARRIED, in this town, on Thursday evening last [i.e. 27 JAN 1831], by the Rev. Mr. Amiss, Mr. WILLIAM H. MAYHEW, of Baltimore Co., to Miss LUCINDA SWANN, eldest daughter of Mr. Nathan Swann. [CG, Sat., 29 JAN 1831, p. 3]

MARRIED, in Washington, on Tuesday evening last [i.e. 25 JAN 1831], Mr. GEO. M. DAVIS, to Miss GEORGIANA REINAGLE, both of that city. [CG, Sat., 29 JAN 1831, p. 3]

MARRIED, in Fredericksburg, Va., on the 21st inst. [i.e. 21 JAN 1831], Mr. HENRY W. WHITEHURST, of Washington City, to Miss ELIZA M. TOWLES, of the former place. [CG, Sat., 29 JAN 1831, p. 3]

DIED, in this town, on Saturday night last, 22d inst. [i.e. 22 JAN 1831], after a long and painful illness of about seven months, WILLIAM SMITH BOOTES, eldest son of Mr. Samuel M. Bootes, aged 17 months. [CG, Sat., 29 JAN 1831, p. 3]

DIED, in Washington, on the 23d inst. [i.e. 23 JAN 1831], FRANCISCO JARDELLA, Sculptor, aged 38 years; born at Carrara, near Florence, in Tuscany. [CG, Sat., 29 JAN 1831, p. 3]

DIED, in Alexandria, on Tuesday night last [i.e. 25 JAN 1831], Dr. SAMUEL CARSON, in the 83d year of his age; a native of Armagh, Ire., but for many years a resident of Alexandria. [CG, Sat., 29 JAN 1831, p. 3]

DIED, in Calvert Co., Md., on the 14th inst. [i.e. 14 JAN 1831], Mrs. BETTY H. MORSELL, relict of the late Mr. James Morsell, in the 71st year of her age. [CG, Sat., 29 JAN 1831, p. 3]

DIED, at Buffalo, N.Y., on the 16th inst. [i.e. 16 JAN 1831], Mrs. AMANDA ROCHESTER, in the 32d year of her age, wife of the Hon. Wm. B. Rochester. [CG, Sat., 29 JAN 1831, p. 3]

DIED, near Basing Ridge, N.J., on the 6th inst. [i.e. 6 JAN 1831], at an advanced age, Mrs. SARAH SOUTHARD, consort of the Hon. Henry Southard, and mother of the Hon. Samuel L. Southard. [CG, Sat., 29 JAN 1831, p. 3]

Georgetown, D.C., **Marriage and Death Notices, 1801-1838**

MARRIED, at White Sulphur Springs, Va., on the 13th ult. [i.e. 13 JAN 1831], Lieut. LEVIN M. POWELL, of the U.S. Navy, to Miss VIRGINIA AUGUSTIN, daughter of James Caldwell, Esq., of that place. [CG, Tues., 1 FEB 1831, p. 3]

MARRIED, in Washington, on the 27th ult. [i.e. 27 JAN 1831], Mr. THOMAS FRANCIS, of Loudoun Co., Va., to Miss SARAH ANN MOUNT. [CG, Tues., 1 FEB 1831, p. 3]

MARRIED, in Norfolk, Va., on the 27th ult. [i.e. 27 JAN 1831], Mr. DANIEL LLOYD, of Alexandria, to Miss MARGARET GOULDEN, of the former place. [CG, Tues., 1 FEB 1831, p. 3]

DIED, at Lexington, Kan., on the 14th ult. [i.e. 14 JAN 1831], Mr. WILLIAM PRENTISS, aged 76, formerly a resident of Boston, Mass. [CG, Tues., 1 FEB 1831, p. 3]

DIED, in Baltimore, on the 28th ult. [i.e. 28 JAN 1831], DAVID WILLIAMSON, aged 78, a native of Scotland, but for the last 60 years a resident of Baltimore. [CG, Tues., 1 FEB 1831, p. 3]

DIED, in Washington, on the 28th ult. [i.e. 28 JAN 1831], Mr. ROBERT KING, in the 56th year of his age. Mr. King was among the earliest inhabitants and assisted in laying out the City. He was afterwards City Surveyor, and for the last eighteen years principal Draughtsman in the General Land Office. [CG, Sat., 5 FEB 1831, p. 3]

DIED, on the 3d inst. [i.e. 3 FEB 1831], after a lingering illness, Dr. JOHN BROWNE CUTTING, aged 76 years. [CG, Sat., 5 FEB 1831, p. 3]

DIED, at the residence of her brother [no date], Robert D. Sewall, Mrs. ANN D. STONE, daughter of the late Robert Sewall, Esq. [CG, Sat., 5 FEB 1831, p. 3]

DIED, in Alexandria, on the 1st inst. [i.e. 1 FEB 1831], after a lingering pulmonary complaint, CRAVEN P. THOMPSON, Esq., in the 49th year of his age. [CG, Sat., 5 FEB 1831, p. 3]

MARRIED, in Washington, on Thursday evening last [i.e. 3 FEB 1831], by the Rev. Mr. Keppler, Mr. JOHN TRETLER, to Miss REBECCA HOUX, both of that city. [CG, Tues., 8 FEB 1831, p. 3]

MARRIED, on Thursday evening last [i.e. 3 FEB 1831], by the Rev. S. Chapin, D.D., Mr. ANDREW ROTHWELL, to Miss ANN, daughter of Col. William Dewees, of that city. [CG, Tues., 8 FEB 1831, p. 3]

DIED, at his residence, in Charles Co., Md., near Charlotte Hall, on the 20th ult. [i.e. 20 JAN 1831], Mr. WILLIAM GOOD, Sen., in the 61st year of his age ... [CG, Tues., 8 FEB 1831, p. 3]

DIED, in Philadelphia, on the 5th inst. [i.e. 5 FEB 1831], Col. EDMUND B. DUVAL, of Md., only son of Judge Duval, in the 42nd year of his age. [CG, Sat., 12 FEB 1831, p. 3]

Georgetown, D.C., **Marriage and Death Notices, 1801-1838**

DIED, in Washington, on the 5th inst. [i.e. 5 FEB 1831], Mr. CHARLES TIMS. [CG, Tues., 15 FEB 1831, p. 3]

DIED, on the 4th inst. [i.e. 4 FEB 1831], Miss MARY DYER, in the 48th year of her age. [CG, Tues., 15 FEB 1831, p. 3]

DIED, at Norfolk, Va., on the 7th inst. [i.e. 7 FEB 1831], after a protracted illness of Paralysis, Com. ARTHUR SINCLAIR, of the U.S. Navy, many years commanding Naval Officer in that station. He was an officer of distinguished gallantry, and skill in his profession, and enjoyed the confidence of the Government in an eminent degree. He entered the Naval service as a Midshipman on the 15th Nov. 1798, and soon after displayed the most intrepid bravery in the action between the *Constellation*, (Com. Truxtun,) and the French frigate *Insurgent*, which reflected so much honor on the naval prowess of our country. He was advanced to the rank of Post Captain, 24th July 1813. As an officer and a citizen, he was highly esteemed, and in all the relations of domestic life, honored and beloved. He has left several children to revere his memory.—*[Norfolk] Beacon*. [CG, Tues., 15 FEB 1831, p. 3]

MARRIED, on Monday evening last [i.e. 14 FEB 1831], by the Rev. Mr. Lucas, Mr. THOMAS W. MAHORNEY, to Miss EMILY B., daughter of Mr. Lemuel Shaw, all of this town. [CG, Thurs., 17 FEB 1831, p. 3]

DIED, in this town, on the morning of the 15th inst. [i.e. 15 FEB 1831], THOMAS AUGUSTINE CLEMENTS, aged eight years and eight months, the third son of B. Clements, Esq. This amiable youth, endeared by many qualifications of a good child, to his parents and to all who knew him, died of the disease commonly called the dropsy of the brain ... [CG, Thurs., 17 FEB 1831, p. 3]

DIED, in Fredericktown, on Saturday morning, the 12th inst. [i.e. 12 FEB 1831], the Rev. JOHN FRANCIS PETERS, S.J., in the 32d year of his age. The deceased was a native of Belgium, and came to this country in 1829. For the last sixteen months he exercised the duties of ministry in this town and its vicinity with great zeal and universal qualification. *Requiescat in pace. Herald.* [CG, Tues., 22 FEB 1831, p. 3]

DIED, at his residence in Fairfax Co., Va., on Thursday morning last [i.e. 17 FEB 1831], aged 62 years, JOHN JACKSON, Esq. [CG, Thurs., 24 FEB 1831, p. 3]

DIED, at Lebanon, Conn., on the 9th ult. [i.e. 9 FEB 1831], Mrs. MARY WILLIAMS, aged 87 years, widow of the late Hon. William Williams, one of the signers of the Declaration of Independence. Mrs. Williams was the daughter of the elder Governor Trumbull, and sister of Col. John Trumbull of N.Y. [CG, Tues., 1 MAR 1831, p. 3]

DIED, in Washington, on Saturday night last [i.e. 27 FEB 1831], after a short illness, the Hon. JAMES NOBLE, aged 48, a Senator in Congress from the State of Indiana, which office he has filled from the time that the State was admitted into the Union. [CG, Tues., 1 MAR 1831, p. 3]

Georgetown, D.C., **Marriage and Death Notices, 1801-1838**

DIED at her residence in Halifax Co., Va., on the 15th ult. [i.e. 15 FEB 1831], Mrs. DOROTHEA WINSTON, widow of the celebrated Patrick Henry. Her last husband was the late Judge Edmund Winston. [CG, Tues., 1 MAR 1831, p. 3]

DIED, at Portsmouth, N.H. [no date], Mr. JOSEPH WATSON, Purser U.S. Navy, aged 28. [CG, Tues., 1 MAR 1831, p. 3]

MARRIED, in Washington, on the 22d ult. [i.e. 22 FEB 1831], the Hon. JOHN MAGEE, member of Congress from N.Y., to Mrs. ARABELLA SNOWDEN, of Washington. [CG, Thurs., 3 MAR 1831, p. 3]

MARRIED, on Monday evening last [i.e. 28 FEB 1831], the Hon. POWHATAN ELLIS, Senator in Congress from the State of Mississippi, to Miss ELIZA WINN, daughter of Timothy Winn, Esq. [CG, Thurs., 3 MAR 1831, p. 3]

MARRIED, on the 15th ult. [i.e. 15 FEB 1831], Mr. THOMAS MacGILL, of Washington, to Miss EMILY WILSON, of Prince George's Co., Md. [CG, Thurs., 3 MAR 1831, p. 3]

MARRIED, at *Oak*, Calvert Co., Md., on the 1st ult. [i.e. 1 FEB 1831], Dr. THOMAS B. HUNGERFORD, to Miss ANN M.C. WILKINSON, only daughter of George Wilkinson, Esq. [CG, Thurs., 3 MAR 1831, p. 3]

MARRIED, in Alexandria, on the 23d ult. [i.e. 23 FEB 1831], Mr. JAMES DUDLEY, to Miss MARGARET ANN SHIELDS, both of that town. [CG, Thurs., 3 MAR 1831, p. 3]

DIED, in this town, on the 22d ult. [i.e. 22 FEB 1831], after a painful illness of four months, Mr. JOHN A. REMINGTON, Printer. [CG, Thurs., 3 MAR 1831, p. 3]

DIED, in Washington, on the 28th ult. [i.e. 28 FEB 1831], Mrs. MARGARET McCUBBIN, wife of Edward McCubbin. [CG, Thurs., 3 MAR 1831, p. 3]

DIED, at *Bloomsbury*, near Fredericktown, Frederick Co., Md., on the 3d inst. [i.e. 3 MAR 1831], Maj. ROGER JOHNSON, in the 83d year of his age, a highly respected citizen, a friend to the poor, a sincere christian, and truly an honest man. [CG, Tues., 8 MAR 1831, p. 3]

DIED, in Washington, on Sunday morning [i.e. 13 MAR 1831], in the 23d year of her age, Mrs. MARIA STRIBLING PRENTISS, wife of Mr. William Prentiss, publisher of the *National Journal*, and daughter of Mr. Jesse Brown. [CG, Tues., 15 MAR 1831, p. 3]

DIED, on the 7th inst. [i.e. 7 MAR 1831], of a paralysis, PHILIP P. ECKEL, in the 63d year of his age. Mr. E. was a native of Germany, but for about forty-eight years past a resident of Baltimore; always bearing the character of an incorruptibly honest man—punctual in his dealings—faithful to his promises—remarkable for the goodness of his heart, extensive liberality, and universal benevolence—and his hand, according to its means, was always ready to record the dictates of his generous feelings. *Baltimore Chronicle*. [CG, Thurs., 17 MAR 1831, p. 3]

Georgetown, D.C., **Marriage and Death Notices, 1801-1838**

MARRIED, in Alexandria, on the 10th inst. [i.e. 10 MAR 1831], by the Rev. Dr. Keith, ROBERT E. SCOTT, Esq., of Warrenton, Va., to Miss ELIZABETH JOHNSON, daughter of Robert I. Taylor, Esq., of Alexandria. [CG, Sat., 19 MAR 1831, p. 3]

MARRIED, in Alexandria, on Tuesday last [i.e. 15 MAR 1831], by the Rev. Wm. Jackson, Mr. WILLIAM P.C. JOHNSON, of Bristol, Pa., to Miss ANN ELIZA WASHINGTON, eldest daughter of Bushrod Washington, Esq., of Va. [CG, Tues., 22 MAR 1831, p. 3]

MARRIED, on the 10th inst. [i.e. 10 MAR 1831], JOSIAH ESSEN, of Washington, to RUTH FLOYD, of Georgetown. [CG, Tues., 22 MAR 1831, p. 3]

DIED, in Washington Co., Md., on the 5th inst. [i.e. 5 MAR 1831], Mr. WILLIAM McGREGORY, aged 102 years. [CG, Tues., 22 MAR 1831, p. 3]

MARRIED, at *Strawberry Hill*, on the 15th inst. [i.e. 15 MAR 1831], Mr. JOHN M. BROWN, merchant of Alexandria, to Miss ANN E., eldest daughter of Capt. Thomas D. Clagett, of Charles Co., Md. [CG, Thurs., 24 MAR 1831, p. 3]

MARRIED, on Thursday last [i.e. 17 MAR 1831], Mr. WILLIAM DIER [Dyer], of Va., to Miss MARY SKINNER, of Alexandria. [CG, Thurs., 24 MAR 1831, p. 3]

DIED, in this town, on Saturday last, the 19th inst. [i.e. 19 MAR 1831], after a long and painful illness, Mrs. ELIZABETH OLIVER, in the 82d year of her age. The deceased was a native of Cooks-town, Ireland, but for the last 30 years of her life was a resident of Georgetown. [CG, Sat., 26 MAR 1831, p. 2]

DIED, on the evening of the 9th inst. [i.e. 9 MAR 1831], at *Pleasant Plains*, near Washington, in the 21st year of her age, Miss SUSAN ELIZA HOLMEAD; and on the 22d inst., Capt. JOHN HOLMEAD, father of the above young lady, in the 71st year of his age. [CG, Sat., 26 MAR 1831, p. 2]

MARRIED, in Alexandria, on the 24th inst. [i.e. 24 MAR 1831], Mr. FRANCIS H. DAVIDSON, to Miss JANE WELBORNE, of that place. [CG, Tues., 29 MAR 1831, p. 3]

MARRIED, on Thursday morning [i.e. 24 MAR 1831], Mr. JOHN M. LISLE, of Philadelphia, to Miss HENRIETTA WHEELER, of Alexandria. [CG, Tues., 29 MAR 1831, p. 3]

DIED [no date], at *Bloomsbury*, the seat of his father, Judge Plater, of an affection of the lungs, JOHN ROUSBY PLATER, Jun., in the 35th year of his age, leaving a wife and three children, with numerous friends and acquaintances, to whom his amiable disposition and unassuming manners endeared him, to mourn their loss under the afflicting dispensation. [CG, Tues., 29 MAR 1831, p. 3]

MARRIED, in Washington, on Monday evening [i.e. 28 MAR 1831], Mr. WILLIAM H. MAURO, of the firm of *P. Mauro & Son*, to Miss ELIZA S., only daughter of the late Mr. James Wharton, of this town. [CG, Thurs., 31 MAR 1831, p. 3]

Georgetown, D.C., **Marriage and Death Notices, 1801-1838**

DIED, in Washington, on the 27th inst. [i.e. 27 MAR 1831], Mrs. SARAH, consort of Wm. Kerr, Jr., in the 38th year of her age, formerly of Boston. [CG, Thurs., 31 MAR 1831, p. 3]

DIED, at Cincinnati, Ohio on the 18th inst. [i.e. 18 MAR 1831], Gen. WILLIAM LYTLE, Surveyor General, in the 61st year of his age. The deceased was one of the pioneers of the West, and for a great number of years a resident of Cincinnati, enjoying in a high degree the respect and confidence of his fellow citizens. [CG, Thurs., 31 MAR 1831, p. 3]

MARRIED, in Baltimore, on Monday last [i.e. 28 MAR 1831], Lieut. RICHARD A. JONES, of the U.S. Navy, son of Com. Jacob Jones, to Miss EMILY, youngest daughter of the late Hon. Wm. Pinkney. [CG, Sat., 2 APR 1831, p. 3]

DIED, in Washington, on the 30th ult. [i.e. 30 MAR 1831], Mrs. ELIZABETH, wife of William A. Davis, in the 52d year of her age. [CG, Sat., 2 APR 1831, p. 3]

MARRIED, on Thursday evening, 31st ult. [i.e. 31 MAR 1831], by the Rev. Mr. Hawley, Mr. JOSEPH PECK, to Miss MARGARETTA, youngest daughter of George Walker, all of the District. [CG, Tues., 5 APR 1831, p. 3]

DIED, at *Montauverd*, the residence of her son-in-law, Maj. George Peter, Montgomery Co., Md., on the 3d inst. [i.e. 3 APR 1831], after a tedious and painful illness, Mrs. SARAH FREELAND, relict of the late James Freeland, Esq., of Petersburg, Va., in the 54th year of her age. [CG, Thurs., 7 APR 1831, p. 3]

MARRIED, in WASHINGTON, on Tuesday last [i.e. 5 APR 1831], Col. FRANCIS W. ARMSTRONG, of Alabama, to Miss ANN M. MILLARD, daughter of Mr. Joshua Millard. [CG, Tues., 12 APR 1831, p. 2]

DIED, in Nashville, on the 23d ult. [i.e. 23 MAR 1831], Gen. ROBERT PURDY, Marshal of the District of West Tennessee. [CG, Tues., 12 APR 1831, p. 2]

DIED, in Philadelphia, on the 4th inst. [i.e. 4 APR 1831], Mrs. ELIZABETH MOORE, in the 60th year of her age, relict of the late Joshua John Moore, of Washington. [CG, Tues., 12 APR 1831, p. 2]

DIED, in Washington, on Thursday last [i.e. 7 APR 1831], Capt. ROBERT TAYLOR, for many years the Captain of a Steamboat on the Potomac River. [CG, Tues., 12 APR 1831, p. 2]

DIED, at Worcester, Mass., on the 4th inst. [i.e. 4 APR 1831], the venerable ISAIAH THOMAS, aged 82, the patriarch of American printers and founder of the American Antiquarian Society. [CG, Tues., 12 APR 1831, p. 2]

MARRIED, in Washington, on Tuesday evening [i.e. 12 APR 1831], Mr. GEORGE H. TUCKER, of Baltimore, to Miss MARGARET DUNNING, of Washington. [CG, Sat., 16 APR 1831, p. 3]

Georgetown, D.C., Marriage and Death Notices, 1801-1838

MARRIED, on Wednesday evening [i.e. 13 APR 1831], Dr. HARVEY KLAPP, of Philadelphia, to Miss ANN P. McKNIGHT, daughter of the late Capt. McKnight of the U.S. Marine Corps. [CG, Sat., 16 APR 1831, p. 3]

MARRIED, in this town, on Thursday evening, 14th inst. [i.e. 14 APR 1831], by the Rev. Mr. Brooke, RICHARD B. MAURY, Esq., of the Navy Department, to Miss ELLEN, daughter of James A. Magruder, all of this place. [CG, Tues., 19 APR 1831, p. 2]

MARRIED, in Washington, on Tuesday evening, the 12th inst. [i.e. 12 APR 1831], by the Rev. W. Matthews, Mr. STEPHEN C. FORD, merchant of Philadelphia and formerly of this town, to Miss ANN R. HOBAN, daughter of Capt. James Hoban of Washington. [CG, Tues., 19 APR 1831, p. 2]

Departed this life, on Monday, the 18th inst. [i.e. 18 APR 1831], in the 33d year of her age, Mrs. MARY ANN MORSELL, consort of James S. Morsell, Esq., Judge of the Circuit Court, and daughter of Mr. William Marbury, of this town. The acquaintances of the family and citizens generally are invited to attend her funeral, from her late residence on West Street, this day (Tuesday) at 4 o'clock, P.M. [CG, Tues., 19 APR 1831, p. 2]

DIED, in Baltimore, on Friday last [i.e. 15 APR 1831], in the 47th year of his age, the Hon. ROLLIN C. MALLARY, a member of the House of Representatives of the U.S. from Vermont, and for the last four or five years Chairman of the committee on Manufactures. [CG, Tues., 19 APR 1831, p. 2]

MARRIED, in Washington, on Monday evening last [i.e. 18 APR 1831], Lieut. FRENCH FORREST, of the U.S. Navy, to Miss EMILY D. SIMMS. [CG, Thurs., 21 APR 1831, p. 3]

MARRIED [no date], Mr. LEVI B. JOHNSON, to Miss EVELINA MAYNARD. [CG, Thurs., 21 APR 1831, p. 3]

MARRIED, in Fredericktown, on the 12th inst. [i.e. 12 APR 1831], by the Rev. J.E. Jackson, the Rev. CHARLES MANN, Rector of Christ Church, Alexandria, D.C., to Miss MARY C. JACKSON, daughter of the Rev. Thomas Jackson. [CG, Thurs., 21 APR 1831, p. 3]

MARRIED, in Washington, on Tuesday evening last [i.e. 19 APR 1831], Col. R.W. WILLIAMS, of Tallahassee, to Miss REBECCA BRANCH, daughter of the Hon. John Branch, of N.C. [CG, Sat., 23 APR 1831, p. 3]

MARRIED, on Wednesday [i.e. 20 APR 1831], Mr. AMBROSE T. MELCHER, of Brunswick, Me., to Miss MARY J. FAYE, of Washington. [CG, Sat., 23 APR 1831, p. 3]

DIED, in Paris, on the 18th ult. [i.e. 18 MAR 1831], Col. JAMES SWANN, formerly of Boston. He had been confined in prison for debt the last 25 years. [CG, Sat., 23 APR 1831, p. 3]

DIED, in Washington, on Sunday night last [i.e. 24 APR 1831], after an illness of about four weeks, Mr. MARCUS LATIMER, in the 40th year of his age. The friends of the deceased, and those of the family, are respectfully invited to attend his funeral, from his late residence, hear the lower bridge, *this afternoon*, at 4 o'clock. [CG, Tues., 26 APR 1831, p. 3]

MARRIED, in this town, on Tuesday evening, 19th inst. [i.e. 19 APR 1831], by the Rev. Mr. Van Lommel, Mr. WILLIAM G. LOVE, to MARY ELIZABETH, eldest daughter of Mr. John Lawrence, all of this place. [CG, Thurs., 28 APR 1831, p. 3]

DIED, in this town, on Tuesday evening last [i.e. 26 APR 1831], in the 22d year of his age, Mr. RICHARD DAVIS, Jr. The friends of the family are respectfully invited to attend the funeral, which will take place this evening at 4 o'clock, from the residence of his father, Mr. Richard Davis, on Bridge street. [CG, Thurs., 28 APR 1831, p. 3]

DIED, in this town, on Tuesday the 20th inst. [i.e. 20? APR 1831], Mrs. CATHERINE KNOWLES, wife of Henry Knowles, Sr., aged 66. Her virtues are attested by the neighboring poor, to whom she was a constant benefactor. [CG, Thurs., 28 APR 1831, p. 3]

DIED, in Penn township, near Philadelphia, on Sunday last [i.e. 24 APR 1831], in the 48th year of his age, the Hon. DANIEL H. MILLER, President of the Bank of Penn township, and late a Representative on Congress from Pa. [CG, Thurs., 28 APR 1831, p. 3]

MARRIED, at Dayton, Ohio, on the 28th ult. [i.e. 28 MAR 1831], Mr. HENRY A. PIERSON, of that place, to Miss ELLEN WARING, of Prince George's Co., Md. [CG, Sat., 30 APR 1831, p. 3]

DIED, at *Mount Eagle*, Fairfax Co., Va., on the 16th inst. [i.e. 16 APR 1831], BUSHROD WASHINGTON, Esq., in the 47th year of his age. [CG, Sat., 30 APR 1831, p. 3]

DIED, in Philadelphia, on the 28th ult. [i.e. 28 APR 1831], Mr. JOHN DUFF, for many years attached to the Theatrical Corps in various parts of the United States. [CG, Thurs., 5 MAY 1831, p. 3]

MARRIED, in Washington, on Monday last [i.e. 2 MAY 1831], Mr. WILLIAM HILL, to Miss ELIZABETH AMBROSE. [CG, Sat., 7 MAY 1831, p. 3]

MARRIED, on Wednesday evening last [i.e. 4 MAY 1831], at *Liberty*, the residence of Col. John Stuart, King George Co., Va., by the Rev. Mr. Goldsmith, EDGAR SNOWDEN, of Alexandria, to Miss LOUISA JANE GRYMES, daughter of the late Benjamin Grymes, Esq., of that County. [CG, Sat., 7 MAY 1831, p. 3]

MARRIED, at the Sand Hills, near Augusta, Ga., on the 7th ult. [i.e. 7 APR 1831], Col. ALFRED IVERSON, of Columbus, to Miss JULIA FORSYTH, daughter of the Hon. John Forsyth. [CG, Sat., 7 MAY 1831, p. 3]

Georgetown, D.C., **Marriage and Death Notices, 1801-1838**

MARRIED, in Charleston, S.C., on the 27th ult. [i.e. 27 APR 1831], JAMES G. ROWE, Esq., of N.C., to Miss MARGARET B., daughter of the Hon. Judge Johnson, of the Supreme Court, U.S. [CG, Sat., 7 MAY 1831, p. 3]

DIED, in Washington, on Wednesday evening [i.e. 4 MAY 1831], after a long illness, Mrs. BELT, wife of Judge Belt, late of Chillicothe, Ohio. [CG, Sat., 7 MAY 1831, p. 3]

MARRIED, on Tuesday evening, the 3d inst. [i.e. 3 MAY 1831], by the Rev. Mr. Amiss, Mr. SAMUEL JONES, to Miss SARAH LIPSCOMB, both of this place. [CG, Tues., 10 MAY 1831, p. 3]

DIED, suddenly, in this town, on Saturday last [i.e. 7 MAY 1831], Mr. JOSEPH ARNY, Confectioner. [CG, Tues., 10 MAY 1831, p. 3]

MARRIED, in Washington, on the 4th inst. [i.e. 4 MAY 1831], Mr. RICHARD GOTT, to Miss ANN E., daughter of William Gordon, Esq., all of Washington. [CG, Thurs., 12 MAY 1831, p. 3]

MARRIED, on the 9th inst. [i.e. 9 MAY 1831], Mr. CHARLES BALLARD, to Miss ELEANOR DOUGHERTY. [CG, Thurs., 12 MAY 1831, p. 3]

MARRIED, at *Oakland*, Fairfax Co., Va., on the 5th inst. [i.e. 5 MAY 1831], ORRIS S. PAINE, Esq., of Washington, to MARY ASHTON, eldest daughter of Capt. George Terrett. [CG, Thurs., 12 MAY 1831, p. 3]

MARRIED, in Alexandria, on the 1st inst. [i.e. 1 MAY 1831], Mr. HOMES TUPPER, to Miss LYDIA MARIA CRABTREE, daughter of Mr. Wm. Crabtree, Jr., all of Savannah. [CG, Thurs., 12 MAY 1831, p. 3]

DIED, in Washington, on Tuesday last [i.e. 10 MAY 1831], Mr. LEWIN TALBURTT, an old inhabitant of the District. [CG, Thurs., 12 MAY 1831, p. 3]

DIED, in Brooklyn, Conn., on the 30th ult. [i.e. 30 APR 1831], Col. DANIEL PUTNAM, aged 71, son of the late Maj. Gen. Putnam. [CG, Thurs., 12 MAY 1831, p. 3]

MARRIED, in Washington, on Tuesday evening last [i.e. 10 MAY 1831], by the Rev. Mr. Danforth, Mr. MICHAEL HOOVER, to Miss MARY TWEEDY, all of that City. [CG, Sat., 14 MAY 1831, p. 3]

MARRIED, on Tuesday evening last [i.e. 10 MAY 1831], by the Rev. Mr. Matthews, WILLIAM C. ORME, to JANE FRANCIS, eldest daughter of Mr. Wm. Ward, Merchant, all of Washington. [CG, Sat., 14 MAY 1831, p. 3]

DIED, in Washington, on Wednesday [i.e. 11 MAY 1831], in the 25th year of his age, Lieut. JOSEPH R. BLAKE, of the U.S. Navy. In the departure of Mr. Blake, the service has been deprived of one of its most devoted and promising officers; and society of an individual of noble and generous spirit, pure and elevated principles, humble and fervent piety. [CG, Sat., 14 MAY 1831, p. 3]

MARRIED, in Fauquier, Va., on the 12th inst. [i.e. 12 MAY 1831], Dr. J.H. LUFBOROUGH, of the District of Columbia, to Miss CAROLINE MORGAN, daughter of James Morgan, deceased. [CG, Tues., 17 MAY 1831, p. 3]

MARRIED, in this town, on Thursday evening last [i.e. 12 MAY 1831], by the Rev. Mr. Tustin, of Charleston, Va., JOHN R. BEALL, Esq., of Jefferson Co., to Miss MARTHA LUCKETT, of Alexandria. [CG, Thurs., 19 MAY 1831, p. 3]

DIED, in Washington, on Monday last [i.e. 16 MAY 1831], in the 76th year of his age, Mr. JOHN PETER MAUL, a native of Germany, and formerly a Messenger in the Department of State. [CG, Thurs., 19 MAY 1831, p. 3]

DIED, in Alexandria, on Friday last [i.e. 13 MAY 1831], Mr. ADAM DIEZ, a native of Germany, aged 49 years. [CG, Thurs., 19 MAY 1831, p. 3]

DIED, in Baltimore, on the 15th inst. [i.e. 15 MAY 1831], Mr. LEMUEL LUDDEN, Merchant, aged 37. [CG, Thurs., 19 MAY 1831, p. 3]

DIED, on Sunday evening last [i.e. 15 MAY 1831], JEFFERSON GLENN, second son of the Hon. Elias Glenn. [CG, Thurs., 19 MAY 1831, p. 3]

MARRIED, in this town, on Tuesday evening last [i.e. 12 MAY 1831], by the Rev. Mr. Young, JAMES R. BRENT, Esq., of Charles Co., Md., to Miss ELEANOR WARING, daughter of Henry Waring, Esq. [CG, Tues., 24 MAY 1831, p. 3]

MARRIED, in Washington, on Wednesday morning [i.e. 18 MAY 1831], Mr. JOHN C. ENGLISH, to Miss ADELIA ANN MORGAN, both of that City. [CG, Tues., 24 MAY 1831, p. 3]

MARRIED, on Tuesday evening [i.e. 17 MAY 1831], Dr. WILLIAM PALMER, to Miss CLEONAH DUVALL, daughter of Dr. Benjamin Duvall, all of Montgomery Co., Md. [CG, Tues., 24 MAY 1831, p. 3]

MARRIED [no date], Mr. WILLIAM W. STEWART, to EVELINE, daughter of Mr. William Wood, all of Washington. [CG, Tues., 24 MAY 1831, p. 3]

MARRIED, in Baltimore, on the 18th inst. [i.e. 18 MAY 1831], Lieut. JOHN B. MAGRULER [sic], of the U.S. Army, to Miss ESTHER HENRIETTA, youngest daughter of the late B.J. Von Kapff. [CG, Tues., 24 MAY 1831, p. 3]

DIED, in this town, on Saturday evening [i.e. 21 MAY 1831], CATHERINE LOUISA SINN, and nine hours after, WILLIAM B. LEWIS SINN, daughter and son of William Sinn, a Clerk in the General Land Office. [CG, Tues., 24 MAY 1831, p. 3]

Georgetown, D.C., **Marriage and Death Notices, 1801-1838**

DIED, at Charleston, S.C., on the 10th inst. [i.e. 10 MAY 1831], JEREMIAH EVARTS, Esq., late Secretary of the American Board of Commissioners for Foreign Missions. Mr. E. left Boston for the Island of Cuba, for the benefit of his health; from thence he came via Savannah to Charleston. Mr. Evarts was the author of the Letters of William Penn, originally published in the *National Intelligencer*, which obtained so great currency and celebrity. [CG, Tues., 24 MAY 1831, p. 3]

DIED, at Detroit, Mich., on the 10th inst. [i.e. 10 MAY 1831], the venerable JOHN TRUMBULL, in the 81st year of his age. He was born at Watertown, Conn., in 1850, graduated at Yale College, practiced law at Hartford, and was appointed to the bench of the highest Court in his native State. [CG, Tues., 24 MAY 1831, p. 3]

Departed this life, on Saturday the 21st inst. [i.e. 21 MAY 1831], in the 68th year of his age, JOSEPH JACKSON, leaving a wife and three children to mourn his loss. As a husband and father, he was kind and affectionate; in his conduct towards his fellow men he proved the correctness of the language of the poet—"An honest man's the noblest work of God." [CG, Thurs., 26 MAY 1831, p. 3]

MARRIED, in this town, on Thursday morning [i.e. 26 MAY 1831], by the Rev. Dr. Balch, JOHN KURTZ, Esq., to Miss SARAH BALTZER. ☞ The Editor acknowledges the receipt of a liberal slice of the Bride's cake, for which &c. [CG, Sat., 28 MAY 1831, p. 3]

MARRIED, on Wednesday evening last [i.e. 25 MAY 1831], by the Rev. Mr. Amiss, Mr. WILLIAM RAMSEY, to Miss CAROLINE DEACONS, all of this place. [CG, Sat., 28 MAY 1831, p. 3]

MARRIED, in Washington, on Tuesday last [i.e. 24 MAY 1831], Mr. REINARD LAMBRRECHT, to Miss JANE A.D. [R]EEVES, both of that place. [CG, Sat., 28 MAY 1831, p. 3]

DIED, at Canajoharrie, in Montgomery Co., N.Y., on Thursday, May 12th [i.e. 12 MAY 1831], Mr. JOHN M'VEAN, editor of the *Canajoharrie Telegraph*, in th 31st year of his age ... His remains were conveyed to Johnstown, (the place of his nativity) and were committed to the grave. [CG, Sat., 28 MAY 1831, p. 3]

MARRIED, in Washington, on Thursday evening [i.e. 26 MAY 1831], Mr. WILLIAM TOWERS, to Miss MARY MITCHELL MOORE, both of that city. [CG, Tues., 31 MAY 1831, p. 3]

MARRIED, in Alexandria, on Thursday last [i.e. 26 MAY 1831], Maj. JOHN FOWLE, of the U.S. Army, to PAULINA, daughter of A.C. Cazenove, Esq. [CG, Tues., 31 MAY 1831, p. 3]

MARRIED, on Thursday last, 26th inst. [i.e. 26 MAY 1831], by the Rev. Thomas J. Dorsey, Mr. WILLIAM T. COLE, of Middleburg, Loudoun Co., Va., to Miss MARY E. TALIAFERRO, of Culpeper Co., Va. [CG, Tues., 31 MAY 1831, p. 3]

Georgetown, D.C., **Marriage and Death Notices, 1801-1838**

DIED, in the City of New York [no date], Mr. WILLIAM HAYMAN, eldest son of Capt. Casper Hayman, of Alexandria. [CG, Tues., 31 MAY 1831, p. 3]

DIED, at his residence in Nottingham twp., N.J., on the 23 inst. [i.e. 23 MAY 1831], suddenly, ROBERT F. HOW, Esq., formerly Chief Clerk in the General Post Office and many years a resident of this town, where he was generally known. [CG, Tues., 31 MAY 1831, p. 3]

MARRIED, in Washington, on Tuesday evening last [i.e. 31 MAY 1831], by the Rev. George Fenwick, of Georgetown, Mr. WILLIAM CLEARY, to Miss HANNAH A., youngest daughter of the late Daniel McLean, all of that place. [CG, Sat., 4 JUN 1831, p. 3]

MARRIED, in Boston, on the 24th ult. [i.e. 24 MAY 1831], by the Rev. Mr. Parkman, THOMAS P. CUSHING, Esq., to Mrs. MARTHA ANN SIGOURNEY, daughter of John Cargill, Esq., of Sussex Co., Va. [CG, Sat., 4 JUN 1831, p. 3]

DIED, a few days since [no date], in the upper part of Queen Anne's Co., Md., Col. ROBERT STEVENS. [CG, Sat., 4 JUN 1831, p. 3]

DIED, at New Haven, Conn., on the 26th ult. [i.e. 26 MAY 1831], the Rev. CLAUDIUS HERRICK, aged 56. Mr. Herrick was extensively known in the country as the founder of a seminary at New Haven, for the education of females, and which he superintended for more than twenty years with great reputation. He was a man of excellent character, distinguished for the amiableness of his disposition, and the most sincere and ardent piety. [CG, Sat., 4 JUN 1831, p. 3]

MARRIED, in Alexandria, on Thursday evening last [i.e. 2 JUN 1831], by the Rev. Isaac Robbins, Mr. RICHARD WALLACE, to Miss ELIZABETH HURST. [CG, Tues., 7 JUN 1831, p. 3]

MARRIED, on Thursday evening last [i.e. 2 JUN 1831], by the Rev. Mr. Cornelius, Mr. EPHRAIM FRANK, to Miss ELLEN LINSAY. [CG, Tues., 7 JUN 1831, p. 3]

MARRIED, on Thursday evening last [i.e. 2 JUN 1831], by the Rev. Mr. Wilson, Mr. JOEL B. SPARKS, to Miss JULIA ANN OGDEN. [CG, Tues., 7 JUN 1831, p. 3]

DIED, suddenly, in this town, on Saturday last [i.e. 4 JUN 1831], Mr. EDWIN MACOMB, a native of the City of New York, and for the last two years a resident of Georgetown. [CG, Tues., 7 JUN 1831, p. 3]

DIED, in Philadelphia, on Friday evening last [i.e. 3 JUN 1831], after a short but painful illness, WILLIAM BAINBRIDGE, Jr., Esq., in the 24th year of his age, only son of Com. Bainbridge, of the U.S. Navy. [CG, Tues., 7 JUN 1831, p. 3]

MARRIED, in Washington, on Tuesday, the 31st May [i.e. 31 MAY 1831], by the Rev. Mr. Matthews, Mr. JOHN McKOWN, to Miss MARGARET WHALER. [CG, Thurs., 9 JUN 1831, p. 3]

Georgetown, D.C., **Marriage and Death Notices, 1801-1838**

MARRIED, at Shepherdstown, Va., on Wednesday evening the 25th ult. [i.e. 25 MAY 1831], by the Rev. E. Hutchinson, GEORGE L. DOUGLASS, Esq., of Washington, to Miss DRUSILLA ANN, daughter of the late Col. V. Rutherford, of Shepherdstown, Va. [CG, Thurs., 9 JUN 1831, p. 3]

DIED, in Philadelphia [no date], JAMES PEALE, Esq., aged 82. Mr. P. was the first proprietor of the Museum in that city. [CG, Thurs., 9 JUN 1831, p. 3]

MARRIED, in Washington, on Tuesday the 7th inst. [i.e. 7 JUN 1831], by the Rev. Wm. Matthews, Mr. JOHN F. CLARKE, to Miss JULIA STETTINUS. [CG, Sat., 11 JUN 1831, p. 3]

MARRIED, on Tuesday last [i.e. 7 JUN 1831], by the Rev. John Smith, Mr. THOMAS NOKES, to Miss ANN RIDGEWAY. [CG, Sat., 11 JUN 1831, p. 3]

MARRIED, in Washington, on Tuesday last [i.e. 7 JUN 1831], Mr. MASON E. CLARK, of Prince George's Co., Md., to Miss RUTH FULLER, daughter of Azariah Fuller, of that City. [CG, Sat., 11 JUN 1831, p. 3]

DIED, in Washington, on Wednesday last [i.e. 8 JUN 1831], after a distressing illness of three months, Mrs. SARAH DEMENT, wife of Richard Dement, Esq., of the General Post Office. [CG, Sat., 11 JUN 1831, p. 3]

DIED, at Fredericksburg, Va., on Monday last [i.e. 13 JUN 1831], Dr. JAMES CARMICHAEL, aged 60, a native of Scotland, greatly respected as a Physician and a gentleman. [CG, Sat., 18 JUN 1831, p. 2]

DIED, in Stafford Co., Va., on the 30th ult. [i.e. 30 MAY 1831], after a long and painful illness, Mrs. MARGARET HOOE, wife of Robert H. Hooe, Esq. [CG, Sat., 18 JUN 1831, p. 2]

DIED, at *Barnaby*, Prince George's Co., Md., on the 6th inst. [i.e. 6 JUN 1831], Mr. OTHO W. CALLIS, in the 38th year of his age, formerly an officer in the army. [CG, Sat., 18 JUN 1831, p. 2]

MARRIED, in Alexandria, on the 9th inst. [i.e. 9 JUN 1831], Mr. HOWISON HOOE, to Miss ANN O'NEAL, all of Alexandria. [CG, Tues., 21 JUN 1831, p. 3]

MARRIED, in Warren, N.C. [no date], the Hon. MARK ALEXANDER, of Mecklenburg, Va. (Representative in Congress) to Miss SALLY TURNER, daughter of the late Governor Turner, of N.C. [CG, Tues., 21 JUN 1831, p. 3]

MARRIED, at Mount Zion, Hancock Co., Ga., on the 30th ult. [i.e. 30 MAY 1831], Lieut. WILLIAM HENRY HARFORD, of the U.S. Topographical Engineers, to Miss MARIA M. BRYAN, daughter of Mr. Joseph Bryan. [CG, Tues., 21 JUN 1831, p. 3]

Georgetown, D.C., **Marriage and Death Notices, 1801-1838**

DIED, in London, on the 6th of May [i.e. 6 MAY 1831], after a few days sickness, with a fever, Rev. SUTHERLAND DOUGLASS, who lately went to Europe for his health. The Rev. Mr. Douglass was formerly Rector of St. John's Church, Georgetown, D.C. [CG, Tues., 21 JUN 1831, p. 3]

MARRIED, on Tuesday evening, 21st inst. [i.e. 21 JUN 1831], by the Rev. Mr. Jones, Mr. S.P. WEBSTER, of Georgetown, D.C., to Miss MARY ELIZABETH, daughter of Maj. James F. Sotheron, of St. Mary's Co., Md. [CG, Tues., 28 JUN 1831, p. 3]

MARRIED, in Washington, on Thursday, 23d inst. [i.e. 23 JUN 1831], by the Rev. Mr. Post, ALFRED M. BADGER, of Portsmouth, N.H., to Miss GRACE ANN GALPIN, of Washington City. [CG, Tues., 28 JUN 1831, p. 3]

MARRIED [no date], by the Rev. Dr. Balch, Dr. BENJAMIN J. WIESTLING, of Harrisburg, Pa., to Miss MATILDA EVELINE, daughter of the late Andrew Ross, Esq., of Georgetown, D.C. [CG, Tues., 28 JUN 1831, p. 3]

Departed this life, on the 26th inst. [i.e. 26 JUN 1831], Lt. JOHN T. RITCHIE, of the U.S. Navy, in the 43d year of his age, after a long and protracted illness, which he bore with uncommon fortitude. In the death of Lt. R. the service has lost a valuable officer, society an ornament and his family a devoted husband, father and friend. [CG, Tues., 28 JUN 1831, p. 3]

MARRIED, in Washington, on Thursday evening, the 23d inst. [i.e. 23 JUN 1831], FERDINAND F. WOOD, of Charles Co., Md., to Mrs. MARY ANN ELIZA SIMMS, daughter of John Nowland of the above city. [CG, Thurs., 30 JUN 1831, p. 3]

MARRIED, in Harford Co., on Thursday evening last [i.e. 23 JUN 1831], Dr. J.M. DEAKINS, of Alexandria, to Mrs. CATHERINE ANN HOLLIS, of Charles Co., Md. [CG, Thurs., 30 JUN 1831, p. 3]

DIED, in Alexandria, on the 25th inst. [i.e. 25 JUN 1831], after a lingering and painful illness, Mr. PETER RHODES, aged 40 years. [CG, Thurs., 30 JUN 1831, p. 3]

DIED, in Portsmouth, Va., on Monday 24th ult. [i.e. 24 JUN 1831], Mr. JOHN Q. ADAMS BOYD, in the 22d year of his age, son of Washington Boyd, Esq., and formerly a Midshipman in the U.S. Navy. [CG, Sat., 2 JUL 1831, p. 3]

DIED, in Alexandria, on the 15th ult. [i.e. 14 JUN 1831], JACOB CHAMBERLAIN, aged 20. [CG, Sat., 2 JUL 1831, p. 3]

MARRIED, at *Arlington House* [no date], by the Rev. Dr. Keith, Lieut. ROBERT LEE, of the U. States Corps of Engineers, to Miss MARY A.R. CUSTIS, only daughter of G.W.P. Custis, Esq. [CG, Thurs., 7 JUL 1831, p. 3]

DIED, in Frederick, Va., on the 26th ult. [i.e. 26 JUN 1831], Mr. WILLIAM W. FITZHUGH, aged 45, formerly of Alexandria. [CG, Thurs., 7 JUL 1831, p. 3]

Georgetown, D.C., **Marriage and Death Notices, 1801-1838**

DIED, in Washington, on the 29th ult. [i.e. 29 JUN 1831], PHILIP HUISSEY, Hair Dresser, aged 57; a native of France, but for seventeen years a resident of Washington. [CG, Thurs., 7 JUL 1831, p. 3]

DIED, in Washington, on Thursday [i.e. 7 JUL 1831], Mr. PATRICK DELANY, aged 40. [CG, Sat., 9 JUL 1831, p. 3]

DIED, at Auburn, N.Y., on the 25th ult. [i.e. 25 JUN 1831], the Hon. GERSHOM POWERS, aged 41, late Member of Congress, and well known as Chairman of the Committee on the District of Columbia. [CG, Sat., 9 JUL 1831, p. 3]

MARRIED, in Georgetown, on the 10th inst. [i.e. 10 JUL 1831], by the Rev. S.B. Balch, Mr. THOMAS W. BROCCHUS, of Washington, to Miss MARY, daughter of the late Capt. John Staunton, of Alexandria. [CG, Tues., 12 JUL 1831, p. 3]

MARRIED, in Washington, on Thursday evening last [i.e. 7 JUL 1831], by the Rev. Mr. Amiss, of Georgetown, Mr. WILLIAM L. CHANDLER, of Fredericksburg, Va., to Miss ADELINE MACKEY, of Washington City. [CG, Tues., 12 JUL 1831, p. 3]

MARRIED, in Alexandria, on Thursday evening last [i.e. 7 JUL 1831], Mr. DOUGALD McFACHRAN, to Miss ANN STEPHENSON, all of that place. [CG, Thurs., 14 JUL 1831, p. 3]

MARRIED, in Washington, on Thursday last [i.e. 7 JUL 1831], by the Rev. Reuben Post, Mr. WILLIAM TAYLOR, of Prince George's Co., Md., to Miss MARTHA E. SMITH, of Alexandria. [CG, Thurs., 14 JUL 1831, p. 3]

MARRIED, in Washington, on Monday evening [i.e. 11 JUL 1831], Dr. ROBERT MAYO, late of Richmond, to Miss ELIZA CATHERINE, eldest daughter of Mr. Joseph Harbaugh, of Washington. [CG, Thurs., 14 JUL 1831, p. 3]

DIED, in Washington, on Tuesday morning [i.e. 12 JUL 1831], after a painful and protracted illness, Mrs. HARRIET SIM, wife of Dr. Thomas Sim. [CG, Thurs., 14 JUL 1831, p. 3]

MARRIED, in Washington, on the 13th inst. [i.e. 13 JUL 1831], by the Rev. Mr. Johns, PHILIP HENRY ECHOLS, Esq., of Monticello, Ga., to Miss MARGARET L.M. BERRIEN, daughter of John MacPherson Berrien, Esq., of Ga. [CG, Sat., 16 JUL 1831, p. 3]

DIED, in Alexandria, on Thursday morning [i.e. 14 JUL 1831], after a severe illness, in the 55th year of his age, SAMUEL SNOWDEN, Esq., for thirty years past proprietor and publisher of the *Alexandria (Phenix) Gazette,* and we believe, the original founder of that paper. His generous heart and cheerful temper acquired the esteem of all who knew him; and, long as he pursued the editorial profession, even in the most exciting times, his political differences never degenerated into rancour or made for him a personal enemy. This tribute is due from us to his memory, as we ourselves, though differing from him in

Georgetown, D.C., **Marriage and Death Notices, 1801-1838**

former times, widely and warmly in politics, never found cause to abate our private esteem or friendly intercourse.—*Intelligencer.* [CG, Sat., 16 JUL 1831, p. 3]

DIED, at his residence in Talbot Co., E.S. Md., on Monday, 11th inst. [i.e. 11 JUL 1831], after a few days illness, of gout in the stomach, His Excellency DANIEL MARTIN, Governor of the state of Md. By his death, George Howard, Esq., of Anne Arundel, President of the Executive Council, becomes acting governor for the remainder of the term. [CG, Sat., 16 JUL 1831, p. 3]

MARRIED, in Washington, on Thursday evening the 14th inst. [i.e. 14 JUL 1831], the Rev. SAMUEL KEPPLER, to Miss MARY JANE, daughter of Basil Waring, Esq., of the Treasury Department. [CG, Tues., 19 JUL 1831, p. 3]

DIED, in Hagerstown, on the 10th inst. [i.e. 10 JUL 1831], Dr. JACOB SCHLEBNY, in the 68th year of his age. The deceased was the third son of Dr. Henry Schlebny, who was one of the first settlers of Washington County [Md.], and endured many of the privations to which the early settlers were subject by the Indians. [CG, Tues., 19 JUL 1831, p. 3]

MARRIED, in this town, on the 12th inst. [i.e. 12 JUL 1831], at the residence of Wm. C. Lipscomb, by the Rev. John Davis, FLEET COX, Esq., of Westmoreland Co., Va., to Miss MARIA ELIZABETH SCOTT, daughter of the late James S. Scott, of Washington City. [CG, Thurs., 21 JUL 1831, p. 3]

MARRIED, in Baltimore, on Monday evening last [i.e. 18 JUL 1831], by the Rev. Mr. Palfrey, of Washington, the Rev. GEORGE WASHINGTON BURNAP, Pastor of the first Independent Church of Baltimore, to Miss NANCY WILLIAMS, only daughter of Amos A. Williams, Esq. [CG, Thurs., 21 JUL 1831, p. 3]

MARRIED, on the 17th inst. [i.e. 17 JUL 1831], Mr. SPENCER WARING, of Washington, to Miss JOSEPHINE HUSSALL, of Baltimore. [CG, Thurs., 21 JUL 1831, p. 3]

MARRIED, at Maysville, Ky., on the 7th inst. [i.e. 7 JUL 1831], RICHARD HENRY LEE, Esq., late Editor of the *Maysville Eagle*, to Miss ELIZA ARMSTRONG, daughter of Mr. John Armstrong, merchant. [CG, Thurs., 21 JUL 1831, p. 3]

DIED, on the 13th inst. [i.e. 13 JUL 1831], on board the U.S. frigate *Potomac*, Mr. LEVI TALBOT, formerly of Alexandria. [CG, Thurs., 21 JUL 1831, p. 3]

DIED, in Alexandria, on Sunday morning [i.e. 17 JUL 1831], Mrs. [Mary Ann] McLEOD, consort of Mr. Daniel McLeod. [CG, Thurs., 21 JUL 1831, p. 3]

DIED, in Fairfax Co., Va., on the 11th inst. [i.e. 11 JUL 1831], CATHERINE EDMONDS, aged 2 years and 7 months; and on the 17th inst., in Alexandria, MARGARET BOYD, aged 9 years and 11 months, daughters of Mr. Thomas W. Hewitt, of that place. [CG, Thurs., 21 JUL 1831, p. 3]

Georgetown, D.C., **Marriage and Death Notices, 1801-1838**

DIED, in Buenos Ayres, on the 2d May [i.e. 2 MAY 1831], Dr. HENRY BOND, a native of Md., and for several years a resident of Baltimore, He was married to the sister of the Governor of Buenos Ayres. [CG, Thurs., 21 JUL 1831, p. 3]

DIED, in this town, on the 23d inst. [i.e. 23 JUL 1831], at the residence of Dr. B.S. Bohrer, the Rev. WILLIAM ALLEN, after an illness of six days, in the 73d year of his age. Mr. Allen was a native of Scotland and a Graduate of the University of Aberdeen, and for the last thirty-one years a highly respectable instructor of youth in this town and its neighborhood. The deceased, with a few harmless eccentricities of deportment, was sincerely anxious to discharge in a becoming manner, the duties of life—above all things he was remarkable for a rigid adherence to truth and honesty, and for an enthusiastic attachment to his personal friends ... [CG, Tues., 26 JUL 1831, p. 3]

MARRIED, in Washington, on Thursday evening last [i.e. 21 JUL 1831], by Rev. Mr. Danforth, Mr. EDWARD HAWKINS, to Miss ELIZABETH KELLY. [CG, Thurs., 28 JUL 1831, p. 3]

MARRIED, on the 10th inst. [i.e. 10 JUL 1831], by the Rev. Mr. Makleheimer, JOHN DUVALL, Esq., to Miss SARAH ANN CLAGETT, youngest daughter of the late Charles Clagett, all of Prince George's Co., Md. [CG, Thurs., 28 JUL 1831, p. 3]

DIED, in Washington, on Friday last [i.e. 22 JUL 1831], in the 63d year of her age, Mrs. SARAH WASHINGTON, widow of the late Henry Washington, of Alexandria. [CG, Thurs., 28 JUL 1831, p. 3]

DIED, on Saturday last [i.e. 23 JUL 1831], HOWARD, infant son of Darius Clagett, of Washington. [CG, Thurs., 28 JUL 1831, p. 3]

DIED, at Vineyard, (Isle of La Mott,) Ver., on the 25th day of June, 1831, of dropsy in the head, Mr. CALVIN HILL, aged 36 years. A widow and eight children are the surviving family. [CG, Thurs., 28 JUL 1831, p. 3]

MARRIED, in Washington [no date], Mr. CHARLES COALE, to Miss JULIA ANN SANFORD. [CG, Sat., 30 JUL 1831, p. 3]

MARRIED, in Philadelphia [no date], Lieut. GEORGE A. MAGRUDER, of the U.S. Navy, to Miss MARIA MARGARETTA SWAN. [CG, Sat., 30 JUL 1831, p. 3]

MARRIED, in Prince George's Co., Md. [no date], Mr. JOHN W. WARD, merchant of Piscataway, to Miss HENRIETTA, daughter of Mr. John Palmer. [CG, Tues., 2 AUG 1831, p. 3]

DIED, in this town, on Saturday morning last [i.e. 30 JUL 1831], Miss ELIZA R. ATKINSON. [CG, Tues., 2 AUG 1831, p. 3]

DIED, in Alexandria, on Friday last [i.e. 29 JUL 1831], Mr. FREDERICK ECKHARDT, aged 29, a native of Germany. [CG, Tues., 2 AUG 1831, p. 3]

Georgetown, D.C., **Marriage and Death Notices, 1801-1838**

DIED, in this town, on Sunday morning, 31 July [i.e. 31 JUL 1831], at the residence of her daughter, (Mrs. Jane Clagett), Mrs. CATHERINE C. HARRISON, at the advanced age of 98 years. [CG, Thurs., 4 AUG 1831, p. 3]

DIED, in Alexandria, on Monday [i.e. 1 AUG 1831], Mr. JAMES SPENCE, aged 37, a native of Scotland. [CG, Thurs., 4 AUG 1831, p. 3]

DIED, at *Buckland*, Va. [no date], Mrs. HANNAH BRENT, in the 73d y ear of her age, widow of the late Capt. William Brent, and mother of George Brent, Esq., Collector of the Port of Alexandria. [CG, Thurs., 4 AUG 1831, p. 3]

DIED, at Alexandria, on the evening of the 28th of July [i.e. 28 JUL 1831], MARY ANN TALBOTT, in the 21st year of her age, eldest daughter of Elisha Talbott, of that place ... [CG, Thurs., 4 AUG 1831, p. 3]

DIED, at his seat in Andalusia, Pa., recently [no date], WILLIAM CHAPMAN, Esq., aged 53 years. Mr. Chapman was a native of Newport-Pagnel, Buckinghamshire, England, and the discoverer of the cure for Stammering. Afflicted to a great degree in his early years, and finding no relief from any course recommended by the faculty of his native country, he was induced to attempt something for himself; he succeeded, and since his arrival in this country, has been the means of imparting relief to many who will look back upon the time they passed with him with gratitude and pleasure. [CG, Thurs., 4 AUG 1831, p. 3]

MARRIED, on the 2d inst. [i.e. 2 AUG 1831], Mr. CHARLES TAYLOE, to Miss VIRGINIA, daughter of the late Richard Turner, Esq., all of King George Co., Va. [CG, Tues., 9 AUG 1831, p. 3]

MARRIED, at Madrid, on the 30th May [i.e. 30 MAY 1831], JAMES I. ROOSEVELT, Jr., Esq., of N.Y., to Miss CORNELIA VAN NESS, daughter of the American Minister to the Court of Spain. [CG, Tues., 9 AUG 1831, p. 3]

DIED, on board the U.S. ship *Brandywine*, at the port of Algeziras, on the 20th June last [i.e. 20 JUN 1831], after a short illness, Lieut. BENJAMIN TALLMADGE, Jr., of Litchfield, Conn., a highly meritorious officer. [CG, Tues., 9 AUG 1831, p. 3]

DIED, at Black Rock, N.Y., on the 27th ult. [i.e. 27 JUL 1831], after a short illness, aged 43, Mrs. LETITIA PORTER, wife of Gen. Peter P. Porter, formerly Secretary of War. [CG, Tues., 9 AUG 1831, p. 3]

DIED, in Alexandria, on Friday [i.e. 5 AUG 1831], Mrs. JULIA ANN STEEL, widow of the late Jonathan H. Steel. [CG, Tues., 9 AUG 1831, p. 3]

MARRIED, in this town, on Monday, the 8th inst. [i.e. 8 AUG 1831], by the Rev. Dr. D.B. Dorsey, Mr. JOSIAH DANIEL McCOY, of Middleburg, Va., to Miss DUANNA BINNS FOX, of Georgetown, D.C. [CG, Thurs., 11 AUG 1831, p. 3]

Georgetown, D.C., **Marriage and Death Notices, 1801-1838**

MARRIED, in Alexandria, on Thursday evening last [i.e. 4 AUG 1831], Mr. JAMES BLACK, to Miss HELEN TALBOT, all of that place. [CG, Thurs., 11 AUG 1831, p. 3]

DIED, in this town, yesterday morning [i.e. 10 AUG 1831], Mrs. STATIRA ELLIOTT, about 70 years of age, widow of the late Lynde Elliott. Her funeral will take place from her residence on Market Space, this afternoon, at 5 o'clock. The friends and acquaintance of the family are respectfully invited to attend. [CG, Thurs., 11 AUG 1831, p. 3]

DIED, on Friday last [i.e. 5 AUG 1831], in Virginia, on her return to Alexandria, Miss CATHERINE B. TAYLOR, daughter of Robert I. Taylor, Esq., of Alexandria, in the 20th year of her age. [CG, Thurs., 11 AUG 1831, p. 3]

DIED, at Pensacola, W. Florida, on Friday, 22d July [i.e. 22 JUL 1831], after a short but painful indisposition, Mrs. HENRIETTA M. DALLAS, consort of Alex'r. J. Dallas, Esq., Commandant of the U.S. Navy Yard at that place, and eldest daughter of the late Richard W. Meade, Esq., formerly of Philadelphia, but more recently of Washington. [CG, Thurs., 11 AUG 1831, p. 3]

MARRIED, at *Kalorama*, in this District, on Tuesday evening the 9th inst. [i.e. 9 AUG 1831], by the Rev. Dr. Laurie, BENJAMIN LINCOLN LEAR, Esq., to LOUISA S. BOMFORD, daughter of Col. George Bomford, of the U.S. Army. [CG, Sat., 13 AUG 1831, p. 3]

DIED, in Washington, on Wednesday [i.e. 10 AUG 1831], after a lingering illness, in the 33d year of his age, Mr. JOHN H. DUFFEY. [CG, Sat., 13 AUG 1831, p. 3]

DIED, at Smith's Farm, Allegany Co., Md., on Sunday the 7th inst. [i.e. 7 AUG 1831], after a long illness, in the 22d year of his age, Mr. CHARLES ALEXANDER PATTERSON, son of Mr. Edgar Patterson, of this town. [CG, Tues., 16 AUG 1831, p. 3]

DIED, suddenly, on Saturday the 13th inst. [i.e. 13 AUG 1831], at the residence of his grandfather Gen. Mason, in this Town, JOHN HENRY MASON, son of John Mason, Jr., aged three years and six months. [CG, Tues., 16 AUG 1831, p. 3]

MARRIED, in Alexandria, on the 14th inst. [i.e. 14 AUG 1831], Mr. WILLIAM H. FOWLE, to Miss ELIZA THACKER, daughter of the late James H. Hooe, Esq., all of that place. [CG, Thurs., 18 AUG 1831, p. 3]

MARRIED, in Norfolk, Va., on the 10th inst. [i.e. 10 AUG 1831], Lieut. JOHN W. WEST, of the U.S. Navy, to Miss MARY C.E. HOLT, eldest daughter of Mr. Henry Holt, of that place. [CG, Thurs., 18 AUG 1831, p. 3]

DIED, in Alexandria, on Tuesday [i.e. 16 AUG 1831], Mrs. MARGARET THOMPSON, in the 63d year of her age. [CG, Thurs., 18 AUG 1831, p. 3]

DIED, in this town, on Tuesday morning last [i.e. 16 AUG 1831], EMILY LOUISA, aged 11 months, infant daughter of Jacob Carter, Jun. [CG, Sat., 20 AUG 1831, p. 3]

Georgetown, D.C., **Marriage and Death Notices, 1801-1838**

DIED, in Washington, on Friday [i.e. 19 AUG 1831], ARTHUR, infant son of Wm. W. Seaton, Esq. [CG, Tues., 23 AUG 1831, p. 3]

DIED, at the residence of Miss Carroll, near Rock Creek, on Thursday, 18th inst. [i.e. 18 AUG 1831], after a short illness, Mrs. HELEN JENIFER, wife of Walter H. Jenifer, of Washington. [CG, Tues., 23 AUG 1831, p. 3]

DIED, at Louisville, Ky., on the 8th inst. [i.e. 8 AUG 1831], Mr. STEPHEN LABILLE, aged 28, son of Mr. Louis Labille, of Washington. [CG, Tues., 23 AUG 1831, p. 3]

DIED, in Baltimore, on Monday the 15th inst. [i.e. 15 AUG 1831], a colored woman, named MARY FREDERICKS, at the advanced age of *one hundred and twelve years*. She retained her faculties unimpaired at the age of 102 years, at which time she become blind, but in all other respects she was capable of work until within a few days of her death. [CG, Tues., 23 AUG 1831, p. 3]

MARRIED, on Tuesday evening last [i.e. 18 AUG 1831], by the Rev. Mr. Clark, Mr. ASA GLADMAN, to Miss ANN PARKER. [CG, Thurs., 25 AUG 1831, p. 3]

MARRIED, in Boston, on the 16th inst. [i.e. 16 AUG 1831], the Rev. REUEL KEITH, D.D., Principal of the Theological seminary near Alexandria, D.C., to Miss ELIZABETH S., eldest daughter of Stephen Higginson, Esq. [CG, Thurs., 25 AUG 1831, p. 3]

MARRIED, on Thursday, the 18th inst. [i.e. 18 AUG 1831], in St. Michael's Church, Trenton, N.J., by the Rev. Dr. Beasley, Prince LUCIEN MURAT, second son of Joachim Murat, the late ex-king of Naples, to CAROLINA GEORGIANA, youngest daughter of the late Maj. Thomas Frazer, of S.C. [CG, Thurs., 25 AUG 1831, p. 3]

DIED, in this town, yesterday [i.e. 24 AUG 1831], FLORIDA, infant twin daughter of Jacob Carter, Junr., aged 11 months and 9 days. The friends of the family are respectfully invited to attend the funeral this afternoon at 5 o'clock. [CG, Thurs., 25 AUG 1831, p. 3]

DIED, on Sunday last [i.e. 21 AUG 1831], at the residence of Mrs. Sarah Perkins, relict of the late James Perkins, Esq., of Boston, an African, who from the time he was purchased at Cape Francois, in the Island of Hispaniola, in 1785, has borne the name of MOUSSE ... (His patronymic name was Deyaha). [CG, Thurs., 25 AUG 1831, p. 3]

DIED, in Washington, on Wednesday evening [i.e. 24 AUG 1831], after a severe illness of two months, Mr. MARK KING, Bookbinder, aged 31 years. [CG, Sat., 27 AUG 1831, p. 3]

DIED, at his residence in Butler Co., Ohio, on the 13th inst. [i.e. 13 AUG 1831], the Hon. JAMES SHIELDS, a member of the last Congress. [CG, Sat., 27 AUG 1831, p. 3]

DIED, at Marseilles, France, on the 16th June last [i.e. 16 JUN 1831], Dr. ROBERT P. MACOMBER, aged 27 years, a native of Rhode Island, and Surgeon of the U.S. ship *Ontario*. [CG, Sat., 27 AUG 1831, p. 3]

Georgetown, D.C., **Marriage and Death Notices, 1801-1838**

DIED, at Baltimore, on the 23d inst. [i.e. 23 AUG 1831], Lieut. FRANCIS SANDERSON, of the U.S. Navy, of a pulmonary disease, in the 30th year of his age. [CG, Sat., 27 AUG 1831, p. 3]

DIED, in Washington, a few days ago [no date], Mrs. ELIZABETH H. CLAGETT, wife of Dr. William H. Clagett, of Piscataway, in the 26th year of her age. [CG, Tues., 30 AUG 1831, p. 3]

DIED, in New Orleans [no date], at the age of 84 years, ANTONIO GONZALOS, upwards of fifty years the proprietor of the old wooden building at the corner of Custom house and Levee streets in that city. The deceased was a man of singular eccentric habits, and although very wealthy, preferred to any higher, the humble occupation of vendor of apples and new laid eggs, for the supply of which he kept a large number of fowls, but was never known to attack his poultry yard for the gratification of his own appetite ... [CG, Tues., 30 AUG 1831, p. 3]

DIED, at his residence in Kanawha Co., Va., on the 10th inst. [i.e. 10 AUG 1831], of apoplexy, Capt. SAMUEL WASHINGTON, aged about 60, a nephew and one of the legatees of Gen. George Washington. [CG, Tues., 30 AUG 1831, p. 3]

DIED, at Charleston, S.C., on the 6th inst. [i.e. 6 AUG 1831], in the 69th year of his age, JOHN ROBERTSON, Esq., for many years Navy Agent on that station, a gentleman of unblemished reputation, an enterprising merchant, and highly respected by all. [CG, Tues., 30 AUG 1831, p. 3]

MARRIED, in Medford, Mass., on the 23d ult. [i.e. 23 AUG 1831], Rev. ISAAC ORR, Editor of the *American Spectator*, to Miss MATILDA H., daughter of Dr. Samuel Kidder. [CG, Thurs., 1 SEP 1831, p. 3]

DIED, in Washington, on Monday [i.e. 29 AUG 1831], Mr. LAWRENCE KROFFT, aged 22. [CG, Thurs., 1 SEP 1831, p. 3]

DIED, in Bath, Me., very suddenly, on the 23d ult. [i.e. 23 AUG 1831], JOHN RUSSELL, Esq., for many years Editor and proprietor of the *Boston Gazette*, aged 69. [CG, Thurs., 1 SEP 1831, p. 3]

DIED, in Hunterdon Co., N.J., on the 14th inst. [i.e. 14 AUG 1831], the Rev. BENJAMIN COLLINS, Minister in the Methodist Episcopal Church. [CG, Thurs., 1 SEP 1831, p. 3]

MARRIED, at Paris [no date], at the house of Mr. Rives, Minister of the U. States at the French Court, NATHANIEL NILES, Esq., Secretary of the American Legation, to Mrs. ROSELLA DeMILHAU, of Baltimore, widow of the late Dr. John Joseph Sue, of Paris. [CG, Sat., 3 SEP 1831, p. 3]

DIED, at Alexandria, on the 30th ult. [i.e. 30 AUG 1831], Mr. WILLIAM CURTIN, aged about 38 years. [CG, Sat., 3 SEP 1831, p. 3]

Georgetown, D.C., **Marriage and Death Notices, 1801-1838**

DIED, at Columbian College, Washington City, on Wednesday [i.e. 31 AUG 1831], of a hemorrhage of the lungs, EPHRAIM R. NELSON, A.B., of Amherst, Mass., Principal of the Classical School, aged 21. [CG, Sat., 3 SEP 1831, p. 3]

MARRIED, in this town, on Thursday evening last [i.e. 1 SEP 1831], by the Rev. Mr. Amiss, Mr. GEORGE PRICE, to Miss MARY ANN ROBINSON, eldest daughter of the late Capt. James Barron, both of Alexandria. [CG, Tues., 6 SEP 1831, p. 3]

MARRIED, on Thursday morning, the 1st inst. [i.e. 1 SEP 1831], by the Rev. Mr. George L. Machenheimer, ZADOCK C. CHESLEY, Esq., of Georgetown, D.C., to Miss MARY CLAGETT, daughter of the late Mr. Charles Clagett, of Prince George's Co., Md. [CG, Tues., 6 SEP 1831, p. 3]

DIED, in this town, on Sunday afternoon [i.e. 4 SEP 1831], after a lingering illness, Mr. HORACE OGLE, about 40 years of age. Mr. Ogle was of a respectable family of Fredericktown, Md., and has left a wife with several small children to lament their loss. [CG, Tues., 6 SEP 1831, p. 3]

DIED, at Baltimore, on Friday morning, 2d September [i.e. 2 SEP 1831], aged nearly 22 years, ROBERT DUER NILES, printer, son of Hezekiah Niles, editor of the *Weekly Register*. [CG, Tues., 6 SEP 1831, p. 3]

DIED, in Baltimore, on Friday last, Sept. 2 [i.e. 2 SEP 1831], at the residence of her father, Alexander Robinson, ANGELICA, wife of Israel Peyton Thompson, of Alexandria, in the 32d year of her age. [CG, Tues., 6 SEP 1831, p. 3]

DIED, in Alexandria, on Monday [i.e. 5 SEP 1831], Mr. THOMAS BUTTS, in the 22d year of his age, son of Mr. Mark Butts. [CG, Thurs., 8 SEP 1831, p. 3]

DIED, on Tuesday [i.e. 6 SEP 1831], ARTHUR T. URIE, in the 32d year of his age. [CG, Thurs., 8 SEP 1831, p. 3]

DIED, at Piscataway, Md., on the 5th inst. [i.e. 5 SEP 1831], Mrs. HENRIETTA WARD, consort of John M. Ward, Esq., of that place. [CG, Thurs., 8 SEP 1831, p. 3]

MARRIED, in Washington, on Tuesday [i.e. 6 SEP 1831], Col. A.W. GOODRICH, to Miss ELIZA JANE THAW, daughter of Mr. Joseph Thaw. [CG, Sat., 10 SEP 1831, p. 3]

MARRIED, in Alexandria, on Tuesday [i.e. 6 SEP 1831], Mr. EDWARD McCUBBIN, of Washington, to Miss SUSAN, eldest daughter of Benjamin Jefferson, of Alexandria. [CG, Sat., 10 SEP 1831, p. 3]

DIED, in Philadelphia, on Wednesday last [i.e. 7 SEP 1831], RICHARD McCALL, Esq., late Navy Agent of the U.S. for the Mediterranean. [CG, Sat., 10 SEP 1831, p. 3]

Georgetown, D.C., **Marriage and Death Notices, 1801-1838**

DIED, at Bethlehem, Pa., on the morning of the 6th inst. [i.e. 6 SEP 1831], WILLIAM JONES, Esq., late Collector of the Port of Philadelphia, and formerly Secretary of the Navy of the U.S. [CG, Sat., 10 SEP 1831, p. 3]

DIED, in Terre Haute, Ind., on the 8th ult. [i.e. 8 AUG 1831], Mrs. SARAH L. BLAKE, wife of the Hon. T.H. Blake, aged 23 years, of pulmonary consumption. [CG, Sat., 10 SEP 1831, p. 3]

MARRIED, at Philadelphia, on the 8th inst. [i.e. 8 AUG 1831], by B.W. Richards, Esq., Mayor, BAZIL B. HOPKINS, of Alexandria, D.C., to Miss ELIZABETH B., eldest daughter of Samuel English, Esq., of Philadelphia. [CG, Tues., 13 SEP 1831, p. 3]

MARRIED, on the 28th January last [i.e. 28 JAN 1831], in Philadelphia, by the Rev. Dr. Abercrombie, GEORGE WILLIAM FEATHERSRONHAUGH, Esq., late of Duanesburgh, in the state of New York, to Miss CHARLOTTE WILLIAMS CARTER, youngest daughter of Bernard M. Carter, Esq., of Va. [CG, Tues., 13 SEP 1831, p. 3]

MARRIED, in Charleston, S.C., on the 1st inst. [i.e. 1 SEP 1831], by the Rev. Mr. Betts, JOSEPH ALFRED VARDEN, of Washington City, to Miss JULIA ANN, eldest daughter of the late Capt. Josiah Phynney, of Charleston. [CG, Tues., 13 SEP 1831, p. 3]

DIED, in this town, early yesterday morning [i.e. 12 SEP 1831], after a short illness, Miss MARIA ELIASON, eldest daughter of Mr. John Eliason, of this place. ☞ The friends of the family are requested to attend her funeral this afternoon, a four o'clock, from the residence of her brother-in-law, Mr. Thomas B. Addison, corner of Congress and Dunbarton streets. [CG, Tues., 13 SEP 1831, p. 3]

DIED, suddenly, in Baltimore, on Sunday, 28th August last [i.e. 28 AUG 1831], HENRY MAYER, Esq., a native of Germany, in the 42d year of his age. For many years a respectable merchant of Georgetown, D.C., from whence he retired to his farm at Sandy Point, Anne Arundel Co., where he lived for the last 10 years, respected and beloved by all who knew him. [CG, Tues., 13 SEP 1831, p. 3]

DIED, in Fredericksburg, on the 8th inst. [i.e. 8 SEP 1831], after a short but severe illness, in the 42d year of his age, WILLIAM A. KNOX, merchant of that place. [CG, Tues., 13 SEP 1831, p. 3]

DIED, at Bellona Arsenal, Va. [no date], after a severe illness, Lieut. LUCIEN J. BIBB, of the U.S. Army. [CG, Tues., 13 SEP 1831, p. 3]

DIED, in Weymouth, Mass., of spasms, on the evening of the 4th inst. [i.e. 4 SEP 1831], and after a sickness of only nine hours, LETITIA BRECKENRIDGE PORTER, aged 11 months and 21 days, only child of Lieut. J.B. Grayson, U.S. Army, formerly a resident of this town. [CG, Tues., 13 SEP 1831, p. 3]

DIED, in Davidson Co., Tenn. [no date], Mr. DAVID RALSTON, aged 90, a patriot of the Revolution, an honest man, and a Christian. [CG, Tues., 13 SEP 1831, p. 3]

DIED, at his residence in Miami township, 20th August [i.e. 20 AUG 1831], PATRICK SMITH, for seven years one of the Associate Judges of the Court of Common Please of Hamilton Co., Ohio. [CG, Tues., 13 SEP 1831, p. 3]

MARRIED, on the 8th inst. [i.e. 8 SEP 1831], by the Rev. Mr. Dubuison, Mr. CHARLES DAVIS, of Charles Co., Md., to Miss MARY ANN HILTON, of this place. [CG, Thurs., 15 SEP 1831, p. 3]

MARRIED, on Sunday the 11th inst. [i.e. 11 SEP 1831], in the City of Washington, by the Rev. Mr. Robb, Mr. ROBERT HUNTER, to Miss MARGARET ANN MERCHANT, both of Alexandria. [CG, Thurs., 15 SEP 1831, p. 3]

DIED, at *Hazel Plain*, her seat in Prince William Co., Va. [no date], after a short illness, Mrs. E.T. HOOE, the widow of the late James H. Hooe, Esq., of Alexandria, in her 51st year. [CG, Thurs., 15 SEP 1831, p. 3]

MARRIED, in Baltimore, on Monday evening [i.e. 12 SEP 1831], by the Rev. Mr. Baer, Mr. JOHN KNOBLOCK, of Washington City, to Miss HARRIET PRICE, of Alexandria, D.C. [CG, Sat., 17 SEP 1831, p. 3]

MARRIED, in Fredericktown, Md., on the 13th inst. [i.e. 13 SEP 1831], by the Rev. Mr. Smalts, Mr. THOS. L. AVERD, to Miss MARTHA ANN ROSE, both of this town. [CG, Sat., 17 SEP 1831, p. 3]

DIED, in Alexandria, on the 12th inst. [i.e. 12 SEP 1831], Mr. JOHN ROACH, aged 52 years, a native of the County of Wexford, Ireland, and for the last 14 years an inhabitant of that town. [CG, Sat., 17 SEP 1831, p. 3]

MARRIED, on Monday, the 5th of September [i.e. 5 SEP 1831], at *Laurel Grove*, Charles Co., Md., by the Rev. Mr. Tachi, Mr. RICHARD B. LLOYD, of Alexandria, to Miss ELIZABETH ELLEN, second daughter of the late Capt. Lawrence Posey, of Charles Co., Md. [CG, Tues., 20 SEP 1831, p. 3]

MARRIED, in Baltimore, on the 13th inst. [i.e. 13 SEP 1831], Mr. JOHN W. WALTERS, of that City, to Miss MARY ANN TALBOT, of Washington City. [CG, Tues., 20 SEP 1831, p. 3]

DIED, in this town, on the 16th inst. [i.e. 16 SEP 1831], in the 16th year of his age, HENRY ROBERTSON, son of Samuel Robertson, dec., late Purser U.S. Navy. [CG, Thurs., 22 SEP 1831, p. 3]

DIED, in Washington, on Sunday night [i.e. 18 SEP 1831], Mrs. ANNE BLAGDEN, relict of the late Mr. George Blagden. [CG, Thurs., 22 SEP 1831, p. 3]

DIED, in Alexandria, on the 19th inst. [i.e. 19 SEP 1831], in the 75th year of her age, Mrs. ESTHER HALLEY, for many years a respectable inhabitant of that town. [CG, Thurs., 22 SEP 1831, p. 3]

Georgetown, D.C., **Marriage and Death Notices, 1801-1838**

MARRIED, in Concord, N.H., on the 14th inst. [i.e. 14 SEP 1831], Capt. JOSEPH MANAHAN, of Washington City, to Miss ELLEN D. MONTGOMERY, daughter of the late Gen. James Montgomery, of Haverhill. [CG, Sat., 24 SEP 1831, p. 3]

DIED, in this town, on Wednesday evening [i.e. 21 SEP 1831], Mr. IGNATIUS PIERCE, aged 52 years; an old inhabitant of Georgetown, who has left a widow and numerous family of children to lament their loss. [CG, Sat., 24 SEP 1831, p. 3]

DIED, in Washington, on Thursday [i.e. 22 SEP 1831], Mrs. SARAH ELLIOT, aged 42, wife of Mr. Jonathan Elliot. [CG, Sat., 24 SEP 1831, p. 3]

DIED, at his residence in Caroline Co., Va. [no date], in the 62d year of his age, Mr. JAMES JONES, leaving an affectionate wife and four children to mourn their irreparable loss. [CG, Sat., 24 SEP 1831, p. 3]

DIED, in Trenton, N.J., on the 15th inst. [i.e. 15 SEP 1831], Dr. WILLIAM C. McCALL, Surgeon, U.S. Navy. [CG, Sat., 24 SEP 1831, p. 3]

MARRIED, in Alexandria, on Friday evening [i.e. 23 SEP 1831], Mr. CHARLES GRAHAM, to Mrs. ELIZABETH KEEFE, both of that place. [CG, Tues., 27 SEP 1831, p. 3]

DIED, in Alexandria, on Friday [i.e. 23 SEP 1831], Mrs. ELIZABETH HAYMAN, in the 45th year of her age, wife of Capt. Caspar Hayman. [CG, Tues., 27 SEP 1831, p. 3]

DIED, at her late residence in Fairfax Co., Va., on Tuesday last [i.e. 20 SEP 1831], Mrs. REBECCA POTTER, in the 93d year of her age. [CG, Tues., 27 SEP 1831, p. 3]

DIED, in Front Royal, Va., on the 16th inst. [i.e. 16 SEP 1831], Dr. PHILIP DODDRIDGE WILLIAMSON, eldest son of the Rev. Wm. Williamson, of Middleburg. [CG, Tues., 27 SEP 1831, p. 3]

DIED, in Fredericktown, Md., on the 16th inst. [i.e. 16 SEP 1831], of a paralytic affection, in the 61st year of her age, Mrs. CATHERINE CONTES TYLER, wife of Dr. John Tyler. [CG, Tues., 27 SEP 1831, p. 3]

DIED, on the 22d inst. [i.e. 22 SEP 1831], Mrs. CATHERINE THOMAS, wife of Dr. John Thomas, and daughter of the late Thomas Turner, Esq., of this town. [CG, Tues., 27 SEP 1831, p. 3]

MARRIED, on the 23d inst. [i.e. 23 SEP 1831], by Rev. C. Mann, Dr. ALEXANDER H. MASON, of Stafford Co., Va., to Miss JANE A., youngest daughter of the late Dr. A.I. SMITH, of Fairfax Co., Va. [CG, Thurs., 29 SEP 1831, p. 3]

DIED, in Washington, on Friday evening, the 23d inst. [i.e. 23 SEP 1831], after a severe illness of nine days, Mrs. HARRIET BUCHLEY, in the 33d year of her age, formerly of St. Mary's Co., Md. [CG, Thurs., 29 SEP 1831, p. 3]

Georgetown, D.C., Marriage and Death Notices, 1801-1838

DIED, in Alexandria [no date], at the house of Mr. Edward Smyth, who had afforded him a refuge in his latter years, PIERRE LaCROIX, in his eighty-eighth year, probably the last surviving soldier who served under Montcalm, the best general of the French, who, with a superior force, defended Quebec against Wolf when they both fell, on the field of the battle. LaCroix was then twelve years of age, a drummer in one of the French regiments. He afterwards served, during the revolutionary war, spoke often of the bravery of Montgomery who fell under the walls of Quebec, but on which side, it is unnecessary now to enquire. He was a soldier and he died a christian ... [CG, Thurs., 29 SEP 1831, p. 3]

DIED, on the 10th July [i.e. 10 JUL 1831], of Yellow Fever, on board the U.S. ship *Vincennes*, at Port Royal, (in the Island of Jamaica), Dr. CALEB W. CLOUD, aged 24 years, assistant Surgeon in the Navy, after an illness of 5 days. [CG, Thurs., 29 SEP 1831, p. 3]

DIED, Capt. JOHN THOMPSON, late of this town, on the night of the 29th inst. [i.e. 29 SEP 1831], in the 69th year of his age. His funeral will move from the residence of his brother, Gen. James Thompson, near the upper bridge on Rock Creek, at three o'clock, this day. His friends and acquaintances are invited to attend without further notice. [CG, Sat., 1 OCT 1831, p. 3]

DIED, in Washington, on Thursday evening [i.e. 29 SEP 1831], in the 67th year of his age, Capt. JOHN COYLE, of the Treasury Department, one of the oldest and most respectable inhabitants of that City. [CG, Sat., 1 OCT 1831, p. 3]

DIED, in Alexandria, on Wednesday last [i.e. 28 SEP 1831], Mrs. ANN CARTWRIGHT, aged 40 years. [CG, Sat., 1 OCT 1831, p. 3]

MARRIED, on the 25th ult. [i.e. 25 SEP 1831], by the Rev. Mr. Amiss, Mr. THOMAS K. SPILMAN, to Miss ELIZABETH BARNHISEL, both of this town. [CG, Tues., 4 OCT 1831, p. 3]

DIED, in Washington, on Saturday, the 1st inst. [i.e. 1 OCT 1831], in the 67th year of her age, Mrs. ELIZABETH McDONALD, consort of Mr. Alex. McDonald. [CG, Tues., 4 OCT 1831, p. 3]

DIED, at the Navy Hospital, Pensacola, on the 14th ult. [i.e. 14 SEP 1831], of yellow fever, Lieut. PAUL H. HAYNE, of the navy, an officer of fine qualities and great promise. [CG, Tues., 4 OCT 1831, p. 3]

DIED, at his place in Baltimore Co., on the 29th ult. [i.e. 29 SEP 1831], CHARLES H. APPLETON, aged 46 years, of a pulmonary complaint. He was a native of Boston and for many years a respectable and enterprising merchant in Baltimore. [CG, Tues., 4 OCT 1831, p. 3]

DIED, at Carlisle, Pa., on Thursday morning last [i.e. 29 SEP 1831], the Hon. WILLIAM RAMSEY, a member of Congress from Pa. [CG, Tues., 4 OCT 1831, p. 3]

Georgetown, D.C., **Marriage and Death Notices, 1801-1838**

MARRIED, in Alexandria, on the 3d inst. [i.e. 3 OCT 1831], Mr. GEORGE W. CUTSHAW, of Jefferson Co., Va., to Miss MARTHA JANE MOXLEY, of Alexandria. [CG, Thurs., 6 OCT 1831, p. 3]

DIED, in Alexandria, on the 2d inst. [i.e. 2 OCT 1831], Miss ARTAMESIA T. REARDON, in the 31st year of her age. [CG, Thurs., 6 OCT 1831, p. 3]

DIED, in Washington, on Friday night last [i.e. 30 SEP 1831], in the 22d year of his age, Mr. EDWIN T. BALL, Stationer. [CG, Thurs., 6 OCT 1831, p. 3]

DIED, on Sunday morning [i.e. 2 OCT 1831], Mrs. SOPHIA DYER, wife of Edward Dyer. [CG, Thurs., 6 OCT 1831, p. 3]

MARRIED, in Washington, on Thursday last [i.e. 6 OCT 1831], by Rev. Mr. Johns, Mr. JOHN W. MAURY, to Miss ISABEL FOYLES, both of that City. [CG, Tues., 11 OCT 1831, p. 2]

DIED, at Fredericksburg, Va., on the 6th inst. [i.e. 6 OCT 1831], THOMAS SEDDON, Esq., Cashier of the Farmers Bank of Virginia in that place. [CG, Tues., 11 OCT 1831, p. 2]

DIED, in Washington, on the 10th inst. [i.e. 10 OCT 1831], in the 54th year of her age, Mrs. ELLEN G. GILLISS, wife of Thomas H. Gilliss, of the Treasury Department. [CG, Thurs., 13 OCT 1831, p. 2]

DIED, on Friday, the 7th inst. [i.e. 7 OCT 1831], Rev. MATTHEW DEAGLE, Pastor of St. Peter's (Catholic) Church in that city [Washington]. [CG, Thurs., 13 OCT 1831, p. 2]

DIED, in Baltimore, on Monday evening [i.e. 10 OCT 1831], Lieut. J.A. DUMESTE, of the U.S. Army. [CG, Thurs., 13 OCT 1831, p. 2]

DIED, in Tallahassee, Middle Florida, on the 21st ult. [i.e. 21 SEP 1831], JAMES G. RINGGOLD, Esq., U.S. District Attorney, a native of Baltimore. [CG, Thurs., 13 OCT 1831, p. 2]

DIED, at Annapolis, on Sunday last [i.e. 9 OCT 1831], the venerable Judge DONE, aged 86 years. [CG, Thurs., 13 OCT 1831, p. 2]

DIED, at Annapolis, Md., on Monday, 3rd inst. [i.e. 3 OCT 1831], ELIZABETH E. GUEST, daughter of the Rev. Job Guest, aged 15 years. [CG, Thurs., 13 OCT 1831, p. 2]

DIED, at Natchitoches, La., on the 13th ult. [i.e. 13 SEP 1831], of a bilious fever, GEORGE KINCAID, formerly of this town. [CG, Thurs., 13 OCT 1831, p. 2]

MARRIED, in Bath, Me. [no date], Lieut. THOMAS T. CRAVEN, of the U.S. Navy, to Miss VIRGINIA A.N. WINGATE, daughter of the Hon. J.F. Wingate. [CG, Thurs., 20 OCT 1831, p. 2]

Georgetown, D.C., **Marriage and Death Notices, 1801-1838**

DIED, at *Vinemount,* near Charleston, Jefferson Co., Va., on the 11th inst. [i.e. 11 OCT 1831], GEORGE BEALL BALCH, Esq., third son of Dr. S.B. Balch of this town. In the death of this amiable, conscientious and pious man, society has sustained a loss. He was universally loved and respected. [CG, Thurs., 20 OCT 1831, p. 2]

DIED, in Alexandria, on Wednesday [i.e. 19 OCT 1831], after a short illness, Mrs. LUCY McGUIRE, consort of Capt. James McGuire, in the 54th year of her age. [CG, Sat., 22 OCT 1831, p. 3]

DIED, on Wednesday [i.e. 19 OCT 1831], Mrs. ELIZABETH BENTER, consort of Mr. William Benter, of West End, Fairfax Co., and formerly of Alexandria. [CG, Sat., 22 OCT 1831, p. 3]

DIED, at his residence near Gloucester Court House, Va., on Sunday last [i.e. 16 OCT 1831], after a short illness, JAMES J. McLANAHAN, Esq., formerly merchant of Baltimore. [CG, Sat., 22 OCT 1831, p. 3]

DIED, at *Hill-Farm,* near Middleburg, on Monday the 10th inst. [i.e. 10 OCT 1831], Mrs. NANCY GIBSON, consort of David Gibson, Esq., in the 66th year of her age. [CG, Sat., 22 OCT 1831, p. 3]

MARRIED, in Alexandria, on Wednesday [i.e. 19 OCT 1831], Mr. SAMUEL KING SHAY, to Miss JANE ELIZA, daughter of the late Capt. David Black, all of that place. [CG, Tues., 25 OCT 1831, p. 2]

MARRIED, on Thursday [i.e. 20 OCT 1831], EDWARD DAINGERFIELD, Esq., to Miss MARGARET B., daughter of John C. Vowell, all of Alexandria. [CG, Tues., 25 OCT 1831, p. 2]

MARRIED, in Falmouth, Va., on Wednesday last [i.e. 19 OCT 1831], JAMES INNIS THORNTON, Esq., Secretary of State for Alabama, to Miss ANN AMELIA, daughter of the late George Smith, Esq., of Dumfries. [CG, Tues., 25 OCT 1831, p. 2]

DIED, in this town, on Saturday the 22d inst. [i.e. 22 OCT 1831], after a short illness, of typhus fever, EDMOND JEFFERSON BEATTY, son of Dr. Charles A. Beatty. [CG, Tues., 25 OCT 1831, p. 2]

DIED, in Washington, on Friday morning [i.e. 21 OCT 1831], Mrs. MARY B. RANDOLPH, wife of Dr. P.G. Randolph, late Chief Clerk of the War Department. [CG, Tues., 25 OCT 1831, p. 2]

DIED, at Pittsburg, Pa., on Sunday, 16th inst. [i.e. 16 OCT 1831], after a long and painful illness, JAMES S. STEVENSON, Esq., one of the Canal Commissioners of Pa., and formerly a representative in Congress from that state. [CG, Tues., 25 OCT 1831, p. 2]

Georgetown, D.C., **Marriage and Death Notices, 1801-1838**

MARRIED, on the 18th inst. [i.e. 18 OCT 1831], at *Glen-Owen*, Loudoun Co., Va., THOMAS S. HOPKINS, to Miss SALLY LEE, daughter of Samuel B. Harris, Esq. all of said county. [CG, Thurs., 27 OCT 1831, p. 3]

DIED, in Alexandria, on Sunday night [i.e. 23 OCT 1831], after a lingering illness, in the 49th year of his age, Mr. SAMUEL MARK, for many years a respectable merchant of that place, and at the time of his death an Inspector of the port of Alexandria. [CG, Thurs., 27 OCT 1831, p. 3]

DIED, in Alexandria, on the 25th inst. [i.e. 25 OCT 1831], AMBROSE VASSE, a native of Languedoc in France, in the 85th year of his age, as near as can be ascertained. He came into this country near the close of the Revolutionary war, was a merchant of some note in the city of Philadelphia for upwards of twenty years, and during one period of this time possessed considerable property. At this time his house and all his purse were open to the wandering stranger from his native land. [CG, Thurs., 27 OCT 1831, p. 3]

DIED, in September last, in the island of St. Helena, Mrs. ELIZABETH HONORIA FRANCIS LAMBE, (relict of the late Sergeant Lambe, of the artillery of the island) at the advanced age of 110 years and four months.—In the year 1731, she was housekeeper in the establishment of Governor Pyke, during his second government, and well remembers having heard that Sir Richard Munden stormed the fort which now bears his name. Twenty-nine personages have filled the seat of Governor of the island during her life time. She was eight times married, had numerous generations (260 of whom are now alive,) and died an example of true piety, in the full persuasion that the Millennium will happen in 1836, and that the carter will be renewed to the Honorable *East India Company.—Liverpool Mer.* [CG, Thurs., 27 OCT 1831, p. 3]

MARRIED, in Washington, on Tuesday evening [i.e. 25 OCT 1831], by the Rev. Mr. Hawley, Capt. CHARLES STEWART McGAULEY, of the U.S. Navy, to LILLA ELIZABETH, eldest daughter of Asbury Dickins, Esq., of the Treasury Department [CG, Sat., 29 OCT 1831, p. 3]

MARRIED, on Tuesday evening [i.e. 25 OCT 1831], by the Rev. Mr. Post, Mr. DANIEL CAMPBELL, to Miss JANE RODBIRD, both of Washington. [CG, Sat., 29 OCT 1831, p. 3]

MARRIED, in Louisville, Ky., on the 15th inst. [i.e. 15 OCT 1831], Capt. J. ROGERS, of the U.S. Army, to Miss JOSEPHINE PRESTON. [CG, Sat., 29 OCT 1831, p. 3]

DIED, at St. Augustine, on the 10th inst. [i.e. 10 OCT 1831], in the 52d year of his age, WATERS SMITH, Esq., Marshal of the U.S. for the District of East Florida. [CG, Sat., 29 OCT 1831, p. 3]

MARRIED, in this town, by the Rev. Mr. Amiss, on the 20th ult. [i.e. 20 OCT 1831], Mr. JOHN S. CARROLL, to Miss HARRIET DIXON, all of this town. [CG, Tues., 1 NOV 1831, p. 3]

Georgetown, D.C., **Marriage and Death Notices, 1801-1838**

DIED, in Alexandria, on Tuesday [i.e. 1 NOV 1831], Mrs. MARGERY MILLS, relict of the late Capt. Wm. Mills, in the 66th year of her age. [CG, Thurs., 3 NOV 1831, p. 3]

DIED, at his residence, *Cameron*, near Alexandria [no date], Mr. DAVID RICKETTS, in the 69th year of his age. [CG, Thurs., 3 NOV 1831, p. 3]

DIED, at Lancaster, Pa., on the 25th ult. [i.e. 25 OCT 1831], after a few hours illness, Mr. JOHN JEFFERSON, son of the celebrated comedian, formerly of the Philadelphia and Washington Theatres. [CG, Thurs., 3 NOV 1831, p. 3]

MARRIED, in Washington, on Tuesday evening last [i.e. 1 NOV 1831], by the Rev. Mr. Johns, Mr. JOHN DAWSON JAMES, to Miss EMILY V. HOLMEAD, all of that city. [CG, Sat., 5 NOV 1831, p. 3]

MARRIED, in Baltimore, on Tuesday evening [i.e. 1 NOV 1831], Lieut. LOUIS M. GOLDSBOROUGH, of the U.S. Navy, to Miss ELIZABETH GAMBLE, second daughter of the Hon. William Wirt. [CG, Sat., 5 NOV 1831, p. 3]

MARRIED, last evening [i.e. 7 NOV 1831], by the Rev. Wm. Ryland, SAMUEL S. RIND, Esq., of this town, to Miss ARAMINTA MARIA KANKEY, of Prince William Co., Va. [CG, Tues., 8 NOV 1831, p. 3]

DIED, in Jefferson Co., Va., on Wednesday the 12th inst. [i.e. 12 OCT 1831], GEORGE B. BALCH, brother of L.P.W. Balch, Esq., of this town ... [CG, Tues., 8 NOV 1831, p. 3]

DIED, at *Susquehanna*, his later residence, in St. Mary's Co., Md., on the 29th ult. [i.e. 29 OCT 1831], Capt. MICHAEL B. CARROLL, aged about 63 years, late of the U.S. Navy. [CG, Tues., 8 NOV 1831, p. 3]

DIED, in Benedict, Charles Co., Md., on Saturday, the 29th ult. [i.e. 29 OCT 1831], Mr. JAMES TURNER, aged about 60 years. [CG, Tues., 8 NOV 1831, p. 3]

DIED, in Boston, on Tuesday night the 1st inst. [i.e. 1 NOV 1831], Hon. JONATHAN MASON, in the 76th year of his age. [CG, Tues., 8 NOV 1831, p. 3]

DIED, at Saratoga Springs, on Wednesday last [i.e. 2 NOV 1831], Dr. JOSHUA PORTER, brother of Gen. Peter B. Porter, late Secretary of War, aged 72. [CG, Thurs., 10 NOV 1831, p. 3]

DIED, in Lexington, Ky., on the 25th ult. [i.e. 25 OCT 1831], after a lingering illness, Mr. JAMES HARPER, Cashier of the U.S. Branch Bank. [CG, Thurs., 10 NOV 1831, p. 3]

DIED, in Washington, on the 7th inst. [i.e. 7 NOV 1831], in the 84th year of her age, Mrs. JANE WATSON, relict of Josiah Watson, for many years a respectable merchant of Alexandria. [CG, Thurs., 10 NOV 1831, p. 3]

Georgetown, D.C., **Marriage and Death Notices, 1801-1838**

DIED, in Philadelphia, on the 7th inst. [i.e. 7 NOV 1831], Mrs. ELIZABETH MacPHERSON, widow of the late Gen. MacPherson, and daughter of the Right Rev. Bishop Whitel. [CG, Sat., 12 NOV 1831, p. 2]

DIED, in N.Y., on Sunday evening [i.e. 6 NOV 1831], Col. JAMES A. DUNLAP, lately appointed U.S. Attorney for the middle District of Florida. [CG, Sat., 12 NOV 1831, p. 2]

MARRIED, in Baltimore, on the 10th inst. [i.e. 10 NOV 1851], by the Rev. W.W. Wallace, Mr. M.S. WINES, of Ind., to Miss ELIZABETH TILLEY, of Georgetown, D.C. [CG, Tues., 15 NOV 1831, p. 3]

MARRIED, at Philadelphia [no date], by the Rev. Dr. Hurley, ROBERT MORRIS, Esq., Editor of the *Philadelphia Inquirer*, to AMANDA LOUISA, youngest daughter of Mr. William Miller, all of Philadelphia. [CG, Tues., 15 NOV 1831, p. 3]

DIED, on Wednesday morning [i.e. 9 NOV 1831], at Annapolis, Mr. FERDINANDO TYDINGS, at an advanced age, long a member of the Methodist Episcopal Church. [CG, Tues., 15 NOV 1831, p. 3]

DIED, in Lenox, Mass. [no date], Judge WM. WALKER, 80 ... He was an officer in the American troops at Cambridge in 1775. Of the Convention that formed the Constitution of Mass. he was a member. For a long time he held the office of Judge of the County Court, and still longer that of Judge of Probate. He took a deep interest in the religious charitable institutions of the last 25 years, and of the Berkshire Bible Society he was President from its organization. [CG, Tues., 15 NOV 1831, p. 3]

Another Revolutionary Patriot Gone! General PHILIP VAN COURTLANDT died at his seat on the North River, at eight o'clock on Sunday evening, 6th inst. [i.e. 6 NOV 1831], at the advanced age of 82 years. [CG, Tues., 15 NOV 1831, p. 3]

DIED, in Otsego, N.Y., on the 14th ult. [i.e. 14 OCT 1831], Mr. SAMUEL HYATT, in the 83d year of his age. Mr. Hyatt was among the first to breast himself against British tyranny, and was in the heat of the battle of Monmouth, and with Gen. Wayne at the storming of Stoney Point. [CG, Tues., 15 NOV 1831, p. 3]

DIED, in Amesbury, Mass. [no date], Mr. BENJA. MERRILL, 84; he was present at the battle of Lexington, and contended on Bunker's Hill, against the strong arm of tyranny and oppression. [CG, Tues., 15 NOV 1831, p. 3]

DIED, in Shelburne, Mass. [no date], Capt. JOHN FELLOWS, 80, a soldier in the Revolution. [CG, Tues., 15 NOV 1831, p. 3]

DIED, in Walpole, N.H. [no date], Capt. JOSEPH FAY, 69, a soldier of the Revolution. [CG, Tues., 15 NOV 1831, p. 3]

DIED, in Mercer, Me. [no date], Capt. BENJ. BAXTER, 74, a revolutionary soldier and pensioner. [CG, Tues., 15 NOV 1831, p. 3]

Georgetown, D.C., **Marriage and Death Notices, 1801-1838**

DIED, in Washington, on the 15th inst. [i.e. 15 NOV 1831], Mrs. ANN CASANAVE, in the 65th year of her age. [CG, Thurs., 17 NOV 1831, p. 3]

MARRIED, in Baltimore, on the 17th inst. [i.e. 17 NOV 1831], by the Rev. Mr. Derbin, DANIEL WESLEY MIDDLETON, of Washington City, to MARGARET CARROL BRICE, daughter of John Brice, Esq., of that place. [CG, Sat., 19 NOV 1831, p. 3]

MARRIED, in Alexandria, on the 11th inst. [i.e. 11 NOV 1831], by the Rev. Dr. Reese, Mr. CHARLES HAWKINS, to Miss LUCINDA V. SUMMERS, all of that place. [CG, Tues., 22 NOV 1831, p. 3]

MARRIED, in the city of New York, on Tuesday last [i.e. 15 NOV 1831], at Christ Church, by the Rev. Mr. Varrella, and afterwards at St. John's Chapel, by the Rev. Mr. Berrian, Mr. V. OBREGON, of Mexico, to Miss MARGARETTA, daughter of the late Mr. Samuel Hurry, of Philadelphia. [CG, Tues., 22 NOV 1831, p. 3]

DIED, at Bladensburg, on Wednesday the 9th inst. [i.e. 9 NOV 1831], Mrs. ELIZABETH B. JACKSON, the wife of Mr. William B. Jackson, and eldest daughter of the late Benjamin Lowndes, Esq. [CG, Tues., 22 NOV 1831, p. 3]

DIED, at his residence in Halifax Co., N.C., on the 10th inst. [i.e. 10 NOV 1831], Mr. GIDEON ALSTON, one of the venerable Counselors of State, in the 65th year of his age. [CG, Tues., 22 NOV 1831, p. 3]

DIED, at Savannah, on the 10th inst. [i.e. 10 NOV 1831], FREDERICK S. FELL, Esq., for many years editor of the *Savannah Republican.* [CG, Tues., 22 NOV 1831, p. 3]

DIED, in Philadelphia, on the 13th inst. [i.e. 13 NOV 1831], in the 76th year of her age, Mrs. SARAH BARRY, relict of the late Com. John Barry, of the U.S. Navy. [CG, Tues., 22 NOV 1831, p. 3]

DIED, in this town, on Monday the 21st inst. [i.e. 21 NOV 1831], after a long and painful illness, Mrs. SARAH PIERCE, in the 61st year of her age. [CG, Thurs., 24 NOV 1831, p. 3]

DIED, at Milledgeville, (Geo.) on the 7th inst. [i.e. 7 NOV 1831], Mrs. LUCINDA BETTON, wife of Capt. Solomon Betton, and sister of the Hon. Charles Fenton Mercer, of Va. [CG, Thurs., 24 NOV 1831, p. 3]

DIED, at Pensacola, on the 28th ult. [i.e. 28 OCT 1831], Mr. JEROME D. MOORE, Printer, formerly of Philadelphia. [CG, Thurs., 24 NOV 1831, p. 3]

DIED, at the Navy Yard near Pensacola, on the 30th ult. [i.e. 30 OCT 1831], Mr. JOHN O'SULLIVAN, Purser's Steward. [CG, Thurs., 24 NOV 1831, p. 3]

DIED, in Boston, on Wednesday, 16th inst. [i.e. 16 NOV 1831], Mr. EDWARD DRAPER, printer, aged 82. Mr. D. was at the time of his decease, probably, the oldest printer in New England ... [CG, Thurs., 24 NOV 1831, p. 3]

Georgetown, D.C., **Marriage and Death Notices, 1801-1838**

MARRIED, in Washington, on Wednesday, the 16th inst. [i.e. 16 NOV 1831], by the Rev. Mr. Charles Polkinhorn, Mr. JAMES TOWLES, of Fredericksburg, Va., to Miss CATHERINE ANN EDMONSTON, of that city. [CG, Sat., 26 NOV 1831, p. 3]

MARRIED, on Tuesday morning last [i.e. 22 NOV 1831], by the Rev. Mr. Matthews, Mr. RICHARD G. BRISCOE, to ANNA MARIA, daughter of Mr. Joseph S. Clarke, merchant, all of that city [Washington]. [CG, Sat., 26 NOV 1831, p. 3]

MARRIED, on Tuesday evening last [i.e. 22 NOV 1831], by the Rev. Mr. Matthews, JAMES HOBAN, Jr., Esq., to Miss MARION B. FRENCH, daughter of Mr. Wm. French, all of that city [Washington]. [CG, Sat., 26 NOV 1831, p. 3]

MARRIED, in Baltimore, on Thursday morning [i.e. 24 NOV 1831], by the Rev. J. Finley, Lieut. ALEXANDER D. McKAY, of the U.S. Army, to Mrs. SARAH M. BANKSON, formerly of this town, and daughter of George Maris, Esq., of Baltimore. [CG, Sat., 26 NOV 1831, p. 3]

MARRIED, at *Aspin Hill*, in Fairfax Co., Va., on Tuesday the 21st inst. [i.e. 22? NOV 1831], by the Rev. Reuel Keith, PROVINCE McCORMICK, Esq., of Winchester, to Miss MARGARETTA, daughter of Wm. Moss, Esq. [CG, Tues., 29 NOV 1831, p. 3]

MARRIED, in this town, on Tuesday evening last [i.e. 29 NOV 1831], by the Rev. Dr. Balch, Mr. EVAN LYONS, to Miss EVELINA BARNES, all of Georgetown. [CG, Thurs., 1 DEC 1831, p. 3]

MARRIED, in Fredericksburg, on Tuesday evening 22d ult. [i.e. 22 NOV 1831], by the Rev. E.C. McGuire, Mr. JOHN H. MADDOX, of Alexandria, to Miss FRANCES S. YOUNG, daughter of the late Mr. James Young, of that place. [CG, Thurs., 1 DEC 1831, p. 3]

DIED, on the 25th inst. [i.e. 25 NOV 1831], at his late residence in Charles Co., Md., RICHARD H. BRANDT, in the 25th year of his age. [CG, Thurs., 1 DEC 1831, p. 3]

MARRIED, in Alexandria, on Thursday evening, 24th ult. [i.e. 24 NOV 1831], Mr. JACOB H. WILSON, to Miss ELIZABETH B. HILLS, both of that place. [CG, Sat., 3 DEC 1831, p. 3]

MARRIED, at *Elmwood*, Frederick Co., the residence of Jacob Poe, Esq., on Wednesday evening last [i.e. 30 NOV 1831], by the Rev. Mr. Jackson, Mr. NEILSON POE, Editor of the *Frederick Examiner*, to Miss JOSEPHINE, youngest daughter of the late Wm. Clemm, Esq., of Baltimore. [CG, Tues., 6 DEC 1831, p. 3]

DIED, in Philadelphia, on the 30th Nov. 1831, in the 82d year of his age, of a protracted and severe illness, JOHN GEYER, formerly a Captain of the Revolutionary Army, and long an useful and respectable citizen of Philadelphia. [CG, Tues., 6 DEC 1831, p. 3]

MARRIED, in Washington, on the 5th inst. [i.e. 5 DEC 1831], Mr. ALLISON NAYLOR, to Miss ELIZABETH GIVEN, both of that city. [CG, Thurs., 8 DEC 1831, p. 3]

Georgetown, D.C., **Marriage and Death Notices, 1801-1838**

MARRIED, in Norfolk, on the 30th ult. [i.e. 30 NOV 1831], Lieut. WM. W. HUNTER, of the U.S. Navy, to Miss JANE VIRGINIA SAUNDERS. [CG, Thurs., 8 DEC 1831, p. 3]

DIED, in Philadelphia, on Sunday the 4th inst. [i.e. 4 DEC 1831], Mrs. SARAH CRAWFORD, relict of Mr. William Crawford. The friends and acquaintances of the family are requested to attend her funeral this evening, at 3 o'clock, from the residence of Mr. Richard Burgess, at the corner of Stoddert and Greene streets. [CG, Thurs., 8 DEC 1831, p. 3]

DIED, in Washington, on the 5th inst. [i.e. 5 DEC 1831], Mr. JOHN BOWEN, in the 47th year of his age. [CG, Thurs., 8 DEC 1831, p. 3]

DIED, in Richmond, on the 1st inst. [i.e. 1 DEC 1831], HANNAH, wife of Mr. William Smyth, and daughter of George Drinker, of Alexandria, D.C. [CG, Thurs., 8 DEC 1831, p. 3]

MARRIED, in Washington, on Tuesday evening last [i.e. 6 DEC 1831], by the Rev. Mr. Hatch, Mr. ROBERT HEWITT, to Miss RUHAMAH, youngest daughter of Griffith Coombe, Esq., all of that city. [CG, Sat., 10 DEC 1831, p. 3]

DIED, in Washington, on the 8th inst. [i.e. 8 DEC 1831], Capt. JAMES HOBAN, aged about seventy-three years. Capt. Hoban was by profession an Architect, and emigrated to this country from Ireland, at the close of the American Revolution. He first settled in Charleston, S.C., from whence he was invited to the City of Washington to superintend the erection of the public buildings. He designed, and obtained the premium for, the President's House, and both built and re-built it. He also superintended the architecture of the Capitol for a considerable time. In private life, Capt. Hoban possessed, in a very high degree, the esteem and confidence of his fellow citizens. He was hospitable, generous, and charitable. In his regard for the just claims and feelings of others, he was scrupulously nice and particular. Such men are blessings to society whilst they live, and, even after death, instruct by example.—*Intelligencer.* [CG, Sat., 10 DEC 1831, p. 3]

DIED, in Rockville, Md., on Wednesday last [i.e. 7 DEC 1831], ZADOC MAGRUDER, Esq., Attorney at Law, in the 37th year of his age. [CG, Sat., 10 DEC 1831, p. 3]

DIED, on the 30th of November last [i.e. 30 NOV 1831], while on a visit in Montgomery county for his health, HENRY RYAN, aged 47 years. For many years a resident of Washington City. [CG, Sat., 10 DEC 1831, p. 3]

MARRIED, in Philadelphia, on the 6th inst. [i.e. 6 DEC 1831], Maj. JOHN ERVING, of the U.S. Army, to EMILY SOPHIA, daughter of the late T.L. Elwyn, Esq., of N.H. [CG, Tues., 13 DEC 1831, p. 3]

DIED, in Boston, on Tuesday last [i.e. 6 DEC 1831], of the prevailing influenza, WILLIAM H. ELIOT, Esq., aged 35, a gentleman of great wealth, enterprise and liberality. [CG, Tues., 13 DEC 1831, p. 3]

Georgetown, D.C., Marriage and Death Notices, 1801-1838

DIED, in Philadelphia, on the 7th inst. [i.e. 7 DEC 1831], Maj. JOSEPH PARKER, of the Revolutionary Army, in the 86th year of his age. [CG, Tues., 13 DEC 1831, p. 3]

DIED, in Washington, on the 31st inst. [i.e. 30? NOV 1831], Mr. CHARLES VENABLE, in the 41st year of his age. [CG, Tues., 13 DEC 1831, p. 3]

DIED, in this place, on the 9th inst. [i.e. 9 DEC 1831], after a long and severe illness which she bore with much patience, LAURETTA, second daughter of Mr. N.S. Dent, of Charles Co., Md. ... [CG, Thurs., 15 DEC 1831, p. 3]

DIED, at his residence in Georgetown, on Monday night last [i.e. 12 DEC 1831], Mr. JOHN EDDES, an old citizen of the place, aged 47 years. [CG, Thurs., 15 DEC 1831, p. 3]

DIED, in Washington, on Tuesday morning [i.e. 13 DEC 1831], suddenly, WILLIAM BENNING, Esq., aged 60 years. [CG, Thurs., 15 DEC 1831, p. 3]

DIED, in Washington City, on Tuesday, the 13th inst. [i.e. 13 DEC 1831], in the 52d year of her age, PHILADELPHIA, the consort of William Costin. She was born at *Mount Vernon*, the seat of the late General Washington. [CG, Sat., 17 DEC 1831, p. 3]

DIED, at the residence of Mrs. E.M. Spalding, in Charles Co., Md., on Monday the 4th inst. [i.e. 4 DEC 1831], Miss ELIZABETH CLEMENTS, at the advanced age, (as it is supposed) of 112 years. This old lady was a native of the county and immediate neighborhood in which she lived and died—retaining her mental faculties nearly unimpaired to the hour of her death, and sufficient bodily strength to render herself every needful assistance. [CG, Sat., 17 DEC 1831, p. 3]

Departed this life on the 10th inst. [i.e. 10 DEC 1831], at his seat near Queen Anne, Prince George's Co., Md., Dr. CLEMENT SMITH, in the seventy-fifth year of his age. [CG, Sat., 17 DEC 1831, p. 3]

DIED, in Rockville, Md., on Monday last [i.e. 12 DEC 1831], Mr. JOHN LANSDALE, aged about 40 years. He was in the vigor of health about an hour before he fell a corpse. [CG, Sat., 17 DEC 1831, p. 3]

DIED, in Alexandria, on Thursday [i.e. 15 DEC 1831], Mrs. PHOEBE HODGKINSON, relict of the late Capt. Anthony Hodgkinson. [CG, Sat., 17 DEC 1831, p. 3]

DIED, at her residence in Georgetown, on Thursday, the 15th inst. [i.e. 15 DEC 1831], in the 65th year of her age, Mrs. MARY P. JOHNS, relict of Aquila Johns, late of Prince George's Co., Md., and the eldest daughter of the late Wm. Bayly ... She has left a numerous connection and many friends ... (The *Hagerstown Torchlight* is requested to copy the above) [CG, Tues., 20 DEC 1831, p. 3]

DIED, in Washington, on the 13th inst. [i.e. 13 DEC 1831], Miss ELIZA VALLETTE, aged 25 years. [CG, Tues., 20 DEC 1831, p. 3]

Georgetown, D.C., **Marriage and Death Notices, 1801-1838**

DIED, in Falmouth, Va., on the 12th inst. [i.e. 12 DEC 1831], ROBERT DUNBAR, Esq., in the 86th year of his age. The deceased was a native of Scotland, but for nearly fifty years had been a highly respected merchant of Falmouth. [CG, Tues., 20 DEC 1831, p. 3]

DIED, in Falmouth, Va., on the 14th inst. [i.e. 14 DEC 1831], Mr. WILLIAM STRINGFELLOW, Inspector of Four for that town. [CG, Tues., 20 DEC 1831, p. 3]

DIED, in Baltimore, on Sunday morning [i.e. 18 DEC 1831], ROSANNA KORN, in the 67th year of her age, widow of John Korn, merchant, formerly of Alexandria. [CG, Tues., 20 DEC 1831, p. 3]

DIED, in Washington, on Tuesday [i.e. 20 DEC 1831], after a short illness, Mr. CHS. H. VARDEN, in the 67 year of his age. [CG, Thurs., 22 DEC 1831, p. 3]

DIED, on the 20th inst. [i.e. 20 DEC 1831], Mrs. MARY BARRON, aged 67 years. [CG, Thurs., 22 DEC 1831, p. 3]

MARRIED, on Tuesday evening, 20th inst. [i.e. 20 DEC 1831], by the Rev. Mr. Stephen L. Dubuisson, Pastor of Trinity Church, Georgetown, ALEXIUS BOON, Esq., of Frederick Co., Md., to Miss NAOMI CLOUD, of this place. [CG, Sat., 24 DEC 1831, p. 3]

MARRIED, in this town, on Wednesday evening [i.e. 21 DEC 1831], by the Rev. Mr. Brooke, Lieut. EDMUND FRENCH, of the U.S. Army, to Miss LOUISA BEALL, daughter of the late Maj. Lloyd Beall, of the U.S. Army. [CG, Sat., 24 DEC 1831, p. 3]

DIED, at Brookline, near Boston, on the 16th inst. [i.e. 16 DEC 1831], Miss HANNAH ADAMS, author of the *History of New England*, the *View of All Religious*, the *History of the Jews*, and other works, at an advanced age. [CG, Sat., 24 DEC 1831, p. 3]

MARRIED, in Alexandria, on the 22d inst. [i.e. 22 DEC 1831], Capt. LEONARD MARBURY, to Miss MARGARET MORRIS, daughter of the late Capt. Francis Dyer, of Alexandria. [CG, Thurs., 29 DEC 1831, p. 3]

DIED, in Washington, on Friday [i.e. 23 DEC 1831], Mr. HENRY TIMS, late Door Keeper of the Senate Chamber. [CG, Thurs., 29 DEC 1831, p. 3]

DIED, on the 22d inst. [i.e. 22 DEC 1831], Mrs. ELIZABETH COOPER, in the 55th year of her age, wife of Mr. Joseph Cooper. [CG, Thurs., 29 DEC 1831, p. 3]

DIED, in this town on Christmas morning [i.e. 25 DEC 1831], Mrs. ELIZA VIRGINIA, wife of Dr. Benjamin S. Bohrer, and eldest daughter of Nathan Lufborough, Esq., of *Grassland*. [CG, Sat., 31 DEC 1831, p. 3]

DIED, in this town, on Thursday [i.e. 29 DEC 1831], after a short illness, Mrs. MARY C. WINTER, in the 43d year of her age. [CG, Sat., 31 DEC 1831, p. 3]

Georgetown, D.C., **Marriage and Death Notices, 1801-1838**

DIED, in Washington, on the 22d inst. [i.e. 22 DEC 1831], Mrs. ELIZA CARBERY, aged about 30 years, wife of Mr. James Carbery. [CG, Sat., 31 DEC 1831, p. 3]

DIED, on the 28th inst. [i.e. 28 DEC 1831], suddenly, Mrs. ELIZABETH B. GIVEN, in the 30th year of her age. [CG, Sat., 31 DEC 1831, p. 3]

DIED, in Washington, on the 5th inst. [i.e. 5 JAN 1832], Mr. JOHN MacDANIEL, aged 52 years, formerly a clerk in the 4th Auditor's Office. [CG, Sat.,7 JAN 1832, p. 3]

DIED, on the 4th inst. [i.e. 4 JAN 1832], JOHN HOLMEAD, aged 17, son of the late Capt. John Holmead. [CG, Sat.,7 JAN 1832, p. 3]

DIED, on Saturday the 30th ult. [i.e. 31? DEC 1831], at his residence in this county, MATTHEW BROWN, Esq., aged about 65 years. Mr. Brown was formerly the editor and one of the proprietors of the *Baltimore Gazette*, which he conducted for 12 years with much ability and success ... [CG, Tues., 10 JAN 1832, p. 3]

DIED, in Alexandria, on the 9th inst. [i.e. 9 JAN 1832], Mr. WILLIAM PATTERSON, in the 81st year of his age. [CG, Thurs., 12 JAN 1832, p. 3]

DIED, on Friday, the 23d Dec. [i.e. 23 DEC 1831], at the residence of Wm. Green, Mecklenburg Co., Va., DOROTHEA RIPLEY, perhaps the most extraordinary woman in the world. We need say more than the truth of her—she was born at Whitby, England, in the year 1767—her parents were pious Methodists, her father one of Wesley's preachers ... [CG, Thurs., 12 JAN 1832, p. 3]

DIED, in Circleville, Ohio, of the prevailing influenza, on the 1st inst. [i.e. 1 JAN 1832], Mr. GEORGE CROOK, formerly of Alexandria, in the 35th year of his age. [CG, Thurs., 12 JAN 1832, p. 3]

DIED, on Thursday 12th inst. [i.e. 12 JAN 1832], Mrs. COMFORT KING, in the 79th year of her age, wife of Mr. Charles King, long a resident of Georgetown ... ☞ The funeral will take place from her late residence on First Street, This Day, at 10 o'clock, immediately after the celebration of High Mass at Trinity Church, to which her friends and acquaintances are respectfully invited. [CG, Sat., 14 JAN 1832, p. 3]

MARRIED, in this town, on Tuesday evening, the 10th inst. [i.e. 10 JAN 1832], by the Rev. Mr. Brooke, Mr. THOMAS HYDE, to Miss ANN MILLER, all of that place. [CG, Tues., 17 JAN 1832, p. 3]

MARRIED, in Washington, on the 12th inst. [i.e. 12 JAN 1832], by the Rev. Mr. McCormick, Mr. EDWARD M. DREW, to Miss MAHALIA ANN, daughter of Mr. John Waters; all of that city. [CG, Tues., 17 JAN 1832, p. 3]

MARRIED, in Baltimore, on Thursday evening last [i.e. 12 JAN 1832], Mr. RICHARD W. VARDEN, of Georgetown, to Miss ANN C. EVANS, of Baltimore. [CG, Tues., 17 JAN 1832, p. 3]

DIED, in Washington, on Saturday last [i.e. 14 JAN 1832], Mr. SAMUEL S. HAMILTON, aged 50 years, clerk in the Indian Bureau, War Department. [CG, Tues., 17 JAN 1832, p. 3]

MARRIED, in Washington, on the 10th inst. [i.e. 10 JAN 1832], by the Rev. Mr. Matthews, Mr. RICHARD LAY, Jr., of Georgetown, to Miss M.S. MATTINGLY, of the former place. [CG, Thurs., 19 JAN 1832, p. 3]

MARRIED, in Washington, on Thursday last [i.e. 12 JAN 1832], by the Rev. Mr. Chalmers, Mr. THOMAS T. BARNES, merchant, to Miss LUCY ANN ORME, of Montgomery Co., Md. [CG, Thurs., 19 JAN 1832, p. 3]

DIED, at his seat, in Caroline Co. [Va.], on Saturday evening last [i.e. 14 JAN 1832], Dr. JOHN TALIAFERRO. [CG, Thurs., 19 JAN 1832, p. 3]

DIED, in Fredericksburg, Va., on Saturday night, 14th inst. [i.e. 14 JAN 1832], Mr. BAILEY BUCKNER, late a resident of Georgetown, D.C. [CG, Thurs., 19 JAN 1832, p. 3]

DIED, on the 9th day of November last [i.e. 9 NOV 1831] at Havana, in the Island of Cuba, VINCENT GREY, Esq., at an advanced age. This gentleman was a native of the State of Virginia, and for more than thirty years had resided at the place of his death, where his memory will be long embalmed in the hearts of his Countrymen ... [CG, Thurs., 19 JAN 1832, p. 3]

DIED, in Washington, on Wednesday, the 4th inst. [i.e. 4 JAN 1832], Mrs. ANN LITTLE, aged 25 years. [CG, Thurs., 19 JAN 1832, p. 3]

DIED, in Washington, on the 11th inst. [i.e. 11 JAN 1832], Mrs. SUSANNA EVANS, relict of John Evans, Esq., and formerly of Portsmouth, N.H. [CG, Thurs., 19 JAN 1832, p. 3]

DIED, after a short illness, at sea, on the 13th ult. [i.e. 13 JAN 1832], while on his passage from Baltimore to New Orleans, Mr. JOHN P. FONDE, late of Washington, aged 37. [CG, Thurs., 19 JAN 1832, p. 3]

MARRIED, in Alexandria, on Thursday evening last [i.e. 19 JAN 1832], Mr. THOMAS E. JACOBS, to Miss SARAH A. MARKLEY, second daughter of the late Capt. Wm. Markley, of Alexandria. [CG, Sat., 21 JAN 1832, p. 3]

MARRIED, on Thursday evening last, in Leesburg, Va. [i.e. 19 JAN 1832], by the Rev. Mr. Clark, Mr. WILLIAM B. PRICE, to Miss SARAH S.P. MARTIN, both of Alexandria. [CG, Sat., 21 JAN 1832, p. 3]

DIED, in Baltimore, on the 18th inst. [i.e. 18 JAN 1832], the Hon. ALEXANDER McKIM, aged 84, Chief Justice of the Orphan's Court and formerly a member of Congress; for sixty years one of the most respected citizens of Baltimore. [CG, Sat., 21 JAN 1832, p. 3]

Georgetown, D.C., **Marriage and Death Notices, 1801-1838**

MARRIED, at Washington City, on the 17th inst. [i.e. 17 JAN 1832], DUDLEY WALKER, Esq., Purser U.S. Navy, to Miss JANE CECILIA, second daughter of Col. Henry Ashton, of that city. [CG, Tues., 24 JAN 1832, p. 3]

DIED, in this town, on Saturday [i.e. 21 JAN 1832], Mr. THOMAS HENSON, aged about 65 years, a native of Lincolnshire, England, and for 15 years a resident of Georgetown. [CG, Tues., 24 JAN 1832, p. 3]

DIED, in Washington, on Saturday last [i.e. 21 JAN 1832], of apoplexy, DANIEL D. ARDEN, Esq., about 40 years of age, a native of N.Y., and for several years, the active partner of the firm of *Yates & McIntyre*, in Washington. [CG, Tues., 24 JAN 1832, p. 3]

DIED, in Washington, on the 16th inst. [i.e. 16 JAN 1832], Mr. WILLIAM ENSEY, aged 72. [CG, Tues., 24 JAN 1832, p. 3]

DIED, in Alexandria, on Wednesday night last, the 18th inst. [i.e. 18 JAN 1832], WILLIAM C. COGINGS, late of Hertford, N.C., and whose near relatives reside in Washington City. His age was 38 years. [CG, Tues., 24 JAN 1832, p. 3]

DIED, on Sunday morning last [i.e. 22 JAN 1832], at the head of Severn, Anne Arundel Co., Mr. JOHN GAITHER, of Rezin. His wife departed this life on the preceding evening. Both were buried in the same grave. Five disconsolate children are left to struggle with adversity. [CG, Thurs., 26 JAN 1832, p. 3]

DIED, at her residence, near Tracy's Landing, in Anne Arundel Co. [no date], Mrs. COMPTON, aged 66, after a short illness. Her neighbor, Mr. JOHN MORTON, attended her funeral, and died suddenly the following night, aged about 40. [CG, Thurs., 26 JAN 1832, p. 3]

DIED, in Washington, on Thursday [i.e. 26 JAN 1832], Miss SUSAN H. SMITH, daughter of Samuel H. Smith. [CG, Sat., 28 JAN 1832, p. 3]

DIED. The last survivor of the Convention which framed the original Republican Constitution of New York, in 1777, THOMAS TREDWELL, Esq., died in Clinton Co., on the 30th ult. [i.e. 30 JAN 1831], aged 88. [CG, Sat., 28 JAN 1832, p. 3]

MARRIED, in Alexandria, on Thursday last [i.e. 26 JAN 1832], Mr. MATTHEW JACKSON, to Miss FRANCIS HENRIETTA WASHINGTON, both of that place. [CG, Tues., 31 JAN 1832, p. 3]

DIED, in Alexandria, on Monday 23d inst. [i.e. 23 JAN 1832], Mr. RICHARD WALLACE, aged 50 year. [CG, Tues., 31 JAN 1832, p. 3]

DIED, in Upper Marlborough, on the 30th ult. [i.e. 30 DEC 1832], RICHARD H. BROOKES, Esq., Cashier of the Planters' Bank of Prince George's Co., in the 30th year of his age. [CG, Sat., 4 FEB 1832, p. 3]

Georgetown, D.C., **Marriage and Death Notices, 1801-1838**

DIED, in Washington, on Thursday last [i.e. 2 FEB 1832], Mrs. ANN R. FORD, wife of Stephen C. Ford, and last daughter of the late Capt. James Hoban. [CG, Tues., 7 FEB 1832, p. 3]

DIED, on Tuesday morning last [i.e. 31 JAN 1832], after a protracted illness, in the 56th year of his age, CHRISTIAN NEWCOMER, Esq., Sheriff of Washington county [Md.]—and his remains were the day after interred in the family burial ground about 3 miles from Hagerstown, in the presence of an unusually large concourse of sympathizing relatives and friends.—*Torch Light.* [CG, Tues., 7 FEB 1832, p. 3]

Departure of the Revolutionary Fathers.
 In Paris, Oneida Co., on the 17th ult. [i.e. 17 JAN 1832], of the influenza, Capt. CHINA SMITH, a Revolutionary patriot, aged 93 years.
 In Western, on the 26th ult. [i.e. 26 JAN 1832], JOSIAH CLEAVELAND, a Revolutionary patriot, aged 73 years.
 In Stow, Mass. [no date], Capt. JUDAH WETHERBEE, a Revolutionary patriot, aged 77 years.
 In Lynn [no date], Dr. JAMES GARDNER, aged 60 years.—He served in the army of the Revolution.
 At Fall River [no date], LEONARD EVANS, aged 80 years, a Revolutionary pensioner.
 In Newstead, on the 23d [i.e. 23 JAN 1832], SAMUEL OWEN, aged 74, a soldier of the Revolution. [CG, Tues., 7 FEB 1832, p. 3]

DIED, in this town, on the 7th inst. [i.e. 7 FEB 1832], in the 72d year of his age, after a short illness, Mr. NICHOLAS WHELAN, for many years a respectable inhabitant of Georgetown.—His funeral will take place at 4 o'clock this day, from his late residence, the house of Mr. Lobin, near Georgetown College. The friends and acquaintances of the deceased are requested to attend without further notice. [CG, Thurs., 9 FEB 1832, p. 3]

DIED, in Washington, on the 5th inst. [i.e. 5 FEB 1832], SARAH ANN, aged 12 years, eldest daughter of Mr. Charles Cruikshank, of this town. On the same day, WALTER H. JENIFER, for several years a clerk in the General Land Office. [CG, Thurs., 9 FEB 1832, p. 3]

MARRIED, on the 7th inst. [i.e. 7 FEB 1832], in this town, by the Rev. Mr. Brooke, WILLIAM B. LIGHTFOOT, of Port Royal, to ROBERTA, daughter of Robert Beverley, of *Blandfield*, all of Virginia. [CG, Sat., 11 FEB 1832, p. 3]

MARRIED, in Washington, on Tuesday evening, 7th inst. [i.e. 7 FEB 1832], by the Rev. Mr. Lucas, Mr. ROBT. F. MILLARD, to Miss MARY H. BROWN, both of that city. [CG, Sat., 11 FEB 1832, p. 3]

DIED, recently [no date], at Williamsburg, Va., FRANCIS LINAEUS SMITH, Esq., aged about 40, formerly a clerk in the Department of State. [CG, Sat., 11 FEB 1832, p. 3]

Georgetown, D.C., **Marriage and Death Notices, 1801-1838**

DIED, on the evening of the 12th inst. [i.e. 12 FEB 1832], at Alexandria, REBECCA, daughter of Elisha Talbott. Thus is another victim added to the many consigned to an early tomb by that formidable destroyer of the young and lovely, pulmonary consumption ... [CG, Tues., 14 FEB 1832, p. 3]

MARRIED, on Tuesday evening, 7th inst. [i.e. 7 FEB 1832], by the Rev. Mr. Johns, Mr. WILLIAM LYNN, of Cumberland, Md., to Miss JANE M., daughter of the late L.M. Johns, of Georgetown. [CG, Thurs., 16 FEB 1832, p. 3]

DIED, in Washington, on Saturday [i.e. 11 FEB 1832], Mrs. DEBORAH BURCH, in the 40th year of her age, wife of Mr. Thomas Burch. [CG, Sat., 18 FEB 1832, p. 3]

DIED, in Philadelphia, on Monday [i.e. 13 FEB 1832], Mrs. MARY R. CHANDLER, wife of Joseph R. Chandler, Editor of the *United States Gazette.* [CG, Sat., 18 FEB 1832, p. 3]

MARRIED, in Washington, on the 14th inst. [i.e. 14 FEB 1832], Mr. STANISLAUS MURRAY, to Miss HARRIET S. HAMILTON, both of that place. [CG, Tues., 21 FEB 1832, p. 3]

MARRIED, at Fort McHenry, near Baltimore, on the 16th inst. [i.e 16 FEB 1832], Lieut. JAMES BARNES, of the U.S. Army, to Miss CHARLOTTE ADAMS. [CG, Tues., 21 FEB 1832, p. 3]

DIED, at Annapolis, on Friday 10th inst. [i.e. 10 FEB 1832], Mrs. ELIZABETH MAYNADIER, consort of Col. Henry Maynadier. [CG, Tues., 21 FEB 1832, p. 3]

DIED, on the 20th inst. [i.e. 20 FEB 1832], in Washington, Miss MARY JANE, eldest daughter of Lawrence L. Van Kleeck, Esq., late of Albany. [CG, Thurs., 23 FEB 1832, p. 3]

DIED, at Annapolis, on Friday last [i.e. 17 FEB 1832], about six o'clock in the evening, JOHN EDELIN, Esq., a Delegate in the General Assembly from Charles County. [CG, Thurs., 23 FEB 1832, p. 3]

MARRIED, on Tuesday evening, the 21st inst. [i.e. 21 FEB 1832], by the Rev. Mr. Brooke, Mr. ANTHONY HYDE, to Miss MARIA SMITH, all of this place. [CG, Sat., 25 FEB 1832, p. 3]

DIED, at Milton, Mass., on the 17th inst. [i.e. 17 FEB 1832], Hon. JONATHAN RUSSELL, aged 60, one of the American Commissioners at Ghent, afterwards Minister to Sweden, Member of Congress &c. [CG, Sat., 25 FEB 1832, p. 3]

MARRIED, in Washington, on the 22d [i.e. 22 FEB 1832], by the Rev. Mr. Hanson, Mr. WILLIAM B. BERRYMAN, to Miss ELIZABETH, second daughter of John Laub, Esq., of this town. [CG, Tues., 28 FEB 1832, p. 3]

Georgetown, D.C., **Marriage and Death Notices, 1801-1838**

MARRIED, on the 23d [i.e. 23 FEB 1832], Mr. WILLIAM GIVENS, to Miss MARY WALLINGFORD. [CG, Tues., 28 FEB 1832, p. 3]

MARRIED, on the 23d [i.e. 23 FEB 1832], Mr. JOHN MARRON, of Ga., to Miss ELIZA ANN, daughter of Mr. Thomas B. Dyer. [CG, Tues., 28 FEB 1832, p. 3]

MARRIED, in Alexandria, on the 23d [i.e. 23 FEB 1832], Mr. JAMES R. HAYMAN, to Miss AGNES BLOXTON. [CG, Tues., 28 FEB 1832, p. 3]

MARRIED, in Alexandria, on the 19th [i.e. 19 FEB 1832], Mr. ZACHARIAH WHITE, to Miss JANE LANE, all of that place. [CG, Tues., 28 FEB 1832, p. 3]

Departed this life on Friday, March 2, 1832, Mr. JOHN LIPSCOMB, in the sixty-fifth year of his age. Mr. Lipscomb was a native of King William, but died a resident of Prince William Co., Va. For twenty-seven years he was a respectable citizen of this town, and one of its most active and industrious mechanics. His veracity was unimpeachable—his honesty questioned by none. For thirty-six years and six months he was an acceptable member of the Methodist Episcopal Church ... The only patrimony he has left a widow and six children is, that of an irreproachable reputation. His remains were interred in the burial ground of the Methodist Episcopal Church in this place on Monday, March 5, 1832, by the side of her who, for thirty five years, was the affectionate companion and willing sharer in the events of his toilsome life. This small tribute is paid by one who knew the deceased long and intimately. Georgetown, D.C., March 5, 1832. [CG, Tues., 6 MAR 1832, p. 3]

MARRIED, on Tuesday the 6th March [i.e. 6 MAR 1832], by the Rev. Mr. Dorsey, Mr. WALTER A. TUTTLE, of Georgetown, to Miss DORCAS ANN WALKER, of Bladensburg, Prince George's Co., Md. [CG, Thurs., 8 MAR 1832, p. 3]

DIED, in Washington [no date], Mr. HEZEKIAH LANGLEY, aged 47. [CG, Sat., 10 MAR 1832, p. 3]

DIED. Hon. OCTAVIUS TANEY, of the Senate of Md. Dr. Taney was a resident of Calvert Co., where he has been successfully engaged in the practice of medicine for many years—he visited Baltimore about ten days ago, and was taken suddenly ill, on the night of his arrival, and died on the 6th inst. [i.e. 6 MAR 1832], in the 39th year of his age, leaving an affectionate wife, brother, and sisters, together with a numerous circle of friends to lament his death. His remains are to be taken to his late residence, attended by a Joint Committee of both branches of the Legislature on Friday morning. [CG, Sat., 10 MAR 1832, p. 3]

DIED, in Rockville, Md., on the 29th ult. [i.e. 29 FEB 1832], JOHN PORTER, in the 31st year of his age, Editor of the *Md. Free Press*. [CG, Sat., 10 MAR 1832, p. 3]

MARRIED, on Sunday evening last [i.e. 11 MAR 1832], by the Rev. D.B. Dorsey, Mr. PETER BERRY, of N.Y., to Miss MARY ANN SMART, of Georgetown, D.C. [CG, Tues., 13 MAR 1832, p. 3]

Georgetown, D.C., Marriage and Death Notices, 1801-1838

DIED, on Saturday morning last [i.e. 10 MAR 1832], in the 58th year of her age, Mrs. ANNE WRIGHT CLAXTON, consort of Mr. John Claxton of this town. The deceased was a native of England, but had been a resident of this town for the last sixteen years ... She has left a widowed husband and six children to bemoan her untimely end ... [CG, Tues., 13 MAR 1832, p. 3]

MARRIED, at Boonville, Mo., on the 14th ult. [i.e. 14 FEB 1832], Mr. JOHN THAW, formerly of Washington City, to Miss JANE, daughter of the late William Hood, Esq. [CG, Tues., 20 MAR 1832, p. 3]

DIED, in Washington, of apoplexy, on the 17th inst. [i.e. 17 FEB 1832], Mrs. MARGARET COLLINS, in the 60th year of her age. [CG, Tues., 20 MAR 1832, p. 3]

DIED, in Baltimore, on Thursday [i.e. 15 MAR 1832], Dr. JAMES PAGE, aged 49, Surgeon in the U.S. Navy. [CG, Tues., 20 MAR 1832, p. 3]

DIED, in Quincy, Mass., on the 12th last [i.e. 12 FEB? 1832], the Hon. THOMAS BOYLESTON ADAMS, aged 59, only brother of Ex-President Adams. [CG, Tues., 20 MAR 1832, p. 3]

DIED, at the Naval Hospital, near Norfolk, Va., on the 17th inst. [i.e. 17 MAR 1832], Lieut. ALEXANDER ESKRIDGE, of the U.S. Navy, aged 39. Lieut. E. was an officer of much merit, and highly respected ... He was attached to the Frigate *Constitution* as a Midshipman, and was on board of her during several memorable conflicts ... [CG, Thurs., 22 MAR 1832, p. 3]

DIED, in Washington City, on Tuesday last [i.e. 20 MAR 1832], in the 18th year of her age, Mrs. ELIZA S., wife of Mr. Wm. H. Mauro, and daughter of the late James Wharton, of this town. [CG, Thurs., 22 MAR 1832, p. 3]

MARRIED, in Washington, on Thursday last [i.e. 22 MAR 1832], Mr. WASHINGTON BOSWELL, to Miss SUSAN MADDOX, all of Prince George's Co., Md. [CG, Tues., 27 MAR 1832, p. 2]

MARRIED, in Alexandria, on Thursday last [i.e. 22 MAR 1832], Mr. JOSIAH S.C. RUTTER, to Miss MARY POLLARD, all of that place. [CG, Tues., 27 MAR 1832, p. 2]

MARRIED [no date], Mr. JOHN MAJOR, Jun., of Fredericksburg, Va., to Miss MARGARET ANN HAND, third daughter of Mr. John Johnson, of Alexandria. [CG, Tues., 27 MAR 1832, p. 2]

DIED, in Washington, on Friday [i.e. 23 MAR 1832], Miss ELIZABETH HANNA, aged 18. [CG, Tues., 27 MAR 1832, p. 2]

DIED, in Washington, on Wednesday the 21st inst. [i.e. 21 MAR 1832], on the 26th anniversary of her birth, Mrs. ELIZABETH M. CARTER, wife of Robert W. Carter, Esq., of

Sabine Hall, and daughter of the late Col. John Tayloe, of *Mount Airy*. [CG, Tues., 27 MAR 1832, p. 2]

DIED, in Alexandria, on Saturday morning last [i.e. 24 MAR 1832], after a short illness, ALBERT C. THOMPSON, aged 21 years. [CG, Tues., 27 MAR 1832, p. 2]

DIED, in Baltimore, on the 25th past [i.e. 25 FEB? 1832], very suddenly, Midshipman DANIEL CARTER, of the U.S. Navy, of Ohio, in the 21st year of his age. [CG, Tues., 27 MAR 1832, p. 2]

MARRIED, in Washington, on the 13th inst. [i.e. 13 MAR 1832], Mr. WILLIAM BALTHIS, to Miss MARGARET ALCINDA GRIM. [CG, Thurs., 29 MAR 1832, p. 3]

DIED, in this town, on yesterday morning [i.e. 28 MAR 1832], after a few hours illness, Mr. JOSEPH SEMMES, in the 85th year of his age. His funeral will take place this evening, at 4 o'clock, from his late residence, which his friends and acquaintances are respectfully invited to attend. [CG, Thurs., 29 MAR 1832, p. 3]

DIED, on Sunday morning, March 25th [i.e. 25 MAR 1832], WILLIAM HENRY, youngest son of Henry G. Wilson, Esq., High Street, aged three years and seven months ... [CG, Thurs., 29 MAR 1832, p. 3]

DIED, in Washington, on the 26th inst. [i.e. 26 MAR 1832], Mr. THOMAS FOYLES, aged 73 years. [CG, Thurs., 29 MAR 1832, p. 3]

MARRIED, in Georgetown, on Thursday evening, 29th inst. [i.e. 29 MAR 1832], by the Rev. Dr. Balch, Mr. HENRY M. SWEENY, of Frederick Co., Va., to Miss MARY S., eldest daughter of Sudley Woodward. [CG, Sat., 31 MAR 1832, p. 3]

MARRIED, on Thursday evening, 29th inst. [i.e. 29 MAR 1832], by the Rev. Thomas Balch, Mr. JOHN TUCKER, to Miss ANN MARIA GORDON, both of Fairfax Co., Va. [CG, Sat., 31 MAR 1832, p. 3]

DIED, in Washington, on Saturday night last [i.e. 31 MAR 1832], at an advanced age, Mrs. MARTHA McLEISH. [CG, Tues., 3 APR 1832, p. 3]

DIED, in Washington, on Saturday last [i.e. 31 MAR 1832], Mr. CHARLES W. PATTERSON, in the 33d year of his age. [CG, Thurs., 5 APR 1832, p. 3]

DIED, in Alexandria, on the 3d inst. [i.e. 3 APR 1832], MORDECAI MILLER, in the 69th year of his age, for many years a respectable Merchant of that town. [CG, Thurs., 5 APR 1832, p. 3]

MARRIED, in Georgetown, on the 29th ult. [i.e. 29 MAR 1832], by the Rev. Dr. Balch, GEORGE McLEISH, to CATHARINE JACKSON, both of Alexandria. [CG, Sat., 7 APR 1832, p. 3]

Georgetown, D.C., **Marriage and Death Notices, 1801-1838**

DIED, in Washington, on the 3d inst. [i.e. 3 APR 1832], Mrs. ELIZA GIBERSON, consort of G.L. Giberson, Esq. [CG, Sat., 7 APR 1832, p. 3]

DIED, in Washington, on the 26th ult. [i.e. 26 MAR 1832], Mrs. ELIZABETH BAYLY, aged 71, wife of Mountjoy Bayly, Sergeant-at-arms of the U.S. Senate. [CG, Sat., 7 APR 1832, p. 3]

DIED, in N.Y., on Wednesday last [i.e. 4 APR 1832], Mrs. JANE HILL, aged 41, wife of Lawrence Hill, formerly of Alexandria. [CG, Sat., 7 APR 1832, p. 3]

MARRIED, in Fairfax, Va., on the 5th inst. [i.e. 5 APR 1832], RICHARD M. SCOTT, Esq., of *Bush Hill*, to Miss LUCINDA, eldest daughter of M.C. Cook, Esq. [CG, Tues., 10 APR 1832, p. 3]

DIED, in Alexandria, on the 5th inst. [i.e. 5 APR 1832], Mrs. ANN RANDALL, in the 54th year of her age, wife of Mr. T. Randall. [CG, Tues., 10 APR 1832, p. 3]

MARRIED, in Georgetown, on the 12th inst. [i.e. 12 APR 1832], by the Rev. Mr. Furlong, Mr. CHARLES MYERS, to Miss SUSANNAH, second daughter of William Parsons, all of this place. [CG, Sat., 14 APR 1832, p. 3]

DIED, at Ellicott's Mills, on the 8th inst. [i.e. 8 APR 1832], at 11 o'clock, A.M., GEORGE ELLICOTT, in the 72d year of his age. [CG, Sat., 14 APR 1832, p. 3]

MARRIED, in Washington, at the Mansion of the President, on the evening of the 10th inst. [i.e. 10 APR 1832], by the Rev. Mr. Hawley, LUCIUS J. POLK, Esq., of Tenn., to Miss MARY A. EASTIN, a member of the President's family. [CG, Tues., 17 APR 1832, p. 3]

MARRIED, in Alexandria, on the 10th inst. [i.e. 10 APR 1832], Mr. WILLIAM H. PARKER, of Washington City, to Miss MARY AUGUSTA, eldest daughter of the late Col. Lewis Hipkins, of the former place. [CG, Tues., 17 APR 1832, p. 3]

MARRIED, in Norfolk, on the 11th inst. [i.e. 11 APR 1832], Capt. ANDREW TALCOTT, of the U.S. Engineer Corps, to Miss HARRIET HACKLEY, of that place. [CG, Tues., 17 APR 1832, p. 3]

DIED, in Georgetown, on the 14th inst. [i.e. 14 APR 1832], Mr. WILLIAM CURREN, in the 72d year of his age. [CG, Tues., 17 APR 1832, p. 3]

DIED, in N.Y., on Thursday last [i.e. 12 APR 1832], JOHN HONE, Esq., in the 68th year of his age, for many years an eminent merchant of that City. [CG, Tues., 17 APR 1832, p. 3]

MARRIED, in Georgetown, on Sunday the 15th inst. [i.e. 15 APR 1832], by the Rev. H. Furlong, Mr. WILLIAM H. COLEMAN, of Baltimore, to Miss GEZENA, eldest daughter of the late Capt. Immohr, of Alexandria. [CG, Thurs., 19 APR 1832, p. 3]

MARRIED, on Tuesday evening last [i.e. 17 APR 1832], by the Rev. Mr. Hanson, E.A. ELIASON, to MARY, eldest daughter of John Lyons. [CG, Thurs., 19 APR 1832, p. 3]

MARRIED, in Washington, on the 17th inst. [i.e. 17 APR 1832], by the Rev. Mr. Hawley, CHARLES McLEAN, M.D., of Baltimore, to Miss MARGARET N. CAMPBELL, of Washington city. [CG, Sat., 21 APR 1832, p. 3]

DIED, on Thursday, the 12th inst. [i.e. 12 APR 1832], ROBERT WILSON, of Baltimore Co., aged 102 years and 11 days. [CG, Sat., 21 APR 1832, p. 3]

MARRIED, in this town on Thursday evening last [i.e. 19 APR 1832], by the Rev. W.C. Lipscomb, Mr. PHINEAS STEER, of Waterford, Va., to Miss ISABELLA, daughter of Mr. Wm. King, of this town. [CG, Tues., 24 APR 1832, p. 3]

MARRIED, in Alexandria, on Thursday evening last [i.e. 19 APR 1832], Mr. ANDREW SULLIVAN, to Mrs. MARTHA GALLAGHER, all of that place. [IA, Tues., 24 APR 1832, p. 3]

DIED, in Philadelphia, on Wednesday evening, the 18th inst. [i.e. 18 APR 1832], SARAH PILMORE POULSON, wife of Charles A. Poulson. [IA, Tues., 24 APR 1832, p. 3]

DIED, in Washington, on Tuesday 24th inst. [i.e. 24 APR 1832], in the 31st year of her age, of consumption, SUSAN DRUET, wife of James Druet. [CG, Thurs., 26 APR 1832, p. 3]

DIED, at Fort Washington, Md., on Friday morning, the 20th of April [1832], Lieut. GEORGE WEBB, of the 1st Regiment U.S. Artillery. [CG, Thurs., 26 APR 1832, p. 3]

DIED, near Bolivar, Tenn., on the 4th inst. [i.e. 4 APR 1832], of consumption, in the 33d year of her age, Mrs. ELIZA ANN FITZHUGH, wife of Dr. Edmund Fitzhugh, and daughter of John Roberts, Esq. [CG, Thurs., 26 APR 1832, p. 3]

Another Revolutionary Hero Gone!—In Philadelphia, on Monday, 23d of April [1832], Mr. JOHN PETERS, aged 100 years 5 months and 22 days. This aged gentleman enjoyed until the last four months of his life all his faculties, and until the end of the last year was out attending to his business every day. He was honest, industrious, and temperate in his habits and rendered his services in times that tried men's souls. He was born in Portugal near Lisbon, and emigrated to this country shortly after the earthquake of 1775. At the commencement of the revolution he was found among the patriots of the day, and assisted in throwing the tea into the river at Boston. He afterwards entered into the army of the United States. He was at the battle of Lexington and Bunker's Hill in which he was wounded and lost one of his fingers. He was engaged in the battles of Monmouth and Princeton, and assisted in capturing the Hessians at Trenton. He was engaged in the capture of Burgoyne and also of Cornwallis, he fought under Washington and Lafayette, at Valley Forge, where he was again wounded, and after serving during the whole war, after the peace of 1782, he was honorably discharged. He has ever since lived in Philadelphia, and has reared a numerous family. [CG, Thurs., 26 APR 1832, p. 3]

Georgetown, D.C., **Marriage and Death Notices, 1801-1838**

MARRIED, on Tuesday evening, 17th inst. [i.e. 17 APR 1832], by the Rev. Wm. Hawley, Mr. JEREMIAH HEPBURN, to Miss ANNA ETTER, both of Washington City. [CG, Sat., 28 APR 1832, p. 3]

MARRIED, on Sunday evening [i.e. 29 APR 1832], by the Rev. Mr. Danforth, Mr. ZACHARIAH DOVE, to Miss ELEANOR TARLTON, all of Washington City. [CG, Thurs., 3 MAY 1832, p. 3]

DIED, on Sunday morning [i.e. 29 APR 1832], Mr. JOHN WOLFENDEN, of Washington city, aged 29 years, son of the late John Wolfenden, Esq., formerly of Baltimore, and lately of Fredericktown, Md. [CG, Thurs., 3 MAY 1832, p. 3]

MARRIED, on the 4th inst. [i.e. 4 MAY 1832], by the Rev. Mr. Matthews, Mr. GEORGE REILLY, to Miss CATHARINE ANN GREEN, both of Baltimore. [CG, Tues., 8 MAY 1832, p. 3]

DIED, at York, Pa., on Tuesday, 1st inst. [i.e. 1 MAY 1832], THOMAS WETHERALD, a distinguished minister of the Society of Friends, and formerly a resident of Washington. [CG, Tues., 8 MAY 1832, p. 3]

MARRIED, on Tuesday evening, 8th inst. [i.e. 8 MAY 1832], by the Rev. Levi R. Reese, Maj. ALEXANDER WAUGH, of Fairfax Co., Va., to Miss MARY T. BUCKY, of Alexandria. [CG, Sat., 12 MAY 1832, p. 3]

DIED, on Wednesday, 18th April [1832], at *Effingham,* the residence of L.G. Alexander, Esq., Mrs. SIGISMUNDA ALEXANDER, widow of the late Col. William Alexander, of Prince William Co., Va., in the 87th year of her age—beloved by all who knew her. [CG, Sat., 12 MAY 1832, p. 3]

DIED, in Washington City, on the 5th inst. [i.e. 5 MAY 1832], after a long illness, Capt. BENJAMIN BURCH, aged seventy-two years, a soldier of the Revolution, and, for twenty-two years, Doorkeeper of the House of Representatives of the United States, a highly responsible, arduous, and honorable office. [CG, Sat., 12 MAY 1832, p. 3]

DIED, at N.Y., on Tuesday last [i.e. 8 MAY 1832], NATHANIEL H. PERRY, Esq., Purser U.S. Navy, and brother of the late Com. Perry. [CG, Sat., 12 MAY 1832, p. 3]

DIED, at Easton, Md., on the 2d inst. [i.e. 2 MAY 1832], THOMAS PERRIN SMITH, founder and proprietor of the *Eastern Star,* aged 56. [CG, Sat., 12 MAY 1832, p. 3]

MARRIED, in Washington, on the 8th inst. [i.e. 8 MAY 1832], THOMAS MURRAY, Jr., of Ark., to MARGARET C., second daughter of C.T. Coote, Esq. [CG, Tues., 15 MAY 1832, p. 3]

MARRIED, in Baltimore, on the 8th inst. [8 MAY 1832], Mr. HENRY D. COOPER, to Miss ANN CHARLOTTE TARLTON, formerly of Alexandria. [CG, Tues., 15 MAY 1832, p. 3]

Georgetown, D.C., **Marriage and Death Notices, 1801-1838**

DIED, in this town, yesterday morning [i.e. 14 MAY 1832], Miss SOPHIA L., daughter of Mrs. Barbara Ringgold. The friends and acquaintance of the family are respectfully invited to attend the funeral, from the residence of her mother on First street, *This afternoon*, at 5 o'clock. [CG, Tues., 15 MAY 1832, p. 3]

DIED, in Baltimore, on Friday 11th inst. [i.e. 11 MAY 1832], the Rev. MICHAEL F. WHEELER, in the 36th year of his age, late Professor of Chemistry in St. Mary's College, Baltimore. Mr. W. was formerly Superior of the Convent of the Visitation, in Georgetown. [CG, Tues., 15 MAY 1832, p. 3]

DIED, in Boston, on the 9th inst. [i.e. 9 MAY 1832], Hon. ISRAEL THORNDIKE. [CG, Tues., 15 MAY 1832, p. 3]

DIED, in Washington, on Monday [i.e. 14 MAY 1832], Hon. JONATHAN HUNT, a Representative in Congress from the state of Vermont. [CG, Thurs., 17 MAY 1832, p. 3]

DIED, in Alexandria, on Monday last [i.e. 14 MAY 1832], Mr. DAVID MARTIN, Bookseller, aged 40. [CG, Thurs., 17 MAY 1832, p. 3]

MARRIED, in Washington, on the 15th inst. [i.e. 15 MAY 1832], Hon. GEORGE POINDEXTER, Senator in Congress from the State of Mississippi, to Miss ANN HEWES, daughter of Samuel Hewes, Esq., of Boston. [CG, Sat., 19 MAY 1832, p. 3]

MARRIED, in Alexandria, on Tuesday last [i.e. 15 MAY 1832], Mr. JAMES P. COLEMAN, to Miss CAROLINE CAROLIN, both of that place. [CG, Sat., 19 MAY 1832, p. 3]

DIED, in Fredericksburg, Va., on the 12th inst. [i.e. 12 MAY 1832], in the 59th year of her age, Mrs. ANN GORDON PATTON, relict of the late Robert Patton, and only daughter of the Revolutionary patriot Gen. Mercer. [CG, Sat., 19 MAY 1832, p. 3]

DIED, in Fairfax Co., Va., on the 12th inst. [i.e. 12 MAY 1832], Mrs. ELIZABETH MITCHELL, consort of the late Benjamin Mitchell, Esq. [CG, Sat., 19 MAY 1832, p. 3]

MARRIED, in Washington, on the 17th inst. [i.e. 17 MAY 1832], by the Rev. Mr. Hildt, Mr. THOMAS PARKER, to Miss CAROLINE, daughter of Mr. Ezekiel Young, all of Washington. [CG, Tues., 22 MAY 1832, p. 3]

DIED, at Philadelphia, on the 16th inst. [i.e. 16 MAY 1832], Mrs. ANN D'WOLF TYNG, aged 27 years and 7 months, wife of Rev. Stephen H. Tyng, Rector of St. Paul's Church, and daughter of the Rt. Rev. Bishop Griswold, of Mass. [CG, Tues., 22 MAY 1832, p. 3]

DIED, at Norwalk, Conn., on the 15th inst. [i.e. 15 MAY 1832], in the 28th year of her age, ANN, wife of the Rev. Jackson Kemper, and only daughter of the late Samuel Rolf, Esq., of Philadelphia. [CG, Tues., 22 MAY 1832, p. 3]

Georgetown, D.C., **Marriage and Death Notices, 1801-1838**

Departed this life on the 20th ult. [i.e. 20 APR 1832], on board the brig *Arctic*, from Rio de Janeiro for Baltimore, off Pernambuco, Lieut. ELIAS C. TAYLOR, of the Navy. [CG, Thurs., 24 MAY 1832, p. 3]

DIED, on Wednesday, 16th inst. [i.e. 16 MAY 1832], at Brentsville, Prince William Co., Va., PHILIP D. DAWE, Esq., Clerk of Prince William County Court, aged 50 years. [CG, Thurs., 24 MAY 1832, p. 3]

MARRIED, in Baltimore, CHARLES H. WINDER, to MARY HARRIS, daughter of the late Gen. Joseph Sterett. [CG, Sat., 26 MAY 1832, p. 3]

MARRIED, ROBERT GILMOR, Jr., to Miss ELLEN, daughter of the late Judge Ward. [CG, Sat., 26 MAY 1832, p. 3]

MARRIED. Mr. THOMAS W. TENANT, to MARY CLARE CARROLL, daughter of B.M. Hodges. [CG, Sat., 26 MAY 1832, p. 3]

MARRIED, in Alexandria, Mr. JOSIAH B. HILLS, to Miss MERCY ANN WILSON. [CG, Thurs., 31 MAY 1832, p. 3]

MARRIED, in Alexandria, Mr. JAMES FADELY, to Miss ANN ROBINSON. [CG, Thurs., 31 MAY 1832, p. 3]

MARRIED, in Alexandria, Mr. PATRICK C. MURRAY, to Mrs. JANE MASSEY, all of Alexandria. [CG, Thurs., 31 MAY 1832, p. 3]

DIED, in Georgetown, on Monday 21st inst. [i.e. 21 MAY 1832], in the 51st year of his age, Mr. STEPHEN T. CONN, a native of Alexandria, but for many years a resident of Abingdon, Va., at which latter place he has children living. Mr. C. was respected by all who knew him, as an honest, industrious and worthy man. [CG, Thurs., 31 MAY 1832, p. 3]

MARRIED, in Washington, on Thursday last [i.e. 31 MAY 1832], by the Rev. Mr. Palfrey, JOSEPH HENRY WHEAT, to Miss ELIZA INGHAM, daughter of Mr. William Greer. [CG, Tues., 5 JUN 1832, p. 3]

MARRIED, on Thursday last [i.e. 31 MAY 1832], by the Rev. F.S. Evans, Mr. SAML. DAVIDSON, of Philadelphia, to Miss MARY STRONG, of Washington. [CG, Tues., 5 JUN 1832, p. 3]

MARRIED, in Alexandria, ROBERT HULL, of N.Y., to HANNAH ANN, eldest daughter of Joseph Janney, of the former place. [CG, Tues., 5 JUN 1832, p. 3]

DIED, in Washington, on Friday morning [i.e. 1 JUN 1832], Mr. JOSHUA MILLARD, in the 56th year of his age. [CG, Tues., 5 JUN 1832, p. 3]

DIED, on Wednesday last [i.e. 30 MAY 1832], ANN HAZELTINE, only daughter of the late Dr. E. Judson. [CG, Tues., 5 JUN 1832, p. 3]

Georgetown, D.C., **Marriage and Death Notices, 1801-1838**

MARRIED, on Tuesday last, the 5th inst. [i.e. 5 JUN 1832], by the Rev. Mr. Laird, THOMAS CORCORAN, Esq., of this place, to EMILY, daughter of Col. William Matthews, of *Federal Hill*, Charles Co., Md. [CG, Sat., 9 JUN 1832, p. 3]

MARRIED, on the 29th ult. [i.e. 29 MAY 1832], Mr. WILLIAM F. DEAKINS, of Prince George's Co., Md., to Miss ELIZABETH NUTT, of Alexandria. [CG, Sat., 9 JUN 1832, p. 3, and Thurs., 14 JUN 1832, p. 3]

MARRIED, in Baltimore, Dr. GEORGE B. MACKENZIE, to Miss RUHAMAH, youngest daughter of the late Adam Ross, of Franklin Co., Pa. [CG, Sat., 9 JUN 1832, p. 3]

MARRIED, [no date], Dr. JAMES G. BREHON, of N.C., to PRISCILLA DORSEY, second daughter of the late Frederick Lindenberger, Balt. [CG, Sat., 9 JUN 1832, p. 3, and Thurs., 14 JUN 1832, p. 3]

MARRIED, [no date], JOSEPH CUSHING, Jr., to ANN, eldest daughter of the late Dr. Colin Mackenzie. [CG, Sat., 9 JUN 1832, p. 3]

MARRIED, [no date], Mr. JOHN LINTON, of Jefferson, Pa., to Miss FRANCES JANE, eldest daughter of Mrs. Ellenor Grier, of Baltimore. [CG, Sat., 9 JUN 1832, p. 3, and Thurs., 14 JUN 1832, p. 3]

DIED, in Washington, on Monday [i.e. 4 JUN 1832], Mr. JOHN G. JOHNSTON, eldest son of the late Christopher Johnston, of Baltimore. [CG, Sat., 9 JUN 1832, p. 3, and Thurs., 14 JUN 1832, p. 3]

DIED, on Thursday evening last [i.e. 7 JUN 1832], Mrs. HELEN LAIRD, wife of William Laird, Esq., of this town. Her funeral will take place *This Morning*, at 10 o'clock. The friends of the family are invited to attend. [CG, Sat., 9 JUN 1832, p. 3, and Thurs., 14 JUN 1832, p. 3]

MARRIED, in St. Mary's Co., Md., on the 7th inst. [i.e. 7 JUN 1832], by the Rev. James Neale, Mr. MATTHEW McLEOD, to Miss ELIZABETH H. MANNING, both of Georgetown. [CG, Thurs., 14 JUN 1832, p. 3]

MARRIED, on Tuesday last, the 5th inst. [i.e. 5 JUN 1832], by the Rev. Mr. Laird, THOS. CORCORAN, Esq., of Georgetown, to EMILY, daughter of Col. William Matthews, of *Federal Hill*, Charles Co., Md. [CG, Thurs., 14 JUN 1832, p. 3]

MARRIED, [no date], in Canandaigua, N.Y., GEORGE W. CLINTON, Esq., son of the late DeWitt Clinton, to Miss LAURA CATHARINE, daughter of the Hon. John C. Spencer. [CG, Thurs., 14 JUN 1832, p. 3]

DIED, in Boston, RICHARD DERBY, Esq., aged 67, formerly Naval Storekeeper at Pensacola, and lately Commander of a Revenue Cutter in the United States service. [CG, Thurs., 14 JUN 1832, p. 3]

Georgetown, D.C., **Marriage and Death Notices, 1801-1838**

MARRIED, on Wednesday evening last [i.e. 13? JUN 1832], by the Rev. Norval Wilson, Mr. JAMES FRASER, of Green Valley, to Miss MARY ANN CAMPBELL, of Alexandria. [CG, Thurs., 21 JUN 1832, p. 3]

DIED, on the 14th inst. [i.e. 14 JUN 1832], at *Mount Vernon*, JOHN A. WASHINGTON, Esq., proprietor of that estate. [CG, Thurs., 21 JUN 1832, p. 3]

MARRIED, on the 26th inst. [i.e. 29 JUN 1832], by the Rev. Mr. McCormick, Mr. SMITH SUIT, of Prince George's Co., Md., to Miss JULIANA GORDON, of Washington Co., D.C. [CG, Tues., 3 JUL 1832, p. 3]

MARRIED, on Friday, the 29th June [i.e. 29 JUN 1832], by the Rev. John Robb, Mr. NATHAN LEAKE, Jr., of Millville, N.J., to Miss ANN LYDIA M'DUELL of Washington. [CG, Tues., 3 JUL 1832, p. 3]

MARRIED, in Harrisburg, Pa., on Tuesday morning last [i.e. 26 JUN 1832], by the Rev. Mr. Stem, the Hon. E. HERRICK, President Judge of the 13th judicial district, fo Miss REBECCA, daughter of the late Andrew Ross, Esq., of Georgetown. [CG, Tues., 3 JUL 1832, p. 3]

MARRIED, on Tuesday evening [i.e. 26 JUN 1832], by the Rev. Mr. Lochman, Mr. HENRY HUEHLER, to Miss MARGARET, daughter of George Wolf, ex-Governor of Pa. [CG, Tues., 3 JUL 1832, p. 3]

DIED, in Georgetown, on the 29th ult. [i.e. 29 JUN 1832], BOLIVAR B., son of Mr. Richard Wells, aged 7 years, 2 months and 25 days. [CG, Tues., 3 JUL 1832, p. 3]

MARRIED, on Tuesday last [i.e. 3 JUL 1832], by the Rev. Mr. Smith, Lieut. W. SEAWELL, of the U.S.A., to Miss MARTHA M. MACKEY, third daughter of William Mackey, Esq., of Georgetown. [CG, Sat., 7 JUL 1832, p. 3]

MARRIED, in Washington, on the 1st inst. [i.e. 1 JUL 1832], by the Rev. Mr. M'Cormick, Mr. EDWARD BURCHHEAD, to Miss MARY A. DOWN, both of that city. [CG, Sat., 7 JUL 1832, p. 3]

DIED, on Monday morning last [i.e. 2 JUL 1832], in Washington city, Mr. F. STEINER. [CG, Sat., 7 JUL 1832, p. 3]

DIED, in Washington, on Thursday night [i.e. 5 JUL 1832], Mrs. JANET LINGAN, relict of the late Gen. James Lingan. [CG, Sat., 7 JUL 1832, p. 3]

DIED, on the 13th ult. [i.e. 13 JUN 1832], at his residence, near Fincastle, Va., at an advanced age, Col. HENRY BOWYER, a soldier of the Revolution, and for many years Clerk of the Court of Botetourt. [CG, Sat., 7 JUL 1832, p. 3]

DIED, at Cumberland, Md., on the 9th Jan. last [i.e. 9 JAN 1832], Mr. FRANCIS DUCHOQUET, the benevolent Indian trader who ransomed Mr. Charles Johnston, of

Georgetown, D.C., **Marriage and Death Notices, 1801-1838**

Botetourt Springs, from captivity by the Indians in the year 1790. [CG, Sat., 7 JUL 1832, p. 3]

DIED, at Norfolk, Va., on Saaturday the 30th June [i.e. 30 JUN 1832], at 7 o'clock, P.M., Lieut. JOHN H. LEE, of the U.S. Navy, in the 36th year of his age. [CG, Sat., 7 JUL 1832, p. 3]

MARRIED, at Baltimore, on Thursday evening [i.e. 5 JUL 1832], by the Rev. Mr. Nevins, Dr. ALEXANDER C. ROBINSON, to ROSA E., daughter of Wm. Wirt, Esq. [CG, Thurs., 12 JUL 1832, p. 3]

MARRIED, at Baltimore, on Monday morning [i.e. 9 JUL 1832], by the Rev. John Finley, STEPHEN J. THOMPSON, to Miss REBECCA R., daughter of Wm. B. Barney, Esq. [CG, Thurs., 12 JUL 1832, p. 3]

MARRIED, on the 7th inst. [i.e. 7 JUL 1832], by the Rev. Mr. Furlong, Mr. BENJAMIN F. ROSE, to Miss REBECCA GIDEON, youngest daughter of Jacob Gideon, Jun., both of Washington City. [CG, Thurs., 12 JUL 1832, p. 3]

MARRIED, in Alexandria, at Friend's meeting-house, on fifth day, 28th ult. [i.e. 28 JUN 1832], JOSEPH H. MILLER, to PHEBE ANN JANNEY, both of that place. [CG, Sat., 14 JUL 1832, p. 3]

DIED, in N.Y., on Tuesday morning [i.e. 10 JUL 1832], of bilious cholic, FRANCIS THOMPSON, in the 56th year of his age. Mr. Thompson belonged to the religious denomination of Friends. He has long been known as an honorable merchant, and especially as one of the original proprietors and constant manger since, of the first Liverpool Packet Line, an enterprize which has done much for the city and the country at large. [CG, Sat., 14 JUL 1832, p. 3]

MARRIED, in N.Y. [no date], Lieut. WILLIAM SETON, of the U.S. Navy, to Miss EMILY, daughter of Nathaniel Prime, Esq. [CG, Tues., 24 JUL 1832, p. 3]

MARRIED, on Thursday morning, the 19th inst. [i.e. 19 JUL 1832], by the Rev. Mr. Mathews, Lieut. JUNIUS J. BOYLE, of the U.S. Navy, to ANN ELIZA, daughter of John McLeod, Esq., of *Shamrock Hill*, Washington Co. [CG, Tues., 24 JUL 1832, p. 3]

DIED, Washington, on Sunday [i.e. 22 JUL 1832], JAMES H. HANDY, of the 4th Auditor's Office. [CG, Tues., 24 JUL 1832, p. 3]

DIED, in Alexandria, on the 14th inst. [i.e. 14 JUL 1832], MARY ELLEN, 4th daughter of William Fowle, in the 15th year of her age. [CG, Tues., 24 JUL 1832, p. 3]

DIED, on Tuesday [i.e. 17 JUL 1832], H.W. CAROTHERS, in his 17th year, eldest son of John Carothers, Esq., of Washington. [CG, Tues., 24 JUL 1832, p. 3]

Georgetown, D.C., **Marriage and Death Notices, 1801-1838**

DIED, at Detroit, on the 15th inst. [i.e. 15 JUL 1832], of fever, Miss ELIZABETH CASS, in the 21st year of her age, eldest daughter of Gov. Cass, Secretary of War. [CG, Thurs., 26 JUL 1832, p. 3]

DIED, on Sunday [i.e. 22 JUL 1832], DANIEL OULD, son of Robert Ould, age 16 years. "Suffer little children to come unto me and forbid them not." [CG, Thurs., 26 JUL 1832, p. 3]

DIED, at Harford twp., Ohio, on the 10th inst. [i.e. 10 JUL 1832], Mrs. MARY HARPER, aged 76, relict of John Harper, Esq., formerly of Alexandria. [CG, Thurs., 26 JUL 1832, p. 3]

DIED, on the 12th inst. [i.e. 12 JUL 1832], at Occoquan, Va., in the 42d year of his age, after a short illness, JOHN MORGAN, for many years a respectable merchant of Alexandria. [CG, Thurs., 26 JUL 1832, p. 3]

MARRIED, in Georgetown, on Tuesday evening last [i.e. 24 JUL 1832], by the Rev. Dr. Balch, Mr. GEORGE THOMSON, to Miss ESTELLE M. JONCHEREZ, all of this town. [CG, Sat., 28 JUL 1832, p. 3]

MARRIED, in Georgetown, on the 31st ult. [i.e. 31 JUL 1832], by the Rev. Dr. Balch, Mr. ELKANAH WATERS, to Miss MARY, second daughter of Wm. Lowry, of Washington. [CG, Tues., 7 AUG 1832, p. 3]

MARRIED, in Baltimore, on Tuesday morning [i.e. 31 JUL 1832], the Hon. RICHARD THOMAS, Speaker of the House of Delegates of Md., to Miss JANE ARMSTRONG, youngest daughter of the late James Armstrong, Esq., of that city. [CG, Tues., 7 AUG 1832, p. 3]

DIED, in Washington, on the 5th inst. [i.e. 5 AUG 1832], RICHMOND, aged 20, eldest son of John G. McDonald. [CG, Tues., 7 AUG 1832, p. 3]

DIED, on Wednesday, 1st inst. [i.e. 1 AUG 1832], Mrs. ISABELLA BROWN, aged 27, wife of Edmund F. Brown, of the Post Office Department. [CG, Tues., 7 AUG 1832, p. 3]

DIED, at N.Y., on the 28th ult. [i.e. 28 JUL 1832], Lieut. MARSHALL LOVE, of the U.S. Marine Corps. [CG, Tues., 7 AUG 1832, p. 3]

DIED, on Monday, the 30th ult. [i.e. 30 JUL 1832], after a severe and protracted illness, departed this life, at New Brunswick, N.J., in the 71st year of his age, the Rev. JOHN CROES, D.D.—for more than thirty years the Rector of Christ Church in that City, and more than sixteen the Head of the Diocese of the Protestant Episcopal Church, in that State. [CG, Tues., 7 AUG 1832, p. 3]

MARRIED, in this town, on Thursday last [i.e. 2 AUG 1832], by the Rev. Mr. Stier, Mr. JOHN M. JOHNSTON, to Miss SARAH ANN MASSI, both of Alexandria. [CG, Thurs., 9 AUG 1832, p. 3]

Georgetown, D.C., **Marriage and Death Notices, 1801-1838**

DIED, in Georgetown, on Saturday [i.e. 4 AUG 1832], WILLIAM, 13 months, youngest son of H.C. Matthews. [CG, Thurs., 9 AUG 1832, p. 3]

DIED, in Washington, on the 14th inst. [i.e. 14 JUL 1832], Mrs. ANNA CUTTS, wife of Richard Cutts, Esq. [CG, Thurs., 9 AUG 1832, p. 3]

DIED, [no date], Miss ELIZA, 15 months, youngest child of Richard Barry. [CG, Thurs., 9 AUG 1832, p. 3]

DIED, at Harrisburg, (Pa.) on the 4th of August [i.e. 4 AUG 1832], in the 57th year of his age, JOSEPH JEFFERSON, Sen., Comedian. Mr. Jefferson was, for many years, a member of the Philadelphia and Baltimore Theatres, and was as much esteemed for his amiability of character and kindness of heart, as he was admired for his professional pre-eminence. [CG, Thurs., 9 AUG 1832, p. 3]

MARRIED, in Alexandria [no date], ELIJAH HOSMAN, of Fairfax Co., to Miss ELIZABETH EDWARDS, of Alexandria. [CG, Tues., 14 AUG 1832, p. 3]

MARRIED, in Alexandria [no date], Mr. CYRUS SIMMONS, to Miss MARY EDWARDS, formerly of Northumberland Co., Va. [CG, Tues., 14 AUG 1832, p. 3]

MARRIED, in Georgetown, at Christ Church, on Thursday evening last [i.e. 16 AUG 1832], by the Rev. C. Colton, HENRY REINTZEL, M.D., to Miss MARY E., daughter of W.S. Nicholls, Esq. [CG, Sat., 18 AUG 1832, p. 3]

DIED, of epilepsy, on the 17th inst. [i.e. 17 AUG 1832], in the 18th year of his age, SYDNEY AUGUSTUS BRADLEY, youngest son of Dr. P. Bradley. For the first five or six years of his life he was a child of uncommon promise, and presented to his fond parents and friends the most favorable prospect they could desire: but for the last eleven years of his earthly pilgrimage the sufferings he endured from epilepsy were perhaps without a parallel. [CG, Tues., 21 AUG 1832, p. 3]

DIED, in Norfolk, on the 13th [i.e. 13 AUG 1832], after a long indisposition, from Pulmonary disease, Mrs. JANE ANDERSON, relict of the late Col. Wm. Anderson, of the Marine Corps, in her 40th year. A lady highly esteemed for her many amiable and benevolent characteristics. [CG, Tues., 21 AUG 1832, p. 3]

DIED, on the 16th [i.e. 16 AUG 1832], after a few days illness, WILLIAM HENRY, son of Alfred D. and Loretta Bladen, formerly of Georgetown, (D.C.) aged 12 years. [CG, Tues., 21 AUG 1832, p. 3]

DIED, at N.Y., on Tuesday evening [i.e. 14 AUG 1832], Mrs. FRANCES NICHOLSON, widow of the late Com. NICHOLSON, in the 89th year of his age. [CG, Tues., 21 AUG 1832, p. 3]

DIED, at New Haven, Conn., on Saturday, 11th [i.e. 11 AUG 1832], HENRY E. DWIGHT, Esq., aged 35, youngest son of the late President Dwight, of Yale College. Mr. Dwight was

Georgetown, D.C., **Marriage and Death Notices, 1801-1838**

well known as an accomplished scholar, an amiable gentleman and sincere christian. [CG, Tues., 21 AUG 1832, p. 3]

DIED, at Paterson, N.J., on the 12th inst. [i.e. 12 AUG 1832], MARIA LOUISA, daughter of the late Gen. Alexander M. Muir, aged 5 years and 6 months. [CG, Tues., 21 AUG 1832, p. 3]

DIED, in Georgetown, after a lingering illness, on the 24th inst. [i.e. 24 AUG 1832], Mr. JOSHUA TENNISON, aged 58, for many years well known as an Inn Keeper in Washington and Georgetown. [CG, Tues., 28 AUG 1832, p. 3]

DIED, in Georgetown, on Sunday 26th inst. [i.e. 26 AUG 1832], Miss ELLEN DOYLE, aged 23. [CG, Thurs., 30 AUG 1832, p. 3]

DIED, in Alexandria, on the 11th inst. [i.e. 11 AUG 1832], ELISHA TALBOT, in the 51st year of his age. [CG, Thurs., 30 AUG 1832, p. 3]

MARRIED, on Tuesday evening, the 28th ult. [i.e. 28 JUL 1832], by the Rev. Mr. Post, Mr. ALEXANDER McINTOSH, of Washington, to Miss MARGARET RAE, recently from Scotland. [CG, Sat., 1 SEP 1832, p. 3]

MARRIED, at Meadville, Pa., by the Rev. J.W. James, on Thursday evening, Aug. 23 [i.e. 23 AUG 1832], Mr. JAMES ROSS DICK, to Miss HARRIET HAWKINS SMITH, daughter of J.K. Smith, Esq., late of Georgetown, D.C. [CG, Sat., 1 SEP 1832, p. 3]

DIED, in this town, on the 28th inst. [i.e. 28 AUG 1832], MARY ELIZABETH PARSONS, daughter of Jenkin Thomas, aged sixteen months and 9 days. [CG, Sat., 1 SEP 1832, p. 3]

DIED, in Baltimore, on Thursday morning [i.e. 30 AUG 1832], MARGARET, consort of the Rev. W.W. Wallace. [CG, Sat., 1 SEP 1832, p. 3]

MARRIED, on the 23d August [i.e. 23 AUG 1832], by the Rev. T.G. Waters, Mr. RICHARD H. CADLE, to Miss MARY E. JACOBS, all of Anne Arundel Co. [CG, Tues., 4 SEP 1832, p. 3]

DIED, at Annapolis on Friday morning [i.e. 31 AUG 1832], of an injury, apparently slight, received on the foot, terminating in lock jaw, Mrs. ANN JACKSON, aged 83 years—the relict of a revolutionary soldier. [CG, Tues., 4 SEP 1832, p. 3]

DIED, on Tuesday 21st inst. [i.e. 21 AUG 1832], near Upper Marlboro', Md., in the 61st year of her age, Mrs. SARAH FORREST, widow of the late Richard Forrest, Esq. [CG, Tues., 4 SEP 1832, p. 3]

DIED, at Norfolk, on the 25th ult. [i.e. 25 AUG 1832], ELEANOR LORETTA VIRGINIA, in the 8th year of her age; and on Monday the 27th, THOMAS JAMES, in his 10th year; both of the prevaililng Cholera,—Children of A.D. Bladen, formerly of this town. [CG, Tues., 4 SEP 1832, p. 3]

DIED, in Frederick, Md., on the 31st ult. [i.e. 31 AUG 1832], after a lingering illness, the Rev. SAMUEL KNOX, in the 76th year of his age, for many years President of the Baltimore College. [CG, Tues., 4 SEP 1832, p. 3]

DIED, in Baltimore, at Hospital No. 3, in the 30th year of her age, Sister MARY FRANCES, daughter of the late Benedict Boarman, of Charles Co., Md. Sister Mary Frances was one of the members of that pious community who have devoted themselves to heroically to attend the suffering under the awful Epidemic, which is now raging among us. She was attacked whilst assisting a poor colored woman who had been brought to the Hospital; her heroism made her forget herself in her ardour to relieve the patient who was under her charge, and she gave no notice of her situation till she was beyond medical relief. She has left the world the first Martyr of Charity among us.—*American*. [CG, Tues., 4 SEP 1832, p. 3]

DIED, in Georgetown, on Friday, 31st ult. [i.e. 31 AUG 1832], aged 13 years and 3 months, WILLIAM HENRY EDMONDSON, grandson of Samuel Bootes. [CG, Tues., 4 SEP 1832, p. 3]

DIED, in Alexandria, on Saturday last [i.e. 1 SEP 1832], Mrs. JEMIMA JENKINS, aged 77 years. [CG, Thurs., 6 SEP 1832, p. 3]

DIED, in Washington, on Tuesday morning [i.e. 4 SEP 1832], of the prevailing epidemic, Mrs. ELIZABETH FRANCE, consort of Mr. John France. [CG, Thurs., 6 SEP 1832, p. 3]

DIED, in Washington, on the 3d inst. [i.e. 3 SEP 1832], of consumption, in the 21st year of her age, Miss MARGARETTA DAVIDSON, eldest daughter of James Davidson, Esq. [CG, Thurs., 6 SEP 1832, p. 3]

MARRIED, in Washington, on Wednesday evening last [i.e. 5 SEP 1832], by the Rev. Mr. Hanson, Mr. JOSEPH HELM, of Georgetown, to Miss JANE MATILDA, daughter of the late Capt. John Holmead, of Washington Co., D.C. [CG, Sat., 8 SEP 1832, p. 3]

DIED, in Philadelphia, on the 14th inst. [i.e. 14 AUG 1832], Mrs. DOROTHY DALE, relict of the late Com. Richard Dale. [CG, Sat., 8 SEP 1832, p. 3]

DIED, in Baltimore, on the 5th [i.e. 5 SEP 1832], BENJAMIN EDES, Esq., Printer; he fought gallantly in 1814 in defence of that city, and had attained the rank of Brigadier General before his death. [CG, Sat., 8 SEP 1832, p. 3]

DIED, at her residence in Birmingham, Broome Co., N.Y., on Monday morning, 7th ult. [i.e. 7 AUG 1832], Mrs. ELIZABETH STUART, wife of William Stuart, Esq., dec., aged 50 years and 7 months. Mrs. S. was the second daughter of Gen. James Clinton, and sister of DeWitt Clinton, formerly Governor of N.Y. [CG, Sat., 8 SEP 1832, p. 3]

Georgetown, D.C., **Marriage and Death Notices, 1801-1838**

DIED, at *Oak Hill*, Va., on the 31st ult. [i.e. 31 AUG 1832], J.A.W. SMITH, Esq., Clerk of the Court of Fauquier Co. [CG, Sat., 8 SEP 1832, p. 3]

MARRIED, at Trenton, N.J. [no date], Lieut. HAMPTON WESTCOTT, of the U.S. Navy, to Miss ELIZABETH GRANT. [CG, Tues., 11 SEP 1832, p. 3]

MARRIED, in Harrisburg, Pa., on Thursday 30th ult. [i.e. 30 AUG 1832], Dr. EDMUND W. ROBERTS, to Miss CAROLINE ROSS, daughter of the late Andrew Ross, Esq., of Georgetown. [CG, Tues., 11 SEP 1832, p. 3]

DIED, in Georgetown, on the 2d inst. [i.e. 2 SEP 1832], after a long illness, at the residence of John Laub, Esq., Miss ELIZA MORRISON, formerly of Philadelphia. [CG, Tues., 11 SEP 1832, p. 3]

DIED, on Thursday last [i.e. 6 SEP 1832], Mrs. MARY ANN OWENS, relict of the late Isaac Owens, Jr., and daughter of Maj. Joel Brown, in the 32d year of her age. Also, Mr. JOHN ESPEY, Turner. Also, Mr. JOSEPH FEARSON, an old citizen. [CG, Tues., 11 SEP 1832, p. 3]

DIED, in Washington, on Friday [i.e. 7 SEP 1832], of the prevailing epidemic, Miss ACHSAH LOMBARD, aged 66, formerly of Boston. [CG, Tues., 11 SEP 1832, p. 3]

DIED, in Washington, on Sunday [i.e. 9 SEP 1832], after a severe and protracted illness, Mrs. [Marcia Burnes] VAN NESS, wife of Gen. J.P. VAN NESS, Mayor of the city. This lady was emphatically the guardian of the Orphan and the friend of the poor. [CG, Tues., 11 SEP 1832, p. 3]

DIED, on the 4th inst. [i.e. 4 SEP 1832], Mrs. HANNAH JOHNSON, aged 56, wife of Mr. John Johnson, formerly of Concord, N.H. [CG, Tues., 11 SEP 1832, p. 3]

DIED, in N.Y., on Tuesday, 4th inst. [i.e. 4 SEP 1832], JOHN FERGUSON, Esq., aged 55, Naval Officer of that port. [CG, Tues., 11 SEP 1832, p. 3]

DIED, in Baltimore, on Friday morning [i.e. 7 SEP 1832], PETER HOFFMAN CRUSE, Esq., Assistant Editor of the *Patriot*, a fine scholar, a gentleman universally esteemed and whose death is deeply regretted. Mr. C. was a native of Alexandria. [CG, Tues., 11 SEP 1832, p. 3]

DIED, in Vandalia, Ill., on the 18th Aug. [i.e. 18 AUG 1832], Mrs. MARY P. HALL, aged 29, wife of the Hon. James Hall, editor of the *Illinois Monthly Magazine*. [CG, Tues., 11 SEP 1832, p. 3]

DIED, on the 2d inst. [i.e. 2 SEP 1832], at the Hot Springs, Va., whither he had gone for his health, Com. C.C.B. THOMPSON, of the U.S. Navy. [CG, Tues., 11 SEP 1832, p. 3]

DIED, in Hagerstown, Md., on the 2d inst. [i.e. 2 SEP 1832], JOHN HENRY, aged 19, eldest son of O.H.W. Stull, Esq. [CG, Tues., 11 SEP 1832, p. 3]

Georgetown, D.C., **Marriage and Death Notices, 1801-1838**

DIED, at his residence in Montgomery Co., Md., on Friday night last [i.e. 7 SEP 1832], after a few days of painful illness, Mr. JAMES ORME, at the advanced age of seventy years. He was born and reared in that community, and the universal sentiment of regret, with which his death has inspired it, is the best evidence of his worth of character and the blameless tenor of his life. Leaving an aged companion and four children to mourn the loss of so kind a husband, and tender and affectionate father. [CG, Tues., 11 SEP 1832, p. 3]

MARRIED, on Tuesday, the 11th inst. [i.e. 11 SEP 1832], by the Rev. Mr. Ryland, Mr. WILLIAM G. RENNER, to Miss JANE, youngest daughter of W.A. Rind, Sr., all of this place. [CG, Thurs., 13 SEP 1832, p. 3]

DIED, in Washington, on Tuesday [i.e. 11 SEP 1832], in the 78th year of his age, Mr. JOHN LLOYD, a native of Ireland. On the 5th inst., Miss SUSAN WELDEN, aged 25 years, eldest daughter of Stephen W. Gray. On Sunday, of the prevailing epidemic, Mr. HUGH TIERNY, a native of Ireland. MARY ELIZABETH, 4 years, daughter of Mr. John Sergeant, Bookbinder. [CG, Thurs., 13 SEP 1832, p. 3]

MARRIED, in Washington, on Tuesday, the 11th inst. [i.e. 11 SEP 1832], by the Rev. Mr. Hildt, Mr. EDWARD BARKER, to Miss JANE ANN SWANN. [CG, Sat., 15 SEP 1832, p. 3]

MARRIED, on Sunday, the 9th inst. [i.e. 9 SEP 1832], by the Rev. Mr. Hawley, Mr. JOHN W. MARTIN, to Miss ELIZABETH TUCKER, all of Washington. [CG, Sat., 15 SEP 1832, p. 3]

MARRIED, in Alexandria [no date], Mr. WALTER H. HANNAN, of Charles Co., Md., to Mrs. JULIA LONGDEN, of the former place. [CG, Sat., 15 SEP 1832, p. 3]

DIED, at his residence in Georgetown [no date], after a short illness of nine days, in the 63d year of his age, JOHN S. HAW, of the Treasury Department ... Mr. Haw has been a resident of Georgetown for the last 30 years, 23 of which he has been a clerk in the Treasury Department, where he has left abundant evidence of his diligence and attention to his duties there ... [CG, Sat., 15 SEP 1832, p. 3]

DIED, on Wednesday morning, the 12th inst. [i.e. 12 SEP 1832], of the cholera, Mrs. MARY OWEN, aged about 52 years. [CG, Sat., 15 SEP 1832, p. 3]

DIED, in Washington, on Thursday [i.e. 13 SEP 1832], Miss HELEN DUFFY. [CG, Sat., 15 SEP 1832, p. 3]

DIED, in Georgetown, on the 11th inst. [i.e. 11 SEP 1832], of the prevailing epidemic, Mrs. BARBARA HURLEY, in the 26th year of her age. [CG, Sat., 15 SEP 1832, p. 3]

MARRIED, in Washington, on the 12th [i.e. 12 SEP 1832], Mr. JAMES W. CAMPBELL, to Miss C.M.V. SHAKES, both of Alexandria. [CG, Tues., 18 SEP 1832, p. 3]

Georgetown, D.C., **Marriage and Death Notices, 1801-1838**

DIED, in Washington, on Saturday [i.e. 15 SEP 1832], Mrs. ANNE DOUGLAS WALLACH, aged 40, consort of Richard Wallach, Esq., and daughter of the late Col. Charles Simms, of Alexandria. [CG, Tues., 18 SEP 1832, p. 3]

DIED, on the 13th [i.e. 13 SEP 1832], Mrs. ELIZABETH SMOOT, in the 36th year of her age, wife of Mr. George Smoot. On the same day, Mr. MARTIN COOK, in the 47th year of his age. [CG, Tues., 18 SEP 1832, p. 3]

DIED, in Lexington, Ky., on the 26th ult. [i.e. 26 AUG 1832], Mrs. SUSANNA HART, relict of the late Col. Thomas Hart, and mother of Mrs. H. Clay, in the 86th year of her age. [CG, Tues., 18 SEP 1832, p. 3]

DIED, about ten o'clock yesterday morning [i.e. 19 SEP 1832], of the prevailing epidemic, Mr. JOHN ELIASON, one of the oldest and most respected inhabitants of this town. ☞ The friends of the deceased and of the family are requested to attend his funeral from his late residence, this afternoon, at 3 o'clock. [CG, Thurs., 20 SEP 1832, p. 3]

DIED, in Washington, on the 15th inst. [i.e. 15 SEP 1832], in the 63d year of his age, Dr. THOMAS SIM. [CG, Thurs., 20 SEP 1832, p. 3]

DIED. On the 17th [i.e. 17 SEP 1832], Mr. ABSALOM RODBIRD, Sen., in the 74th year of his age. [CG, Thurs., 20 SEP 1832, p. 3]

DIED. On the 18th [i.e. 18 SEP 1832], Mr. JAMES WALKER, Butcher, aged 30. [CG, Thurs., 20 SEP 1832, p. 3]

MARRIED, in Gosport, Va., on the 12th inst. [i.e. 12 SEP 1832], Dr. JOHN R. CHANDLER, of Georgetown, Surgeon in the U.S. Navy, to Miss ELIZABETH PAGE. [CG, Sat., 22 SEP 1832, p. 3]

MARRIED, on the 18th inst. [i.e. 18 SEP 1832], Maj. CHARLES S. WILLIAMS, of the General Post Office, to Miss MARY E.F., daughter of Col. Wm. Hamilton, of Charles Co., Md. [CG, Sat., 22 SEP 1832, p. 3]

Departed this life, on Thursday, 20th inst. [i.e. 20 SEP 1832], at 6 o'clock in the morning, ROBERT BARRY, Jr., aged 32 years. He has left a disconsolate wife and two children ... His body will be interred this day, (Saturday) at 10 o'clock forenoon. His friends and acquaintances are respectfully invited to attend his funeral from his house in Market Street. [CG, Sat., 22 SEP 1832, p. 3]

DIED, at *Cedar Shelter*, Charles Co., Md., on the 8th inst. [i.e. 8 SEP 1832], WILLIAM R.A. SKINNER, in the 19th year of his age, beloved and respected by all who knew him; thus cut off in the prime of life ... [CG, Sat., 22 SEP 1832, p. 3]

DIED, at *Locust Hill*, Charles Co., Md., on the 7th inst. [i.e. 7 SEP 1832], of cholera, in a few hours, Mr. —CHUNN, an old and respectable citizen, and member of the Baptist Church. "Blessed are they that die in the Lord." [CG, Sat., 22 SEP 1832, p. 3]

DIED, in Washington, on Tuesday [i.e. 18 SEP 1832], Mrs. CATHERINE HOUX, 48, formerly of Frederick, Md. [CG, Sat., 22 SEP 1832, p. 3]

DIED. On Friday the 14th [i.e. 14 SEP 1832], ANNE S., 11, daughter of the late Thomas Wilson. [CG, Sat., 22 SEP 1832, p. 3]

DIED. On Tuesday [i.e. 18 SEP 1832], Mrs. JULIA CLARK, wife of Mr. John F. Clark. [CG, Sat., 22 SEP 1832, p. 3]

DIED, in Georgetown, on Wednesday [i.e. 19 SEP 1832], Miss ELIZABETH GOLDTHWAIT, aged 16, daughter of James L. Edwards, Esq. [CG, Sat., 22 SEP 1832, p. 3]

DIED, on the 12th inst. [i.e. 12 SEP 1832], at *Grampion*, St. Mary's Co., Md., Miss MARGARET FENWICK, of Georgetown. [CG, Sat., 22 SEP 1832, p. 3]

MARRIED, in Georgetown, on the 19th [i.e. 19 SEP 1832], SAMUEL DAVIDSON KING, to Miss MATILDA SOPHIA HOLTZMAN, daughter of John Laub, Esq. [CG, Tues., 25 SEP 1832, p. 3]

DIED, at the residence of Mrs. Sarah Plater, Prince George's Co., Md., Mrs. ANNE REINTZEL, relict of the late Daniel Reintzel, Esq., of this town. She had long laboured under disease, but on the morning of the 19th [i.e. 19 SEP 1832], the sudden rupture of a blood vessel terminated her mortal existence ... [CG, Tues., 25 SEP 1832, p. 3]

DIED, at Fairfax Court House, Va., on the 17th [i.e. 17 SEP 1832], Dr. SIMEON DRAPER, in the 47th year of his age. [CG, Tues., 25 SEP 1832, p. 3]

DIED, in Washington [no date], after a long illness, Mr. JOHN M. POWERS, Inn-keeper, in the 29th year of his age. [CG, Tues., 25 SEP 1832, p. 3]

DIED. Of the prevailing disease, on Friday [i.e. 21 SEP 1832], Mrs. ANNE ALLEN, widow of Thomas Allen, ship carpenter. [CG, Tues., 25 SEP 1832, p. 3]

DIED [no date]. Mr. CHARLES DAVIS, Sen., aged 80 years and 9 months. [CG, Tues., 25 SEP 1832, p. 3]

DIED. On Saturday, 15th [i.e. 15 SEP 1832], Mrs. ELIZABETH BUGH, in the 46th year of her age. [CG, Tues., 25 SEP 1832, p. 3]

DIED, near Piscataway, Md., on the 19th [i.e. 19 SEP 1832], Mr. ROBERT T. WASHINGTON, son of Lund Washington, Senr. [CG, Tues., 25 SEP 1832, p. 3]

DIED, in Washington, on Friday [i.e. 21 SEP 1832], of the prevailing epidemic, Mrs. JULIA ANN CROWLEY, wife of Mr. P. Crowley, Printer. [CG, Tues., 25 SEP 1832, p. 3]

Georgetown, D.C., **Marriage and Death Notices, 1801-1838**

DIED. On the 19th [i.e. 19 SEP 1832], Mr. THOMAS SINON, aged 38, a native of Ireland. [CG, Tues., 25 SEP 1832, p. 3]

DIED [no date]. JAMES HAMELY, Maltster, from Cornwall, England. [CG, Tues., 25 SEP 1832, p. 3]

DIED. On Thursday, 20th [i.e. 20 SEP 1832], ISABEL M., only child of John Little, 9 months. [CG, Tues., 25 SEP 1832, p. 3]

DIED [no date]. GEORGE OWEN, 2 months, infant son of E.F. Brown. [CG, Tues., 25 SEP 1832, p. 3]

DIED [no date]. ELIZA CATHCART, 6 months, infant daughter of James Hutton. [CG, Tues., 25 SEP 1832, p. 3]

DIED, in Boston [no date], Maj. THOMAS MELVILLE, 82, a hero of the Revolution, and one of those concerned in the destruction of Tea in Boston harbor; he is almost the last of the "cocked hats." [CG, Tues., 25 SEP 1832, p. 3]

MARRIED, in Georgetown on Tuesday last [i.e. 25 SEP 1832], by the Rev. Frederick Stier, Mr. GEORGE B. BARNES, to Miss JULIA ANN BAKER. And on the same day, Mr. CLEMENT WOODWARD, to Miss SARAH P. WOOLS. [CG, Thurs., 27 SEP 1832, p. 3]

MARRIED, in Washington, on Tuesday 18th [i.e. 18 SEP 1832], Mr. PHILIP WILLIAMS, to Mrs. SARAH ANN MARKWARD. [CG, Thurs., 27 SEP 1832, p. 3]

MARRIED, on Sunday last [i.e. 23 SEP 1832], Mr. RAPHAEL L. EDELEN, of Georgetown, to Miss CHARLOTTE ARTHELLA, daughter of George H. Lanham, Esq., of Prince George's Co., Md. [CG, Thurs., 27 SEP 1832, p. 3]

DIED, in Washington, on the 21st [i.e. 21 SEP 1832], Mrs. SARAH TERESA HOLTZMAN, aged 38, wife of Mr. Samuel Holtzman, and youngest daughter of the late Mrs. Mary Sweeny. [CG, Thurs., 27 SEP 1832, p. 3]

DIED, on Saturday [i.e. 22 SEP 1832], CLARISSA PAULA, in the 8th year of her age, daughter of Edward Dyer. [CG, Thurs., 27 SEP 1832, p. 3]

DIED, on Tuesday [i.e. 25 SEP 1832], Mr. SAMUEL STEWART, aged 53. [CG, Thurs., 27 SEP 1832, p. 3]

DIED, in New Port, Ky., on the 17th inst. [i.e. 17 SEP 1832], Mr. STEPHEN R. KEAN, formerly of Washington. [CG, Thurs., 27 SEP 1832, p. 3]

DIED, in this town, on Tuesday morning [i.e. 2 OCT 1832], Mr. ROBERT A. SLYE. [CG, Thurs., 4 OCT 1832, p. 3]

Georgetown, D.C., **Marriage and Death Notices, 1801-1838**

DIED. On the 18th ult. [i.e. 18 SEP 1832], Mrs. MARY SLYE, wife of Thomas G. Slye, Esq. [CG, Thurs., 4 OCT 1832, p. 3]

DIED, in Washington City, on Monday morning last [i.e. 1 OCT 1832], BENJAMIN LINCOLN LEAR, Esq., a highly respected member of the Bar of Washington Co. [CG, Thurs., 4 OCT 1832, p. 3]

DIED, in Washington City, on the 27th ult. [i.e. 27 SEP 1832], in the 85th year of her age, ELEANOR CAMPBELL (a coloured woman). Her life and death exemplified the christian, in the fullest sense. Though her skin was unchanged, her soul was spotless. [CG, Thurs., 4 OCT 1832, p. 3]

DIED, in Washington [no date], Mr. WILLIAM KNOWLES, age 67, one of the oldest and most respected inhabitants of that city. [CG, Sat., 6 OCT 1832, p. 3]

DIED, at N.Y., on the morning of the 1st inst. [i.e. 1 OCT 1832], Mrs. SARAH DYER, consort of Mr. Samuel Dyer. The deceased lady has left a family of small and interesting children, together with a large circle of relations and friends, to regret her death, and long remember her social, kind and friendly virtues. [CG, Sat., 6 OCT 1832, p. 3]

DIED, on Tuesday evening last [i.e. 2 OCT 1832], of the prevailing epidemic, Miss ELIZABETH PETER, of Jefferson Co., formerly of Georgetown. [CG, Tues., 9 OCT 1832, p. 3]

DIED, on Tuesday evening last [i.e. 2 OCT 1832], of the prevailing epidemic, Mr. THOMAS B. PETER, son of Maj. John Peter, of Jefferson Co., in the 22d year of his age. [CG, Tues., 9 OCT 1832, p. 3]

DIED, at Philadelphia [no date], after a lingering and painful illness, on Thursday night, the 4th inst., at 11 o'clock, the Rev. Dr. JOHN GLENDY, aged 77 years, formerly Pastor of the Second Presbyterian Church of Baltimore, where he will be long remembered with affectionate regard for his many virtues. [CG, Tues., 9 OCT 1832, p. 3]

DIED, on the 6th inst. [i.e. 6 OCT 1832], at *Bradford's Rest*, Montgomery Co., Md., RICHARD THOMAS, aged eighteen months and twenty-two days, youngest child of Thomas G. Good, of this town. [CG, Thurs., 11 OCT 1832, p. 3]

DIED, in Washington, on the 6th inst. [i.e. 6 OCT 1832], of the prevailing epidemic, Mrs. REBECCA PERKINS. [CG, Thurs., 11 OCT 1832, p. 3]

DIED, in Washington, on Thursday last [i.e. 4 OCT 1832], of a lingering illness, Mr. JOHN ALEXANDER FRENCH. [CG, Thurs., 11 OCT 1832, p. 3]

MARRIED, in this town, on Thursday evening last, by the Rev. Mr. Lipscomb, Mr. JAMES B. BROWN, to Miss MARY F. AVARD. [CG, Sat., 13 OCT 1832, p. 3]

Georgetown, D.C., **Marriage and Death Notices, 1801-1838**

MARRIED, on Thursday evening last [i.e. 11 OCT 1832], by the Rev. Mr. Brooke, Capt. PETER BARGY, Jr., of Herkimer Co., N.Y., to Miss HANNAH JOHNSON, youngest daughter of the late Jesse Baily, of this place. [CG, Sat., 13 OCT 1832, p. 3]

DIED, at Stockholm (Sweden) on the 7th of August last [i.e. 7 AUG 1832], LAURA SOPHIA, wife of Christopher Hughes, Esq., Charge des Affairs of the U.S.A., and daughter of Gen. Samuel Smith, of Baltimore. [CG, Sat., 13 OCT 1832, p. 3]

DIED, on Sunday night the 14th inst. [i.e. 14 OCT 1832], after a short and severe illness, JULIA MARIA, only child of Capt. Walter B. Chew, aged 12 months and 12 days. [CG, Thurs., 18 OCT 1832, p. 3]

DIED, in Norfolk, on Saturday last [i.e. 13 OCT 1832], JOHN E. HOLT, Esq., for nearly twenty years Mayor of the borough; and a gentleman of most estimable character. [CG, Thurs., 18 OCT 1832, p. 3]

MARRIED, in this town, on Tuesday evening last [i.e. 16 OCT 1832], Mr. P. FARRIS, to Miss JULIAN BECRAFT. [CG, Sat., 20 OCT 1832, p. 2]

DIED, in this town, on Tuesday evening last [i.e. 16 OCT 1832], after a protracted sickness, MOORE DICKSON, a native of the County of Down, Ireland, but a resident of this town for more than nine years. [CG, Sat., 20 OCT 1832, p. 2]

MARRIED, in Washington, on Sunday morning last [i.e. 21 OCT 1832], by the Rev. O.B. Brown, Mr. CHANSTAUN H. LAURIE, of the U.S. Navy, to Miss MARGARET A. McCUTCHEN. [CG, Tues., 23 OCT 1832, p. 3]

MARRIED [no date], by the Rev. Dr. Balch, Midshipman, DANIEL F. DULANY, Jr., to Miss MARGARET ANN GANTT, both of Fairfax Co., Va. [CG, Tues., 23 OCT 1832, p. 3]

MARRIED, on Tuesday morning last [i.e. 16 OCT 1832], at Hyde Park, (N.Y.) by the Rev. Mr. Johnson, Mr. JARED SPARKS, of Boston, to Miss FRANCES ALLEN, daughter of William Allen, Esq., of Hyde Park. [CG, Tues., 23 OCT 1832, p. 3]

DIED, in Washington, on Tuesday last [i.e. 23 OCT 1832], of consumption, Mrs. ANN, wife of Mr. George Bede, aged 30 years. [CG, Thurs., 25 OCT 1832, p. 3]

Obituary. Died, at Washington, Miss. [no date], Maj. JOHN HOLBROOK, Principal of the Collegiate Institution at that place, aged 32 years ... He has left a wife and one child, to lament his premature death.—They were formerly from Hartland, Ver.—*Railroad Journal.* [CG, Thurs., 25 OCT 1832, p. 3]

DIED, in Brooklyn, (N.Y.) on the 21st inst. [i.e. 21 OCT 1832], Mrs. AMELIA F., wife of Capt. John T. Newton, of the U.S. Navy, in the 35th year of her age. [CG, Sat., 27 OCT 1832, p. 3]

Georgetown, D.C., **Marriage and Death Notices, 1801-1838**

DIED, on Friday evening, 19th [i.e. 19 OCT 1832], in Baltimore, in the 66th year of his age, Mr. WILLIAM WARREN, for many years a manager of the Baltimore, Philadelphia and Washington Theatres. [CG, Sat., 27 OCT 1832, p. 3]

MARRIED, in Burlington, N.J., on the 22d inst. [i.e. 22 OCT 1832], Rev. CHAUNCEY COLTON, of Washington City, to ANN, daughter of the late William Coxe, Esq., of Burlington. [CG, Tues., 30 OCT 1832, p. 3]

DIED, in Georgetown, D.C., on Thursday morning, 1st Nov. [i.e. 1 NOV 1832], LEWIS GRANT DAVIDSON, Esq., long a highly respected resident of this place. [CG, Sat., 3 NOV 1832, p. 2]

MARRIED, in Georgetown, on Wednesday evening last [i.e. 31 OCT 1831], by the Rev. Mr. Brooke, Mr. GEORGE P. FORREST, to Mrs. ELEANOR M. YATES, daughter of the late Henry H. Chapman, Esq., all of Georgetown. [CG, Tues., 6 NOV 1832, p. 3]

MARRIED, at Norfolk, on Wednesday evening last [i.e. 31 OCT 1831], by the Rev. Mr. Wingfield, Lieut. SAMUEL BARRON, of the U.S. Navy, to Miss IMOGENE WRIGHT, of Norfolk. [CG, Tues., 6 NOV 1832, p. 3]

MARRIED, in Middlebury, (Vt.) on the evening of October 8th [i.e. 8 OCT 1832], by the Rev. McDonald, the Rev. Mr. CHAUNCEY W. FITCH, of Gambier, Ohio, to Miss MARGARET S. HENSHAW, daughter of the late Daniel Henshaw of that place. [CG, Thurs., 8 NOV 1832, p. 3]

DIED, on Thursday last [i.e. 1 NOV 1832], MARY EDGAR, eldest daughter of Mr. Edgar Patterson of this town. The friends and acquaintances of the family are invited to attend her funeral this afternoon at half past 3 o'clock. [CG, Thurs., 8 NOV 1832, p. 3]

DIED, on Monday the 5th [i.e. 5 NOV 1832], MARGARET ISABELLA, third daughter of William Morton, Georgetown, D.C., in the 13 year of her age. [CG, Sat., 10 NOV 1832, p. 3]

DIED, in Washington, Ky., on the 25th Oct. [i.e. 25 OCT 1832], in the 71st year of his age, Dr. JOHN JOHNSTON, (father of the Hon. Josiah S. Johnston, Senator from La.) The deceased was a native of Conn., and removed to Ky. in 1789; for 40 years he has been a respectable and successful practitioner of Washington and its vicinity—was esteemed by all who knew him, and died as he lived, an honest man. [CG, Sat., 10 NOV 1832, p. 3]

DIED, in Fredericksburg, Va., on Tuesday last [i.e. 6 NOV 1832], Lieut. JAMES G. BOUGHAN, of the U.S. Navy, aged 37 years. [CG, Sat., 10 NOV 1832, p. 3]

DIED, in Georgetown, D.C., on the 13th Oct. [i.e. 13 OCT 1832], of cholera, Mrs. SARAH R. BERRY, aged 35, formerly of Boston, Mass., and wife of Mr. Noble F. Berry. ☞ Editors in Boston will please insert this. [CG, Sat., 10 NOV 1832, p. 3]

Georgetown, D.C., **Marriage and Death Notices, 1801-1838**

DIED, in Maysville, Ky., on the 28th Oct. [i.e. 28 OCT 1832], Mr. JAMES MORRISON, Merchant, in the 50th year of his age, after a short but severe attack of cholera. [CG, Sat., 10 NOV 1832, p. 3]

MARRIED, in Norfolk, Va., on the 6th inst. [i.e. 6 NOV 1832], Lieut. JOHN McCLELLAN, of the U.S. Army, to Miss GEORGIANA A. TAYLOR, of Norfolk. [CG, Tues., 13 NOV 1832, p. 3]

MARRIED, in Shelbyville, Ky., on the 29th ult. [i.e. 29 OCT 1832], HENRY E. THOMAS, of Louisville, to MARY GRAFTON, daughter of the late Thomas G. Addison, of Md. [CG, Tues., 13 NOV 1832, p. 3]

MARRIED, at Columbia, Mo. [no date], Hon. WILLIAM H. ASHLEY, Representative in Congress, to Mrs. WILCOX, daughter of James W. Moss, Esq. [CG, Tues., 13 NOV 1832, p. 3]

DIED, in Washington, on the 4th inst. [i.e. 4 NOV 1832], Lieut. THOMAS McKEAN BUCHANAN, of the U.S. Navy. [CG, Tues., 13 NOV 1832, p. 3]

DIED, in N.Y., on the 4th [i.e. 4 NOV 1832], Mid. WILLIAM F. IRVING, of the U.S. Navy, aged 23. [CG, Tues., 13 NOV 1832, p. 3]

DIED, at Fort Jackson, La., on the 2d Oct. [i.e. 2 OCT 1832], in the 27th year of his age, Dr. E.J. COLLINS, of Baltimore, Acting Assistant Surgeon in the Army. [CG, Tues., 13 NOV 1832, p. 3]

DIED, in N.Y., on the 7th inst. [i.e. 7 NOV 1832], Dr. JAMES MANN, Surgeon U.S. Army, and an officer in the Revolutionary Army. [CG, Tues., 13 NOV 1832, p. 3]

DIED, on the 9th inst. [i.e. 9 NOV 1832], Capt. JAMES T. LEONARD, of the U.S. Navy, aged 54. [CG, Tues., 13 NOV 1832, p. 3]

DIED, in Alexandria, on Sunday [i.e. 11 NOV 1832], Mr. ROBERT S. BLACKLOCK. [CG, Tues., 13 NOV 1832, p. 3]

DIED, at Bedford, Pa., on the 5th inst. [i.e. 5 NOV 1832], Mrs. AMELIA, wife of Walter Lowrie, Esq., Secretary of the U.S. Senate. [CG, Tues., 13 NOV 1832, p. 3]

DIED, in Lafayette Co., Mo., on the 21st Sept. [i.e. 21 SEP 1832], JONATHAN S. FINDLAY, Esq., in the 55th year of his age, a native of Pa., and formerly a resident of Washington city. [CG, Tues., 13 NOV 1832, p. 3]

DIED, in Georgetown, on Tuesday last [i.e. 13 NOV 1832], VALENTINE BOGENREIFF, in the 65th year of his age. Mr. B. was a member of the Presbyterian Church for many years, and an humble follower of his Lord and Master. [CG, Thurs., 15 NOV 1832, p. 3]

Georgetown, D.C., **Marriage and Death Notices, 1801-1838**

MARRIED, in Washington, on the 13th inst. [i.e. 13 NOV 1832], by the Rev. Mr. Chalmers, Mr. ORLANDO DELPHY, of Baltimore, to Miss JANE GROVES, of Alexandria. [CG, Sat., 17 NOV 1832, p. 2]

DIED, at Washington, yesterday morning [i.e. 16 NOV 1832], Mr. EDWARD J. COALE, Bookseller, formerly of Baltimore. [CG, Sat., 17 NOV 1832, p. 2]

MARRIED, in Washington, on Thursday evening last [i.e. 15 NOV 1832], by the Rev. Mr. Hawley, the Hon. JOHN G. WATMOUGH, a Representative in Congress from the State of Pa., to MATILDA, eldest daughter of Stephen Pleasanton, Esq., 5th Auditor of the Treasury Department. [CG, Tues., 20 NOV 1832, p. 2]

MARRIED, at *Walnut Grove*, near Vansville, Md., on Thursday morning last [i.e. 15 NOV 1832], Lieut. ARCHIBALD B. FAIRFAX, of the U.S. Navy, to SARAH [CARLYLE], second daughter of the Hon. John C. Herbert. [CG, Tues., 20 NOV 1832, p. 2]

MARRIED, on Sunday morning last [i.e. 18 NOV 1832], Mr. WILLIAM L. WEEMS, of Tenn., to Miss POLLY HATTON, daughter of Henry Hatton, Esq., late of Prince George's Co., Md. [CG, Tues., 20 NOV 1832, p. 2]

MARRIED, at N.Y., on the 13th inst. [i.e. 13 NOV 1832], Capt. D. WILCOX, U.S. Army, to Mrs. SARAH J. DAVIS, of Boston. [CG, Tues., 20 NOV 1832, p. 2]

MARRIED, in Norfolk, on the 14th inst. [i.e. 14 NOV 1832], Lieut. MARTIN BURK, of the 3d Regiment U.S. Artillery, to Miss MATTE TAYLOR, daughter of the late Francis Taylor, Esq., of Norfolk. [CG, Tues., 20 NOV 1832, p. 2]

MARRIED, in Richmond, on the 13th inst. [i.e. 13 NOV 1832], Lieut. Wm. H. KENNON, of the U.S. Navy, to Miss NANCY, daughter of Beverly Randolph, of that city. [CG, Tues., 20 NOV 1832, p. 2]

DIED, in Salem, Mass. [no date], Mr. JOSEPH VINCENT, age 96 years and 7 months. When the news of the battle of Bunker Hill reached Salem, he immediately repaired to the field of action ...When the sloops of war were built at Newburyport, Mr. Vincent was called upon to furnish the cordage for them. This article at that time, was not easily to be obtained, and he refused to sell to the merchants here using these words, "My Country first—until she is supplied, I have nothing for you." He took the promise to pay of the State of Mass., rather than the Merchants' gold—this promise to pay was never fulfilled—he never received an adequate compensation, being compelled to take Continental money. In 1777, a number of apprentices, and a colored servant in his family, wishing to enter the army, he equipped them at his own expense. He afterwards joined the army under Washington as a volunteer. [CG, Tues., 20 NOV 1832, p. 2]

DIED, at Covington, (La.) [no date], Dr. JAMES EWELL, (author of the *Medical Companion*) recently of N. Orleans and formerly of Washington City, D.C. [CG, Tues., 20 NOV 1832, p. 2]

Georgetown, D.C., **Marriage and Death Notices, 1801-1838**

MARRIED, on the 18th inst. [i.e. 18 NOV 1832], at *Friendship,* Prince George's Co., Md., Mr. EDWARD COLLIGE, of Washington, to Miss E.A. BOWIE, daughter of the late John B. Bowie. [CG, Thurs., 22 NOV 1832, p. 3]

Departed this life in Georgetown, on the 18th inst. [i.e. 18 NOV 1832], in the 13th year of her age, after a long illness, MARIE LOUIS MASON, eldest daughter of Maj. Milo Mason; Commandant of Fort Washington ... [CG, Thurs., 22 NOV 1832, p. 3]

DIED, on Monday evening [i.e. 19 NOV 1832], suddenly, at Brown's Hotel in Washington city, the Hon. PHILIP DODDRIDGE, a Representative in Congress from the State of Virginia, aged about 60 years ... [CG, Thurs., 22 NOV 1832, p. 3]

MARRIED, in Philadelphia, on Tuesday last [i.e. 20 NOV 1832], before Joseph Watson, Esq., ROBERT B. FOWLER, of Georgetown, to MARIA LEEKENS, of Philadelphia. [CG, Sat., 24 NOV 1832, p. 3]

DIED, in Georgetown, on the 16th inst. [i.e. 16 NOV 1832], ANN ELIZABETH, in the 13th year of her age, eldest child of Stephen Gough, of St. Mary's Co., Md. [CG, Sat., 24 NOV 1832, p. 3]

MARRIED, in Anne Arundel Co., Md., on Thursday evening [i.e. 22 NOV 1832], by the Rev. Mr. Humphrey, Mr. JOHN B. PATTERSON, of Georgetown, to Miss ELIZA—daughter of the late Joseph M'Ceney, Esq., of that county. [CG, Tues., 27 NOV 1832, p. 3]

MARRIED, in Annapolis, on Thursday evening [i.e. 22 NOV 1832], Mr. DANIEL LLOYD, Talbot Co., to Miss VIRGINIA UPSHER, of Georgetown, D.C. [CG, Tues., 27 NOV 1832, p. 3]

DIED, in Georgetown, on the 22d inst. [i.e. 22 NOV 1832], after a short illness of one week, of the Scarlet Fever, FRANCES S. AFFORDBY, aged 6 years, 11 months and 13 days; eldest daughter of the late Lieut. John T. Ritchie, U.S. Navy; and on the 23d [i.e. 23 NOV 1832], after a few hours illness, of the same disease, her only brother, JOHN THOMAS, aged 14 months and 17 days. [CG, Tues., 27 NOV 1832, p. 3]

DIED, in Norfolk, on Wednesday, 21st Nov. [i.e. 21 NOV 1832], Col. WILLIAM C. HOLT, in the 49th year of his age, President of the Farmers' Bank, and for several years Speaker of the Senate of Virginia. A gentleman highly and universally respected. [CG, Tues., 27 NOV 1832, p. 3]

DIED, of the cholera, on the 3d inst. [i.e. 3 NOV 1832], on board the steamboat *Express,* on his way from Louisville to St. Louis, Col. WM. MACREA, of the 2d regiment of U.S. Artillery, aged 65 years, upwards of 41 of which had been passed in the service of his country. [CG, Tues., 27 NOV 1832, p. 3]

MARRIED, on Tuesday, the 20th [i.e. 20 NOV 1832], by the Rt. Rev. Bishop Meade, Mr. SYDNOR EDMUNDS, of Fauquier Co., to Miss MARGARET B.—daughter of Elias Edmunds, Esq., of Berryville, Frederick Co., Va. [CG, Thurs., 29 NOV 1832, p. 3]

Georgetown, D.C., **Marriage and Death Notices, 1801-1838**

MARRIED, on Wednesday the 21st inst. [i.e. 21 NOV 1832], by the Rev. David Elliott, Dr. PHINEAS BRADLEY, of Washington City, late Assistant Postmaster General, to Mrs. ANN McDONALD, relict of the late John McDonald, of Alexandria, D.C. [CG, Thurs., 29 NOV 1832, p. 3]

MARRIED, in Martinsburg, Va., on Tuesday evening, 20th inst. [i.e. 20 NOV 1832], by the Rev. Mr. Johnson, Mr. JOHN G. CHAPMAN, to MARY ELIZABETH—eldest daughter of the late Capt. Fielder Luckett, of Alexandria. [CG, Thurs., 29 NOV 1832, p. 3]

DIED, in Alexandria, on the 24th inst. [i.e. 24 NOV 1832], WILLIAM H. HURDLE, son of Lawrence Hurdle, aged 17 years and 7 months. [CG, Thurs., 29 NOV 1832, p. 3]

DIED, in Alexandria, on Tuesday, Oct. 9th [i.e. 9 OCT 1832], LUCY EUGENIA—and at *Clifton*, Fairfax Co., Va., on Wednesday, Oct. 10th, JUNIA SURVILLA, third and fourth daughters of the late James H. Hooe—the former in the 19th, the latter in the 16th year of her age. [CG, Thurs., 29 NOV 1832, p. 3]

DIED, of the yellow fever, in New Orleans, on Wednesday, 31st Oct. [i.e. 31 OCT 1832], Mr. CHARLES A. LANCASTER, a native of Charles Co., Md. [CG, Thurs., 29 NOV 1832, p. 3]

DIED, in Washington [no date], Mrs. ELLEN JUDSON, widow of Dr. E. Judson, formerly of the U.S. Navy. [CG, Thurs., 29 NOV 1832, p. 3]

DIED, at *Waterloo*, Va., on the 24th inst. [i.e. 24 NOV 1832], Miss SIDNEY ALEXANDER—daughter of the late Gerard Alexander, of Prince William Co. [CG, Thurs., 29 NOV 1832, p. 3]

DIED, in Dumfries, Va., on Sunday the 25th inst. [i.e. 25 NOV 1832], of pulmonary consumption, WILLOUGHBY W. TEBBS. [CG, Thurs., 29 NOV 1832, p. 3]

MARRIED, in Washington, on Thursday, 29th ult. [i.e. 29 NOV 1832], the Hon. HUGH L. WHITE, Senator in Congress from the State of Tenn., to Mrs. ANN PEYTON. [CG, Thurs., 6 DEC 1832, p. 2]

MARRIED, on Thursday evening, 29th ult. [i.e. 29 NOV 1832], at the President's House, ALPHONSO PAGEOT, Esq., Secretary to the French Legation, to Miss MARY ANN LEWIS, daughter of William B. Lewis, Esq., 2d Auditor of the Treasury. Mr. Pageot is the brother of Madame Seurrureur, the lady of the French Minister. [CG, Thurs., 6 DEC 1832, p. 2]

MARRIED, at *Hayes*, Montgomery Co., Md., on the 27th ult. [i.e. 27 NOV 1832], by the Rev. Mr. Mines, Dr. JOHN M. THOMAS, of Washington City, to HARRIET MARGARET, daughter of the late James Dunlop, Esq., of Georgetown. [CG, Thurs., 6 DEC 1832, p. 2]

Georgetown, D.C., **Marriage and Death Notices, 1801-1838**

DIED, in Georgetown, on Monday the 3d inst. [i.e. 3 DEC 1832], after an illness of the cholera of thirty-four hours, THOMAS A., son of Lewis Carbery, aged nine years, four months and twenty-one days. [CG, Thurs., 6 DEC 1832, p. 2]

DIED, in Washington, on Monday evening, the 3d inst. [i.e. 3 DEC 1832], after a protracted and painful illness, PETER LENOX, Esq., in the 62 year of his age. [CG, Thurs., 6 DEC 1832, p. 2]

DIED, in Philadelphia, on Friday [i.e. 30 NOV 1832], in the 51st year of his age, Gen. THOMAS J. ROGERS, formerly a member of Congress from Pa. [CG, Thurs., 6 DEC 1832, p. 2]

DIED, at Savannah, on the 19th Nov. [i.e. 19 NOV 1832], EDWARD E. TATNALL, Esq., formerly a member of Congress from Ga. [CG, Thurs., 6 DEC 1832, p. 2]

DIED, on the 25th of Oct. [i.e. 25 OCT 1832], in the Island of St. Thomas, West Indies, of a rapid consumption, HENRIETTA, consort of John M. Lyle, Esq., of Philadelphia, and formerly of Alexandria, D.C. [CG, Thurs., 6 DEC 1832, p. 2]

MARRIED, on Tuesday, Nov. 28th [i.e. 28 NOV 1832], by the Rev. Mr. Smith, Mr. SAMUEL SUTTON, to Miss NANCY LEACH, both of Alexandria. [CG, Sat., 8 DEC 1832, p. 3]

MARRIED, in Baltimore, on Tuesday evening last [i.e. 4 DEC 1832], Lieut. I.S. STERETT, (U.S.N.) to Miss JANE S., daughter of J. Smith Hollins, both of that city. [CG, Sat., 8 DEC 1832, p. 3]

MARRIED, on Tuesday evening, 4th inst. [i.e. 4 DEC 1832], Mr. GEORGE W. NORRIS, to Miss LYDIA C., second daughter of Dennis A. Smith, all of Baltimore. [CG, Sat., 8 DEC 1832, p. 3]

MARRIED, in Norfolk [no date], Dr. JAMES CORNICK, of the U.S. Navy, to Miss CATHERINE B. MOSELEY. [CG, Sat., 8 DEC 1832, p. 3]

DIED, in Georgetown, on Friday afternoon [i.e. 7 DEC 1832], SUSAN ELIZA, daughter of the late John S. Compton, aged 8 years and 5 months. The friends and acquaintances of the family are invited to attend her funeral at half past 3 o'clock this afternoon at Mr. Brawner's, Bridge Street. [CG, Sat., 8 DEC 1832, p. 3]

DIED, in Washington, on Tuesday evening, the 4th inst. [i.e. 4 DEC 1832], after a lingering illness, Mr. THOMAS HOWARD, in the 54th year of his age, and for the last thirty years a resident of this city. [CG, Sat., 8 DEC 1832, p. 3]

DIED, on the 29th ult. [i.e. 29 NOV 1832], at *Rosehill*, the residence of the Rev. John Mines, near Rockville, Md., Mrs. SUSAN SHIPPEN MINES, wife of the Rev. J. Addison Mines, late of Philadelphia, aged 27 years. [CG, Sat., 8 DEC 1832, p. 3]

Georgetown, D.C., **Marriage and Death Notices, 1801-1838**

MARRIED, on the 29th ult. [i.e. 29 NOV 1832], Mr. WILKERSON G. WILLIAMS, to Miss MARY M. NASH, and on Thursday evening last [i.e. 6 DEC 1832], WILLIAM LANPHIER, Jr., to Miss ELIZABETH McDOUGALL, all of Alexandria. [CG, Tues., 11 DEC 1832, p. 3]

MARRIED, in Washington on the 6th inst. [i.e. 6 DEC 1832], LEWIS KRUMBHAAR, Jr., Esq., of Philadelphia, to SOPHIA, youngest daughter of the late Andrew Ramsay, Esq. [CG, Tues., 11 DEC 1832, p. 3]

DIED, in Washington, on the 4th inst. [i.e. 4 DEC 1832], Maj. E.S. LAMBERT, in the 34th year of his age, formerly of the U.S. Army, and for the last six years a resident of the District of Columbia. [CG, Tues., 11 DEC 1832, p. 3]

DIED, at Fort Armstrong, Ill., on the 26th Oct. [i.e. 26 OCT 1832], Maj. THOMAS J. BEALL, of the U.S. Army. [CG, Tues., 11 DEC 1832, p. 3]

MARRIED, in Washington, on Sunday evening last [i.e. 9 DEC 1832], by the Rev. Mr. Hanson, Mr. OBADIAH MOSS, to Miss ELIZABETH ORME, both of Washington. [CG, Thurs., 13 DEC 1832, p. 3]

MARRIED, on the 9th inst. [i.e. 9 DEC 1832], at *Brook Grove*, Prince George's Co., Md., by the Rev. Mr. Mackenheimer, JONATHAN PROUT, Esq., of Washington City, to Miss ANNA LOWNDES, daughter of the late Thomas T. Gantt, Esq. [CG, Thurs., 13 DEC 1832, p. 3]

DIED, in Georgetown, on Monday last, the 10th inst. [i.e. 10 DEC 1832], of scarlet fever, GEORGE M., and a few hours thereafter, ANNA ELIZABETH, children of Otho M. Linthicum, Esq., the former aged five, and the latter seven years, after a few days illness ... [CG, Thurs., 13 DEC 1832, p. 3]

DIED, in Georgetown, on Tuesday evening [i.e. 11 DEC 1832], at 10 o'clock, Mrs. JANE MATILDA HELM, consort of Mr. Joseph Helm. For more than two years, Mrs. Helm had made a profession of experimental religion, and preserved a high standing as a member of the Methodist Episcopal Church ... The friends and acquaintances of the family are respectfully invited to attend the funeral this morning, at 10 o'clock from her late residence on West Street. [CG, Thurs., 13 DEC 1832, p. 3]

DIED, in Washington, on the 10th inst. [i.e. 10 DEC 1832], ALEXANDER KERR, Esq., Cashier of the Bank of the Metropolis. [CG, Thurs., 13 DEC 1832, p. 3]

MARRIED, on Thursday the 6th inst. [i.e. 6 DEC 1832], by the Rev. Mr. Lumbsden, JOHN H. WINEMILLER, Esq., to Miss ELIZA ANN, second daughter of Mr. James Magruder, all of Montgomery Co., Md. [CG, Sat., 15 DEC 1832, p. 2]

MARRIED, on the 6th inst. [i.e. 6 DEC 1832], at *Retreat*, the residence of George D. Parnham, Esq., Charles Co., Md., by the Rev. Mr. Laird, the Rev. HENRY B. GOODWIN, Rector of St. Paul's Parish, Prince George's Co., to SUSAN A., daughter of the late Dr. Parnham. [CG, Sat., 15 DEC 1832, p. 2]

Georgetown, D.C., Marriage and Death Notices, 1801-1838

MARRIED, at Round Hill, on Thursday, 12th inst. [i.e. 13? DEC 1832], by the Rev. Mr. Wilson, Mr. LEOLIN NICHOLSON, of Alexandria, to Miss MARGARET S.—daughter of William and Maria Lindsay, of Fairfax Co., Va. [CG, Thurs., 20 DEC 1832, p. 3]

DIED, in Georgetown, on Sunday last, the 16th inst. [i.e. 16 DEC 1832], JOHN—son of Dr. Otho M. Linthicum, aged three years ... [CG, Thurs., 20 DEC 1832, p. 3]

DIED, in Georgetown, on Monday the 17th [i.e. 17 DEC 1832], after a short illness, in the 14th year of her age, SUSAN F., daughter of Henry Waring, Esq. ... [CG, Thurs., 20 DEC 1832, p. 3]

DIED, in Washington, on Monday [i.e. 17 DEC 1832], AMIE HOUSTON, in the 15th year of her age, eldest daughter of Joseph P. McCorkle. [CG, Thurs., 20 DEC 1832, p. 3]

MARRIED, in Easton, Pa. [no date], HORACE E. WOLF, of the city of Washington, son of Gov. Wolf, to SABINA, daughter of the late Michael Simon, Esq., of Easton. [CG, Sat., 22 DEC 1832, p. 2]

MARRIED, at Chelsea [no date], Mr. ROBERT BROOK, to Miss BARBARA ANN BERRY, daughter of the late J. Berry, Esq., both of said county. [CG, Sat., 22 DEC 1832, p. 2]

MARRIED, in Norfolk [no date], Mr. WM. D. PORTER, of the U.S. Navy, to Miss JANE E. MARCHANT, of that Borough. [CG, Sat., 22 DEC 1832, p. 2]

DIED, at *Poplar Hill*, Charles Co., Md. [no date], JAMES GARDINER, Esq., in the 59th year of his age. [CG, Sat., 22 DEC 1832, p. 2]

DIED, at Natchitoches, La., on the 14th ult. [i.e. 14 NOV 1832], aged 57, the Hon. JOHN C. CARR, Parish Judge of the parish of Natchitoches. He was a native of Liverpool, Eng.—a man of superior education and sterling integrity. [CG, Sat., 22 DEC 1832, p. 2]

DIED, at N.Y., Dec. 3d [i.e. 3 DEC 1832], Mr. LOUIS MOREAU LISLET, the oldest member of the bar in that city, and much respected by the community. Mr. M.L. was born at Cape Francois, St. Domingo, in 1767. [CG, Sat., 22 DEC 1832, p. 2]

DIED, on Tuesday morning [i.e. 18 DEC 1832], after a short illness, STEPHEN HONEYWELL, Esq., Treasurer of the Maryland Savings Institute of Baltimore, in the 46th year of his age. [CG, Sat., 22 DEC 1832, p. 2]

DIED, on the River St. Johns, near St. Augustine, East Florida, on the 26th of Nov. [i.e. 26 NOV 1832], Col. JOHN LAWRENCE LEWIS, aged 54. [CG, Sat., 22 DEC 1832, p. 2]

DIED, in Hagerstown [no date], BENJAMIN YOE, Esq., merchant, aged 60. [CG, Tues., 25 DEC 1832, p. 2]

DIED, at Albany, on Wednesday, the 19th [i.e. 19 DEC 1832], of apoplexy, WILLIAM JAMES, Esq., in the 63d year of his age ... [CG, Tues., 25 DEC 1832, p. 2]

Georgetown, D.C., **Marriage and Death Notices, 1801-1838**

GARDINER GREEN, Esq., President of the U.S. Branch Bank in Boston, died on Wednesday morning [i.e. 19 DEC 1832] in the 79th year of his age. Mr. Green has long had the reputation of being the most opulent man in New-England. He resigned his office of the President of the Branch a few days since, and William Appleton, Esq., is elected to fill the vacancy. The amount of Mr. Green's estate is estimated at about 8,000,000.—*Boston Atlas.* [CG, Tues., 25 DEC 1832, p. 2]

MARRIED, on Thursday, the 3d of January [i.e. 3 JAN 1833], at the Presbyterian Church in F Street, by the Rev. Dr. Laurie, HENRY JACKSON, of the Treasury Department, to Mrs. LAVINIA LYNE, daughter of Wm. Hunter, Esq. [CG, Sat., 5 JAN 1833, p. 2]

MARRIED, on Tuesday, January 1st [i.e. 1 JAN 1833], by the Rev. Mr. Matthews, Mr. EDWARD HOBAN, to Miss MARY ANN WILLIAMS, both of Washington. [CG, Sat., 5 JAN 1833, p. 2]

MARRIED, on Thursday evening, the 3d inst. [i.e. 3 JAN 1833], by the Rev. Mr. Hildt, Mr. JOSEPH COOPER, to Mrs. PHEBE ANN SANDIFORD, all of Washington. [CG, Sat., 5 JAN 1833, p. 2]

MARRIED, in Washington, on Monday [i.e. 31 DEC 1832], by the Rev. Mr. Hildt, Mr. JOSEPH BUTLER, to Miss MARTHA F. HUDSON. [CG, Sat., 5 JAN 1833, p. 2]

MARRIED, on Tuesday [i.e. 1 JAN 1833], by the Rev. J. Laurie, Mr. ANDREW GRAHAM, to Miss ADELIA SOPHIA TSCHIFFELY. [CG, Sat., 5 JAN 1833, p. 2]

MARRIED, in Prince George's Co., Md., on Thursday evening, 20th ult. [i.e. 20 DEC 1832], by the Rev. Mr. Smallwood, Mr. WILLIAM TRUNNELL, of Georgetown, D.C., to Miss CHRISTIANA ALLDRIDGE, of the former place. [CG, Sat., 5 JAN 1833, p. 2]

MARRIED, near Natchez, Miss. [no date], J.B.H. LATROBE, Esq., of Baltimore, to Miss CHARLOTTE VIRGINIA CLAIBORNE, only daughter of the late Gen. F.L. Claiborne. [CG, Sat., 5 JAN 1833, p. 2]

DIED, at N.Y., on Wednesday morning [i.e. 2 JAN 1833], after a short illness, JONATHAN OGDEN, in the 65th year of his age. [CG, Sat., 5 JAN 1833, p. 2]

DIED, at Norfolk, Va., a few days ago [no date], JAMES NIMMO, Esq., Attorney at Law, aged 78 years, one of the most venerable and esteemed citizens of that community. [CG, Sat., 5 JAN 1833, p. 2]

DIED, at Louisville, Ky., on the 24d ult. [i.e. 24 DEC 1832], EDWARD SHIPPEN, Esq., Cashier of the Branch Bank of the United States of that place. [CG, Sat., 5 JAN 1833, p. 2]

DIED, in Washington, on Tuesday [i.e. 1 JAN 1833], in the 15th year of her age, ANN FENTON LEE, daughter of John D. Simms. On the same day, Mr. JOHN ROBERTSON, in the 30th year of his age. [CG, Sat., 5 JAN 1833, p. 2]

Georgetown, D.C., **Marriage and Death Notices, 1801-1838**

DIED, on the 30th ult. [i.e. 30 DEC 1832], Mr. BENJAMIN B. MYERS. [CG, Sat., 5 JAN 1833, p. 2]

DIED, suddenly, at West Point, on Monday evening, 24th ult. [i.e. 24 DEC 1832], THOMAS GIMBREDE, Instructor of Drawing in the Military Academy, West Point, aged 51. [CG, Sat., 5 JAN 1833, p. 2]

DIED, in N.Y., on the 29th ult. [i.e. 29 DEC 1832], Maj. CHARLES B. TALLMADGE, Paymaster U.S. Army. [CG, Sat., 5 JAN 1833, p. 2]

DIED, in New Haven, Conn., on the [blank], Hon. JAMES HILLHOUSE, at an advanced age, formerly of the U.S. Senate. [CG, Sat., 5 JAN 1833, p. 2]

DIED, at New Orleans, on the 5th Nov. [i.e. 5 NOV 1832], of malignant cholera, Mr. JOHN T. LIPSCOMB, in the 37th year of his age, a native of Washington, and for many years a resident of Georgetown. [CG, Sat., 5 JAN 1833, p. 2]

DIED, at Fort Gibson, Miss., early in Nov., Col. JOHN P. DECATUR, of typhus fever, formerly Naval Storekeeper at Portsmouth, N.H. and brother of the late Com. Decatur. [CG, Sat., 5 JAN 1833, p. 2]

DIED, in Leesburg, Va., on the 24th Dec. [i.e. 24 DEC 1832], Mr. JOSIAH L. DREAN, aged 33. [CG, Sat., 5 JAN 1833, p. 2]

MARRIED, on Thursday last [i.e. 3 JAN 1833], by the Rev. Thomas Burges, Mr. RICHARD H. TOLER, one of the Editors of the *Lynchburg Virginian*, to Miss MARY ANN FRANCES, daughter of Maj. William Duval, of Buckingham County. [CG, Tues., 8 JAN 1833, p. 2]

DIED, at *Bloomsbury*, St. Mary's Co., on Friday night the 28th ult. [i.e. 28 DEC 1832], Mrs. ELIZABETH, relict of the late Judge Plater, in the sixty-first year of her age. [CG, Tues., 8 JAN 1833, p. 2]

DIED, on Tuesday night, 1st January [i.e. 1 JAN 1833], Mrs. ANN PRISCILLA, wife of Robert Manning, Esq., of St. Mary's Co., Md. [CG, Tues., 8 JAN 1833, p. 2]

MARRIED, in this town, on the 6th inst. [i.e. 6 JAN 1833], by the Rev. Mr. H. Furlong, Mr. WILLIAM H. PECKHAM, of Washington, to Miss SARAH ANN RETALLACK, of Georgetown, D.C. [CG, Thurs., 10 JAN 1833, p. 3]

MARRIED, in Washington, on Sunday, January 6th [i.e. 6 JAN 1833], by the Rev. Mr. Post, Mr. GEORGE F. MILES, of Georgetown, to Miss SOPHIA GALPIN, of New Haven, Conn. [CG, Thurs., 10 JAN 1833, p. 3]

DIED, in Washington, on Tuesday morning, the 8th inst. [i.e. 8 JAN 1833], Miss ANN RILEY. [CG, Thurs., 10 JAN 1833, p. 3]

Georgetown, D.C., **Marriage and Death Notices, 1801-1838**

DIED, on Tuesday evening last [i.e. 8 JAN 1833], in the 38th year of his age, Mr. JOHN P. DENNY, of the General Post Office Department. [CG, Thurs., 10 JAN 1833, p. 3]

DIED, in Alexandria, on Tuesday [i.e. 8 JAN 1833], WILLIAM HENRY GRAYSON, son of the late Capt. Grayson, of that place. [CG, Thurs., 10 JAN 1833, p. 3]

DIED, on Sunday, Jan. 6 [i.e. 6 JAN 1833], VIRGINIA, infant daughter of Wm. D. Nutt. [CG, Thurs., 10 JAN 1833, p. 3]

DIED, in Washington, on Monday, 7th inst. [i.e. 7 JAN 1833], Mr. JAMES SESSFORD, aged 48. [CG, Sat., 12 JAN 1833, p. 3]

DIED, near Port Tobacco, Charles Co., Md., in October last [i.e. OCT 1832], Dr. JOHN N. WEEMS, in the 42d year of his age. [CG, Sat., 12 JAN 1833, p. 3]

DIED, on the 4th inst. [i.e. 4 JAN 1833], near Piscataway, Prince George's Co., Mr. JOSEPH EDELIN, Sen., in the 78th year of his age. [CG, Sat., 12 JAN 1833, p. 3]

DIED, at Cincinnati, Ohio, on the 1st inst. [i.e. 1 JAN 1833], Mrs. SARAH ANN MILFORD, aged 23 years, wife of James Milford, Printer, and eldest daughter of Mr. James Broadwell, formerly of Georgetown, D.C. [CG, Sat., 12 JAN 1833, p. 3]

MARRIED, in Georgetown, on the 15th inst. [i.e. 15 JAN 1833], by the Rev. Mr. Brook, Mr. HENRY M. CHEW, of Prince George's Co., Md., to ELIZABETH ANN, youngest daughter of John S. Haw, deceased. [CG, Thurs., 17 JAN 1833, p. 3]

DIED, in Washington, on Tuesday, 15th inst. [i.e. 15 JAN 1833], Maj. WILLIAM GAMBLE, aged 78, an officer of the Revolutionary Army. [CG, Thurs., 17 JAN 1833, p. 3]

DIED, in Boston, on Thursday, 10th inst. [i.e. 10 JAN 1833], Col. AMOS BINNEY, aged 65, formerly Navy agent at that port. [CG, Thurs., 17 JAN 1833, p. 3]

MARRIED, in Georgetown, on the 17th inst. [i.e. 17 JAN 1833], by the Rev. Mr. Pool, Mr. HENRY CARTER, to Miss MARY LANG, all of Georgetown. [CG, Sat., 19 JAN 1833, p. 3]

MARRIED, on Thursday evening last [i.e. 17 JAN 1833], by the Rev. Norval Wilson, Mr. LEONARD C. ADAMS, to Miss MARGARET E. BALL, all of Alexandria. [CG, Sat., 19 JAN 1833, p. 3]

MARRIED, in Washington, on Thursday evening the 17th inst. [i.e. 17 JAN 1833], by the Rev. Mr. Hildt, Mr. PEREGRINE WARFIELD BROWNING, to Miss MARGARET ANN WOOD, all of Washington. [CG, Sat., 19 JAN 1833, p. 3]

MARRIED, on the 8th inst. [i.e. 8 JAN 1833], at *Clamber Hill*, Charles Co., Md., by the Rev. J. Combes, Mr. COURTNEY JENKINS, Esq., of Baltimore, to Miss CAROLINE A. JENKINS, eldest daughter of John J. Jenkins, Esq. [CG, Sat., 19 JAN 1833, p. 3]

Georgetown, D.C., **Marriage and Death Notices, 1801-1838**

DIED, in this town, on Sunday, the 13th inst. [i.e. 13 JAN 1833], Mr. BARNABAS YOUNG, in the 52d year of his age, for many years a resident of this place. [CG, Sat., 19 JAN 1833, p. 3]

MARRIED, on Thursday evening the 17th inst. [i.e. 17 JAN 1833], by the Rev. Dr. Balch, Dr. CHARLES H. LAUB, to ANN ELIZA, eldest daughter of Robert Getty, Esq., all of Georgetown. [CG, Tues., 22 JAN 1833, p. 2]

MARRIED, at Columbia, S.C., on the 3d inst. [i.e. 3 JAN 1833], by the Rev. Mr. Henry, Mr. A.P. CALHOUN, eldest son of the Hon. J.C. Calhoun, to Miss EUGENIA CHAPPELL, eldest daughter of Col. J.J. Chappell. [CG, Tues., 22 JAN 1833, p. 2]

DIED, in Georgetown, on Sunday last [i.e. 20 JAN 1833], Miss JANE ABBOTT, youngest daughter of Mr. John Abbott, of Georgetown, D.C. ... [CG, Tues., 22 JAN 1833, p. 2]

DIED, in Georgetown, D.C., on Thursday the 17th inst. [i.e. 17 JAN 1833], ANN LEEKE HEPBURN, aged 12 years, the second daughter of John M. Hepburn, Esq., after an illness of only two days. [CG, Tues., 22 JAN 1833, p. 2]

DIED, in Washington on the 19th inst. [i.e. 19 JAN 1833], SUSANNA BARRY, relict of the late Capt. Edward Barry. [CG, Tues., 22 JAN 1833, p. 2]

MARRIED, at *Mount Ida*, near Alexandria, on the 17th inst. [i.e. 17 JAN 1833], RICHARD JOHNSON, Esq., of Beaufort, S.C., to Miss ANN MANN SMITH, youngest daughter of the late Col. Caleb Smith, of King George Co., Va. [CG, Thurs., 24 JAN 1833, p. 3]

DIED, in Alexandria, on Tuesday morning [i.e. 22 JAN 1833], in the 27th year of her age, Mrs. JANE ELIZABETH, wife of William Davis, Esq., Merchant of that place. [CG, Thurs., 24 JAN 1833, p. 3 (twice)]

DIED, on the 13th [i.e. 13 JAN 1833], in Bryan Town, Charles Co., Md., in the 18th year of her age, Miss JULIA POSEY, daughter of Mrs. Sarah E. Posey. [CG, Thurs., 24 JAN 1833, p. 3]

MARRIED, at Pittsfield, Mass., on the 1st inst. [i.e. 1 JAN 1833], ORRIN WRIGHT, M.D., to Mrs. FRANCES PEASE, of Washington, D.C. [CG, Sat., 26 JAN 1833, p. 2]

DIED, in Georgetown, on Wednesday, January 23 [i.e. 23 JAN 1833], Mrs. DEWANN B. McCOY, in the 25th year of her age. The deceased has been afflicted for more than a year past with a wasting consumption ... [CG, Sat., 26 JAN 1833, p. 2]

DIED, in Leesburg, on Saturday, 26th inst. [i.e. 26 JAN 1833], SAMUEL POSTON, aged about 40 years, after a protracted illness.—The deceased was formerly of Washington City, but had resided in Leesburg for the last three years. [CG, Tues., 29 JAN 1833, p. 3]

Georgetown, D.C., **Marriage and Death Notices, 1801-1838**

DIED, in Madison, C.H., Va., on the 10th inst. [i.e. 10 JAN 1833], Mrs. ANN SWIFT, aged 65, relict of the late Jonathan Swift, Esq., of Alexandria, D.C. [CG, Tues., 29 JAN 1833, p. 3]

DIED, in Washington, on Monday night [i.e. 28 JAN 1833], at half past 11 o'clock, WEBSTER ERLES, the infant son of Mr. Azariah Fuller, aged 10 months and 10 days. [CG, Thurs., 31 JAN 1833, p. 3]

DIED, on the 24th inst. [i.e. 24 JAN 1833], JOHN LEWIS DENNEY, son of the late John P. Denney, aged one year and nine months. [CG, Thurs., 31 JAN 1833, p. 3]

DIED, a few days since [no date], in Botetourt Co., CHAS. JOHNSTON, Esq., proprietor of the Botetourt Springs. [CG, Tues., 5 FEB 1833, p. 3]

MARRIED, in Washington, on Tuesday evening, the 5th inst. [i.e. 5 FEB 1833], by the Rev. Mr. Schriber, ROBERT FITZHUGH, Esq., of the U.S. Navy, to MARIA, daughter of Daniel Carroll, Esq., of *Duddington.* [CG, Sat., 9 FEB 1833, p. 3]

MARRIED, in Pensacola, (Fla.) on the 10th ult. [i.e. 10 JAN 1833], ISAAC HULSE, Surgeon of the U.S. Hospital of that station, to Miss MELANIA, daughter of John Innerarity, Esq., of Pensacola. [CG, Sat., 9 FEB 1833, p. 3]

DIED, on Wednesday, the 6th inst. [i.e. 6 FEB 1833], in the 23d year of her age, Mrs. ISOBEL RITTENHOUSE, wife of Mr. Benjamin F. Rittenhouse, and daughter of the Rev. Dr. Laurie, of this city ... [CG, Sat., 9 FEB 1833, p. 3]

DIED, on Friday morning last [i.e. 8? FEB 1833], after a short but severe illness, RICHARD PARKER, the eldest son of Thomas B. Dashiell, aged 4 years and 4 months. [CG, Sat., 9 FEB 1833, p. 3]

DIED, on Sunday morning, February 3d [i.e. 3 FEB 1833], ELIZABETH, daughter of Mr. Christopher Cammack, aged 2 years and ten months. [CG, Sat., 9 FEB 1833, p. 3]

DIED, on Thursday [i.e. 7 FEB 1833], JOSEPH FRANKLIN, youngest child of Mr. Moses Marson, printer, formerly of Boston, aged 13 months. [CG, Sat., 9 FEB 1833, p. 3]

DIED, at Alexandria, on Sunday, Jan. 27 [i.e. 27 JAN 1833], JOHN RICHARDS, aged 3 years and 9 months; and on Monday, February 4, THOMAS BROCCHUS, aged 7 years and 2 months, sons of Richard Stanton. [CG, Sat., 9 FEB 1833, p. 3]

DIED, at Baltimore [no date], Miss MARY M. FRAILEY, the much beloved and affectionate daughter of L. Frailey, in the 22d year of her age. [CG, Sat., 9 FEB 1833, p. 3]

DIED, on Tuesday afternoon, the 5th inst. [i.e. 5 FEB 1833], in the 31st year of her age, SARAH, wife of James Harwood, and daughter of the late Bishop Kemp. [CG, Sat., 9 FEB 1833, p. 3]

Georgetown, D.C., **Marriage and Death Notices, 1801-1838**

DIED, at Philadelphia, at the house of his father, on the 22d of Jan. last [i.e. 22 JAN 1833], Don Carlos M. BERNABUE, son of the Consul General of Spain, for the United States of America. [CG, Sat., 9 FEB 1833, p. 3]

MARRIED, on Thursday evening last [i.e. 7 FEB 1823], by the Rev. Elias Harrison, CHARLES H. TRIPLETT, to ESTHER ANN, youngest daughter of the late Wm. Dunlap, all of Alexandria. [CG, Tues., 12 FEB 1833, p. 2]

MARRIED, in Baltimore, on Thursday evening [i.e. 7 FEB 1823], by the Rev. Mr. Morris, Mr. TOBIAS NIXDORFF, merchant, formerly of Georgetown, to Miss ANGELINA AMELIA, daughter of the late David Bixler, of Baltimore. [CG, Tues., 12 FEB 1833, p. 2]

DIED. Departed this life last night [i.e. 11 FEB 1823], after a distressing and painful illness in sure hope of a blissful immortality, Mrs. SUSAN KENNEDY, in the 57th year of her age ... The friends and acquaintances of the family are respectfully invited to attend her funeral tomorrow afternoon at half past three o'clock. [CG, Tues., 12 FEB 1833, p. 2]

DIED, in Washington, on Monday [i.e. 11 FEB 1833], WALTER B. BEALL, of the General Land Office, aged 63. [CG, Tues., 12 FEB 1833, p. 2]

DIED, in Washington, on Friday, 8th inst. [i.e. 8 FEB 1833], DECIMUS EUGENE, in the 14th year of his age, son of Dr. T. Watkins. [CG, Tues., 12 FEB 1833, p. 2]

DIED, in Alexandria, on Sunday morning, the 3d inst. [i.e. 3 FEB 1833], in the 42d year of her age, Mrs. SARAH MOUNT, wife of Mr. Thomas Mount, and eldest daughter of Mr. Joseph Smith. [CG, Tues., 12 FEB 1833, p. 2]

DIED, in Hagerstown, Md., on Tuesday last [i.e. 5 FEB 1833], in the 39th year of his age, Lieut. WM. POTTENGER, of the United States Navy. [CG, Tues., 12 FEB 1833, p. 2]

DIED, at his residence in Warrenton, N.C., on the 29th ult. [i.e. 29 JAN 1833], the Hon. JOHN HALL, recently Judge of the Supreme Court of that State, after a lingering indisposition of about twelve months, in the 64th year of his age. [CG, Tues., 12 FEB 1833, p. 2]

DIED, at his residence, at Pleasant Hill, in Warren Co., N.C., on the 28th ult. [i.e. 28 JAN 1833], Col. PHILEMON HAWKINS, the last of the signers of the Constitution of the State of North Carolina in 1776. [CG, Tues., 12 FEB 1833, p. 2]

DIED, in Pitt Co., N.C., on the 1st inst. [i.e. 1 FEB 1833], Mrs. ELIZABETH MOORE, in the 101st year of her age. [CG, Tues., 12 FEB 1833, p. 2]

MARRIED, on Tuesday evening, the 12th inst. [i.e. 12 FEB 1833], by the Rev. Mr. Dubuisson, at the residence of Com. Cassin, in Georgetown, D.C., EDWARD DYER, Esq., of Washington, to Miss HENRIETTA A., youngest daughter of the late Capt. Joseph Tarbell, of the U.S. Navy. [CG, Thurs., 14 FEB 1833, p. 3]

Georgetown, D.C., **Marriage and Death Notices, 1801-1838**

DIED, at half past 6 o'clock, yesterday morning, (Feb. 13th) in the 44th year of his age, Mr. GIDEON DAVIS, of the War Department. In the death of this worthy man, society at large has sustained a great loss—the Methodist Protestant Church, of which he was an active and most exemplary member, a greater—but his amiable family the greatest of all. ☞ His friends particularly, and the public generally are respectfully invited to attend his funeral, which will move from his residence on Bridge street, Georgetown, D.C., tomorrow afternoon at 4 o'clock. [CG, Thurs., 14 FEB 1833, p. 3]

DIED, in Georgetown, on the 9th inst. [i.e. 9 FEB 1833], Miss JANE BRENT, aged 61, formerly of Charles Co., Md. [CG, Thurs., 14 FEB 1833, p. 3]

DIED, in Georgetown, on the 8th inst. [i.e. 8 FEB 1833], Mrs. ELEANOR ORME, wife of Mr. Jeremiah Orme, of this place, leaving behind an affectionate husband with a family of little children to mourn her loss ... Mrs. Orme was a subject of long and great affliction ... *[lengthy religious commentary continues]* [CG, Thurs., 14 FEB 1833, p. 3]

MARRIED, in Dayton, Ohio, on the 15th ult. [15 JAN 1833], GEORGE W. SMITH, Esq., of that place, to Miss LUCINDA WESTON, daughter of the late Capt. Weston, of Alexandria, D.C. [CG, Sat., 16 FEB 1833, p. 3]

DIED, in Washington, on Sunday morning [i.e. 17 FEB 1833], after an illness of little more than twenty-four hours, Mr. ROBERT CLARKE, aged fifty years. [CG, Tues., 19 FEB 1833, p. 2]

Extensive listing of all local government officials. [CG, Thurs., 21 FEB 1833, p. 1]

DIED, in Boston, on Sunday, 10th inst. [i.e. 10 FEB 1833], Mrs. MARIA THERESA APPLETON, aged 46 years, wife of the Hon. Nathan Appleton, member of Congress, from Mass., and daughter of the late Thomas Gold, Esq., of Pittsfield. Mr. A. passed through New York, on his way home, on the day of Mrs. A's death. [CG, Thurs., 21 FEB 1833, p. 3]

MARRIED, in Washington, on Tuesday morning, 26th inst. [i.e. 26 FEB 1833], by the Rev. Mr. Hatch, EBENEZER J. HUME, Esq., of Nashville, Tenn., to Miss BARBARA ELLEN BERRY, of this city. [CG, Sat., 2 MAR 1833, p. 3]

DIED, in Washington, on Monday the 25th ult. [i.e. 25 FEB 1833], in the 34th year of her age, after a lingering disease of 15 months, Mrs. ALICE MILBURN, the wife of Mr. George Milburn, of this city. [CG, Sat., 2 MAR 1833, p. 3]

DIED, at Quebec, on the 14th ult. [i.e. 14 FEB 1833], Monseigneur BERNARD CLAUDE PANET, Bishop of Quebec, aged 80 years. He succeeded the late Bishop Plesis in December 1825, and resigned the administration of the Diocese in October last to Monseigneur Joseph Signay, who succeeded to the Bishopric. [CG, Sat., 2 MAR 1833, p. 3]

Georgetown, D.C., **Marriage and Death Notices, 1801-1838**

DIED, at *Lucky-Hit farm*, on Tuesday the 26th inst. [i.e. 26 FEB 1833], RICHARD KIDDER MEADE, in the 50th year of his age ... On the morning of the 26th our friend was in the enjoyment of his usual health. At 12 o'clock he repaired to the meeting-house, at the White Post, and with a fervor of zeal peculiar to himself, was prepared to take an active part in the proceedings of a temperance society, which he himself had been greatly instrumental in forming a few months previous, and to the success of which he seemed to devote the energies of his mind and body. The society being organized, the president read some very beautiful and appropriate extracts from the addresses of Judge Cranch and others ... his brother, Bishop Meade, inquired for his resolutions ... [CG, Tues., 5 MAR 1833, p. 2]

DIED, in Washington on Saturday evening last, 2d inst. [i.e. 2 MAR 1833], in the 22d year of her age, Mrs. HARRIET MURRAY, wife of Mr. Stanislaus Murray. [CG, Tues., 5 MAR 1833, p. 3]

DIED [no date], after an illness of several years, proceeding from a cancer in the face, Mrs. MARY ANN GREER, consort of James Greer, formerly of Georgetown. [CG, Tues., 5 MAR 1833, p. 3]

DIED, on the 4th inst. [i.e. 4 MAR 1833], after an illness of only a few hours, Mrs. JANE MARIA TABBS, daughter of the late Charles Carroll, of *Bellevue*, and wife of Moses Tabbs, Esq. [CG, Tues., 5 MAR 1833, p. 3]

MARRIED, on Tuesday evening last [i.e. 5 MAR 1833], by the Rev. Mr. Hanson, Mr. ROBERT HARRESTON, of Philadelphia, to Miss JANE E. WILLIAMS, of Washington. [CG, Thurs., 7 MAR 1833, p. 3]

MARRIED, in Washington on Monday evening, the 4th inst. [i.e. 4 MAR 1833], by the Rev. Mr. Palfrey, Hon. JOHN KING, of N.Y., to Mrs. SARAH S. BRANNAN, of that city. [CG, Thurs., 7 MAR 1833, p. 3]

DIED, at Dayton, Ohio, on Thursday night last [i.e. 28 FEB 1833], Col. THOMAS J. McARTHUR, eldest son of Gov. MacArthur, in the 31st year of his age. [CG, Thurs., 7 MAR 1833, p. 3]

Departed this life, at *Oak Hill*, Prince George's Co., Md., on the 26th ult. [i.e. 26 FEB 1833], Mrs. MARY E. MORAN, wife of Samuel C. Moran, and eldest daughter of Mr. Benjamin Burns, of Washington. [CG, Thurs., 7 MAR 1833, p. 3]

DIED, on Tuesday afternoon [i.e. 12 MAR 1833], at 2 o'clock, Mr. JOHN B. PATTERSON, in the 27th year of his age. He has left a young and amiable widow, to whom he had been married not quite four months, to mourn, with his parents, brothers, sisters, and friends, the untimely death of this truly amiable young man. His friends and acquaintances, and those of the family, are invited to attend his funeral, from the residence of his father, Mr. Edgar Patterson, on Third street, this afternoon at 4 o'clock. [CG, Thurs., 14 MAR 1833, p. 3]

Georgetown, D.C., **Marriage and Death Notices, 1801-1838**

DIED, in Washington City, on Sunday morning last [i.e. 17 MAR 1833], WILLIAM L., son of Col. Wm. L. Brent. [CG, Tues., 19 MAR 1833, p. 2]

DIED, in Georgetown, on Sunday morning last [i.e. 17 MAR 1833], at 4 o'clock, of rapid consumption, occasioned by the rupture of a blood vessel, Mrs. MARIA DUNCAN, wife of Mr. Joseph M. Duncan, and daughter of the late John W. Durant, Esq., of Philadelphia. [CG, Thurs., 21 MAR 1833, p. 2]

DIED, in Hagerstown, Md., on the 20th inst. [i.e. 20 MAR 1833], after a short illness, FREDERICK STULL, only son of O.H.W. Stull, Esq. This is the third son Mr. Stull has lost within a few months. [CG, Tues., 26 MAR 1833, p. 2]

MARRIED, in Washington City, on Tuesday evening last, 26th inst. [i.e. 26 MAR 1833], by the Rev. Mr. Brooke, Mr. GEO. D. ABBOT, of Georgetown, to Miss MARY D., third daughter of John N. Moulder, Esq. [CG, Thurs., 28 MAR 1833, p. 2]

DIED, in Portsmouth, (Va.) on Thursday last [i.e. 21 MAR 1833], Dr. THOS. F. WIESENTHAL, late Surgeon in the U.S. Navy, aged 43 years. [CG, Thurs., 28 MAR 1833, p. 2]

DIED, at Bristol, (Pa.) on Tuesday (19th inst.) [i.e. 19 MAR 1833], after a very protracted illness, MARY, daughter of the late Maj. Farlie, and wife of Thomas A. Cooper, Tragedian. [CG, Thurs., 28 MAR 1833, p. 2]

MARRIED, on Thursday evening last [i.e. 28 MAR 1833], by the Rev. Mr. Hanson, the Rev. GEORGE HILDT, of the Methodist Episcopal Church, to Miss HARRIET STUBBS, of Ohio. [CG, Sat., 30 MAR 1833, p. 3]

DIED, on Tuesday last [i.e. 26 MAR 1833], in this city, MICHAEL HOGAN, Esq., in the 68th year of his age. He came to this country about twenty-five years ago, with a splendid estate, the most of which was lost, not by folly, but by misfortune. But such were his amiable and estimable qualifies, that the reverse lost him not a friend, and few individuals have had the happiness of enjoying the friendship of so many worthy and intelligent men. [CG, Sat., 30 MAR 1833, p. 3]

DIED, on Wednesday week [i.e. 20? MAR 1833], at Fredericktown, Md., Mrs. CATHARINE C. M'PHERSON, wife of Dr. Wm. S. M'Pherson, in the 35th year of her age. This is the fifth time, within one year, that Death has visited this family—four children, and their mother. [CG, Sat., 30 MAR 1833, p. 3]

Georgetown, D.C., **Marriage and Death Notices, 1801-1838**

THE POTOMAC ADVISOR AND METROPOLITAN INTELLIGENCER
July 13, 1837 to December 31, 1837, and
January 1, 1838 to February 12, 1838

DIED. On Thursday night last [i.e. 27 JUL 1837], Mrs. VINSON, wife of Mr. Charles Vinson, late of Washington city, but now resident in Georgetown, leaving an afflicted husband and numerous children to lament her death. [PA, Mon. 31 JUL 1837, p. 3]

MARRIED. On Thursday the 27th ult. [i.e. 27 JUL 1837], by the Rev. Henshaw, JOHN BARCROFT, of the Post Office Department, Washington city, to SARAH W., daughter of the late Samuel Byrnes, of Baltimore. [PA, Fri. 4 AUG 1837, p. 3]

DIED. On Saturday morning the 29th ult. [i.e. 29 JUL 1837], at 5 o'clock, RACHEL ANN, infant daughter of Joseph O'D. and Elizabeth Ann Bowen, aged five months, after an illness of a few days. [PA, Fri. 4 AUG 1837, p. 3]

MARRIED. On Thursday evening the 3rd inst. [i.e. 3 AUG 1837], by the Rev. Henry Slicer, the Rev. LEWIS JANNEY, of the Ebe [sic] Conference, to Miss MARTHA A., eldest daughter of Thomas Brown, Esq., of this place. [PA, Mon. 7 AUG 1837, p. 3]

DIED. At Edinburg, on May 8th [i.e. 8 MAY 1837], R.H. BARCLAY, of the Royal Navy, who commanded the British fleet in the engagement with Com. Perry, on Lake Erie. [PA, Wed. 16 AUG 1837, p. 3]

DIED. During the past week, at Berkeley Springs, Va., GWINN HARRIS, Esq., late one of the Executive Counsel of Maryland and long a Purser in the United States Navy. To the older inhabitants of our town, Mr. H. was well known, and his sterling merits as a gentleman and friend were fully appreciated by them. His death will be by all such much regretted. [PA, Mon. 21 AUG 1837, p. 3]

DIED. On Monday morning [i.e. 21 AUG 1837], in this place, Mr. DAVID BANGS. He had his residence here for many years and was regarded as a worthy, industrious, and good citizen, and esteemed by many. He has left a wife and several children to lament his loss ... [Note: Paper of 30 AUG 1837, page 3, gives notice by Elizabeth Banks, widow, that she continues on the business of her deceased husband, on Bridge street, a few doors below the Union Tavern.] [PA, Wed. 23 AUG 1837, p. 3]

DIED. On Saturday the 19th inst. [i.e. 19 AUG 1837], after a lingering illness, Capt. BENEDICT J. JENKINS, in the 49th year of his age, formerly captain in the employment of some of the most respectable merchants of the city, and of late years master of the steamboat *Fredericsburgh*, in Baltimore. [PA, Wed. 23 AUG 1837, p. 3]

DIED. At his residence on Pennsylvania Avenue, Washington city, on Thursday morning, the 7th inst. [i.e. 7 SEP 1837], after a short illness, Dr. THOMAS SCOTT, in the 51st year of his age. [PA, Mon. 11 SEP 1837, p. 3]

Georgetown, D.C., **Marriage and Death Notices, 1801-1838**

DIED. In this town, on Saturday, the 9th inst. [i.e. 9 SEP 1837], Mr. MESHACK CAMPBELL, late a cooper, aged about 59 years. Apparently in health on Friday night, next morning numbered with the cold clouds of the valley! How necessary is it then, that all should be prepared to meet that awful, yet certain visitation of God. [PA, Mon. 18 SEP 1837, p. 3]

DIED. At his residence on Pennsylvania Avenue, on 17th inst. [i.e. 17 SEP 1837], of a pulmonary affection, Dr. BERNARD J. MILLER, which he bore with patience and submission to Him who, in His wisdom, thought fit thus early to call him from this world. The deceased was estimable and manly; rich in the benevolence of his nature, and strictly tenorious of all those charities which elevate, endear, and give excellence to character. For several years, he held the appointment of surgeon Major in the Columbian Navy, the duties of which he discharged with skill and fidelity. On his return to the United States, he resumed the practice of Medicine, and gave high promise of usefulness in his career ... The friends of the family are respectfully invited to attend his funeral this afternoon at 4 o'clock. [PA, Wed. 20 SEP 1837, p. 3]

MARRIED. On Sunday evening, the 17th inst. [i.e. 17 SEP 1837, by the Rev. Mr. Lucas, Mr. ALEXANDER RATCLIFF, to Miss MARY DELOZIER, both of this place. [PA, Fri. 22 SEP 1837, p. 3]

MARRIED. On Thursday evening, the 21st inst. [i.e. 21 SEP 1837], by the Rev. Mr. Slicer, Mr. GEORGE NALLEY, to Miss ANN ELIZABETH WORRELL, both of Rockville, Md. [PA, Fri. 22 SEP 1837, p. 3]

DIED. In Washington, on Wednesday morning [i.e. 20 SEP 1837], in the sixty second year of his age, JOHN LAUB, for many years a respected and valued citizen of this town. He came here we believe with the Government, and for many years past has been known as the faithful and efficient chief clerk, in the office of the First Comptroller of the Treasury. He was believed to be more familiar with our revenue system than any other many connected with the Treasury Department. His loss to his particular department will be long felt. [PA, Fri. 22 SEP 1837, p. 3]

DIED. In New Orleans, on the 11th inst. [i.e. 11 SEP 1837], of Yellow Fever, Mr. WM. H. THOMPSON, in the 27th year of his age, formerly merchant of this place. Mr. Thompson was a native of Alexandria, where he was generally known and highly respected. [PA, Fri. 22 SEP 1837, p. 3]

DIED. Near New Orleans on the 12th inst. [i.e. 12 SEP 1837], Mr. JOHN POPHAM, formerly merchant of this place. Mr. P. has been cut off in the prime of life, and in the midst of usefulness, and his death will be long lamented by his relatives and friends. [PA, Fri. 22 SEP 1837, p. 3]

DIED. In Philadelphia, on Sunday night last [i.e. 10 SEP 1837], Mr. JOHN B. GRUBB, a merchant of that city, and a native of Alexandria—where he has many friends and connexions who mourn his loss. [PA, Fri. 22 SEP 1837, p. 3]

Georgetown, D.C., **Marriage and Death Notices, 1801-1838**

DIED. In Newton, Mass., on the 10th [i.e. 10 SEP 1837], Mrs. ELIZA S. LADD, consort of Mr. John H. Ladd, formerly of this place. [PA, Fri. 22 SEP 1837, p. 3]

DIED. In New Orleans, on Sunday morning last [10 SEP 1837], Mr. JAMES TATE, late of Washington City, aged about 23. The deceased was a young man in the prime of life, possessed of all the amiable qualities which endear man to his fellows. He had been in this city but a few weeks, when he was attacked with the yellow fever, which could not be made to yield to the best of medical treatment. His friends did everything which lay in their power, and while they lamented his untimely exit, they followed his remains in the cemetery, where he was decently interred ... [PA, Fri. 22 SEP 1837, p. 3]

MARRIED. Mr. WM. S. SCOTT, of the Thorpe, near Horncastle, England, but late of Fairfax Co., Va., to ALICE, daughter of the late John Bonner, Esq., of Langton, near Horncastle, a celebrated farmer and grazier. [PA, Fri. 29 SEP 1837, p. 3]

DIED. At his residence, near Crawfordsville, Ind., on the 9th inst. [i.e. 9 SEP 1837], after a very short illness, GUSTAVUS HALL SCOTT, Esq., late of Fairfax Co., Va., in the 52d year of his age. [PA, Fri. 29 SEP 1837, p. 3]

DIED. With unfeigned sorrow we announce the death of Mrs. SUSAN B. COXE, wife of Richard S. Coxe, Esq., of Washington. She died on Sunday night last [i.e. 17 SEP 1837], after an illness of six or seven days ... [PA, Fri. 29 SEP 1837, p. 3]

MARRIED. On Thursday the 28th inst. [i.e. 28 SEP 1837], by the Rev. Dr. Johns, Dr. ALEXANDER H. TYSON, of Baltimore Co., to Mrs. REBECCA A. HOWARD, of this city. [PA, Wed. 4 OCT 1837, p. 3]

MARRIED. In Washington on Tuesday evening last [i.e. 3 OCT 1837], by the Rev. Henry Slicer, Mr. GEORGE M. DANIEL, to Miss JANE GROVES. [PA, Mon. 9 OCT 1837, p. 3]

MARRIED. In Georgetown, on the Tuesday evening last [i.e. 3 OCT 1837], by the Rev. Henry Slicer, Mr. JOHN REINTZEL, to Miss ELIZA CHICK. [PA, Mon. 9 OCT 1837, p. 3]

MARRIED. In Washington City, on Tuesday evening, the 10th inst. [i.e. 10 OCT 1837], by the Rev. Mr. Reese, Mr. GEORGE S. GIDEON, to Miss CATHARINE C. DRAKE, daughter of Mr. Willard Drake, all of this city. [PA, Fri. 13 OCT 1837, p. 3]

DIED. In Georgetown, on the evening of the 10th inst. [i.e. 10 OCT 1837], having just completed her 12th year, CATHARINE W. PEARSON, the second daughter of the late Joseph Pearson, Esq. ... [PA, Fri. 13 OCT 1837, p. 3]

DIED. Suddenly at *Northview*, heights of Georgetown, on the night of the 6th inst. [i.e. 6 OCT 1837], JOHN PETERS, a principal clerk in the Second Auditor's office, aged 57 years. [PA, Fri. 13 OCT 1837, p. 3]

DIED. In New Orleans on the 5th inst. [i.e. 5 OCT 1837], at half past five o'clock of the prevailing epidemic, URIAH FORREST HYDE, aged 32 years. The deceased, a native,

Georgetown, D.C., **Marriage and Death Notices, 1801-1838**

and resident till within a few years passed, of this place—was well known and highly esteemed by numbers of our citizens, and numerous friends, we are sure, will lament that the hand of death has thus early been laid upon him. [PA, Mon. 16 OCT 1837, p. 3]

DIED. On board ship *Lotus*, on the evening of the 4th October [i.e. 4 OCT 1837], Mr. WM. ROBINSON, a native of Newburyport, Mass., and for some time a resident of Georgetown, D.C., but lately of N.Y. ... (*New Orleans True American*) [PA, Mon. 16 OCT 1837, p. 3]

MARRIED. On Thursday, the 12th inst. [i.e. 12 OCT 1837], by the Rev. Mr. Owens, HENRY BRADLEY, to MARY, youngest daughter of the late William Prout, all of Washington. [PA, Wed. 18 OCT 1837, p. 3]

MARRIED. At *Bel-Air*, Prince George's Co., Md., on Tuesday morning, the 10th inst. [i.e. 10 OCT 1837], by the Rev. Dr. Marbury, Rev. UPTON BEALL, to LOUISA OGLE, daughter of Benjamin Ogle, Esq. [PA, Wed. 18 OCT 1837, p. 3]

MARRIED. On Tuesday evening, the 17th inst. [i.e. 17 OCT 1837], by the Rev. Mr. Levy, Mr. FRANCIS J. KELLENBERGER, to Miss MARY ELLEN HILLEARY, both of this town. [PA, Fri. 20 OCT 1837, p. 3]

DIED. At New Orleans, on the 24th of September [i.e. 24 SEP 1837], JOHN DAVIDGE LINDENBERGER, son of the late Frederick Lindenberger, of Baltimore, in the 21st year of his age. [PA, Fri. 20 OCT 1837, p. 3]

DIED. In New Orleans, on the 17th [i.e. 17 SEP 1837], WM. E. WATKINS, of Va., deeply deplored by a numerous circle of friends. [PA, Fri. 20 OCT 1837, p. 3]

DIED. In New Orleans, on the 16th [i.e. 16 SEP 1837], JOHN A. KIRK, formerly of Alexandria, D.C. [PA, Fri. 20 OCT 1837, p. 3]

DIED. Suddenly at his residence in Baltimore, on the 16th inst. [i.e. 16 OCT 1837], Lieut. JOHN CASSIN, of the United States Navy; eldest son of Com. Cassin, and formerly an inhabitant of this place ... [PA, Mon. 23 OCT 1837, p. 3]

MARRIED. At the Navy Yard, by the Rev. Mr. Brewer, BENJAMIN H. BELL, to Miss R. BRYANANT, grand-daughter of Mr. Benjamin Bryanant. [PA, Wed. 25 OCT 1837, p. 3]

DIED. On the 15th inst. [i.e. 15 OCT 1837], in Washington city, D.C., Mrs. MARY WESTERFIELD, wife of David Westerfield, in the 47th year of her age. In the death of this amiable lady, the poor, the destitute, and the afflicted have lost an amiable and sincere advocate and friend. She was an affectionate wife, a tender and doting mother, and a faithful friend. May God rest her soul—praise cannot soothe the dull cold ear of death. [PA, Wed. 25 OCT 1837, p. 3]

MARRIED. In this city on Thursday evening, 26th inst. [i.e. 26 OCT 1837], by the Rev. Mr. Hawley, CHARLES B. FISK, Esq., Engineer in Chief of the Chesapeake and Ohio Canal,

Georgetown, D.C., **Marriage and Death Notices, 1801-1838**

to Miss MARY ELIZABETH, daughter of Maj. George Bender, late of the U.S. Army. [PA, Wed. 1 NOV 1837, p. 3]

MARRIED. In this city, at the residence of C. Hill, Esq., on Thursday 26th inst. [i.e. 26 OCT 1837], by the Rev. J.P. Donellan, Mr. JOHN PLANT, to Miss MARTHA STREBECK, all of this city. [PA, Wed. 1 NOV 1837, p. 3]

DIED. In this town, on last Sabbath night [i.e. 29 OCT 1837], Mrs. JANE McVEAN, wife of the Rev. James McVean of this place ... [also see 3 NOV 1837, page 3, which describes her death due to a pulmonary complaint she had for two or three years] [PA, Wed. 1 NOV 1837, p. 3]

MARRIED. In this town, at the residence of Raphael Semmes, on the 9th inst. [i.e. 9 NOV 1837], at 8 o'clock A.M., by the Rev. J.F.M. Lucas, THOMAS SEMMES, of Washington, Ga., to CATHARINE T.H., daughter of the late Richard H. Winter, of Charles Co., Md. [PA, Mon. 13 NOV 1837, p. 3]

MARRIED. On Tuesday evening, the 7th inst. [i.e. 7 NOV 1837], by the Rev. John Owen, ISAAC CANFIELD SMITH, of N.Y., to ROSALIE MARTHA, daughter of N.B. Van Zandt, Esq., of Washington city. [PA, Mon. 13 NOV 1837, p. 3]

MARRIED. On Tuesday evening last [i.e. 7 NOV 1837], by the Rev. Mr. McLean, ROBERT HARPER WILLIAMSON, of Wood Co., Va., to MATILDA, daughter of the late Charles Glover, Esq., of Washington city. [PA, Mon. 13 NOV 1837, p. 3]

MARRIED. On Tuesday, the 17th ult. [i.e. 17 OCT 1837], by the Rev. George Lemmon, THOMAS O. CARTER, Esq., of Prince William Co., Va., to Miss JUDITH T. CARTER, of Fauquier. [PA, Mon. 13 NOV 1837, p. 3]

MARRIED. By Rev. George Lemmon, on Tuesday the 31st ult. [i.e. 31 OCT 1837], JOHN H. GOODWIN, Esq., of Fredericksburg, to Miss MARY A. HART, of Fauquier. [PA, Mon. 13 NOV 1837, p. 3]

MARRIED. On the 1st inst. [i.e. 1 NOV 1837], near Princess Anne, Md., by the Rev. Mr. Crosdell, JOHN WOOLFORD, Esq., to Miss ELLEN GILLISS POLK, daughter of the late Samuel Polk, Esq., all of Somerset Co., Md. [PA, Mon. 13 NOV 1837, p. 3]

MARRIED. At Georgetown, on the 24th of October [i.e. 24 OCT 1837], by the Rev. Mr. Rodney, JOHN H. BARNES, to ADELAIDE CHARDON, daughter of the late Anthony Chardon, Esq. By this connexion, he becomes the brother-in-law of his own son, and uncle and grandfather to his own son's children; and she becomes aunt and grandmother to her sister's children, and mother-in-law to her sister. [PA, Mon. 13 NOV 1837, p. 3]

DEATHS. At his residence, on Wednesday, 8th inst. [i.e. 8 NOV 1837], in the 64th year of his age, SAMUEL WIMSATT, a native of Md., and for nearly twenty years a resident of Washington city. In his death his numerous and afflicted family have met with an irreparable loss—their main and almost only support; and the world has also lost at least an *honest man*. [PA, Mon. 13 NOV 1837, p. 3]

DIED. On Sunday, the 5th inst. [i.e. 5 NOV 1837], Mrs. ELIZABETH VEITCH, widow of the late Richard Veitch, for many years a respectable inhabitant of Alexandria. [PA, Mon. 13 NOV 1837, p. 3]

MARRIED. On Thursday evening, the 9th inst. [i.e. 9 NOV 1837], by the Rev. Mr. Lucas, Mr. SAMUEL RAINEY, to Miss LUCY BEALL OFFUTT, both of this place. [PA, Wed. 15 NOV 1837, p. 3]

DIED. Lately, at Middletown, Conn., at an advanced age, EBENEZER JACKSON, Esq. He was the survivor of five children, all sons, of the late Gen. Michael Jackson, who commanded the regiment of the Mass. line, afterwards known as "Brooks Regiment," Gen. Jackson commenced his career at Lexington and Bunker Hill, and continued in active service, until disabled by a severe wound. He brought into the war all his sons, thus affording a remarkable example of the devotion to liberty which influenced the patriots of that day. [PA, Fri. 17 NOV 1837, p. 3]

Death of a Revolutionary Hero—Capt. RICHARD BOHUN BAKER, the last survivors of the band of the heroes engaged during the Revolutionary war, in the defense of Fort Moultrie, died on Monday night week [i.e. 13 NOV 1837], at that post, the scene of his gallant conduct, aged 80 years and two months. [PA, Mon. 13 NOV 1837, p. 3]

DIED. At Flat Rock, Buncombe Co., N.C., on the 8th ult. [i.e. 8 OCT 1837], ISAAC CORSE, Esq., in the 78th year of his age. Mr. Course was a native of Philadelphia, but for 58 years a resident of South Carolina, and a greater part of that time an active, intelligent, and respectable merchant of Charleston, S.C. [PA, Mon. 13 NOV 1837, p. 3]

DIED. At his residence, in Anne Arundel Co., Md., on Tuesday, the 7th inst. [i.e. 7 NOV 1837], in the 44th year of his age, Mr. SAMUEL DOVE, for thirty years a resident of this city. [PA, Mon. 13 NOV 1837, p. 3]

MARRIED. On Thursday evening the 16th inst. [i.e. 16 NOV 1837], by the Rev. Mr. Hamilton, Mr. JAMES LUSBY, to Mrs. ADELINE WILLIAMS, all of this city. [PA, Mon. 20 NOV 1837, p. 3]

MARRIED. On Thursday afternoon, the 16th inst. [i.e. 16 NOV 1837], at Trinity Church, by the Rev. John Owen, Rector thereof, MARSHALL BROWN, of this city, to LOUISA STUART STITH, second daughter of the late Griffin Stith, of Prince William Co., Va. [PA, Mon. 13 NOV 1837, p. 3]

DIED. On the morning of the 17th inst. [i.e. 17 NOV 1837], Mrs. ELLEN PICKETT, wife of Jas. C. Pickett, Esq., 4th Auditor, in the 37th year of her age, leaving an infant three weeks old. [PA, Mon. 13 NOV 1837, p. 3]

Georgetown, D.C., **Marriage and Death Notices, 1801-1838**

DIED. In Boston, on Saturday evening [i.e. 18 NOV 1837], of apoplexy, THOMAS GREEN FESSENDEN, Esq. He was a man of most amiable character, of excellent principles, and of extensive information. His literary attainments were highly respectable, and he is author of several useful publications, well known to the Public, and had been for many years the editor of that valuable weekly publication, *The New England Farmer.* [PA, Mon. 13 NOV 1837, p. 3]

MARRIED. On Tuesday evening, 14th inst. [i.e. 14 NOV 1837], at *Mount Pleasant,* Prince George's Co., Md., by the Rev. Mr. Woodley, Dr. RICHARD CLAGETT, to Miss GRACE, daughter of the late Col. Henry Warring, all of that county. [PA, Fri. 24 NOV 1837, p. 3]

MARRIED. On the same evening [i.e. 14 NOV 1837], by the Rev. Mr. Marbury, Rev. WILLIAM HODGES, of Va., to Miss CORNELIA L., third daughter of the late John Hodges of this village. *Upper Marlboro Gazette.* [PA, Fri. 24 NOV 1837, p. 3]

The intelligence, which reached us on Friday evening last, of the death of the Hon. JOSEPH KENT—the high minded and patriotic Senator of the United States, from the state of Maryland brought with it, much sorrow ... [PA, Mon. 27 NOV 1837, p. 3]

DIED. In Georgetown, on the 19th inst. [i.e. 19 NOV 1837], at the residence of Mr. John Clements, Mrs. ELENOR SHIPLEY, consort of Rezin Shipley, in the sixty-sixth year of her age, and for the last thirty five years a resident of this place. [PA, Mon. 27 NOV 1837, p. 3]

DIED. On the night of the 30th ult. [i.e. 30 NOV 1837], MARY BANKSON WILSON, third daughter of James C. and Anne E.B. Wilson, aged 10 years and 13 days ... [PA, Mon. 4 DEC 1837, p. 3]

MARRIED. On Thursday evening last [i.e. 30 NOV 1837], by the Rev. Mr. Levy, Mr. FRANCIS DUER, to Miss CATHARINE KALDENBACH, both of this place. [PA, Wed. 6 DEC 1837, p. 3]

DIED. On Friday last [i.e. 1 DEC 1837], at his late residence, on Beall street, Mr. JOHN HOLTZMAN. The deceased, having long resided here, was well known and highly esteemed by the citizens at large; and his death is lamented by a large circle of relatives and friends. He for several years held the responsible office of collector of this Corporation, and faithfully (and at the same time with lenity toward the debtors to the Corporation) discharged its duties. He was several times elected, by his fellow citizens, to serve them in the councils of the town, and satisfactorily discharged its duties. At the time of his death he held the commission from the Executive, of Justice of the Peace for the county of Washington, D.C. In a word, in all the relations of life he sustained a character well worthy of imitation from others. [PA, Fri. 8 DEC 1837, p. 3]

MARRIED. On Thursday evening last, 30th ult. [i.e. 30 NOV 1837], by the Rev. B.M. Miller, Mr. BENJAMIN ATWELL, of Anne Arundel Co., to SARAH ANN, daughter of Mr. John Dodson, of Prince George's county. [PA, Mon. 11 DEC 1837, p. 3]

Georgetown, D.C., **Marriage and Death Notices, 1801-1838**

DIED. In Munceytown, Ind., on the 26th November last [i.e. 26 NOV 1837], in the 22d year of his age, WILLIAM RENNER, Esq., formerly of this District. Mr. Renner emigrated to the West about three years ago, and in that short space of time had so far acquired the confidence of his fellow citizens as to be elected to the Legislature of his adopted State. He was a young gentleman of talents and acquirements, and was last rising to eminence in his profession when he was cut off by the disease incident to a change of climate. [PA, Mon. 11 DEC 1837, p. 3]

MARRIED. On Thursday, the 7th inst. [i.e. 7 DEC 1837], in Aldie, Va., by the Rev. Mr. Adie, Mr. WILLIAM GADSBY, of Washington, to Miss JANE K., daughter of the late James Smith, Esq., of Richmond. [PA, Fri. 15 DEC 1837, p. 3]

MARRIED. On Thursday evening, the 7th inst. [i.e. 7 DEC 1837], by the Rev. Dr. Hawley, Lieut. MURRY MASON, of the United States Navy, to CLARA C., daughter of the Hon. John Forsyth. [PA, Fri. 15 DEC 1837, p. 3]

DIED. At Piqua, Ohio, on the night of the 29th ult. [i.e. 29 NOV 1837], of billious colic, Mr. GIDEON B. BEALL, aged about 33 years, formerly a resident of Washington, and a clerk in the office of the Treasurer of the U. States. [PA, Fri. 15 DEC 1837, p. 3]

MARRIED. On Thursday, 14th inst. [i.e. 14 DEC 1837], by the Rev. Mr. Levy, Mr. BENJAMIN REISS, to Miss MARIA E. SIMPSON, daughter of John Simpson, all of this place. [PA, Wed. 20 DEC 1837, p. 3]

DIED. On Monday evening last [i.e. 18 DEC 1837], Mrs. ANN B. REDIN, wife of Wm. Redin, Esq., of this place. Her funeral will take place tomorrow (Thursday) morning, at eleven o'clock, from her late residence on Gay street. The friends of Mr. Redin, and the public, are invited to attend. [PA, Wed. 20 DEC 1837, p. 3]

MARRIED. In Washington city, on Tuesday evening the 19th inst. [i.e. 19 DEC 1837], by the Rev. Mr. Hawley, JOSEPH REYNOLDS, Esq., of this place, to MARY LEVINA, eldest daughter of Judge Belt of that city. [PA, Fri. 22 DEC 1837, p. 3]

MARRIED. On Saturday evening the 16th inst. [i.e. 16 DEC 1837], in this city, by the Rev. Mr. Hawley, Mr. CHRISTOPHER HAGER, to Miss FREDERICA CLOAK, all of this city. [PA, Wed. 20 DEC 1837, p. 3]

MARRIED. At Alexandria, D.C., on Thursday, 14th inst. [i.e. 14 DEC 1837], at noon, by the Rev. Mr. Dana, RANDOLPH COYLE, of the City of Washington, to JANE J. MOORE, daughter to Alexander Moore, Esq., of Alexandria. [PA, Wed. 20 DEC 1837, p. 3]

MARRIED. On Monday evening last, 11th inst. [i.e. 11 DEC 1837], by the Rev. Mr. Hawley, The Rev. E.Y. HIGBEE, of N.Y., to Miss FANNY LEAR, eldest daughter of the late Com. Jno. D. Lenly, of the U.S. Navy. [PA, Wed. 20 DEC 1837, p. 3]

Georgetown, D.C., **Marriage and Death Notices, 1801-1838**

MARRIED. In Baltimore, On Tuesday evening, 12th inst. [i.e. 12 DEC 1837], by the Rev. John M. Duncan, THORNTON A. JENKINS, of the U.S. Navy, to ANNA, daughter of Jno. Power, Esq. [PA, Wed. 20 DEC 1837, p. 3]

DIED. In Richmond, on the 10th inst. [i.e. 10 DEC 1837], Mrs. MARGARET ANN WHITE, wife of Thomas W. White, Esq., editor of the *Southern Literary Messenger*, aged 43 years. [PA, Wed. 20 DEC 1837, p. 3]

DIED. At his residence, *Catoctin Valley*, Frederick Co., on the 2nd inst. [i.e. 2 DEC 1837], ROBERT PATTENGALL, Esq., a native of the Parish of Rannois, County of Norfolk, England, in the 72d year of his age. [PA, Wed. 20 DEC 1837, p. 3]

DIED. In N.Y., on Friday the 19th inst. [i.e. 19 DEC 1837], after a severe illness of four weeks, of Scarlet Fever, PHILIP H. WADSWORTH, son of John and Caroline Wadsworth, and grandson of Francis Massi of Washington City, aged 3 years and 6 months ... [PA, Mon. 25 DEC 1837, p. 3]

DIED. At the Parsonage of Rock Creek Church, D.C., on Thursday the 4th inst. [i.e. 4 DEC 1837], after a lingering and painful illness of two years, GEORGE BATES, youngest son of Wm. Jones, late of Cincinnati, Ohio. [PA, Fri. 5 JAN 1838, p. 3]

DIED. At her residence in Georgetown, on the 4th inst. [i.e. 4 JAN 1838], in the 28th year of her age, Mrs. ELIZA ANN ESSEX, leaving a husband and five small children to deplore her loss, and also deeply regretted by an extensive circle of relatives and friends. [PA, Wed. 10 JAN 1838, p. 3]

DIED. At his residence in Georgetown, at 5 o'clock, on Friday morning the 5th inst. [i.e. 5 JAN 1838], after a protracted illness of several months, THOMAS G. WATERS, an old and highly respected citizen, aged 58 years. [PA, Fri. 12 JAN 1838, p. 3]

Obituary. Departed this life on Friday, the 5th inst. [i.e. 5 JAN 1838], at his residence in Montgomery Co., the Rev. THOS. READ, (father of Mr. Robert Read of this town) in the 90th year of his age. The deceased was educated and received ordination as Deacon and Priest, in England, at an early age. For nearly forty years, he held the Rectorship of Prince George's Parish in this Co., which he resigned on the 7th February, 1814; having been only thirty months absent from it in all that time. At the time of his death and for some time previous, he was the oldest Minister of any grade in the Protestant Episcopal Church, in the U. States ... *Md. Journal.* [PA, Mon. 15 JAN 1838, p. 3]

DIED. In Georgetown, D.C., on Sunday morning, 14th of January 1838, after a painful illness, SOPHIA M., daughter of Anthony and Middleton Smith, in the 17th year of her age. [PA, Wed. 17 JAN 1838, p. 3]

Another Soldier of the Revolution Gone! Died on the 8th inst. [i.e. 8 JAN 1838], Col. WILLIAM LAMAR, of Allegany Co., in the 83d year of his age. Col. Lamar was a native of Frederick Co., Md., and has been a resident amongst us, for more than thirty years past. He entered the Revolutionary army shortly after the declaration of

Georgetown, D.C., **Marriage and Death Notices, 1801-1838**

independence, in the 21st year of his age. He was appointed an ensign at the age of 21, and not long afterwards, he was promoted to the rank of lieutenant—then made quartermaster—and finally promoted to the rank of captain of the 7th Md. regiment ... Col. Lamar received several wounds in the battles of the Revolution. He was shot in the thigh at Guilford, and in the breast at Eutaw ... [PA, Fri. 19 JAN 1838, p. 3]

DIED. In Washington City, on the 13th inst. [i.e. 13 JAN 1838], after a lingering illness, THOMAS ARBUCKLE, Esq., for many years a faithful clerk in the Post Office Department. Respected in life for his many virtues, and supported in death by the consolations of that religion which governed his progress through life, he has left many friends and acquaintances, who, on their own account, will long regret the loss they have sustained by his decease. [PA, Fri. 19 JAN 1838, p. 3]

DIED. On Wednesday evening last [i.e. 17 JAN 1838], MARIA DALLAS, daughter of Col. Croghan, aged six years and five months. [PA, Mon. 22 JAN 1838, p. 3]

DIED. On Monday last [i.e. 22 JAN 1838], at the residence of Capt. Cooper, in this place, after a long and most distressing illness, Mrs. VIRGINIA MASON, wife of George Mason, Esq., of *Hollin Hall*, Va., and daughter of Gen. John Mason. Her funeral takes place from the residence of Capt. Cooper, this day at half past 3 o'clock, P.M. [PA, Wed. 24 JAN 1838, p. 3]

DIED.— Some time in the latter part of October last [1837], at Natchez, Miss., Mr. SAMUEL THOMAS TURNER, in the 22nd year of his age. The deceased was a native of this town, and resided here until about twelve months ago ... After some weeks travel and examination of various places, he finally settled himself in Natchez, where, unhappily, the fever of the Southern country, put an end to his earthly career ... His sisters and brothers, in him, have lost a most affectionate and kind brother, and long will lament his early and untimely fate. [PA, Wed. 24 JAN 1838, p. 3]

MARRIED. In Washington, on Tuesday [i.e. 23 JAN 1838], by the Rev. Mr. Owen, Rev. JOSEPH PACKARD, Professor in the Theological Seminary, Va., to Miss ROSINA, daughter of Gen. Walter Jones. [PA, Fri. 26 JAN 1838, p. 3]

DEATHS. On Saturday last [i.e. 20 JAN 1838] about noon, at *Rose Hill*, the residence of his father, near Rockville, the Rev. T.J. ADDISON MINES, after a protracted illness. In the death of this gentleman the Presbyterian Church has lost one of her ministers ... His remains were attended by a very large concourse to the Presbyterian Church in Rockville, where a sermon was preached from Jeremiah 22.10 ... [PA, Fri. 26 JAN 1838, p. 3]

DIED.— At the *Retreat*, his place of residence in Charles Co., Md., on the 6th of January [1838], WILLIAM P. COMPTON, in the 29th year of his age, leaving an only son, and a large number of friends and warmly attached connexions to regret his loss. [PA, Fri. 26 JAN 1838, p. 3]

Georgetown, D.C., **Marriage and Death Notices, 1801-1838**

DIED.—On the 17th inst. [i.e. 17 JAN 1838], at *Bromont*, in Charles Co., Md., Miss MARGARET CLERKLEE, daughter of the late James Clerklee, Esq. [PA, Fri. 26 JAN 1838, p. 3]

MARRIED. On the 25th inst. [i.e. 25 JAN 1838], by the Rev. Mr. Levy, Mr. SAMUEL HEIN, to Miss HENRIETTA SARAH, third daughter of Mr. John Simpson, of this town. [PA, Wed. 31 JAN 1838, p. 3]

DIED. Departed this life on the 24th inst. [i.e. 24 JAN 1838], after an illness of 24 days, which he bore with christian fortitude, Mr. GEORGE A. KELLENBURGER, in the 41st year of his age. [PA, Wed. 31 JAN 1838, p. 3]

DIED. In Washington City, on Tuesday morning [i.e. 30 JAN 1838], after a short illness, in the 30th year of her age, Mrs. MARY JOSEPHINE WRIGHT, wife of Edward Wright, and only daughter Mr. William V. Jenkins, of Baltimore. [PA, Fri. 2 FEB 1838, p. 3]

DIED.—In Baltimore, on the 28th ult. [i.e. 28 JAN 1838], Mrs. HANNAH JENNINGS, wife of the Rev. Dr. Samuel K. Jennings, of that city ... [PA, Fri. 2 FEB 1838, p. 3]

DIED. At his residence in Delaware Co., Pa., on the 12th of January last [i.e. 12 JAN 1838], JOSHUA HUMPHREYS. The subject of this brief sketch was born in that part of Chester Co., now Delaware, in June 1851; and at the time of his decease was in his 87th year. In the early part of his life, his parents moved to Philadelphia, when he was apprentices to James Penrose, a ship builder of the highest reputation ... In the Revolutionary War he built the frigate *Randolph*, afterwards commanded by Capt. N– ... a member of the Society of Friends ... [PA, Wed. 7 FEB 1838, p. 3]

DEATHS. At his residence in the village of Westfield, N.Y., on the 8th of January [i.e. 8 JAN 1838], of a pulmonary complaint, Capt. CHARLES C. TUPPER, of the United States Marines, aged 43 years. [PA, Fri. 9 FEB 1838, p. 3]

DIED.— On the 2d inst. [i.e. 2 FEB 1838], at *Chatham*, near Fredericksburg, Va., JOHN COALTER, Esq., formerly a Judge of the Court of Appeals of Virginia, and long one of the most distinguished men in that Commonwealth. [PA, Fri. 9 FEB 1838, p. 3]

DIED, at *Summer Hill*, Anne Arundel Co., Md., on the 23d of January [i.e. 23 JAN 1838], after a short but distressing illness of six days, Mrs. ELIZABETH ORME, relict of the late Moses Orme, Esq., in the 64th year of her age ... *National Intelligencer*. [PA, Fri. 9 FEB 1838, p. 3]

Georgetown, D.C., **Marriage and Death Notices, 1801-1838**

Index

A

Abbett
  Thomas B., 176
Abbot
  George D., 256
Abbott
  Henry R., 152
  Jane, 251
  John, 251
  Mary Ann, 152
Abercrombie
  Rev., 63, 108, 199
Aberdeen, Scot., 48
Abingdon, Va., 225
Accomack Co., Va., 1, 8
accountants, 12, 33
Adams
  Charles Francis, 116
  Charlotte, 217
  Elizabeth, 92
  Ex-President, 116, 219
  George A., 86
  Hannah, 212
  Hetty R., 152
  John, 27, 77
  John Alexander, Rev., 156
  John, Jr., 152
  Joseph Thornton, 162
  Leonard C., 250
  Matilda, 152
  Rev., 78
  Samuel W., 175
  Thomas Boyleston, 219
  William Godfrey, 9
  William, Dr., 137
Addison
  Anthony, 136
  Francis K., 142
  Henrietta Maria, 153
  Mary Grafton, 241
  Thomas B., 199
  Thomas G., 153, 241
  Walter Dulany, Rev., xi, 14-18, 20, 23, 27, 30, 34, 36, 38, 46, 50, 57, 64, 73, 78, 84, 86, 89, 94, 96, 98, 100, 124, 125, 142

Addison's Chapel, 2
Adie
  Rev., 264
Adylott
  Rev., 62
African Church, xii
agents, 108, 138, 197, 198, 250
Alabama, 57, 104, 182, 204
Albany, N.Y., 39, 40, 62, 68, 115, 119, 152, 155, 174, 217, 247
Albemarle Co., Va., 145, 165
Albion, Ill., 119
Alcock
  Elizabeth, 104
Alden
  John, 48
aldermen, 133, 151
Aldie, Va., 264
Alexander
  Gerard, 244
  James W., Rev., 155
  Lawrence G., 223
  Mark, Hon., 189
  Sidney, 244
  Sigismunda, 223
  William, Col., 223
Alexandria Co., D.C., 11, 65, 74
Alexandria, D.C., 4, 9, 12, 14, 16, 25-27, 31, 32, 39, 44, 45, 47, 48, 50, 51, 53, 55, 56, 65, 68-70, 72, 74, 76, 79, 85, 89, 101, 104, 105, 114, 116, 118-123, 125, 127, 131, 132, 134-146, 148-150, 152-156, 158, 160, 162-178, 180, 181, 183-206, 208-215, 217-235, 241, 242, 244-247, 250-254, 258, 260, 262, 264
Alexandria, Pa., 25
Algeziras, 194
Algiers, 77

Alldridge
  Christiana, 248
Allegany Co., Md., 195, 265
Alleghany Co., Va., 130
Allen
  Anne, 236
  David, 71
  Ethan, xi
  Ethan, Rev., 143
  Frances, 239
  Frederick, 71
  George, 54
  Lt., 68
  Rev., 75, 84, 156
  Thomas, 236
  Thomas G., Rev., 70, 90
  William, 239
  William, Rev., 193
Alsop
  Mrs., 52
Alston
  Gideon, 208
Ambrose
  Elizabeth, 184
Amelia Co., Va., 38, 173
American Antiquarian Society, 182
American Colonization Society, 116
Amesbury, Mass., 207
Amherst, Mass., 109, 198
Amherst, N.Y., 137
Amiss
  John L., Rev., xi, 150, 174, 176, 185, 187, 191, 198, 202, 205
  Rev., 177
Amos
  Isaac R., 141
  Sarah, 141
Analostan Island, D.C., 100
Anciaux
  Eliza, 7
  Nicholas, 7
Andalusia, Pa., 194
Anderson
  Euphemia, 156
  James, Dr., 12
  Jane, 230
  John, 103

Joseph, Sr., 156
William, 130
William, Col., 153, 230
Andrews
  Christopher, 21
  George, 36
  Wells, xi
Annapolis, Md., 2, 12, 64, 71, 89, 90, 111, 156, 164, 165, 174, 203, 207, 217, 231, 243
Anne Arundel Co., Md., 80, 82, 101, 121, 126, 127, 152, 170, 192, 199, 215, 231, 243, 262, 263, 267
apothecaries, 103
Appler
  D., 176
  Mary Ann, 176
Appleton
  Charles H., 202
  Maria Theresa, 254
  Nathan, Hon., 254
  William, 248
apprentices, 242
Arbuckle
  Thomas, 266
archbishops, 20, 43, 103, 124
Archipelago, 125
architects, 210
Arden
  Daniel D., 215
Arkansas, 103, 169, 223
Armagh, Ire., 177
Armstrong
  Eliza, 192
  Elizabeth, 29
  Francis W., Col., 182
  James, 229
  Jane, 229
  John, 29, 192
  Rev., 131
Arnold
  Susan, 80
  William, 68
Arny
  Elizabeth, 56
  Joseph, 56, 62, 185
Asbury
  Francis, Rev., 34
Ash
  Robert, Rev., 153

Ashby
  Samuel, 32
Ashley
  William H., Hon., 241
Ashton
  Henry, Col., 215
  Jane Cecilia, 215
Ashworth
  Mary A., 59
Associated Methodist Church, 174
Athens, Ga., 57
Athens, N Y., 34
Atkinson
  Eliza R., 193
attorneys, 7, 29, 35, 109, 117, 121, 127, 128, 130, 136, 139, 163, 167, 172, 203, 207, 208, 210, 238, 247, 248
Atwell
  Benjamin, 263
  William, 127
Auburn, N.Y., 191
Auchmuty
  Juaria M., 22
  Robert N., 22
auditors, 262
Augusta, Ga., 146, 151, 184
Austin
  Eliza, 40
  Matilda, Mrs., 127
authors, 27, 126, 187, 212, 242
Aux Cayes, Hayti, 108
Avard
  Mary F., 238
Averd
  Thomas L., 200
Avery
  Ann, 154
Avignon, Md., 108

B
Babcock
  Elisha, 47
Bacon
  Washington, 126
Badger
  Alfred M., 190
Baer
  Rev., 200

Bagget
  Alexander, 134
  Jane, 134
Baggett
  James, 132
Bailey
  Elizabeth, 24
  Theodorus, Lt., 155
  William L., 174
Baily
  Hannah Johnson, 239
  Jesse, 239
Bainbridge
  Com., 188
  Comm., 37
  John T., 37
  William, Jr., 188
Bainbridge, Ohio, 152
Baker
  Daniel, xi
  Frances P., 105
  George S., 57
  James, 79
  John R., 107
  Julia Ann, 237
  Nelson R., 156
  Rev., 69, 77, 101
  Richard Bohun, Capt., 262
  Sabre Jet, 46
  Samuel Hanson, 25, 105
  Thomas, 28
  Virginia H., 138
  Zachariah, 46
Balch
  Anna E.B., 31
  George B., 206
  George Beall, 204
  Harriot, 14
  Jane Whann, 73
  L.P.W., 206
  Rev., 4, 7, 8, 11, 13-17, 22, 24, 25, 35, 36, 40, 41, 43, 53, 55, 56, 64, 66, 69, 75, 76, 78, 90, 93, 94, 97, 101, 110, 142, 145, 158, 187, 190, 209, 220, 229, 239, 251
  Stephen Bloomer, Rev., xi, 2, 9, 17, 31, 41, 42, 46, 49, 50, 52,

270

73, 74, 80, 133, 170,
 191, 204
Thomas Bloomer, Rev,
 xi, 46, 59, 220
Balfour
 George, Dr., 162
Ball
 Edwin T, 203
 Margaret E., 250
 William Lee, Hon, 77
Ballard
 Charles, 185
 James H., Capt., 68
Balthis
 William, 220
Baltimore Co., Md., 124,
 177, 202, 222, 259
 Carroll's Manor, 28
Baltimore College, 232
Baltimore, Md., 14, 17, 19,
 20, 30, 31, 35-37,
 41-44, 46, 50, 51, 55,
 56, 58-60, 62, 70, 71,
 73, 78, 85, 89, 92,
 95, 100, 102-108,
 111, 113-115, 117,
 118, 120-127,
 130-132, 134, 135,
 137, 139-141, 143,
 145-147, 150,
 152-154, 156,
 159-162, 165, 169,
 171, 172, 175, 176,
 178, 180, 182, 183,
 186, 192, 193,
 196-200, 202-204,
 206-209, 212-214,
 217-226, 228-233,
 238-242, 245, 247,
 248, 250, 252, 253,
 257, 259, 260, 265,
 267
 hospital No 3, 232
Baltzer
 Elizabeth, 22
 George, 12
 Sarah, 187
Bangs
 Benjamin, 125
 David, 257
 Elizabeth, 257
 Mary, 125
Bank of Columbia, 38, 91
Bank of Orleans, 113

Bank of the Metropolis, 114,
 246
Bank of Virginia, 171
bankers, 30, 184
Banks
 Elizabeth, 257
Bankson
 Sarah M, 209
Banning
 Anthony, 93
Barbadoes, 6, 19
Barber
 John P, 68
Barbour
 Maria, 91
 Thomas, Col., 86
Barboursville, Va., 86
Barclay
 Francis, Rev., 14
 Mrs, 14
 R.H., 257
 R.H., Mr., 257
 Thomas, Col., 148
Barcroft
 John, 257
Bard
 David, Rev., 25
Barge
 Catharine, 68
Bargy
 Peter, Jr, Capt., 239
Barker
 Edward, 234
 Quinton, 132
Barkley
 Samuel, 44
Barnes
 Barnaby, 38
 Elizabeth, 154
 Evelina, 209
 George A., 46
 George B, 237
 James, Lt., 217
 John, 60, 91, 97
 John H, 261
 Margaret, 166
 Mr., 84
 Rev, 87
 Richard, Col., 8
 Thomas T, 214
Barnet
 Isaac Cox, 142
Barney
 John H., 115

Margaret, 115
Rebecca R., 228
William B., 228
Barnhisel
 Elizabeth, 202
Barnstable, Mass., 21
Barnum
 Mr., 160
Barrand
 Phillip, Dr, 173
Barren
 Jeannet, 42
Barron
 Charlotte A., 87
 Henry, 84
 James, Capt., 198
 James, Com., 113, 125
 Mary, 212
 Mary A.A., 113
 Mary Ann Robinson, 198
 Samuel, Com., 18
 Samuel, Lt, 240
Barrott
 Wm. D., 85
Barry
 Capt., 108
 Com., 7
 Edward, Capt., 137, 149,
  251
 Eleanor, 137
 Eliza, 230
 John, Com., 208
 Richard, 230
 Robert, Jr., 235
 Sarah, 208
 Susanna, 251
Bartgis
 Matthias, 85
Bartlett
 Peter Q., 171
Barton
 Benjamin Smith, 30
Basing Ridge, N J., 177
Bateman
 Elizabeth, 83
Bates
 Lydia, 166
Bath, Eng, 147
Bath, Me., 197, 203
Bath, Va, 81
Baton Rouge, La., 128, 137
Battle of Brandywine, 112
Battletown, Va., 105

271

Baum
   John Christian, 3
Baxley
   Henry W., Dr., 124
Baxter
   Benjamin, Capt., 207
   R., Rev., 101
   Roger, xi
Bayard
   Chevalier, 165
Bayles
   Robert, 153
   Susan Ann, 153
Bayley
   Ann, 1
   Thomas, Col., 1
Baylor
   Gwynn, 94
   Roberta, 94
Bayly
   Elizabeth, 221
   M., Gen., 57
   Mary Rebecca, 57
   Mountjoy, 221
   Rebecca, 20
   William, 20, 211
Bazlin
   Peter, 58
Beall
   Ann Rebecca, 132
   Basil W, 72
   Deborah, 43
   Elizabeth, 59
   George, 132
   Gideon, 85
   Gideon B, 264
   John R., 186
   Lloyd, Maj., 212
   Louisa, 212
   Maria, 86
   Mary, 42
   Mary B, 38
   Ninian, 12
   Robert B., 59
   Susana Vulinda, 36
   Thomas J., Maj, 246
   Upton, Col., 99
   Upton, Rev., 260
   Walter B., 253
   William Dent, Col, 122
Beanes
   Sarah, 62
   William, Dr, 62

Bear
   John, xi
Beard
   George, 102, 132
Beasley
   Rev., 196
Beatty
   Charles, 10
   Charles A., Dr., 204
   Edmond Jefferson, 204
   Henry T., 75
   James, Jr., 120
   Maj., 36
   Mrs., 36
   R H, Dr., 97
   Thomas, 25
Beaufort, S.C, 35, 251
Beck
   James, Sr., 54
   Margaret, 169
   Nicholas F., 155
   Rebecca, 64
   Rezin, 67
   Sarah, 45
   Trueman, 62
   Truman, 169
Becker
   Henry, Capt, 137
Beckwith
   A.D., 156
Becraft
   Julianna, 239
Bede
   Ann, 239
   George, 239
Bedford Co., Va., 131
Bedford, Pa, 114, 115, 144, 241
Bedford, Va., 31
Beeding
   Craven P., 35
Belfast, Me., 52
Belgium, 179
Bell
   Benjamin H., 260
   Henry, 28
   John, 123
   John L., 118
   Rev., 109
   Sally, 29
   Thomas, 29
   Walter, 29
Bellefontaine, Mo, 118
Bellona Arsenal, Va., 199

Bellows
   Ellen, 68
Belt
   Benjamin, 9
   Judge, 185, 264
   Mary Levina, 264
   Mrs., 185
   Otho, 117
   Parmelia, 9
   William S., Jr., 19
Belville, Tenn., 6
Bench
   Rev., 78
Bender
   George A., 161
   George, Maj., 261
   Mary Elizabeth, 261
Benedict, Md., 78, 206
Benham
   J.S., 155
Bennett
   Alfred, Rev., 53
   John, 123
   Sarah, 123
Benning
   William, 211
Benson
   Joseph, Rev, 52
Benter
   Elizabeth, 204
   William, 204
Bentz
   Mr., 74
Berch
   Balaam, 65
Berkeley Co, Va, 25, 111
Berkeley Springs, Va., 257
Berkeley, Va., 45
Berkshire Bible Society, 207
Bermuda, 1
Bernabue
   Don Carlos M., 253
Berret
   John J, 161
Berrian
   Rev., 208
Berrien
   John MacPherson, 191
   Macpherson, 7
   Margaret L M., 191
Berry
   Ann Maria, 172
   Barbara Ann, 247
   Barbara Ellen, 254

Benjamin, 38
Benjamin S., Sr., 59
  J., Mr., 247
  Miss, 7
  Noble F., 240
  Peter, 218
  Sarah R., 240
  Zachariah, 8
Berryman
  William B., 217
Berryville, Va, 243
Bethlehem, Pa, 199
Betterton
  Benjamin, 8
  Eliza, 8
Betton
  Lucinda, 208
  Solomon, Capt., 208
Betts
  Rev., 199
Between-the-Logs, 99
Beverley
  Harriott, 16
  Maria, 17
  Robert, 16, 17, 216
  Roberta, 216
Beverly
  Carter, 21
  Jane, 21
  Jane Bradshaw, 14
  Robert, 14
Bey of Tunis, 26
Bibb
  Lucien J, Lt., 199
Bingham
  Mrs., 1
  William, Hon., 1
Binney
  Amos, Col., 250
Birckhead
  Solomon, Dr., 141
Bird
  Edward, Rev, 61
  Mary, Mrs, 120
  William, 127
Birkhead
  Jane, 117
  Solomon, Dr., 117
Birmingham, Eng, 77
Birmingham, N.Y., 232
Biscoe
  Josiah, 116
Bishop
  John, 6

Samuel, 6
bishops, 1, 101, 107, 170, 207, 254
Bixler
  Angelina Amelia, 253
  David, 253
Black
  David, Capt., 175, 204
  James, 195
  Jane Eliza, 204
Black Rock, N.Y., 194
Blackburn
  Edward, 3
Blackford
  Francis G., 135
Blacklock
  Robert S, 241
Bladen
  A.D., 232
  Alfred D., 230
  Eleanor L.V, 231
  Loretta, 230
  Thomas James, 231
  William Henry, 230
Bladen Co, N.C., 112
Bladensburg, Md., 6, 10, 12, 24, 25, 37, 66, 132, 150, 168, 208, 218
Blagden
  Anne, 200
  George, 200
Blagrove
  Gracy Ann, 62
  Henry B., 43, 62
Blair
  Hugh, Rev., 1
  Samuel, Rev., 56
  Susan, 56
  William, 167
Blake
  George S., Lt., 113
  Glorvina, 169
  James H., Dr., 169
  Joseph R., Lt., 185
  Sarah L, 199
  T.H., Hon, 199
  Thomas Holdsworth, Hon., 154
Blasdell
  Capt., 72
Bleecker Street Presbyterian Church, 116
Bliss
  Abbey W., 93

Bloxton
  Agnes, 218
Blunt
  Capt, 173
  Mary Ann, 173
Blydenburg
  Eliza M., 108
  Samuel, 108
Boardly
  J.R., 105
Boarman
  Benedict, 232
  Mary Louisa, 17, 23
  Miss, 232
  Sarah T., 23
  T C, 23
  Thomas C., 17
Bodely
  Thomas, 58
Boehm
  Charles G, 62
Bogenreiff
  Valentine, 241
Bohrer
  Abraham, 74
  B S., Dr, 193
  Barbara, 49
  Benjamin S., Dr., 212
  Eliza Virginia, 212
  Harriet, 74
  Mary M., 49
Bolivar, Tenn., 222
Bolling
  Lucy Ann, 71
  Robert, 71
Bomberger
  Jacob, 111
Bomford
  George, Col., 195
  Louisa S., 195
Bonaparte
  Jerome, 124
  Jerome Napoleon, 124
  Napoleon, 81
Bond
  Henry, Dr, 193
  Phineas, 33
Bonham
  Marcellea, 136
Bonner
  John, 259
  Alice, 259
  John, 259
bookbinders, 196, 234

273

Booke
   Alonzo, 106
bookkeepers, 38
booksellers, 9, 22, 117, 224,
   242
Boon
   Alexius, 212
Boone
   Arnold, 12
Boonville, Mo , 219
Boose
   John, 87
   Sarah Ann, 18
Bootes
   Samuel, 232
   Samuel M., 177
   William Smith, 177
Bordeaux, Fra., 50
Bordley
   John, 31
   John Beale, 31
Boston
   Charles, 102
Boston Tea Party, 108
Boston Theatre, 95
Boston, Mass., 3, 6, 11, 22,
   24, 31, 39, 45, 50,
   53, 54, 66, 67, 90,
   95, 108, 116,
   124-127, 130, 132,
   133, 144, 148,
   157-159, 163, 166,
   170, 172, 178, 182,
   183, 187, 188, 196,
   197, 202, 206, 208,
   210, 212, 222, 224,
   226, 233, 237, 239,
   240, 242, 248, 250,
   252, 254, 263
   harbor, 108, 237
Boswell
   Benjamin, 42
   Eliza, 175
   Leonard, 113
   Rev., 15
   Washington, 219
   William H., 53
Botetourt Co., Va., 227, 252
Botetourt Springs, 228, 252
Boughan
   James G , Lt , 240
Boughton
   Theodosius, Sir, 142

Bouis
   Joseph, 165
Bouldin
   Jeru, Col., 150
   John, 110
Boulware
   John, 116
Boush
   Wilson, Capt , 128
Bowen
   Elizabeth Ann, 257
   John, 210
   Joseph O'D., 257
   Rachel Ann, 257
Bowery Presbyterian
   Church, 143
Bowie
   E.A., Miss, 243
   Elizabeth, 5
   John B., 243
   Mary, 84
   Robert, 92
   Walter, 5
   Washington, 84
Bowman
   Rev., 174
Bowyer
   Henry, Col., 227
Boxborough, 39
Boyd
   Archibald, 7
   Capt , 19
   David, 85
   John P , 166
   John Q. Adams, 190
   Miss, 7
   Washington, 190
Boyle
   Junius J., Lt., 228
Bradford
   C., Capt , 90
   Catharine A., 90
   Cornelius, 175
Bradley
   Abraham, Jr., 59, 166
   Charles, 86
   Hannah, 59
   Henry, 260
   Mary G., 166
   P., Dr., 230
   Phineas, Dr , 244
   Sydney Augustus, 230
Brady
   Peter, 57

Brainerd, 53
Branch
   John, Hon., 167, 183
   Margaret, 167
   Rebecca, 183
Brandt
   Richard H., 209
Brandywine, 138
Brannan
   Sarah S., 255
Branson
   Margaret, 46, 50
Brashears
   Richard Wells, 7
Brawner
   Bazil, 153
   E.A., Mrs., 47
   Mr., 245
   Robert, 47
Braxton
   George, 1
Brearley
   David, Col., 124
   Eleanor Jones, 124
Breckenridge
   John, xi
   Rev., 58
Bredin
   John, 109
Brehon
   James G., Dr., 226
Brent
   George, 194
   Hannah, 194
   James R , 186
   Jane, 254
   Robert Y., 20, 159
   William L., 256
   William L , Col., 256
   William, Capt., 194
Brenton
   Mereah (C), 56
Brentsville, Va., 225
Brewer
   George G., 89
   Rev., 260
Brice
   John, 208
   Margaret Carrol, 208
bricklayers, 102
Bridge Street Presbyterian
   Church, xi
Bridgeport, Conn , 58

Bridges
  James S., 42
  John, 60
Brien
  Bernard, 47
Brinkman
  Margaret, 32
Briscoe
  Caroline, 71
  Richard G., 209
Bristol, Conn., 22
Bristol, Pa., 131, 181, 256
Bristol, R.I., 108, 120
British Army, 6
Brittany, Fra., 95
Broad Creek, Md., 35
Broadhead
  Rev., 111
Broadus
  William, Maj., 167
Broadwell
  James, 250
Brocchus
  Thomas W., 191
Brodhag
  Charles, 4
  Elizabeth, 4
Brodie
  J.W., 106
Brogden
  William, Maj., 82
Bromsgrove, Eng., 56
Bronaugh
  Frances, 149
  Jeremiah W., 17
  William I., 72
  Wm. I., Jr., 40
Bronson
  Mary, 54
Brook
  Mary, 99
  Rev., 250
  Robert, 247
Brooke
  Clement, 78
  Edmund, 88
  Harriet, 88
  John Thompson, xi
  Letitia, 29
  Mary M., 78
  Rev., 122, 123, 136, 151, 153, 170, 183, 212, 213, 216, 217, 239, 240, 256
  T.E., Miss, 88
  Thomas, 5
  Thomas A., 83
  William, Gen., 115
Brookes
  Richard H., 215
Brookline, Mass., 212
Brooklyn, Conn., 185
Brooklyn, N.Y., 121, 175, 239
  navy yard, 107
Brooks
  Abby, 116
  Elizabeth, 133
  John B., 90
  John T., 48
  Joseph, 90
  Lewis I., 121
  Peter C., Hon., 116
Brookville, 90
Brookville, Md., 64
Broome Co., N.Y., 232
Brough
  Eliza, 71
  Robert, 74
  William, 71
Brown
  Abbe, 140
  Ann, 168
  C.R., Rev., 89
  Catherine S., 143
  E.F., 237
  Edmund F., 229
  Eliza, 124
  Eliza A., 84
  George, 237
  Gustavus Richard, Dr., 10
  Isabella Brown, 229
  Jacob, Gen., 140
  Jacob, Maj. Gen., 84, 106
  James B., 238
  James, Hon., 168
  Jesse, 124, 180
  Joel, Maj., 233
  John D., 150
  John M., 181
  Maj. Gen., 23
  Marshall, 262
  Martha, 41
  Martha A., 257
  Mary E., 147
  Mary H., 216
  Matthew, 213
  Michael, 262
  O.B., Rev., 28, 79, 147, 176, 239
  Obadiah Bruen, xi
  Pamela, 106
  Paoli, 58
  Rev., 20, 24, 31, 120
  Richard, Dr., 16
  Robert, 148
  Samuel, 140, 168
  Sophia, 167
  Stewart, Jr., 152
  Thomas, 257
  William, 16
Brown's Hotel, 243
Browne
  Elizabeth B., 129
  James, 129
Browning
  Peregrine Warfield, 250
Brownville, N.Y., 106, 140
Bruen
  Matthias, Rev., 116
Bruff
  Dr., 51
  Mary, 47, 51
  William, 56
Bruley
  Margaret, 79
Bruner
  Katharine, 53
Brunet
  John B., 128
  P., 67
Brunswick Co., Va., 36
Brunswick, Me., 113, 176, 183
Brunswick, N.J., 125
Brush Hill, 59
Bryan
  John Randolph, 137
  Joseph, 189
  Maria M., 189
Bryan Town, Md., 251
Bryanant
  Benjamin, 260
  R., Miss, 260
Buchanan
  Dr., 26
  Joseph, Dr., 117
  Thomas McKean, Lt., 241

Buchley
  Harriet, 201
Buckanan
  John, 153
Buckingham Co., Va , 116, 249
Buckingham, Pa., 60
Buckinghamshire, Eng , 194
Buckner
  Bailey, 214
Bucks Co., Pa., 121
Bucky
  Mary T., 223
Buddy
  Charles, 96
Buenos Ayres, Bra , 81, 121, 193
Buffalo, N Y., 164, 177
Buffalo, Pa., 39
Buford
  Maria, 156
Bugh
  Elizabeth, 236
Bull
  David, 15
Bullard
  Ann Frances, 138
Buncombe Co., N.C., 262
Bunker's Hill, 35, 207, 222, 262
  battle of, 242
Bunn
  Rev., 9
  Seely, xi
Burch
  Benjamin, Capt., 223
  Deborah, 217
  Rev., 38, 43
  Thomas, xi, 217
Burchan
  John, 9
Burchhead
  Edward, 227
Burges
  Thomas, Rev , 249
Burgess
  Dawson P., 27
  James Crawford, 83
  Judson Coolidge, 9
  Richard, 83, 210
Burgoyne
  Mr., 138, 222

Burk
  Cornelis Frances, Mrs., 94
  Martin, Lt., 242
Burke
  James, 148
  R.S., 141
  Sarah, 148
Burlington, N J., 6, 65, 240
Burnap
  George W., Rev., 192
Burne
  Levi, 132
Burnes
  Marcia, 4
Burneston
  Hannah, 57
  Isaac, 55
Burnett
  Charles A , 114
Burns
  Benjamin, 177, 255
  Ellen, 177
  Thomas, 69
Burr
  Col , 9
  Mima, 58
  Samuel, 58
Burrows
  Col , 6
  Frances Harriett, 38
  John, 83
  Mary, 5
  Miss, 6
  Robert, Capt , 167
  W W., Col., 5
Burton
  Caroline, Mrs., 89
burying grounds, 38, 146, 153, 165, 187, 215, 216, 259
  Catholic, 3, 80, 102
  M.E. Church, Pr. Wm Co., 218
  Pere LaChaise, 126
  Presbyterian, 2, 3, 9, 14
  public, 10
  Rock Creek, 7
  Share's (Harrisburg, Pa.), 111
Bush Hill, Pa., 129
Bushby
  Mr., vi
Bushwick, L I , 119

Busquet
  Catalina, 164
  Gen., 164
Bussard
  Daniel, 7, 151
  Philip, 16
  William, 102
Butcher
  Job, 12
  Jonathan, 12
  Rebecca, 11
butchers, 235
Butler
  Edward, Capt., 6
  Joseph, 248
  Mrs., 8
  Thomas, Maj., 6
Butler Co., Ohio, 196
Butt's Hill, 159
Butts
  Mark, 198
  Thomas, 198
Byrd
  Maria C , 105
  Thomas Taylor, 105
Byrne
  Christopher, 35
Byrnes
  Samuel, 257
  Sarah W., 257

C
Cabell
  Elizabeth C., 155
  George, Dr., 155
Cadle
  Richard H., 231
Caesar's Creek, Fla., 124
Cahaba, Ala , 53
Cahoone
  Henry, Capt., 142
Cain
  Anna, 52
Calder
  Martha, 50
  William, 50, 82
Caldwell
  Elias B , 7, 86
  James, 178
  John, 5
  Mr , 39
  Virginia Augustin, 178

Calhoun
  A.P., Mr., 251
  J.C., Hon , 251
Callao, 121
Callis
  Otho W., 189
Calnan
  John, 172
Calvert
  George, 170
  Rosalie Eugenia, 170
Calvert Co , Md., 6, 115,
  136, 145, 147, 177,
  180, 218
Camalier
  Catharine, 163
  Vincent, 163
Cambridge, Mass , 49, 207
Cambridge, Md., 151
Camden, S.C., 109, 138
Cammack
  Christopher, 252
  Elizabeth, 252
  Hannah, 101
Campbell
  Daniel, 205
  Eleanor (C), 238
  Fenneth, 112
  James W., 234
  John, 39
  John N., xi
  John N., Rev., 71
  Margaret N , 222
  Mary, 112
  Mary Ann, 227
  Meshack, 258
  Nicholas, 108
  Rebecca W., 127
  Rev., 71, 88, 115, 125,
    133
  William, 127
Cana
  Frederick, 65
Canada, 5, 61
Canajoharrie, N.Y., 187
canal commissioners, 204
Canandaigua, N.Y , 23, 40,
  226
Cannon
  John B., 127
  Minos, Sr , 112
Cantelo
  Mrs., 63
Canterbury, Eng , 68

Canton, Conn., 153
Cantwell
  Simon, 150
Cape Breton, 59
Cape Francois, 196, 247
Cape Henry, Hayti, 44
Capitol Hill, 9
Carberry
  John B., 16
  Susanna, 16
  T., Capt., 96
Carbery
  Eliza, 213
  Henry, Gen., 61
  James, 213
  Lewis, 245
  Thomas A., 245
Carey
  M.B , Mrs., 120
  Margaret, 166
  Mathew, 120
Cargill
  John, 188
  Martha Ann Sigourney,
    188
Carlin
  Sarah H., 138
Carlisle, Pa., 89, 202
Carmichael
  Alexander, 93
  George F., Dr., 136
  James, Dr., 189
  Mrs., 91
Carmick
  Daniel, 39
Carnahan
  Hannah M , 167
  James, Rev., 167
Carolin
  Caroline, 224
Caroline Co., Va., 115, 201,
  214
Carothers
  H.W., Master, 228
  John, 228
  Massa Ann, 151
Carpenter
  Abel, 93
  Miss, 8
carpenters, 4
Carr
  John C., Hon , 247
  Mary Jane, 145
Carrara, Italy, 177

Carrere
  Eliza L., 20
  John, 20
Carrico
  Ann Elizabeth, 139
Carrington
  Henry, 155
Carrol
  Mary, 104
Carrol, Va., 107
Carroll
  Ann, 165
  Archbishop, 20
  Bishop, 14, 95
  Charles, 1, 255
  Daniel, 252
  Henry James, 23
  John S., 205
  John, Rev , 30, 44
  Maria, 252
  Michael B., Capt., 206
  Miss, 1, 196
  Nicholas, 165
  Rev., 1
Carson
  Samuel, Dr , 177
Carter
  Adelaide, 156
  Alfred G., 174
  Benjamin, Capt., 138
  Bernard M , 199
  Betty, 148
  Charles, 148
  Charles H., 170
  Charlotte Williams, 199
  Daniel, 220
  Elizabeth L., 174
  Elizabeth M., 219
  Emily Louisa, 195
  Florida, 196
  Henry, 250
  Hill, 67
  Jacob, Jr., 195, 196
  Judith T., 261
  Lucy, 67
  Nathaniel H., 141
  Robert W., 219
  Thomas O., 261
Cartwright
  Ann, 202
Carusi
  Ignatius, 171
  Samuel, 141

Cary
  Rebecca, 70
  Wilson Miles, 70
Casanave
  Ann, 208
cashiers, 20, 56, 113, 156,
    171, 203, 206, 215,
    246, 248
Cass
  Elizabeth, 229
  Gov., 229
  Jonathan, Maj., 164
Cassin
  Capt., 67
  Com., 253, 260
  James, 19
  John, Lt., 260
  Margaret, 154
  Stephen, Com., 154
Cassine
  Rais Bel, 87
Catawissa, N Y., 111
Cathcart
  James Leander, 72
Catlett
  Ann E., 66
  Hanson, Dr., 66
Catoctin Valley, Md., 265
Caton
  Mary, 134
Cautre
  Louis, 51
Cavanly
  Alfred W., 164
Cawood
  Benjamin, 104
Cazenove
  A.C., 187
  Anna Maria, 74
  Anthony Charles, 74
  Paulina, 187
Cebrular
  Eliza C , 41
Cecil Co., Md., 23, 92, 103,
    161
Chalmers
  John, Rev , xi, 69, 97,
    157, 214, 242
  Mary Jane, 157
Chamberlain
  Jacob, 190
Chambersburgh, Pa., 62
Chamblin
  Charles, 164

  E S., 164
Chandler
  Eliza, 64
  Jane, 96
  John R., Dr., 235
  Joseph R , 217
  Lucy, 78
  Mary R , 217
  Walter S., 78, 86
  William L., 191
Chaney
  Abraham, 143
Chapelier
  John, 46
Chapin
  Gurdin, 51
  S., Rev., 178
Chapman
  David L., 91
  G T., Rev., 61
  Henry H , 21, 91, 240
  Henry Hendley, 57
  John G., 244
  John Henry, 21
  S.H., 108
  William, 194
Chapofa, Fla., 116
Chappell
  Eugenia, 251
  J.J., Col., 251
Chardon
  Adelaide, 261
  Anthony, 261
Charles
  Eliza, 65
Charles City Co., Va , 104
Charles Co., Md., 5, 9, 12,
    13, 15, 16, 21, 23,
    25, 39, 44, 47, 53,
    78, 87, 105, 110,
    125, 126, 148, 151,
    154, 162-164, 168,
    178, 181, 186, 190,
    200, 206, 209, 211,
    217, 226, 232, 234,
    235, 244, 246, 247,
    250, 251, 254, 261,
    266, 267
Charleston, 68
Charleston City Gazette, 68
Charleston, Mass , 6
Charleston, S.C., 4, 15, 27,
    44, 103, 109, 123,
    127, 128, 145, 148,

    185, 187, 197, 199,
    210, 262
Charleston, Va., 153, 186,
    204
Charlestown, 166
Charlestown, Md., 103
Charlestown, N.H , 71
Charlotte Hall, Md., 46, 126,
    178
Charlotte, Va , 155
Chartres, Fra., 57
Chase
  Matilda, 111
  Thomas, 111
Chasteau
  Louis, 60
Chatham
  Fanny, 173
  Henry, 173
Chatham, Va , 137
Chauncey
  Anna, 107
  Com , 107
Cheesely
  Joseph, 46
Cheetham
  James, 18
Chelmsford, Eng., 50
Chelsea, 247
Chenango Co., N.Y., 113
Cherokee Indians, 58
Cherry
  Eliza, 61
Chesapeake & Ohio Canal,
    260
Chesapeake & Ohio Canal
    Co , 130
Chesley
  Zadock C , 198
Chester
  Emeline M., 114
Chester Co., Pa., 115, 267
Chester Town, Md , 23, 57
Chester, N.H., 59
Chester, Pa., 130
Chestertown, Md., 87
Chew, 125
  Henry M , 250
  Julia Maria, 239
  Walter B., Capt , 239
Chicago, Ill., 172
Chichester
  George Mason, Capt.,
    84

278

Chick
  Eliza, 259
Child
  Henry, 109
Childs
  Ann, 169
  John, xi
  Samuel, 78
  Sarah A , 45
  Timothy, Hon., 175
Chili, 121
Chillicothe, Mo., 16
Chillicothe, Ohio, 111, 185
Chilton
  Thomas, Capt., 12
Chisholm
  Eleanor, 19
Christ Church, 48, 116, 120, 183, 208, 229, 230
Christ Episcopal Church, xi
Christmas
  Joseph S., Rev., 143
Chunn
  Mr , 235
Cicle
  Thomas, 92
Cincinnati, Ohio, 108, 129, 155, 157, 158, 161, 169, 182, 250, 265
Circleville, Ohio, 213
City Hotel, 159
City Point, Va , 128
Clagett
  Ann E., 181
  Charles, 193, 198
  Darius, 193
  Elizabeth H., 197
  Horatio, 135
  Howard, 193
  Jane, 194
  John Marshall, 135
  Mary, 198
  Richard, Dr., 263
  Sally, 35
  Sarah Ann, 193
  Thomas D , Capt., 181
  William H., Dr , 197
  Wm. W , 27
Clagget
  Elizabeth Ann, 170
  Nathaniel, 170
  William, 84
Claggett
  Rev , 7, 26

Claiborne
  Betsey, 104
  Charlotte Virginia, 248
  Dandridge, 104
  F L , Gen., 248
Claremont, N H , 162
Clark
  Alexander, 52
  Christine, Mrs , 133
  George, Dr., 17
  Jane, 93
  John B., Capt., 131
  John F., 236
  Julia, 236
  Mason E , 189
  Rev., 196, 214
  Samuel, Rev , 93
  William, Gen., 165
Clarke
  Anna Maria, 209
  Benjamin, 76
  George, Dr , 64
  Isaac, 127
  John F., 189
  Joseph S., 209
  Mrs., 165
  Rev , 41
  Robert, 254
  Thomas, 105
  Wm., 66
Clarkson
  Jacob, 41
  Rev., 2
Clavier
  Mary Catharine, 109
Claxton
  Anne Wright, 219
  John, 219
  Martha B., 160
  Richard W , 123
Clay
  H., Mrs., 235
  Henry, 61, 132
  Mathew, 27
  Susan H., 61
Cleary
  William, 188
Cleaveland
  Josiah, 216
Clements
  B., 179
  Bennett, 107, 171
  Bluntt, 44
  Catherine, 171

  Elizabeth, 211
  John, 263
  John Thomas, 133
  Thomas Augustine, 179
Clementson
  Edward, 133
  George, 91, 96
  Mr , 74
  Sarah, 31
Clemm
  Josephine, 209
  William, 209
Clerklee
  James, 267
  Margaret, 267
clerks, 2, 37, 99, 117, 144, 167, 186, 188, 204, 214, 216, 227, 233, 234, 259, 266
Clifton
  Alfred Wharton, 134
  Franklin, Col., 134
Cline
  Mary Ann, 104
  Peter, 104
  William, 174
Clingan
  William, Rev , 6
Clinton
  Ann Dewitt, 171
  DeWitt, 226, 232
  George W., 226
  James, Gen., 171, 232
Clinton Co., N Y., 215
Clitherall
  George C., Dr., 127
Cloak
  Frederica, 264
Clokey
  John, 172
Cloreviere
  Rev., 86
Cloud
  Caleb W., Dr., 202
  Naomi, 212
Coale
  Charles, 193
  Edward J., 242
Coalter
  Elizabeth, 137
  Henry, 90
  John, 267
  Judge, 137
  Lydia Ann, 90

Coats
  Ann Jane, 116
Cobb
  Daniel, Hon., 148
  Susan, 79
  Thomas W., Hon., 140
Cochran
  James, 41
Cocke Co., Tenn., 121
Coffer
  Jane Catherine, 132
Coggeshell
  Merea (C), 56
Cogings
  William C., 215
Cohagen
  John F., 105
Cohen
  David I., 161
  Dr., 161
  Harriet T, 161
  Jacob, 161
  Philip I, 91
Cokely
  Philip, 78
Cokendeffer
  Catharine, 3
Colborn
  James, 88
Cole
  Margaret C., Mrs., 127
  William T., 187
Coleman
  James P., 224
  William, 105
  William H, 221
Coles
  Isaac A., Col., 145
Coliflower
  George, 139
  Mrs., 139
Collard
  James S., 175
collectors, 6, 164, 194, 199, 263
College of New Jersey, 5, 167
Colley
  Eliza Ann, 41
Collige
  Edward, 243
Collingwood
  S, Mr, 56

Collins
  Benjamin, Rev., 197
  E.J., Dr., 241
  Edward W., 160
  Lewis, 153
  Louisa, 59
  Margaret, 219
Colner
  Catharine, 149
Colombia, So. Amer., 112
Colrain, Mass., 29
Colston
  Edward, 25
  Jane, 25
Coltman
  Charles, 103
Colton
  C., Rev, 230
  Chauncey, Rev., 240
Columbia Co., N Y, 62, 111
Columbia, Mo., 241
Columbia, S.C., 251
Columbian College, 116, 129, 198
Columbian Navy, 258
Columbus, 184
Colvert
  Louisa, 38
Combes
  J., Rev., 250
comedians, 108, 206, 230
commissioners, 105, 159
Compton
  John S., 245
  Mrs., 215
  Susan Eliza, 245
  William P., 266
comptrollers, 258
Concord, N.H, 201, 233
Cone
  Spencer Houghton, xi
confectioners, 185
Congressional Examiner, 63
Conn
  Stephen T., 225
Connecticut, 133, 240
Connell
  John, 133
Connelly
  Mr., 147
Conner
  Valentine, 165
Connolly
  Bridget, 154

Connor
  Thomas, 100
Contee
  Benjamin, Rev, 19
  Sarah Russel, 19
Continental money, 120, 242
Convent of the Visitation, 95, 224
Conway
  James H., 38
Conwell
  Rev., 46, 49, 101
Cook
  Catharine, Mrs, 121
  Daniel P., 134
  Julia, 134
  Lucinda, 221
  M.C., 221
  Martin, 235
  Sarah, Mrs., 107
  Septimus J, Dr, 132
  Thomas, 55, 94
  William, 42
Cookesey
  Mary, 43
Cooks-town, Ire, 181
Cool Springs, Md., 80
Coolidge
  Charles, 11
  Mrs, 24
Coombe
  Griffith, 210
  Ruhamah, 210
Coons
  Elijah, Dr., 151
Cooper
  Capt., 266
  Elizabeth, 212
  George, Capt., 109
  Henry D., 223
  Ira, 58
  Isaac, 47
  Joseph, 212, 248
  Mary, 158
  Samuel, Lt, 100
  Thomas, 130
  Thomas A., 256
coopers, 258
Cooperstown, N Y., 162
Coosawatchie, 123
Coote
  C.T., Mr., 223
  Margaret C, 223

Corbin
  James P., 136
Corcoran
  Hannah, 70
  Sarah, 57
  Thomas, 57, 70, 136, 226
Corebin
  Caroline R.H., 122
  Robert, 122
Cork, Ire., 108
Cornelius
  Rev., 188
  S., Rev., 121, 134, 146
  Samuel, xi
Corner
  James J., 125
Cornick
  James, Dr., 245
Cornwall, 77
Cornwall, Eng., 237
Cornwallis
  Lord, 130, 138, 222
  Mr., 222
Cornwallis's Neck, Md., 15
Corse
  Isaac, 262
Cortland Co., N.Y., 53
Corwin
  Mathias, 119
Costin
  Philadelphia, 211
  William, 211
Cotton
  John, 103
Cougnacq
  Charles Francis, 1
Courcey
  Nell (C), 46
Courter
  Alice E., 137
Couzins
  Keziah A., 17
Cover
  Ann Sophia, 158
  George, 158
Covington, La., 242
Cox
  Fleet, 192
  John Chandler, 23
  John, Col., 124
  Mathilda, 124
  Miss, 6
  Mrs, 41

  William, 41, 158
Coxe
  Ann, 240
  Richard S., 259
  Susan B., 259
  William, 240
Coyle
  John, Capt., 202
  Randolph, 264
Cozens
  Dr., 54
  Lewis, 54
  W.R., Dr., 74
Crabtree
  Lydia Maria, 185
  William, Jr., 185
Crachami
  Miss, 81
Craig
  Caroline, 129
  Henrietta, Mrs., 27
  John D., 151
  Margaret, 151
Crain
  Peter Wood, 163
  Robert, 125
Cramphin
  Thomas, 173
Cranch
  Ann Ellen, 48
  Judge, 255
  William, Hon., 48
Crandell
  Jane, 154
  Lucinda Constantia, 154
Craney Island, 67
Cranston
  John, 119
Cravan
  Eleanor, 15
Craven
  Elijah R., Dr., 71
  Elisha, Dr., 76
  Thomas T., Lt., 203
Crawford
  Eliza, 46, 50
  James, 81
  Mrs., 176
  Sarah, 210
  William, 38, 46, 50, 210
Crawford Co., Ind., 59
Crawfordsville, Ind., 259
Creek Indians, 31, 58

Creighton
  Ann, 59
Crey
  Christina, 150
  Frederick, 150
Croes
  John, Rev., 229
Croghan
  Col., 266
  Maria Dallas, 266
Cronise
  Mary, 139
Crook
  George, 213
Crosby
  Henry, 71
Crosdell
  Rev., 261
Cross
  Joseph, Col., 165
Crossfield
  Jehiel, 11
Crowley
  Julia Ann, 236
  P., Mr., 236
  Thomas, 87
Crown
  Joseph, 48, 52
  Mary, 48, 52
Cruikshank
  Ann, 36
  Charles, 41, 216
  John, 38
  Richard, Capt., 145
  Sarah Ann, 216
Cruse
  Mary, 114
  Peter Hoffman, 233
Cruttenden
  Harriet L., 142
  Joel, 142
Cuba, 103, 187, 214
Culpeper Co., Va., 27, 102, 126, 138, 149, 163, 167, 187
Cumberland Co., Md., 33
Cumberland Co., Pa., 151
Cumberland, Md., 14, 217, 227
Cunigin
  Archibald, 84
Cunningham
  Hugh, 137
  Robert B., Lt., 147

Curren
   William, 221
Curtin
   William, 197
Cushing
   Joseph, Jr., 226
   Thomas H., 43
   Thomas P., 188
   William, Hon., 18
Custis
   G.W.P., 190
   George W.P., 9
   Mary A.R., 190
Cutshaw
   George W., 203
Cutting
   John Browne, Dr , 178
Cutts
   Anna, 230
   Augustus, Lt., 103
   Richard, 230

D

D'Agrella
   Manuel Teixeira, 112
D'Arbel
   Dominique, 157
D'Wolfe
   James, 22
   Mary Ann, 22
Dabney
   William B , 140
Dade
   Hon., 94
   Townsend, xi
   William A G , Hon , 122
Daingerfield
   Edward, 204
Dale
   Dorothy, 232
   Elizabeth, 106
   Richard, 106
   Richard, Com , 232
Dallas
   Alexander J., 195
   Alexander James, 40
   Henrietta M., 195
Dana
   Rev., 264
Dandridge
   William, 171

Danforth
   Joshua N., Rev., xi, 108, 109, 172, 185, 193, 223
Daniel
   George M , 259
Danneny
   J.G.S.A., 155
Darby
   Sarah, 6
Dargen
   Margaret, 94
Darley
   Susan, 149
Darnall
   Henry, 15
Dashiel
   Mary, 60
   T.B., 38
   Thomas B., 17, 60
Dashiell
   George W., 43
   Richard Parker, 252
   Thomas B., 252
Dashiells
   Rev., 26
Daukins
   E., Gen , 158
   Susan, 158
Daul
   John, 45
Davenport, Eng., 93, 97
Davidge
   John Beale, 113
Davidson
   Francis H., 181
   James, 121, 232
   John, Maj., 135
   Lewis G., 46
   Lewis Grant, 50, 240
   Margaret, 121
   Margaretta, 232
   Samuel, 18, 225
   W.J., 54
Davidson Co., Tenn., 199
Davis
   Aurelia, 161
   Charles, 200
   Charles A., Rev., 79
   Charles, Sr., 236
   David, 23
   Elizabeth, 182
   Elizabeth H., 49
   Frances Rebecca, 67

   George A., 141
   George M , 177
   Gideon, 50, 254
   Helen, 110
   Ignatius, 67
   Jane Elizabeth, 251
   John, xi, 58, 125
   John W., 133
   John, Rev., 192
   Martha Ann, 102
   Mary E., 125
   Naylor, 23
   Rev., 2, 7, 100
   Richard, 184
   Richard, Jr., 184
   Samuel H., xi
   Samuel H., Rev , 63
   Sarah J., 242
   Solomon, 60
   Thomas, Rev., 9
   William, 251
   William A., 182
Davy
   Humphrey, Sir, 110
Daw
   Joseph, 174
Dawe
   Philip D., 225
Dawes
   Benjamin, 83
   Joseph H , 129
   Mrs., 83
Dawson
   Charles W., 66
   Thomas, 94
Day
   Rev., 31
Dayton, Ohio, 79, 157, 172, 184, 254, 255
de Walewski
   M., 133
deacons, 155, 265
   Caroline, 187
Deagle
   Matthew, Rev., xi, 124, 203
Deakins
   J M , Dr., 190
   Leonard, 19
   T., Miss, 19
   William F., 226
Dean
   Frances, 3
   William, 130

Dearborn
   Charles, Capt , 148
DeButts
   Samuel, 24
   Sophia, 73
Decatur
   Com., 153, 249
   John P., Col., 249
Decheaux
   Rev., 47
Declaration of
   Independence, 179
DeClaville
   Constantine Petit, 57
DeCloriviere
   Joseph Peter Picot, 95
DeGilse
   Godfrey L , 148
DeGilsie
   Dorothy, 76
DeGreuhm
   Mr., 75
deKrafft
   Charles, 9
Delany
   Patrick, 191
Delaplane
   Joseph, 19, 22
   Mrs., 19
DeLaRouche
   Harriet F.B , 106
Delaware, 2, 4
Delaware Co., N Y., 133
Delaware Co , Pa., 130, 267
Delozier
   Mary, 258
Delphia, N.Y., 133
Delphy
   Orlando, 242
Dement
   Richard, 189
   Sarah, 189
   Wm , Jr., 25
DeMilhau
   Rosella, 197
Demure
   Rev , 85
Denney
   John Lewis, 252
   John P., 252
Denny
   James, 68
   John P., 154, 250
   John, Capt., 68

John, Dr., 119
Dent
   Lauretta, 211
   N.S., Mr., 211
dentists, 163
Denty
   John, 91
Derbin
   Rev., 208
Derby
   Richard, 226
Detau
   Rev., 59
Deteaux
   Rev , 68
Detheu
   Rev , 83
Dethroux
   Rev., 50
Detroit, Mich , 5, 187, 229
Deutz
   M , 126
Deviny
   Ann, 80
   Charles, 80
Devonshire, Eng., 158
Dewdney
   John, 101
Dewees
   Ann, 178
   Jesse, 10
   William, Col., 178
Dewey
   Eliza C., 113
Dexter
   Samuel, 34
Deyaha
   Mousse (C), 196
Dick
   James Ross, 231
   Thomas, 6
Dickey
   Mary, 107
Dickins
   Asbury, 205
   Lilla Elizabeth, 205
Dickinson
   Edward, Dr , 147
   Louisa S., 175
Dickson
   John, 23
   Moore, 239
Didenhover
   Mary C , 176

Dier
   William, 181
Dieskau
   Baron, 119
Diez
   Adam, 186
Digges
   William Dudley, 135
Disney
   Jane, 132
Dixon
   Elizabeth, 80
   Harriet, 205
   Jane, 137
   John, 84
   T., Mr., 8
   Teresa, 13
   Thomas, 91
Dobbin
   Archibald, 135
Dobbyn
   John, 116
Doddridge
   Philip, Hon , 243
Dodge
   Emily, 114
Dodson
   John, 263
   Sarah Ann, 263
Doll
   John, 85
   Mr., 101
   Susan, 85
Doncastle
   Elizabeth, 10
Done
   John, 24
   Judge, 203
   William, 24
Donellan
   J P., Rev., 261
Donelson
   Daniel S , Gen., 167
Donnellan
   Capt , 142
Donohoo
   John A , 70
Doolittle
   Betsy, 54
   Joseph, 54
   Lemuel, 54
   Roswell, 54
door keepers, 212, 223

Dorchester Co., Md., 59, 71, 93, 153
Dorsett
  Fielder R., 44
Dorsey
  Clement, Hon , 133
  D.B., Rev., 194, 218
  Harriet, 26
  Rev., 218
  Sally Maria, 133
  Thomas J., Rev , 131, 187
  Wm. I., 90
Dougherty
  Eleanor, 185
  Rev., 90, 94
Douglass
  Elizabeth, 129
  George L , 189
  Richard H., 123
  Sutherland, Rev., xi, 190
Dove
  Samuel, 262
  Sarah Y., 15
  Zachariah, 223
Down
  Mary A., 227
Down Co , Ire , 239
Downs
  Hamilton M., 112
  Malcolm, 112
Dox
  Myndert M., 164
Doxe
  Emily, 65
  William, 65
Doyle
  Ellen, 231
Doyne
  Joseph, 55
draftsmen, 9
Drake
  Catharine C., 259
  Willard, 259
Draper
  Edward, 208
  Simeon, Dr , 236
draughtsmen, 178
Drean
  Josiah L., 249
Drew
  Edward M , 213
Drewry
  James, 59

Drinker
  George, 210
Druet
  James, 222
  Susan, 222
Drummond
  Mary Ann, 103
  Thomas F., 103
Duanesburgh, N Y., 199
Dublin, Ire., 81, 126, 139, 152, 153
DuBois
  Mr., 57
Dubuisson
  Stephen L., Rev., xi, 88, 200, 212, 253
Duchoquet
  Francis, 227
Dudden
  J., 125
Dudley
  James, 180
Duer
  Francis, 263
Duff
  John, 184
Duffey
  Capt., 101
  John H., 195
Duffy
  Helen, 234
Dufief
  Jeremiah, 16
Dugan
  Caroline, 132
Duke of Tuscan, 53
Dulaney
  James H., 55
Dulany
  Daniel F., Jr., 239
Dullatur, Scot., 80
Dumbarton Methodist Church, xi, xii
Dumeste
  J.A., Lt., 203
Dumfries, Va., 31, 51, 94, 172, 204, 244
Dunbar
  Robert, 212
Duncan
  John M., Rev., 265
  Joseph M., 256
  Maria, 256
  Mary Ann, 46, 49

Samuel J., 116
  William, 46, 49
Dundore
  Henry, 139
Dunham
  Thornton C., 137
Dunlap
  Esther Ann, 253
  James A , Col., 207
  William, 253
Dunlop
  Harriet Margaret, 244
  Hellen, 64
  James, 64, 69, 244
Dunn
  J S., Dr., 153
  James C , 63
  Rev., 84
Dunning
  Margaret, 182
Duplin Co., N.C., 83
Duport
  P.L., 30
Durald
  Martin, 61
Durant
  John W., 256
Duryee
  Abraham I., Dr., 60
Dusan
  Dorothy, 8
Duval
  Edmund B , Col., 178
  Edward W., 169
  Judge, 178
  Mary Ann Frances, 249
  William, Maj., 249
Duvall
  Benjamin, Dr , 186
  Cleonah, 186
  John, 163, 193
Dwight
  Henry E., 230
  President, 230
Dyall
  Joshua, 28
Dye
  Mary, 102
  R., Capt., 102
Dyer
  Clarissa Paula, 237
  Edward, 203, 237, 253
  Eliza Ann, 218
  Francis, Capt , 212

Margaret Morris, 212
Mary, 179
Mrs., 4
Samuel, 238
Sarah, 238
Sophia, 203
Susan, 157
Thomas B., 218
William, 4, 181
William B., Capt., 135
William, Capt, 157
Dyson
John, Dr., 13
Walter, 126

E

Earl of Carhampton, 52
East Feliciana, 161
East Florida Herald, 68
East Haddam, Conn., 69
East India Co , 205
East Indies, 57
East Randolph, Ver., 115
Eastbradford, 49
Eastern Shore Maryland, 57
Eastin
  Mary A., 221
Easton
  Jane, 31
Easton, Md., 82, 170, 223
Easton, Pa., 247
Eatonton, Ga , 122
Echols
  Philip Henry, 191
Eckel
  Philip P., 180
Eckhardt
  Frederick, 193
Ecklin
  Leonard, 79
Eddes
  John, 211
Edelen
  John A., 107
  Raphael L., 237
Edelin
  James, 132
  John, 217
  Joseph, 250
Edenton, N C , 108, 120
Edes
  Benjamin, 232
  William H., 122

Edgell
  Dr., 125
  Mrs., 125
Edinburgh, Scot., 1, 80, 257
editors, 3, 18, 19, 23, 105,
  109, 118, 130, 136,
  162, 187, 192, 197,
  198, 207-209, 217,
  218, 233, 240, 249,
  265
Edmondson
  William Henry, 232
Edmonston
  Catherine Ann, 209
Edmunds
  Elias, 243
  Margaret B., 243
  Sydnor, 243
Edson
  Elizabeth, 120
Edwards
  Elizabeth, 230
  Elizabeth Goldthwait, 236
  James L., 236
  Mary, 230
Egan
  Michael DuBourg, Rev., 107
Egbert
  Capt., 29
Eichelberger
  Lewis, Rev., 140
elders, 32
Eliason
  E.A , Mr., 222
  John, 199, 235
  Maria, 199
Eliot
  William H., 210
Elizabeth Town, N J , 72
Elk Ridge, 118
Elk Ridge, Md., 162
Elkridge Landing, 91
Elkton Bank of Maryland, 20
Elkton, Md , 20
Ellicott
  George, 221
Ellicott's Mills, Md., 221
Elliot
  Elizabeth E , 74
  Ellen, 125
  Jonathan, 201
  Sarah, 201

  William, 74
Elliott
  David, Rev , 244
  John, 129
  Jonathan, 78
  Lynde, 195
  Mary Ann, 78
  Statira, 195
  Stephen, 145
Ellis
  Ariane, 108
  Powhatan, Hon., 180
  Robert, 78
Ellsworth
  Oliver, 11
Elwyn
  Emily Sophia, 210
  T L , 210
Emack
  William, 175
Emerson
  Labina, 171
Emmit
  Thomas Addis, 102
Emmitsburg, Md , 57, 107, 158
Emory
  John, xi
Emperor of Austria, 53
engineers, 108, 133, 143,
  169, 189, 190, 221, 260
England, 8, 30, 37, 50, 52,
  58, 77, 86, 95, 101,
  104, 111, 119, 123,
  152, 157, 215, 219,
  237, 259, 265
English
  David, Jr , 39, 93
  Elizabeth B., 199
  James, 143, 160
  John C., 186
  Mary O., 93
  Samuel, 199
Ensey
  William, 215
Entriken
  Mrs , 49
Entwisle
  James, 27
Erie Co , N.Y , 137
Ermantinger
  John, 85

Erving
  John, Maj., 210
Eskridge
  Alexander, Lt., 219
Espey
  John, 233
Essen
  Josiah, 181
Essex
  Eliza Ann, 265
Essex Co., Va., 64
Estep
  Rezin, 152
Etter
  Anna, 223
Europe, 48, 190
Eutaw, 266
Eutaw Springs, 138
Evans
  Ann C , 213
  E., 168
  Elizabeth, 6
  Elizabeth Ann, 168
  Evan, 6
  F.S., Rev , 166, 225
  French S., xi
  French, Rev., 107
  John, 214
  John T., 135
  Leonard, 216
  Samuel, 66
  Susanna, 214
  T., 30
Evarts
  Jeremiah, 187
Eveleth
  Sarah, Mrs., 122
Everitt
  Mary Augusta, 127
  Thomas, 127
Eversfield
  Charles, 27
Ewell
  James, Dr., 242

F

Fadely
  Jacob, Jr , 67
  James, 225
Fagan
  John, 168
Fahey
  Bridget, 147

Fairbanks
  Gerry, Col., 126
Fairclough
  Joseph William, Rev., xi, 72, 134
Fairfax
  Archibald B., Lt., 242
  Brian, Rev , 4
Fairfax C.H., Va , 236
Fairfax Co.
  West End, 204
Fairfax Co., Va , 7, 21, 72, 76-78, 82, 97, 102, 105, 118, 123, 133, 134, 140, 141, 151, 164, 174, 175, 179, 184, 185, 192, 201, 209, 220, 223, 224, 230, 239, 244, 247, 259
Fairfax Co , Va. , 201
Fairfax, Va., 163, 221
Fall River, 216
Falling Spring, Va., 130
Falmouth, Va., 204, 212
Farlie
  Maj., 256
  Mary, 256
Farmer's Tavern, 30
farmers, 259
Farmers Bank of Virginia, 203
Farmers' and Mechanics Bank, 67
Farmers' Bank, 48, 243
Farmers' Bank of Maryland, 69
Farmington, Conn , 119
Farrell
  Maria, 35
  Rev , 20
Farrigue
  Edward, 159
Farris
  P., Mr., 239
Fauntleroy
  Rebecca P.F , Mrs., 138
Fauquier Co., Va., 32, 98, 134, 135, 171, 186, 233, 243, 261
Faw
  Abraham, 166
  Sophia E., 166

Fay
  Joseph, Capt., 207
Faye
  Mary J., 183
Fayetteville, N.C., 156
Fearson
  Joseph, 233
  Samuel, 83
Feathersronhaugh
  George William, 199
Fechtig
  Lewis R , Rev., xi, 73
Fell
  Frederick S , 208
Fellows
  John, Capt , 207
Fendall
  B.T., Capt., 173
  Eliza C., 173
Fennall
  Thomas, 138
Fenno
  John Ward, 3
Fenwick
  Ann, 158
  Benedict J , xi
  Enoch, xi
  Francis I., 90
  George, Rev., 188
  John, Rev., 12
  Margaret, 236
  Rev., 8, 17, 44
  Richard, 158
Ferdinand 3d, 53
Ferguson
  Alexander, 39
  John, 233
Ferriar
  Dr , 112
  John, Col , 112
Fessenden
  Thomas Green, 263
Fielding
  Windford, 42
Fields
  Horace, Maj., 175
Fillebrown
  Thomas, Jr., 106
  William Henry, 106
Fincastle, Va , 227
Findlay
  Jonathan S., 241
Findley
  J.S., Mr , 94

Finley
  J., Rev., 209
  John, Rev., 228
Finn
  Henry J., 95
Fire Place, L.I., 29
First Baptist Church, xi, xii
Fisher
  Alexander, 29
  James, 138
  Nathaniel W., Rev., 109
Fisk
  Charles B., 260
Fitch
  Chauncey W., Rev., 135, 240
  Ebenezer, Rev., 43
  Lucy, 43
  Mary W., 135
Fitzhugh
  Edmund, Dr., 222
  Eliza Ann, 222
  Hannah E., Mrs., 4
  Mary Ann, Mrs., 122
  Molly, 9
  Richard H., 36
  Robert, 252
  Samuel, 19
  William H., 151
  William Henry, 107
  William W., 190
  Wm., 9
Flagg
  A.C., 143
Flat Rock, N C., 262
Fleet
  Warrington (C), 163
Fleete
  Henry (C), 77
Fletcher
  Elizabeth H., 53
Flisset
  Catharine, 16
Florence, Italy, 53, 177
Florida, 8, 205, 207
Floris
  Charles, 39
Flower
  Richard, 119
Floyd
  Ruth, 181
Folsom
  Ezekiel, 43

Fonde
  John P., 214
Foote
  Ebenezar, Hon., 133
  William H., 152
Force
  Almira, 58
Ford
  Ann, 43
  Ann R., 216
  Athanasius, 49
  Isabella, 1
  Sally, 57
  Stephen C., 183, 216
  Susanna Maria, 38
  William, 129
Forman
  Ann E., 105
Forrest
  Ann, 23
  French, Lt., 183
  George P., 240
  Joseph, 73
  Julius, 117
  Richard, 117, 231
  Sarah, 231
  Uriah, 23
Forsyth
  Clara C., 264
  John, Hon., 184, 264
  Julia, 184
Fort
  William, 132
Fort Armstrong, 161
Fort Armstrong, Ill., 246
Fort Gibson, Miss., 249
Fort Jackson, La., 241
Fort McHenry, 37, 217
Fort Montgomery, 35
Fort Mott, 138
Fort Moultrie, 262
Fort Nelson, 88
Fort Norfolk, 132
Fort St Mark, 68
Fort Stanwix, 174
Fort Warren, 40
Fort Washington, Md., 175, 222, 243
Fort William Henry, 119
Fortress Monroe, 122
Fortune
  James, 156
Foundry Chapel, 77

Foundry Methodist Church, xi
Fountain Rock, 122
Fourth Presbyterian Church, 109
Fourth Street Methodist Church, xi, xii
Fowle
  John, Maj., 187
  Jonathan, 114
  Mary Ellen, 228
  William, 228
  William H., 195
Fowler
  Daniel, 2
  Elizabeth Jenifer, 163
  Fanny P., 151
  John, 49
  Lt., 151
  Robert B., 243
  Thomas M., 163
Fox
  B., 31
  C., 31
  Duanna Binns, 194
Foxall
  Henry, Rev., xi, 16, 32, 77
  Margaret, 32
Foyles
  Isabel, 203
  Thomas, 220
Frailey
  L., 252
  Mary M., 252
France, 69, 81, 95, 128, 133, 155, 157, 168, 175, 191, 205
  Elizabeth, 232
  John, 232
Francis
  Thomas, 178
Frank
  Ephraim, 188
  John, 16
Franklin Co., 12
Franklin Co., Pa., 62, 151, 226
Franklin, N Y., 109
Franks
  Samuel D., Hon., 146
Franzoni
  Eurydice, 152

Fraser
  James, 227
Frazer
  Anthony, 74
  Carolina Georgiana, 196
  Thomas, 65
  Thomas, Maj., 196
Frederick Co., Md , 4, 26, 31, 47, 61, 67, 70, 180, 209, 212, 265
Frederick Co., Va., 105, 148, 220, 243
Frederick, Md , 85, 136, 232, 236
Frederick, Va., 190
Fredericks
  Mary (C), 196
Fredericksburg, Va., 34, 48, 78, 105, 110, 118, 120, 126, 131, 136, 138, 145, 146, 156, 162, 163, 167, 170, 177, 189, 191, 199, 203, 209, 214, 219, 224, 240, 261, 267
Fredericktown, Md., 25, 27, 38, 70, 78, 81, 118, 137, 139, 179, 180, 183, 198, 200, 201, 223, 256
Freeland
  James, 182
  Sarah, 87, 182
Freeman
  Ann, 78
  Frances, 78
  Thomas, 57
French
  Caroline, 45
  Charles, 170
  Edmund, Lt., 212
  George, 92
  John Alexander, 238
  Margaret H.W., 92
  Marion B., 209
  Mary Virginia, 170
  V., Mr , 45
  William, 209
French Town, Md , 20
Friend's Meeting House, 12, 141, 228, 255
Front Royal, Va., 201
Frost
  Amariah, 2

  Esther, 2
Fryman
  Ann, 80
Fuller
  Azariah, 189, 252
  Ruth, 189
  Webster Erles, 252
Fullterton
  Matthew M., Rev., 150
Fulton
  Elizabeth, 176
  Robert, 25
Furlong
  Henry, Rev., xi, 221, 228, 249

G

Gadsby
  William, 264
Gaedike
  Helmuth J., 130
Gagne
  Magdaline Morin, 155
  Nouvelle B.J., 155
Gaillard
  Cornelia Ann, 155
Gaither
  Ann R., 45
  Frederic R., 75
  George R., 59
  Greenbury, 79
  Harriet T., 17
  Henry, 40
  John, 215
  Maria, 75
  Mary, Mrs., 17
  Rezin, 215
  Samuel R., 75
Gale
  John, Dr., 161
Gales
  Ann Eliza, 64
  Joseph, 64
Gallagher
  Martha, 222
  Martha, Mrs , 222
Gallatin
  Albert, Hon., 146
  Frances, 146
Galpin
  Grace Ann, 190
  Sophia, 249

Galt
  Gabriel, 129
Gamage
  William, 49
Gambier, Ohio, 135, 240
Gamble
  Charlotte S., 14
  Col., 121
  James, 107
  John, 14
  Mary Hamilton, 107
  William, Maj , 250
gamblers, 114
Gannon
  Mary Eleanor, 172
Gansevoort
  Peter, Gen., 174
Gantt
  Anna Lowndes, 246
  Edward, xi
  Edward B., 96
  Edward, Rev., 2, 6-8
  Eliza, 4
  Levi, 4
  Margaret Ann, 239
  Thomas T , 246
Gardiner
  George W., Capt., 151
  H.S., Lt., 87
  James, 247
  William, 176
Gardner
  Charles K , 41
  James, 54
  James, Dr., 216
  Jane, 2
  Lucy, 54
  Mary, 33
  William, 127
Garnett
  James, Sr , Rev., 149
Garretson
  Isaac, 137
Gaston
  Wm., Hon., 36
Gates
  Mr., 138
  Susan, 166
Geintzel
  Anne, 236
  Daniel, 236
General Land Office, 1, 46, 178, 186, 216, 253

General Post Office, 167,
  168, 188, 189, 235,
  250
Geneva, N.Y., 116
Geneva, Switz., 9, 110
George
  Enoch, Rev., 32
  Mary, 32
Georgetown College, 90,
  129, 216
Georgetown, Del., 145
Georgia, 6, 140, 152, 191,
  218
Germantown, Pa., 54, 55,
  96, 138
Germany, 1, 65, 85, 101,
  180, 186, 193, 199
Gerry
  Eldridge, 24
  Thomas R., Lt., 155
Gettinger
  Rebecca, 137
Getty
  Ann Eliza, 251
  Robert, 12, 251
Getz
  Daniel, 80
Geyer
  John, 209
Ghent, 217
Gholson
  Thomas, Hon., 36
  Wm., 36
Gibbon
  Elizabeth, 101
  Rev., 133
Gibbs
  A.C., 134
  Margaret, 66
  Theodore, 139
Giberson
  Eliza, 221
  G.L, Mr., 221
Gibson
  Ann S., 168
  David, 204
  Joseph, 135, 168
  Margaret Vanhorn, 135
  Mary A.C., 172
  Nancy, 204
  Rev., 20
  William Lewis, xi
Gideon
  George S., 259

Jacob, Jr., 228
Rebecca, 228
Gifford
  Fortune, 147
  Mr., 147
Gilbert
  David, 136
Giles
  Amelia, 20
  Augusta, 38
  Thomas, 20
  William B, 38, 173
Giles, Va, 33
Gilles
  Rev., 78
Gilliam
  Rev., 71
Gillingham
  Elizabeth, 141
  George, 95
  Jacob, 131
  Matthias, 131
  Moses, 131
Gillis
  Ellen G., 203
  Irving, Miss, 9
  Leah Ann, 117
  Thomas H, 117, 203
Gilliss
  L.I., Rev., 173
Gilman
  Nicholas, Hon., 22
Gilmor
  Robert, Jr, 225
Gimbrede
  Thomas, 249
Gist
  Thomas, 26
Given
  Elizabeth, 209
  Elizabeth B., 213
Givens
  William, 218
Gladman
  Asa, 196
Glasgow
  Catharine A., 153
  George, 170
Glendy
  John, Rev., 238
  Rev., 38, 71
Glenn
  Elias, Hon., 186
  Jefferson, 186

Rachel, 38
Thomas, 38
Gloucester C.H., Va., 204
Gloucester Co, Va, 66
Gloucester Twp., N J., 66
Glover
  Charles, 261
  Matilda, 261
Gloyd
  Elizabeth, 14
Godman
  John D., 147
  Samuel T., 52
Gold
  Thomas, 254
Goldsborough
  Charles, Jr, 82
  Louis M, Lt., 206
Goldsmith
  Catharine, 60
  Rev., 184
Gonzalos
  Antonio, 197
Good
  Richard Thomas, 238
  Thomas G, 238
  William, Sr, 178
Goodenough
  Betsey, 58
Gooding
  Mr., 102
Goodrich
  A.W., Col., 198
Goodwin
  Henry B, Rev., 246
  John H., 261
  Juliet, 87
Gordon
  Ann E., 185
  Ann Maria, 220
  Juliana, 227
  William, 108, 185
  William A, 169
Gorham
  Benjamin, Hon., 127
Gosport, Va, 18, 113, 125,
  129, 235
Gossum
  Charity Ann, 67
Goszler
  Anthony, 100
  Christiana, 82
  George A., 82
  Henry, 100

Gott
  Richard, 185
Gough
  Ann Elizabeth, 243
  Stephen, 243
Gould
  Hannah Greene, 155
  Peter P., 155
Goulden
  Margaret, 178
Governors, 106, 153, 164, 179, 205, 229, 247
  Buenos Ayres, 193
  Kentucky, 167
  Louisiana, 120, 144
  Maryland, 192
  Massachusetts, Lt., 132, 148
  New Jersey, 4
  New York, 232
  North Carolina, 189
  Ohio, 255
  Pennsylvania, 162, 227
  Virginia, 173
Gracie
  Archibald, 111
Graeff
  Henry G., 57
Graenacher
  Charles J., 158
Graff
  Andrew, 31
Graham
  Alexander, 31
  Andrew, 248
  Charles, 201
  George, 87, 159
Grant
  Catharine, 69
  Elizabeth, 233
Grassi
  John A., Rev., xi, 36, 43
Graves
  Martha Maria, 109
  Rufus, 109
Gray
  Catharine, 120
  Eliza, 103
  Francis B., 142
  Horatio Nelson, Rev., 116
  John B., 164
  John G., 142
  Margaret Elizabeth, 164
  Rebecca A., 164
  Robert, 131
  Stephen W., 103, 234
  Susan Welden, 234
  Thomas K., 169
  Thomas W., 126
  Thomas, Col., 121
  William, Hon., 90
Grayson
  Alexander, 73
  Capt., 250
  J.B., Lt., 199
  Letitia Breckenridge Porter, 199
  William, 16
  William Henry, 250
graziers, 259
Great Britain (see England), 68
Greatrake
  Eloisa, 72
  Lawrence, 72
Greece, 125, 144
Green
  Catharine Ann, 223
  Charles, 162
  Gardiner, 248
  John, 23, 70
  Nathan, 149
  Rev., 100
  Sarah, 12
  William, 213
Green Castle, 12
Green Valley, Va., 227
Greene
  George Washington, 142
Greenland, 51
Greenleaf's Point, 28
Greenlief
  Joseph, 22
Greensboro, Ga., 140
Greentree
  Matthew, 137
  Rev., 25, 36, 42
Greenwell
  Joseph W., 90
Greer
  Eliza Ingham, 225
  James, 255
  Mary Ann, 255
  William, 225
Gresham
  Sterling, 46
Greuhm
  Baroness, 86
Grey
  H.H., xi
  Vincent, 214
Grier
  Ellenor, 226
  Frances Jane, 226
Griffin
  Ellen, 77
  Peter, 71
Griffith
  David, Capt., 118
  Elizabeth, 90
  Lyde, Col., 90
  Rebecca, 118
  Rev., 45
  Thomas, 90, 123
Grim
  Margaret Alcinda, 220
Grimes
  Joseph, 166
Griswold
  A.V., Rev., 120
  Ann D'Wolf, 224
  Bishop, 224
  George, Rev., 120
grocers, 47
Grosvenor
  Mary Jane, 30
  Thomas P., 30, 42
  Thomas P., Hon., 25
Groves
  Jane, 242, 259
  Rachel, 12
Grubb
  John B., 258
  Samuel S., 164
Gruber
  John, 127
Grundick
  Rev., 139
Grymes
  Benjamin, 184
  Louisa Jane, 184
  Wyndham, 5
Guatemala, 81
Guest
  Elizabeth E., 203
  Job, xi
  Job, Rev., 203
  Rev., 85, 86, 89, 92
  Robert, 105
  Sarah E., 105

Guilford, 266
Gulick
  John, 25
Gunnell
  James S., Dr., 89
Gurley
  Felicia L.B., 116
  H.H., Hon., 128, 137
  Lucy, 137
  Miss, 128
  R.R., Rev., 116
Gustine
  Anne Taylor Green, 34
  Dr , 34, 41

H
Hackett
  Eliza, 146
Hackley
  Harriet, 221
Hadley, Mass., 147
Hagan
  Francis, 174
Hager
  Christopher, 264
Hagerstown, Md., 7, 27, 28, 58, 74, 108, 111, 139, 146, 150, 161, 192, 211, 216, 233, 247, 253, 256
Hagerty
  Rev., 41
hair dressers, 39, 191
Haislip
  Elizabeth Jane, 162
Hales
  Charles, Col., 161
  Jemima, 161
  Mary, 94
Halifax C H , Va., 27
Halifax Co., N.C , 208
Halifax Co., Va., 180
Halifax, N.S., 93
Hall
  Christopher, 105
  E , Rev , 58
  Elijah, Hon., 154
  Elizabeth B., Mrs., 26
  James, Hon., 233
  John, Hon., 253
  Mary G., 166
  Mary P., 233
  Peter, 166

Susan, 45
William J., 166
Haller
  Catherine, 52
Halley
  Esther, 200
Halliday
  Margaret, 156
  Robert, 156
Haman
  John, 7
Hamely
  James, 237
Hamersley
  Thomas S , Lt., 168
Hamilton
  Alexander, Gen., 9
  Harriet S., 217
  James, 44, 126
  John, 42
  Mary E.F., 235
  Miss, 101
  Paul, Hon., 35
  Rev., 79, 262
  Samuel S., 214
  William, xii
  William, Col., 235
  Wm , Rev , 79
Hamilton Co., Ohio, 200
Hamiltonian system, 126
Hamme
  Frederick, 8
Hammer
  John Godfrey, 101
Hammett
  J., 130
Hammond
  Camilla A., 170
  Denton, 170
Hampshire Co., Va., 1
Hampton, Va., 18, 45, 71, 106
Hamtramck
  John F., Col., 5
Hancock Co , Ga , 189
Hancock, Md., 97
Hancock, Ver., 58
Handy
  James H , 228
Hanna
  Elizabeth, 219
Hannan
  Walter H., 234
Hannan's Town, Jam , 37

Hanover, 89
Hanover Co., Va., 144, 165
Hansford
  Cary H., Lt., 166
Hanson
  Alexander C , 30
  Alexander Contee, 42
  Charles W., 25
  Elizabeth B., 5
  Isaac K , 28
  James M., xii
  Mary J , 25
  Rev., 217, 222, 232, 246, 255, 256
  Samuel, 174
  Samuel, Col., 174
  Samuel, Maj., 5
Harbaugh
  Eliza Catherine, 191
  Joseph, 191
Harden
  Rachel, 124
  Samuel, 124
Harding
  Caroline F , 31
  Edward, 31
  Philip, 20
Hardy
  William, 176
Harford
  William Henry, Lt., 189
Harford Co., Md , 49, 115, 141, 190
Harford twp., Ohio, 229
Harkness
  Samuel, 148
Harman
  Abigail, 60
  Jacob, 60
Harmon
  William True, 176
Harper
  James, 206
  John, 229
  Mary, 229
  Robert Goodloe, 1
Harper's Ferry, Va., 63, 167
Harpeth, Tenn., 112
Harreston
  Robert, 255
Harriman
  Orlando, 111
  Rebecca, 111

Harris
  E., Mrs., 76
  Gwinn, 257
  John B., 112
  Joseph, 37
  Sally Lee, 205
  Samuel, 67
  Samuel B., 205
Harrisburg, Pa , 111, 190,
  227, 230, 233
Harrison
  Ann, 11
  Catherine C., 194
  Elias, xii
  Elias, Rev., 253
  F., 108
  Gessner, Dr , 174
  Hall, 162
  James, 7
  Jane R., 127
  John Cleves Symmes, 170
  Jonathan, 127
  Louisa, 63
  Mary E., 148
  Rev., 74
  Richard, 11, 63, 128
  Samuel, 171
  William H., Gen., 170
Harrison & Sterett, 162
Harrott
  Elias, 89
  Ellen, 89
Harry
  John, 74
Harrystown, Md., 139
Hart
  Dennis, 17
  Hart, Col., 235
  Mary A., 261
  Susanna, 235
Hartford, Conn., 15, 47, 54, 187
Hartland, Ver., 239
Hartwell
  Anna W , 118
Harwood
  James, 252
  Sarah, 252
  Susan Ann, 89
Hasell
  Wm. S., 29
Haskins
  John B., 48, 52

Haslet
  Andrew, 44
Hatch
  Rev , 210, 254
Hathwell
  Matilda, 78
  Mr., 78
  hatters, 169
Hatton
  Henry, 242
  John, 106
  Martha, 106
  Polly, 242
Havana, 108, 140
Havana, Cuba, 39, 214
Haven
  Joshua, 163
Haverhill, Mass., 59, 70, 201
Haw
  Elizabeth Ann, 250
  Henry, Dr., 124
  John S., 159, 234, 250
  Mary Ann, 159
Hawkins
  Charles, 208
  Edward, 193
  Philemon, Col., 253
  Samuel, 141
Hawley
  Rev., 43, 71, 76, 79, 80,
    84, 85, 92, 167, 182,
    205, 221, 222, 234,
    242, 260, 264
  William H., xii
  Wm., Rev., 223
Hay
  Charles, 78
  George, 104
  George, Hon., 165
  Hortensia Monroe, 104
Hayden
  Eliza L., 134
  H H., Dr., 134
Hayes
  Lionel Augusta, 118
Hayley
  William, 50
Hayman
  Caspar, Capt., 201
  Casper, Capt , 188
  Elizabeth, 201
  James R., 218
  William, 188
  Wm , Jr., 61

Hayne
  Col , 138
  Paul H., 202
Haynie
  Charlotte, 24
Hayti, 44
Hayward
  Dr., 157
Haywood
  Sarah Ann, 61
Hazel
  Henry, 71
  Margaret, 16
Hazerentine
  John, 37
Heabner
  Mr., 50
Heard
  Edward I., 164
  Mary G., 164
Heaton
  Catharine Van
    Rencelear, 88
Hedges
  Mary, 61
  Nicholas, 61
Hein
  Samuel, 267
Heiskell
  John, Capt , 4
Helfenstein
  Jonathan, Rev., 118
Hellen
  Walter, 29
Helm
  Jane Matilda, 246
  Joseph, 232, 246
  Meredith, Dr., 89
  Sophia Western, 28
  Thomas, 28
Helmuth
  J.C.H , Rev., 85
Hemphill
  Andrew, Rev., xii, 36
Henderson
  Alexander, 31
  Archibald, Col., 74
  Elizabeth Jane, 138
  James, 138
  John, 12
  Mary, 31
  Tarlton T., 82
Heneman
  Mary Ann, 144

Heney
  Thomas, 107
Henry
  Dorothea, 180
  Patrick, 180
  Rev., 251
Henshaw
  Daniel, 240
  Margaret S , 240
  Rev., 60, 85, 257
Henson
  Sarah C., 73
  Thomas, 215
Hepburn
  Ann Leeke, 251
  James, 66
  Jeremiah, 223
  John M., 251
Herbert
  John C., Hon., 242
  Lucinda, 154
  Maurice, 158
  Sarah Carlyle, 242
  Thomas, 158
  Thomas S., M.D., 170
Herkimer Co., N.Y , 239
Hernsmon
  Matthias A., 1
Heron
  James, 115
Herrick
  Claudius, Rev , 188
  E., Hon., 227
Hersant
  Michel Esperance, 69
Hertford, N.C , 215
Hesselius
  John, 154
  Rachel B , 154
Heughes
  Anne, 11
  Arie Ann, 40
Hevner
  Frederick, 43
Hewes
  Ann, 224
  Samuel, 224
Hewitt
  Catherine Edmonds, 192
  Margaret Boyd, 192
  Robert, 210
  Thomas W., 192
Heyer
  Ann Duryea, 150

Garrett, 35
Isaac, 150
Hickey
  James, 157
  Mary Ann, 157
Hicks
  Elias, 142
Hide
  William, 56
Higbee
  E.Y., Rev., 264
Higgins
  James B., 155
  James, Rev., 26
  Lauraner, 155
Higginson
  Elizabeth S., 196
  Stephen, 196
Higham, Mass., 17
Higinbotham
  Miss, 5
Hildt
  George, Rev., xii, 224, 256
  Rev., 234, 248, 250
Hill
  Aaron, Hon., 172
  C , 261
  C., Mr., 261
  Calvin, 193
  Clement B., 172
  Gibson F , 122
  Jane, 221
  Lawrence, 221
  Russel, 103
  William, 184
Hilleary
  Mary Ellen, 260
Hillhouse
  James, Hon., 249
Hills
  Elizabeth B., 209
  Josiah B., 225
  Prudence, 120
  Samuel, 120
Hillsanders
  Ann, 18
Hillsborough, Va., 156
Hilton
  Mary Ann, 200
  Samuel, Capt., 141
Hindman
  James, Col., 141

Hines
  John, 28
Hingston
  Nicholas, 158
Hinkle
  Juliana, 22
  Samuel, 22
Hipkins
  Lewis, Col., 221
  Mary Augusta, 221
Hirschel
  Solomon, Rev., 161
Hispaniola, 196
Hoban
  Ann R., 183
  Edward, 248
  James, Capt., 151, 183, 210, 216
  James, Jr., 209
  Martha, 151
Hobkirk-hill, 138
Hoboken, N J , 9
Hobson
  George, 120
Hoburg
  Richard, 19
Hodges
  B.M , 225
  Cornelia L , 263
  John, 263
  Mary Clare Carroll, 225
  Thomas C , 55
  William, Rev., 263
Hodgkin
  Ann M., 127
  Daniel, 51
Hodgkinson
  Anthony, Capt , 211
  Phoebe, 211
Hodson
  Thomas J., 153
Hoff
  John F., xii
Hoffman
  John, Rev., 118
  Mr. & Mrs , 14
  Peter, 114
  Sarah, 14
Hogan
  Michael, 256
Holbrook
  John, Maj , 239
  P.M., 150

Holleywood
　Mary Jane, 171
Holliday
　Mary L , 14
Hollingsworth
　Samuel, 150
Hollins
　J. Smith, 245
　Jane S , 245
　John, 145
Hollis
　Catherine Ann, 190
Hollman
　Mr., 44
Holme's Hole, Me , 115
Holmead
　Emily V., 206
　Jane Matilda, 232
　John, 213
　John B , 167
　John, Capt., 181, 213, 232
　Susan Eliza, 181
Holmes
　Gabriel, Gen., 121
　Henry, Rev , 108
Holt
　Henry, 195
　John E , 239
　Mary C.E , 195
　William, 70
　William C., Col , 243
Holtzman
　Harriet, 83
　Isabella, 27
　John, 35, 83, 263
　Mary, 44
　Samuel, 237
　Sarah Teresa, 237
　Thomas, 82
　William, 27
Holy Trinity Catholic Church, xii
Homans
　Benjamin, 76, 165
　Benjamin F , 76
　Isaac Smith, 152
　James T., Lt , 115
　John, 165
Homer
　William H., Lt., 125
Homer, N.Y , 53
Hone
　John, 221

Honeywell
　Stephen, 247
Hood
　Jane, 219
　William, 219
Hooe
　Bernard, Sr., 29
　E.T., Mrs., 200
　Eliza Thacker, 195
　Howison, 189
　James H., 195, 200, 244
　Junia Survilla, 244
　Lucy Eugenia, 244
　Margaret, 189
　Mary S.C , 29
　Robert H., 189
Hoover
　Andrew, 16
　Clarissa, 146
　Michael, 146, 185
Hopgood
　Mr., 39
Hopkins
　Bazil B., 199
　David, 1
　John, 2
　Molly, 2
　Thomas S., 205
Hopkinson
　Francis, 73, 161
　Francis, Hon., 73
　Laura, 161
Hord
　Peter, 120
Horncastle, Eng., 259
Horner
　Inman, 31
　Lydia, 26
　Phebe, 122
Horrell
　Thomas, Rev., 45
horsemen, 2
Hoskins
　Melinda, 36
　Rev., 18
Hoskinson
　Rev , 67
Hosman
　Elijah, 230
Hot Springs, Va., 233
Hotchkiss
　Henry N., Rev., 116
　Rev., 93
house numbering system, ix

house keepers, 47, 205
Houx
　Catherine, 236
　Rebecca, 178
Hovey
　Stephen S., 53
How
　Robert F., 188
Howard
　Elisha, 45
　George, 192
　Henry, 32
　John Eager, Col , 102
　Joseph, 56
　Rebecca A., 259
　Thomas, 245
　Thomas Gassaway, 103
Howard Co , Mo , 82
Howe
　John, 54
　Mary, 104
Howel
　Richard, 4
Howell
　Honoria, 106
　William, 106
Howland
　Gardiner G., 104
Hubble
　William, 118
Hubhall
　Eliza, 165
Hudson
　Martha F., 248
Hudson River, 35
Hudson Square, 102
Huehler
　Henry, 227
Huggins
　Mr., 39
Hughes
　Christopher, 239
　Hannah, 78
　Laura Sophia, 239
Hughs
　Walter, 86
Hugle
　George F., 138
Huissey
　Philip, 191
Hull
　John G., 145
　Oliver, 111
　Robert, 225

Hulse
  Isaac, 252
Hume
  Ebenezer J., 254
Humphrey
  Rev., 243
Humphreys
  Ann F., 133
  Correl, 153
  Joshua, 267
Hungerford
  Thomas B., Dr., 180
Hunt
  Allen, 93
  Jonathan, Hon., 224
  Thomas F., Capt, 125
Hunter
  Archibald, Capt., 65
  Elizabeth Wake, 146
  John H., Col, 147
  John W., Col., 146
  Narsworthy, Hon., 3
  Rev., 44
  Robert, 200
  Sarah, 101
  William, 248
  William W, Lt., 210
Hunterdon Co., N J, 197
Huntingfield, Md., 124
Huntt
  Henry, Dr., 125
Hurdle
  Lawrence, 244
  Levi, 152
  William, 92
  William H., 244
Hurley
  Barbara, 234
  Rev., 207
Hurlihy
  Maurice, 134
Hurry
  Margaretta, 208
  Samuel, 208
Hurst
  Elizabeth, 188
  Grace, 106
  John, 106
Husler
  Joseph, 58
Hussall
  Josephine, 192
Hutchins
  Charles, 165

Hutchinson
  John S, 99
  Rev. E., 189
  Samuel, 82
  Sarah, 89
Hutton
  Eliza Cathcart, 237
  Eliza W, 72
  James, 72, 237
Huygens
  Adelaide C.W., 157
  Chevalier, 157
Hyatt
  Ann, 60
  Samuel, 207
  Seth, Sr., 60
Hyde
  Anthony, 217
  Eliza, 44
  Ellinor, 92
  Rebecca, 110
  Thomas, 92, 110, 213
  Uriah Forrest, 259
Hyde Park, N.Y., 239
Hyer
  Harriet, 78

I

Illinois, 134, 164
Immohr
  Capt., 221
  Gezena, 221
Indian agents, 123, 169, 172
Indian Bureau, 214
Indian Key, 124
Indian traders, 227
Indiana, 93, 154, 179, 207
  Legislature, 264
Indians, 111, 119, 138, 192, 228
  Cherokee, 77, 169
  Choctaw, 103
  Wyandot, 99
Ingle
  Edward, 85, 159
Inglis
  Mary, 111
inn keepers, 231, 236
Innerarity
  John, 252
  Melania, 252
inspectors, 205
  flour, 212

instructors, 249
Iredell Co., N.C., 113, 145
Ireland, 21, 37, 52, 54, 82, 116, 135, 139, 143, 148, 153, 176, 177, 181, 210, 234, 237, 239
Irons
  Thomas, 126
Ironside
  George, 168
  Mary H, 168
Irvine
  Armstrong, 40
  Brig Gen., 40
Irving
  Leah, 154
  Levin, Dr., 154
  William F., 241
Irwin
  David, 117
  John, 59
Isaacs
  Ralph, 28
Island of Timos, 125
Isle of La Mott, Ver., 193
Isle of Wight Co, Va., 106
Italy, 51
Iverson
  Alfred, Col, 184

J

Jack
  John, 4
  Letitia, 4
Jackson
  Ann, 231
  Ann R., 118
  Catharine, 220
  Ebenezer, 262
  Elizabeth B., 208
  Elizabeth P, 146
  Ellen, 118
  Gen., 31
  Henry, 248
  J E, Rev., 183
  James J., Rev, 63
  Jane S., 82
  John, 179
  Joseph, 31, 187
  Mary C., 183
  Matthew, 215
  Michael, Gen., 262

Rev., 29, 104, 209
Spencer, 118
Thomas, Rev., 183
William B., 208
William M , xii
William, Rev., 134, 181
Jacob
　George P., Dr , 105
Jacobs
　George, 45
　Hannah, 170
　Maria Louisa, 48
　Mary, 137
　Mary E., 231
　Philip, 48
　Thomas E , 214
Jamaica, 1, 106, 202
James
　Daniel, 118
　J.W., Rev., 231
　John Dawson, 206
　John Waller, xii
　William, 247
Jamison
　C.C., 43
　Richard, 79
Janney
　Hannah Ann, 225
　John H., 171
　Joseph, 225
　Lewis, Rev., 257
　Phebe Ann, 228
　Samuel H., 177
　Thomas, 150
Janvier
　Thomas, 109
Jarboe
　Nelson, 164
Jardella
　Francisco, 177
Jarvis
　Leonard, Dr., 162
　Susan P., 162
Jefferson
　Benjamin, 198
　Elizabeth, 108
　Jane, 176
　John, 206
　Joseph, 94, 108
　Joseph, Sr., 176, 230
　Susan, 198
　Thomas, 27, 83, 86
　Thomas, Hon., 147

Jefferson Co., Va., 14, 22,
　151, 186, 203, 204,
　206, 238
Jefferson, Pa., 226
Jemeson
　Teresia C., 44
Jenifer
　Helen, 196
　W H., 123
　Walter H., 196, 216
Jenkins
　Alexander G., 137
　Benedict J , Capt., 257
　Caroline A , 250
　Courtney, 250
　Jemima, 232
　John J , 250
　Lydia R., 152
　Thornton A., 265
　Uriah, Capt., 152
　William V., 267
Jennings
　Hannah, 267
　Robert C., 105
　Robinsonova, 105
　Samuel K , Rev., 267
　Samuel X., Jr., 51
Jephson
　Maria Farquhar, 133
　Mr., 133
Jericho, L.I., 142
Jerusalem, Palestine, 175
Jessop
　William, Sr., 118
Jessup
　Eliza Hancock, 87
　Gen , 87
Jesup
　Elizabeth Croghan, 154
　Gen., 154
jewellers, 171
Jinkins
　Mary Josephine, 100
　William V , 100
Johns
　Aquila, 211
　Jane M , 217
　John, 63
　John Johnson, 63
　L.H., Mr., 81
　L.M., 217
　Mary P , 211
　Rev., 191, 203, 206,
　　217, 259

Johnson
　Alexander M., 104
　Ann E.M., 43
　Dennis, Capt., 104
　Edward J., Lt., 114
　Elijah, 117
　Gov., 153
　Hannah, 233
　Henry, Hon., 120, 144
　Jane, 63
　John, 69, 219, 233
　Jonathan, 63
　Levi B., 183
　Lewis, 30
　Margaret Ann Hand, 219
　Margaret B., 185
　Noble, 148
　Rev., 76, 102, 239, 244
　Richard, 251
　Roger, Maj., 180
　Sally, 69
　Thomas, 13
　William, 148
　William P.C , 181
Johnson Co., N D., 132
Johnston
　Charles, 227, 252
　Christopher, 226
　James, 173
　John G., 226
　John M., 229
　John, Dr., 240
　Josiah S., Hon., 240
　Robert, Gen., 12
　William, Sir, 138
Johnstown, N.Y., 63, 187
Joncherez
　Estelle M., 229
Jones
　Abby P., 62
　Ann, 59
　Catharine, 147
　Charity Margaretta, 136
　Edward, 2, 3, 5, 117,
　　123, 147
　Elizabeth, 7
　Evan D., 123
　Francis Burdett, 169
　George Bates, 265
　Harriet R., 161
　Horatio, 136
　Isaac, 132
　Jacob, Com., 182
　James, 201

John Coffin, 124
John Coffin, Hon., 127
Joseph H., xii
Maria, 3
Maria H., 28
Matilda, 62
Mordecai Clinton, 29
Mrs., 2, 3
Paul, 154
Rev., 102, 133, 190
Richard, 113
Richard A., Lt., 182
Rosina, 266
Samuel, 62, 143, 185
Samuel, Jr., 105
Sarah, 105
Walter, Gen., 266
William, 57, 199, 265
Jordan
  Mrs., 52
Joyce
  Ann, Mrs., 126
Judd
  Rev., 12
  William H., Rev., 114
judges, 31, 35, 48, 104, 105, 111, 116, 122, 123, 125, 128-130, 132, 133, 136, 137, 140, 144, 146, 147, 159, 165, 167, 178, 180, 181, 185, 200, 203, 207, 225, 227, 247, 249, 255, 264, 267
  Circuit Court, 183
  county court, 207
  Orphans Court, 214
  probate court, 207
  supreme court, 253
Judson
  Ann Hazeltine, 225
  E., Dr., 225, 244
  Ellen, 244
Jullien
  Honore, 175
jurists, 102
justices, 22
justices of the peace, 263

K

Kaldenbach
  Catharine, 263

Kaldenback
  C., Miss, 8
Kanawha Co., Va., 197
Kankey
  Araminta Maria, 206
  Rebecca Montgomery, 147
  Zebulon, Rev., 147
Kay
  Elizabeth, 115
  James, 115
Kean
  Gilbert D., 161
  Stephen R., 237
Kearnes
  Francis, 4
Kearney
  James, Col., 169
  Stephen N., Maj., 165
Keefe
  Elizabeth, 201
Keele
  Henry, Capt., 81
Keeler
  Noah B., 75
Keep
  Samuel, 159
Keerl
  Nancy, 126
Keffer
  Caroline E., 134
Keightly
  Archibald, 162
  Isabella, 162
Keith
  Marietta, 148
  Reuel, xii
  Reuel, Rev., 148, 196, 209
  Rev., 98, 181, 190
Kellenberger
  Francis J., 260
Kellenburger
  George A., 267
Kellog
  Allen, 140
Kelly
  Elizabeth, 193
  John, 166
  Thomas, 28
Kemp
  Bishop, 252
  Rev., 25, 37

Kemper
  Ann, 224
  Jackson, Rev., 224
  Peter, 108
Kendal
  Caroline J., 54
Kenne
  Lucretia, 132
Kennedy
  Ann Catharine, 155
  Henry W., Capt., 121
  James A., 79
  Julia E., 25
  Robert, 155
  Susan, 253
  William L., 123
Kennon
  Beverly, Capt., 104
  William H., Lt., 242
Kent
  Daniel, 115, 136
  Joseph, Hon., 263
Kent Co., Md., 23, 31, 93, 124, 161
Kentucky, 69, 129, 135, 167, 174, 240
Kenyon College, 120, 131, 135
Keplinger
  William, 104
Keppler
  Samuel, Rev., 157, 178, 192
Kerr
  Alexander, 246
  Sarah, 182
  William, Jr., 182
Key
  Elizabeth, 120
  Francis S., 71
  Loisa E., 153
  Maria Lloyd, 71
  Mary Brent, 175
  Philip B., 144, 153, 175
  Philip Barton, 120
Key West, Fla., 130, 150
Kidder
  Matilda H., 197
  Samuel, Dr., 197
Kidwell
  James, 72
  John H., 132
  Mary, 133

Kielly
  Rev., 89
Kilbourn
  James E., 107
Kincaid
  George, 203
  James, 97
King
  Ann, 41
  Charles, 38, 115, 213
  Comfort, 213
  Cyrus, 42
  Ezekial, 125
  George, 38, 115
  George, Sr., 55
  Hannah, 168
  Henry, 94
  Isabella, 34, 222
  James D , 149
  John, 102, 255
  John A., 149
  John H., 89
  John W., 169
  Jonas, Rev., 125
  Joseph, 26
  Margaretta, 57
  Mark, 196
  Mary, 26
  Nicholas, 57
  Rebecca, 149
  Robert, 178
  Rufus, Hon., 100
  Samuel Davidson, 236
  Sarah M., 115
  William, 222
  William, Jr., 34
  Wm., 222
King & Queen Co., Va , 116, 138
King Charles, of France, 95
King George Co., Va., 79, 138, 184, 194, 251
King Louis XVI, 95
King Louis XVIII, 95
King of Prussia, 75
King William Co., Va., 104, 218
Kingston, Jam., 37
Kingston, N J , 153
Kinsey
  Hon., 6
  Mary, 6
Kirby
  Edmond, 84

Kirk
  Andrew M., 173
  John A., 260
  M.T., 97
  Mary, 97
Kitchell
  John, 109
Kittera
  John Wilkes, 1
Kittery, Me., 103
Klapp
  Harvey, Dr., 183
Knight
  John L., 146
knights, 155
Knoblock
  John, 200
Knowle
  Catharine, 7
Knowles
  Catherine, 184
  George B., 155
  Henry, 32, 72
  Henry, Sr., 184
  John, 45, 72
  Sarah, 32
  Thomas, 67
  William, 42, 238
Knowlton
  John S C., 118
Knox
  Benjamin L., 130
  Samuel, Rev., 232
  William A., 199
Konkle
  Peter C., 72
Koontz
  Margaret, 136
Korn
  John, 212
  Rosanna, 212
Krofft
  Lawrence, 197
Krumbhaar
  Lewis, Jr., 246
Kuhn
  Caroline Catharine, 173
  Joseph L., Capt , 173
Kurtz
  Daniel, 22
  Elizabeth, 15
  John, 187
  Rev , 59, 60, 62, 89
  Sarah, 35

Thomas, 93

L

La Fourche, La., 144
Labille
  Lewis C , 72
  Louis, 196
  Stephen, 196
LaBruce
  Mary Ann, 127
Lacey
  Charles, 81
Lackland
  James, 35, 45
  Jane Lynn, 45
  Rosetta L., 35
LaCroix
  Pierre, 202
Lacy
  John, 42
Ladd
  Eliza S., 259
  John H., 259
Ladico
  George T., 164
  Maria Rusi, 164
Lafayette
  Marquis de, 174, 222
Lafayette Co., Mo., 94, 241
Laird
  Helen, 226
  John, 10, 64, 90
  Mary, 10
  Rev., 226, 246
  William, 64, 90, 226
Lake Erie, 257
Lake George, 119
Lamar
  Elizabeth, 78
  William, Col., 265
Lamb
  Rebecca, 41
  Robert, 24
  William, 109
Lambe
  Elizabeth Honoria Francis, 205
  Serg , 205
Lambert
  David, 43
  E.S , Maj , 246
  Eliza, 92
  Mary, 96

Morris, 92, 96
Lambrecht
  Reinard, 187
Lamden
  Thomas S., 59
Lammond
  Alexander, 168
Lamson
  Henry, 70
Lancaster
  Adeline G., 139
  Charles A., 244
  Stephen, 45
Lancaster and Philadelphia turnpike, 101
Lancaster Co., Pa., 2, 4, 111, 113
Lancaster, Eng , 68
Lancaster, Pa., 1, 31, 57, 158, 206
Landreth
  John, 71, 151
  Sarah E., 71
Lane
  Hardage, 5
  Jane, 218
  Joanna, 61
  Samuel, 60, 61
Lang
  Mary, 250
Langley
  Hezekiah, 218
Langton, Eng., 259
Languedoc, Fra., 205
Lanham
  Aquilla, 114
  Charles E , 75
  Charlotte Arthella, 237
  Elisha, 59, 75
  Eliza, 114
  George H , 237
  Marcia M., 114
  Margaret, 28
Lanphier
  John, 174
  William, Jr., 246
Lansdal
  Christopher, 171
Lansdale
  John, 211
Larkin
  Jacob, Rev., 104
  Joshua W., 121
  Lionel James, 41

Rev., 153
  Samuel, 121
Larner
  Eliza, Mrs., 133
Lathrop
  John, Rev , 31
Latimer
  Marcus, 183
  Rebecca, 84
  Samuel, 87
Latrobe
  B.H., Mr., 12
  J.B.H., Mr., 248
  Miss, 12
Laub
  Andrew M , 80
  Charles H., Dr., 251
  Elizabeth, 217
  John, 217, 233, 236, 258
  Matilda Sophia, 236
Laurenson
  Elizabeth, 120
  Philip, 120
Laurie
  Chanstaun H., 239
  J., Rev , 248
  James, Rev., xii, 11, 26, 103
  Rev., 59, 79, 159, 195, 248, 252
Laval
  Col., 20
  Jacint, Col., 63
Lavalette
  Gen., 94
Law
  John, 64
Lawless
  Luke Edward, 86
Lawrence
  James, 34
  John, 184
  Mary Elizabeth, 184
Lay
  Richard, Jr., 214
Layland
  Nancy, 17
Leach
  Nancy, 245
Leake
  Nathan, Jr., 227
Leakin
  Jesse, 39

Lear
  Benjamin Lincoln, 195, 238
Lebanon Springs, N Y , 62
Lebanon, Conn., 66, 179
Lebanon, Ohio, 104, 119
LeBaron
  Francis, Dr , 103
Lee
  Ann H., 107
  Ann Kinloch, 98
  Ann Matilda, 127
  Daniel, 74
  Francis L., 21
  Henry, Gen., 98, 107
  John H , Lt., 228
  Presha, 74
  Richard, 127
  Richard Henry, 192
  Robert E., 190
  Thomas, 169
  William, 170
  Wm , 14
Leekens
  Maria, 243
Leesburg, Va., 19, 36, 73, 104, 112, 214, 249, 251
Leitch
  John, 131
Lemmon
  George, Rev., 261
  Rev., 31
Lenly
  Fanny Lear, 264
  Jno. D , Comm., 264
Lenox
  Angelica, 69
  Julia, 159
  Peter, 245
  Peter, Capt , 159
Lenox, Mass., 207
Leonard
  Jacob, 123
  James T., Capt., 241
  Juliana W., 122
  Sophia E , 166
Lethaux
  Rev., 65
Levely
  H , 106
  William, 65
Levering
  Lydia Rebecca, 108

Peter, 108
Levy
   Rev., 260, 263, 264, 267
Lewis
   Andrew, 175
   Edward S , 117
   Edward Simmons, 30
   H.C., 65
   John Lawrence, Col , 247
   Joseph, 109
   Mary Ann, 109, 244
   William B., 244
Lexington, Kan , 178
Lexington, Ky., 20, 61, 128, 206, 235
Lexington, Mass., 222, 262
   battle of, 207, 222
Lexington, Mo., 94
Lexis
   Peter, 18
Lightfoot
   William B., 216
Limerick, Ire., 150
Limington, Me , 104
Lincoln
   Benjamin, Maj. Gen , 17
Lincoln Co , Me., 116
Lincolnshire, Eng , 215
Lindenberger
   Frederick, 226, 260
   John Davidge, 260
   Priscilla Dorsey, 226
Lindsay
   Margaret S., 247
   Maria, 247
   Mr., 134
   Thomas, 164
   William, 247
Lingan
   Gen., 35
   James, Gen , 227
   Janet, 227
   Sarah, 34
Linn
   James, 49
Linsay
   Ellen, 188
Linthicum
   Anna Elizabeth, 246
   George M., 246
   John, 247
   Otho M , 246
   Otho M., Dr , 73, 247

Linton
   John, 226
   Sarah, 154
Linvill
   James, 42
Lipscomb
   Ann, 84
   John, 218
   John T , 249
   Rev., 238
   Sarah, 185
   W.C., Rev., 222
   William C., 192
Lisbon, Port., 222
Lisle
   John M., 181
Lislet
   Louis Moreau, 247
Litchfield, Conn., 140, 194
Litle
   Richard H , 85
Littig
   Caleb B., 127
Little
   Ann, 214
   Annabella, 124
   Isabel M , 237
   John, 237
   John P , 167
   Peter, Col., 124, 140
   Rev , 73
   Robert, Rev., 74
Little Falls, D.C., 54
Littleton, Mass., 118
Litton
   Mary D., 70
Liverpool, Eng., 101, 144, 162, 247
Livingston, 62
   Chancellor, 143
   Edward S., 66
   Henry, Gen., 71
   John H , Rev., 84
Livingston, N.Y., 71
Lloyd
   Daniel, 178, 243
   Edward, Hon., 93
   John, 168, 234
   Richard B , 200
   Sarah S., 93
   Selina, 168
Lobin
   Mr., 216

Lochman
   Rev., 227
Locke
   Andrew, 101
   Prudence D., 126
Lodge
   Emily M , 42
Logan
   Rev., 38
Logan Co., Ohio, 139
Lomax
   Michael, 162
Lombard
   Achsah, 233
London, Eng , 33, 42, 52, 68, 81, 109, 110, 124, 142, 162, 190
Long
   Maj., 138
Longden
   John, 144
   Julia, 234
Longworth
   Mary, 158
   Nicholas, 158
Lord Cornwallis, 138
Lord Fairfax, 4
Lord Finlater, 48
Lord Stirling, 174
Lord Wellington, 37
Loring
   Israel, 3
Lorman
   Mary, 135
   William, 135
Loudoun Co., Va., 4, 12, 20, 31, 40, 61, 67, 72, 73, 76, 78, 82, 84, 96, 104, 110, 132, 142, 156, 164, 165, 168, 178, 187, 205
Louisburg, 119
Louisiana, 120, 145, 169
Louisville, Ky , 65, 117, 128, 196, 205, 241, 243, 248
Love
   Ann, 2
   Charles, 11
   Marshall, Lt , 229
   Nancy, 11
   William G , 184
Lovell
   Dorcas L , Mrs., 125

Low
  Samuel, Rev., 48, 51
Lowe
  John F.M , 166
Lowndes
  Benjamin, 12, 24, 208
  Charles, Lt., 93
  Dorotha, 24
  Francis, 27
  Francis, Sr., 105
  Jane, 105
  Rebecca, 103
  William, 68
  William, Hon., 103
Lowrie
  Amelia, 241
  Walter, 241
Lowry
  Mary, 229
  William, 229
Lucas
  Fielding, 126
  J.F.M., Rev., 261
  James, xii
  Rev., 70, 179, 216, 258, 262
  Sarah W., 126
Luckett
  Catharine Ann, 123
  Fielder, Capt., 14, 244
  Ignatius, Capt., 123
  Martha, 186
  Mary Elizabeth, 244
Ludden
  Lemuel, 186
Ludlow
  Israel L., 155
Lufborough
  David, 75
  J H , Dr., 186
  Nathan, 212
Lumpkins
  Moore, 132
Lumsdon
  William O., Rev., 123, 129, 246
Lusby
  James, 262
Luttrell
  Col., 53
Lutz
  John, 80
  Mary Ann, 80
Lycoming Co., Pa , 149

Lyle
  Henrietta, 245
  John M., 245
Lyles
  Col., 35
  Sidney, 35
Lymington, Md., 119
Lynch
  Ann, 123
Lynchburg, Va , 249
Lyndall
  Sarah Rowen, 111
Lyndeborough, N H , 149
Lyne
  Lavinia, 248
Lynn
  Nancy, 133
  William, 217
Lynn, Mass , 216
Lyon
  Mary, 22
  Stephen, 41
  Teresa, Mrs., 17
Lyons
  Evan, 209
  James, Dr., 144
  John, 222
  Mary, 222
Lyons, France, 175
Lytle
  William, Gen., 182

M' (also see Mc)
M'Arthur
  Duncan, Gen., 151
  Effe, 151
M'Candless' tavern, 147
M'Cann
  Mary Ann, 124
M'Caskey
  Hugh, 113
M'Ceney
  Eliza, 243
  Joseph, 243
M'Clean
  John, Hon., 100
M'Cleary
  William, Lt., 1
M'Cleish
  James, 68
M'Clure
  Francis, 10

M'Connell
  Mary, 60
M'Cord's Ferry, 138
M'Corkle
  Joseph P , 157
  Maria, 157
M'Cormack
  Rev , 1
M'Cormick
  Rev., 9, 10, 12, 32, 35, 36, 40, 42, 52, 101, 227
M'Donald
  John, 10
M'Duell
  Ann Lydia, 227
M'Elroy
  Joseph, Rev., 66
  Rev., 52, 70
M'Fadon
  John, 126
  Margaret, 126
M'Fee
  Mrs., 11
M'Ivaine
  Rev., 70
M'Kelden
  Andrew, 38
M'Kenny
  Thomas L., 57
M'Kenzie
  James, 118
M'Kim
  Mary, 42
M'Lean
  Ann Eliza, 41
  Arabella E , 100
  John, 41, 129
  John, Hon , 157
  Sarah Ann, 157
  William Monroe, 129
M'Leod
  Matthew, 97
M'Mahon
  Sarah, 14
  William, 14
M'Mechen
  John, Hon., 147
  Judge, 105
M'Phail
  Anna, 106
  John, 106
M'Pherson
  Catharine C., 256

Josias H., Dr., 5
William S., Dr., 256
M'Rea
   Ann, 44
M'Sheery
   Dr., 41
M'Vean
   John, 187

Mc (also see M')
McCall
   Richard, 198
   William C , Dr., 201
McCann
   James, xii
   James, Rev., 77, 80, 82, 84
McClean
   Charles, M.D , 222
McCleland
   George, 109
   Nancy, 109
McClellan
   John, Lt , 241
McClelland
   Margaret, 158
McCloskey
   Michael, 74
McConnico
   Andrew J , Col., 172
McCorkle
   Amie Houston, 247
   Joseph P., 247
McCormick
   Alexander, xii
   Province, 209
   Rev., 30, 46, 65, 71, 139, 213, 227
McCoy
   Dewann B., 251
   Josiah Daniel, 194
McCubbin
   Edward, 180, 198
   Ellen, 154
   Margaret, 180
McCutchen
   Jacobina, 166
   Margaret A., 239
McCutcheon
   Elizabeth, 90
McDenick
   Mary Ann, 141

McDonald
   Alexander, 202
   Ann, 244
   Elizabeth, 202
   John, 244
   John G., 229
   Rev , 240
   Richmond, 229
   W.K., 167
McDougall
   Elizabeth, 246
McDuffie
   George, Hon., 165
   Mary Rebecca, 165
McElroy
   John, Rev., xii, 47, 48, 57
McFachran
   Dougald, 191
McGauley
   Charles Stewart, Capt., 205
McGee
   Mary Ann, 104
McGehee
   George W., 123
McGlassin
   George, Maj., 62
McGregory
   William, 181
McGuire
   E.C., Rev., 209
   Edward C., Rev., 126, 209
   James, Capt , 204
   Lucy, 204
McIlvaine
   Charles P., Rev., xii, 54, 57, 61, 65, 67, 69, 74, 76, 78, 83
McIntire
   Margaret Ann, 168
   Nancy, 140
   Rufus, Hon., 140
   Samuel, 99
McIntosh
   Alexander, 231
   Echie, 143
McKann
   Rev , 75
McKay
   Alexander D , Lt., 209
McKim
   Alexander, Hon , 214

McKinsty
   John, Col., 62
McKnew
   Zadok, 168
McKnight
   Ann P., 183
   Capt , 183
   George B., Dr., 117
McKown
   John, 188
McLanahan
   James J., 204
McLean
   Adeline S., 141
   Ann, 170
   Charles, M.D., 222
   Daniel, 188
   Hannah A., 188
   John, 141, 170
   John, Hon., 168
   Rev., 261
McLeish
   George, 220
   Martha, 220
McLellan
   William, Maj., 103
McLeod
   Ann Eliza, 228
   Daniel, 192
   John, 228
   Mary, 47
   Mary Ann, 192
   Matthew, 226
McNeill
   Francis A., Rev., 139
McPhearson
   Maria, 166
McPherson
   Margaret, 63
   Wm , Gen., 63
McRim
   Nathaniel, 59
McVaugh
   Townshend, 76
McVean
   James, Rev , xii, 261
   Jane, 261

MacArthur
   Thomas J , Col., 255
MacCubbin
   John S., 125
Macdaniel
   Ezekiel, 122

John, 213
Mary Ann, 122
Macdonald & Ridgely, 131
MacGill
   Juliet A.C., Mrs., 134
   Thomas, 134, 180
Machenheimer
   George L., Rev, 193, 198
Machin
   Thomas, 35
Mackall
   Anna Maria, 92
   Benjamin, 92
   Hellen M, 89
   Leonard, Capt., 89
   Rebecca (Bayly), 20
Mackenzie
   Ann, 226
   Colin, Dr., 226
   George B., Dr, 226
   James, Capt., 104
Mackey
   Adeline, 191
   Alexander, 26, 34
   Ann Jane, 145
   Martha M., 227
   Mary, 79
   Sarah, 26
   William, 79, 145, 227
   William, Jr., 87
Macomb
   Alexander, 176
   Alexander, Gen., 64
   Alexander, Maj. Gen., 97
   Catherine, 100
   Edwin, 188
   Maj Gen., 100, 176
   Mrs., 64
Macomber
   Robert P, Dr, 196
Macon
   Edgar, Col., 130
MacPherson
   Elizabeth, 207
   Gen, 207
Macrae
   John, 135
Macrea
   William, Col, 243
Mactier
   Alexander, 152
   Grace, 152

Maddox
   John H., 209
   Susan, 219
Madeira, 5, 112
Madison
   Ex-President, 130
Madison, C.H., Va., 251
Madrid, Spa., 194
Maffitt
   Ann B., 174
Magee
   John, Hon., 180
Magruder
   Alexander C., 24
   Ann E., 73
   Edward, 58
   Eliza Ann, 246
   Ellen, 183
   George A, Lt, 193
   George B., 73
   George, Col., 72
   Hezekiah, Dr., 142
   James, 246
   James A., 183
   James, Jr., 173
   Ninian, Dr., 69
   Rebecca B, 24
   Rebecca D., 58
   Robert B., 63
   Thomas, 160
   Zadoc, 210
Magruler
   John B., Lt., 186
Maguire
   Joseph, 29
Mahorney
   Thomas W., 179
Maine, 42, 130, 140
Major
   Ann Jane, 142
   John, 142
   John, Jr., 219
Malbro
   John, 94
   Susannah, 94
Malcolm
   James Peller, 27
Mallary
   Rollin C., Hon., 183
Malta, 108
maltsters, 237
Manahan
   Joseph, Capt, 201
Manchester, Eng., 112

Manchester, S.C., 165
Mann
   C., Rev., 201
   Charles, Rev., 183
   Elizabeth, 177
   James, Dr., 241
   Samuel, 177
Manners
   Thomas, 7
Manning
   Ann Priscilla, 249
   Elizabeth H., 97, 226
   Ignatius, Capt, 11
   Mary H., 96
   Mary T., 144
   Robert, 249
Mansfeld
   Jared, Col., 140
Mansion Hotel, 143
Marbury
   Eliza, 167
   John H., 173
   Leonard, Capt., 212
   Luke (C), 76
   Mary Ann, 36, 122
   Rev., 260, 263
   William, 122, 183
March
   John, 9
Marchant
   Jane E., 247
Marcilly
   Josephine, 70
Marden
   Nathaniel, 80
Marie, Can., 155
Marion
   Gen., 138
Maris
   George, 209
Mark
   John, 75
   Samuel, 205
Marker
   Kitty, 2
Markley
   Capt., 148
   Elizabeth, 148
   Sarah A., 214
   William, Capt., 214
Marks
   Maria Sophia, 52
Markward
   John B, 160

Sarah Ann, 237
Marlborough, Md., 117
Marron
   John, 218
   Rev., 142
Marseilles, Fra., 81, 107,
   141, 196
Marshall
   Charles, 25
   Jane, 25
   John, 95
   William, 35
   William Louis, Rev., 98
marshals, 1, 166, 182, 205
Marson
   Joseph Franklin, 252
   Moses, 252
Martin
   Ann G., 174
   Catharine, 146
   Daniel, Hon., 192
   David, 224
   Eliza, 20
   Honore, 20
   John W., 234
   Judge, 123
   Philip, 159
   Sarah S.P., 214
   William D., Hon., 133
Martinsburg, Va., 20, 135,
   137, 138, 140, 244
Maryland, 5, 33, 35, 42, 57,
   67, 82, 94, 95, 104,
   106, 112, 123, 133,
   156, 167, 178, 193,
   241, 257, 261, 263
   Executive Counsel, 257
   House of Delegates, 229
   Legislature, 161, 218
   Levy Court, 161
Maryland Savings Institute,
   247
Masi
   Seraphim, 90
Mason
   Alexander H., Dr., 201
   Ann, 110
   Ann Thornton, 114
   Armistead, 114
   Gen., 195
   George, 63, 266
   John, 43
   John Henry, 195
   John M., Rev., 131

John, Gen., 100, 266
John, Jr., 100, 195
Jonathan, Hon., 206
Louisa, 63
M A, Mrs., 27
Marie Louis, 243
Maynadier, 170
Milo, Maj., 243
Mr., 8
Mrs., 115
Murry, Lt., 264
Richard B., 114, 115
Sarah Maria, 100
Stephens T., Gen., 5
Virginia, 115, 266
Massachusetts, 22, 34, 68,
   113, 130, 148, 156,
   224, 262
   constitution of, 22
Massey
   Jane, Mrs., 225
Massi
   Francis, 265
   Sarah Ann, 229
Massie
   Henry, 130
   Mary L., 130
Matanzas, 156
Matheson
   Ellen, 146
Mathews
   Rev., 13, 29, 87, 228
Matlock
   Simeon, 15
Matthews
   Emily, 226
   H.C., 230
   Jacob, 83
   James, 167
   Mussendine, Maj., 145
   Rev., 21, 44, 69, 96,
   141, 170, 185, 188,
   209, 214, 223, 248
   Tobias, 18
   W., Rev., 133, 183
   William, xii, 230
   William, Col., 226
   William, Rev., 189
Mattingly
   M.S, Miss, 214
Mattoom
   Duodema, 54
Maul
   John Peter, 186

Maund
   John James, 4
Maupin
   Baptise, 16
Mauro
   Alexander, 105
   Eliza S., 219
   Jonathan, 105
   William H., 181, 219
Maury
   James, 144
   John W., 203
   Mrs., 144
   Richard B., 183
Maws
   Louisa, 5
Maxwell
   James, Capt., 135
   Jesse, 56
Mayer
   Catharine, 146
   Henry, 199
   J., Rev., 80
   Philip F, Rev., 78
Mayfield
   Benjamin, 69
Mayhew
   William H., 177
Maynadier
   Elizabeth, 217
   Henry, Col., 217
   William M., 143
   William, Lt, 122
Maynard
   Evelina, 183
Mayo
   Robert, Dr., 191
mayors, 136, 140, 199, 233
Maysville, Ky., 153, 192, 241
Meade
   Bishop, 255
   Rev., 243
   Richard W., 195
Meadville, Pa, 231
Mechlin
   William, 78
Mecklenburg C.H, Va., 8
Mecklenburg Co., Va., 145,
   189, 213
Medfield, Mass, 155
Medford, Mass., 116, 197
Mediterranean Sea, 18, 87,
   198

Meem
  Peter, 11
Meigs
  Josiah, 63
Meim
  Ann E., 85
Melcher
  Ambrose T., 183
Melville
  Thomas, Maj., 237
Mengus
  Ann Aspasia, 125
Mennis
  Calohill, 131
Mercer
  Ann Gordon, 224
  Charles Fenton, Hon , 208
  Gen., 224
Mercer Co., Ky , 167
Mercer, Me., 207
Merchant
  Margaret Ann, 200
merchants, 2, 3, 5, 7, 9, 10, 12, 14, 15, 18, 19, 28, 31, 35, 39, 42, 45, 47, 50, 54-56, 58, 59, 71, 78, 82, 83, 85, 87, 89, 90, 92, 103-107, 109-111, 120, 123-125, 129-131, 136, 139, 150-152, 160, 162, 163, 167, 172, 181, 183, 185, 186, 192, 193, 197, 199, 202, 204-206, 209, 212, 214, 220, 221, 228, 229, 241, 242, 247, 251, 253, 257, 258, 262
Meredith
  J., 104
  Louisa, 104
Merrick
  Samuel, 107
Merrill
  Benjamin, 207
messengers, 133, 186
Methuen, Mass., 113
Mexico, 100, 103, 208
Michal
  Seligman, 126
Middleborough, Mass., 48

Middleburg, Va., 20, 82, 153, 168, 174, 187, 194, 201, 204
Middlebury, Ver., 240
Middlemore
  W., 30
Middlesex, Eng., 12
Middlesex, Ver., 71
Middleton
  Daniel Wesley, 208
  Henry O., 20
Middleton, N Y , 41
Middletown, Conn., 262
Milburn
  Alice, 254
  George, 254
Miles
  George F., 249
Milford, 132
  James, 250
  Sarah Ann, 250
Milford, Md., 84
Mill Creek, S.C., 164
Millard
  Ann M , 182
  Edward, 83
  Joshua, 182, 225
  Robert F., 216
Milledgeville, Ga., 208
Miller
  Amanda Louisa, 207
  Ann, 213
  B.M., Rev., 263
  Benjamin M., 170
  Bernard J , Dr , 258
  Catharine, 92
  Daniel H., Hon., 184
  Eliza, 90, 159
  Frederick, Maj., 137
  Gen., 68
  John, 140
  John William, 70
  Joseph H., 228
  Lucius, 146
  Mary, 139
  Mary Ann, 140
  Mordecai, 220
  Peter, 90
  Sarah Ann, 170
  Thomas R , Maj., 146
  William, 207
Mills
  Margery, 206
  Peter, Capt , 167

  William, Capt., 206
Millville, N.J., 227
Milton
  James, 151
Milton, Mass., 217
Mincher
  Anne, 24
Minchin
  Harriet, 70
Minden
  battle of, 35
Mines
  J. Addison, Rev , 245
  John, xii
  John, Rev., 245
  Rev., 244
  Susan Shippen, 245
  T J Addison, Rev., 266
Minor
  Sarah A , 163
Mississippi, 180, 224
Mississippi Territory, 3
Missouri, 82, 165
Mitchel
  Ichabod, Capt., 113
  Matilda, 77
  Ruben, 93
  Ruth, 93
Mitchell
  Alexander C., 93
  Alexander, Dr , 10
  Benjamin, 224
  Elizabeth, 224
  Elizabeth H , 17
  J., Mr., 93
  James, Capt , 76
  John, 20, 127, 136
  John, Capt., 17
  Mary Ann, 7
  Mary C., 40
  Mary, Mrs., 20
  Matilda Jane, 127
  Thomas, 62, 132
Mix
  Charles E., 110
  E , 88
  Elijah, 85
  Maria Clarissa, 85
Mobile, Ala., 114
Moegan Indians, 61
Mogadore, 87
Mohalby
  Garafilia, 144

Molden
  Jane Eliza, 174
Molton
  John, 49
Monahan
  Charles T., 108
Monmouth Co., N.J., 152
Monmouth, N.J , 222
  battle of, 207, 222
Monroe
  James, 104, 165
  James, President, 89
  Joseph Jones, 82
  Mrs., 165
  President, 167
Monroe, Va , 33
Montague Square, 162
Montcalm
  Mr., 202
Montgomery
  Ellen D., 201
  James, 71
  James, Gen., 201
  Mr., 202
Montgomery C.H., Md., 63
Montgomery Co , Md., 2, 5,
  6, 12, 20, 21, 26, 28,
  31, 35, 45, 52, 60,
  64, 69, 70, 72, 74,
  75, 84, 87, 97, 99,
  102, 107, 110, 114,
  131, 135, 138, 149,
  158, 170, 173, 182,
  186, 210, 214, 234,
  238, 244, 246, 265
Montgomery Co , N Y , 187
Montgomery, Ala., 117
Montgomery, N Y , 65
Monticello, Ga , 191
Montoya
  J M., 103
Montpelier, Fra., 110
Moor
  David, 133
Moore
  Alexander, 264
  Cathrine, 164
  Elizabeth, 141, 182, 253
  Francis, Rev , 22
  James, 124
  Jane J., 264
  Jeremiah, xii
  Jeremiah, Rev , 6
  Jerome D , 208

John O., 164
Joshua John, 182
Margaret, 124, 129
Mary Mitchell, 187
Rev , 67
Thomas, 64
William S., 162
Moran
  Mary E., 255
  Samuel C , 255
Morgan
  Adelia Ann, 186
  Caroline, 186
  James, 186
  John, 148, 229
  Mary Ann, 148
  Mordecai M., 37
  Mr., 138
  William, 148
  William, Jr., 65
Morice
  Davis F., 124
Morin
  Magdaline, 155
Morris
  Rev , 253
  Robert, 129, 207
  Samuel, 149
  Valentine, 27
Morrison
  Eliza, 233
  James, 241
  James, Col., 69
  John, 30
  Mary, 111
  William S., 138
Morsell
  Betty H., 177
  James, 177
  James S., 183
  James S , Hon., 122
  Mary Ann, 183
Morton
  John, 215
  Margaret Isabella, 240
  William, 240
Moseley
  Arthur, 116
  Catherine B., 245
Mosher
  James, Jr., 89
  Jeremiah, 158
Moss
  James W., 241

Margaretta, 209
Obadiah, 246
Polly, 54
Samuel, 54
William, 209
Moulder
  Elizabeth U., 115
  J.N., 115
  John N., 92, 256
  Mary, 92
  Mary D., 256
Mount
  Sarah, 253
  Sarah Ann, 178
  Thomas, 253
Mount Holly, N.J., 151
Mount Hope, Conn., 22
Mount Pleasant, N Y , 88
Mount St. Mary's Seminary,
  107
Mount Terling, Ind., 59
Mount Vernon Tavern, 101
Mount Vernon, Ohio, 131
Mount Vesuvious, 51
Mount Zion, Ga., 189
Mountz
  Catherine, 16
  George, 19
  Jacob, 9
  John, Jr., 16
Moxley
  Martha Jane, 203
Moyers
  Charlotte, 61
Mughlenburg
  Frederick Augustus, 1
Muhollen
  M A., 28
Muir
  Alexander M., 231
  Elizabeth, 142
  James, Rev., xii, 26, 31,
    142
  John, 171
  Mary Louisa, 231
Mull
  Alexander M., Lt , 157
Munceytown, Ind , 264
Muncy twp., Pa., 149
Munday
  William, 131
Munden
  Richard, Sir, 205

Munroe
 Col., 119
 Frances W., 164
 Thomas, 164
Murat
 Joachim, 196
 Lucien, Prince, 196
Murdock
 William, 113
Murfreesborough, N.C., 39, 73, 147
Murphy
 Catherine, 53
 Lawrence, 143
Murray
 A., Com., 161
 Comm., 55
 Gen., 81
 Harriet, 255
 James, 12
 Katharine, 161
 Lemuel N., 104
 Patrick C., 225
 Stanislaus, 217, 255
 Thomas, Jr., 223
Muse
 Alexander A., 146
Mustin
 Thomas, 28
Myers
 Augusta, 91
 Barbara, 148
 Benjamin B., 249
 Charles, 221
 Charlotte, 79
 John, 79
 John, Capt., 172
 Michael, 85
 Moses, 91, 172

N

Naftel
 Mary, 50
Nagle
 Pierce, 108
Nairn
 Mary, 128
Nalley
 George, 258
Nally
 Eleanor, 169
 Mr., 91
Nanjemoy, Md., 168

Nansemond Co., Va., 173
Nantucket, 45, 71
Naples, 66, 196
Nash
 Mary M., 246
 Patrick F., 154
Nashville, Tenn., 6, 182, 254
Natchez, M.T., 44
Natchez, Miss., 248, 266
Natchitoches, 49, 123
Natchitoches, La., 203, 247
Navy Yard, 108, 260
 Brooklyn, N.Y., 107, 121
 Gosport, Va., 125, 129
 Pensacola, Fla., 208
 Washington, D.C., 70, 108, 135, 149, 163
Navy Yard Hill, 148, 165
Naylor
 Allison, 209
 Lettice M., 3
Neal
 Francis, Rev., 38
 Rev., 8, 23, 36
Neale
 Francis Ignatius, xii
 Francis, Rev., 17, 32
 Henry, 30
 James, Rev., 97, 226
 Leonard, Rev., 43
 Rev., 11, 41
Necker
 Mons, 9
Nelson
 Ephraim R., 198
 James, 54
 John, 38
 Lucy, 165
 Madison, 70
 Mary, 104
 Roger, 27
 Thomas, Gen., 165
 William, 129
Nestell
 Peter, Maj., 43
Netherlands, 157
Nevil
 Mary, 49
Neville
 Frederick A., Lt., 155
Nevins
 Rev., 228
New Berlin, N.Y., 113

New Brunswick, N.J., 84, 229
New England, 48, 208, 248, 263
New Hampshire, 22, 119, 157, 210
New Harmony, 93
New Harmony, Ind., 97
New Haven, Conn., 6, 58, 86, 106, 110, 140, 188, 230, 249
New Jersey, 27, 139, 164
New London, Conn., 114, 173
New Market, Md., 47
New Mills, N.J., 81
New Orleans, La., 39, 53, 54, 56, 61, 62, 75, 101, 113, 118, 161, 169, 197, 214, 242, 244, 249, 258-260
New Port, Ky., 237
New York, 3-5, 14, 18, 25, 28, 35, 37, 41, 45, 48, 52, 60, 62, 85, 86, 91, 100, 104, 105, 107-109, 111, 114-116, 119, 130, 131, 133, 138, 141-143, 146, 148-150, 152, 155, 157, 160, 167-169, 174-176, 179, 180, 194, 207, 215, 218, 221, 223, 225, 228-230, 233, 238, 241, 242, 247-249, 254, 255, 260, 261, 264, 265
 constitution of, 215
 Governor, 232
New York, N.Y., 12, 48, 103, 105, 112, 188, 208
Newburgh, 171
Newburyport, Mass., 41, 44, 75, 109, 118, 242, 260
Newcastle, Del., 109
Newcomer
 Christian, 216
Newell
 Mr., 131
 Thomas M., 152
Newell's Hotel, 131

307

Newport, R.I., 3, 22, 56, 129
Newport-Pagnel, Eng., 194
Newstead, 216
Newton
  Amelia F., 239
  James H., 47, 50
  John T., Capt., 239
  Mary A., 41
  Miss, 35
  Susan, 88
  Walter, 91
Newton, Mass., 259
Nicholas
  John S., Lt, 145
Nicholls
  I.S., 102
  Mary E, 230
  Sarah S., 102
  William S., 230
Nichols
  Samuel T., 84
Nicholson
  Com., 230
  Frances, 230
  Joseph Hopper, Hon, 42
  Leolin, 247
Niles
  Hezekiah, 198
  Nathaniel, 197
  Robert Duer, 198
Nimmo
  James, 248
Nivison
  John, 8
Nixdorff
  Julianna, 163
  Tobias, 163, 253
Noble
  James, Hon., 179
Nokes
  Thomas, 189
Noland
  D.P., 31
  Emily A., 168
  Lloyd, 20
Norfleet
  John P, 120
Norfolk Co., Mass, 132
Norfolk Co., Va., 74, 129
Norfolk, Eng., 265
Norfolk, Va, 8, 18, 38, 43, 45, 48, 51, 55, 63, 74, 81, 86-88, 91, 104, 105, 120, 122, 125, 128, 131, 147, 153, 162, 166, 172, 173, 175, 178, 179, 195, 210, 221, 228, 230, 231, 239-243, 245, 247, 248
Naval Hospital, 219
Norris
  George W., 245
  Margaret, 130
  Mary, 23
  Oliver, xii
  Rev., 28, 79
  Thomas, 118, 130
Norriss
  John, 149
North Bend, Ohio, 170
North Carolina, 8, 36, 42, 61, 121, 138, 142, 143, 183, 185, 189, 226
  constitution of, 253
North Kingstown, 54
North River, 207
Northampton Co., Va, 8, 105
Northamptonshire, Eng., 123
Northrop
  John P., 77
  Sally B, 77
Northumberland Co., Va., 230
Norton
  John T., 119
  Mary H, 119
Norwalk, Conn., 224
Norwich, Eng., 91
Nottingham twp, N.J., 188
Nottingham, Eng., 30
Nottingham, Md, 163
Nottoway C.H, Va., 88
Nourse
  John R., 171
  Michael, Col., 171
Nowlan
  Elizabeth, 65
Nowland
  John, 190
  William P, 23
Nuckolls
  W.T., Hon, 158
Nutt
  Elizabeth, 226
  Virginia, 250

William D, 250

O

O'Brien
  Eliza, Mrs., 47
  Mary, 158
  Mrs., 158
  Richard, 77
O'Conner
  Michael, 139
O'Donoghue
  T., Mr., 89
O'Meara
  Barry, 142
  Lee, Lady, 142
O'Neal
  Ann, 134, 189
  Mary, 72
O'Neale
  Georgiana Clinton, 107
  Sarah, 84
  William, 107
  Wm., 84
O'Reily
  Henry, 169
  Louisa, 169
O'Sullivan
  John, 208
Obregon
  V, Mr., 208
Occoquan, Va., 229
Offley
  John Holmes, 88
Offutt
  Lucy Beall, 262
  Zachariah M, 97
Ogden
  Jonathan, 248
  Julia Ann, 188
  Mrs., 141
Ogden, N Y, 109
Ogilvie
  James, 48
Ogle
  Benjamin, 260
  Horace, 198
  Louisa, 260
Oglethorpe
  Gen., 58
Ohio, 113, 119, 151, 152, 155, 220, 256
Ohio Co, Va., 107
Old Point Comfort, 81, 134

Oliver
  Elizabeth, 181
  John, 71
Oneida Co., N.Y., 110, 216
Ontario Co., N.Y., 43
Orange Co., N.Y., 41
Order of the Red Eagle, 75
Orme
  Eleanor, 254
  Elizabeth, 246, 267
  James, 3, 234
  Jeremiah, 92, 254
  Lucy Ann, 214
  Moses, 267
  Patrick, 170
  Rezin, 36
  Thomas, 35
  William C., 185
Orndorff
  Elizabeth, 89
Orr
  Isaac, Rev., 166, 197
  James, 37
  Mary, 166
Orwigsburg, Pa, 146
Osborn
  Sarah, 87
Osborne
  Charlotte, 8
Otis
  James, Hon., 21
  Samuel Allyne, Hon., 21
Otsego, N.Y., 207
Ott
  John, 36
  John, Dr., 97
  Mary C., 97
Ould
  Daniel, 229
  Henry, 52
  Robert, 229
Overn
  Margaret, 106
Owen
  Edward W., 170
  John, Rev, 261, 262
  Mary, 234
  Rev., 266
  Samuel, 216
Owens
  Charles, 147
  Isaac, Jr., 82, 233
  Mary Ann, 233
  Rev., 260

S.A W., 105
Singleton, 41
Owings
  Elizabeth H., 51
Oxford, Eng., 52
Oxford, N.Y, 61

P

P. Mauro & Son, 181
Pacific Ocean, 165
Packard
  Joseph, Rev., 266
Page
  Ann, 27
  Charles, 27
  Elizabeth, 235
  James, Dr., 219
Pageot
  Alphonso, 244
Paine
  Orris S., 185
  Robert Treat, Hon., 22
  Thomas, 77
Pairo
  Jane J., 167
  Thomas W., 167
Palfrey
  Rev., 192, 225, 255
Palmer
  Catherine, 143
  Edward, 143
  Henrietta, 193
  John, 193
  William, Dr, 186
Palmyra, N.Y., 23
Panet
  Bernard Claude, 254
Pannell
  George, 105
Paris, Fra., 50, 81, 126, 142, 183, 197
Paris, N.Y., 216
Parke
  Benjamin, 105
Parker
  Ann, 196
  Copeland, 173
  Joseph, Maj., 211
  Thomas, 224
  William H., 221
Parkman
  Rev., 188

Parnham
  Dr., 246
  George D., 246
  Susan A., 246
Parrott
  Jane, 170
Parsons
  Eliza, 150
  Harriet Josephine, 130
  Mary Elizabeth, 125
  Moses, 115
  Mrs., 47
  Solomon, 156
  Susannah, 221
  Theodore, 115
  William, 47, 150, 221
Parsonsfield, Me, 140
Paskin
  John, 76
Passage
  Adelaide, 134
  John, 134
Pasto, Colombia, 112
pastors, 116, 128, 140, 142, 143, 238
Paterson, N.J, 231
Pattengall
  Robert, 265
Patterson
  Charles Alexander, 195
  Charles W., 220
  Edgar, 2, 149, 195, 240, 255
  John B., 243, 255
  Joseph, 114
  Mary, 240
  William, 124, 213
Patterson's Creek, 1
Patton
  Ann Gordon, 224
  Catharine, 123
  James, 97, 123
  John B., 11
  Mary Ann S., 97
  Robert, 163, 224
Paxton
  James, 10
paymasters, 167
Payne
  Ann, 123, 129
  Jacob, 129
  James, 78
Peabody
  John, Gen, 75

Sophia, 75
Peale
　Ann C., 114
　James, 114, 189
Pearce
　Dutee J., Hon., 129
Pearse
　Sarah H., 157
Pearson
　Catharine W., 259
　George F., Lt., 118
　Joseph, 46, 50, 259
　Lawson, 135
Pease
　Frances, 251
Peaslee
　Daniel, Hon., 68
Pechin
　Catherine, 159
　Christiana, 38
　Julia, 85
　William, 38
　William, Col., 159
　Wm., Col., 85
Peck
　Joseph, 182
Peckham
　William H., 249
Peerce
　William, 17
Peers
　Valentine, Maj., 153
Peirce
　Elizabeth C., 52
Pelton
　Mary, 89
Pendleton
　Edmund, 7
　John B., 108
Penn
　Anne, 162
　John, 162
　William, 187
Pennington
　James, 24
Pennsylvania, 40, 77, 85, 153, 164, 227, 241
Penny
　Isabella, 55
　John, 55
Pensacola, Fla., 104, 112, 130, 159, 166, 195, 208, 226, 252
　Navy hospital, 202

Navy Yard, 208
pensioners, 207, 216
Peper
　Lucy, 68
Perkins
　James, 196
　Rebecca, 238
　Sarah, 196
　William H., 157
Pernambuco, 225
Perry
　Christopher R., 173
　Com., 223, 257
　Comm., 257
　Nathaniel H., 223
　O H., Com., 173
　Raymond H.J., 22
　Sarah, 173
Peru, 121
Peter
　America Pinkney, 94, 98
　Ann, 20
　Elizabeth, 238
　George, 20, 21
　George, Capt., 15
　George, Col., 87
　George, Maj., 138, 182
　Jane, 17
　John P C., 138
　John, Maj., 238
　Mary, 172
　Robert, Jr., 15
　Thomas, 94, 98
　Thomas B., 238
　William, 172
　William H., 160
Peters
　John, 222, 259
　John Francis, Rev., 179
　William, 141
Petersburg, Va., 71, 103, 182
Petigru
　Thomas, Lt., 127
Peyton
　Ann, 244
Philadelphia, Pa., 1, 5-9, 12, 17, 21, 22, 27-31, 33, 34, 37, 38, 43, 46, 47, 49, 50, 54-56, 62, 63, 65, 68, 72, 75, 78, 79, 81, 83, 91, 94-96, 100, 101, 106-111, 114,

116-122, 128-130, 132, 133, 136, 143, 147, 152, 155, 156, 159, 161, 163, 168, 170, 171, 176, 178, 181-184, 188, 189, 193, 195, 198, 199, 205-211, 217, 222, 224, 225, 230, 232, 233, 238, 240, 243, 245, 246, 253, 255, 256, 258, 262, 267
　alms house, 8
Philips
　Ann, 46
Phillips
　Elizabeth, 157
　George, 133
　Horatio G., 157
　Janett B., 133
　John, 162
　Letitia, 162
　Susan C., 46
philosophers, 110
Phynney
　Josiah, Capt., 199
　Julia Ann, 199
Physic
　Henry W., 56
physicians, 1, 111, 124, 138, 144, 147, 173, 189
Piatt
　Benjamin M., 139
　H.J., 139
Pickens
　Andrew, Col., 104
Pickett
　Ellen, 262
　James C., 262
　Jas C., 262
Pierce
　George, 78
　Ignatius, 201
　Sarah, 208
　Susanna, Mrs., 93
Pierson
　Henry A., 184
Pigman
　Benne S., 85
Pike
　Z.M., Gen., 170
Pindall
　James, Hon., 121
　Ruhamah, 121

Pinebush, N.Y., 65
Pinkney
  Elizabeth, 69
  Emily, 182
  Jonathan, 69
  William, Hon., 182
Pintard
  John M., 5
Pippenger
  Wesley E., vii
Piqua, Ohio, 264
pirates, 68
Piscataway, Md., 132, 193, 197, 198, 236, 250
Pise
  Rev., 100
Pitkin
  Timothy, Hon., 119
Pitt Co., N.C., 253
Pittman
  John, 118
Pitts
  John, xii, 47
Pittsburg, Pa., 5, 66, 95, 204
Pittsfield, Mass., 251, 254
Pittsylvania Co., Va., 132
Plaistow, N.H., 109
Plant
  John, 261
Planters' Bank, 215
Plater
  Ann, 15
  Elizabeth, 249
  John Rousby, Jr., 181
  Martha, 82
  Rebecca, 64
  Sarah, 236
  Thomas, 15, 21, 64, 82
  Thomas, Col., 149
Platt
  Sarah Ann, 155
Pleasant Hill, N C, 253
Pleasant twp., Ohio, 107
Pleasanton
  Augustus J, 132
  Matilda, 242
  Stephen, 2, 242
Pleasants
  John H., 130
Pleury
  Elie Peter, 8
Plummer
  Rachael, 31
  Yate, 31

Plymouth Rock, 48
Plymouth, Mass., 142
Poe
  David, 37
  Jacob, 209
  James, Capt., 62
  Neilson, 209
Poindexter
  George, Hon, 224
police officers, 146
Polk
  Ellen Gilliss, 261
  Lucius J., 221
  Samuel, 9, 261
Polkinhorn
  Charles, Rev., 209
Pollard
  Mary, 219
Pomery
  William, 134
Pool
  Rev., 250
Poole
  Sarah Ann, 17
Poolsville, Md., 100
Poor
  John, 87
Poor House, 91
Popham
  John, 258
Port Mahon, 125, 164
Port Royal, Jam., 202
Port Royal, Va., 216
Port Tobacco, Md., 10, 13, 110, 133, 167, 250
Port-au-Prince, S.D., 37
Porter
  James, Sr., 68
  John, 218
  Joshua, Dr., 206
  Letitia, 194
  P.B., 23
  Peter B., Gen., 206
  Peter P., Gen, 194
  William D., 247
Portland, Me., 54, 58
Portobello, Scot, 111
Portsmouth, N.H., 121, 129, 154, 157, 159, 163, 168, 180, 190, 214, 249
Portsmouth, Va., 125, 129, 190, 256
Portugal, 222

Posey
  Elizabeth Ellen, 200
  Julia, 251
  Lawrence, Capt., 200
  Sarah E, 251
Post
  Reuben, Rev., xii, 73, 103, 110, 190, 191, 205, 231, 249
Post Office Department, 229, 257, 266
postmasters, 107, 136, 172, 244
Poston
  John, 142
  Samuel, 251
Potomac Bridge, 28
Potomac River, 67
Pottenger
  William, Lt., 253
Potter
  Rebecca, 201
Potts
  Floride, 80
  Samuel J., 41, 80
Poughkeepsie, N.Y, 44, 146
Poulson
  Charles A., 222
  Sarah Pilmore, 222
  Susannah, 136
  Zachariah, 136
Powel
  Grafton, 100
Powell
  Ann W, 20
  Burr, 20
  Charles L., 168
  Eleanor, Mrs., 133
  Elizabeth, 95
  Levin M., Lt, 178
  Snelling, 95
Power
  Anna, 265
  John, 265
Powers
  Elizabeth, 160
  Gershom, Hon., 191
  John M., 236
  Thomas, 117
Prather
  Overton, 139
Prentiss
  Maria Stribling, 180
  William, 178, 180

Presbury
  George G., 103
  Sarah, 103
Presbyterian Church, 15, 91, 266
  burying ground, 9
Presidents, 104, 130
  Jefferson, 147
  Monroe, 165, 167
Preston
  Josephine, 205
Preston, Eng , 55
Prettyman
  Thomas G., 89
Prevost
  James Marcus, 121
  John B., 121
Price
  George, 198
  Harriet, 200
  Matilda R , 146
  William B , 214
priests, 265
Prime
  Emily, 228
  Nathaniel, 228
Prince
  James, 50
Prince Fredericktown, Md., 145
Prince George's Co., Md., 2, 4, 5, 8, 9, 18, 20, 23-25, 28, 29, 36, 38, 45, 46, 52, 54, 58-60, 62, 67, 78, 92, 100, 107, 108, 113, 117, 122, 127, 132, 135, 136, 139, 158, 160, 165, 166, 170-173, 175, 180, 184, 189, 191, 193, 198, 211, 215, 218, 219, 226, 227, 236, 237, 242, 243, 246, 248, 250, 255, 260, 263
  Piscataway Forest, 27
  woodyard, 26
Prince George's Parish, Md., 265
Prince of Hayti, 44
Prince William Co , Va , 29, 62, 84, 87, 88, 122, 133, 147, 150, 170, 172, 200, 206, 218,
223, 225, 244, 261, 262
  county court, 225
Princess Anne, Md., 261
Princess Maria Ferdinanda Amelia Xaifre, 53
Princeton College, N.J., 20
Princeton, N.J., 5, 25, 62, 134, 138, 153, 167
  battle of, 222
principals, 198
printers, 3, 10, 11, 28, 30, 35, 47, 103, 110, 120, 123, 148, 156, 167, 180, 182, 198, 208, 232, 236, 250, 252
  King's, 124
Printing Office, 10
prisoners, 183
professors, 1, 30, 113, 123, 135, 140, 147, 148, 157, 159, 171, 174, 266
Prout
  Eliza B , 175
  Jonathan, 175, 246
  Martha H., 117
  Mary, 260
  William, 260
Providence, R.I., 114, 157
Provoost
  Samuel, Rev., 28
Provost
  Rev , 5
Prussia, 75
Pryse
  Thomas, 7
publishers, 11, 180, 191
Purcell
  Thomas Francis, 124
Purdy
  Robert, Gen., 182
Putnam
  Daniel, Col , 185
  Maj. Gen., 185
Pye
  Charles, 15
Pyke
  Gov., 205
Pynchon
  Edward, 144

Q
Quakers, 228
Quarles
  Roger, Capt , 131
Quebec, Can., 155, 202, 254
Queen Anne, Md., 211
Queen Anne's Co., Md., 76, 188
Queen's Chapel, 79
Queenston Heights, N.Y., 23
Quincy, Mass., 219
Quinn
  William, 69
Quynn
  William, 46, 50

R
rabbis, 126
Radcliffe
  Jacob, 48
  William S., 48
Radford
  Mary, 165
Radnor twp., Pa., 115
Rae
  Margaret, 231
Ragan
  Basil, 123
  Cecelia, 165
  Sarah, 176
Rahauser
  Rev., 7
Rainey
  S., 147
  Samuel, 262
Rainsford
  Ann, 57
Raleigh, N.C., 64, 143
Ralston
  A.G., 110
  David, 199
Ramsay
  Andrew, 246
  David, 27
  George D., Lt , 164
  Robert T , 167
  Sophia, 246
Ramsburgh
  Catharine, 138
Ramsey
  William, 187

William, Hon., 202
Randall
  Ann, 221
  T., Mr., 221
Randolph
  Beverly, 242
  David Meade, 166
  John, Hon., 147
  Judith, 33
  Mary B., 204
  Nancy, 242
  P.G., Dr., 204
  Richard, 33
  Thomas Mann, 33
  William, 147
  Wm. Beverley, 34
Randolph, Ver., 120
Rankin
  H. Thompson, 145
  Julia Ann, 145
  Robert, Lt , 2
Rannois Parish, Eng , 265
Rappine
  Daniel, 8
Ratcliff
  Alexander, 258
  Eliza, 63
  Joseph, 122
  Martha, 122
Ratcliffe
  Gracy N., 43
  Joseph, 39
  Mrs., 84
  T.F., 39
Ratrie
  William, 102
Ravenscroft
  John Stark, Rev , 143
Rawlings
  Samuel, 88
Ray
  Alexander, 66
  Diane Maria, 6
  James, 6
  Mary, 101
Raymond
  Daniel, 141
  Jane, 71
Rea
  John, 58
Read
  George C., Capt., 106
  Rev., 20, 46
  Robert, 45, 67, 265

  Susannah, 26
  Thomas, Rev., 26, 45, 67, 265
Reardon
  Artamesia T., 203
recorders, 35
rectors, 116, 120, 161, 183, 190, 224, 229, 246, 262, 265
Red River, 49
Redheiffer
  Charles, 47, 50
Redin
  Ann B., 264
  William, 264
Redman
  James, 75
  Rev., 28
Redmond
  Rev., 31
Reed
  Conrad, 79
  Philip, Gen., 124
  Rev., 2, 45, 59
  Thomas B., Hon., 128
  William Fleming, 13
Reeder
  John, 37
  Rachel, 75
  William A., 160
Reese
  Ann Margaret, 118
  John, 118
  Levi R , Rev , 223
  Rev., 208, 259
Reeves
  J., 124
  Jane A D., 187
  Randolph B , 125
register of deeds, 144
Rehoboth, 93
Reid
  James, Rev , 133
  John, 31
  Maria, 32
Reilly
  George, 223
Reily
  Rev., 90
Reinagle
  Ann, 30
  Georgiana, 177
Reintzel
  Henry, M.D., 230

  John, 259
Reiss
  Benjamin, 264
Relpp
  George, 109
Remington
  Eliza Ann, 97
  John A., 125, 180
  Wm., 97
Renfrewshire, Scot., 95
Renner
  Daniel, 2, 136
  Helen, 2
  John, 40
  Maria, 146
  William, 264
  William G., 234
Renshaw
  Sally, 9
Repiton
  Joseph A., 71
representatives, 33, 242, 243
residences
  Analostan, 43
  Arlington House, 190
  Aspin Hill, 209
  Audley, 148
  Barnaby, 189
  Barnaby Manor, 136
  Bel-Air, 260
  Bellevue, 255
  Belmont, 42
  Belville, 6
  Berkley, 104
  Bizarre, 33
  Blandfield, 216
  Bloomingdale, 88
  Bloomsbury, 116, 180, 181, 249
  Bradford's Rest, 238
  Bromont, 267
  Brook Grove, 246
  Buckland, 194
  Buckmarsh, 4
  Burleath, 16
  Bush Hill, 2, 137, 152, 221
  Cameron, 206
  Carroll's Manor, 28
  Carrollton, 1
  Catoctin Valley, 265
  Cedar Hill, 92, 150
  Cedar Point, 53

Cedar Shelter, 235
Chatham, 267
Clamber Hill, 250
Clifton, 244
Clifton Lodge, 97
Clover Hill, 83
Duddington, 252
Effingham, 223
Elmwood, 209
Farley Vale, 136
Federal Hill, 226
Friend's-Loss, 102
Friendship, 170, 243
Glen-Owen, 205
Grampion, 236
Grassland, 75, 212
Green Hill, 21, 135
Greenwood, 15
Hayes, 69, 244
Hayfield, 152
Hazel Plain, 200
Hill-Farm, 204
Hollin Hall, 266
Honey-wood, 25
Kalorama, 195
Kingston Hall, 23
Laneville, 138
Laurel Grove, 200
Liberty, 184
Liberty Hall, 104
Locust Grove, 29, 163
Locust Hill, 235
Long Meadows, 139
Lowe's Rest, 12
Lucky-Hit farm, 255
Milton Hill, 164
Montauverd, 138, 182
Morven, 112
Mount Air, 132
Mount Airy, 25, 220
Mount Eagle, 4, 184
Mount Erin, 152
Mount Ida, 251
Mount Pleasant, 263
Mount Vernon, 128, 211, 227
Mount Welby, 24
Neabsco, 147
Nomony-Hall, 4
Northview, 259
Oak, 180
Oak Hill, 104, 233, 255
Oakland, 83, 185
Ossian Hall, 140

Park House, 119
Perrywood, 78
Pleasant Plains, 181
Poplar Hill, 175, 247
Poplar Plain, 115
President's House, 210, 221, 244
Ravensworth, 107, 151
Retreat, 246, 266
Rich Hill, 23
Rock Hill, 167
Rose Hill, 67, 266
Rosedale, 23
Rosehill, 245
Sabine Hall, 220
Sallisbury, 2
Shamrock Hill, 228
Shirley, 67
Smith's Farm, 195
Solona, 174
Stepney, 88
Stonington, 135
Stony Point, 166
Strawberry Hill, 181
Sully, 21
Summer Hill, 267
Summerseat, 133
Susquehanna, 206
Tuckahoe, 33
Tudor Place, 94, 98
Vansville, 62
Vinemount, 204
Walnut Grove, 242
Waterloo, 244
Weston, 57
Wilua, 92
Worton, 31
Retallack
    Sarah Ann, 249
Retter
    Peter, 17
Reves
    Edward, 112
Revolutionary War, 7, 15, 18, 21, 22, 25, 35, 37, 43, 49, 50, 55-57, 61, 63, 68, 77, 82, 86, 91, 95, 102, 107-109, 112, 113, 115, 116, 119, 122, 124, 129-131, 136-138, 144, 145, 148, 153, 154, 159, 160, 165-167, 174,

176, 199, 202, 205, 207, 209-211, 216, 222-224, 227, 231, 237, 241, 250, 262, 265-267
Rex
    Mary Ann, 141
Reynolds
    George, 41
    Joseph, 264
    Richard, 114
Rhode Island, 119, 142, 159, 196
Rhodes
    Maria W., 50
    Peter, 190
    Rosanna, 74
    William, 74
    Wm., 50
Rice
    Elizabeth, 19
    Luther, xii
Richards
    B W., 199
    G., Mr., 36
    George, Rev., 21
Richardson
    Catherine, 132
Richmond Co., Va., 64
Richmond, Va., 5, 7, 14, 29, 33, 43, 44, 61, 115, 135, 144, 145, 155, 191, 210, 242, 264, 265
    theatre, 70
Ricketts
    David, 206
    John Thomas, 119
    Mary, 119
Ridenour
    Jacob, 139
    Mrs , 139
Ridge
    John R., 77
Ridgely
    Charles, 106
    Charles G., 143
    Charles G , Com , 112
    Charles S , Col., 101
    Charles, Capt., 95
    Cora Florida, 112
    Cornelia L., 143
    Nicholas G., 131
    Nicholas, Hon., 145

Samuel H., Lt., 101
Sophia, 116
Sophia P., 116
William G., 116
Ridgeway
  Ann, 189
  E., Lt., 164
Rigden
  Elizabeth, 68
  Stephen, 14
Riggs
  Alice, Mrs., 42
  Elisha, 42
  Elizabeth A T., 173
Riley
  Ann, 249
  Capt., 69, 87
Rind
  Child, 11
  Jane, 234
  Rebecca M.K., 169
  Samuel S , 147, 169, 206
  W.A., Sr., 234
  William A , 11
  William A , Sr., 169
Ringgold
  Ann Maria, 125
  Barbara, 224
  Elizabeth, 23
  James G., 203
  Maria, Mrs., 93
  Richard, 23
  Samuel, Gen , 122
  Sophia L., 224
  Tench, 125
Rio de Janeiro, Bra , 140, 225
Riordan
  John T., 146
Ripley
  Dorothea, 213
  Eleazer W., Gen , 161
Riswick
  Mary Ann Ellen, 89
Ritchie
  Abner, 53
  Frances S. Affordby, 243
  John T., Lt , 190, 243
  John Thomas, 243
  Mary Ann, 156
  William, 78
Rittenhouse
  Benjamin F., 252

Isobel, 252
John R., 16
rivers, 222
  Hudson, 35
  Mississippi, 103
  North, 91, 207
  Potomac, 67, 182
  Red, 49
  Sassafras, 161
  Savanna, 58
  Severn, 215
  South, 121
  St. Johns, 247
  Tennessee, 57
  Western, 102
Rives
  Mr., 197
Roach
  John, 200
Robb
  John, Rev., 227
  Rev., 157, 200
Robbins
  Edward H., Hon., 132
  I., Rev., 72, 131, 134
  Isaac, xii
  Isaac, Rev., 69, 188
  Jane Prince, 131
  Judge, 59
  Margaret, 59
  Rev., 26
Roberts
  Edmund W., Dr., 233
  Eliza Ann, 222
  John, 222
  Rev., 46, 50
  Robert R , xii
  Susanna P., 40
Robertson
  Eliza, 86
  Henry, 200
  John, 197, 248
  Lelia, 145
  Mary, 177
  Samuel, 86, 200
  Sarah, 56
  Susan R., 90
  Thomas, 14
Robey
  Pricilla, 132
Robinson
  Alexander, 198
  Alexander C., Dr., 228
  Ann, 225

Horatio N., 164
John C., 65
Lydia, 171
Mary Ann, 198
Rev , 48
William, 260
Wm., 260
Rochambeau
  Gen., 63
Rochester
  Amanda, 177
  William B , Hon., 177
Rock Creek, 196
  bridge on, 202
Rock Creek Church, 7, 265
Rock Hill, 2
Rockaway, N.Y., 44
Rocklesstown, N.J , 131
Rockville, Md., 20, 42, 45, 67, 90, 99, 107, 155, 171, 174, 210, 211, 218, 245, 258, 266
Rodbird
  Absalom, Sr., 235
  Jane, 205
Rodney
  Caesar A , 81
  Rev., 261
Rogers
  Capt., 119
  J , Capt , 205
  Lloyd N., 104
  Thomas, 164
  Thomas J., Gen , 245
Rolf
  Ann, 224
  Samuel, 224
Roman
  Zenon, 169
Rome, Italy, 142
Roosevelt
  James I., Jr., 194
  Nicholas, 12
Rose
  Benjamin F , 228
  Martha Ann, 200
  Samuel, 129
Ross
  Adam, 226
  Andrew, 58, 66, 190, 227, 233
  Caroline, 233
  Edward C., Lt., 171
  Gen., 37

Hannaett, 66
John L., 129
Mary Ann, 41
Matilda Eveline, 190
Rebecca, 227
Reuben, Maj., 147
Richard, 91
Robert, 52
Ruhamah, 226
Thomas, 146
Rossburg, Md., 110
Roszel
  G S., Rev., 51
  Rev., 32
  Stephen George, xii
Roszell
  S.C., 157
  Stephen C., 73
Rotch
  Susan, Mrs , 127
Rothwell
  Andrew, 178
Round Hill, Va., 247
Rouzie
  Reuben, 133
Rowan
  Rev., 50
Rowe
  James G., 185
  Lazarus, 119
Rowles
  Joseph E., 4
Roxbury, Mass , 158
Royal Navy, 257
Rozzell
  Octavia, 36
Runkle
  Ralph, 139
Runnells
  John H., 163
Rupert
  Leonard, 111
  Philip, 111
Rush
  Dr., 7
  Mary, 7
  Richard, 96
  Richard, Hon , 96
Russell
  John, 197
  Jonathan, Hon., 217
Rustick
  John, 144

Rutgers
  Henry, Col , 141
Rutherford
  Alexander, 51
  Drusilla Ann, 189
  Eunice, 51
  Francis, 166
  V., Col., 189
Rutledge
  E.C., Lt., 103
Rutter
  Josiah S C., 219
Ryan
  Henry, 210
Ryland
  Rev., 35, 40, 42-45, 100, 160, 234
  William, xii
  William, Rev., 107, 206
  Wm., Rev., 85
Rynearson
  John, 149

S

Sacket's Harbor, N.Y., 118
Sahara Desert, 69
Sailer
  William, 66
sailing masters, 149
Salem, Mass., 1, 53, 242
Salisbury, 44
Salomon
  E., Mr., 56
Sampson Co., N.C., 121
Sand Hills, Ga., 184
Sanders
  Beverley C., 169
Sanderson
  Francis, Lt., 197
Sandiford
  Phebe Ann, 248
Sandusky, Ohio, 99
Sandwich Islands, 162
Sandwich, Mass., 22
Sandy Point, Md , 199
Sane
  Mary, 156
Sanford
  Alexander, 131
  Elizabeth, 8
  Henrietta C , 131
  John W., 156
  Julia Ann, 193

Sarah Eveleth, 118
Thomas, 118
Sangston
  John A , Capt., 163
  Susan B., 163
Saratoga Springs, 206
Sargent
  Thomas F., Rev., xii, 11, 12
Sassafras Neck, Md., 23
Saul
  William M , 113
Saunders
  Ann B., 36
  Caroline, 45
  Emily, 78
  Jane Virginia, 210
Savannah, Ga., 1, 7, 58, 185, 187, 208, 245
Saxony, 53
Sayrs
  John Johnson, Rev., xii, 11
Scattergood
  Joseph, 80
Schaffer
  George, 157
Schenectady, N.Y., 138, 143
Schlebny
  Henry, Dr., 192
  Jacob, Dr., 192
Schoharie Co., N.Y., 35
Schohariekill, N.Y , 137
Schriber
  Rev., 252
Schwartze
  Augustus J., Jr., Dr., 105
Scituate, Mass., 18, 129
Scotland, 1, 10, 61, 76, 80, 102, 111, 151, 166, 167, 178, 189, 193, 194, 212, 231
Scott
  Caroline, 56
  Clarinda, 172
  D.W , 152
  Edward, Hon., 121
  Eleanor, 8
  Eleanor Douglass, 137
  Elizabeth, 2
  George, 93, 97
  Gustavus, 2
  Gustavus Hall, 259
  Henry D., 141

Henry D., Lt., 87
Horatio, 56
James S., 192
Jesse, 172
John C., 2, 102
M , Rev., 5
Maria Elizabeth, 192
Mary, 152
Mary Ann, 102
Richard K., 58
Richard M., 137, 152, 221
Robert E , 181
Thomas, 134
Thomas, Dr., 257
Upton, Dr , 21
William L , 150
William S., 259
Wm. S., 259
Scrivner
   Margaret Ann, 100
sculptors, 177
Seal
   William, 130
Searle
   Rev , 42
Seaton
   Arthur, 196
   W.W., 95
   William, 95
   William W., 196
Seawell
   Francis, 79
   W., Lt , 227
Second Baptist Church, xii
Second Presbyterian Church, xi
Seddon
   Thomas, 203
Seixas
   Rev., 91
Selby
   Brice, 2
   Brig, 45
Selecman
   Margaret, 134
   Thomas, 134
   William D , 134
Selvy
   Adeline, 134
Semmes
   Benedict I , Dr , 132
   Caroline, 132
   Eleanor H , 153

Joseph, 28, 36, 55, 220
Raphael, 261
Sarah D., 28
Thomas, 261
Semple
   Robert, 8
senators, 5, 128-130, 133, 137, 139, 140, 142, 147, 148, 154, 158, 161, 168, 175, 179, 180, 218, 224, 240, 241, 244, 263
Seneca, Md., 6
Sengstack
   C.P., 52
Sergeant
   John, 234
   Mary Elizabeth, 234
sergeant-at-arms, 221
servants, 242
Sessford
   James, 250
Sessums
   Isaac, 112
Seton
   William, Lt., 228
Seurrureur
   Madame, 244
Seven Buildings, 2
Severn River, 215
Sewall
   Bennet H , 144
   C., Capt., 11
   Mary, 11
   Robert, 175, 178
   Robert D., 175, 178
   Samuel, Hon , 22, 35
Seymour
   William, 132
Shakes
   C.M.V., 234
Shane
   Rev., 91
Shanklin
   Robert H., 62
Shanks
   Elizabeth Jordan, 85
   Elizabeth Trueman, 174
   William, 174
Sharp
   Maria, 10
Sharpsburg, Md., 156
Shaw
   Elizabeth, Mrs , 44

Emily B., 179
Lemuel, 179
William P , 172
Wm., 69
Shawneetown, Ill , 168
Shay
   Samuel King, 204
Sheafe
   James, 129
Sheckell
   Richard R., 74
Sheekleton
   Mr., 81
Shekell's Tavern, 65
Shelburne, Mass., 207
Shelbyville, Ky., 241
Shepherd
   Elizabeth, 168
   Thomas, Capt., 168
Shepherdstown, Va., 140, 189
Sheppard
   Nathan, 106
   Sarah, 152
   Thomas, Col., 152
   William B , 163
Shepperd
   Augustine H., Hon., 142
Sherburne
   J.S , Hon., 159
   Jonathan W., Lt., 171
sheriffs, 138, 216
Sherley
   Elizabeth, 32
Sherlock
   John, 17
Sherman
   Charles R., 104
Shields
   James, Hon , 196
   Margaret Ann, 180
Shindler
   William R , 140
Shinn
   Asa, xii
ship carpenters, 168, 236
ship masters, 128, 131
Shipley
   Elenor, 263
   Rezin, 263
Shippen
   Edward, 248
   William, 56

ships
- Anacreon, 128
- Brandywine, 194
- brig Arctic, 225
- brig Laura, 101
- brig Mentor, 58
- brig Olympia, 101
- brig Patriot, 103
- Constallation, 179
- Delaware, 125
- frigate Brandywine, 121
- frigate Constallation, 88
- frigate Constitution, 219
- frigate Guerriere, 165
- frigate Insurgent, 179
- frigate Macedonian, 153
- frigate Potomac, 192
- frigate United States, 1, 153
- Guerriere, 146
- Hornet, 81
- Liverpool packet, 228
- Lotus, 260
- Moss, 68
- Ontario, 196
- Peacock, 156
- privateer Roger, 131
- Ranger, 154
- revenue cutter, 226
- revenue cutter Alert, 142
- revenue cutter Wasp, 104
- Richmond packet, 29
- schooner Alligator, 68
- schooner Hamilton, 19
- sloop, 174
- sloop of war Peacock, 67
- Sloop Sally, 81
- sloop Spendid, 124
- steamboat, 28, 182
- steamboat Express, 243
- steamboat Fredericsburgh, 257
- Tom Bowline, 92
- Vincennes, 121, 202

Shittle
- Mary, 156
- Thomas, 156

Shoemaker
- Betsey, 12
- Charles F., 88
- Rebecca, 62

Shore
- Harriet W, 145

Harvey, 145
Shrewsbury Parish, 161
Sibald
  Capt, 6
Siffert
  Harriet, 35
Signay
  Joseph, 254
silversmiths, 123, 171
Sim
  Harriet, 191
  Thomas, Dr., 191, 235
Simkins
  Eli, 43
Simmonds
  Matilda, 89
  Robert, 89
Simmons
  Cyrus, 230
  Mrs., 12
  William, 12
  Wm., 44
Simms
  Ann Fenton Lee, 248
  Charles, Col., 235
  Elexius, 152
  Emily D., 183
  John D., 248
  Mary Ann Eliza, 190
Simon
  Michael, 247
  Sabina, 247
Simonds
  Robert J, 155
Simons
  Charles W, Col., 113
Simpson
  Elizabeth, 97
  Henrietta Sarah, 267
  Joel, 69
  John, 264, 267
  Maria E., 264
  Tobias (C), 139
Sims
  Joseph, 122
Sinclair
  Arthur, Com, 179
  James, 78
Singleton
  Richard, 165
Sinn
  Catherine Louisa, 186
  Henry, 139
  William, 186

William B. Lewis, 186
Sinon
  Thomas, 237
Sister Mary Frances, 232
Sister Mary James, 172
Sitgreaves
  Samuel, Hon., 161
  Samuel, Rev., 161
Skinner
  Elizabeth L., 95
  I.L., Rev., 171
  Lucretia C., 171
  Mary, 181
  William R A., 235
Skippon
  John, 103
Skipwith
  H., 145
Slacum
  George W., 155
  Helen Adela, 155
Slade
  Mary, 39
Slater
  David, 29
Slaughter
  Gabriel, Col., 167
  John, Col., 138
  N.G.C., 104
  Philip, xii
Slemmers
  Rev., 24
Slicer
  Henry, Rev., 257-259
Sligo, Ire., 24
Slorzosi
  Carlotta, 142
  Louis, 142
Slow
  Baron, 95
Slye
  Mary, 238
  Mary Alphonsa, 149
  Robert A, 94, 237
  Thomas G., 149, 238
Small
  Abraham, 117
Smallwood
  Enoch W., 133
  Rev., 248
  Samuel N., 175
  William A., Rev., 124
Smalts
  Rev., 200

Smart
  Mary Ann, 218
Smerna, 88
Smith
  A.I., Dr , 201
  Alexander, Hon , 147
  Ann, 42
  Ann Amelia, 204
  Ann E., 47
  Ann Mann, 251
  Anthony, 265
  Benjamin P., 146
  Caleb, Col., 251
  Caroline Laurens, 20
  Catherine, 83
  China, Capt., 216
  Clement, Dr., 211
  David (C), xii
  Dennis A., 245
  Dr., 58
  E., 50
  Eliza, 5
  Esther, 21
  Francis Linaeus, 216
  George, 204
  George W., 254
  Harriet Hawkins, 231
  Hugh Charles, 162
  Isaac Canfield, 261
  J., Gen , 42
  J., Lieut , 57
  J.A.W., 233
  J.K , 231
  J.L., 75
  James, 264
  Jane A , 201
  Jane K., 264
  John, 28
  John A., 134
  John R., 171
  John W., 127
  John, Rev., 189
  Joseph, 253
  Louis F , 171
  Lydia C., 245
  Maria, 217
  Martha E., 191
  Middleton, 265
  Patrick, 200
  Rev , 5, 77, 87, 89, 97,
    102, 245
  Richard, 47, 50, 83
  Samuel H , 171, 215
  Samuel S., Rev., 20
Samuel, Gen., 239
Sarah (Hoffman), 14
Sidney W., Dr., 154
Sophia Covington, 134
Sophia M., 265
Sophronia A., 162
Susan H., 215
Susanna B., 121
Thomas Perrin, 223
Thomas, Rev , 93
Walter, 21
Walter, Maj , 14
Waters, 205
William M , Gen., 172
Smith's Inlet, 29
Smithville, N.C., 127
Smoot
  Alexander, 71
  Eliza Virginia, 71
  Elizabeth, 235
  George, 235
  George H., 121
Smyrna, 125
Smyth
  Edward, 202
  Hannah, 210
  William, 210
Snelson
  Nathaniel, 71
Snethen
  Nicholas, xii
Snow Hill, Md., 59, 69
Snowden
  Arabella, 180
  Edgar, 184
  John, 127
  Rachael, 127
  Rezin Hammond, 126
  Samuel, 191
Society of Friends, 50, 64,
  80, 142, 267
  minister of, 223
  soldiers, 18, 49, 54, 56, 57,
    102, 109, 113, 115,
    116, 119, 129, 131,
    132, 137, 138, 144,
    148, 150, 202, 207,
    216, 223, 227, 231,
    265
Somers Town, Eng , 27
Somerset Co., Md., 9, 23,
  24, 61, 71, 151, 154,
  261
Somervell
  Ann, 45
  Thomas T , 45
Somerville
  David, 19
Sotheron
  James F., Maj., 190
  Mary Elizabeth, 190
Sothoron
  Mary, 46
Soulnier
  John, 110
  Sarah Wilson, 110
South America, 112
South Carolina, 41, 53, 133,
  158, 164, 196, 262
  Secretary of State, 164
South River, 121
Southall
  Mary Anna, 163
Southard
  Henry, Hon., 177
  Samuel L., Hon., 177
  Sarah, 177
Souther
  John, Capt , 101
Sowers
  Ann, 4
  Jacob, 4
Spain, 194, 253
Spalding
  Bernard, 43
  E.M , Mrs , 211
Spanish Army, 164
Sparks
  Jared, 239
  Joel B., 188
Spaulding
  Enoch, 83
  Winifred, 147
Speake
  Ellenor, 16
  Rufus H., Dr., 131
Speed
  John, 65
Spence
  Andrew, 129
  Irving, 59
  James, 194
Spencer
  Benjamin F., Capt , 120
  John C., Hon., 226
  Laura Catharine, 226

Sperry
  Jacob, 133
Spicer
  Frederick, 156
Spilman
  Thomas K., 202
Spotsylvania Co., Va., 137
Sprigg
  W.O., Mr., 4
Springer
  Ann, 46
Springfield, Mass., 144
Springfield, Md., 59
St Andre
  Durant, 155
  Marie Alexandrine, 155
St. Andrew's Square, 129
St Augustine, Fla., 205, 247
St. Clair
  Gen , 6
St Clairsville, Ohio, 117
St. Domingo, 37, 94, 247
St. Francisville, 161
St. Helena, 205
St John's Chapel, 208
St John's Church, 190
St. John's Church, N.Y., 63
St. John's Episcopal Church,
  xi, xii
St. Johns River, 247
St. Joseph's Church, Phila , 94
St. Louis, Mo., 39, 86, 130, 243
St. Mary's Catholic Church, xi
St. Mary's Church, Eng., 68
St. Mary's Co., Md., 5, 8, 11, 29, 30, 46, 48, 52, 80, 83, 85, 91, 97, 116, 190, 201, 206, 226, 236, 243, 249
  William & Mary Parish, 14
St Mary's College, Baltimore, 224
St. Michael's Church, 85, 162, 196
St. Patrick's Catholic Church, xii
St. Paul's Church, 109, 224
St Paul's Episcopal Church, xi, xii
St. Paul's Parish, 246

St. Peter's Catholic Church, xi
St. Peter's Church, 203
St. Steven's Parish, 161
St. Thomas, V.I., 70, 81, 245
Stabler
  Edward, 176
Stafford Co., Va., 48, 189, 201
Stahl
  Jacob, 89
Stanard
  Edward Carter, 19
Standage
  Marcia, 172
Stanton
  John Richards, 252
  Richard, 252
  Thomas Brocchus, 252
Staples
  Samuel J., 120
Stark
  Ann H., 147
  Robert B., Dr., 147
  Robert, Hon., 164
State Department, 186, 216
stationers, 9, 203
Staughton
  Rev., 87
  William, Rev., 114, 129
Staunton
  John, Capt , 191
  Mary, 191
steamboat captains, 182
Steed
  Robert E , 122
Steel
  Catherine, 141
  Jonathan H., 194
  Julia Ann, 194
Steele
  Henry M , 71
  Horatio N., 101
Steer
  Phineas, 222
Steiner
  F., Mr., 227
Steingasser
  Joseph, 89
Stelle
  Mary B., 118
Stem
  Rev., 227

Stenger
  Charlotte A.M., 13
Stephenson
  Ann, 191
Sterett
  I.J., Lt., 245
  Joseph, Gen., 225
  Mary Harris, 225
Stettinius
  John, 158
  Joseph, 110
Stettinus
  Julia, 189
Stevens
  Byam Kerby, 146
  Robert, Col., 188
Stevenson
  James S., 204
  Rev., 49
Stewart
  C.S., Rev., 162
  Charles S., Rev., 62
  Eleanor Campbell, 76
  Harriet, 162
  Henry, 73
  Hugh, 7
  Israel, 169
  Miss, 7
  Samuel, 237
  William, 161
  William W , 186
  William Y., Capt., 127
Stier
  Frederick, Rev., 237
  Rev., 229
Still Water, 138
Stinchcomb
  Aquilla S , 59
Stirling
  Lord, 174
Stith
  Griffin, 262
  Louisa Stuart, 262
Stockholm, Swe., 239
Stoddart
  Christopher, 55
Stoddert
  Benjamin, Maj , 2
  Rebecca, 2
Stone
  Ann D., 178
  Anna Maria, 135
  Milly, 145
  Thomas, 53

William S., 145
stone cutters, 130
Stoney Point, 207
store keepers, 129, 132, 155, 226, 249
Storer
   John Langdon, Col., 168
Story
   Lydia, Mrs., 6
   William, 6
Stout
   Eban, 73
   John, 40
Stow, Mass., 216
Straham
   Col., 6
Strahan
   Charles, 170
Stratton
   Benjamin H., Dr., 151
   John, 8
Strebeck
   Martha, 261
Street
   John, 157
   Upper George, 162
streets
   Beall, 176, 263
   Bridge, 17, 58, 67, 76, 88, 136, 184, 245, 254, 257
   Cherry, 169
   Cherry Alley, 173
   Congress, 199
   Darby Road, 128
   Dunbarton, 199
   F, 248
   First, 176, 213, 224
   Frederick, 154
   Gay, 264
   Greene, 210
   High, 30, 130, 147, 163, 220
   Jefferson, 34, 62, 141
   list of, viii
   Market, 154, 235
   Market Space, 195
   Nassau, 141
   Pennsylvania Ave., 257, 258
   Stoddert, 210
   Third, 151, 255
   West, 183, 246

Streight
   Rev., 14
Stricker
   Gen., 145
Stringfellow
   William, 212
Strode
   John, 20
Strong
   Hepzibah, 66
   Mary, 225
Stuart
   Daniel, Dr., 140
   Elizabeth, 232
   John, Col., 184
   Mary Fell, 33
   Philip, 33
   Philip, Gen., 160
   Stuart, 140
   William, 232
Stubbs
   Harriet, 256
Stull
   Catharine, 76
   Frederick, 256
   John Henry, 233
   Major, 76
   O H W., 233, 256
Sue
   John Joseph, Dr., 197
   Rosella, 197
Suit
   Smith, 227
Sullivan
   Andrew, 222
   Edward, 123
   Maj. Gen., 159
   Margaret Virginia, 127
Summerfield
   J., Rev., 88
   William, 88
Summers
   Lucinda V., 208
Sumter
   Gen., 138
surgeon dentists, 163
surgeons, 119, 127, 130, 161, 196, 201, 202, 219, 235, 241, 252, 256, 258
surveyors, ix, 9, 12, 140, 150, 173, 178, 182
Sussex Co., Va., 188

Suter
   Alexander, 17, 26
   John, 146
   Margaret, 2
   Robert, 17
Sutton
   Samuel, 245
Swan
   Caleb, 15
   Maria Margaretta, 193
Swann
   James, Col., 183
   Jane Ann, 234
   John, 112
   Lucinda, 177
   Nathan, 177
Swansea, Wales, 161
Sweden, 58, 217, 239
Sweeny
   George, 29, 170
   Henry M., 220
   Margaret, 109
   Mary, 237
   Susan H., 170
Sweet Springs, Va., 160
Sweeting
   Henry W., 154
Swift
   Ann, 252
   Delano, 116
   J.G., Gen., 116, 143
   James F., 133
   James Foster, 143
   John, 23
   Jonathan, 252
Switzerland, 61
Swope
   David, 146
Symington
   Peter, 53

T

T. & G.M. Lee, 169
Tabbs
   Elizabeth, 134
   Jane Maria, 255
   Moses, 255
Tachi
   Rev., 200
Talbot
   Elisha, 231
   Helen, 195
   Levi, 192

Mary Ann, 200
Talbot Co., Md , 82, 170, 192, 243
Talbott
  Elisha, 194, 217
  Mary Ann, 194
  Rebecca, 217
Talburtt
  Lewin, 185
Talcott
  Andrew, Capt , 221
Taliaferro
  John, Dr., 214
  Mary E , 187
Talien
  M., 50
Tallahassee, Fla., 116, 183, 203
Tallmadge
  Benjamin, Jr., Lt., 194
  Charles B., Maj., 249
Taney
  Dr , 218
  Octavius, Hon , 218
Taneytown, Md., 6, 118
Tarbell
  Henrietta A., 253
  Joseph, Capt., 253
Tarlton
  Ann Charlotte, 223
  Eleanor, 223
  Henry, 121
Tate
  James, 259
Tatnall
  Edward E , 245
Tatsapaugh
  Rosetta, 174
Tayler
  John, 44
Tayloe
  Catharine, 79
  Charles, 194
  John, 25, 79
  John, Col , 220
  Rebecca P., 25
  William, 152
Taylor
  Catherine B., 195
  Charles, 126, 174
  Elias C., Lt , 225
  Elizabeth Johnson, 181
  Francis, 242
  Georgiana A., 241

  John, 53
  Josias, 143
  Matte, 242
  Robert I., 181, 195
  Robert, Capt , 182
  William, 191
Tebbs
  Foushee, 51
  Nancy R., 51
  Willoughby W., 244
tellers, 114
Temple Cloud, 125
Templeman
  Hetty, 11
Tenant
  Thomas W., 225
Tenly Town, Md , 110
Tennessee, 121, 167, 182, 221, 242, 244
Tennessee River, 57
Tennesson
  Samuel, 175
Tennison
  Elizabeth, 107
  Joseph B., 60
  Joshua, 72, 231
  Walker, 72
Terre Haute, Ind., 154, 199
Terrel
  Mr., 5
Terrett
  George, Capt., 185
  Mary Ashton, 185
Thaw
  Eliza Jane, 198
  John, 219
  Joseph, 8, 11, 198
theatre, 27, 37, 52, 70, 78, 83, 86, 94, 95, 156, 176, 184, 230, 240
  Baltimore, Md., 230, 240
  Charleston, S C., 44
  Philadelphia, Pa., 206, 230, 240
  Washington, D.C., 206, 240
Thecker
  Elizabeth, 83
Theological Seminary, 148, 196, 266
Thibodeauxville, Miss., 153
Thomas
  Ann, 114
  Benjamin, 177

Caroline, 52
Catherine, 201
Gardner, 119
George, 114
Henry E., 241
Isaiah, 182
Jenkin, 150, 231
John, 52
John Hanson, 27
John M., Dr., 70, 244
John V., 70
John, Dr., 201
Margaret, 36
Mary Eliz. Parsons, 231
Richard, Hon., 229
Thomas Janney & Co., 150
Thompson
  Albert C., 220
  Andrew E., 97
  Angelica, 198
  Ann, 103
  C.C.B., Com., 233
  Craven P., 178
  Francis, 228
  George, 61
  Gustavus, 76
  James, Col., 69
  James, Gen., 202
  James, Lt., 6
  John, Capt., 202
  Margaret, 76, 195
  Mary Cecilia, 69
  Mr., 29
  Nancy, 76
  Peyton, 198
  Richard, 26
  Stephen J., 228
  William, 159
  William H., 258
  Wm. H , 258
  Wm , Sr , 75
Thompson's Island, 72
Thompson's Tavern, 29
Thomson
  George, 229
  Sarah Ellen, 69
  Wm., 22
Thorn
  William, 168
Thorndike
  Israel, Hon., 224
Thornton
  George F , 79
  James Innis, 204

S., Mrs., 68
Thorpe, Eng., 259
Three Fingered Jack, 37
Threlkeld
  Elizabeth, 98
  John, 16, 98, 161
  Mary, 16
Thrift
  Karen H., 76
Throop
  Benjamin, Col., 61
Thurston
  William, 66
Tierny
  Hugh, 234
Tiffany
  Harriet B., 62
Tiffin
  Edward, Dr., 111
Tilden
  John, 87
  Rebecca, 87
Tilghman
  Edward, 29
  Judge, 100
Tilley
  Elizabeth, 207
  H.W., 141
  Henry T., 66
  Mary, 55
  Mr., 47
Tilson
  Martin L., 142
Timberlake
  Lewis, 115
  Louisa, 115
Tims
  Charles, 179
  Henry, 212
Timsbury, Ire , 125
Tinslar
  Benjamin R., Dr , 146
Tippett
  Charles B., xii
Tod
  John, Hon , 144
Todd
  Charles W., 136
  S.J., 117
  William, 149
Toler
  Frances, 166
  Richard H., 249
Tolland, Conn., 106

Tolson
  Ann H., 20
  Francis, 20
Tompkins
  Judge, 49
Tomson
  Tommy (C), 110
Tone
  Theobald Wolfe, 80
Toulson
  Francis, 132
  Margaret, 132
Towers
  William, 187
Towle
  Rev., 22
Towles
  Eliza M., 177
  James, 209
Townley
  James, 32
  Joshua, 72
Townsend
  Jeremiah Atwater, 85
  Lemuel, 113
  Mary, 113
  Rebecca A., 72
Tracy
  James Francis, 152
Tracy's Landing, Md., 215
tragedians, 256
Travers
  John, 56
treasurers, 144, 247, 264
Treasury Department, 2, 3, 9, 11, 40, 58, 60, 63, 71, 72, 78, 85, 88-90, 92, 96, 112, 117, 124, 133, 149, 170, 173, 192, 202, 203, 205, 234, 242, 244, 248, 258, 264
Treat
  Samuel, 3
Tredwell
  Thomas, 215
Tredyffrin twp., 49
Trenton, N J , 4, 10, 49, 138, 155, 196, 201, 222, 233
Tretler
  John, 178
Trevett
  Samuel R., Jr , 67

Trimble
  William, Maj., 107
Trinity Catholic Church, xi
Trinity Church, 34, 212, 213, 262
Trinity College, 153
Trinity Methodist Episcopal Church, xii
Trinque
  Pierre, 94
Triplett
  Charles H., 253
  Margaret E.T., 11
Tripoli, 18
Trotter
  Matthew, Gen , 174
Trueheart
  Daniel, 44
  Maria D., 44
Trumbull
  Gov., 179
  John, 187
  John, Col., 179
Trunnell
  William, 248
Truxtun
  Com., 150, 179
  William, 150
Tschiffeley
  Louis S., 90
Tschiffely
  Adelia Sophia, 248
Tubman
  Henry, 5
Tucker
  Eliza, 174
  Elizabeth, 234
  George, 174
  George H., 182
  James, 123
  John, 220
  Samuel, 36
  St George, 70
Tuel
  Sarah, 157
Tunnicliff
  Mary, 9
  William, 9
Tupper
  Charles C., Capt., 267
  Homes, 185
Turk's Island, 19
Turnbull
  Eliza, 8

Turner
  Catharine C., 70
  Gov., 189
  James, 206
  James B.B , 43
  John, 15
  Martha, 142
  Richard, 194
  Sally, 189
  Samuel, 43, 142
  Samuel Thomas, 266
  Samuel, Dr., 60
  Thomas, 33, 70, 201
  Virginia, 194
turners, 233
Tuscany, Italy, 177
Tuscumbia, Ala., 151
Tustin
  Rev., 186
Tuston
  Septimus, Rev., 97
tutors, 116, 120
Tutte
  Walter A., 218
Tuttle
  Mary, 16
Tweedy
  Mary, 185
  Sidney, 148
Twiggs
  David E., 146
Twine
  Daniel B , 92
Twyford
  Smith, 53
Tydings
  Ferdinando, 207
Tyler
  B.O , Mr , 90
  Catherine Cecelia, 172
  Catherine Contes, 201
  Elizabeth Ann Maria, 90
  George, 23
  Isaac Hughes, 128
  John, Dr., 201
  Lydia Ann, 60
  Mary B., 23
Tyng
  Ann D'Wolf, 224
  Dudley A., Hon., 109
  Rev., 53, 55, 78, 92
  Stephen Higginson,
    Rev., xii, 109, 224
Tyrone Co., Ire., 153

Tyson
  Alexander H., Dr., 259
  Jesse, 171
  John S., 127
  Margaret, 171

U

U.S. Army, 4, 5, 7, 84, 119,
  124, 132, 133, 146,
  189, 216, 222, 242,
  246, 261
  apothecary, 103
  brigadier general, 166
  captain, 6, 125, 138,
    164, 205, 209, 242
  colonel, 5, 41, 60, 115,
    122, 138, 195, 265
  lieutenant, 57, 66, 79,
    98, 100, 106, 122,
    131, 164, 186, 199,
    203, 209, 212, 217,
    227, 241
  major, 31, 118, 153, 165,
    187, 210-212, 246,
    250, 261
  major-general, 97
  officer, 8, 48, 189
  paymaster, 15, 249
  private, 131
  surgeon, 161, 241
U.S Branch Bank, 56, 156,
  171, 206, 248
  President, 171
U.S. Congress, 3, 4, 8, 25,
  27, 33, 36, 42, 49,
  53, 77, 87, 91, 120,
  121, 127-130, 133,
  137, 140, 142, 147,
  148, 154, 158, 161,
  168, 175, 179, 180,
  183, 184, 189, 191,
  196, 202, 204, 214,
  217, 224, 241, 243
  Georgia, 245
  Massachusetts, 254
  Pennsylvania, 242, 245
  Tennessee, 244
  Virginia, 5
U.S. House of
  Representatives, 1,
  3, 24, 42, 49, 114,
  119, 148, 183, 223

U.S. Marine Corps, 1, 2, 6,
  22, 39, 74, 87, 100,
  121, 132, 153, 173,
  183, 229, 230, 267
  captain, 22, 121, 132,
    173, 183, 267
  clerk, 37
  colonel, 153, 230
  commandant, 6, 74
  lieutenant, 1, 2, 87, 229
  major, 39
  paymaster, 6
  quarter master, 100
U.S. Military Academy, 171
U.S. Navy, 18, 22, 34, 35,
  72, 76, 86, 87, 94,
  117, 146, 152, 162,
  165, 183, 233,
  239-241, 244, 245,
  247, 252, 265
  accountant, 33
  agent, 197, 198, 250
  captain, 104, 106, 205,
    206, 241, 253
  clerk, 76, 78
  commandant, 125, 195
  commodore, 113, 143,
    150, 154, 173, 179,
    188, 208, 233, 260,
    264
  flag, 7
  hospital, 202
  lieutenant, 81, 88, 93,
    103, 113-115, 118,
    141, 145, 147, 154,
    155, 157, 164, 166,
    168, 171, 178, 182,
    183, 185, 190, 193,
    195, 197, 202, 203,
    206, 210, 219, 225,
    228, 233, 240-243,
    253, 260, 264
  master commandant,
    175
  midshipman, 104, 130,
    137, 156, 157, 160,
    190, 220, 239, 241
  officer, 55, 233
  post captain, 28
  purser, 119, 137, 180,
    200, 215, 223, 257
  purser's steward, 208
  sailing master, 62
  secretary, 2, 167, 199

store keeper, 129, 249
storekeeper, 226
surgeon, 67, 119, 127,
    130, 201, 202, 219,
    235, 256
U.S. Senate, 21, 24, 241,
    249
    Speaker, 243
Ulrick
    George, 62
Underwood
    Jane, 19
Union Mills, Md., 45
Union Tavern, vi, 18, 38,
    257
University of Aberdeen, 193
University of Edinburgh, 1
University of Georgia, 123
University of Maryland, 113,
    159
University of Pennsylvania,
    30
University of Virginia, 115,
    174
Upfold
    George, Rev., 133
Upper Marlborough, Md., 7,
    58, 62, 215, 231, 263
Upperman
    Catharine S., 110
    Eliza, 80
    Henry, 54, 110
    Henry, Sr., 66
    Mary Ann, 54
Upsher
    Virginia, 243
Urie
    Arthur T , 198

V

Vallette
    Eliza, 211
Valley Forge, Pa , 138, 222
Valparaiso, 121, 146, 165
Van Benthuysen
    Jane Catalina, 146
    John, 146
Van Courtlandt
    Philip, Gen., 207
Van Horn
    Rezin B , Dr., 150
Van Horne
    Espy, 114

Van Kleeck
    Lawrence L., 217
    Mary Jane, 217
Van Lomel
    Rev., 158
Van Lommel
    Rev., 184
Van Ness
    Cornelia, 194
    David, 79
    John P., 4
    John P., Gen , 233
    Marcia (Burnes), 233
Van Rensselaer
    Catharine, 152
    Stephen, Hon., 152
Van Wyck
    John C , 147
    Sidney Jane, 147
Van Zandt
    N.B., 261
    N.B., Mr., 261
    Rosalie Martha, 261
Vandalia, Ill., 233
Vanderhoof
    Daniel, 110
Vanlomell (etc)
    Rev., 144, 149, 165, 172
Vansville, Md., 62, 242
Varden
    Chs. H., 212
    Joseph Alfred, 199
    Richard W., 213
Varnell
    George W , 172
Varrella
    Rev , 208
Vasse
    Ambrose, 205
Veitch
    Elizabeth, 262
    Richard, 262
Venable
    Charles, 211
Venango Co , N.Y , 109
Vera Cruz, 110
Vermont, 75, 183, 193, 224
Verren
    A., Rev., 157
Villard
    A.J., 20
    R.H.L., 28
    Sophie, 20

Vincent
    Joseph, 242
    Margaret, 153
    Willis, 153
Vincent's Orphan Asylum,
    172
Vineyard, Ver., 193
Vinson
    Charles, 257
    Eliza W., 131
    John, 131
    Mrs., 257
Vinton
    D.H., Lt., 106
    R.S., Rev., 123
    Rev , 122, 129
    Robert S., xii
Violett
    Louisa E , 143
    Robert G., 143
Virginia, 1, 5, 35, 36, 41, 42,
    56, 77, 86, 102, 110,
    121, 122, 124, 129,
    147, 170, 171, 181,
    195, 208, 214, 216,
    243, 260, 263
    Court of Appeals, 7, 267
    Eastern District, 165
    Governor, 173
    Superior Court, 163
Von Kapff
    B.J., 186
    Esther Henrietta, 186
Von Weisenske
    Caroline Henrietta, 62
Vowell
    John C., 204
    Margaret B., 204

W

Wadsworth
    Caroline, 265
    John, 265
    Philip H , 265
Wagner
    George, 78
    Sophia, 78
Wainwright
    Robert D., 22
Waite
    Obed, 140
Walch
    B.A., 158

Walker
  David, 97
  Dorcas Ann, 218
  Dudley, 215
  Elizabeth Ann, 67
  George, 182
  James, 97, 158, 235
  Margaretta, 182
  Nathan, 67
  William, Hon., 207
Wall
  Albert G., Lt., 88
Wallace
  Margaret, 231
  Richard, 188, 215
  W.W , Rev., 160, 163, 207, 231
  William W , Rev., 123
Wallach
  Anne Douglas, 235
  Richard, 235
Wallingford
  Mary, 218
Walpole, N.H., 207
Walsh
  Harriet B., 97
  Rev., 97
  Robert, 176
Walter, 96
  Thomas R., 37
Walters
  John W., 200
Wapatomaka, Ohio, 164
War Department, 12, 28, 106, 169, 214, 254
  clerk, 84, 204
Ward
  Ellen, 225
  Henrietta, 198
  Jane Francis, 185
  John M., 198
  John W., 193
  Judge, 225
  Ulysses, 36
  William, 185
Warder
  Walter, 168
Ware
  Rev , 47
Waring
  Basil, 123, 192
  Basil H., 123
  Eleanor, 186
  Ellen, 184

  Henry, 186, 247
  Mary Jane, 192
  Spencer, 192
  Susan F., 247
Warner
  Eliza L., 140
  John, 140
Warren
  William, 240
Warren Co , N C., 253
Warren Co., Ohio, 119
Warren, N.C., 189
Warrenton, N.C., 253
Warrenton, Va., 181
Warring
  Grace, 263
  Henry, Col., 263
Warterman
  Barclay, 106
Washington
  Ann, 128
  Ann Eliza, 181
  Baily, Dr., 127, 128
  Bushrod, 181, 184
  Bushrod, Hon , 128
  Francis Henrietta, 215
  Gen., 15
  George, Gen., 5, 17, 121, 132, 133, 148, 197, 211, 222, 242
  Henry, 193
  John, 128
  John A., 227
  Lund, 30, 60, 69
  Lund, Jr , 64
  Lund, Sr , 236
  Mrs , 128
  Peter Grayson, 63
  Robert T., 236
  Samuel, Capt., 197
  Sarah, 193
  Susan Jean, 30
  Susan Monroe, 60
  William Augustine, Col., 18
  William Grayson, 64
Washington Co., D C , 122, 227, 228, 232, 238
Washington Co., Md., 7, 89, 92, 181, 192, 216
Washington Federalist, vi
Washington Society, 126
Washington, D.C., v, 2, 4, 6-9, 11, 12, 106,

257-261, 263, 264, 266, 267
Washington, Ga., 261
Washington, Ky., 240
Washington, Miss., 57, 239
Washington, Pa., 39
Washington, Ver., 68
Waterford, Va., 69, 222
Waterhouse
  Alice L , 168
Waters
  Deborah, 86
  Elizabeth, 83
  Elkanah, 229
  John, 213
  Mahalia Ann, 213
  Richard, Col., 115
  T.G., Rev , 231
  Thomas G., 265
  Wm., Rev., 38
Watertown, Conn , 187
Wathen
  Frances, 151
Watkins
  Decimus Eugene, 253
  Elizabeth, 132
  Henry, 132
  T., Dr., 253
  William, 55
  William E., 260
  Wm. E., 260
Watmough
  John G., Hon., 242
Watrous
  Sarah, 100
Watson
  James, 65, 87
  Jane, 206
  Jane Love, 87
  John, 134
  Joseph, 180, 243
  Josiah, 206
Watters
  William, xii
Watts
  Elizabeth A.K , 105
Waugh
  Alexander, Maj., 223
  Beverley, Rev , xii, 53, 61, 63, 64
Way
  Mr , 10
Waymouth
  William W., 45

Wayne
  Gen., 207
Wayson
  Eliza, 169
Weaver
  Catharine, 79
Webb
  Benjamin Y., 158
  George, Lt., 222
  Henrietta Maria, 21
  Susanna, 12
  Thomas, 12, 21
Webster
  Charlotte, 169
  Daniel, Hon., 130
  Rev., 59
  S P., 190
  Toppan, 169
Weed
  E.J., 100
Weeks
  John, 51
Weems
  Gregory, Dr , 124
  John N., Dr , 250
  M.L., Rev., 5
  Midshipman, 75
  Richard, 25
  William, 6
  William L., 242
Weightman
  John, 35
  William, 32
Weis
  John, 139
Welborne
  Jane, 181
Welch
  Joseph, Col., 109
Wellford
  Horace, Dr , 64
  Jane C., 136
  John S , 136
  Mary C., 136
  William N., 138
Wellington
  Lord, 37
Wells
  Bolivar B , 227
  George, Jr., 162
  George, Rev , 174
  Janetta, 162
  Jemima B , 100
  John D., Dr , 159

John, Jr., 88, 89
Joshua, xii
Julia Ann, 171
Mary Geraldine, 89
Mary, Mrs., 16
Richard, 24, 227
Samuel, Rev., 73
Thomas Hyde, 88
Wells, Ver., 113
Wendell
  Cathalina, 40
  John H., 40
  John H., Gen., 174
Wentworth
  Martha, 115
Wertenbaker
  William, 115
West
  Eliza, 139
  George, 33
  Hannah, 26
  John, 92
  John W., Lt., 195
West Indies, 67, 245
West Point, 94, 101, 140, 249
West Point, N.Y., 35
West River, Md., 161
Westcott
  Hampton, 233
Westerfield
  David, 260
  Mary, 260
Western, 216
Western River, Va., 102
Westfield, N.Y , 267
Westham, Eng , 12
Westmoreland C.H., Va., 4
Westmoreland Co., Va., 192
Weston
  Ann F., 85
  Capt., 85, 254
  Lucinda, 254
Wetherald
  Thomas, 223
Wetherbee
  Judah, Capt , 216
Wetherel
  John P., 69
Wetherill
  Samuel, 119
Wetherspoon
  Daniel, 151

Wetzel
  Wm. Y., 44
Wexford, Ire., 37, 200
Weyborn
  Horace, 149
Weymouth, Mass., 199
Whaler
  Margaret, 188
Wharton
  Eliza S., 181
  James, 159, 181, 219
  Rev., 6, 65
  William L., Dr , 124
Wheat
  Joseph Henry, 225
Wheeler
  Elizabeth, 72
  Henrietta, 181
  Michael F., Rev., 224
Wheeling, Va., 105, 117
Whelan
  Emily E., 103
  Nicholas, 216
Whetcroft
  Sarah A , 164
Whilden
  Jane J., Mrs., 109
Whipple
  Gen., 159
Whips
  Reuben, 17
Whisler
  John, Maj., 118
Whitall
  Emeline N., 151
  Samuel, 151
Whitby, Eng., 213
White
  Hugh L., Hon., 244
  John, 73, 158
  John Jackson, 157
  Margaret Ann, 265
  Peregrine, 48
  Rev., 7, 22, 170
  Thomas W., 265
  Zachariah, 218
White Post, the, 255
White Sulphur Springs, Va., 178
Whitehurst
  Henry W., 177
Whitel
  Rev., 207

Whiteside
  Peter, 129
whitesmiths, 37
Whitfeld
  Elizabeth, 132
Whitfield
  James, Rev., 124
  Rev., 103
Whiting
  Cecilia B., 140
  John, 59
  John, Col., 18
Whittemore
  Benjamin B., 110
Whittington
  Louisa R., 69
Wickham
  Edmond F., 67
Wiesenthal
  Thomas F., Dr., 256
Wiestling
  Benjamin J., Dr, 190
Wiggin
  Eliza, 110
  Timothy, 110
Wight
  Elizabeth Ann, 125
  Jonathan, 155
Wightt
  Susan, 53
Wilcox
  Charles G., 136
  D., Capt., 242
  Mrs., 241
Wilet
  Marinus, Col., 160
Wiley
  David, 34
  David, Rev, 25
  Gerardus, 34
  John, 35
  Margaret Y., 25
  Mary, 40
  Rev, 5, 14
Wilkes
  Mr., 52
Wilkins
  Gouverneur Morris, 152
Wilkinson
  Ann M C., 180
  George, 180
Willcoxen
  Horatio, 45

Willet
  Marinus, Col, 174
Willey
  Calvin, 106
  James M., 106
William and Mary Parish, 116
Williams
  Adeline, 262
  Adeline, Mrs., 262
  Amanda M.F., 61
  Amos A., 192
  Benjamin, 124
  Brook, 64
  Charles S., 235
  Charlotte, 79
  Elie E., 107
  Elie, Col., 67
  Elijah, Jr., 125
  George P., 120
  Harriet Eliza, 74
  James, 80, 89
  Jane E., 255
  Jeremiah, 7
  Lemuel, 166
  Mary, 179
  Mary Ann, 248
  Nancy, 192
  Philip, 237
  Prudence, 106
  R.W., Col., 183
  Susan May, 124
  W.G., Lt., 94, 98
  Wilkerson G., 246
  William J., 106
  William, Hon., 179
Williams College, 43
Williamsburg, Va., 70, 71, 216
Williamsburgh, Md., 2
Williamson
  David, 178
  Philip Doddridge, Dr, 201
  Robert Harper, 261
  William, 73
  William, Rev., 201
  Wm, Rev., 20
Williamson Co., Tenn., 112
Williamsport, Pa., 114
Willingford, Conn, 54
Willis
  Elizabeth, 14
  Mr., 140

Richard, 14
Williston
  Rev, 45
Willsholt
  Mr., 55
Wilmer
  William Holland, Rev., xii, 20, 27, 44
Wilmington
  N.C., 112
Wilmington Gazette, 29
Wilmington, Del, 46, 56, 164
Wilmington, Ver, 41
Wilmot
  Margaret, 12
Wilson
  Agnes S., 236
  Anne E.B., 263
  Catharine, Mrs., 55
  Clarissa, 87
  Emily, 180
  George, 87
  Harriet B, Mrs., 97
  Henry G., 220
  Jacob H., 209
  James, 52, 110, 167
  James C., 31, 263
  James Joseph, 110
  Jane, Mrs., 84
  John, 125
  John R, 14
  John, Jr, 61
  John, Sr., 102
  Joseph S., 115
  Margaret K., 109
  Mary Ann, 125
  Mary Bankson, 263
  Mercy Ann, 225
  Norval, xii
  Norval, Rev., 227, 250
  Norwell, Rev., 101
  Rev., 102, 188, 247
  Robert, 222
  Sarah, 84
  Thomas, 80, 109, 236
  William, 78, 109
  William Henry, 220
Wimsatt
  Samuel, 261
Winchester
  Samuel G, Rev., 152
Winchester, N.Y., 27

Winchester, Va., 14, 28, 140, 209
Winder
  Charles H., 225
  Levin, Gen , 61
  Mrs., 61
  William H., Gen , 79
Windsor
  Rosanna N., 174
Windsor, Conn , 11
Windsor, Pa , 4
Windsor, Ver , 95
Winemiller
  John H., 246
Wines
  M.S., Mr., 207
Wing
  Desire, 53
Wingard
  Abraham, 46
  Mary Eliza, 46
Wingate
  J.F., Hon., 203
  Virginia A.N., 203
Wingfield
  Rev., 240
Winn
  Eliza, 180
  Timothy, 180
Winston
  Dorothea, 180
  Edmund, Hon., 180
Winter
  Catharine T.H., 261
  John, 47
  Mary C , 212
  Richard H., 261
Winters
  Mary, 37
Wirt
  Agnes Cabell, 175
  Elizabeth Gamble, 206
  John, 9
  John Henry, 141
  Rosa E , 228
  William, 175, 228
  William, Hon , 206
Wiscasset, Me., 22
Wise
  John Francis, 173
  Mary Ann, 173
  Nathaniel S., 136
  Richard, 139

Wolcott
  Alexander, Dr., 172
Wolf
  George, 227
  Horace E., 247
  Margaret, 227
  Mr., 202
Wolfenden
  John, 223
Wood
  Charles F., 108
  Eveline, 186
  Ferdinand F., 190
  John, 61
  Mary Ann, 250
  William, 186
Wood Co., Va , 261
Woodbury, 66
Woodford Co , Ky , 132
Woodley
  Rev., 263
Woodman
  Edward, 49
Woods
  Mrs., 40
  Nathaniel, 39
Woodside
  Eliza, 11, 112
  John, 11, 112
Woodstock, Mass , 58
Woodstock, Va., 80, 92
Woodville, Va , 138
Woodward
  Clement, 237
  Mary S., 220
  Sudley, 220
  Thomas, 36
  W , 105
Woolford
  John, 261
Wools
  Sarah P., 237
Worcester
  Samuel, Rev., 53
Worcester Co., Md., 69
Worcester, Mass., 182
Worcestershire, Eng., 56
Worley
  Louisa, 137
Worrell
  Ann Elizabeth, 258
Worthington
  Catherine, 46, 50
  Charles, 46, 50

  Eliza, 36
  John G., 157
  Thomas, Dr., 141
Wright
  Daniel, 156
  Edward, 267
  Emily, 76
  Harriet, 169
  Imogene, 240
  John, 69
  Mary Josephine, 267
  Orrin, M.D., 251
  Richard, 100
  Susanna, 69
  T.C., Mr., 76
  Thomas C., 135
  W.H C'C., 140
Wrigley
  Francis, 120
Wyatt
  Mary, 113
  Rev., 113

Y

Yager
  Joseph, 92
Yale College, 187, 230
Yamasee Indians, 58
Yates
  Eleanor M , 240
  John R., 124
Yates & McIntyre, 215
Yeaton
  Julia Ann Eliza, 79
  Wm., 79
Yoe
  Benjamin, 247
Yokey
  Henry, 137
Yomacraw, Ga., 58
York Co., Va., 105
York, Pa., 223
York, Va., 108
York-Haven, 55
Yorktown, Va., 112, 130, 166
Young
  Barnabas, 251
  Benjamin A., xii
  Caroline, 224
  Elizabeth, 149
  Ezekiel, 224
  Frances S., 209

James, 209
Jane, 143
Notley, 3
Rev., 35, 186
Young Ladies Academy, 10

Z
Zimmerman
Emeline, 149

[ ]
Basil (C), 145
Mousse (C), 196
Nancy, 47
Sarah (C), 46
Yarrow (C), 68

ABOUT THE AUTHOR

Wesley E. Pippenger is an active member in a number of historical and genealogical societies in Virginia, and is past-President of the Board of Governors of the Virginia Genealogical Society. He has been employed by the Federal Government for over 27 years, and is a management analyst with the Office of Inspector General, National Aeronautics and Space Administration in Washington, D.C. He resides in Arlington, Virginia.

Mr. Pippenger has been active in genealogical research since 1970. Shortly after moving from Colorado to Virginia in 1982, he began to locate, study, catalog, and have data published about cemeteries in the Alexandria, Virginia area. Subsequent published works, now numbering upwards of 60 items, include abstracts of court records, vital records, acts of the Virginia Assembly, newspapers, land, probate, and legislative petition records, and more. His current landmark project, published in series by the Virginia Genealogical Society, is to inventory all estate-related documents for the period 1800-1865, for the entire state of Virginia.

Other Heritage Books by Wesley E. Pippenger:

Alexandria (Arlington) County, Virginia Death Records, 1853-1896

Alexandria City and Arlington County, Virginia Records Index: Vol. 1

Alexandria City and Arlington County, Virginia Records Index: Vol. 2

Alexandria County, Virginia Marriage Records, 1853-1895

Alexandria Virginia Marriage Index, January 10, 1893 to August 31, 1905

Alexandria, Virginia Marriages, 1870-1892

Alexandria, Virginia Town Lots, 1749-1801
Together with the Proceedings of the Board of Trustees, 1749-1780

Alexandria, Virginia Wills, Administrations and Guardianships, 1786-1800

Alexandria, Virginia 1808 Census (Wards 1, 2, 3, and 4)

Alexandria, Virginia Death Records, 1863-1896

Alexandria, Virginia Hustings Court Orders, Volume 1, 1780-1787

Connections and Separations: Divorce, Name Change and Other Genealogical Tidbits from the Acts of the Virginia General Assembly

Daily National Intelligencer *Index to Deaths, 1855-1870*

Daily National Intelligencer, *Washington, District of Columbia Marriages and Deaths Notices (January 1, 1851 to December 30, 1854)*

Dead People on the Move: Reconstruction of the Georgetown Presbyterian Burying Ground, Holmead's (Western) Burying Ground, and Other Removals in the District of Columbia

Death Notices from Richmond, Virginia Newspapers, 1841-1853

District of Columbia Ancestors, A Guide to Records of the District of Columbia

District of Columbia Death Records: August 1, 1874-July 31, 1879

District of Columbia Foreign Deaths, 1888-1923

District of Columbia Guardianship Index, 1802-1928

District of Columbia Interments (Index to Deaths)
January 1, 1855 to July 31, 1874

District of Columbia Marriage Licenses, Register 1: 1811-1858

District of Columbia Marriage Licenses, Register 2: 1858-1870

District of Columbia Marriage Records Index
June 28, 1877 to October 19, 1885: Marriage Record Books 11 to 20
Wesley E. Pippenger and Dorothy S. Provine

District of Columbia Marriage Records Index
October 20, 1885 to January 20, 1892: Marriage Record Books 21 to 30

District of Columbia Probate Records, 1801-1852

District of Columbia: Original Land Owners, 1791-1800

Early Church Records of Alexandria City and Fairfax County, Virginia

Georgetown, District of Columbia 1850 Federal Population Census (Schedule I) and 1853 Directory of Residents of Georgetown

Georgetown, District of Columbia Marriage and Death Notices, 1801-1838

*Husbands and Wives Associated with Early Alexandria, Virginia
(and the Surrounding Area), 3rd Edition, Revised*

Index to District of Columbia Estates, 1801-1929

*Index to Virginia Estates, 1800-1865
Volumes 4, 5 and 6*

John Alexander, a Northern Neck Proprietor, His Family, Friends and Kin

Legislative Petitions of Alexandria, 1778-1861

Pippenger and Pittenger Families

Proceedings of the Orphan's Court, Washington County, District of Columbia, 1801-1808

The Georgetown Courier *Marriage and Death Notices:
Georgetown, District of Columbia, November 18, 1865 to May 6, 1876*

*The Georgetown Directory for the Year 1830: to which is appended, a Short Description
of the Churches, Public Institutions, and the Original Charter of Georgetown, and
Extracts of the Laws Pertaining to the Chesapeake and Ohio Canal Company*

The Virginia Gazette and Alexandria Advertiser:
Volume 1, September 3, 1789 to November 11, 1790

The Virginia Journal and Alexandria Advertiser:
Volume I (February 5, 1784 to January 27, 1785)

Volume II (February 3, 1785 to January 26, 1786)

Volume III (March 2, 1786 to January 25, 1787)

Volume IV (February 8, 1787 to May 21, 1789)

The Washington and Georgetown Directory of 1853

Tombstone Inscriptions of Alexandria, Volumes 1-4

Other Heritage Books by Dorothy S. Provine:

Alexandria County, Virginia Free Negro Register, 1797-1861

*Compensated Emancipation in the District of Columbia:
Petitions under the Act of April 16, 1862*

District of Columbia Free Negro Registers

District of Columbia Indentures of Apprenticeship, 1801-1893

*District of Columbia Marriage Records Index
June 28, 1877 to October 19, 1885: Marriage Record Books 11 to 20*
Wesley E. Pippenger and Dorothy S. Provine

District of Columbia Marriage Records, 1870-1877

Index to District of Columbia Wills, 1921-1950